SAS® Language: Reference

Version 6
First Edition

SAS Institute Inc.
SAS Campus Drive
Cary, NC 27513

The correct bibliographic citation for this manual is as follows: SAS Institute Inc., *SAS® Language: Reference, Version 6, First Edition* Cary, NC: SAS Institute Inc., 1990. 1042 pp.

SAS® Language: Reference, Version 6, First Edition

ISBN 1-55544-381-8

1st printing, March 1990
2nd printing, June 1992

Note that text corrections may have been made at each printing.

DOC S18, Ver 1.66W, 012290

Contents

Part 3 Special Features 965

Part 4 Appendices 975

Illustrations

Figures

Tables

Credits

Documentation

Composition	Jim Byron, Gail C. Freeman, Cynthia M. Hopkins, Amanda G. Lemons, Pamela A. Troutman, Denise L. Truelove, David S. Tyree
Graphic Design	Creative Services Department
Proofreading	Kevin A. Clark, Gwen T. Colvin, Jennifer M. Ginn, Beth A. Heiney, Hanna P. Hicks, Beryl C. Pittman, Josephine P. Pope, Toni P. Sherrill, John M. West, Susan E. Willard, Anna B. Williams
Technical Review	Technical review is performed not only by the primary developers of the base SAS software features documented here but also by members of the following divisions at the Institute: Applications, Education, Host Research and Development (including Quality Assurance), and Technical Support. The Publications Division wishes to express its appreciation of the work provided by these reviewers.
Writing and Editing	Deborah S. Blank, Cathy Cameron Carter, Amy S. Glass, Christina N. Harvey, Stacy A. Hilliard, J. Renee Hurt, Brenda C. Kalt, Carol Austin Linden, Susan H. McCoy, Sonja R. Moore, Len Olszewski, Kathryn A. Restivo, Helen Weeks, Judith K. Whatley, John S. Williams

Software

Development

The portable language features of Release 6.06 base SAS software were developed by the Core Division. Product development includes design, programming, debugging, support, and providing source material for documentation. In the following list, the SAS Institute staff member whose name is followed by an asterisk has primary responsibility for the feature; others give specific assistance.

Credits for host-specific features appear in the SAS documentation for that operating system. Credits for procedures appear in the *SAS Procedures Guide, Version 6, Third Edition*. Credits for other development divisions that are associated with specific products are listed in the manuals for those products.

DATA Step	Jeffrey A. Polzin,* Mark V. Schaffer, Mark Watson
Source Management and Development Support	Jim H. Boone, Karen H. Cross, Andrew T. Fagan, Thomas Gyori, Robert P. Janka, Walt Martin, Edward McGee, David V. Phillips
Display Manager	Tracy C. Byrd, Claire S. Cates,* Jeff Shaughnessy

Formats and Informats	David M. DeLong, Richard D. Langston*
Functions	Marc-david Cohen, David M. DeLong, Georges H. Guirguis, Warren F. Kuhfeld, Jeffrey A. Polzin, Randal K. Whitehead*
Internal Documentation	Elizabeth Bales
I/O Systems: Engine Supervisor	Stephen Beatrous, John S. Wallace
I/O Systems: Base Engine	Billy Clifford, Barbara Foster, Karen L. Armstrong, Rebecca Perry, John S. Wallace
I/O Systems: XPORT and Tape Engines	Fred Levine
I/O Systems: BMDP, OSIRIS, and SPSS Engines	Richard D. Langston
Macro Facility	Bruce Tindall,* Susan M. O'Connor
Parsing	Richard D. Langston, Jeffrey A. Polzin, Bruce Tindall
Printing and Messages	Claire S. Cates, Jeffrey A. Polzin, Randal K. Whitehead*
Procedure Interface	Richard D. Langston
Supervisor Integration	Claire S. Cates,* Jeffrey A. Polzin
System Options	Richard D. Langston, Mark V. Schaffer

Testing

I/O System Testing	John T. Stokes, Kevin L. Mosman, Cynthia Grant
Developmental Testing	David C. Berger, Elizabeth C. Langston, Caroline Quinn, Deanna T. Tawiah, Amanda W. Womble, Ann L. Yang
Quality Assurance	Marilyn Adams, Patricia L. Berryman, Oita C. Coleman, Deborah J. Johnson, Joy Polzin, Richard A. Ragland, Scott Sweetland

Technical Support

Full-Screen Products	Ann E. Carpenter, Jim Goodling, Annette T. Harris,* Yvonne Selby
Statistical Procedures	Donna O. Fulenwider, Eddie Routten,* David Schlotzhauer, Mike Stockstill, Donna E. Woodward
Base SAS Software	Johnny B. Andrews, Greg Cooper, David A. Driggs, Lynn H. Patrick,* Thomas J. Hahl, Christina A. Keene, Meg Pounds

Minicomputer Systems Interface	Ginny Dineley,* Ann Ferraro, Maureen Hayes, Ken Larsen, Mark Moorman, Toby Trott, Maggie Underberg, Stephen A. Vincent
Mainframe Systems Interface	Chuck Antle, Martha Hall, Greg Hester, Kevin Hobbs, Charles A. Jacobs, Bradley W. Klenz, Marty Light, Mark J. Lochbihler, Jason Moore, Terry D. Poole, Joy Reel,* Katrina Rempson, Jeff Simpson, Michael Williams, Thomas W. Zack

Using This Book

Purpose

SAS Language: Reference, Version 6, First Edition provides complete reference information for all portable language features in Release 6.06 base SAS software. In this context, *portable* includes features that work the same across all host operating systems. (In contrast, host-specific features are those which are meaningful only under specific host operating systems or which work differently under different host operating systems. This book usually abbreviates the term host operating system to host system.) *Language* includes all aspects of base SAS software that are not procedures.*

This book replaces the following documentation:

- *SAS User's Guide: Basics, Version 5 Edition*
- SAS Technical Report P-146, *Changes and Enhancements to the Version 5 SAS System*
- SAS Technical Report P-168, *Changes and Enhancements to the Version 5 SAS System under VMS™*
- SAS Technical Report P-175, *Changes and Enhancements to the SAS System, Release 5.18, under OS and CMS*
- SAS Technical Report P-182, *Changes and Enhancements to the SAS System, Release 5.18, under VMS*
- SAS Technical Report P-183, *Changes and Enhancements to the SAS System, Release 5.18, under AOS/VS and PRIMOS®.*

"Using This Book" is your guide to using *SAS Language: Reference*. It describes what you should know in order to benefit from using this book; how the book is organized; which sections you should read if you have specific goals; and the typographical, syntax, and coding conventions used. In addition, the final section describes other SAS documentation that may be helpful to you.

Audience

SAS Language: Reference is written for users who either have previous experience in using the SAS System or who have at least an intermediate level of experience with another programming language and understand the fundamentals of programming logic. Such users may include end users, applications developers, or systems programmers.

---

* The SAS macro facility is briefly outlined in this book. For complete documentation, see the *SAS Guide to Macro Processing, Version 6, Second Edition*

Prerequisites

The following table summarizes the SAS System concepts you need to understand in order to use *SAS Language: Reference.*

You need to know how to	Refer to
invoke the SAS System at your site	instructions provided by the SAS Software Consultant at your site
use base SAS software; you need varying amounts of familiarity with the SAS System depending on which features you want to use	*SAS Introductory Guide* for a brief introduction and *SAS Language and Procedures: Usage, Version 6, First Edition* for a more thorough introduction
manage files on your operating system	SAS documentation for your host operating system or vendor documentation for your host system

How to Use This Book

This section provides an overview of the information in this book and describes what you should read in particular situations.

Organization

This book begins with the changes and enhancements for Version 6 base SAS software. Later parts contain background information on the SAS language, reference entries for individual items in the language, special topics, and appendices. Each part is described briefly here.

Part 1: Description of the SAS System

Part 1 describes how the SAS language works as a whole; how components of the language (such as statements and functions) work, along with tables that list and compare individual items; how different parts of the language work together; and how the SAS Display Manager System and the SAS Text Editor work.

Chapter 1, "Essential Concepts"

Chapter 2, "The DATA Step"

Chapter 3, "Components of the SAS Language"

Chapter 4, "Rules of the SAS Language"

Chapter 5, "SAS Output"

Chapter 6, "SAS Files"

Chapter 7, "SAS Display Manager System"

Chapter 8, "SAS Text Editor"

Part 2: Reference

This part contains reference entries for individual items in the SAS language.

Chapter 9, "SAS Language Statements"

Chapter 10, "SAS Operators"

Chapter 11, "SAS Functions"

Chapter 12, "SAS CALL Routines"

Chapter 13, "SAS Informats"

Chapter 14, "SAS Formats"

Chapter 15, "SAS Data Set Options"

Chapter 16, "SAS System Options"

Chapter 17, "SAS Display Manager Windows"

Chapter 18, "SAS Display Manager Commands"

Chapter 19, "SAS Text Editor Commands"

Part 3: Special Features

Chapter 20, "SAS Macro Facility," contains a brief outline of the SAS macro facility in Release 6.06.

Part 4: Appendices

The appendices describe additional features available with base SAS software.

Appendix 1, "SAS Notes"

Appendix 2, "SAS Sample Library"

Appendix 3, "Stored Program Facility"

What You Should Read

Depending on your level of experience with base SAS software, you should read different parts of this book first. The following table shows the experience levels and the suggested reading for users of that level.

If you are	You should read
an experienced SAS user	"Changes and Enhancements" to find the summary of changes and enhancements to the language for Release 6.06. You should then look at the individual reference entries to find more details on the new features and the background chapters to find overall explanations of the items you are interested in.
new to the SAS System: experienced programmer	Chapter 1, which serves as an overview of SAS processing; the first part of Chapter 2, which describes the DATA step; and Chapter 5, which describes the output of SAS programs and how to interpret it. Then scan the tables in Chapter 3 to determine the elements you need to write your program, and use the reference entries for those elements as you write your program. **Note:** *SAS Language and Procedures: Usage* is a faster intermediate-level introduction to the SAS System than this reference book.
new to the SAS System: inexperienced computer user	either the *SAS Introductory Guide* or *SAS Language and Procedures: Usage*. This book is a reference book, not a tutorial. If you have only this book, follow the directions for experienced programmers who are new to the SAS System.

Reference Aids

SAS Language: Reference will be easier to use if you are familiar with the following features of the book. They are listed in order of appearance within the book.

inside front cover graphic
: illustrates the different parts of the SAS System, organized by function.

table of contents
: lists the chapter titles, major subheadings, and the page number for each.

list of illustrations
: consists of three lists: displays (for representations of terminal displays), figures (for illustrations), and tables (for titled tables). Each list provides the page numbers for the items listed.

Changes and Enhancements
: provides information about changes and new features in base SAS software since Release 5.18.

chapter tables of contents	give the titles and page numbers of sections within chapters. Chapter tables of contents appear in all chapters and appendices.
host information notes	identify places in which more specific information about a feature is available in the SAS documentation for your operating system or, in some cases, in the vendor's documentation. You should consult that documentation for a complete explanation before using the feature.
Glossary	defines the major terms used in this book.
Index	provides the page numbers where specific topics are discussed. Page ranges indicate discussions that cover several pages.
inside back cover graphic	illustrates the parts of base SAS software and the major categories of features within each.

Two other features make the reference entries easier to use. First, all reference entries within a single chapter appear in one alphabetical list, rather than being divided by category. In addition, some previously complex entries in "SAS Language Statements" have been divided into individual entries. For example, the INPUT and PUT statements each consist of five entries (general, column, formatted, list, and named), rather than single large entries.

Conventions

This section explains the various conventions used in presenting text, SAS language syntax, file and library references, examples, and printed output in this book. The following terms are used in discussing syntax:

keyword	is a literal that is a primary part of the SAS language. (A literal must be spelled exactly as shown although it can be entered in uppercase or lowercase.) Keywords in this book include names of SAS language statements and functions and macro language statements and functions.
argument	is an element that follows a keyword. It is either literal or user-supplied. It has a built-in value or has a value assigned to it. Arguments that you must use are required arguments. Other arguments are optional arguments, or more simply, options.
value	is an element that supplies a quantity for an argument. It may be a literal or a user-supplied value.

Typographical Conventions

SAS Language: Reference uses several type styles and related conventions in presenting information. The following list explains the meaning of the conventions in general. Conventions used in presenting syntax appear in the following section.

roman
: is the standard type style used for most text in this book.

UPPERCASE ROMAN
: is used for literal elements of the SAS language and variable names in text.

italic
: is used to define new terms and to emphasize important information.

`monospace`
: is used to show examples of SAS code set off from the text. In most cases, this book uses lowercase type for SAS code, with the exception of some title characters. Within the text, monospace is used to show the values of character variables.

ƀ
: is used to represent the blank character when it is necessary to show a precise number of blanks.

Although this book follows the conventions listed here, you can enter your own SAS code in lowercase, uppercase, or a mixture of the two. (As a general rule, the SAS System changes all source statements submitted to uppercase except for character variable values and text within quoted strings, such as titles.*) The following examples illustrate these typographical conventions:

- An operator written with letters, such as EQ for =, is called a *mnemonic operator*.
- Use the TRIM function in the concatenation operation as follows:

```
data namegame;
   length color name $8;
   color='black';
   name='jack';
   game=trim(color)||name;
run;
```

  This example produces a value of `blackjack` for the variable GAME.
- Since trailing blanks are ignored in a comparison, `fox` is equivalent to `foxƀƀƀ`.

---

* The CAPS system option in Chapter 16, "SAS System Options," describes the rules precisely.

Syntax Conventions

Type styles have special meanings when used in the presentation of base SAS software syntax in this book. The following list explains the style conventions for the syntax sections:

UPPERCASE BOLD identifies SAS keywords such as the names of statements and functions (for example, **INPUT**).

UPPERCASE ROMAN identifies arguments and values that are literals (for example, FIRSTOBS=, PAGE).

italic identifies arguments or values that you supply. Items in italic can represent user-supplied values that are either

- □ nonliteral values assigned to an argument (for example, *variable* in END=*variable*)
- □ nonliteral arguments (for example, *label* in LINK *label*).

In addition, an item in italics can be the generic name for a list of arguments from which the user can choose (for example, *attribute-list*). If more than one of an item in italics can be used, the items are expressed as *item-1* through *item-n*.

The following symbols are also syntax conventions:

< > (angle brackets) identify optional arguments. Any argument not enclosed in angle brackets is required.

| (vertical bar) indicates that you can choose one value from a group. Values separated by bars are mutually exclusive.

. . . (ellipsis) indicates that the argument or group of arguments following the ellipsis can be repeated any number of times. If the ellipsis and the following argument are enclosed in angle brackets, they are optional.

The following examples illustrate the syntax conventions described in this section. These examples contain selected syntax elements, not complete syntax.

FOOTNOTE<*n*> <'*text*' | "*text*">;

- □ FOOTNOTE is in uppercase bold because it is the name of the statement.
- □ *n* and *text* are in italics because they are optional arguments you can supply.
- □ You can supply *text* surrounded with either single or double quotes, but not both.

BY <DESCENDING> <GROUPFORMAT> *variable-1* . . .
<<DESCENDING> <GROUPFORMAT> *variable-n*>;

- BY is in uppercase bold because it is the name of the statement.
- DESCENDING and GROUPFORMAT are in uppercase roman because they are optional literal arguments.
- *Variable* is in italics because it is an argument you supply.
- You must specify at least one *variable* (*variable-1*), and you can specify either the DESCENDING option, the GROUPFORMAT option, or both before it.
- The ellipsis followed by the bracketed group of arguments on the second line indicates that you can repeat the entire group of arguments any number of times.

Conventions for Referencing SAS Data Libraries and External Files

Many SAS statements and other elements of the SAS language refer to SAS data libraries and external files. In Release 6.06, you can usually choose whether to make the reference through a logical name (a libref or fileref) or to use the physical filename enclosed in quotes. If you use a logical name, you usually have a choice of using a SAS statement (LIBNAME or FILENAME) or the operating system's control language to make the association. As a result, many methods of referring to SAS data libraries and external files are available, and some of them depend on the host operating system.

In examples that use external files, this book uses the italicized phrase *file-specification*. You must see the SAS documentation for your host system for the rules for referencing external files on your host. Similarly, examples refer to SAS data libraries with the convention *SAS-data-library*. The following example illustrates an INFILE statement that refers to an external file:

```
infile file-specification obs=100;
```

Conventions for Examples and Output

Most of the programs in this book were run using the following SAS system options:

- NODATE
- LINESIZE=76
- PAGESIZE=60
- NOSTIMER.

SAS programs that use only these options do not contain an OPTIONS statement. However, any SAS program that uses other options or specifies different values for these options includes an appropriate OPTIONS statement.

Your output may differ from the output shown in the book if you run the example programs with different options or different values for those options. In addition, decimal values in your output may differ slightly from the output shown in this book. This difference is a function of the processor used in your computer, rather than a problem with the software.* In all situations, the differences should be minor.

Additional Documentation

SAS Institute provides many publications about products of the SAS System and how to use them on specific hosts. For a complete list of SAS publications, you should refer to the current *Publications Catalog*. The catalog is produced twice a year. You can order a free copy of the catalog by writing to

SAS Institute Inc.
Book Sales Department
SAS Campus Drive
Cary, NC 27513

To order any of the books listed below see ordering information in the back of this book.

Base SAS Software Documentation

In addition to *SAS Language: Reference*, you will find these other documents helpful when using base SAS software:

- *SAS Language and Procedures: Introduction, Version 6, First Edition* (order #A56074) provides information for users who are unfamiliar with the SAS System or any other programming language.
- *SAS Procedures Guide, Version 6, Third Edition* (order #A56080) provides detailed reference information about procedures in base SAS software.
- *SAS Language and Procedures: Usage, Version 6, First Edition* (order #A56075) provides task-oriented examples of the major features of base SAS software.
- *SAS Guide to Macro Processing, Version 6, Second Edition* (order #A56041) provides a tool for extending and customizing your SAS programs.
- SAS documentation that provides information about the host-specific features of the SAS System for your operating system is listed in the back of this book under "Operating System Documentation for the SAS System."

Documentation for Other SAS Software

The SAS System includes many software products in addition to the base SAS System. Several books that may be of particular interest to you are listed here:

- *SAS/ASSIST Software: Your Interface to the SAS System* (order #A56086) provides information on using the SAS System in a menu-driven windowing environment that requires no programming.
- *SAS/FSP Software: Usage and Reference, Version 6, First Edition* (order #A56001) provides information on using interactive procedures for creating SAS data sets and entering and editing data or for creating, editing, and printing form letters and reports.

* "Details of Numeric Precision" in Chapter 3 describes numeric precision in general.

□ *SAS/AF Software: Usage and Reference, Version 6, First Edition* (order #A56011) provides tutorial and reference information about the applications development facilities available in SAS/AF software.

□ *SAS/GRAPH Software: Reference, Version 6, First Edition, Volume 1* and *Volume 2* (order #A56020) provides information on creating presentation graphics to illustrate relationships of data.

Changes and Enhancements

Introduction

This section summarizes the major changes and enhancements to the base SAS software for Release 6.06 since Release 5.18. It is intended for users who have previous experience with base SAS software. Changes and enhancements are grouped here by the chapter organization of this reference guide. Complete information on these topics can be found in their respective chapters.

One major change to the design of the software is that the micro-to-host link is no longer part of base SAS software. This capability is still available, but it is now offered as a separate product called SAS/CONNECT software in Release 6.06.

Note: Although many of the features described here are new for all hosts, certain features have been available previously on some hosts.

Chapter 1, "Essential Concepts"

Because of the new Multiple Engine Architecture (MEA), different types of SAS data sets are now available and, in addition to the DATA step, you can use the SQL procedure and SAS/ACCESS software to create SAS data sets.

Chapter 5, "SAS Output"

Error recovery has been enhanced. It now provides the SAS System with the ability to correct some misspellings of keywords and to continue processing the step where the error occurred.

Chapter 6, "SAS Files"

The most dramatic change for Release 6.06 base SAS software is the use of logical data models and engines to access SAS files. The first half of Chapter 6 details the structure of the SAS file system, introduces terminology for SAS data sets and engines, introduces engines, and describes the logical data model for SAS data sets and SAS data libraries.

The second half of the chapter describes the features of SAS data sets for Release 6.06, which include

- □ indexes for WHERE-expression and BY-group processing
- □ compressed observations
- □ performance options
- □ damaged file recovery.

Chapter 9, "SAS Language Statements"

The following features are now available in statements with Release 6.06 base SAS software:

- The ARRAY statement now accepts _TEMPORARY_ arrays made up of temporary data elements. The SAS System ignores the automatic variables _N_ and _ERROR_ when _ALL_ is specified for arrays of character variables.
- The BY statement applies to preceding SET, MERGE, or UPDATE statements only. It no longer applies to all SET, MERGE or UPDATE statements in a DATA step.
- The iterative DO statement enables you to specify variables as well as constants in a series of items for iterative processing.

  A WHILE or UNTIL clause in an iterative DO statement no longer controls all the iterations.
- The FILE statement contains two new options: FILENAME= and FILEVAR=. The FILENAME= option defines a character variable that the SAS System sets to the value of the physical name of the file that is currently open for PUT statement output. The FILEVAR= option enables you to close the current output file and open a new one. The FILE statement now enables you to access a file from an aggregate storage location by specifying the name of the file in parentheses after a fileref that points to the aggregate storage location.
- The FILENAME statement enables you to associate a valid SAS name (called a fileref for file reference) with a single external file, an aggregate storage location, or an output device. It also enables you to write to the log the attributes of one or more external files and to disassociate a fileref from a file.
- The FORMAT statement enables you to specify default formats for both character and numeric data within a DATA step.
- The %INCLUDE statement now enables you to access a file or files from an aggregate storage location by specifying the name of the file or files in parentheses after a fileref that points to the aggregate storage location.
- The INFILE statement contains several new options: EXPANDTABS, FILENAME=, FILEVAR=, PRINT, and SHAREBUFFERS. The EXPANDTABS option replaces the TABS option on hosts that previously supported TABS. The FILENAME= option defines a variable that the SAS System sets to the value of the physical name of the currently open input file. The FILEVAR= option enables you to close the current input file and open a new one. The PRINT option enables you to use a print file as input to a DATA step without removing the carriage control characters. The SHAREBUFFERS option enables you to easily update an external file in place.

  The INFILE statement now enables you to access a file from an aggregate storage location by specifying the name of the file in parentheses after a fileref that points to the aggregate storage location.
- The INFORMAT statement enables you to specify default informats for both character and numeric data within a DATA step.
- The LIBNAME statement has new options that enable you to specify engines and engine/host options, clear a libref, and list the characteristics of SAS data libraries.

- □ The MISSING statement now accepts lowercase as well as uppercase characters for special missing values.
- □ The PUT statement now includes the ability for you to specify field alignment with a format. You can also specify a quoted character in a format list.
- □ The SELECT statement accepts multiple expressions in WHEN clauses.
- □ The WHERE statement enables you to select observations from input SAS data sets before they are read into the program data vector.
- □ The WINDOW and DISPLAY statements create and display customized windows in the DATA step.

Chapter 10, "SAS Operators"

The IN operator compares a value on the left side of the operator to a list of values on the right side.

Chapter 11, "SAS Functions"

The following functions are new for Release 6.06 base SAS software:

- □ BYTE
- □ HBOUND (new for mainframe environments)
- □ LBOUND (new for mainframe environments)
- □ ORDINAL
- □ RANK
- □ TRIGAMMA.

The INPUT and PUT functions now include the question mark (?) and double question mark (??) arguments that enable you to suppress printing of input data lines and error messages.

The RESOLVE function is not available in Release 6.06.

Chapter 12, "SAS CALL Routines"

The EXECUTE CALL routine is not available in Release 6.06 base SAS software.

Chapter 13, "SAS Informats"

The following informats are new to one or more host systems supported by Release 6.06 base SAS software:

$ASCII*w.*	MSEC*w.*	S370FPD*w.d*
$BINARY*w.*	OCTAL*w.d*	S370FPIB*w.d*
$EBCDIC*w.d*	PDTIME*w.*	S370FRB*w.d*
$OCTAL*w.*	PERCENT*w.*	TODSTAMP*w.*
BINARY*w.d*	RMFSTAMP*w.*	TU*w.*
BITS*w.d*	SMFSTAMP*w.*	VAXRB*w.d*
COMMAX*w.d*	S370FIB*w.d*	

The following informats have been changed:

- □ The $VARYING*w.* informat now reads zero-length records.
- □ The date and time informats now include a special use of the YEARCUTOFF= system option. This option enables you to override the default system date and specify a date range.

Chapter 14, "SAS Formats"

The following numeric and character formats are new to one or more host systems supported by Release 6.06 base SAS software:

$ASCII*w.*	COMMAX*w.d*	PK*w.d*
$BINARY*w.*	DOLLARX*w.d*	S370FIB*w.d*
$EBCDIC*w.*	NEGPAREN*w.d*	S370FPD*w.d*
$OCTAL*w.*	OCTAL*w.*	S370FPIB*w.*
BINARY*w.*	PERCENT*w.*	S370FRB*w.d*

The following date formats are also new with Release 6.06 base SAS software:

DAY*w.*	MONTH*w.*	YYMM*xw.*
DOWNAME*w.*	QTR*w.*	YYMON*w.*
JULDAY*w.*	QTRR*w.*	YYQ*xw.*
MMYY*xw.*	WEEKDAY*w.*	YYQR*xw.*
MONNAME*w.*	YEAR*w.*	

The $VARYING format now can write zero-length records.

Chapter 15, "SAS Data Set Options"

The following data set options are new and provide you greater control when you are working with SAS data sets:

- □ The BUFNO=, BUFSIZE=, COMPRESS=, and REUSE= data set options enable you to use and store SAS data sets more efficiently.
- □ The WHERE= data set option enables you to select observations from input SAS data sets before they are read into the program data vector.
- □ The CNTLLEV= data set option controls the level at which shared update access is denied.

Chapter 16, "SAS System Options"

The following system options are new to one or more host systems supported by Release 6.06 base SAS software:

ALTLOG=	DBCSTYPE=	REMOTE=
ALTPRINT=	DMR	REUSE=
AUTOEXEC=	ECHOAUTO	SASAUTOS=
BUFNO=	ENGINE=	SASHELP=
BUFSIZE=	FORMDLIM=	SASMSG=
CARDIMAGE	FORMS=	SITEINFO=
CATCACHE=	GWINDOW	SYSLEAVE=
CLEANUP	MAUTOSOURCE	VERBOSE
COMAMID=	MRECALL	WORKTERM
COMPRESS=	PAGENO=	YEARCUTOFF=
CONFIG=	PRINT=	
DBCSLANG=	PROCLEAVE=	

The following system options have changed for Release 6.06 base SAS software. For details, see Chapter 16, "SAS System Options," and the SAS documentation for your host system.

- ERASE (see WORKINIT and WORKTERM)
- INTERACTIVE (see BATCH)
- KANJI (see DBCS)
- LEAVE= (see SYSLEAVE= and PROCLEAVE=)
- MACROGEN (see MPRINT)
- SASNEWS= (see NEWS=).

The DQUOTE and TEXT82 system options are obsolete. Their functions are now a part of Release 6.06 base SAS software.

The C60/C48/C96 and SKIP= system options are not supported in Release 6.06 base SAS software.

Chapter 17, "SAS Display Manager Windows"

The new features listed here are available within the SAS Display Manager System:

- The PMENU facility provides an additional way to execute commands.
- Dialog boxes are part of the PMENU facility.
- Requestor windows appear in response to an action on your part and require that you confirm, modify, or cancel the action.
- The attention sequence interrupts execution of certain display manager commands.
- Scroll bars are tools that enable you to control vertical and horizontal scrolling.

In addition, the SAS Display Manager System has several new windows and many new commands. Some windows now have selection-field commands. All Release 6.06 windows are new except the LOG, PROGRAM EDITOR, and OUTPUT windows.

Chapter 18, "SAS Display Manager Commands"

Release 6.06 base SAS software reflects many changes and enhancements to the SAS Display Manager System, including many new and enhanced commands. These changes and enhancements include the following features:

- You can now change the sizes of display manager windows and reposition them on the display. Any number of windows can appear on the display at a single time.
- The FILE command now copies the contents of a window into an external file.
- The INCLUDE command now copies an external file into a window.
- In Version 5 base SAS software, the COPY command was used to copy an external file into a window; it is now used to copy a catalog entry into a window.
- In Version 5, the SAVE command was used to copy the contents of a window into an external file; it is now used to copy the contents of a window to a catalog entry.
- Version 5 color commands have been condensed into a single COLOR command with various arguments.
- A cut-and-paste facility is available.

The following display manager commands are no longer available:

- the SPLIT command
- the / command (now replaced by the *n* command).

Chapter 19, "SAS Text Editor Commands"

Numerous new commands have been added to the SAS Text Editor. A spell checker is available, as is the UNDO command.

Chapter 20, "SAS Macro Facility"

The autocall facility is available on all host systems.

The following macro statements are new:

- %DISPLAY
- %SYSEXEC
- %WINDOW.

The following macro functions have been enhanced:

- The %BQUOTE function in Release 6.06 combines the actions of the Version 5 %BQUOTE and %QUOTE functions.
- The %NRBQUOTE function in Release 6.06 combines the actions of the Version 5 %NRBQUOTE and %NRQUOTE functions.
- The %SUPERQ function in Release 6.06 now quotes mnemonic operators. This function was formerly an autocall macro.

Appendix 3, "Stored Program Facility"

The SAS System now enables you to store compiled DATA step programs and execute them at another time.

Description of the SAS® System

PART 1

CHAPTER 1 Essential Concepts

Introduction

This chapter introduces you to the SAS System in general and to base SAS software specifically. It provides an overview of the software, defines basic concepts and terminology, and describes the methods of operation available for using the SAS System.

What Is the SAS System?

The SAS System is an integrated system of software products. The SAS System enables you to perform

- □ data entry, retrieval, and management
- □ report writing and graphics
- □ statistical and mathematical analysis
- □ business forecasting and decision support
- □ operations research and project management
- □ applications development.

The core of the SAS System is base SAS software. It consists of

□ the *SAS language*, a programming language that you use to manage your data

□ procedures that are software tools for data analysis and reporting

□ a macro facility

□ a windowing environment called the SAS Display Manager System.

This book documents only the SAS language and the windowing environment. See "Using This Book" for a list of documentation on other features of base SAS software. The rest of this chapter introduces some terms and concepts fundamental to the SAS language.

Overview of Base SAS Software

This section addresses topics that pertain to base SAS software as a whole, including the SAS data set, Multiple Engine Architecture, the DATA step, SAS procedures, and files.

The SAS Data Set

Before you can analyze your data and produce a report with SAS software, the data must be in a form the SAS System can recognize. This form is called a *SAS data set*, and it consists of the following:

□ descriptor information

□ data values.

The descriptor information describes the contents of the SAS data set to the SAS System. The *data values* are the data that have been collected or calculated. They are organized into a rectangular structure containing rows called observations and columns called variables. An *observation* is a collection of data values that usually relate to a single object. A *variable* is the set of data values that describe a given characteristic. Figure 1.1 illustrates the structure of a SAS data set.

Figure 1.1 *Structure of a SAS Data Set*

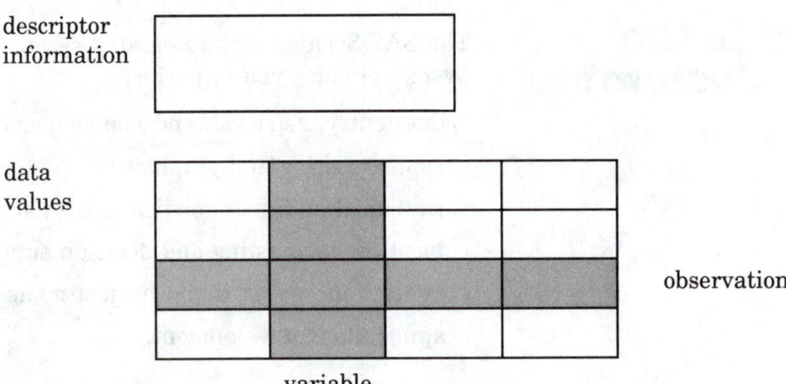

In general, an observation is the data associated with an entity such as an inventory item, a regional sales office, a client, or a patient in a medical clinic. Variables are characteristics of these entities, such as the list price, sale price, number in stock, originating vendor, and so on.

The collection of data values in a SAS data set has a rectangular shape even when created from incomplete data because the SAS System recognizes *missing values*. For example, the following data lines show data that do not form a rectangular shape:

```
Atlanta      173     125     148      111
Dallas       102     113     122       99
Detroit      195     163     117
Seattle      187
```

When the data are read into a SAS data set, however, each row becomes an observation, each column is given a variable name, and the data are given a rectangular structure because absent data values are recorded as missing. The periods in the following SAS data set represent missing values.*

```
OBS   OFFICE       JAN     FEB     MAR      APR

 1    Atlanta      173     125     148      111
 2    Dallas       102     113     122       99
 3    Detroit      195     163     117        .
 4    Seattle      187       .       .        .
```

Multiple Engine Architecture

Prior to Release 6.06 of base SAS software, only one kind of SAS data set was available. It had the logical structure described in the previous section, stored descriptive information as well as data values, and had a particular set of physical attributes. To create a SAS data set from raw data with base SAS software, you had to use a group of SAS language statements called a *DATA step*.**

The DATA step is still available and is a central part of base SAS software. *Multiple Engine Architecture*, however, has made available new ways to create SAS data sets and different implementations of the SAS data set. Through internal groups of instructions called *engines*, SAS software is able to read and process different implementations of a SAS data set, instead of the single kind of SAS data set available in earlier releases.

Using a DATA step, you can create a SAS data set in which data values are physically stored. Using the SQL procedure and SAS/ACCESS software, you can produce two kinds of SAS data sets: one that stores values and one that stores the information necessary to obtain the data values from other SAS data sets or files formatted by other vendors' software. See Figure 1.2.

---

* Reading missing values from input data and coding and storing missing values with special meanings are discussed in Chapter 2, "The DATA Step."

** Other SAS software procedures, such as the MEANS procedure in base SAS software and some procedures in SAS/FSP software, supply other ways to create SAS data sets.

Figure 1.2 *Creating a SAS Data Set: From Data to Results of Analysis*

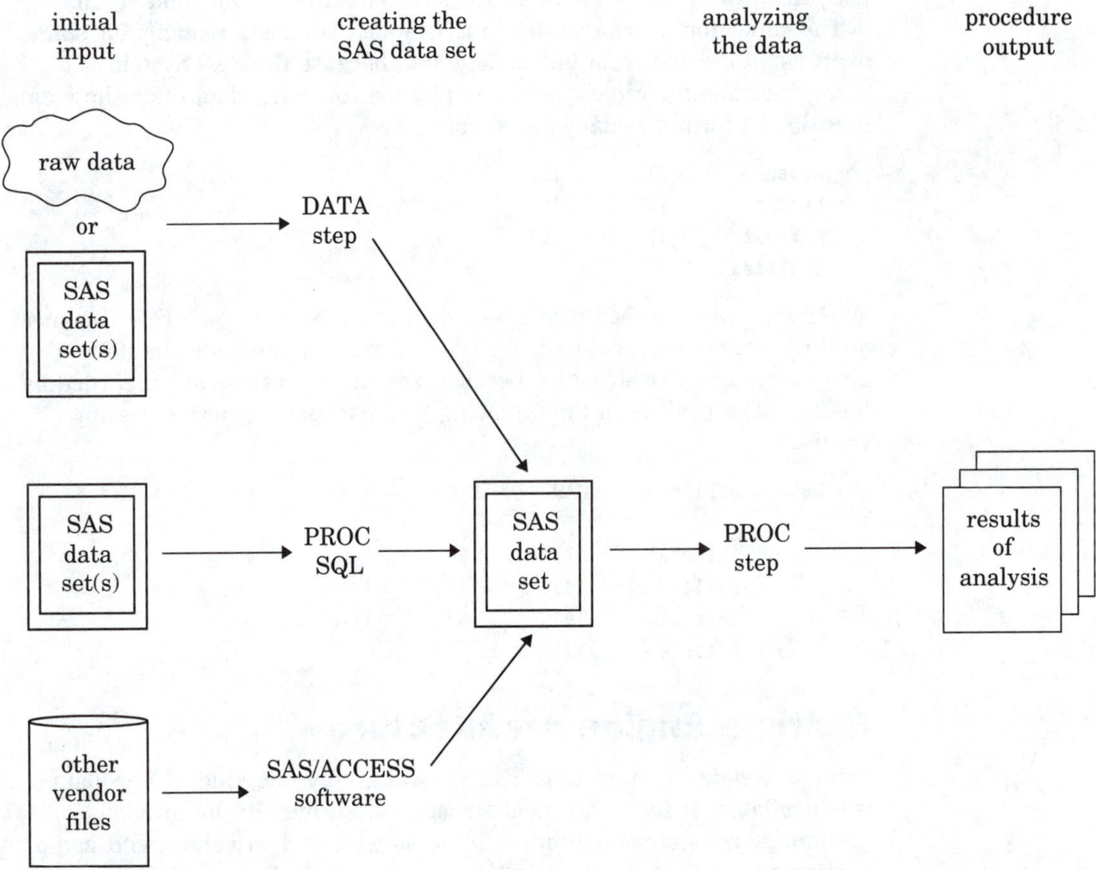

The DATA step, the SQL procedure, and SAS/ACCESS software are described in the following sections. Additional features of Multiple Engine Architecture, including the relationships of different implementations of the SAS data set and advanced performance features, are discussed in Chapter 6, "SAS Files."

The DATA Step

A DATA step consists of a group of statements in the SAS language that read raw data or existing SAS data sets to create a SAS data set. The kind of SAS data set created in a DATA step is called a *SAS data file.* A SAS data file is a SAS data set in which data values are physically stored. With a DATA step, you can read your raw data or other existing SAS data sets and perform the calculations or manipulation necessary so that you can analyze your data and create reports with *SAS procedures.* DATA step programming is discussed in Chapter 2.

The SQL Procedure

The SQL procedure enables you to use Structured Query Language (SQL™) to access and manipulate data stored in multiple SAS data sets. You do this by creating a SAS data view or a SAS data file. A SAS data file stores actual data values. A *SAS data view,* however, does not actually store data

SQL is a trademark of International Business Machines Corporation.

values. Instead, it stores the information necessary to obtain the data values from other SAS data files and SAS data views.

PROC SQL is also a data analysis procedure. It adds the power of the SAS System to the flexibility of data manipulation based on SQL. PROC SQL is documented in the *SAS Guide to the SQL Procedure: Usage and Reference, Version 6, First Edition.*

SAS/ACCESS Software

SAS/ACCESS software enables users of many of the most widely used database management systems (DBMSs) or other interface products to read information directly from their files. You can use this software to create a SAS data view that describes the data from a file such as a DBMS table to the SAS System. SAS/ACCESS software enables you to use information stored in other vendors' software files without the expense of storing it in a SAS data file. A set of fill-in-the-blank menus prompts you for information that is then used to construct a SAS data view.* SAS/ACCESS software also enables you to create and load other vendors' files using data from a SAS data file or a SAS data view. For more information on SAS/ACCESS software, see the SAS documentation for the available interfaces to other vendors' software.

SAS Procedures

Once your data are accessible as a SAS data set, you can analyze the data and write reports using a set of utilities known as SAS procedures. A group of procedure statements is called a *PROC step*. SAS procedures analyze data in a SAS data set for producing univariate descriptive statistics, frequency tables, crosstabulation tables, tabular reports consisting of descriptive statistics, charts, plots, and so on. Other procedures provide ways to manage SAS files.

Procedures in base SAS software are documented in two books.

□ *SAS Procedures Guide, Version 6, Third Edition*

□ *SAS Guide to the SQL Procedure: Usage and Reference*

Files Used with the SAS System

When working with the SAS System, you use files created and maintained by the SAS System as well as files that are created and maintained by your host system and have no special characteristics related to the SAS System. Data files organized in particular formats or structures known to the SAS System are referred to as *SAS files*. Data files not in a structure known to the SAS System and from which you can read data and to which you can route output in your SAS jobs are called *external files*.**

---

* You also have the option of creating a SAS data file from the SAS data view.

** The SAS System uses special SAS/ACCESS files to read data from other vendors' files, such as DBMS tables. These files are not external files in this context.

SAS Files

Three SAS files are briefly described in this section:

□ SAS data file

□ SAS data view

□ SAS catalog.

The most used SAS file is the SAS data file, a type of SAS data set in which data values are physically stored. Chapter 2 describes the SAS DATA step, which you use to create a SAS data file. In addition to the SAS data file, several other kinds of SAS files can be created and used in SAS jobs.

A SAS data view is also a type of SAS data set. It enables you to look at information stored in one or more SAS data sets or in other vendors' software files. You can create a SAS data view with the SQL procedure in base SAS software or with SAS/ACCESS software.* A SAS data view, unlike a SAS data file, does not actually store data values. A SAS data view is instead a set of instructions to the SAS System. These instructions construct a logical SAS data set, enabling you to treat parts of other vendors' files or one or more SAS data sets as a single SAS data set. SAS data views enable you to create logical SAS data sets without using the storage space required by additional SAS data files.

A *SAS catalog* is a type of SAS file that stores many different kinds of information to be used in a SAS job. For example, a SAS catalog can contain instructions for reading and printing data values and function key settings that you use in the windowing environment available in the SAS System.

See Chapter 6 for a complete discussion of all SAS files.

External Files

External files are files not maintained or specially structured by the SAS System that you use during your SAS session for storing

□ raw data that you want to read into a SAS data file

□ SAS program statements

□ procedure output.

In Chapter 2, you learn more about external files and about how to reference them in your SAS jobs.

■ **Host Information** .... Refer to the SAS documentation for your host system for details on characteristics of external files on your own host system.

.... ■

* See "Multiple Engine Architecture" earlier in this chapter.

The SAS Data Library

All SAS files reside in a *SAS data library*. On some host systems, a SAS data library is a physical relationship among files; on other host systems, it is a logical relationship among files. See Chapter 6 for a complete discussion of SAS data libraries.

■ **Host Information** .... Refer to the SAS documentation for your host system for details on the characteristics of SAS data libraries.

Running the System

This section discusses how to begin your SAS session, the various ways you can execute SAS programs, and techniques for automatically customizing your SAS session.

Starting a SAS Session

You start a SAS session with the SAS command. The SAS command follows the rules for other commands on your host system. On some hosts, you embed the SAS command in a file of system commands or control statements; on other hosts, you enter the command at the system prompt. The form of the SAS command depends on your

- □ host system
- □ method of executing SAS programs.

Methods of Operation

Several methods of running SAS programs are possible in Release 6.06 of the SAS System:

- □ display manager mode
- □ interactive line mode
- □ noninteractive mode
- □ batch (or background) mode.*

Each of these methods is introduced in the following sections. In addition, SAS/ASSIST software provides a menu-driven system for running your SAS program. For information about SAS/ASSIST software, see *SAS/ASSIST Software: Your Interface to the SAS System.*

Display Manager Mode

Using the SAS Display Manager System, you execute SAS programs in a windowing environment. In *display manager mode*, you can edit and execute programming statements, display the SAS log, display procedure output, display online help, set function keys, and more. See Displays 1.1 and 1.2 for examples of the LOG, PROGRAM EDITOR, and OUTPUT windows available in display manager. See Chapter 7, "SAS Display Manager System," for a discussion of display manager.

* Note that batch mode is not supported on all host systems.

■ **Host Information** .... See the SAS documentation for your host system for the form of the SAS command to use to invoke the SAS System using the windowing environment. ■

Display 1.1 *The LOG and PROGRAM EDITOR Windows*

```
LOG
Command ===>

NOTE: Copyright(c) 19xx SAS Institute Inc., Cary, NC 27512-8000, U.S.A.
NOTE: SAS (r) Proprietary Software Release 6.xx
      Licensed to SAS Institute Inc., Site xxxxxxxx.
```

```
PROGRAM EDITOR
Command ===> submit

00001 data region;
00002    input office $12. jansales febsales marsales;
00003    cards;
00004 Atlanta     144091.83 251079.52 293052.03
00005 Louisville  93072.59 99062.49 104069.39
00006 Richmond    87095.61 92059.37 98061.43
```

Display 1.2 *The OUTPUT Window*

```
OUTPUT
Command ===>

                      Region I: First Quarter Sales                        1

         OBS     OFFICE        JANSALES     FEBSALES     MARSALES

          1     Atlanta        144091.83    251079.52    293052.03
          2     Louisville      93072.59     99062.49    104069.39
          3     Richmond        87095.61     92059.37     98061.43
```

Interactive Line Mode

In *interactive line mode*, program statements are entered in sequence in response to prompts from the SAS System. DATA and PROC steps execute when

□ a RUN, QUIT, or CARDS statement is entered

□ another DATA or PROC statement is entered

□ the ENDSAS statement is entered.

By default, the SAS log and output are displayed on the screen immediately following the programming statements.

Output 1.1 shows a sample interactive line mode SAS session.* The SAS System prompts you with a number and a question mark to enter SAS statements. (You can enter more than one SAS statement per line.) If you use a CARDS statement in a DATA step, the prompt changes to a number and a greater-than (>) symbol. This prompt indicates that the SAS System expects you to enter data before you enter more SAS statements. Notes from the SAS log and output from PROC steps are displayed as well as the programming statements and data that you enter.

Output 1.1 *Sample Interactive Line Mode Session*

```
NOTE: Copyright(c) 19xx SAS Institute Inc., Cary, NC 27512-8000, U.S.A.
NOTE: SAS (r) Proprietary Software Release 6.xx
      Licensed to SAS Institute Inc., Site xxxxxxxx.

  1? data region;
  2? input office $12. jansales febsales marsales;
  3? cards;
  4> Atlanta        144091.83 251079.52 293052.03
  5> Louisville     93072.59 99062.49 104069.39
  6> Richmond       87095.61 92059.37 98061.43
  7> ;
NOTE: The data set WORK.REGION has 3 observations and 4 variables.

  8? title 'Region I: First Quarter Sales';
  9? proc print; run;
                        Region I: First Quarter Sales                         1

          OBS       OFFICE        JANSALES     FEBSALES      MARSALES

            1     Atlanta        144091.83    251079.52     293052.03
            2     Louisville      93072.59     99062.49     104069.39
            3     Richmond        87095.61     92059.37      98061.43

 10? endsas;
```

Noninteractive Mode

In *noninteractive mode*, SAS program statements are stored in an external file. The statements in the file execute immediately when you issue a SAS command referencing the file. Depending on the host system and the SAS system options you use, the SAS log and output from the noninteractive program are either written to separate external files or displayed.

■ **Host Information** ....

Refer to the SAS documentation for your host system for information on how these files are named and where they are stored.

.... ■

Batch Mode

You can run SAS jobs in *batch mode* under host systems that support batch or background execution. Place your SAS statements in a file and submit them for execution along with the control statements and system commands required at your site.

When you submit a SAS job in batch mode, one file is created to contain the SAS log for the job and another file to hold output produced in a PROC step or, when directed, output produced in a DATA step by a PUT statement.

* Note that details in appearance may vary among hosts.

■ **Host Information** .... Refer to the SAS documentation for your host system for information about executing SAS jobs in batch mode. Also see documentation specific to your site for local requirements for running jobs in batch and for viewing output from batch jobs. ■

Customizing Your SAS Session

There are different ways to customize your SAS session. One way is to store system options with the settings you want in a *configuration file.* When you invoke the SAS System, these settings are in effect, according to your specifications. Another way to customize your SAS session is to use an *autoexec file* to execute SAS statements automatically each time you invoke the SAS System and begin your session. Both of these methods are discussed in the following sections.

The Configuration File

Each time you invoke the SAS System, it looks for a configuration file. This file contains settings for SAS system options, which are used to configure your session. SAS system options determine, among other things, how the SAS System initializes its interfaces with your computer hardware and the host system, how it reads and writes data, and how the output appears.

By placing SAS system options in a configuration file, you can avoid repeatedly specifying the options at invocation. For example, if you do not want the time and date of your session to appear at the top of each page of output, you can specify the NODATE option in your configuration file.

See Chapter 3, "Components of the SAS Language," and Chapter 16, "SAS System Options," for discussion and descriptions of SAS system options.

■ **Host Information** .... See the SAS documentation for your host system for more information about the configuration file. On some hosts, you can use both a system-wide and a user-specific configuration file. ■

The Autoexec File

You can cause SAS statements to execute automatically immediately after the system is initialized by storing them in a file designated as the autoexec file. This file is created using the AUTOEXEC= system option. See Chapter 16 for details of the option.

Any SAS statement can be included in an autoexec file. For example, you can use FILENAME and LIBNAME statements to reference frequently used external files and SAS data libraries. You can use DM statements to execute SAS display manager commands that affect how the windowing environment is configured.

■ **Host Information** .... See the SAS documentation for your host system for information on how autoexec files should be set up so that they can be located by the SAS System. ■

CHAPTER 2 The DATA Step

Introduction

As was discussed in Chapter 1, “Essential Concepts,” data must be accessed through a SAS data set before you can process them with the SAS System. This chapter describes the DATA step, the primary method for creating a SAS data set with base SAS software.* A DATA step creates a *SAS data file*, a type of SAS data set which actually stores data values. For the purposes of this chapter, the broader term SAS data set will be used. For details about different implementations of SAS data sets, see Chapter 6, "SAS Files."

A DATA step is a group of SAS language statements that begins with a DATA statement. The DATA statement is followed by programming statements that perform the manipulations necessary to build the data sets. Report writing, file management, and information retrieval can all be handled in a DATA step. You can use the DATA step for these purposes:

- retrieval, that is, getting your input data into a SAS data set
- editing, that is, checking for errors in your data and correcting them
- computing the values for new variables
- printing reports and writing disk or tape files, according to your specifications
- producing new SAS data sets from existing ones by subsetting, merging, and updating the old data sets
- data manipulation, that is, rearranging data in a SAS data set for use with a SAS procedure.

The topics in this chapter fall into two large categories: DATA step processing and reading raw data in a DATA step. Reading SAS data sets in a DATA step is discussed in "Combining SAS Data Sets" and "BY-Group Processing" in Chapter 4, "Rules of the SAS Language."

DATA Step Processing

When you submit a DATA step to the SAS System for execution, it is first compiled and then executed. Figure 2.1 shows the flow of action in a typical SAS DATA step. In the next sections, each of these phases is discussed and a sample DATA step provides a step-by-step description. Major features of the DATA step are also discussed, such as creating step boundaries and stopping a DATA step, as well as the process by which some values are set to missing at the beginning of the DATA step and for each iteration.

* In addition to the DATA step, several procedures in base SAS software create a SAS data set as part of their output. The FSEDIT and FSVIEW procedures in SAS/FSP software can be used to create and edit SAS data sets.

Figure 2.1 *Flow of Action in a Typical SAS DATA Step*

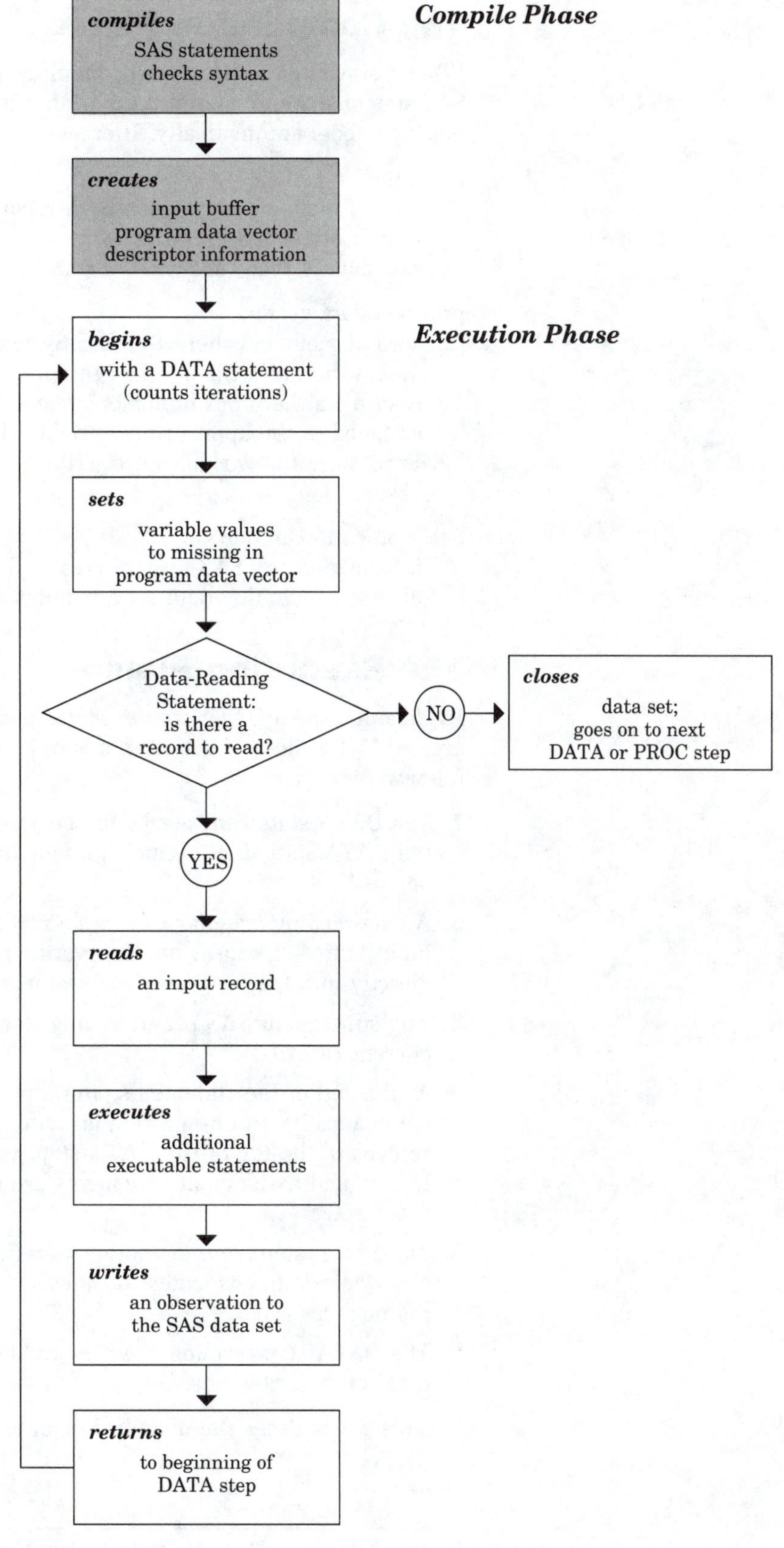

The Compilation Phase

When you submit a DATA step, the SAS System checks the syntax of the SAS statements and compiles them, that is, translates the statements into machine code, automatically. It creates three items at this time:*

input buffer
: area of memory into which each record of raw data is read when an INPUT statement executes. Note that this buffer is created only when raw data is read, not when a SAS data set is read.

program data vector
: area of memory where the SAS System builds your data set, one observation at a time. When the program executes, data values are read from the input buffer or created by SAS language statements and assigned to the appropriate variables in the program data vector. From here the variables are written to the SAS data set as a single observation.

descriptor information
: information the SAS System creates and maintains about each SAS data set, including data set attributes and variable attributes.

The Execution Phase

By default, a SAS DATA step executes once for each observation being created.** The flow of action in a simple DATA step is described as follows:

1. The DATA statement marks the beginning of a DATA step. Each time the DATA statement executes, a new iteration of the DATA step begins.***
2. A data-reading statement causes a record of data to be read into the input buffer or causes an observation from a SAS data set to be read directly into the program data vector.
3. Any subsequent SAS programming statements are executed for the current record.
4. At the end of the statements, an output, return, and reset occur automatically: an observation is written to the SAS data set; the system returns to the top of the DATA step; values of variables created by INPUT and assignment statements are reset to missing in the program data vector.
5. The SAS System counts another iteration, reads in the next record or observation, and executes the subsequent programming statements for the next record.
6. The DATA step terminates when end-of-file is encountered in a SAS data set or a raw data file.

Table 2.1 outlines the default flow of action in a DATA step.

---

* Note that the input buffer and program data vector are logical concepts that are independent of the physical implementation.

** Overriding this default action is discussed later in "Variations on the Basic DATA Step."

*** See _N_, the automatic variable whose value is set to the number of times the DATA step has iterated, in "Automatic Variables" later in this chapter.

Table 2.1 *Default Flow in the Execution Phase of a DATA Step*

Structure of a DATA Step	Action Taken
DATA statement	begins step counts iterations
Optional data-reading statement:	
INPUT	reads a record from input data
or	
SET, MERGE, or UPDATE	reads one observation at a time from input SAS data set
Optional SAS programming statements, for example:	further process the data for the current observation
`qtr1=jan+feb+mar;`	computes the value for QTR1 for the current observation
`if price<500;`	subsets by value of variable PRICE for the current observation
Default actions:	
At end of DATA step:	
Automatic write	writes observation to data set
Automatic return	returns to DATA statement
At top of DATA step:	
Automatic reset	resets values to missing in program data vector

A Sample DATA Step

The following statements provide a simple example of a DATA step that reads raw data:

```
data weight(keep=idno loss);
   input idno $ week1 week16;
   loss=week1-week16;
   cards;
2477 195  163
2431 220  198
2456 173  155
2412 135  116
;
```

When the statements are compiled, the input buffer and the program data vector are built. The program data vector contains all the variables created in the DATA step statements and two variables, _N_ and _ERROR_, that are automatically generated for every DATA step.* See Figure 2.2.

* See "Automatic Variables" later in this chapter for details about these variables.

Figure 2.2 *Input Buffer and Program Data Vector*

input buffer

```
----+----1----+----2----+----3----+----4----+----5----+----6----+----7----+----8
```

program data vector

IDNO	WEEK1	WEEK16	LOSS	_N_	_ERROR_
	.	.	.	1	0
K	D	D	K	D	D

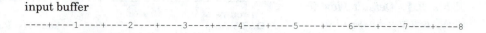

Note the initial values of the variables in the program data vector. Variables created by the INPUT and assignment statements (IDNO, WEEK1, WEEK16, and LOSS) are set to missing initially. The automatic variable _N_ is set to 1; the automatic variable _ERROR_ is set to 0.

Note also that the variable names are marked with either a K (for kept) or a D (for dropped) in Figure 2.2. Variables that are kept are part of the observation written to the SAS data set. Dropped variables are not written to the SAS data set. IDNO and LOSS are kept because they are specified in the KEEP= *data set option* in the DATA statement. WEEK1 and WEEK16 are dropped because they are not specified with the KEEP= option. The _N_ and _ERROR_ variables are dropped because automatic variables are never written to the output data set.

The first data line is read into the input buffer. The input *pointer*, which the SAS System uses to keep its place as it reads data from the input buffer, is positioned at the beginning of the input buffer, ready to read the data record. See Figure 2.3.

Figure 2.3 *Position of Input Pointer in Input Buffer before Data Are Read*

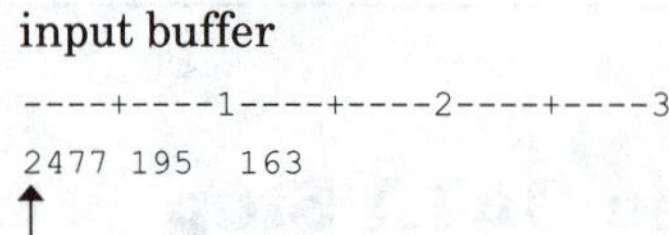

Then the INPUT statement reads *data values* from the record in the input buffer and writes them to the program data vector where they become *variable* values. See Figure 2.4.

Figure 2.4 *Values Are Read from the First Record into the Input Buffer*

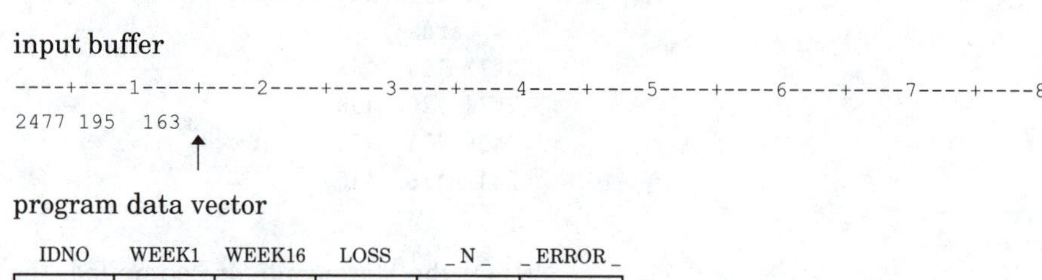

IDNO	WEEK1	WEEK16	LOSS	_N_	_ERROR_
2477	195	163	.	1	0
K	D	D	K	D	D

When the INPUT statement has read a value for each variable, the assignment statement is executed, and a value for the variable LOSS is computed and written to the program data vector. See Figure 2.5.

Figure 2.5 *Value is Computed and Assigned to Variable LOSS in the Program Data Vector*

program data vector

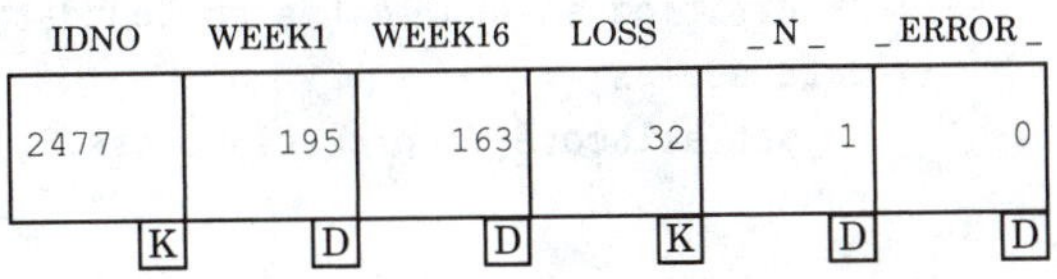

IDNO	WEEK1	WEEK16	LOSS	_N_	_ERROR_
2477	195	163	32	1	0
K	D	D	K	D	D

observation output to SAS data set

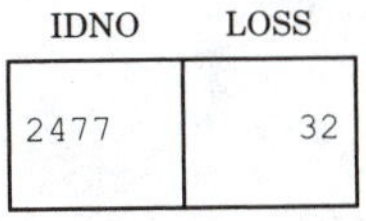

IDNO	LOSS
2477	32

When the last statement in the step has executed, three things happen automatically:

1. All values in the program data vector, except those marked to be dropped, are output as a single observation to the data set WEIGHT.
2. The SAS System returns to the DATA statement to begin the next iteration.
3. The values of variables in the program data vector are reset. The values of variables created by the INPUT and assignment statements are reset to missing. The values of automatic variables are not reset to missing: _ERROR_ is reset to 0; _N_ is incremented by 1.*

Step Boundary

It is important to understand what creates a step boundary in SAS programming so that you know when statements are put into effect. For example, consider the following DATA steps:

```
/* using a default step boundary */
data scores;
   set allscore(drop=score5-score7);
   options firstobs=5 obs=55;      /* affects both DATA steps */

data test;                         /* first step boundary     */
   set alltests;
run;
```

The OPTIONS statement in this example specifies that the first observation read from the input data set should be the 5th and the last one read should be the 55th. These settings are in effect for the first DATA step as well as the second because the OPTIONS statement appears *before* the boundary of the first DATA step.

---

* See "Automatic Variables" and "When Variable Values are Set to Missing Automatically" later in this chapter.

If a RUN statement is inserted immediately before the OPTIONS statement, the first DATA step reaches its boundary before the OPTIONS statement is encountered. The OPTIONS statement settings, therefore, are put into effect only for the second DATA step, as in the following example:

```
/* creating an explicit step boundary */
data scores;
   set allscore(drop=score5-score7);
run;                          /* first step boundary       */

options firstobs=5 obs=55;    /* affects only 2nd DATA step*/

data test;
   set alltests;
run;
```

Following the statements in a DATA (or PROC) step with a RUN statement is the simplest way to make the step begin to execute, but a RUN statement is not always necessary. The SAS System recognizes several step boundaries for a DATA step:

- a RUN statement
- the semicolon (when a CARDS statement is used) or four semicolons (when a CARDS4 statement is used) after data lines
- a DATA statement, which begins a new DATA step
- a PROC statement, which begins a PROC step
- an ENDSAS statement
- in noninteractive or batch mode, the end of an input file containing SAS programming statements.

When you submit a DATA step to the SAS System during interactive processing, it does not begin running until a step boundary is crossed. This fact enables you to submit statements as you write them while preventing a step from executing until you have entered all the statements.

Types of DATA Steps

The type of input data used in a DATA step determines what data-reading statements you use. There are four basic types of simple DATA steps, categorized by the source of the input data: those that read

- data from an external file
- instream data
- data from existing SAS data sets
- no data but generate data from programming statements.

Most DATA steps read input data records from only one of the first three sources of input. Some DATA steps use the fourth method, and a few combine some or all of the sources.

Finally, a DATA step can be used for the sole purpose of reading and writing data (for example, generating a report) without creating a data set. The reserved data set name _NULL_ is used to prevent the creation of a data set.

The structure and primary statements used in each of the types of DATA steps are outlined in the following sections.

Reading Data from an External File

The components of a DATA step that produces a SAS data set from raw data stored in an external file are outlined here.

DATA statement
: marks the beginning of the DATA step and gives a name to the SAS data set(s) being created.

INFILE statement
: identifies the external file that contains the data. This statement has options that control how the records are read.

INPUT statement
: describes your input by giving a name to each variable and identifying its location in the data record. It causes a data record to be read.

Other SAS statements
: enable you to modify the data, create new variables, and so on.

Reading Instream Data

The components of a DATA step that produces a SAS data set from data lines in the job stream are outlined here.

DATA statement
: marks the beginning of the DATA step and gives a name to the SAS data set(s) being created.

INFILE statement
: specifies options that control reading of instream data lines. This statement is optional. When the INFILE statement is used with instream data, CARDS or CARDS4 must be used as the file specification.

INPUT statement
: describes your input by giving a name to each variable and identifying its location in the data record.

Other SAS statements
: enable you to modify the data, create new variables, and so on.

CARDS or CARDS4 statement
: marks the end of the programming statements and the beginning of the data.

Data lines
: are records of data values.

; or ;;;;
: marks the end of the data lines. A single semicolon is used with a CARDS statement; four are required if a CARDS4 statement is used. (The examples in this book use a single semicolon in column 1 as a convention.)

Reading Data from Existing SAS Data Sets

The components of a DATA step that produces a SAS data set from one or more existing data sets are outlined here.

DATA statement
: marks the beginning of the DATA step and gives a name to the SAS data set(s) being created.

SET, MERGE or UPDATE statement
: identifies the existing SAS data sets used as input in the current DATA step. No description of the data values is needed; the descriptor portion of the existing SAS data set provides the necessary information about variables.

BY statement
: specifies the identifying variables for the SET, MERGE, or UPDATE statement. This statement is optional with a SET or a MERGE statement but is required with an UPDATE statement.

Other SAS statements
: enable you to modify the data, create new variables, and so on.

Using DATA step programming with existing SAS data sets is discussed in Chapter 4.

Generating Data from Programming Statements

It is possible to create data for a SAS data set by generating observations with programming statements, such as DO loops and assignment statements, rather than by reading data. A DATA step that reads no input goes through only one iteration. The components of a DATA step without input are outlined here.

DATA statement
: marks the beginning of the DATA step and gives a name to the SAS data set(s) being created.

Programming statements
: generate data, as with DO loops and assignment statements.

An example of a DATA step that has no input follows:

```
data invest;
   do year=1990 to 2009;
      capital+2000 + .07*(capital+2000);
      output;
   end;
   put _n_;
run;
```

The statements within the DO loop in this example are executed 20 times. The DATA step, however, has only one iteration, as shown by the value of the _N_ variable (1), which the PUT statement writes to the log in this example.

Writing a Report with a DATA Step

A DATA step can be used for the sole purpose of generating a report without creating a data set. The components of a DATA step that produces a report with PUT statements are outlined here.

DATA _NULL_;
: begins the DATA step, using the reserved data set name _NULL_, indicating that no SAS data set be created.

Data-reading or data-generating statements
: read data from an external file, instream data, or a SAS data set, or generate data, respectively.

FILE statement
: specifies the file to which the report is to be written.

Other SAS statements
: enable you to modify the data, to create new variables, and so on.

PUT statement(s)
: writes lines of the report to the file specified or to the SAS log.

Variations on the Basic DATA Step

You are not limited to the default flow of action in a DATA step, as described earlier in "The Execution Phase." These default actions can be overridden in many ways, as outlined here.

- □ You can read from more than one record to create a single observation. See the INPUT statement in Chapter 9, "SAS Language Statements," for information about line pointer controls.
- □ You can read from more than one external file with multiple INFILE and INPUT statements or with the FILEVAR= option in an INFILE statement.
- □ You can use the POINT= option in the SET statement to permit random access of a SAS data set.
- □ You can use a RETAIN statement to prevent variable values in the program data vector from being reset to missing for each iteration of the DATA step.
- □ You can create more than one SAS data set in a single DATA step by specifying the name of more than one SAS data set name in the DATA statement.
- □ You can create more than one observation in a single iteration of the DATA step. See Chapter 9 for a description of the OUTPUT statement.
- □ You do not have to execute each statement for each observation. You can use a conditional statement and, based on its result, further process the observation, output it, or delete it. See descriptions of the following statements in Chapter 9: subsetting IF, IF-THEN, SELECT, DELETE, and OUTPUT.
- □ You can output an observation before the end of the DATA step is reached. Note that if you use an OUTPUT statement in the course of the DATA step, you turn off the automatic output, the default action taken at the end of a DATA step.

- You are not required to output each observation created. You can test a variable value for a condition, and delete the observation or output it, based on the outcome of the test. See descriptions of the following statements in Chapter 9: subsetting IF, IF-THEN, SELECT, DELETE, and OUTPUT.
- When creating more than one output SAS data set, you can write an observation to different SAS data sets, depending on the outcome of the test for a condition, by specifying the output SAS data set name in the OUTPUT statement. See descriptions of the following statements in Chapter 9: subsetting IF, IF-THEN, and OUTPUT.
- You can use multiple output files and control which file is written to by PUT statements with multiple FILE statements. You can also use the FILEVAR= option in an FILE statement to open and close multiple output files.

How to Stop the DATA Step

This section discusses what causes a DATA step to stop execution and how to alter the flow of a DATA step for a given observation.

What Causes a DATA Step to Stop Executing

A DATA step that does not contain a data-reading statement (an INPUT, SET, MERGE or UPDATE statement) stops after only one iteration. Most DATA steps, however, do read input. They automatically cease execution under certain conditions, depending on the source of input data.

- A DATA step that reads raw data from instream data lines stops after the last data line is read.
- A DATA step that reads raw data from a single external file stops when end-of-file is reached.
- A DATA step that reads raw data from more than one external file stops when end-of-file is reached on any one of the input data files.
- A DATA step that reads observations from a SAS data set stops after the last observation is read.
- A DATA step that reads observations from more than one SAS data set with a single SET, MERGE, or UPDATE statement stops when all of the input data sets have been exhausted.
- A DATA step that reads observations from multiple SAS data sets with multiple SET, MERGE, or UPDATE statements stops when end-of-file is encountered by any of the data-reading statements.
- A DATA step that reads observations from a SAS data set with a SET statement that uses the POINT= option has no way to detect the end of the input SAS data set. (This method is called direct or random access.) Such a DATA step usually requires a STOP statement.

A DATA step also stops when it executes a STOP or ABORT statement. Some system options and data set options, such as OBS=, may cause a DATA step to stop earlier than it would otherwise.

Stopping the Flow for a Given Observation

There are many ways to alter the flow of the DATA step for a given observation.

□ A subsetting IF statement stops the current iteration and causes a return to the top of the DATA step when a certain condition is not met.

□ An IF-THEN RETURN statement stops the current iteration and causes a return to the top of the DATA step when a certain condition is met.

□ DO loops cause parts of the DATA step to be executed multiple times.

□ The LINK and RETURN statements alter the flow of control, execute statements following the label specified, and return control of the program to the next statement following the LINK statement.

□ The HEADER= option in the FILE statement alters the flow of control whenever a PUT statement causes a new page of output to begin; statements following the label specified in the HEADER= option are executed until a RETURN statement is encountered, at which time control returns to the point from which the HEADER= option was activated.

□ GO TO statements or the EOF= option in an INFILE statement cause the flow of execution to be altered.

□ The _N_ variable can be used to cause parts of the DATA step to execute only for particular iterations, as shown in this example.

```
if _n_=1 then
   do;
      SAS statements
   end;
```

□ A SELECT statement conditionally executes one of a group of SAS statements.

□ An OUTPUT statement in an IF-THEN construct outputs an observation before the end of the DATA step based on a condition.

□ A DELETE statement in an IF-THEN construct deletes an observation before the end of the DATA step based on a certain condition and causes a return to the top of the DATA step.

□ An ABORT statement in an IF-THEN construct can stop the execution of the DATA step and instruct the SAS System to resume execution with the next DATA or PROC step. It can also stop executing a step altogether, depending on the options specified in the ABORT statement and on the method of operation.

□ A WHERE statement or the WHERE= data set option causes certain observations to be read, based on one or more specified criteria.

Automatic Variables

Some variables are created automatically by the DATA step or by particular DATA step statements. These variables are added to the program data vector but are not output to the data set being created. The values of automatic variables are retained from one iteration of the DATA step to the next, rather than set to missing.

Automatic variables created by individual statements are documented with those statements. See the BY statement, the WINDOW statement, and "Implicit Array, Reference" in Chapter 9.

Two automatic variables are created for each DATA step: _N_ and _ERROR_. Their definitions follow:

_N_
: is initially set to 1. Each time the DATA step loops past the DATA statement, the variable _N_ is incremented by 1. The value of _N_ represents the number of times the DATA step has iterated.

ERROR
: is 0 by default but is set to 1 whenever an error is encountered, such as an input data error, a conversion error, or a math error, as in division by 0 or a floating point overflow. You can read the value of this variable to help locate errors in data records and to print an error message to the SAS log.

For example, either of the two following statement writes the contents of an input record in which an input error is encountered to the SAS log during each iteration of the DATA step:

□ `if _error_=1 then put _infile_;`

□ `if _error_ then put _infile_;`

When Variable Values Are Set to Missing Automatically

The values of all variables in the program data vector, except for automatic variables, are initially set to missing before the first iteration of the DATA step. Thereafter, when variables are set to missing depends on the source of the input, whether raw data or other SAS data sets. Each of these cases is described in the following sections.

When Reading Raw Data

At the beginning of each iteration of the DATA step, the SAS System sets the value of each variable you create in the DATA step to missing, with the following exceptions:

□ variables named in a RETAIN statement

□ variables created in a SUM statement

□ data elements in a _TEMPORARY_ array

□ any variables created with options in the FILE or INFILE statements

□ automatic variables.

The SAS System replaces the missing values as it encounters values you assign to the variables. Thus, if you use program statements to create new variables, their values in each observation are missing until you assign the values in an assignment statement, as shown in the following DATA step:

```
data new;
   input x;
   if x=1 then y=2;
   cards;
4
1
3
1
;
```

This DATA step produces a SAS data set with the following variable values:

OBS	X	Y
1	4	.
2	1	2
3	3	.
4	1	2

When X equals 1, the value of Y is set to 2. Since no other statements set Y's value when X is not equal to 1, Y remains missing (.) for those observations.

When Reading a SAS Data Set

When variables are read with a SET, MERGE, or UPDATE statement, the SAS System sets the values to missing only before the first iteration of the DATA step. (If a BY statement is present, the variable values are also set to missing when the BY group changes.) Thereafter, the variables retain their values until new values become available: for example, through an assignment statement or through the next execution of the SET, MERGE, or UPDATE statement. Variables created with options in the SET, MERGE, and UPDATE statements also retain their values from one iteration to the next.

When a data set in a match-merge operation (with a BY statement) exhausts its observations, the variables it contributes to the output data set retain their values as described earlier. That is, as long as the BY value in effect when the data set exhausts its observations does not change, the variables it contributes to the output data set retain their values from the final observation. FIRST.*variable* and LAST.*variable*, the automatic variables generated by the BY statement, both retain their values. Their initial value is 1.

When the BY value changes, the variables are set to missing and remain missing because the data set contains no more observations to provide replacement values. When a data set in a one-to-one merge operation (without a BY statement) exhausts its observations, variables it contributes to the output data set are set to missing and remain missing.

See the MERGE, SET, UPDATE, and BY statements in Chapter 9. See also the discussion of reading SAS data sets in a DATA step in "Combining SAS Data Sets" and "By-Group Processing" within Chapter 4.

Reading Raw Data

Raw data are data that do not have associated descriptor information that can be used by the SAS System.* You can use a DATA step to read raw data into a SAS data set from two sources: the job stream (that is, immediately following a CARDS or CARDS4 statement) or an external file. Raw data from either source are read with an INPUT statement.

Data Entered Instream

If you enter data in the job stream, you must use a CARDS statement. The CARDS statement and data lines occur at the end of the DATA step, following all other statements. A semicolon must appear on the line following the last data line.** An example is shown here.

```
data weight;
   input idno $ week1 week8 week16;
   loss=week1-week16;
   cards;
2477 195  177  163
2431 220  213  198
2456 173  166  155
2412 135  125  116
;
```

If your data contain semicolons, use a CARDS4 statement to precede the data lines and follow the data lines with a line containing four semicolons.

Data Stored in an External File

If your data are already stored in a file, you can specify that file in an INFILE statement in the DATA step. The INFILE statement must be executed before the INPUT statement that reads from it. The following DATA step reads data from a file specified in an INFILE statement:

```
data weight;
   infile file-specification;
   input idno $ week1 week8 week16;
   loss=week1-week16;
run;
```

■ **Host information** .... Using external files with your SAS jobs entails host-specific information. See the SAS documentation for your host system. ■

* Raw data do not include DBMS files. Data stored in DBMS files cannot be read into a SAS data file with an INPUT statement. You can use SAS/ACCESS software to read data in DBMS files and create a *SAS data view*. See "Multiple Engine Architecture" in Chapter 1.

** A semicolon appearing alone on the line immediately following the last data line is the convention used in this book. However, a PROC statement, DATA statement, or global statement ending in a semicolon on the line immediately following the last data line is sufficient.

Kinds of Data

Data values are either *character* or *numeric*. A character value is simply a sequence of characters. It can contain letters, numbers, and special characters: for example, underscores (_), pound signs (#), and ampersands (&). A numeric value usually contains only numbers, including numbers in E-notation, and sometimes a decimal point or minus sign. (You can use formatted input to enable the SAS System to read values containing certain other characters as numbers.) When read into a SAS data set, numeric values are stored in floating-point format native to the host.

Both character and numeric data can appear on data lines in standard or nonstandard form. *Standard data* are stored with one digit or character per byte. (One column in a display or printout is equivalent to one byte.) Standard data can be read with list, column, and formatted input. See "Styles of Input" later in this chapter. Examples of simple, standard data include

```
ARKANSAS
1166.42
```

Data that are not in standard form can be read only with the aid of informats. Examples of *nonstandard data* include numeric values containing commas and dollar signs, date/time values, and hexadecimal and binary values.

A value read with an INPUT statement is assumed to be numeric unless one of the following three things is true:

□ A dollar sign follows the variable name in the INPUT statement.

□ A character informat is used.

□ The variable has been previously defined as character: for example, in a LENGTH statement, by an assignment statement, or in an expression.

If a data value is read that is incompatible with the type specified for that variable, the SAS System takes the action described in "Invalid Data and How They Are Handled" later in this chapter.

Numeric Data

Numeric data can be represented in several ways. For example, the standard numeric data values 23 and −23 can be expressed as shown in Table 2.2. Standard numeric data values and negative data values, as shown in the table, can be read without any special instructions to the system.

Table 2.2 *Standard Numeric Data*

Data Description	Data	Result
input right aligned	23	23
input not aligned	23	23
input left aligned	23	23
input with leading zeros	00023	23
input with decimal point	23.0	23
in E-notation, $2.3 x 10^{1}$	2.3E1	23
in E-notation, $230 x 10^{-1}$	230E−1	23
minus sign for negative numbers	−23	−23

Numeric data in forms such as fractions, integer binary and real binary, and hexadecimal can be read only with the instructions provided by SAS informats. You also must use informats to read time and date values as well as numeric data containing special embedded characters ($, %, (), commas, and blanks) or blanks which must be read as zeros. For a complete list of numeric data items that you must read with SAS informats, see "Numeric Informats" in Chapter 3, "Components of the SAS Language."

Table 2.3 shows examples of numeric input data that either must be read with an informat or are invalid. See "Invalid Data and How They Are Handled" later in this chapter for information on how the SAS System handles invalid numeric input.

Table 2.3 *Nonstandard and Invalid Numeric Data*

Data	Reason
2 3	embedded blank requires COMMA. or BZ. informat
− 23	embedded blank requires COMMA. or BZ. informat
2,341	comma requires COMMA. informat
(23)	parentheses require COMMA. informat
C4A2	hexadecimal value requires HEX. informat
1MAR90	date requires DATE. informat
23−	invalid numeric data; sign should precede the number
..	invalid numeric data; missing value is a single period
J23	invalid numeric data; not a number

Remember the following points when reading numeric data:

- □ A minus sign preceding the number (without an intervening blank) indicates a negative value.
- □ Leading zeros and the placement of a value in the input field do not affect the value assigned to the variable. Leading zeros and leading and trailing blanks are not stored with the value. Unlike some languages, FORTRAN for example, the SAS System does not read trailing blanks as zeros by default. To cause trailing blanks to be read as zeros, use the BZ. informat described in Chapter 13, "SAS Informats."
- □ Numeric data can have leading and trailing blanks but cannot have embedded blanks (unless read with a COMMA. or BZ. informat).
- □ To read decimal values from input lines that do not contain explicit decimal points, indicate where the decimal point belongs by a decimal parameter with column input or an informat with formatted input. See the INPUT statement in Chapter 9 for more information. An explicit decimal point in the input data overrides any decimal specification in the INPUT statement.

Character Data

Input data can include any character. However, be careful when your input data include one of the following:

- □ leading blanks
- □ semicolons when data follow a CARDS statement.

Character values beginning with blanks can cause problems with list input because leading and trailing blanks are trimmed from a character value before the value is assigned to a variable. To read values with leading blanks, use formatted input with the $CHAR. informat. For more information, see the $CHAR. informat in Chapter 13 and the INPUT statement in Chapter 9.

If your data contain semicolons, you must use the CARDS4 statement and signify the end of the data with four consecutive semicolons. See the CARDS and CARDS4 statements in Chapter 9 for more information.

Invalid Data and How They Are Handled

An input value is invalid if it

- □ requires an informat that is not available
- □ does not conform to the informat specified
- □ cannot be read with the input style specified
- □ is read as standard numeric data (no dollar sign or informat) and does not conform to the rules for standard SAS numbers
- □ is out of range (too large or too small).

■ **Host Information** .... The range for numeric values is host-dependent. See the SAS documentation for your host system. ■

When an error in an input value is encountered, the SAS System

- □ sets the value of the variable being read to missing or to the value specified with the INVALIDDATA= system option.
- □ prints an invalid data note in the SAS log.
- □ prints the input line and column number containing the invalid value in the SAS log. If a line contains unprintable characters, it is printed in hexadecimal form. A scale is printed above the input line to help determine column numbers.
- □ sets the automatic variable _ERROR_ to 1 for the current observation.

Styles of Input

The INPUT statement reads raw data into a SAS data set. The different styles of input available in an INPUT statement are documented in detail in Chapter 9. Here the basic concepts of reading raw data are presented.

There are four styles of input available for reading raw data from external files or instream data. The style you select depends on the layout of the data values in the data records. You are not limited to one style of input; you can combine whatever styles you need in a single INPUT statement. For details about column, formatted, list, and named input, see Chapter 9.

List Input

List input uses a scanning method for locating data values. Data values are not required to be aligned in columns but must be separated by at least one blank (or other defined delimiter). List input requires only that you specify the variable names and a dollar sign if defining a character variable. You do not have to specify the location of the data fields.

An example of simple list input follows:

```
data scores;
   length name $ 12;
   input name $ score1 score2;
   cards;
Riley 1132 1187
Henderson 1015 1102
;
```

Simple list input places several restrictions on the type of data that can be read:

- □ Input values must be separated by at least one blank, the default delimiter, or by the delimiter specified with the DELIMITER= option in the INFILE statement.
- □ Missing values, both numeric and character, must be represented by periods, not blanks.
- □ Character input values can be no longer than 8 bytes unless a statement prior to the INPUT statement, such as a LENGTH statement, defines the variable with a longer length. (A longer character value can be read, but only 8 bytes will actually be stored.)
- □ Character values cannot contain embedded blanks.
- □ Fields must be read in order.
- □ Data must be in standard numeric or character format.

Modifying list input List input can be made more flexible by the addition of format modifiers; input of this kind is called modified list input. Format modifiers enable you to use list input to read nonstandard data that require the additional instructions provided by SAS informats in order to be read by the SAS System.

The & (ampersand) format modifier enables you to read character values containing embedded blanks with list input and to specify a character informat. The : (colon) format modifier enables you to use list input but also to specify an informat after a variable name, whether character or numeric. See Chapter 9 for more information about list input.

Column Input

Column input enables you to read standard data values that are aligned in columns in the data records. Specify the variable name, follow it with a dollar sign if it is a character variable, and specify the columns within which the data values are to be located in each record, as in the following example:

```
data scores;
   input name $ 1-12 score1 17-20  score2 27-30;
   cards;
Riley           1132       1187
Henderson       1015       1102
;
```

To be read with column input, data values must be

- □ in the same field on all the input lines
- □ in standard numeric or character form.

Features of column input include the following:

□ Character values can contain embedded blanks.

□ Character values can be from 1 to 200 characters long.

□ No placeholder, such as a single period, is required for missing data.

□ Input values can be read in any order, regardless of their position in the record.

□ Values or parts of values can be reread.

□ Both leading and trailing blanks within the field are ignored.

□ Values need not be separated by blanks or other delimiters.

Formatted Input

Formatted input enables you to read nonstandard data for which the SAS System requires additional instructions. Formatted input is typically used with pointer controls that give you control over the position of the input pointer in the input buffer when reading data. The INPUT statement in the following DATA step uses formatted input and pointer controls. Note that $12. and COMMA5. are informats and +4 and +6 are column pointer controls.

```
data scores;
   input name $12. +4 score1 comma5. +6 score2 comma5.;
   cards;
Riley           1,132      1,187
Henderson       1,015      1,102
;
```

Formatted input combines the flexibility of using informats with many of the features of column input. Important points about formatted input include the following:

□ Characters values can contain embedded blanks.

□ Character values can be from 1 to 200 characters long.

□ No placeholder, such as a single period, is required for missing data.

□ With the use of pointer controls to position the pointer, input values can be read in any order, regardless of their position in the record.

□ Values or parts of values can be reread.

□ Formatted input enables you to read data stored in nonstandard form, such as packed decimal or numbers with commas.

Named Input

Named input is used to read records in which data values are preceded by the name of the variable and an equal sign, as in the following example:

```
name=riley score1=1132 score2=1187
```

The following INPUT statement can read this line of data:

```
input name=$ score1= score2=;
```

Note that when an equal sign follows a variable in an INPUT statement, the SAS System expects that data remaining on the input line contain only named input values. You cannot switch to another form of input in the same INPUT statement after using named input.

Additional Data-reading Features

In addition to different styles of input, there are many tools to meet the needs of different data-reading situations. You can use options in the INFILE statement in combination with the INPUT statement to give you additional control over the reading of data records. For example with list input, the DELIMITER= option in the following INFILE statement enables the SAS System to read data values separated by a delimiter other than a blank, the default:

```
data one;
   infile file-specification delimiter=',';
   input idno score1 score2 score3;
run;
```

Note that the INFILE statement can be used to control the reading of data lines whether they are read from an external file or from instream data. Use the CARDS option in the INFILE statement when reading instream data, as shown in this example:

```
data one;
   infile cards delimiter=',';
   input idno score1 score2 score3;
   cards;
4956,121,223,421
4948,119,111,398
;
```

Table 2.4 lists common data-reading tasks and the appropriate features available in the INPUT and INFILE statements. For complete details on these and other data-reading features, see the INFILE and INPUT statements in Chapter 9.

Table 2.4 *Data-reading Tasks and SAS Tools*

Data-reading Tasks	SAS Tools
Read multiple records to create a single observation	#*n* or / line pointer control in the INPUT statement
Read a single record to create more than one observation	trailing @@ in the INPUT statement trailing @ with multiple INPUT and OUTPUT statements
Read variable-length data fields and variable-length records	LENGTH= option in INFILE statement $VARYING*w*. informat in INPUT statement
Read from more than one input file; control program flow when the end of an input file is reached	EOF= option in INFILE statement END= option in INFILE statement multiple INFILE and INPUT statements FILEVAR= option in an INFILE statement
Read a file with varying record layouts	IF-THEN statements with multiple INPUT statements, using trailing @ as necessary
Read hierarchical files	IF-THEN statements with multiple INPUT statements, using trailing @ as necessary
Read and maintain, instead of truncate, leading blanks	$CHAR. informat in INPUT statement
Read with list input data that contain a delimiter other than blanks	DELIMITER= option in INFILE statement
Control the length of the data lines available to the input pointer	LINESIZE= option in INFILE statement
Specify first and last observations to be read	FIRSTOBS= and OBS= data set options
Specify the first and last record to be read	FIRSTOBS= and OBS= options in the INFILE statement
Control action taken when INPUT statement reads past end of input line (because of missing values or errors in data)	FLOWOVER, MISSOVER, and STOPOVER options in INFILE statement
Read data that contain the standard tab character	EXPANDTABS option in INFILE statement

Missing Values in Input Data

Most collections of data include some missing values. These values can be recognized as missing at the time the SAS System reads them. Missing values can be coded with a blank or a single period, depending on the style of input you use. Numeric data can contain characters that represent special missing values when you want to distinguish between types of missing values.

Coding Missing Values

You can represent missing values on data lines for numeric and character variables with either blanks or single periods. If list input is not used to read data, columns containing missing values can simply be left blank, as in the following example:

```
data testscor;
   input name $ 1-6 pretest 8-9 posttest 11-12;
   cards;
ANN    92 96
SUSAN 84
BILL   81 95
more data lines
;
```

The value for POSTTEST in the second observation is blank and is recorded as missing.

List input requires that missing values for both numeric and character data be represented with periods. With list input, the SAS System begins reading the next data value at the next nonblank column; therefore, if a missing value is simply left blank, the SAS System reads the value of the following variable in place of the value that is missing.* To read the same data lines with list input, you must code the missing value in the second record with a period, as in this example:

```
data testscor;
   input name $ pretest posttest;
   cards;
ANN    92 96
SUSAN 84 .
BILL   81 95
more data lines
;
```

Missing Values with Special Meanings

The SAS System enables you to differentiate among classes of missing values in numeric data. For numeric variables only, you can designate up to 27 special missing values (the letters A through Z and the special character underscore (_)) when you want to differentiate among missing values. When data values contain characters in numeric fields that you want the SAS System to interpret as special missing values, use a MISSING statement to specify those characters.

---

* To read a single period as the value of a character variable instead of a missing value, use the $CHAR. informat.

In the survey data shown in the following example, the letter R could be used to indicate that a respondent refused to respond to a question, and the letter X could indicate that the response is invalid. The MISSING statement in the following DATA step causes the values R and X to be read as special missing values:

```
data survey;
   missing r x;
   input id questn1;
   cards;
8401 2
8402 R
8403 1
8404 X
8405 2
more data lines
;
```

The value for the numeric variable QUESTN1 is stored as an R for the second observation and as an X for the fourth.

Without the MISSING statement, this example would have the following results:

- □ The values R and X would be read as invalid numeric values.
- □ Messages about invalid numeric data would be written to the SAS log.
- □ Values for the variable QUESTN1 would be stored as missing, not as R and X, in the second and fourth observations of the data set SURVEY.

Note that missing values can also be represented as a single period, followed by the special missing value character, as in the following data lines:

```
8401 2
8402 .R
8403 1
8404 .X
8405 2
```

Reading Binary Data

The SAS System can read data stored in binary form with the special instructions supplied by SAS informats. You can use formatted input and specify the informat in the INPUT statement. The informat you choose is determined by three factors:

- □ the type of number being read: integer binary, packed decimal, positive integer binary, or real binary
- □ the type of machine on which the program will run
- □ whether you want to be able to run the program on more than one machine.

Different computers store numeric binary data in different forms. IBM® 370, Hewlett-Packard® 9000, Data General MV ECLIPSE®, and PRIME 50 Series™ computers store bytes in one order. IBM-compatible microcomputers and VAX™ computers store bytes in a different order called byte-reversed. The SAS System provides a number of informats for reading binary data and corresponding formats for writing binary data. Some of these informats read data in native mode: that is, the byte-ordering system that is standard for the machine. Other informats force the data to be read by the IBM 370 standard, regardless of the native mode of the machine. The informats that read in native or IBM 370 mode are listed in Table 2.5.

Table 2.5 *SAS Informats for Reading Binary Data*

Description	Native Mode Informats	IBM 370 Mode Informats
Integer Binary	IB*w.d*	S370FIB*w.d*
Packed Decimal	PD*w.d*	S370FPD*w.d*
Positive Integer Binary	PIB*w.d*	S370PIB*w.d*
Real Binary	RB*w.d*	S370FRB*w.d*

If a SAS program that reads binary data will be run on only one type of machine, you can use the native mode informats and formats. However, if you want to write SAS programs that can be run on multiple machines using different byte-storage systems, use the IBM 370 informats. The IBM 370 informats enable you to write SAS programs that can read data in this format and that can be run in any SAS environment, regardless of the standard for storing numeric data.* The IBM 370 informats can also be used to read data originally written with the corresponding native mode formats on an IBM mainframe.

For more information on binary data, see "Numeric Values" in Chapter 3. For a complete description of the informats, see Chapter 13. For a discussion of how numeric binary data are written, see Chapter 14, "SAS Formats."

Reading Column-Binary Data

Column-binary data storage is an older form of data storage that is no longer widely used and is not needed by most SAS users. Column-binary data storage compresses data so that more than 80 items of data can be stored on a single punched card. The obvious advantage is that this method enables you to store more data in the same amount of space. There are disadvantages, however. Special card readers are required and difficulties are frequently encountered when such data are read. Because multi-punched decks and card-image data sets remain in existence,

---

IBM is a registered trademark of International Business Machines Corporation.

Hewlett-Packard is a registered trademark of Hewlett-Packard Company.

ECLIPSE is a registered trademark of Data General Corporation

PRIME 50 Series is a trademark of Prime Computer, Inc.

VAX is a trademark of Digital Equipment Corporation.

* For example, using this informat you could download data from a mainframe to a PC and use the IBM 370 informats to read the data.

however, the SAS System provides informats for reading column-binary data. This section is provided for the small audience that still needs to read data stored in column-binary or multi-punched form.

The next section discusses the SAS tools that you need to know to read column-binary data. A detailed explanation of column-binary data storage follows.

How to Read Column-Binary Data

To read column-binary data with the SAS System, you need to know the following:

- □ how to select the appropriate SAS column-binary informat
- □ how to set the LRECL= option in the INFILE statement
- □ how to use pointer controls.

Table 2.6 lists and describes SAS column-binary informats.

Table 2.6 *SAS Informats for Reading Column-Binary Data*

Informat Name	Description
$CB*w*.	reads standard character data from column-binary files
CB*w*.	reads standard numeric data from column-binary files
PUNCH.*d*	reads whether a row is punched
ROW*w.d*	reads a column-binary field down a card column

Because each card column of column-binary data is expanded to two bytes before the fields are read, set the LRECL= to 160 in the INFILE statement for the input file of column-binary data. For example, to read column-binary data from a file, use an INFILE statement in the following form before the INPUT statement that reads the data:

```
infile file-specification lrecl=160;
```

Note that the expansion of each column of column-binary data into two bytes does *not* affect the position of the column pointer. For example, using the absolute column pointer control @ is done as usual because the informats automatically compute the true location on the doubled record. If a value is in column 23, use the pointer control @23 to move the pointer there.

Description of Column-Binary Data Storage

The arrangement and numbering of rows in a column on punched cards originated with the Hollerith system of encoding characters and numbers. It is based on using a pair of values to represent either a character or a numeric digit. This pair of values is related to the arrangement of rows on a punched card since each value in the pair corresponds to a physical punch in a particular area of the card column. The zone component of the pair can have the values 12, 11, 0 (or 10), or not punched. The zone portion of the punched card is the first three rows. The digit component of the pair can have the values 1 through 9, or not punched. The digit portion of the card is the fourth through the twelfth rows. Thus, in the Hollerith system, each column on a card has a maximum of two punches, one punch in the zone portion and one in the digit portion. These punches correspond to a pair of values, and each pair of values corresponds to a specific alphabetic character, or to a sign and a numeric digit.

Figure 2.6 shows the multi-punch combinations corresponding to letters of the alphabet.

Figure 2.6 *Columns and Rows in a Punched Card*

	row	A	B	C	D	E	F	G	H	I	J	K	L	M	N	O	P	Q	R	S	T	U	V	W	X	Y	Z
zone portion	12	X	X	X	X	X	X	X	X	X	-	-	-	-	-	-	-	-	-	-	-	-	-	-	-	-	-
	11	-	-	-	-	-	-	-	-	-	X	X	X	X	X	X	X	X	X	-	-	-	-	-	-	-	-
	10	-	-	-	-	-	-	-	-	-	-	-	-	-	-	-	-	-	-	X	X	X	X	X	X	X	X
digit portion	1	X	-	-	-	-	-	-	-	-	X	-	-	-	-	-	-	-	-	-	-	-	-	-	-	-	-
	2	-	X	-	-	-	-	-	-	-	-	X	-	-	-	-	-	-	-	X	-	-	-	-	-	-	-
	3	-	-	X	-	-	-	-	-	-	-	-	X	-	-	-	-	-	-	-	X	-	-	-	-	-	-
	4	-	-	-	X	-	-	-	-	-	-	-	-	X	-	-	-	-	-	-	-	X	-	-	-	-	-
	5	-	-	-	-	X	-	-	-	-	-	-	-	-	X	-	-	-	-	-	-	-	X	-	-	-	-
	6	-	-	-	-	-	X	-	-	-	-	-	-	-	-	X	-	-	-	-	-	-	-	X	-	-	-
	7	-	-	-	-	-	-	X	-	-	-	-	-	-	-	-	X	-	-	-	-	-	-	-	X	-	-
	8	-	-	-	-	-	-	-	X	-	-	-	-	-	-	-	-	X	-	-	-	-	-	-	-	X	-
	9	-	-	-	-	-	-	-	-	X	-	-	-	-	-	-	-	-	X	-	-	-	-	-	-	-	X
alphabetic character		A	B	C	D	E	F	G	H	I	J	K	L	M	N	O	P	Q	R	S	T	U	V	W	X	Y	Z

The SAS System stores each column of column-binary data in two bytes. Since each column has only 12 positions and since 2 bytes contain 16 positions, the 4 extra positions within the bytes are located at the beginning of each byte. Figure 2.7 shows the correspondence between the rows of a punched card and the positions within 2 bytes that the SAS System uses to store them. The SAS System stores a punched position as a binary 1 bit and an unpunched position as a binary 0 bit.

Figure 2.7 *Column-Binary Representation on a Punched Card*

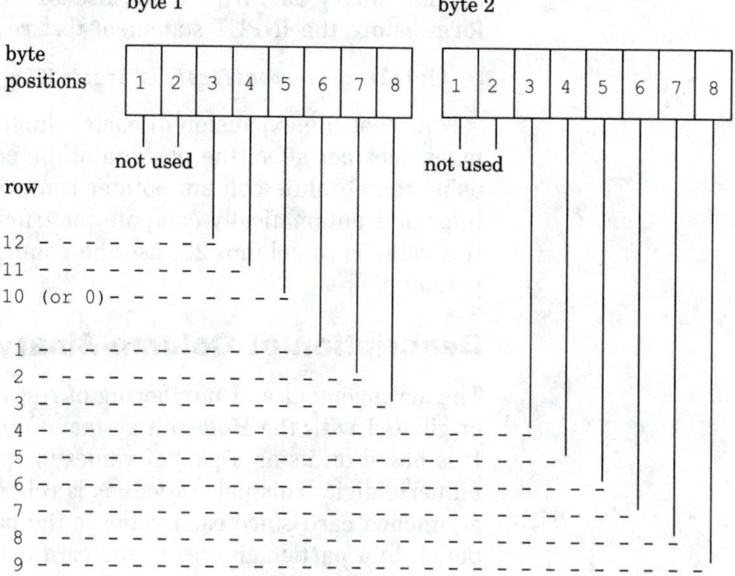

External Files

The following sections define external files and explain how to read from or write to these files in a SAS job.

Definition

At times during your SAS session, you will want to be able to use *external files*: that is, files that contain data or text or files in which you want to store data or text. These files are not organized and managed by the SAS System.* For example, you use external files in a SAS session to

□ read data already stored in a file as input to a SAS DATA step

□ store printed reports created by a SAS procedure in a file

□ store the SAS log from your session in a file

□ submit a file containing SAS programming statements for processing by the SAS System

□ identify a file containing SAS programming statements that you want to be executed automatically each time you invoke the SAS System

□ write data with PUT statements.

SAS programming statements, records of raw data, and procedure output created by SAS procedures are all stored in files that are managed and maintained by the host system, not by the SAS System. These files are referred to as external files throughout SAS documentation.

SAS Statements to Use with External Files

To read from or write to an external file in a SAS job, reference the file in the appropriate SAS statement either directly or indirectly. To reference a file directly, simply specify in quotes its physical name, the name by which the operating system recognizes it. To reference one indirectly, first identify the file to the SAS System and assign it a *file reference* with a FILENAME statement.** Then specify the file reference, called a *fileref*, in a statement that identifies a file that will be read from or written to in your SAS job.

■ **Host information** .... Using external files with your SAS jobs entails significant host-specific information. Refer to the SAS documentation for your host system. .... ■

* External files do not include database management system (DBMS) files.

** Under some host systems, you can also use a host command to assign a fileref.

The following statements control reading and writing of external files.

□ DATA Step Statements

INFILE
: identifies the external file containing raw input data to be read by an INPUT statement in the DATA step.

FILE
: identifies the external file where lines are to be written by PUT statements in a DATA step.

□ Global Statements

%INCLUDE
: reads into your SAS program SAS statements and data lines from external files and executes the statements.

FILENAME
: associates a SAS file reference (fileref) with the name of an external file.

As an example, you can use an INFILE statement to refer directly to an external file that contains raw data, as in this example:

```
infile 'external-file';
```

You can also use an INFILE statement in combination with a FILENAME statement, or a host command that assigns a fileref, for the same task, as in this example:

```
filename fileref 'external-file';
infile fileref;
```

Note that a physical filename is enclosed in quotes in a SAS statement. A fileref is not enclosed in quotes.

When using many files from the same aggregate storage location (such as a directory, partitioned data set (PDS), or MACLIB), you can use a single fileref, followed by a filename enclosed in parentheses, to access many files. Assign a fileref to an aggregate storage location with a FILENAME statement or with an appropriate host command. Then in a FILE, INFILE, or %INCLUDE statement, specify the fileref followed by, in parentheses, the name of a file that resides in that location, as shown here:

```
filename fileref 'aggregate-storage-location';
infile fileref(file);
```

For more details about using external files, see the FILENAME statement in Chapter 9 and the SAS documentation for your host system.

CHAPTER 3 Components of the SAS® Language

(continued on next page)

(continued from previous page)

Introduction

This chapter introduces the components of the SAS language for which reference entries appear in Part 2, Reference. Those components include statements, functions, CALL routines, informats, formats, data set options, and system options. This chapter provides general information about each component. It also discusses three other components of the SAS language: numeric values, character values, and variables.

SAS Statements

A *SAS statement* is a series of items that may include keywords, SAS names, special characters, and operators. All SAS statements end with a semicolon. A SAS statement either requests the SAS System to perform an operation or gives information to the system.

This book covers two kinds of SAS statements:

- □ those used in DATA step programming
- □ those that are global in scope and can be used anywhere in a SAS program.

The *SAS Procedures Guide, Version 6, Third Edition* gives detailed descriptions of the SAS statements that are specific to each SAS procedure.

DATA Step Statements

DATA step statements are those that can appear in the DATA step. They can be either executable or declarative. *Executable statements* result in some action during individual iterations of the DATA step; *declarative statements* supply information to the SAS System and take effect when the system compiles program statements.

Table 3.1 shows the SAS executable and declarative statements that can be used in the DATA step.

Table 3.1 *Executable and Declarative Statements in the DATA Step*

Executable Statements	Declarative Statements
ABORT	ARRAY
assignment	ATTRIB
CALL	BY
DELETE	CARDS
DISPLAY	CARDS4
DO	DATA
ERROR	DROP
FILE	END
GO TO	FORMAT
IF	INFORMAT
IF-THEN/ELSE	KEEP
INFILE	LABEL
INPUT	LENGTH
LINK	RENAME
LIST	RETAIN
LOSTCARD	statement label
MERGE	WHERE
OUTPUT	WINDOW
PUT	
RETURN	
SELECT	
SET	
STOP	
SUM	
UPDATE	

In addition to being either executable or declarative, SAS DATA step statements can be grouped into four categories, depending on their function. This grouping is just a convenient way of thinking about various types of programming statements. The groupings do not affect the way the statements work. The four categories of DATA step statements are

- □ action statements that let you
  - □ create and modify variables
  - □ select only certain observations to process in the DATA step
  - □ look for errors in the input data
  - □ work with observations as they are being created.
- □ control statements that let you
  - □ skip statements for certain observations
  - □ change the order that statements are executed
  - □ transfer control from one part of a program to another.
- □ file-handling statements that let you
  - □ work with files used as input to the data set
  - □ work with files to be written by the DATA step.

□ information statements that let you

  □ give the SAS System additional information about the program data vector

  □ give the SAS System additional information about the data set or data sets being created.

Table 3.2 lists and briefly describes the DATA step statements by category. For descriptions of individual statements, see Chapter 9, "SAS Language Statements."

Table 3.2 *Categories and Descriptions of DATA Step Statements*

Category	Statements	Description
Action	ABORT	stops execution of the current DATA step, SAS job, or SAS session.
	assignment	evaluates an expression and stores the result in a variable.
	CALL	invokes a SAS CALL routine.
	DELETE	stops processing of the current observation and excludes it from any data set being created.
	ERROR	sets _ERROR_ to 1 and, optionally, writes a message to the SAS log.
	LIST	writes to the SAS log the input data records for the observation being processed.
	LOSTCARD	resynchronizes the input data when the SAS System encounters a missing record in data with multiple records per observation.
	null	acts as a placeholder. *
	OUTPUT	writes the current observation to a SAS data set.
	STOP	stops execution of the current DATA step.
	subsetting IF	causes the DATA step to continue processing only the observations that meet a condition specified on the IF statement.
	sum	adds the result of an expression to an accumulator variable.
	WHERE	selects observations from SAS data sets that meet a particular condition.
Control	DO	designates a group of statements to be executed as a unit.
	iterative DO	causes the statements between the DO and END statements to be executed repetitively, based on the value of an index variable.
	DO OVER	executes the statements in a DO loop for the elements in an implicit array.
	DO UNTIL	executes the statements in a DO loop repetitively until a condition is true.

(continued)

Table 3.2 *(continued)*

Category	Statements	Description
	DO WHILE	executes the statements in a DO loop repetitively while a condition is true.
	END	ends a DO group or SELECT group.
	GO TO	moves execution immediately to the statement label indicated.
	IF-THEN/ELSE	executes a SAS statement for observations meeting specific conditions and optionally provides an alternative when the condition is not satisfied.
	LINK	causes the SAS System to jump to a labeled statement in the step and continue execution until it encounters a RETURN statement.
	RETURN	stops executing statements at the current point in the DATA step and returns to a predetermined point.
	SELECT	conditionally executes one of several SAS statements or groups of statements.
	statement label	identifies a statement referred to by another statement.
File-handling	BY	controls the operation of a SET, MERGE, or UPDATE statement and sets up special grouping attributes.
	CARDS	indicates to the SAS System that data lines follow.
	CARDS4	indicates to the SAS System that data lines containing semicolons follow.
	DATA	begins a DATA step and provides names for any output SAS data sets.
	DISPLAY	displays a window created with the WINDOW statement. The DISPLAY statement shares some characteristics of information statements.
	FILE	specifies the current output file for PUT statements.
	INFILE	identifies an external file containing raw input data to be read by subsequent INPUT statements.
	INPUT	describes the arrangement of values in an input record and assigns input values to corresponding SAS variables.
	MERGE	joins observations from two or more SAS data sets into single observations.
	PUT	writes lines to the SAS log, to the SAS procedure output file, or to the external file specified in the most recent FILE statement.
	SET	reads observations from one or more SAS data sets.
	UPDATE	updates a master file by applying transactions. Both transaction and master files are SAS data sets.
Information	ARRAY	temporarily defines a set of variables to be processed the same way.
	ATTRIB	associates a format, informat, label, and length with one or more variables.
	DROP	excludes variables from output SAS data sets.
	FORMAT	associates formats with variables in a DATA step.

(continued)

Table 3.2 *(continued)*

Category	Statements	Description
	INFORMAT	associates informats with variables.
	KEEP	includes variables in output SAS data sets.
	LABEL	associates descriptive labels with variables.
	LENGTH	specifies the number of bytes for storing the values of SAS variables.
	RENAME	specifies new names for variables in output SAS data sets.
	RETAIN	causes a variable created by an INPUT or assignment statement to retain its value from one iteration of the DATA step to the next.
	WINDOW	creates customized windows for applications. The WINDOW statement shares some characteristics of file-handling statements.

* Because it can be branched to, the null statement is considered an executable statement in the DATA step. However, the null statement can appear anywhere in a SAS program.

Global Statements

Global statements can be used anywhere in a SAS program. They generally provide information to the SAS System, request information or data, move between different modes of execution, or set values for system options. Global statements are not executable; they take effect as soon as the SAS System compiles program statements.

Other SAS software products have additional global statements that are used with those products. For information, see the SAS documentation for those products.

Table 3.3 lists and describes SAS global statements, organized by function into five categories:

□ data identification statements that associate reference names or values with other libraries, files, or input data values.

□ log control statements that enable you to alter the appearance of the SAS log.

□ host system statements that enable you to access the host system directly.

□ output control statements that enable you to add titles and footnotes to your SAS output.

□ program control statements that govern the way the SAS System processes your SAS program. For instance, program control statements enable you to include data lines or statements from other files, issue SAS display manager commands, or change system options from within the SAS code.

Table 3.3 *Categories and Descriptions of Global Statements*

Category	Statements	Description
Data Identification	FILENAME	temporarily associates a valid SAS name with an external file or an output device.
	LIBNAME	temporarily associates a SAS library reference (libref) with the physical name of a SAS data library.
	MISSING	assigns characters in input data to represent special missing values for numeric data.
Log Control	comment	documents the purpose of the job.
	PAGE	skips to a new page in the SAS log.
	SKIP	skips a number of lines you specify in the SAS log.
Host System	X	issues a host system command from within a SAS session.
Output Control	FOOTNOTE	prints up to ten lines of text at the bottom of the procedure output.
	TITLE	prints up to ten lines of text at the top of each page of SAS output.
Program Control	DM	submits SAS display manager or text editor commands as SAS statements.
	ENDSAS	terminates a SAS job or session after the current DATA or PROC step.
	%INCLUDE	accesses SAS statements and data lines in an external file, from earlier lines in the same session, or from the keyboard, and submits the statements for execution.
	%LIST	lists lines entered earlier in the current session.
	OPTIONS	temporarily changes the value of one or more SAS system options.
	RUN	executes the previously entered SAS statements or RUN group.
	%RUN	ends source statements following a %INCLUDE statement, when the include operation specifies keyboard-entry source.

SAS Functions

A *SAS function* returns a value from a computation or system manipulation that requires zero or more arguments. Although most functions use arguments supplied by the user, a few obtain their arguments from the host operating system. The syntax of a function consists of a function name and function arguments; the arguments must be enclosed in parentheses. For example, use the following form for a function with two arguments:

function-name(*argument-1*,*argument-2*)

Parentheses must always be supplied even if the function does not require an argument.

A function must be used as part of a SAS statement. SAS functions are used in DATA step programming statements and in some statistical procedures.

Consider the following examples of functions and arguments:

- `dollars=int(cash);`
- `if sum(cash,credit)>1000 then put company ' is profitable';`
- `least=min(sum(of x1-x10),y);`

SAS functions fall into a number of categories: arithmetic, array, truncation, mathematical, trigonometric and hyperbolic, probability, quantile, sample statistics, random number, financial, character, date and time, state and ZIP code, and special functions. The functions are listed by category later in this chapter.

Some other SAS products also offer DATA step functions. Refer to the documentation pertaining to the specific SAS product for additional information about these functions.

Using Function Arguments

Function arguments can be variable names, constants, or expressions, including expressions involving other functions, as shown in the following examples:

- `x=max(cash,credit);`
- `x=sqrt(1500);`
- `s=repeat('----+',16);`
- `x=min((enroll-drop),(enroll-fail));`

Functions with More Than One Argument

Function arguments must be preceded by the word OF or separated by commas. Normally, arguments are separated by commas when functions contain more than one argument. Variable lists preceded by OF and arrays are compact ways of supplying arguments for functions, as shown in the following examples:

function-name(OF *variable-1–variable-n*)
function-name(OF *variable-1 variable-2 variable-3* . . .)
function-name(OF *array-name*{*})
function-name(OF *_NUMERIC_*)
function-name(OF *variable-–variable*)

Note: The two dashes or double minus signs appearing in the last function in the previous list are not misprints. The function must contain both symbols. See Chapter 4, "Rules of the SAS Language," for more information on SAS variable lists.

Consider the following examples:

- `a=sum(of x1-x100 y1-y100);`
- `a=sum(of x  y  z);`

□ `a=sum(x1,x2,x3,x4);`

□
```
array y{10} y1-y10;
x=sum(of y{*});
z=sum(of y1-y10);
```

Note that the two assignment statements in the last example produce the same result. Both explicit and implicit arrays can be used in this way. Note that the asterisk cannot be used with _TEMPORARY_ arrays. See Chapter 4 and the "Explicit ARRAY Statement" in Chapter 9 for more information on array processing.

Restrictions on Arguments

Some functions require that their arguments be restricted within a certain range; for example, the argument of the LOG function must be greater than 0. Most functions do not permit missing values as arguments. Some of the exceptions are the sample statistics functions and some of the financial functions. If the value of an argument is invalid (for example, missing or outside a certain range), the SAS System prints an error message and sets the result to a missing value.

In general, the allowed range of the arguments is machine-dependent (for example, as with the EXP function). Note also that for some probability functions, combinations of extreme values can cause convergence problems. When this occurs, a missing value is returned and an error message is printed.

Characteristics of Target Variables

Some character functions produce resulting variables, or *target variables*, with a default length of 200 bytes. Numeric target variables have default lengths of 8. Character functions to which the default target variable lengths do not apply are shown in Table 3.4:

Table 3.4 *Target Variables*

Function	Target Variable Type	Target Variable Length (bytes)
BYTE	character	1
COMPRESS	character	length of first argument
INPUT	character	width of informat
	numeric	8
LEFT	character	length of argument
PUT	character	width of format
REVERSE	character	length of argument
RIGHT	character	length of argument
SCAN	character	200
SUBSTR	character	length of first argument
TRANSLATE	character	length of first argument
TRIM	character	length of argument
UPCASE	character	length of argument

Notes on Sample Statistic Functions

The SAS System contains 15 functions whose results are sample statistics of the values of the arguments. The functions correspond to the statistics produced by the MEANS procedure. The computing method for each statistic is discussed in Chapter 1, "SAS Elementary Statistics Procedures," in the *SAS Procedures Guide*. In each case, the statistic is calculated for the nonmissing values of the arguments.

Notes on Random Number Functions

Random number functions return variates generated from various distributions. These random numbers are controlled by an initial seed value specified by the user. The given seed is used to obtain the first observation in the stream of random numbers. It is not possible to control the seed values and, therefore, the random numbers after the initialization.

On the first execution of a function, a nonpositive argument for *seed* indicates that a seed equal to the computer clock time at execution is to be used. With each execution, the random number function returns an observation and internally updates the seed. Although the current seed changes internally each time the function is executed, the value of the seed argument remains unchanged.

The CALL routines are SAS System alternatives to generate random numbers. With CALL routines, the user has a greater control of the seed and random number streams. For details on individual CALL routines, see Chapter 12, "SAS CALL Routines."

Notes on Financial Functions

The SAS System contains ten functions that compute depreciation. Each DEP*xxx* function computes the depreciation for a single time period. Each DACC*xxx* function computes the accumulated depreciation up to the period specified.

The period argument can be fractional for all of the functions except DEPDBSL and DACCDBSL. For fractional arguments, the depreciation is prorated between the two consecutive time periods preceding and following the fractional period.

▶ ***Caution:** Verify the depreciation method for fractional periods.*

You must verify whether this method is appropriate to use with fractional periods because many depreciation schedules, specified as tables, have special rules for fractional periods.

Functions by Category

SAS functions are grouped into the categories shown in Table 3.5.

Table 3.5 *Categories and Descriptions of Functions*

Category	Function	Description
Arithmetic	ABS	returns the absolute value.
	MAX	returns the largest value.
	MIN	returns the smallest value.
	MOD	returns the remainder value.
	SIGN	returns the sign of a value.
	SQRT	returns the square root of a value.
Array	DIM	returns the number of elements in an array.
	HBOUND	returns the upper bound of an array.
	LBOUND	returns the lower bound of an array.
Character	BYTE	returns one character in the ASCII or EBCDIC collating sequence.
	COLLATE	returns an ASCII or EBCDIC collating sequence character string.
	COMPRESS	removes specific characters from character expressions.
	INDEX	searches the source for the character string specified by the excerpt.
	INDEXC	locates the first occurrence in the source of characters present in any of the excerpts.
	LEFT	left aligns a SAS character expression.
	LENGTH	returns the length of an argument.
	RANK	returns the position of a character in the ASCII or EBCDIC collating sequence.
	REPEAT	repeats a character expression.
	REVERSE	reverses a character expression.
	RIGHT	right aligns a character expression.
	SCAN	returns a given "word" from a character expression.
	SUBSTR	extracts a substring from an argument or replaces character value contents.
	TRANSLATE	replaces specific characters in a character expression with other specific characters.
	TRIM	removes trailing blanks from character expressions.
	UPCASE	converts all letters in an argument to uppercase.
	VERIFY	returns the position of the first character unique to an expression.

(continued)

Table 3.5 *(continued)*

Category	Function	Description
Date and Time	DATE	returns the current date as a SAS date value.
	DATEJUL	converts a Julian date to a SAS date value.
	DATEPART	extracts the date from a SAS datetime value.
	DATETIME	returns the current date and time of day.
	DAY	returns the day of the month from a SAS date value.
	DHMS	returns a SAS datetime value from date, hour, minute, and second.
	HMS	returns a SAS time value from hour, minute, and second values.
	HOUR	returns the hour from a SAS time or datetime value.
	INTCK	returns the number of time intervals in a given time span.
	INTNX	advances a date, time, or datetime value by a given interval.
	JULDATE	returns the Julian date from a SAS date value.
	MDY	returns a SAS date value from month, day, and year values.
	MINUTE	returns the minute from a SAS time or datetime value.
	MONTH	returns the month from a SAS date value.
	QTR	returns the yearly quarter from a SAS date value.
	SECOND	returns the second from a SAS time or datetime value.
	TIME	returns the current time of day.
	TIMEPART	extracts a time value from a SAS datetime value.
	TODAY	returns the current date as a SAS date value.
	WEEKDAY	returns the day of the week from a SAS date value.
	YEAR	returns the year from a SAS date value.
	YYQ	returns a SAS date value from the year and quarter.
Financial	COMPOUND	returns the missing argument from a compound interest calculation.
	DACCDB	returns the accumulated declining balance depreciation.
	DACCDBSL	returns the accumulated declining balance converting to a straight-line depreciation.
	DACCSL	returns the accumulated straight-line depreciation.
	DACCSYD	returns the accumulated sum-of-years-digits depreciation.
	DACCTAB	returns the accumulated depreciation from specified tables.
	DEPDB	returns the declining balance depreciation.
	DEPDBSL	returns the declining balance converting to a straight-line depreciation.
	DEPSL	returns the straight-line depreciation.
	DEPSYD	returns the sum-of-years-digits depreciation.
	DEPTAB	returns the depreciation from specified tables.
	INTRR	returns the internal rate of return as a fraction.
	IRR	returns the internal rate of return as a percentage.
	MORT	returns the amortization parameters.

(continued)

Table 3.5 *(continued)*

Category	Function	Description
	NETPV	returns the net present value as a fraction.
	NPV	returns the net present value.
	SAVING	returns the future value of a periodic saving.
Mathematical	DIGAMMA	returns the derivative of the logarithm of the GAMMA function.
	ERF	returns the probability that a normally distributed random variable with mean 0 and standard deviation 1 will take on a value less than X.
	ERFC	returns the complement to the ERF function.
	EXP	raises the constant *e* to the given power.
	GAMMA	calculates $(x-1)!$.
	LGAMMA	returns the natural logarithm of the GAMMA function.
	LOG	returns the natural logarithm.
	LOG2	returns the logarithm to the base 2.
	LOG10	returns the logarithm to the base 10.
	ORDINAL	returns the largest value of a part of a list.
	TRIGAMMA	returns the derivative of the DIGAMMA function.
Probability	POISSON	returns a probability from the Poisson distribution.
	PROBBETA	returns a probability from the beta distribution.
	PROBBNML	returns a probability from the binomial distribution.
	PROBCHI	returns a probability from the chi-square distribution.
	PROBF	returns a probability from the *F* distribution.
	PROBGAM	returns a probability from the gamma distribution.
	PROBHYPR	returns a probability from the hypergeometric distribution.
	PROBNEGB	returns a probability from the negative binomial distribution.
	PROBNORM	returns a probability from the standard normal distribution.
	PROBT	returns a probability from the *t* distribution.
Quantile	BETAINV	returns the *p* quantile from the beta distribution.
	CINV	returns the *p* quantile from the chi-square distribution.
	FINV	returns the *p* quantile from the *F* distribution.
	GAMINV	returns the *p* quantile from the gamma distribution.
	PROBIT	returns the *p* quantile from the standard normal distribution.
	TINV	returns the *p* quantile from the *t* distribution.
Random Number	NORMAL	returns a random variate from a normal distribution.
	RANBIN	returns a random variate from a binomial distribution.
	RANCAU	returns a random variate from a Cauchy distribution.

(continued)

Table 3.5 *(continued)*

Category	Function	Description
	RANEXP	returns a random variate from an exponential distribution.
	RANGAM	returns a random variate from a gamma distribution.
	RANNOR	returns a random variate from a normal distribution.
	RANPOI	returns a random variate from a Poisson distribution.
	RANTBL	returns a random variate from a tabled probability distribution.
	RANTRI	returns a random variate from a triangular distribution.
	RANUNI	returns a random variate from a uniform distribution.
	UNIFORM	returns a random variate from a uniform distribution.
Sample Statistic	CSS	returns the corrected sum of squares of the nonmissing arguments.
	CV	returns the coefficient of variation of the nonmissing arguments.
	KURTOSIS	returns the kurtosis statistic or 4th moment of the nonmissing arguments.
	MAX	returns the largest value.
	MIN	returns the smallest value.
	MEAN	returns the arithmetic mean or average.
	N	returns the number of nonmissing arguments.
	NMISS	returns the number of missing values.
	RANGE	returns the difference between the largest and smallest of the nonmissing arguments.
	SKEWNESS	returns the skewness statistic of the nonmissing arguments.
	STD	returns the standard deviation of the nonmissing arguments.
	STDERR	returns the standard error of the mean of the nonmissing arguments.
	SUM	returns the sum of the nonmissing arguments.
	USS	returns the uncorrected sum of squares of the nonmissing arguments.
	VAR	returns the variance of the nonmissing arguments.
Special Functions	DIF	returns the difference between the argument and its *n*th lag.
	INPUT	returns a value using a specified informat.
	LAG	returns lagged values from a queue.
	PUT	returns a value using a specified format.
	SYMGET	returns the value of a macro variable during DATA step execution.

(continued)

Table 3.5 *(continued)*

Category	Function	Description
State and ZIP Code	FIPNAME	converts FIPS codes to state names in uppercase.
	FIPNAMEL	converts FIPS codes to state names in uppercase and lowercase.
	FIPSTATE	converts FIPS codes to two-character postal codes.
	STFIPS	converts state postal codes to FIPS state codes.
	STNAME	converts state postal codes to state names (all uppercase).
	STNAMEL	converts state postal codes to state names in uppercase and lowercase.
	ZIPFIPS	converts ZIP codes to FIPS state codes.
	ZIPNAME	converts ZIP codes to state names (all uppercase).
	ZIPNAMEL	converts ZIP codes to state names in uppercase and lowercase.
	ZIPSTATE	converts ZIP codes to state postal codes.
Trigonometric and Hyperbolic	ARCOS	returns the arccosine of the argument.
	ARSIN	returns the arcsine of the argument.
	ATAN	returns the arctangent of the argument.
	COS	returns the trigonometric cosine of the argument.
	COSH	returns the hyperbolic cosine of the argument.
	SIN	returns the trigonometric sine of the argument.
	SINH	returns the hyperbolic sine of the argument.
	TAN	returns the trigonometric tangent of the argument.
	TANH	returns the hyperbolic tangent of the argument.
Truncation	CEIL	returns smallest integer>=argument.
	FLOOR	returns largest integer<=argument.
	FUZZ	returns nearest integer if the argument is within 1E−12.
	INT	returns the integer value.
	ROUND	rounds to the nearest round-off unit.
	TRUNC	truncates a numeric value to a specified length.

SAS CALL Routines

The SAS System provides a series of CALL routines that alter variable values or perform other system functions. Table 3.6 lists these CALL routines and their descriptions.

Table 3.6 *Categories and Descriptions of CALL Routines*

Category	CALL Routines	Description
Random Number Routines	RANBIN	returns a random variate from a binomial distribution.
	RANCAU	returns a random variate from a Cauchy distribution.
	RANEXP	returns a random variate from an exponential distribution.
	RANGAM	returns a random variate from a gamma distribution.
	RANNOR	returns a random variate from a normal distribution.
	RANPOI	returns a random variate from a Poisson distribution.
	RANTBL	returns a random variate from a tabled probability distribution.
	RANTRI	returns a random variate from a triangular distribution.
	RANUNI	returns a random variate from a uniform distribution.
Other Routines	LABEL	assigns variable label to specified character variable.
	SYMPUT	passes DATA step information to a macro variable.
	SYSTEM	issues host system commands.
	VNAME	assigns variable name as value of specified variable.

Notes on Random Number Routines

The SAS System contains a CALL routine that corresponds to every random number function. CALL routines give the user greater control over the seed stream and the random number stream than their function counterpart.

Random-number-generating routines are invoked with CALL statements. The general form of a CALL statement is as follows:

CALL *routine(seed,<argument,>variate);*

Routine can be the name of any SAS random-number-generating function, except NORMAL and UNIFORM (see RANNOR and RANUNI). *Seed* and *variate* must be valid SAS variable names. The seed variable holds the current seed values, and *variate* holds the generated variates. *Argument* can be any additional list of parameters as required by the specific distribution.

The seed variable should be initialized prior to the first execution of the CALL statement. After each execution of the CALL statement, *seed* contains the current seed in the stream (that is, the seed that will generate the next number), and *variate* contains the generated number. After each execution, the user has the option of altering the seed, which therefore alters the random number stream.

SAS Informats

An *informat* is an instruction that the SAS System uses to read data values into a variable. For example, the following value contains a dollar sign, a blank, and commas:

```
$ 1,000,000
```

You can use the COMMA*w.d* informat to instruct the SAS System to remove the unwanted characters from the value before reading the remaining numeric value into a variable.

Unless you explicitly define a variable first, the SAS System uses the informat to determine whether the variable is numeric or character. The SAS System also uses the informat to determine the length of character variables.

SAS informats have the following form:

<*$*>*informat*<*w*>.<*d*>

The *$* indicates a character informat, its absence indicates a numeric format. *Informat* is the name of an informat. The informat can be one of the SAS informats or an informat you define yourself using the INVALUE statement in the FORMAT procedure. (For details see Chapter 19, "The FORMAT Procedure," in the *SAS Procedures Guide.*) The *w* is the width value, which for most informats is the number of columns in the input data. The *d* is an optional decimal scaling factor in numeric informats. Note that all informats *must* contain a period as a part of the name.

If you omit the *w* and *d* values from the informat, the SAS System uses default values. If you specify a *d* value for data containing decimal points, the SAS System reads the number of decimal places that are actually in the data, regardless of the *d* value.

If you specify a width too narrow to read all the columns in your data lines, you can get unexpected results. The problem occurs most often with date and time informats. Remember that blanks or special characters between the day, month, year, or time increase the width of the input field, so you should adjust accordingly the width you specify with an informat. If the width you specify puts a special character in the last column the SAS System reads, the result is an invalid data message. (For details about date and time values, see Chapter 4.)

If you use an incompatible informat, such as using a numeric informat to read alphabetic characters, the SAS System prints an error message in the SAS log describing the problem and gives the variable a value of missing. (For more information about missing values, see Chapter 2, "The DATA Step.")

Using SAS Informats

There are four ways to use informats in base SAS software. They are

- □ in an INPUT statement
- □ with the INPUT function
- □ in an INFORMAT or ATTRIB statement in a DATA step
- □ in an INFORMAT or ATTRIB statement in a PROC step.

The simplest way to use an informat to read values into a variable is by using it in an INPUT statement after the variable name. For example, the following INPUT statement uses $*w*. character informat to read values into the variable STYLE and the *w.d* numeric informat to read values into the variable PRICE:

```
input @15 style $3. @21 price 5.2;
```

You can use informats with the INPUT function. The INPUT function reads any character or numeric variable or constant with any valid informat, and returns the resulting value. Thus, the INPUT function is useful for converting data, and informats increase its versatility, as in this example:

```
tempchar='98.6';
tempnumr=input(tempchar,4.);
```

Here, the INPUT function in combination with the *w.d* informat converts the character value of TEMPCHAR to a numeric value and assigns the numeric value 98.6 to TEMPNUMR.

You can also use the INPUT function to read numeric values with character informats (thereby converting numeric values to character values), but this practice can produce misleading results. If you use the INPUT function to convert numeric values to character, an implicit conversion takes place. The result of the conversion is right aligned and padded with blanks if necessary. Numbers exceeding the width of the field you allow can be misrepresented, as in this example:

```
x=2557897;
y=input(x,$3.);
put y;
```

These statements result in the value

```
255
```

A better way to convert numeric values to character values is to use the PUT function with a SAS format. See "Using SAS Formats" for an example of numeric-character conversion using the PUT function and SAS formats.

If you use the INFORMAT statement to associate an informat with a variable, the SAS System uses the informat you specify in any subsequent INPUT statement to read values into the variable. For example, in the following statements, the INFORMAT statement associates the variables BIRTHDAT and INTERVW with the DATE*w*. informat:

```
informat birthdat intervw date6.;
input @63 birthdat intervw;
```

Informats associated with variables using an INFORMAT statement behave like informats used with a colon modifier. The SAS System reads the variables using list input, but with an informat. In modified list input, the SAS System

□ does not use the *w* value in an informat to specify column positions or input field widths in an external file

□ uses the *w* value in an informat to specify the length of character variables

□ ignores the *w* value in numeric informats

□ uses the *d* value in an informat in same way it usually does for numeric informats

□ treats blanks embedded in input data as delimiters unless you change this with a DELIMITER= option specification on an INFILE statement.

See Chapter 2 for a discussion of reading raw data with modified list input.

You can also associate an informat with a variable by using the ATTRIB statement. The ATTRIB statement enables you to associate several different attributes with one or more variables, including an informat. For example, in the following statements, the ATTRIB statement associates the variables BIRTHDAT and INTERVW with the DATE*w*. informat:

```
attrib birthdat intervw informat=date6.;
input @63 birthdat intervw;
```

Permanent Versus Temporary Associations

Using an INFORMAT statement or an ATTRIB statement in the DATA step permanently associates an informat with a variable by affecting the descriptor information of the SAS data set containing the variable. However, using these statements in a PROC step associates an informat with a variable for that PROC step, as well as in any output data sets the procedure creates containing the variable. See the *SAS Procedures Guide* for more information about using informats in procedures.

Note: Permanently associating an informat with the variable does not imply that the informat is stored in the same location as the variable. The informats supplied with base SAS software are always available to variables, but if you permanently associate a user-created informat (discussed under "Categories of Informats," later in this chapter) with a variable, you must ensure that the informat is available to the variable. Therefore, storing user-created informats is an important consideration if you associate them with variables in permanent SAS data sets, if you use them in programs that run on a regular basis, or if you share these programs or data sets with other users.

When the FMTERR option is in effect, the SAS System produces an error message if it cannot find a user-defined informat; then the current DATA step stops. When the system option NOFMTERR is in effect, the SAS System continues processing if it cannot find a user-defined informat, substituting a default informat. Although the NOFMTERR option enables the SAS System to work with a variable, you lose the information supplied by the user-defined informat. If the user-defined informat is involved, a DATA step may misread data and produce incorrect results.

To avoid losing the informats you create, always give directions for accessing stored informats with directions for accessing any data sets or SAS program files referring to them. If you ship a tape containing a SAS data set or program file referring to user-defined informats to a SAS user at another installation, be sure that one file on the tape contains any user-defined informats to which the data set or program file refers.

Informat Aliases

There are several SAS informats that operate identically but have different names. Table 3.7 lists all such informat aliases. The reference text contains complete descriptions of the operation of each primary informat but not of its alias.

Table 3.7 *SAS Informats with Aliases*

Primary Informat Name	Informat Alias(es)
COMMA*w.d*	DOLLAR*w.d*
COMMAX*w.d*	DOLLARX*w.d*
w.d	BEST*w.d*, D*w.d*, F*w.d*, E*w.d*
$*w.*	$F*w.*

Categories of Informats

There are five categories of informats in the SAS System. They are

- □ numeric informats that instruct the SAS System to read numeric data values into numeric variables.
- □ character informats that instruct the SAS System to read character data values into character variables.
- □ date and time informats that instruct the SAS System to read data values into variables that represent dates, times, and datetimes.
- □ column-binary informats that instruct the SAS System to read data stored in column-binary or multi-punched form into character and numeric variables. (For details about reading and writing column-binary data, see Chapter 2.)
- □ user-defined informats developed with the FORMAT procedure. See the *SAS Procedures Guide* for more information.

Table 3.8 provides brief descriptions of the SAS informats. For more detailed descriptions, see the reference material in Chapter 13, "SAS Informats."

Table 3.8 *Categories and Descriptions of SAS Informats*

Category	Informat	Description
Character	$ASCII*w.*	converts ASCII character data to native format.
	$BINARY*w.*	converts binary values to character values.
	$CHAR*w.*	reads character data with blanks.
	$CHARZB*w.*	converts binary 0s to blanks.
	$EBCDIC*w.*	converts EBCDIC character data to native format.

(continued)

Table 3.8 *(continued)*

Category	Informat	Description
	$HEX*w.*	converts hexadecimal data to character data.
	$OCTAL*w.*	converts octal data to character data.
	$PHEX*w.*	converts packed hexadecimal data to character data.
	$VARYING*w.*	reads varying-length character values.
	$*w.*	reads standard character data.
Date and time informats	DATE*w.*	reads data values (*ddmmmyy*).
	DATETIME*w.*	reads date and time values (*ddmmmyy hh:mm:ss.ss*).
	DDMMYY*w.*	reads day-month-year (*ddmmyy*).
	JULIAN*w.*	reads Julian dates (*yyddd* or *yyyyddd*).
	MMDDYY*w.*	reads month-day-year (*mmddyy*).
	MONYY*w.*	reads month and year (*mmmyy*).
	MSEC*w.*	reads TIME MIC values.
	NENGO*w.*	reads Japanese dates values (*r.yymmdd*).
	PDTIME*w.*	reads packed decimal time of SMF and RMF records.
	RMFDUR*w.*	reads the duration of RMF measurement intervals in RMF records.
	RMFSTAMP*w.*	reads time and date fields of RMF records.
	SMFSTAMP*w.*	reads time-date values of SMF records.
	TIME*w.*	reads hours, minutes, and seconds (*hh:mm:ss.ss*).
	TODSTAMP*w.*	reads 8-byte time-of-day stamp.
	TU*w.*	reads timer units.
	YYMMDD*w.*	reads year, month, and day (*yymmdd*).
	YYQ*w.*	reads quarters of the year.
Column binary	$CB*w.*	reads standard character data from column-binary files.
	CB*w.d*	reads standard numeric values from column-binary files.
	PUNCH.*d*	reads whether a row of column-binary data is punched.
	ROW*w.d*	reads a column-binary field down a card column.
Numeric	BINARY*w.d*	converts positive binary values to integers.
	BITS*w.d*	extracts bits.
	BZ*w.d*	converts blanks to 0s.
	COMMA*w.d*	removes embedded commas, decimal points, and parentheses.

(continued)

Table 3.8 (continued)

Category	Informat	Description
	COMMAX*w.d*	removes embedded commas, decimal points, and parentheses; decimal point and comma are reversed.
	E*w.d*	reads scientific notation.
	HEX*w.*	converts hexadecimal values to fixed- or floating-point values.
	IB*w.d*	reads integer binary (fixed-point) values.
	OCTAL*w.d*	converts positive octal values to integers.
	PD*w.d*	reads packed decimal data.
	PERCENT*w.*	converts percentages into numeric values.
	PIB*w.d*	reads positive integer binary (fixed-point) values.
	PK*w.d*	reads unsigned packed decimal data.
	RB*w.d*	reads real binary (floating-point) data.
	S370FIB*w.d*	reads integer binary data in IBM mainframe format.
	S370FPD*w.d*	reads packed decimal data in IBM mainframe format.
	S370FPIB*w.d*	reads positive integer binary data in IBM mainframe format.
	S370FRB*w.d*	reads real binary (floating-point) data in IBM mainframe format.
	VAXRB*w.d*	reads real binary (floating-point) data in VMS format.
	w.d	reads standard numeric data.
	ZD*w.d*	reads zoned decimal data.
	ZDB*w.*	reads zoned decimal data with blanks.

SAS Formats

A *format* is an instruction that the SAS System uses to write data values. For example, the WORDS*w.* numeric format, which converts numeric values to their equivalent in words, writes the value 692 in words, as `six hundred ninety-two`.

SAS formats have the following form:

<$>*format*<*w*>.<*d*>

$ indicates a character format; its absence indicates a numeric format. *Format* is the name of a format. The format can be one of the SAS formats or a format you define yourself using the FORMAT procedure. (For details see Chapter 19, "The FORMAT Procedure," in the *SAS Procedures Guide*.) The *w* is the width value, which for most formats is the number of columns in the output data. The *d* is an optional decimal scaling factor in numeric formats. Note that all formats *must* contain a period as a part of the name.

For example, in DOLLAR10.2, the *w* value of 10 specifies a maximum of 10 columns for the value. The *d* value of 2 specifies that two of these columns are for the decimal part of the value, which leaves eight columns for all the remaining characters in the value, including the decimal point, the remaining numeric value, a minus sign if the value is negative, the dollar sign, and commas, if any.

If you omit the *w* and *d* values from the format, the SAS System uses default values. The *d* value you specify with a format tells the SAS System to display that many decimal places, regardless of how many decimal places are in the data. Formats never affect or truncate the stored data values they are used to represent.

If you specify a format width too narrow to represent a value, the SAS System tries to squeeze the value into the space available. Character formats truncate values on the right. Numeric formats sometimes revert to the BEST*w*. format, causing the SAS System to print asterisks if the value is too large for the format to represent adequately, or 0 if the value is too small.

If you use an incompatible format, such as using a numeric format to write character values, the SAS System first attempts to use an analagous format of the other type. If this is not feasible, it prints an error message in the SAS log describing the problem.

Using SAS Formats

There are four ways to use formats in base SAS software. They are

□ in a PUT statement,

□ with the PUT function

□ in a FORMAT or ATTRIB statement in a DATA step

□ in a FORMAT or ATTRIB statement in a PROC step.

The simplest way to use a format to write a variable is by using it in a PUT statement after the variable name, as follows:

```
amount=1145.32;
put amount dollar10.2;
```

These statements use the DOLLAR*w.d* format in a PUT statement to produce the following result, a numeric value written as a dollar amount:

```
$1,145.32
```

You can also use formats with the PUT function. The PUT function writes a numeric or character variable or constant with any valid format and returns the resulting character value. For example, the following statement converts the values of the numeric variable CC into a three-character hexadecimal representation:

```
cchex=put(cc,hex3.);
```

CCHEX contains the same characters as those written by the following statement:

```
put cc hex3.;
```

The PUT function is useful for converting a numeric value to a character value or for changing the character format associated with a variable or value.

You can associate a format with a variable with the FORMAT statement. Once you do this, the SAS System uses the format you specify in any subsequent use of PUT to write the values of the variable you specify. For example, the following statement associates the COMMA*w.d* numeric format with the variables SALES1 through SALES12:

```
format sales1-sales12 comma10.2;
```

Formats you specify in a PUT statement behave differently than those you associate with a variable in a FORMAT statement. The major difference is that with specified formats, the PUT statement preserves leading blanks with formats that have leading blanks, and with associated formats, the PUT statement always trims leading blanks.

You can also associate a format with a variable with the ATTRIB statement. The ATTRIB statement enables you to associate several different attributes with one or more variables, including a format. For example, in the following statement the ATTRIB statement associates the variables SALES1 through SALES12 with the COMMA*w.d* format:

```
attrib sales1-sales12 format=comma10.2;
```

Permanent Versus Temporary Association

Using a FORMAT statement or an ATTRIB statement in the DATA step permanently associates a format with the variable by affecting the descriptor information of the SAS data set containing the variable. However, using these statements in the PROC step associates a format with a variable for that PROC step, as well as in any output data sets the procedure creates that contain the variable or variables. See the *SAS Procedures Guide* for more information about using formats in procedures.

Note: Permanently associating a format with the variable does not imply that the format is stored in the same location as the variable. The formats supplied with base SAS software are always available to variables, but if you permanently associate a user-created format (discussed under "Categories of Formats" later in this chapter) with a variable, you must ensure that the format is available to the variable. Therefore, storing user-created formats is an important consideration if you associate them with variables in permanent SAS data sets, if you use them in programs which run on a regular basis, or if you share these programs or data sets with other users.

When the FMTERR option is in effect, the SAS System produces an error message if it cannot find a user-defined format; then the current DATA step stops. When the system option NOFMTERR is in effect, the SAS System continues processing if it cannot find a user-defined format and substitutes a default format, usually the BEST*w.* or $*w.* format. Although the NOFMTERR option enables the SAS System to work with the variable, you lose the information supplied by the missing user-defined format.

To avoid losing the formats you create, always give directions for accessing stored formats with directions for accessing any data sets referring to them. If you ship a tape containing a SAS data set referring to user-defined formats to a SAS user at another installation, be sure that one file on the tape contains any user-defined formats to which the data set refers.

Format Aliases

There are two sets of SAS formats that operate identically but have different names. Table 3.9 shows both sets of format aliases. The reference text contains complete descriptions of the operation of each primary format but not of its alias.

Table 3.9 *SAS Formats with Aliases*

Primary Format Name	Format Alias
w.d	F*w.d*
$*w.*	$F*w.*

Categories of Formats

There are four categories of formats in the SAS System. They are

□ numeric formats that instruct the SAS System to write numeric data values from numeric variables.

□ character formats that instruct the SAS System to write character data values from character variables.

□ date and time formats that instruct the SAS System to write data values from variables that represent dates, times, and datetimes.

□ user-defined formats created with the FORMAT procedure. See the *SAS Procedures Guide* for more information.

You can store the formats you create with the FORMAT procedure for later use. Storing formats is an important consideration if you associate formats with variables in permanent SAS data sets, especially those shared with other users.

Table 3.10 provides brief descriptions of the SAS formats. For more detailed descriptions, see the reference material in Chapter 14, "Formats."

Table 3.10 *Categories and Descriptions of SAS Formats*

Category	Format	Description
Character	$ASCII*w.*	converts native format character data to ASCII representation.
	$BINARY*w.*	converts character values to binary representation.
	$CHAR*w.*	writes standard character data.
	$EBCDIC*w.*	converts native format character data to EBCDIC representation.
	$HEX*w.*	converts character values to hexadecimal representation.
	$OCTAL*w.*	converts character values to octal representation.
	$VARYING*w.*	writes varying-length character values.
	$*w.*	writes standard character data.

(continued)

Table 3.10 *(continued)*

Category	Format	Description
Date and Time Formats	DATE*w.*	writes data values (*ddmmmyy*).
	DATETIME*w.d*	writes datetime values (*ddmmmyy:hh:mm:ss.ss*).
	DAY*w.*	writes day of month.
	DDMMYY*w.*	writes date values (*ddmmyy*).
	DOWNAME*w.*	writes name of day of the week.
	HHMM*w.d*	writes hours and minutes.
	HOUR*w.d*	writes hours and decimal fractions of hours.
	JULDAY*w.*	writes Julian day of the year.
	JULIAN*w.*	writes Julian dates (*yyddd* or *yyyyddd*).
	MMDDYY*w.*	writes month-day-year (*mmddyy*).
	MMSS*w.d*	writes minutes and seconds.
	MMYY*xw.*	writes month and year separated by a character. (MMYY*xw.* is a set of formats.)
	MONNAME*w.*	writes name of month.
	MONTH*w.*	writes month of year.
	MONYY*w.*	writes month and year (*mmmyy*).
	NENGO*w.*	writes Japanese dates (*r.yymmdd*).
	QTR*w.*	writes quarter of year.
	QTRR*w.*	writes quarter of year in Roman numerals.
	TIME*w.d*	writes hours, minutes, and seconds.
	TOD*w.*	writes the time portion of datetime values.
	WEEKDATE*w.*	writes day of week and date (*day-of-week, month-name dd yy*).
	WEEKDATX*w.*	writes day of week and date (*day-of-week, dd month-name yy*).
	WEEKDAY*w.*	writes day of week.
	WORDDATE*w.*	writes date with name of month, day, and year (*month-name dd, yyyy*).
	WORDDATX*w.*	writes date with day, name of month, and year (*dd month-name yyyy*).
	YEAR*w.*	writes year part of date value.
	YYMM*xw.*	writes year and month, separated by a character. (YYMM*xw.* is a set of formats.)
	YYMMDD*w.*	writes year-month-day (*yymmdd*).
	YYMON*w.*	writes year and month abbreviation.
	YYQ*xw.*	writes year and quarter separated by a character. (YYQ*xw.* is a set of formats.)
	YYQR*xw.*	writes year and quarter in Roman numerals separated by a character. (YYQR*xw.* is a set of formats.)

(continued)

Table 3.10 *(continued)*

Category	**Format**	**Description**
Numeric	BEST*w.*	chooses best notation.
	BINARY*w.*	converts numeric values to binary representation.
	COMMA*w.d*	writes numeric values with commas and decimal points.
	COMMAX*w.d*	writes numeric values with commas and decimal points; comma and decimal point are reversed.
	DOLLAR*w.d*	writes numeric values with dollar signs, commas, and decimal points.
	DOLLARX*w.d*	writes numeric values with dollar signs, commas, amd decimal points; comma and decimal point are reversed.
	E*w.*	writes values in scientific notation.
	FRACT*w.*	converts values to fractions.
	HEX*w.*	converts numeric values to hexadecimal representation.
	IB*w.d*	writes integer binary values.
	NEGPAREN*w.d*	displays negative values in parentheses.
	OCTAL*w.*	converts numeric values to octal representation.
	PD*w.d*	writes packed decimal data.
	PERCENT*w.d*	prints numbers as percentages.
	PIB*w.d*	writes positive integer binary values.
	PK*w.d*	writes unsigned packed decimal data.
	RB*w.d*	writes real binary (floating-point) data.
	ROMAN*w.*	writes Roman numerals.
	SSN*w.*	writes Social Security numbers.
	S370FIB*w.d*	writes integer binary data in IBM mainframe format.
	S370FPD*w.d*	writes packed decimal data in IBM mainframe format.
	S370FPIB*w.d*	writes positive integer binary data in IBM mainframe format.
	S370FRB*w.d*	writes real binary (floating-point) data in IBM mainframe format.
	w.d	writes standard numeric data.
	WORDF*w.*	converts numeric values to words.
	WORDS*w.*	converts numeric values to words, with decimals as fractions.
	Z*w.d*	writes leading 0s.
	ZD*w.d*	writes data in zoned decimal format.

SAS Data Set Options

Data set options are those that appear after SAS data set names. They specify actions that apply only to the processing of the SAS data set with which they appear and let you perform such operations as

- □ renaming variables
- □ specifying variables to be included or dropped in later processing
- □ selecting only the first or last *n* observations for processing.

Output options in the DATA step can only appear in the DATA statement, not in the OUTPUT statement.

SAS data set options used with the DATA step or SAS procedures are listed in Table 3.11. The table gives the name of each option, a brief description, and whether it can be used in an input (or update) data set only, an output data set only, or in both. For a detailed description of each option, see Chapter 15, "SAS Data Set Options."

Table 3.11 *SAS Data Set Options*

Data Set Option	Description	Data Set Where Used
BUFNO=	specifies the number of buffers for processing a SAS data set.	Both
BUFSIZE=	specifies a permanent buffer size for output SAS data sets.	Output
CNTLLEV=	specifies the level of shared access to SAS data sets.	Input
COMPRESS=	compresses observations in an output SAS data set.	Output
DROP=	excludes variables from processing or from output SAS data sets.	Both
FILECLOSE=	specifies how a tape is positioned when a SAS file on the tape is closed.	Both
FIRSTOBS=	causes processing to begin at a specified observation.	Input
IN=	creates a variable that indicates whether the data set contributed data to the current observation (DATA step only).	Input
KEEP=	specifies variables for processing or writing to output SAS data sets.	Both
LABEL=	specifies a label for the data set.	Both

(continued)

Table 3.11 *(continued)*

Data Set Option	Description	Data Set Where Used
OBS=	causes processing to end with the *n*th observation.	Input
RENAME=	changes the name of a variable.	Both
REPLACE=	overrides the REPLACE system option.	Output
REUSE=	specifies whether new observations are written to free space in compressed SAS data sets.	Output
TYPE=	specifies the data set type for a specially structured SAS data set.	Both
WHERE=	selects observations that meet the specified condition.	Input

Using Data Set Options

Data set options are specified in parentheses after the SAS data set name in DATA step statements or PROC statements, for example,

```
data new(drop=year);
```

The DROP= option specifies that a variable called YEAR used during DATA step execution not be written to the SAS data set called NEW.

You can specify several data set options after a data set name in one DATA statement. Separate each option with at least one space, as in this example:

```
set new(drop=age firstobs=3);
```

The following examples show data set options in SAS statements:

- □ `proc print data=new(drop=year);`
- □ `set master(keep=name address);`
- □ `update master(rename=(a=z)) newdata;`

Many data set options control the processing of variables in a data set; therefore, they are relevant only to the DATA step or procedure where they are used. However, data set options that affect the physical characteristics of a data set, such as the BUFSIZE= or the COMPRESS= option, remain in effect for the life of the data set, controlling how the data are stored by the system. To change or cancel these options, you must re-create the data set in a new DATA statement.

Some SAS data set options, such as the BUFSIZE= and the COMPRESS= options, are only meaningful when creating a SAS data set. They can be ignored or can generate a warning message when used to access an existing SAS data set. There may be restrictions on using data set options with certain data sets, depending on how the data set is created. See the description of the individual data set options in Chapter

15 for details. For information on the engines used to create SAS data sets, read Chapter 6, "SAS Files."

Input Versus Output Data Sets

Most SAS data set options can apply to either input or output SAS data sets when used in a DATA step or SAS procedure. If a data set option is associated with an input data set (for example, one specified in a SET, MERGE, or UPDATE statement), the action applies to the data set being read. If the option is specified with a data set in the DATA statement, the SAS System applies the action to the output data set.

You can use data set options in the same DATA step on both input and output data sets. When you do so, keep in mind that the SAS System applies data set options specified with input data sets before it evaluates program statements or applies data set options specified for output data sets. See "Dropping, Keeping, and Renaming Variables" in Chapter 4.

In some instances, data set options conflict when they are used in the same statement. For example, you cannot specify both the DROP= and KEEP= options for the same data set in the same statement.

Comparisons

The SAS System uses two other kinds of options in addition to data set options:

- *Statement options* are specified only in a given SAS statement or statements, and they affect only that statement or step. For example, the HEADER= option in the FILE statement is a statement option.
- *System options* are instructions that control the way the SAS System performs operations, for example, SAS System initialization, hardware and software interfacing, and the input, processing, and output of jobs. SAS system options differ from SAS data set and statement options in that once you invoke system options, they remain in effect for all DATA and PROC steps in a SAS job or session unless you respecify them. For example, the CENTER system option affects all of the output from a SAS job, regardless of how many DATA and PROC steps the job contains.

  Some SAS system options and data set options share the same name and have the same function. You can specify these data set options on data sets to override the system settings. Specifically, the BUFNO=, BUFSIZE=, COMPRESS=, FIRSTOBS=, OBS=, REUSE= and REPLACE= data set options take precedence over settings established with the system options of the same name.

SAS System Options

System options are instructions that affect the entire SAS session and control the way the SAS System performs operations, for example, SAS System initialization, hardware and software interfacing, and the input, processing, and output of jobs.

There are eight system options that have equivalents as data set options. They are BUFNO=, BUFSIZE=, COMPRESS=, FIRSTOBS=, LABEL, OBS=, REPLACE, and REUSE=. SAS data set option settings override equivalent SAS system option settings. For more information about data set options, see Chapter 15.

SAS system options differ from SAS data set and statement options in that once you invoke system options, they remain in effect for all DATA and PROC steps in a SAS job or session unless you respecify them. For example, the CENTER system option affects all of the output from a SAS program, regardless of how many DATA and PROC steps the program contains.

Table 3.11 lists SAS system options by functional categories. The sections that follow address how to determine what settings are in effect, how to change settings, how DATA and PROC step boundaries delimit system option settings, how SAS system options compare with SAS data set options and statement options, and how the SAS System determines order of precedence of system option settings.

SAS system options are divided by function into the following categories:

- □ Initialization options are instructions to the SAS System that control SAS System initialization and hardware and software interfacing.
- □ Reading and writing data options control the ways in which data are input to and output from the SAS System.
- □ Log and procedure output control options specify the ways in which SAS System output is written to the SAS log and procedure output file.
- □ SAS data set control options specify how SAS data sets are input, processed, and output.
- □ Error-handling options specify how the SAS System reports on and recovers from error conditions.
- □ Macro facility options control aspects of the macro facility of base SAS software.
- □ Product interface options specify how base SAS software interfaces with other SAS software products.

■ **Host Information** ......

In addition to these categories, the SAS System includes host-specific SAS system options. For details on SAS system options that apply to your host system, refer to the SAS documentation for your host system.

.... ■

Table 3.12 *Categories and Descriptions of SAS System Options*

Category	Option	Description
Initialization	ALTLOG=	specifies a destination to which a copy of the SAS log is written.
	ALTPRINT=	specifies a destination to which a copy of the SAS print file is written.
	AUTOEXEC=	specifies the autoexec file. The autoexec file is a file containing SAS statements that are executed automatically whenever the SAS System is invoked.
	BATCH	specifies whether the batch set of SAS system option default values is in effect when the SAS System executes.
	CONFIG=	specifies the name of your configuration file. The configuration file contains SAS system options that are executed automatically whenever the SAS System is invoked. The SAS System supplies a default configuration file, but you can create your own configuration file and store it in your choice of location. The name of the configuration file is host specific.
	DMR	invokes a remote SAS session on a host computer in order to run SAS/CONNECT software.
	DMS	specifies whether the primary windows of the SAS Display Manager System are to be active in a SAS session.
	ECHOAUTO	echoes autoexec input to the SAS log.
	INITSTMT=	specifies a SAS statement or statements to be executed before any SAS statements from the SYSIN file and after any statements in the autoexec file.
	LOG=	specifies a destination to which the SAS log is written when executing SAS programs in modes other than display manager.
	NEWS=	specifies a file that contains messages to be written to the SAS log. Typically, the file contains information for users such as news items about the system.
	OPLIST	writes the settings of SAS System options given at SAS invocation to the SAS log.
	PRINT=	specifies the destination to which SAS output is written when executing SAS programs in modes other than display manager.
	REMOTE=	specifies the kind of communications device used for SAS/CONNECT software.

(*continued*)

Table 3.12 *(continued)*

Category	Option	Description
	SASHELP=	specifies the location of the SASHELP library, which is where help files are stored.
	SASMSG=	specifies the external library that contains SAS messages.
	SASUSER=	specifies the name of the SASUSER library, which contains a user's profile catalog. The library and catalog are created automatically by the SAS System; you do not have to create them explicitly.
	SETINIT	allows alteration of site license information.
	SITEINFO=	specifies a file that contains site-specific information. If the SITEINFO command and the SITEINFO= system option are specified, site-specific information is displayed in the SITEINFO window.
	SYSIN=	specifies a file containing a SAS program. This option is applicable only when you are using noninteractive SAS execution mode and can be specified only at SAS invocation.
	TERMINAL	specifies whether a terminal is attached at SAS invocation. The SAS System defaults to the appropriate setting for the TERMINAL system option based on whether the session is invoked in the foreground or background.
	VERBOSE	writes the settings of all SAS System options in the configuration file. Some hosts may list additional information, such as the name of the configuration file.
	WORK=	specifies the name of the SAS WORK library.
	WORKINIT	controls whether the WORK data library is initialized at SAS System invocation.
Reading and Writing Data	CAPS	specifies whether lowercase characters input to the SAS System from SAS source statements and data lines are translated to uppercase.
	CARDIMAGE	specifies whether to process SAS source and data lines as 80-byte cards.
	CHARCODE	enables users to substitute character combinations for special characters not on the keyboard.
	DBCS	specifies whether the SAS System recognizes double-byte character sets (DBCS).
	DBCSLANG=	specifies which double-byte character set (DBCS) language is being used.
	DBCSTYPE=	specifies the type of double-byte character set (DBCS) encoding method.

(continued)

Table 3.12 *(continued)*

Category	Option	Description
	ENGINE=	specifies the default engine to be associated with a SAS library.
	INVALIDDATA=	specifies the value that the SAS System is to assign to a variable when invalid numeric data are encountered with an input format, such as in an INPUT statement or the INPUT function.
	PARM=	specifies a parameter string passed to an external program.
	PARMCARDS=	specifies the file reference of the file that is opened when a PARMCARDS statement is encountered in a procedure.
	PROBSIG=	controls the number of significant digits of *p*-values in some statistical procedures
	S=	specifies the length of statements, exclusive of sequence numbers, on each line of a SAS source statement and the length of data, exclusive of sequence numbers, on lines following a CARDS statement.
	S2=	specifies the length of secondary source statements, such as %INCLUDE statements, autoexec files, and autocall macro files.
	SEQ=	specifies the length of the numeric portion of the sequence-number field on SAS source lines.
	YEARCUTOFF=	specifies the first year of a 100-year span used as the default by various DATE and DATETIME informats and functions.
Log and Procedure Output Control	CENTER	controls whether SAS procedure output is centered.
	DATE	controls whether the date and time that the SAS job began are printed at the top of each page of the SAS log and any print file created by the SAS System.
	FORMCHAR=	specifies the default output formatting characters for your output device. Formatting characters are used to construct tabular output outlines and dividers for various procedures, for example, the CALENDAR, FREQ, and TABULATE procedures.
	FORMDLIM=	specifies a character that is used to delimit page breaks in SAS output.
	FULLSTIMER	specifies whether all the performance statistics of your computer system that are available to the SAS System are written to the SAS log.
	LABEL	permits SAS procedures to use labels with variables. A label is a string of up to 40 characters that can be written by certain procedures in place of the variable name.
	LINESIZE=	specifies the line size (printer line width) for the SAS log and the SAS procedure output file used by the DATA step and procedures.

(continued)

Table 3.12 *(continued)*

Category	Option	Description
	MISSING=	specifies the character to print for missing numeric variable values.
	NOTES	controls whether notes are written to the SAS log.
	NUMBER	controls whether the page number prints on the first title line of each page of printed output.
	OVP	controls whether output lines printed by the SAS System can be overprinted.
	PAGENO=	specifies a beginning page number for the next page of printed output.
	PAGESIZE=	specifies the number of lines that can be printed per page of SAS output.
	SOURCE	controls whether SAS source statements are written to the SAS log.
	SOURCE2	controls whether secondary source statements from files included by %INCLUDE statements are written to the SAS log.
	SPOOL	controls whether SAS statements are written to a utility data set in the WORK data library for later use by a %INCLUDE *n:m* statement or %LIST statement.
	STIMER	specifies whether performance statistics of your computer system are written to the SAS log.
SAS Data Set Control	BUFNO=	specifies the number of buffers to be allocated for processing a SAS data set.
	BUFSIZE=	specifies the permanent size of input/output buffers for SAS data sets.
	CATCACHE=	specifies the number of SAS catalogs to keep open.
	COMPRESS=	specifies whether observations in a newly created SAS data set are to be compressed (variable-length records) or uncompressed (fixed-length records). The record type is a permanent attribute of the data set.
	FIRSTOBS=	causes the SAS System to begin reading at a specified observation in a data set. If the SAS System is processing a file of raw data, the FIRSTOBS= system option causes the SAS System to begin reading at a specified line of data.
	LAST=	specifies the name of the most recently created data set.
	OBS=	specifies the last observation from a data set or the last record from a raw data file that the SAS System is to read.
	REPLACE	specifies whether permanently stored SAS data sets are replaced.

(continued)

Table 3.12 *(continued)*

Category	Option	Description
	REUSE=	specifies whether free space is tracked and reused in newly created compressed SAS data sets when adding new observations. If space is reused, observations added to the SAS data set are inserted wherever enough free space exists instead of at the end of the SAS data set.
	TAPECLOSE=	specifies the default CLOSE disposition (volume position) to be performed when a SAS data library on tape is closed.
	USER=	specifies the name of the default permanent SAS data library. If this option is specified, you can use one-level names to reference permanent SAS files in SAS statements.
	WORKTERM	specifies whether SAS WORK files, such as data sets, are erased from the current SAS WORK data library at the end of the SAS session.
Error Handling	CLEANUP	specifies how the SAS System handles an out-of-memory or a disk-full condition.
	DSNFERR	controls whether the SAS System generates an error message when an input or update SAS data set specified in a job is not found.
	ERRORABEND	forces the SAS System to abend when most errors occur that would normally cause it to issue only an error message.
	ERRORS=	controls the maximum number of observations for which complete error messages are printed.
	FMTERR	controls whether the SAS System generates an error message when the system cannot find a format to associate with a variable.
	PROCLEAVE=	specifies the amount of memory to leave unallocated so that a procedure can terminate normally when error recovery code is initiated.
	SYSLEAVE=	specifies the amount of memory to leave unallocated so that the SAS System can terminate normally when error recovery code is initiated.
	VNFERR	specifies whether the SAS System sets the error flag (_ERROR_=1) for a missing variable when a _NULL_ data set (or a data set that is bypassed by the operating system control language) is used in a MERGE statement of a DATA step.
Macro Facility	IMPLMAC	controls whether macros defined as statement-style macros can be invoked with statement-style macro calls or if the call must be a name-style macro call.
	MACRO	specifies whether the SAS macro language, the SYMGET function, and the SYMPUT routine are available.

(continued)

Table 3.12 *(continued)*

Category	Option	Description
	MAUTOSOURCE	controls whether the macro autocall feature is available.
	MERROR	controls whether the SAS macro language compiler issues a warning message if the macro processor cannot match a macro-like name (%*name*) to an appropriate macro keyword.
	MLOGIC	specifies whether the macro language processor traces its execution.
	MPRINT	specifies whether SAS statements generated by macro execution are displayed.
	MRECALL	specifies whether the macro processor searches the autocall libraries for a file that was not found during an earlier search.
	SASAUTOS=	specifies the autocall library or libraries.
	SERROR	controls whether a warning message is issued when the SAS System encounters a macro variable reference that cannot be matched with an appropriate macro variable.
	SYMBOLGEN	specifies whether the macro processor displays the result of resolving macro variable references.
	SYSPARM=	specifies a character string that can be passed to SAS programs. The character string specified can be accessed in a SAS DATA step by the SYSPARM() function or anywhere in a SAS program by using the automatic macro variable reference &SYSPARM.
Product Interface	COMAMID=	specifies the communications access method for SAS/CONNECT and SAS/SHARE software.
	DEVICE=	specifies a terminal device driver for SAS/GRAPH software.
	FORMS=	specifies the name of the default form used to customize the appearance of interactive windowing output.
	FSDEVICE=	specifies the interactive windowing device driver for your terminal.
	GWINDOW	displays SAS/GRAPH software that is sent to your terminal to be displayed in the GRAPH window of the SAS Display Manager System.
	SORTPGM=	specifies the name of the system sort utility to be invoked by the SAS System.

Determining What Settings Are in Effect

There are four ways to determine what settings are in effect for SAS system options. They are the

□ VERBOSE system option

□ OPLIST system option

□ OPTIONS window

□ OPTIONS procedure.

This section provides background information about each of these ways. For details on the VERBOSE and OPLIST system options, see Chapter 16, "SAS System Options." For details on the OPTIONS window, see Chapter 17, "SAS Display Manager Windows." For details on the OPTIONS procedure, see the *SAS Procedures Guide*.

■ **Host Information** .... All SAS system options are initialized with default settings when the SAS System is invoked. However, the default settings for some SAS system options vary across host systems and sites. For details, refer to the SAS documentation for your host system. ■

Using the VERBOSE System Option

You specify the VERBOSE system option at SAS invocation to determine the settings of SAS system options that were set at SAS invocation. The VERBOSE system option writes the settings to the terminal if the SAS System is invoked at a terminal or to the batch log if the SAS System is invoked as a batch job. The VERBOSE system option is not valid as a part of an OPTIONS statement or as an entry in the OPTIONS window.

Using the OPLIST System Option

You specify the OPLIST system option at SAS invocation to determine the settings of SAS system options that were set at SAS invocation. The OPLIST system option writes the settings to the SAS log. The OPLIST system option is not valid as a part of an OPTIONS statement or as an entry in the OPTIONS window.

Using the OPTIONS Window

You can use the OPTIONS window of the SAS Display Manager System to determine some of the settings of SAS system options that can be changed during your SAS session. The OPTIONS window does not list SAS system options that can be specified only at invocation or ones that are specific to your host system.

Unlike the VERBOSE and OPLIST system options, you can use the OPTIONS window to change some system option settings that affect your SAS session. See "Specifying Settings in the OPTIONS Window" later in this chapter. You invoke the OPTIONS window itself by entering OPTIONS on a command line while in display manager or while running an interactive windowing procedure such as FSEDIT.

Using the OPTIONS Procedure

You can use the OPTIONS procedure to determine the settings of all SAS system options. The OPTIONS procedure displays all SAS system option settings including those specified at SAS invocation, those that can be changed during your SAS session, and those that are host specific. You cannot change SAS system option settings with the OPTIONS procedure.

The OPTIONS procedure includes an option that enables you to specify either a long or short version of the list of settings. If you specify LONG or omit the option, each system option is listed on a separate line and is followed by a brief description. If you specify SHORT, the SAS System produces a compressed list of the system options without the descriptions.

The OPTIONS procedure writes to the SAS log, not the procedure output file.

Changing SAS System Option Settings

At invocation, the SAS System provides default settings for all SAS system options. However, there are several ways to override the default settings. Depending on the function of the system option, you can specify a setting in one or more of the following ways:

- □ on the command line during SAS invocation
- □ as a statement in the configuration file
- □ as a part of an OPTIONS statement
- □ as an entry in the OPTIONS window.

Some system options can be specified only during SAS invocation—either on the command line or as a statement in the configuration file. One system option, the CONFIG= system option, which specifies the name of the configuration file, can be specified only on the command line during SAS invocation. Other system options can be specified on the command line, in the configuration file, as a part of an OPTIONS statement, and as an entry in the OPTIONS window. Others can be specified on the command line, in the configuration file, and as a part of an OPTIONS statement.

■ **Host Information** .... For details on which SAS system options must be set at invocation and host-specific default options settings, refer to the SAS documentation for your host system. ■

The following sections provide background information about specifying SAS system options. For details on individual system options, including where a particular system option can be specified, see Chapter 16.

Specifying Settings on the Command Line During SAS Invocation

You can specify any SAS system option setting on the command line during SAS invocation. However, many SAS system option settings can be specified only during SAS invocation. For example, the AUTOEXEC= system option, which specifies the autoexec file, is valid only during SAS invocation. In other words, you cannot specify a setting for the AUTOEXEC= system option as a part of an OPTIONS statement or as an entry in the OPTIONS window.

■ **Host Information** .... The syntax for specifying SAS system options on the command line during SAS invocation is generally consistent with the command-line syntax of your host system. However, some host systems may require or exclude certain characters when you specify SAS system options on the operating system command line. In addition, some host systems require you to specify an alias for some SAS system options. (An alias is an abbreviated form of a SAS system option.) For details, refer to the SAS documentation for your host system. ■

Specifying Settings in a Configuration File

A configuration file is an external file that can contain any SAS system options except the CONFIG= system option, which names the configuration file. If you use the same option settings frequently, it is convenient to specify the options in a configuration file.

By default, each time the SAS System is invoked, it checks for a configuration file. When the SAS System finds a configuration file, it uses the system option settings specified in that file instead of the SAS system option default settings.

■ **Host Information** ....

The name of a configuration file and the syntax used to store statements there depend on your host system. Some host systems allow you to specify more than one configuration file per session. Although the syntax for specifying SAS system options in a configuration file is generally consistent with the command-line syntax of your host system, some systems may require or exclude certain characters when you specify SAS system options on the operating system command line. For more information, refer to the SAS documentation for your host system. ■

Specifying Settings as Part of an OPTIONS Statement

Within a SAS program or during a SAS session, you can specify SAS system options in an OPTIONS statement. For example, the following OPTIONS statement specifies three system options:

```
options nodate center linesize=75;
```

You can specify an OPTIONS statement at any time during a session or program except within data lines or parmcard lines. Settings remain in effect throughout the session or program unless you reset them with another OPTIONS statement or change them in the OPTIONS window.

For details on the OPTIONS statement, see Chapter 9.

Specifying Settings in the OPTIONS Window

You can specify settings for some SAS system options in the OPTIONS window of the SAS Display Manager System. The OPTIONS window displays an option column that lists the names of the SAS system options that can be changed during your SAS session and a value column that lists the current settings. (The OPTIONS window does not list SAS system options that can be specified only at invocation or ones that are specific to your host.) You can change a setting by typing over the existing setting in the value column and pressing the ENTER or RETURN key. (You do not include an equal sign as a part of the value.)

You invoke the OPTIONS window itself by entering OPTIONS on a command line while in display manager or while running an interactive windowing procedure such as FSEDIT.

Changes to system options made in the OPTIONS window take effect immediately and remain in effect throughout the session unless you reset them with an OPTIONS statement or change them in the OPTIONS window.

For more information on the OPTIONS window, see Chapter 17.

Delimiting System Option Settings with Step Boundaries

When you specify a SAS system option setting within a DATA or PROC step, the setting applies to that step and to all subsequent steps for the duration of the SAS session or until you respecify the setting. For example, the following program segment contains a DATA step, an OPTIONS statement, and two PROC steps:

```
data temp;
   set items(drop=old borrowed);
run;

options obs=5;

proc sort;
   by new;
run;

proc print;
   var new blue;
run;
```

Notice that the OPTIONS statement appears after the RUN statement that ends (sets the boundary of) the DATA step. Therefore, the system option OBS= does not apply to the DATA step; it is outside the boundary of the DATA step.

If you remove the RUN statement that ends the DATA step, the OPTIONS statement will be within the boundary of the DATA step, and the OBS= system option will apply to the DATA step as well as all subsequent steps.

For more information on step boundaries, see "Step Boundary" in Chapter 2.

Order of Precedence

You can specify the same SAS system option in more than one place. The order of precedence that determines which setting takes effect is as follows:

- □ If the same system option is specified in the SAS command and in a configuration file, the setting established with the SAS command overrides the setting in the configuration file.
- □ If a system option is specified in a configuration file, as a part of an OPTIONS statement, as a statement in the OPTIONS window, or on the command line during SAS invocation, its setting overrides the default setting.
- □ Settings specified in an OPTIONS statement or the OPTIONS window override settings specified on the SAS command. The order of execution determines if settings specified through the OPTIONS window or OPTIONS statement are in effect.
- □ The last setting specified overrides an earlier setting.

The following list shows the order of precedence of SAS system options from the highest (item 1) to the lowest (item 4):

1. OPTIONS statement and OPTIONS window
2. command line specification
3. configuration file specification
4. SAS System default settings.

Numeric Values

This unit on numeric values contains two sections. "Overview of Numeric Processing" provides general information on how the SAS System reads and writes numeric data and performs numeric-character conversions. "Details of Numeric Precision" provides detailed information on how the SAS System stores numbers and performs numeric computations.

Overview of Numeric Processing

This section contains summary information about the following topics:

- □ reading numeric data
- □ representing numeric data in SAS programs
- □ writing numeric data
- □ using SAS date and time values
- □ making numeric-character conversions.

Detailed information about these subjects can be found in the references given at the end of the individual sections.

Reading Numeric Data

The SAS System can read numeric data from the following sources:

- □ a SAS data set by using either a SET, MERGE, or UPDATE statement
- □ the job stream by using a CARDS or CARDS4 statement
- □ an external file by using an INFILE statement
- □ data entry in interactive windowing procedures such as FSEDIT
- □ Screen Control Language (SCL).

Almost any form of numeric input can be accepted by the SAS System including *standard* and *nonstandard data*. Standard numeric data are written with one digit per byte and can be read into the SAS System without any special instructions.

Nonstandard numeric data must be read using a SAS informat. SAS informats exist that can read nonstandard numeric data, such as fractions, hexadecimals, scientific notation (E-notation), binary (integer), and floating-point (real binary) data. SAS informats also exist that can read numeric data containing blanks that must be read as zeroes or special characters, such as dollar signs or commas.

Missing values can be recognized as missing at the time the SAS System reads them. Missing values can be coded with a blank or a single period, depending on the type of input you use. In addition, numeric data can contain characters that represent special missing values that allow you to distinguish between types of missing values.

For more information on reading numeric data, including details about missing values in input data and how the SAS System handles invalid data, see "Reading Raw Data" in Chapter 2.

Representing Numeric Data in SAS Programs

Numeric data can be represented in SAS programs as constants in standard numeric, scientific, and hexadecimal notation. Ordinary numeric missing values are represented as single periods. Special missing values can be represented as a period followed by one of the characters A through Z or the underscore character (_).

Bit masks can be used in bit testing to compare internal bits in a value's representation.

For more information on how to represent numeric data in SAS programs, including the details of bit testing, see "SAS Constants" in Chapter 4.

Writing Numeric Data

The *w.d* format is the default format for writing numeric data. However, there are numerous other SAS formats you can use in a FORMAT, an ATTRIB, or a PUT statement for writing numeric data.

If the value of a variable does not fit into the width of the format you are using, the SAS System tries to squeeze the value into the space available, in which case numeric formats may revert to the BEST*w*. format. If it is not possible to represent the value in some fashion, the SAS System prints asterisks. Even if the SAS System truncates or rounds a value of a numeric variable during the printing routine, the complete value is maintained and is stored intact by the system. (You can use the PROBSIG= system option to control the precision of statistical procedures.)

For information on individual formats, see Chapter 14. For information on the PROBSIG= system option, see Chapter 16.

Using SAS Date and Time Values

The SAS System represents date, time, and datetime values as numbers using the following rules:

- A date is represented by the number of days between January 1, 1960 and that date.
- A time is represented as the number of seconds between midnight and that time of day.
- A datetime is represented by the number of seconds between midnight, January 1, 1960 and that datetime.

The SAS System has a number of informats that read date and time values and convert them to SAS date and time values. The SAS System also has a number of formats that write date and time values in a variety of ways.

SAS dates are valid back to A.D. 1582 and ahead to A.D. 20,000. Leap year, century, and fourth-century adjustments are handled correctly. However, leap seconds are ignored, and the SAS System does not adjust for daylight saving time.

For more information on SAS date and time values, see Chapters 4, 13, and 14.

Making Numeric-Character Conversions

If the type of a variable is already established and you try to assign a value to the variable that is not of the same type, the SAS System converts the value to the expected type. For a listing of the rules by which the SAS System automatically converts character variables to numeric variables and vice-versa, see "SAS Constants" in Chapter 4.

Details of Numeric Precision

This section contains detailed information on how the SAS System stores numbers and performs computations. The following topics are discussed:

- floating-point representation
- precision versus magnitude
- computational considerations of fractions
- numeric comparison considerations
- using the LENGTH statement and the TRUNC function
- double-precision versus single-precision floating-point numbers
- transferring data between host systems.

Floating-Point Representation

To store numbers of large magnitude and to perform computations that require many digits of precision to the right of the decimal point, the SAS System stores all numeric values using *floating-point* (real binary) representation. Floating-point representation is an implementation of what is generally known as scientific notation, in which values are represented as numbers between 0 and 1 times a power of 10. For example, 1234 is .1234 times 10 to the 4th power. The *base* is the number raised to a power; in this example, 10. The *mantissa* is the number multiplied by the base; in this example, .1234. The *exponent* is the power to which the base is raised; in this example, 4.

Floating-point representation is a form of storing in scientific notation, except that on most operating systems the base is not 10, but is either 2 or 16.

Under most situations, the way the SAS System stores numeric values does not affect you as a user. However, floating-point representation can account for anomalies you may notice in SAS program behavior. This section identifies the types of problems that can occur and how you can anticipate and avoid them.

On IBM Mainframe and Data General MV ECLIPSE Operating Systems Floating-point representations are not necessarily related to a single operating system. IBM mainframe host systems (MVS, CMS, and VSE) and Data General's AOS/VS host system all use the same representation made up of 8 bytes as follows:

```
SEEEEEEE MMMMMMMM MMMMMMMM MMMMMMMM MMMMMMMM MMMMMMMM MMMMMMMM MMMMMMMM

 byte 1   byte 2   byte 3   byte 4   byte 5   byte 6   byte 7   byte 8
```

This representation corresponds to bytes of data with each character being 1 bit. The S in byte 1 is the sign bit of the number. A value of 0 in the sign bit is used to represent positive numbers. The seven E characters in byte 1 represent a binary integer known as the characteristic. The characteristic represents a signed exponent and is obtained by adding the bias to the actual exponent. The bias is defined as an offset used to allow for both negative and positive exponents with the bias representing 0. If a bias was not used, an additional sign bit for the exponent would have to be allocated. For example, IBM mainframes and Data General MV ECLIPSE machines employ a bias of 64 (base 10) or 40 (base 16). A characteristic with the value 66 (base 10) represents an exponent of +2, while a characteristic of 61 represents an exponent of -3.

The remaining M characters in bytes 2 through 8 represent the bits of the mantissa. The mantissa is the fractional portion of the number. There is an implied *radix point* before the most significant bit of the mantissa, which also implies that the mantissa is always strictly less than 1. The term radix point is used instead of decimal point because decimal point implies that we are working with decimal (base 10) numbers, which may not be the case. The radix point can be thought of as the generic form of decimal point.

The exponent has a base associated with it. Do not confuse this with the base in which the exponent is represented. The exponent is always represented in binary, but the exponent is used to determine what power of the exponent's base should be multipled by the mantissa. In the case of the IBM mainframes and Data General MV ECLIPSE machines, the exponent's base is 16. For other machines, it is commonly either 2 or 16.

Each bit in the mantissa represents a fraction whose numerator is 1 and whose denominator is a power of 2. For example, the most significant bit in byte 2 represents 1 / 2 ** 1, the next most significant bit represents 1 / 2 ** 2, and so on. In other words, the mantissa is the sum of a series of fractions such as 1/2, 1/4, 1/8, and so on. Therefore, for any floating-point number to be represented exactly, you must be able to express it as the previously mentioned sum. For example, 100 is represented as the following expression:

```
(1/4 + 1/8 + 1/64) * (16 ** 2)
```

To illustrate how the above expression is obtained, two examples follow. The first example is in base 10. In decimal notation, the value 100 is represented as follows:

```
100.
```

The period in this number is the radix point. The mantissa must be less than 1; therefore, you normalize this value by shifting the number three places to the right, which produces the following value:

```
.100
```

Because the number was shifted three places to the right, 3 is the exponent, which results in the following expression:

```
.100*10**3=100
```

The second example is in base 16. In hexadecimal notation, 100 (base 10) is written as follows:

```
64.
```

The period in this number is the radix point. Shifting the number two places to the right, produces the following value:

```
.64
```

Shifting the number two places also indicates an exponent of 2. Rewriting the number in binary produces the following value:

```
.01100100
```

Finally, the value .01100100 can be represented in the following expression:

$$\frac{1}{2^2}+\frac{1}{2^3}+\frac{1}{2^6}=\frac{1}{4}+\frac{1}{8}+\frac{1}{64}$$

In this example, the exponent is 2. To represent the exponent, you add the bias of 64 to the exponent. The hexadecimal representation of the resulting value, 66, is 42. The binary representation is as follows:

```
01000010 01100100 00000000 00000000 00000000 00000000 00000000 00000000
```

On the VMS™ operating system The SAS System under VMS stores numeric values in the D-floating format, which has the following scheme:

```
MMMMMMMM MMMMMMMM MMMMMMMM MMMMMMMM MMMMMMMM MMMMMMMM SEEEEEEE EMMMMMMM

 byte 8   byte 7   byte 6   byte 5   byte 4   byte 3   byte 2   byte 1
```

In D-floating format, the exponent is 8 bits instead of 7, but uses a base 2 instead of base 16 and a bias of 128, which means the magnitude of the D-floating format is not as great as the magnitude of the IBM representation. The mantissa of the D-floating format is, physically, 55 bits. However, all floating-point values under VMS are normalized, which means it is guaranteed that the high-order bit will always be 1. Because of this guarantee, there is no need to physically represent the high-order bit in the mantissa. The high-order bit is hidden.

For example, the decimal value 100 represented in binary is as follows:

```
01100100.
```

This value can be normalized by shifting the radix point as follows:

```
0.1100100
```

Because the radix was shifted to the left seven places, the exponent, 7 plus the bias of 128, is 135. Represented in binary, the number is as follows:

```
10000111
```

To represent the mantissa, subtract the hidden bit from the fraction field:

```
.100100
```

You can combine the sign (0), the exponent, and the mantissa to produce the D-floating format:

```
MMMMMMMM MMMMMMMM MMMMMMMM MMMMMMMM MMMMMMMM MMMMMMMM SEEEEEEE EMMMMMMM

00000000 00000000 00000000 00000000 00000000 00000000 01000011 11001000
```

VMS is a trademark of Digital Equipment Corporation.

On the PRIMOS®operating system The PRIMOS operating system represents floating-point values in base 2 with a bias of 128. There are 16 bits for the exponent, but only 47 bits for the mantissa; PRIMOS represents a larger range of numbers at the expense of precision.

Floating-point values on the PRIMOS look like this:

```
SMMMMMMM MMMMMMMM MMMMMMMM MMMMMMMM MMMMMMMM MMMMMMMM EEEEEEEE EEEEEEEE

 byte 1   byte 2   byte 3   byte 4   byte 5   byte 6   byte 7   byte 8
```

Using the IEEE standard The Institute of Electrical and Electronic Engineers (IEEE) representation is used by many operating systems, including PC DOS®, OS/2®, SUN-3™UNIX®, and HP UNIX systems. The IEEE representation uses an 11-bit exponent with a base of 16 and bias of 1023, which means that it has much greater magnitude than the IBM mainframe representation, but at the expense of 3 bits less in the mantissa. Note that the PC DOS and OS/2 operating systems store the floating-point numbers in the opposite order of most of the other operating systems listed. For example, the value of 1 represented by the IEEE standard is as follows:

```
3F F0 00 00 00 00 00 00  (most operating systems)
00 00 00 00 00 00 F0 3F  (PC DOS and OS/2)
```

Summary Table 3.13 summarizes various representations of floating-point numbers that are stored in 8 bytes.

Table 3.13 *Summary of Floating-Point Numbers Stored in 8 Bytes*

Representation	Base	Bias	Exponent Bits	Max Mantissa Bits
IBM mainframe	16	64	7	56
VAX/VMS	2	128	8	56
AOS/VS	16	64	7	56
PRIMOS	2	128	16	47
IEEE	16	1023	9	52

The SAS System allows for truncated floating-point numbers via the LENGTH statement, which effectively reduces the number of mantissa bits. For more information on the effects of truncated lengths, see "Using the LENGTH Statement" later in this chapter.

Precision Versus Magnitude

As discussed in the previous section, floating-point representation allows for numbers of very large magnitude (numbers such as 2 to the 30th power) and high degrees of precision (many digits to the right of the decimal place). However, operating systems differ on how much precision and how much magnitude to allow.

PRIMOS is a registered trademark of Prime Computer, Inc.

OS/2 and PC DOS are registered trademarks of International Business Machines Corporation.

SUN-3 is a trademark of Sun MicroSystems, Inc.

UNIX is a registered trademark of AT&T

Refer to Table 3.13. You can see that the number of exponent bits and mantissa bits varies. The more bits that are reserved for the mantissa, the more precise the number; the more bits that are reserved for the exponent, the more magnitude the number can have.

Whether precision or magnitude is more important depends on the characteristics of your data. For example, if you are working with physics applications, very large numbers may be needed, and magnitude will probably be more important. However, if you are working with banking applications where every digit is important but the number of digits is not great, then precision is more important. Most often, SAS applications need a moderate amount of both precision and magnitude, which is sufficiently provided by floating-point representation.

Computational Considerations of Fractions

Regardless of how much precision is available, there is still the problem that some numbers cannot be represented exactly. In the decimal number system, the fraction 1/3 cannot be represented exactly in decimal notations. Likewise, most decimal fractions (for example, .1) cannot be represented exactly in base 2 or base 16 numbering systems. Therein lies the principal reason for difficulty in storing fractional numbers in floating-point representation.

Consider the IBM mainframe representation of .1:

```
40 19 99 99 99 99 99 99
```

Notice the trailing 9 digit, similar to the trailing 3 digit in the attempted decimal representation of 1/3 (.3333...). This lack of precision is aggravated by arithmetic operations. Consider what would happen if you added the decimal representation of 1/3 several times. When you add .33333.... to .99999....., the theoretical answer is 1.33333....2, but in practice, this answer is not possible. The sums become imprecise as the values continue.

Likewise, the same process happens when the following DATA step is executed:

```
data _null_;
   do i=-1 to 1 by .1;
      if i=0 then put 'AT ZERO';
   end;
run;
```

The AT ZERO message in the above DATA step is never printed because the accumulation of the imprecise number introduces enough error that the exact value of 0 is never encountered. The number is close, but never exactly 0. This problem is easily resolved by explicitly rounding with each iteration, as the following statements illustrate:

```
data _null_;
   i=-1;
   do while(i<=1);
      i=round(i+.1,.001);
      if i=0 then put 'AT ZERO';
   end;
run;
```

Numeric Comparison Considerations

As discussed in the previous section, imprecision can cause problems with computations. Imprecision can also cause problems with comparisons. Consider the following example in which the PUT statement is not executed:

```
data _null_;
   x=1/3;
   if x=.33333 then put 'MATCH';
run;
```

However, if you add the ROUND function, as in the following example, the PUT statement is executed:

```
data _null_;
   x=1/3;
   if round(x,.00001)=.33333 then put 'MATCH';
run;
```

In general, if you are doing comparisons with fractional values, it is good practice to use the ROUND function.

Using the LENGTH Statement

As discussed earlier in "Floating-Point Representation," the SAS System allows for numeric values to be stored on disk with less than full precision. That is, the LENGTH statement can be used to dictate the number of bytes that are used to store the floating-point number. The LENGTH statement must be used carefully to avoid significant data loss.

For example, the IBM mainframe representation uses 8 bytes for full precision; you can store as few as 2 bytes on disk. The value 1 is represented as 41 10 00 00 00 00 00 00 in 8 bytes. In 2 bytes, it would be truncated to 41 10. You still have the full range of magnitude because the exponent remains intact; there are simply fewer digits involved. A decrease in the number of digits means either fewer digits to the right of the decimal place or fewer digits to the left of the decimal place before trailing zeroes must be used.

For example, consider the number 1234567890, which would be (in decimal) .1234567890 to the 10th power of 10. If you have only five digits of precision, the number becomes 123460000 (rounding up). Note that this is the case regardless of what power of 10 is used (.12346, 12.346, .0000012346, and so on).

The only reason to truncate length by using the LENGTH statement is to save disk space. All values are expanded to full size to perform computations in DATA and PROC steps. In addition, you must be careful in your choice of lengths, as the previous discussion shows.

Consider a length of 2 bytes on an IBM mainframe system. This value allows for 1 byte to store the exponent and sign and 1 byte for the mantissa. The largest value that can be stored in 1 byte is 255. Therefore, if the exponent is 0 (meaning 16 to the 0th power or 1 multiplied by the mantissa), then the largest integer that can be stored with complete certainty is 255. Complete certainty refers to the fact that some larger integers can be stored because they are multiples of 16. For example, consider the 8-byte representation of the numbers 256 to 272 in the following table:

Value	Sign/Exp	Mantissa1	Mantissa2-7	
256	43	10	000000000000	(trailing zeros; multiple of 16)
257	43	10	100000000000	(extra byte needed)
258	43	10	200000000000	
259	43	10	300000000000	
.				
.				
.				
271	43	10	F00000000000	
272	43	11	000000000000	(trailing zeros; multiple of 16)

The numbers from 257 to 271 cannot be stored exactly in the first 2 bytes; a third byte is needed to store the number precisely. Therefore, the following code produces misleading results:

```
data temp;
   length x 2;
   x=257;
   y1=x+1;
run;

data _null_;
   set temp;
   if x=257 then put 'FOUND';
   y2=x+1;
run;
```

The PUT statement is never executed because the value of X is actually 256 (the value 257 truncated to 2 bytes). Recall that 256 is stored in 2 bytes as 4310, but 257 is also stored in 2 bytes as 4310, with the third byte of 10 truncated.

You receive no warning that the value of 257 is truncated in the first DATA step. Note, however, that Y1 will indeed have the value of 258. Y1 has the value of 258 because the values of X are kept in full, 8-byte floating-point representation in the program data vector. Only when being stored in a SAS data set is the value truncated. Y2 has the value of 257 because X is truncated before the number is read into the program data vector.

▶ ***Caution:** Using the LENGTH statement can affect numeric precision.*

Only use the LENGTH statement to truncate values when disk space is limited. If you do use the LENGTH statement, refer to the length table in your host system documentation for maximum values. Also, if the variable values are not always integers, do not use the LENGTH statement. Fractional numbers lose precision if truncated.

Using the TRUNC Function The TRUNC function truncates a number to a requested length and then expands the number back to full length. The truncation and subsequent expansion duplicate the effect of storing numbers in less than full length and then reading them. For example, if the variable

```
x=1/3;
```

is stored with a length of 3, then the following comparison is not true:

```
if x=1/3 then ...;
```

However, adding the TRUNC function makes the comparison true, as in the following:

```
if x=trunc(1/3,3) then ...;
```

You can use the TRUNC function to determine the minimum number of bytes needed to store a value accurately. For example, the following program finds the minimum length of bytes (MINLEN) needed for numbers stored in a native SAS data set named NUMBERS. The data set NUMBERS contains the variable VALUE. VALUE contains a range of numbers, in this example, from 269 to 272:

```
data numbers;
   input value;
   cards;
269
270
271
272
;

data temp;
   set numbers;
   x=value;
   do L=8 to 1 by -1;
      if x NE trunc(x,L) then
      do;
         minlen=L+1;
         output;
         return;
      end;
   end;
run;

proc print noobs;
   var value minlen;
run;
```

Output 3.1 shows the results from this code.

Output 3.1 *Using the TRUNC Function*

```
                    The SAS System                                   1

                 VALUE    MINLEN

                  269        3
                  270        3
                  271        3
                  272        2
```

Note that the minimum length required for the value 271 is greater than the minimum required for the value 272. This fact illustrates that it is possible for the largest number in a range of numbers to require fewer bytes of storage than a smaller number. Therefore, if precision is needed for all numbers in a range, you should obtain the minimum length for all the numbers, not just the largest one.

Double-Precision Versus Single-Precision Floating-Point Numbers

You may have data created by an external program that you want to read into a SAS data set. If the data are in floating-point representation, you can use the RB*w.d* informat to read in the data. However, there are exceptions.

The RB*w.d* informat may truncate double-precision floating-point numbers if the *w* value is less than the size of the double-precision floating-point number (8 on all the operating systems discussed in this chapter). Therefore, the RB8. informat corresponds to a full 8-byte floating point. The RB4. informat corresponds to an 8-byte floating point truncated to 4 bytes, exactly the same as a LENGTH 4 in the DATA step.

An 8-byte floating point that is truncated to 4 bytes may not be the same as *float* in a C program. In the C language, an 8-byte floating-point number is called a *double*. In FORTRAN, it is a REAL*8. In IBM's PL/I, it is a FLOAT BINARY(53). A 4-byte floating-point number is called a *float* in the C language, REAL*4 in FORTRAN, and FLOAT BINARY(21) in IBM's PL/I.

On the IBM mainframes, AOS/VS, and VAX running VMS, a single-precision floating-point number is exactly the same as a double-precision number truncated to 4 bytes. On the operating systems using the IEEE standard, this is not the case. A single-precision floating-point number uses a different number of bits for its exponent and uses a different bias, which means that reading in values using the RB4. informat does not produce the expected results.

Transferring Data between Operating Systems

The problems of precision and magnitude when using floating-point numbers are not confined to a single operating system. Additional problems can arise when moving from one operating system to another unless caution is observed. This section discusses factors to consider when transporting data sets with very large or very small numeric values, using the UPLOAD and DOWNLOAD procedures, the CPORT and CIMPORT procedures, or transport engines.

Refer to Table 3.13, which shows the maximum number of digits of exponent and mantissa and the exponent base. Because there are differences in the maximum values that can be stored on different hosts, there may be problems in transferring your data in floating point from one machine to another. Consider, for example, transporting data between an IBM mainframe and an IBM PC.

The IBM mainframe has a range limit of approximately .54E−78 to .72E76 (and their negative equivalents and 0) for its floating-point numbers. Other machines, such as the IBM PC, have wider limits (the IBM PC has an upper limit of approximately 1E308). Therefore, if you are transferring numbers in the magnitude of 1E100 from a PC to a mainframe, you lose that magnitude. During data transfer, the number is set to the minimum or maximum allowable on that operating system, so 1E100 on a PC is converted to a value that is approximately .72E76 on an IBM mainframe.

▶ ***Caution:*** *Transfer of data between machines can affect numeric precision*

If you are transferring from an IBM mainframe to a PC, notice that the number of bits for the mantissa is 4 less than that for an IBM mainframe, which means you lose 4 bits when moving to an IBM PC. This precision and magnitude difference is a factor when moving from one host to any other where the floating-point representation is different.

Character Values

Character values are values that contain alphabetic characters, numeric digits 0 through 9, and other special characters. This section summarizes information about character values.

Reading Character Values

To read character variables from data lines, place a dollar sign ($) after the variable name in the INPUT statement. By default, character data read from data lines remain in original case. If you want the SAS System to read data as uppercase, use the CAPS system option.

When an INPUT statement reads character fields in data lines, the SAS System reads the entire input field and removes any leading blanks before assigning the value to the variable. Therefore, character values read with an INPUT statement are left aligned. Use the $CHAR*w*. informat to maintain leading blanks.

If the value is shorter than the length of the variable, the SAS System adds blanks to the end of the value to make the value have the length specified. This process is known as padding the value with blanks.

Using Character Values

Character values are used in

- □ character expressions
- □ values of some options
- □ descriptive strings
- □ filenames and other information that the SAS System passes directly to the host system.

Character Expressions

Character expressions can appear in assignment statements, in selection statements (for example, IF-THEN/ELSE statements), and in pointer controls. The most important point to remember is that character constants are enclosed in quotes, but names of character variables are not. Refer to the following statements:

□ `x='abc';`

□ `x=abc;`

□ `if x=' ' then do;`

□ `if name='Smith' then do;`

□ `if name=Smith then do;`

In the second and fifth examples, the SAS System searches for variables ABC and SMITH, instead of a constant. You should represent missing character values in assignment statements with a blank surrounded by quotes, as shown in the third example.

The SAS System distinguishes between uppercase and lowercase letters when comparing SAS values. For example, the character variable values `Smith` and `SMITH` are not equivalent. Use the UPCASE function to produce uppercase values for comparison. Note that the CAPS system option does not translate existing values to uppercase.

To create a character expression, see "SAS Expressions" and "SAS Functions" in Chapter 4.

Option Values

Many system options and statement options take character values. In some cases, the value can be a character constant or the name of a character variable. Again, it is important to remember that character constants are enclosed in quotes, while the names of character variables are not. For example, the following sets of statements are equivalent:

□ `infile` *file-specification* `delimiter=',';`

□ `com=',';`
`infile` *file-specification* `delimiter=com;`

Descriptive Strings

Descriptive strings include character constants used as titles, footnotes, variable labels, and similar items. Enclose character constants in quotes as shown here:

□ `title 'Status Report';`

□ `footnote 'Meeting Agenda';`

□
```
label gross='Revenue before taxes'
      net='Revenue after taxes';
```

For compatibility with previous releases, the SAS System accepts some simple character constants in statements like these without quotes. In new programs, you should always surround character constants in descriptive strings with quotes.

Host Strings

SAS System programs can contain some strings in the form required by the host system. The most common examples are host file names and host system commands. Host file names or library specifications can appear in the areas shown in the lists in this section.

The following statements use host file specifications:

FILE
FILENAME
INFILE
%INCLUDE
LIBNAME

The following display manager commands use host file specifications:

FILE
INCLUDE
PRINT
PRTFILE

The following SAS system options use host file specifications:

ALTLOG=	SASMSG=
ALTPRINT=	SASUSER=
AUTOEXEC=	SITEINFO=
LOG=	SORTPGM=
NEWS=	SYSIN=
PRINT=	USER=
SASAUTOS=	WORK=
SASHELP=	

Host system commands can appear in the X statement and the X display manager command. Consider the following example:

```
x 'system command';
```

Enclose strings to be passed to the host in quotes.

■ **Host information** .... For details, refer to the documentation provided by the vendor for your host system.

.... ■

Using Quotes

The SAS System accepts single quotes (apostrophes) or double quotes (quotation marks). If the value itself contains a single quote, the simplest way to produce the textual single quote is to surround the value with double quotes. In addition, the system interprets two consecutive single quotes as a textual quote rather than a string delimiter when the string is surrounded by single quotes. Therefore, it also is acceptable to use two single quotes to represent a single textual quote within a value surrounded by single quotes.

▶ ***Caution:*** *Matching quotes properly is important.*

Missing or extraneous quotes cause the SAS System to misread both the erroneous statement and the statements that follow it.

The following examples illustrate how to use quotes:

□ `name="O'Brien";  /* correct use   */`

□ `name='O''Brien'; /* correct use   */`

□ `name='O'Brien';  /* incorrect use */`

Note: In the third example, `O` is the character value of NAME, `Brien` is extraneous, and `';` begins another quoted string.

Note that macro variable references (*&name*) and other macro facility items are resolved within double quotes but not within single quotes. Refer to the *SAS Guide to Macro Processing, Version 6, Second Edition* for more information about macro variables.

Character Variable Length

The SAS System determines the length of a variable from its first occurrence in the DATA step, as described in Chapter 2. Therefore, you must allow for the longest possible value in the first statement that mentions the variable. Use the LENGTH statement to determine the length of a character variable both in the program data vector and in the data set being created. (In contrast, a LENGTH statement determines the length of a numeric variable only in the data set being created.) The maximum length of any character variable in the SAS System is 200 bytes.

When the SAS System assigns a value to a variable, it pads the value with blanks or truncates the value on the right side, if necessary, to make it match the length of the target variable. Consider the following statements:

```
length address1 address2 address3 $ 200;
address3=address1||address2;
```

Because the length of ADDRESS3 is 200 bytes, only the first 200 bytes of the concatenation (the value of ADDRESS1) are assigned to ADDRESS3.

Character values often contain trailing blanks. If that is the case, use the TRIM function to remove trailing blanks from ADDRESS1 before performing the concatenation, as follows:

```
address3=trim(address1)||address2;
```

Alignment of Values in Character Variables

When you assign a character value in an assignment statement, the SAS System stores the value as it appears in the statement. The SAS System does not perform any alignment. Output 3.2 illustrates the character value alignment produced by the following program:

```
data aircode;
   input city $1-13;
   length airport $ 10;
   if city='San Francisco' then airport='SFO';
   else if city='Honolulu' then airport='HNL';
   else if city='New York' then airport='JFK or EWR';
   else if city='Miami' then airport='   MIA    ';
   cards;
San Francisco
Honolulu
New York
Miami
;

proc print data=aircode;
run;
```

Output 3.2 *Output from the PRINT Procedure*

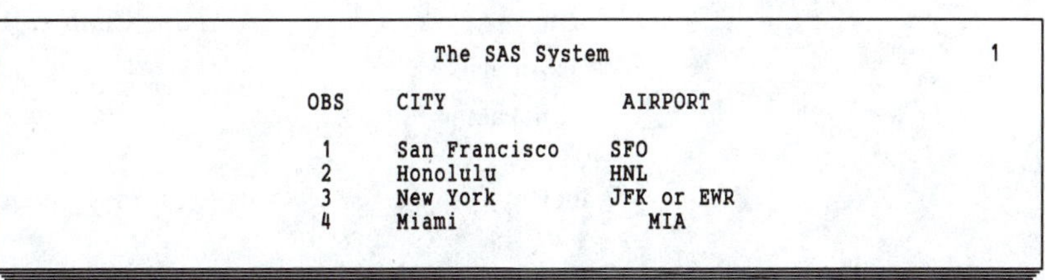

```
                    The SAS System                          1

          OBS    CITY             AIRPORT

           1     San Francisco   SFO
           2     Honolulu        HNL
           3     New York        JFK or EWR
           4     Miami              MIA
```

Working with Character Values

The SAS System provides several features and system options to assist you in working with character values. See Chapter 4 for a description of SAS operators, concatenation, and the comparison of SAS values and magnitudes assigned to individual characters. A description of SAS character functions is located in "SAS Functions" earlier in this chapter.

Variables

Variable Attributes

SAS variables can have the attributes listed in Table 3.14.

Table 3.14 *Variable Attributes*

Attribute	Possible Values	Default Value
Name	Any valid SAS name	None
*Type	Numeric Character	Numeric
*Length		
Numeric	2 to 8 bytes or 3 to 8 bytes **	8 8
Character	1 to 200 bytes	*
Informat	See Chapter 13	
Numeric		*w.d*
Character		$*w.*
Format	See Chapter 14	
Numeric		BEST12.
Character		$*w.*
Label	Up to 40 characters	None
Position in observation	NA	NA
Index part	0, 1, 2, or 3	0

* If not explicitly defined, a variable's type and length are implicitly defined by its first occurrence in a DATA step.

** The minimum length is 2 bytes on some host systems, 3 on others. See the SAS documentation for your host system.

Variable attributes listed in Table 3.14 are defined as follows:

Name
: identifies a variable by its name, the identifying attribute. A variable name must conform to SAS naming rules. A SAS name can be up to eight characters long. The first character must be a letter (A,B,C, . . . ,Z) or underscore(_). Subsequent characters can be letters, digits (0 to 9), or underscores. Note that no blanks are allowed.

  The names _N_, _ERROR_, _I_, _MSG_, and _CMD_ are reserved for the variables that are generated automatically for a DATA step. See "Automatic Variables" in Chapter 2.

Type
: identifies a variable as numeric or character. It is assumed within a DATA step to be numeric unless character is indicated. Numeric values represent numbers, can be read in a variety of forms, and are stored in floating-point format. For a complete discussion of standard and nonstandard numeric values, see "Kinds of Data" in Chapter 2 and "Numeric Values" earlier in this chapter.

  Character values can contain letters, numbers, and special characters and can be from 1 to 200 characters long.

Length
: refers to the number of bytes used to store each of the variable's values in a SAS data set. You can use a LENGTH statement to affect the length of both numeric and character variables. In the program data vector, all numeric variables have a length of 8 during processing, so that variable lengths specified in a LENGTH statement affect the length of numeric variables only in the output data set. Lengths of character variables specified in a LENGTH statement affect both. In an INPUT statement, you can also assign a length other than the default to character variables. A variable appearing for the first time on the left side of an assignment statement has the same length as the result of the expression on the right side of the assignment statement.

Informat
: refers to the instructions that the SAS System uses when reading data values. If no informat is specified, the default informat for a numeric variable is *w.* and $*w.* for a character variable. You can assign SAS informats to a variable in the INFORMAT or ATTRIB statement. You can use the FORMAT procedure to create your own informat for a variable.

Format
: refers to the instructions that the SAS System uses when printing the variable values. If no format is specified, the default format for a numeric variable is BEST*w.* and $*w.* for a character variable. You can assign SAS formats to a variable in the FORMAT or ATTRIB statement. You can use the FORMAT procedure to create your own format for a variable.

Label
: refers to a descriptive label up to forty characters long. A variable label, which can be printed by some SAS procedures, is useful in report writing. You can assign a label to a variable with a LABEL or ATTRIB statement.

Position in observation
: is determined by the order in which the variables are defined in the DATA step. You can find the position of a variable in the observations of a SAS data set with the CONTENTS procedure. This attribute is generally not important within the DATA step except in variable lists like the following:

```
var rent--phone;
```

  See "SAS Variable Lists" in Chapter 4 for more information.

  The position of variables in a SAS data set affects the order they appear in the output of SAS procedures, unless you control the order

(Position in observation continued)

with a VAR statement. See the *SAS Procedures Guide* for more information.

Index part
indicates whether the variable is part of the index for the data set. Possible values and definitions are listed as follows:

Value	Definition
0	none
1	regular index
2	composite index
3	regular and composite index

Indexes are discussed in the section "SAS Indexes" in Chapter 6.

Automatic Variables

Several variables can be automatically created by the DATA step in various circumstances. They exist within the program data vector but are not output to the data set being created. They include the following:

_N_	_CMD_	FIRST.*variable*
ERROR	_MSG_	LAST.*variable*
_I_		

Only _N_ and _ERROR_ are always created within a DATA step. The others are created by specific statements.

_N_ is the number of iterations of a DATA step. The SAS System increments the value of _N_ by one each time the DATA step loops past the DATA statement and begins the next iteration.

ERROR is set to 0 by default, but the SAS System gives it a value of 1 if it encounters an error within a DATA step. Errors that cause the SAS System to assign _ERROR_ a value of 1 include input data errors, data conversion errors, failure of the POINT= option, or function call errors.

The SAS System generates FIRST.*variable* and LAST.*variable* only when input is from one or more SAS data sets and you use a BY statement.

See "By-Group Processing" in Chapter 4 for a discussion of FIRST.*variable* and LAST.*variable*. Also, see the WINDOW statement in Chapter 9 for a discussion of the _CMD_ and _MSG_ variables. See the Implicit ARRAY Statement in Chapter 9 for a discussion of the _I_ variable.

Variables in Assignment Statements

A variable appearing for the first time in a DATA step on the left side of an assignment statement has the same type (character or numeric) as the result of the expression on the right side of the statement.

If you define a numeric variable and assign the result of a character expression to it, the SAS System tries to convert the character result of the expression to a numeric value and execute the statement. If the conversion is not possible, the SAS System issues an error message, assigns the numeric variable a value of missing, and sets the automatic variable _ERROR_ to 1. See "SAS Constants" in Chapter 4 for more information.

If you define a character variable and assign the result of a numeric expression to it, the SAS System tries to convert the numeric result of the expression to a character value using the BEST*w*. format, where *w* is the width of the character variable and has a maximum value of 12. The SAS System then tries to execute the statement. If the character variable you use is not sufficiently long to contain a character representation of the number, the SAS System issues an error message and assigns the character variable asterisks if the value is too large. The SAS System provides no error message and assigns the character variable the character zero (0) if the value is too small. Consider the two DATA steps in the SAS log shown in Output 3.3.

Output 3.3 *Automatic Variable Type Conversions*

```
4
5           data _null_;
6             x= 3626885;
7             length y $ 4;
8             y=x;
9             put y;

36E5
NOTE: Numeric values have been converted to character
      values at the places given by: (Number of times) at (Line):(Column).
      1 at 8:5
10          data _null_;
11            xl= 3626885;
12            length yl $ 1;
13            yl=xl;
14            xs=0.000005;
15            length ys $ 1;
16            ys=xs;
17            put yl= ys=;
18          run;

NOTE: Invalid character data, XL=3626885.00 , at line 13 column 6.
YL=* YS=0
XL=3626885 YL=* XS=5E-6 YS=0 _ERROR_=1 _N_=1
NOTE: Numeric values have been converted to character
      values at the places given by: (Number of times) at (Line):(Column).
      1 at 13:6
      1 at 16:6
```

In the first DATA step of the example, the SAS System was able to fit the value of Y into a 4-byte field by representing its value in scientific notation. See Chapter 14 for a discussion of the BEST*w*. format.

In the second DATA step of the example, the SAS System could not fit the value of YL into a 1-byte field, and it displayed a value of an asterisk (*) instead.

If a variable appears for the first time on the right side of an assignment statement, the SAS System assumes that it is a numeric variable and that its value is missing. A note is printed in the SAS log that the variable is uninitialized. (A RETAIN statement initializes a variable and can assign it a value, even if the RETAIN statement appears after the assignment statement. For more information on the RETAIN statement, see Chapter 9.)

A variable appearing for the first time on the left side of an assignment statement has the same length as the result of the expression on the right side of the assignment statement. A subsequent LENGTH statement can change the length of a numeric variable, but not the length of a character variable. (For more information on the LENGTH statement, see Chapter 9.) For information on the length of values returned by SAS functions, see "SAS Functions" earlier in this chapter and the descriptions of the individual functions in Chapter 11, "SAS Functions."

Table 3.15 gives the length of a result variable produced by various types of expressions when the length is not explicitly set.

Table 3.15 *Length Produced by Various Expressions*

Resulting Type	Expression	Resulting Length	Example
Numeric variable	Numeric variable	Default numeric length (8 bytes unless otherwise specified)	`length a 4;` `x=a;` `*X has length 8;`
Character variable	Character variable	Length of source variable	`length a $ 4;` `x=a;` `*X has length 4;`
Character variable	Character literal	Length of first literal encountered	`x='ABC';` `x='ABCDE';` `*X has length 3;`
Character variable	Concatenation of variables	Sum of the lengths of all variables	`length a $ 4 b $ 6 c $ 2;` `x=a||b||c;` `*X has length 12;`
Character variable	Concatenation of variables and literal	Sum of the lengths of variables and literals encountered in first assignment statement	`length a $ 4;` `x=a||'CAT';` `x= a||'CATNIP';` `*X has length 7;`

CHAPTER 4 Rules of the SAS® Language

(continued on next page)

(continued from previous page)

Introduction

Like any language, the SAS language has its own vocabulary and syntax: that is, words and the rules for putting them together. You define your data and the questions you have about them using the SAS language; this sequence of SAS statements is called a SAS program.

This chapter describes the individual pieces that make up SAS program code, including words in the SAS language, SAS expressions, SAS constants, SAS operators, and the rules for naming and describing SAS program elements. It also discusses date and time values, BY-group processing, and rules for combining SAS data sets.

Words in the SAS Language

Like other languages, the SAS language is composed of several kinds of words. A word in the SAS language is a collection of characters that communicates a meaning to the SAS System and is not divisible into smaller units capable of independent use. Each word in the SAS language belongs to one of several general categories. Understanding the types of words that comprise the SAS language makes the rules governing their syntax and use easier to follow.

The following sections describe how the SAS System recognizes words, what categories of words there are, what makes a word valid within a category, and how the SAS System expects you to use specific kinds of words.

How the SAS System Recognizes Words

The SAS statements in a program first appear to the SAS System as a continuous series of characters. The SAS System divides the characters into words, also known as tokens, as it scans each statement for the first time.

The SAS System classifies tokens into four basic types: names, literals, numbers, and special characters.

□ A name token is a series of characters beginning with a letter or an underscore. Later characters can include letters, underscores, and digits. In most SAS processing, the maximum length of a name is 8 characters. However, that restriction comes from other parts of the SAS System, not from the rules for tokenization. A name token can contain up to 200 characters. Examples of name tokens include

```
data        _new          yearcutoff
year_99     descending    _n_
```

□ A literal token consists of 1 to 200 characters enclosed in single or double quotes. The SAS System does not store the surrounding quotes as part of the literal token; it simply marks the token as a literal. Examples of literals include

```
'Chicago'           "1990-91"
'Amelia Earhart'    "Report for the Third Quarter"
```

□ A number token in general is composed entirely of numeric digits, with an optional decimal point and a leading plus or minus sign. The SAS System also recognizes numbers in scientific (E−) notation, numbers in hexadecimal notation, missing value symbols, and date and time literals as number tokens. Examples of number tokens include

```
5683    2.35     0b0x
-5      5.4E-1   '24aug90'd
```

□ A special-character token is usually a single keyboard character, excluding letters, numbers, the underscore, and the blank. In general, each special character is a single token, although some two-character operators, such as ** and <=, form single tokens. The blank can end a name or a number token, but it is not a token. Examples of special-character tokens include

```
=        ;        ,
+        @        /
```

A token ends when the SAS System encounters one of the following:

- □ the beginning of a new token
- □ a blank after a name or a number token
- □ the ending quote of a literal token.

No token can have more than 200 characters.

Placement and Spacing of Words in SAS Statements

You can begin SAS statements in any column of a line and write several statements on the same line. You can begin a statement on one line and continue it on another line, but you cannot split a word between two lines.

The rules for recognizing the boundaries of tokens determine the use of spacing in SAS programs. Consider the following two statements:

```
total=x+y;
input group 15 room 20;
```

In the first statement, the SAS System can determine the boundary of every token by examining the beginning of the next token. The first special-character token, the equal sign, marks the end of the name token TOTAL. The plus sign, another special-character token, marks the end of the name token X. The last special-character token, the semicolon, marks the end of the Y token. Therefore, blanks are not needed to end any tokens (though you may add blanks for readability).

In the second statement, the SAS System recognizes the end of the individual tokens by the presence of blanks. Without blanks, the entire statement up to the semicolon fits the rules for a name token: it begins with a letter or underscore, contains letters, digits, or underscores thereafter, and is less than 200 characters long. Therefore, the second statement requires blanks to distinguish individual name and number tokens.

Note that a blank is not treated as a character in a SAS statement unless it is enclosed in quotes as a literal or part of a literal. Therefore, you can put multiple blanks any place in a SAS statement where you can put a single blank, with no effect on the syntax. For example, the following statements are equivalent:

```
total2=total+10;
total2  =  total + 10 ;
```

Although the SAS System does not have rigid spacing requirements, SAS programs are easier to read if you consistently indent statements. The examples in this book illustrate good spacing conventions.

SAS Keywords

A SAS keyword is a word or symbol in a SAS statement that defines the statement type to the SAS System. Keywords are a fixed part of the SAS language, and their form and meaning are also fixed.

Generally, you use keywords within SAS statements to indicate the specific kind of processing you want the SAS System to perform and to modify, generalize, limit, or put conditions on that processing.

Many SAS statements begin with a keyword to identify the statement type. Each of the following SAS statements begins with a SAS keyword:

□ `put x;`

□ `data one;`

□ `format value1 abcd.;`

□ `proc means data=store.supply maxdec=3;`

□ `infile rawdata;`

The keyword names each statement. The list includes a PUT statement, a DATA statement, a FORMAT statement, a PROC statement, and an INFILE statement.

In several kinds of SAS statements, the keyword defining the statement type is a symbol, or a combination of symbols, which does not necessarily begin the statement. Examples include

□ assignment statements, where the equal sign (=) in combination with the syntax of the statement defines the statement type

□ sum statements, which require a plus sign (+)

□ comments and comment statements, which are enclosed by the keywords slash asterisk and asterisk slash (/*, */) or asterisk and semicolon (*, ;)

□ null statements, which consist of a single semicolon (;).

In most cases, the SAS System does not prohibit you from using a keyword as simply a name in other situations. Here is an example:

```
data _null_;
data=365;
```

In this example, the character string DATA is a keyword in the first line and a valid variable name in the second line. The second line is an example of an assignment statement.

SAS Names

A *SAS name* is a name token assigned to

variables	arrays
SAS data sets	statement labels
formats or informats	SAS macros or macro variables
SAS procedures	SAS catalog entries
options	librefs or filerefs

There are two kinds of names in the SAS System: names supplied by SAS System users and names of elements of the SAS language.

Names Supplied by Users

SAS names supplied by users must meet the following requirements:

□ Names can be up to eight characters long.

□ The first character must be a letter (A, B, C, . . ., Z) or underscore (_). Subsequent characters can be letters, numeric digits (0, 1, . . ., 9), or underscores. With regard to user-supplied SAS names, the SAS System is not case sensitive and converts all names to uppercase during processing.

- Blanks cannot appear in SAS names.
- Special characters, except for the underscore, are not allowed. The dollar sign ($), pound sign (#), and at sign (@) are allowed in filerefs only.
- Names of special SAS automatic variables and variable list names (for example, _N_, _ERROR_, _NUMERIC_, and _ALL_) cannot be assigned as user-supplied variable names.
- Names the SAS System reserves for particular libraries should not be used as names for user-supplied librefs. These include

LIBRARY	SASUSER
SASCAT	USER
SASHELP	WORK
SASMSG	

- The SAS System reserves three names for special data sets: _NULL_, _DATA_, and _LAST_. Do not assign these names to a new data set.

Names of Elements of the SAS Language

Certain elements of the SAS language have names that are easily recognizable because of their special syntax. These elements include

- special SAS variables or variable lists that both begin and end with an underscore: for example, _N_, _ERROR_, _NUMERIC_, _CHARACTER_, and _ALL_. See "SAS Variable Lists" later in this chapter for more information about variable list names.
- SAS formats and informats. Character formats and informats always begin with a dollar sign ($). All formats and informats always end with either a decimal point, or a decimal point and a numeric digit. The characters after the dollar sign (if any) and preceding the decimal point follow the rules for user-supplied SAS names.
- macro keywords. A percent sign (%) always precedes these names, but it is not part of the keyword name.
- macro variable references. An ampersand (&) always precedes these names, but it is not part of the macro variable name.
- procedure and option names. In some cases, these names are longer than eight characters.

Just as the SAS System recognizes keywords from position and context, it also recognizes names in the same way. If the SAS System sees a word that meets the requirements for a user-supplied SAS name and that is not used in a syntax that defines it as anything else, it assumes the word is a variable name.

Some examples of names in SAS statements follow:

- In the following PUT statement, X is a user-supplied variable name and $CHAR5. is the name of a SAS character format:

```
put x $char5.;
```

- ONE is the user-supplied name of the SAS data set that this DATA step creates:

```
data one;
```

□ In this FORMAT statement, VALUE1 is a user-supplied variable name and ABCD. is a user-supplied format name:

```
format value1 abcd.;
```

□ In the following statement, MEANS is the name of a SAS procedure. STORE.SUPPLY consists of two user-supplied names: STORE is a user-supplied libref, a name referring to a SAS data library; SUPPLY is a user-supplied SAS data set name, referring to a SAS data set within the SAS library specified by the libref.

```
proc means data=store.supply maxdec=3;
```

□ In this INFILE statement, RAWDATA is a user-supplied fileref, a name referring to an external data file.

```
infile rawdata;
```

Comments in SAS Code

You can insert comments in SAS code in either of two ways:

□ wherever a single blank can appear (except within a quoted literal string), as in these examples:

□
```
   /* sort the data set */
proc sort;
```

□
```
proc sort /* sort the data set */;
```

□ as a separate comment statement, as in this example:

```
   * sort the data set;
proc sort;
```

As the previous examples illustrate, two sets of delimiters are acceptable:

```
* comment;
```

```
/* comment */
```

Only the latter form can appear within an existing SAS statement.

Refer to Chapter 9, "SAS Language Statements," for a complete description of comments.

SAS Variable Lists

A SAS *variable list* is a list of variable names following a specific form. There are three kinds of variable lists:

□ numbered range lists

□ name range lists

□ special SAS name lists.

Within a DATA step, the SAS System keeps track of active variables in the order the compiler encounters them, whether they are read from existing data sets or an external file, or created in the step. The order that the SAS System uses to keep track of variables is the same order that the variables appear in SAS variable lists.

You can use abbreviated variable lists in many SAS statements, including those which define variables. Abbreviated variable lists are especially useful *after* you define all of the variables you will use in a SAS program.

You can use three kinds of abbreviated variable lists:

□ Numbered range lists require you to have a series of variables with the same name, except for the last character or characters, which are consecutive numbers. For example, the following two lists refer to the same variables:

- □ `x1,x2,x3,...,xn`
- □ `x1-xn`

In a numbered range list, you can begin with any number and end with any number as long as you do not violate the rules for user-supplied variable names and the numbers are consecutive and ascending.

□ Name range lists rely on the position of variables on the program data vector, as in these examples:

- □ `x--a`
- □ `x-numeric-a`
- □ `x-character-a`

The first list includes all variables, in the order they are on the program data vector, from X to A inclusive. The second list includes all numeric variables from X to A inclusive. The third list includes all character variables from X to A inclusive.

□ Special SAS name lists include

NUMERIC	specifies all numeric variables already defined in the current DATA step.
CHARACTER	specifies all character variables currently defined in the current DATA step.
ALL	specifies all variables currently defined in the current DATA step.

For example, consider the following INPUT statement:

```
input idnum name $ weight pulse chins;
```

In later statements you can use these abbreviated forms:

□
```
      /* keep the variables idnum weight and pulse */
keep idnum-numeric-pulse;
```

□
```
      /* keep the variables name weight and pulse */
keep name--pulse;
```

Suppose you decide to give some of the numeric variables sequential names, as in VAR1, VAR2, and so on. Then, you can write the INPUT statement as follows:

```
input idnum name $ var1-var3;
```

Note that although the character variable NAME is not included in this abbreviated list, variables in a numbered list need not be all character or all numeric variables.

Other examples of abbreviated variable lists are shown throughout this book. Note that abbreviated variable lists are allowed in most SAS data set options, including the DROP= and KEEP= options. They are not allowed in the RENAME= option. See Chapter 15, "SAS Data Set Options," for more details.

SAS Expressions

An *expression* is a sequence of operands and operators forming a set of instructions that are performed to produce a result value. The *operands* are variable names or constants, and they can be numeric, character, or both. The *operators* are special-character operators, functions, and grouping parentheses. A single variable name, constant, or function is also a valid expression. See Chapter 11, "SAS Functions," for a complete discussion of SAS functions. Refer to "SAS Operators" later in this chapter for a general discussion of operators. Chapter 10, "SAS Operators," contains a table of operators and explains the order in which the SAS System evaluates operators in SAS expressions.

The following examples show valid SAS expressions:

- `3`
- `x`
- `log(y)`
- `x+1`
- `part/all*100`
- `1-exp(n/(n-1))`
- `age<100`
- `state='NC'|state='SC'`
- `trim(last)||', '||first`

Use expressions in SAS programming statements for transforming variables, creating new variables, conditional processing, calculating new values, and assigning new values.

SAS expressions can resolve to numeric values, character values, or Boolean values. See "Logical (Boolean) Operators and Expressions" later in this chapter for a discussion of SAS expressions that resolve to Boolean values.

SAS Constants

A SAS *constant* is a number or a character string that indicates a fixed value. Constants can be used in many SAS statements, including assignment and IF-THEN statements. They can also be used as values for certain options. Constants are also called *literals*.

This section discusses the forms and uses of the two basic types of SAS constants: numeric and character. When values for both numeric and character constants are missing, they can be represented with missing values. Both numeric and character constants may be the subject of bit testing, a special use of SAS constants. SAS date and time constants are also discussed.

Numeric Constants

A *numeric constant* is a number that appears in a SAS statement. Numeric constants can be presented in a variety of forms including standard notation, scientific (E) notation, hexadecimal notation, and special SAS date and time values.

Standard Notation

Most numeric constants are written just as numeric data values are. The numeric constant in the following expression is 100:

```
part/all*100
```

Numeric constants expressed in standard notation can be integers, can be specified with or without a plus or minus sign, and can include decimal places, as in these examples:

- `1`
- `1.23`
- `01`
- `-5`

Scientific Notation

In scientific notation, the number before the E is multiplied by the power of ten indicated by the number after the E. For example, 2E4 is the same as $2x10^4$ or 20,000. Numeric constants larger than $(10^{32})-1$ must be specified in scientific notation. Additional examples include

- `1.2e23`
- `0.5e-10`

Hexadecimal Notation

Numeric constants can be expressed as hexadecimal values in SAS statements. A numeric hex constant starts with a numeric digit (usually 0), can be followed by more hexadecimal digits, and ends with the letter X. If the constant does not begin with a numeric digit, the SAS System can treat it as a variable name. The constant can contain up to 16 valid hexadecimal digits (0 to 9, A to F). Here are some examples of numeric hex constants:

```
0c1x 0b37x 322x 0c4x 9x
```

Numeric hex constants can be used in a DATA step as follows:

```
data test;
   input abend pib2.;
   if abend=0c1x or abend=0b0ax then do;
   more SAS statements
run;
```

Character Constants

A *character constant* consists of 1 to 200 characters and must be enclosed in quotes. Character constants can also be represented in hexadecimal form. In the following SAS statement, **Tom** is a character constant:

```
if name='Tom' then do;
```

If a character constant includes a single quote, surround it with double quotes. For example, if you want to specify the character value **Tom's** as a constant, you enter

```
name="Tom's"
```

You can also write a single quote as two consecutive single quotes and the SAS System treats it as one. You can then surround the character constant with single quotes, as follows:

```
name='Tom''s'
```

The same principle holds true for double quotes, as the following example shows:

```
name="Tom""s"
```

Hexadecimal Notation

SAS character constants can be expressed in hexadecimal notation. A character hex constant is a string of an even number of hex characters enclosed in single or double quotes, followed immediately by an X, as in this example:

```
'534153'x
```

A comma can be used to make the string more readable, but it is not part of and does not alter the hex value. If the string contains a comma, the comma must separate an even number of hex characters within the string, as in this example:

```
if value='3132,3334'x then do;
```

Date and Time Constants

You can create a *SAS date constant* or a *SAS time constant* by writing the date or time enclosed in single or double quotes, followed by a D (date), T (time), or DT (datetime) to indicate the type of value. Use the following patterns to create date and time constants:

'*ddmmm<yy>yy*'D
"*ddmmm<yy>yy*"D

represent a SAS date value. Refer to the following examples:

- □ `date='1jan1990'd;`
- □ `date='01jan89'd;`

'*hh:mm<:ss.s>*'T
"*hh:mm<:ss.s>*"T

represent a SAS time value. Refer to the following examples:

- □ `time='9:25't;`
- □ `time='9:25:19't;`

'ddmmm<yy>yy: hh:mm<:ss.s>'DT
"ddmmm<yy>yy: hh:mm<:ss.s>"DT
represent a SAS datetime value. Refer to the following examples:

□ `dtime='18jan89:9:27:05'dt;`

□ `if begin='01may90:9:30:00'dt then`
`end='31dec90:5:00:00'dt;`

Refer to Chapter 13, "SAS Informats," Chapter 14, "SAS Formats," and the YEARCUTOFF= system option in Chapter 16, "SAS System Options," for related information.

Numeric-Character Conversion

If a value does not match the type called for, the SAS System attempts to convert the value to the expected type. The SAS System automatically converts character variables to numeric variables and numeric variables to character variables, according to the following rules:

□ If you use a character variable with an operator (for example, the plus sign) that requires numeric operands, the SAS System converts the character variable to numeric.

□ If you use a comparison operator (for example, the equal sign) to compare a character variable and a numeric variable, the character variable is converted to numeric.

□ If you use a numeric variable with an operator (for example, the concatenation operator) that requires a character value, the numeric value is converted to character using the BEST12. format. Because the SAS System stores the results of the conversion beginning at the rightmost byte, you must store the converted values in a variable of sufficient length to accommodate the BEST12. format.

□ If you use a numeric variable on the left side of an assignment statement and a character variable on the right, the character variable is converted to numeric. In the opposite situation, where the character variable is on the left and the numeric is on the right, the SAS System converts the numeric variable to character using the BEST*n*. format, where *n* is the length of the variable on the left.

Whenever the SAS System performs an automatic conversion, it prints a message in the SAS log warning that the conversion took place. If converting a character variable to numeric produces invalid numeric values, the SAS System assigns a missing value to the result, prints an error message in the log, and sets the value of the automatic variable _ERROR_ to 1.

Bit Masks

Bit masks are used in bit testing to compare internal bits in a value's representation. The general form of the operation is

expression comparison-operator bit-mask

Each component of the bit-testing operation is described here:

expression
: can be any valid SAS expression. Both character and numeric variables can be the subject of bit testing. When testing a character value, the SAS System aligns the leftmost bit of the mask with the leftmost bit of the string; the test proceeds through the corresponding bits, moving to the right. When the SAS System tests a numeric value, the value is truncated from a floating-point number to a 32-bit integer. The rightmost bit of the mask is aligned with the rightmost bit of the number, and the test proceeds through the corresponding bits, moving to the left.

▶ ***Caution:** Truncation can occur when comparing with a bit mask.*

If the expression is longer than the bit mask, the SAS System truncates the expression before it makes the comparison with the bit mask. A false comparison may result. An expression's length (in bits) must be less than or equal to the length of the bit mask. If the bit mask is longer than a character expression, the SAS System writes a warning in the log stating that the bit mask is truncated on the left and continues processing.

comparison-operator
: compares an expression with the bit mask. Refer to "Comparison Operators" later in this chapter for a discussion of operators.

bit-mask
: is a string of 0s, 1s, and periods in quotes that is immediately followed by a B. Zeros test whether the bit is off; 1s test whether the bit is on; and periods ignore the bit. Commas and blanks can be inserted in the bit mask for readability without affecting its meaning.

Here is an example of a test of a character variable:

```
if a='..1.0000'b then do;
```

If the third bit of A (counting from the left) is on, and the fifth through eighth bits are off, the comparison is true and the expression results in 1. Otherwise, the comparison is false and the expression results in 0.

Here is another example:

```
data test;
   input @88 bits $char1.;
   if bits='10000000'b then category='a';
   else if bits='01000000'b then category='b';
   else if bits='00100000'b then category='c';
run;
```

Note: Bit masks cannot be used as bit literals in assignment statements. For example, the following statement is not valid:

```
x='0101'b;        /* incorrect */
```

The $BINARYw. and BINARYw. formats and the $BINARYw., BINARYw.d, and BITSw.d informats can be useful in bit testing. Use them for converting character and numeric values to their binary values, and vice versa, and for extracting specified bits from input data. See Chapter 13 and Chapter 14 for descriptions and examples of these informats and formats.

Missing Values

Missing values are often present in the data you use in your SAS programs. To check data for missing values, or to work with these values, you can assign missing values to variables in programming statements. In certain situations, the SAS System generates missing values.

This section describes how you assign missing values, how the SAS System handles missing values, and how and when the SAS System generates missing values. For information about how the SAS System reads missing values in input data, see "Missing Values in Input Data" in Chapter 2, "The DATA Step."

How to Represent Missing Values

You inform the SAS System about the type of missing value with which you are working by using standard missing value notations for numeric, character, and special numeric missing values.

numeric missing values
: are represented by a single decimal point (.).

character missing values
: are represented by a blank enclosed in quotes (' ').

special numeric missing values
: are represented by two characters: a decimal point followed by either a letter (for example, .B) or an underscore (._). Thus, 27 special missing values are possible.

Note: Previous releases of SAS software required that you use the uppercase form of a letter to represent special missing values; the SAS System now accepts either uppercase or lowercase letters.

▶ *Caution: If you do not begin a special numeric missing value with a period, the SAS System identifies it as a variable name.*

To use a special numeric missing value in a SAS expression or assignment statement, you must begin the value with a period, followed by the letter or underscore.

When the SAS System prints a special missing value, it prints only the letter or underscore.

Ordering of Missing Values

When sorting the data in your SAS program, it is important to understand how the SAS System orders missing values.

Numeric variables Within the SAS System, a missing value for a numeric variable is smaller than all numbers: if you sort your data set by a numeric variable, observations with missing values for that variable appear first in the sorted data set. For numeric variables, you can compare special missing values with numbers and with each other. Table 4.1 shows the sorting order of numeric values.

Table 4.1 *Missing Value Sort Order*

Sort Order	Symbol	Description
smallest	_	underscore
	.	period
	A–Z	special missing values A (smallest) through Z (largest)
	$-n$	negative numbers
	0	zero
largest	$+n$	positive numbers

For example, the numeric missing value (.) is sorted before the special numeric missing value .A, and both are sorted before the special missing value .Z. The SAS System does not distinguish between lowercase and uppercase letters when sorting special numeric missing values. This sorting order is true for both ASCII and EBCDIC systems.

Character variables Missing values of character variables are smaller than any printable character value. When you sort a data set by a character variable, observations with missing (blank) values of the sorting variable always appear before observations in which values of the sorting variable contain only printable characters. However, some usually unprintable characters (for example, machine carriage-control characters, and real or binary numeric data that have been read in error as character data) have values less than the blank. Therefore, when your data include unprintable characters, missing values may not appear first in a sorted data set.

Missing Values in Expressions

Missing value constants used in SAS expressions or assignment statements are helpful for checking missing values in your data. You can also assign special numeric missing values to help analyze the data.

Missing values in assignment statements You can set values to missing within your DATA step with program statements such as this one:

```
if age<0 then age=.;
```

This statement sets the value of AGE to an ordinary missing value if AGE has a value less than 0.

The following example assigns a special missing value. Suppose that you are checking the ages that people report for themselves in a survey by subtracting their date of birth from the date of the interview and comparing that with their answer to the question on age. If the subtraction gives a different age from what they report, you assign a value of .D (for discrepancy) to AGE as indicated here:

```
data survey;
   input survdate birthdat age;
   if (survdate-birthdat) ne age then age=.d;
   cards;
1990 1950 40
1990 1960 33
more data lines
;
```

Missing values in comparison operations When you check for ordinary missing numeric values, your code might look as follows:

```
if numvar=. then do;
```

If your data contain special missing values, you can check for ordinary and special missing values of a variable with the following statement:

```
if numvar<=.z then do;
```

To check for missing character values, you might use the following code, where ' ' is a blank literal for character variables:

```
if charvar=' ' then do;
```

In each case, the SAS System checks to see if the variable's value in the current observation is equal to the missing value specified. If it is, the SAS System executes the DO group.

Missing values in logical operations Missing values and zero have a value of `false` when you use them with logical operators such as AND or OR. All other values have a value of `true`. See "Logical (Boolean) Operators and Expressions" later in this chapter for more information on logical operators.

Missing Values Generated by the SAS System

In addition to the missing values that are present in your data and that you assign in program statements, the SAS System can assign missing values to protect you from problems arising in three common computing situations:

- □ using missing values in calculations
- □ performing illegal operations
- □ converting character values to numeric when the character variable contains nonnumerical information.

Missing values in calculations If you use a missing value in an arithmetic calculation, the SAS System sets the result of that calculation to missing. Then, if you use that result in another calculation, the next result is also missing. This action is called *propagation of missing values.* Propagation of missing values is important because the SAS System continues working at the same time that it lets you know, via warning messages, which arithmetic expressions have missing values and at what point it created them.

The result of any numeric missing value in a SAS expression is a period. Thus, special missing values and ordinary numeric missing values both propagate as a period. For example, the following DATA step results in a period being written to the log:

```
data a;
   x=.d;
   y=x+1;
   put y=;
run;
```

If you do not want missing values to propagate in your arithmetic expressions, you can use the sample statistic functions described in Chapter 11 to omit missing values from the computations. For example, consider the following DATA step:

```
data test;
   x=.;
   y=5;
   a=x+y;
   b=sum(x,y);
run;
```

The value of X is missing; the value of Y is 5. Adding X and Y together in an expression produces a missing result, so the value of A is missing. However, since the SUM function ignores missing values, the value of B is 5.

Illegal operations If you try to perform an illegal operation (for example, dividing by zero, taking the logarithm of zero, or using an expression to produce a number too large to be represented as a floating-point number known as overflow), the SAS System prints a warning message and assigns a missing value to the result.

Illegal character-to-numeric conversions The SAS System automatically converts character values to numeric values if a character variable is used in an arithmetic expression. If a character value contains nonnumerical information and the SAS System tries to convert it to a numeric value, an error message is printed and the result of the conversion is set to missing.

SAS Operators

SAS operators are symbols that request a comparison, a logical operation, or an arithmetic calculation. The SAS System uses two major kinds of operators: prefix operators and infix operators.

A *prefix operator* is an operator that is applied to the variable, constant, function, or parenthesized expression immediately following it, for example, −6. The plus sign (+) and minus sign (−) can be used as prefix operators. The word NOT and its equivalent symbols are also prefix operators (see "Logical (Boolean) Operators and Expressions" later in this chapter). Some examples of prefix operators used with variables, constants, functions, and parenthesized expressions are shown here:

- `+y`
- `-25`
- `-cos(angle1)`
- `+(x*y)`

An *infix operator* applies to the operands on each side of it, for example, 6<8. There are four general kinds of infix operators: arithmetic; comparison; logical or Boolean; and others, such as minimum, maximum, and concatenation. When used to perform arithmetic operations, the plus and minus signs are infix operators.

A SAS expression with no more than one operator is called a *simple expression*. When an expression includes several operators, it is called a *compound expression*. When the SAS System encounters a compound expression, it follows certain rules to determine the order in which to evaluate each part of the expression. Chapter 10 contains a complete discussion of the rules for evaluating compound expressions.

The SAS System also contains several other operators that are used only with certain SAS statements or display manager windows. The WHERE statement uses a special group of SAS operators, valid only when used with WHERE expressions. See the WHERE statement in Chapter 9, "SAS Language Statements," for a discussion of these operators. The CALCULATOR display manager window uses a unique set of operators, in addition to standard arithmetic operators. For details, see the CALCULATOR window in Chapter 17, "SAS Display Manager Windows."

Arithmetic Operators

Arithmetic operators indicate that an arithmetic calculation is performed. The arithmetic operators are shown here:

Symbol	Definition
**	exponentiation
*	multiplication
/	division
+	addition
−	subtraction

For example, A**3 means raise the value of A to the third power. The expression 2*Y means multiply 2 by the value of Y.

Note: The asterisk (*) is always necessary to indicate that multiplication is performed; thus, 2Y and 2(Y) are not valid expressions.

If a missing value is an operand for an arithmetic operator, the result is a missing value. See "Missing Values Generated by the SAS System" earlier in this chapter for a discussion of propagation of missing values.

Comparison Operators

Comparison operators propose a relationship between two quantities and ask the SAS System to determine whether or not that relationship holds. If it does hold (in other words, if it is true), the result of carrying out the operation is the value 1; if it does not hold (in other words, if it is false), the result is the value 0.

Definition of Comparison Operators

Comparison operators can be expressed as symbols or written with letters. An operator written with letters, such as EQ for =, is called a *mnemonic operator*. The symbols for comparison operators and their mnemonic equivalents are shown in the following table:

Symbol	Mnemonic Equivalent	Definition
=	EQ	equal to
^=	NE*	not equal to
¬=	NE	not equal to
~=	NE	not equal to
>	GT	greater than
<	LT	less than
>=**	GE	greater than or equal to
<=	LE	less than or equal to
	IN	equal to one of a list

* The symbol you use for NE depends on your terminal.
** The symbols =< and => are also accepted for compatibility with previous releases of the SAS System.

You can add a colon (:) modifier to any of the operators to compare only a specified prefix of a character string. See "Character Comparisons" later in this chapter for details.

The IN operator compares a value produced by an expression on the left of the operator to a list of values given on the right. The result is 1 if the value on the left matches a value in the list and 0 otherwise. The form of the comparison is

expression IN (*value-1*<. . . ,*value-n*>)

The components of the comparison are as follows:

expression
: can be any valid SAS expression but is usually a variable name when used with the IN operator.

value
: must be a SAS constant.

Examples of using the IN operator are included in the following sections, "Numeric Comparisons" and "Character Comparisons."

Numeric Comparisons

The SAS System makes numeric comparisons based on the values of the numbers. A missing numeric value compares smaller than any other numeric value, and missing numeric values have their own sort order (see "Ordering of Missing Values" earlier in this chapter). A false comparison may result when numeric values of different lengths are compared because values less than 8 bytes have less precision than those longer than 8 bytes. Rounding also affects the outcome of numeric comparisons. See "Numeric Values" in Chapter 3, "Components of the SAS Language," for a complete discussion of numeric precision.

Consider the expression A<=B. If A has the value 4 and B has the value 3, then A<=B has the value 0 (false). If A is 5 and B is 9, then the expression has the value 1 (true). If A and B each have the value 47, then again the relationship holds and the expression has the value 1.

Comparison operators appear frequently in IF-THEN statements, as in this example:

```
if x<y then c=5;
else c=12;
```

Comparisons are also used in expressions in assignment statements. For example, the preceding statements can be recoded as follows:

```
c=5*(x<y)+12*(x>=y);
```

Since quantities inside parentheses are evaluated before any operations are performed on them, the expressions (X<Y) and (X>=Y) are evaluated first and the result (1 or 0) is substituted for the expressions in parentheses. Therefore, if X=6 and Y=8, the expression evaluates as follows:

```
c=5*(1)+12*(0)
```

The result of this statement is C=5.

Use the IN operator to determine whether a value is among a specified range of numbers. The following statements are equivalent:

- □ `if num in (1,3,5) then output;`
- □ `if num=1 or num=3 or num=5 then output;`

Character Comparisons

Comparisons are performed on character as well as numeric operands, although the comparison always yields a numeric result (1 or 0). Character operands are compared character-by-character from left to right. Character order is determined by machine *collating sequence*. Two character values of unequal length are compared as if blanks were attached to the end of the shorter value before the comparison is made. A missing character value compares smaller than any other printable character value.

You can also compare only a specified prefix of a character string using a colon (:) after the comparison operator. The SAS System then truncates the longer value to the length of the shorter value for the comparison. Note that the SAS System truncates and extends values only during the comparison. The values themselves keep their lengths.

For example, in the EBCDIC and ASCII collating sequences, `G` is greater than `A`; therefore, the expression `Gray>Adams` is true. Because `.` is less than `h`, expression `C. Jones<Charles Jones` is also true.

Since trailing blanks are ignored in a comparison, `fox` is equivalent to `foxbbb` (where `b` is the symbol for the blank character). However, because blanks at the beginning and in the middle of a character value are significant to the SAS System, `fox` is not equivalent to `bbbfox`.

The following statement selects observations that have the single letter `S` as a value for the variable LASTINIT:

```
if lastinit='S';
```

In the following example, the colon modifier after the equal sign tells the SAS System to look at only the first character of values of the variable LASTNAME and to select the observations with names beginning with the letter S:

```
if lastname=:'S';
```

Since printable characters are greater than blanks, the following statements select observations with values of LASTNAME that are greater than or equal to the letter S:

```
□ if lastname>='S';
□ if lastname>=:'S';
```

These operations show how to compare the beginnings of character strings. Several SAS character functions (for example, the INDEX function) are helpful for searching strings and extracting values.

Use the IN operator to determine whether a variable's value is among a list of character values. The following statements produce the same results:

```
□ if state in ('NY','NJ','PA') then region2+1;
□ if state='NY' or state='NJ' or state='PA' then region2+1;
```

Logical (Boolean) Operators and Expressions

Logical operators, also called *Boolean operators,* are usually used in expressions to link sequences of comparisons. The logical operators are shown in the following table.

Symbol	Mnemonic Equivalent
&	AND
|	OR
¬	NOT *
^	NOT
~	NOT

* The symbol you use for NOT depends on your terminal.

In addition, a numeric expression without any logical operators can serve as a Boolean expression.

The AND Operator

If *both* of the quantities linked by AND are 1 (true), then the result of the AND operation is 1; otherwise, the result is 0. For example, examine the following comparison:

```
a<b & c>0
```

The result is true (has the value 1) only when both A<B *and* C>0 are 1 (true): that is, when A is less than B and C is positive.

Two comparisons with a common variable linked by AND can be condensed with an implied AND. For example, the following two subsetting IF statements produce the same result:

- `if 16<=age and age<=65;`
- `if 16<=age<=65;`

The OR Operator

If *either* of the quantities surrounding an OR is 1 (true), then the result of the OR operation is 1 (true); otherwise, the OR operation produces a 0. For example, examine the following comparison:

```
a<b|c>0
```

The result is true (has the value 1) when A<B is 1 (true) regardless of the value of C. It is also true when the value of C>0 is 1 (true), regardless of the values of A and B. Therefore, it is true when either or both of those relationships hold.

Be careful when using the OR operator with a series of comparisons (in an IF, SELECT, or WHERE statement, for instance). Remember that only one comparison in a series of OR comparisons needs to be true to make a condition true, and any nonzero, nonmissing constant is always evaluated as true. (See "Boolean Numeric Expressions" later in this chapter.) Therefore, the following subsetting IF statement is always true:

```
if x=1 or 2;
```

The SAS System first evaluates X=1, and the result can be either true or false; however, since the 2 is evaluated as nonzero and nonmissing (true), the entire expression is true. In this statement, however, the condition is not necessarily true:

```
if x=1 or x=2;
```

Either comparison can evaluate as true or false.

You can also use the IN operator with a series of comparisons. The following statements are equivalent:

- `if x in (2, 4, 6);`
- `if x=2 or x=4 or x=6;`

The NOT Operator

The prefix operator NOT is also a logical operator. The result of putting NOT in front of a quantity whose value is 0 (false) is 1 (true). That is, the result of negating a false statement is 1 (true). For example, if X=Y is 0 (false) then NOT(X=Y) is 1 (true). The result of NOT in front of a quantity whose value is missing is also 1 (true). The result of NOT in front of a quantity with a nonzero, nonmissing value is 0 (false). That is, the result of negating a true statement is 0 (false).

For example, the following two expressions are equivalent:

- `not(name='SMITH')`
- `name ne 'SMITH'`

Furthermore, NOT(A&B) is equivalent to NOT A | NOT B, and NOT(A | B) is the same as NOT A&NOT B. For example, the following two expressions are equivalent:

□ `not(a=b & c>d)`

□ `a ne b | c le d`

Boolean Numeric Expressions

In computing terms, a value of true is a 1 and a value of false is a 0. In the SAS System, any numeric value other than 0 or missing is true; a value of 0 or missing is false. Therefore, a numeric variable or expression can stand alone in a condition. If its value is a number other than 0 or missing, the condition is true; if its value is 0 or missing, the condition is false.

For example, suppose that you want to fill in variable REMARKS depending on whether the value of COST is present for a given observation. You can write the IF-THEN statement as follows:

```
if cost then remarks='Ready to budget';
```

This statement is equivalent to

```
if cost ne . and cost ne 0 then remarks='Ready to budget';
```

A numeric expression can be simply a numeric constant, as follows:

```
if 5 then do;
```

The numeric value returned by a function is also a valid numeric expression:

```
if index(address,'Avenue') then do;
```

Other Operators

This section describes the following three operators:

□ MIN (><)

□ MAX (<>)

□ concatenation (||).

The MIN and MAX Operators

The MIN and MAX operators are used to find the minimum or maximum value of two quantities. Surround the operators with the two quantities whose minimum or maximum value you want to know. The MIN (><) operator returns the lower of the two values. The MAX (<>) operator returns the higher of the two values. For example, if A<B, then A><B returns the value of A.

If missing values are part of the comparison, the SAS System uses the sorting order for missing values described earlier in this chapter. For example, the maximum value returned by .A<>.Z is the value .Z.

The Concatenation Operator

The concatenation operator (||) concatenates character values. The results of a concatenation operation are usually stored in a variable using an assignment statement. The length of the resulting variable is the sum of the lengths of each variable or constant in the concatenation operation.

The concatenation operator does not trim leading or trailing blanks. If the variable is padded with trailing blanks, check the lengths of both variables and use the TRIM function to trim trailing blanks from values before concatenating them. Use the LEFT function to trim leading blanks. See Chapter 11 for descriptions and examples of character functions.

For example, in this DATA step, the value that results from the concatenation contains blanks because the length of the COLOR variable is eight:

```
data namegame;
   length color name $8;
   color='black';
   name='jack';
   game=color||name;
   put game=;
run;
```

The value of GAME is `blackbbbjack`.

To correct this problem, use the TRIM function in the concatenation operation as follows:

```
game=trim(color)||name;
```

This statement produces a value of `blackjack` for the variable GAME.

The following examples demonstrate other uses of the concatenation operator:

- If A has the value `fortune`, B has the value `five`, and C has the value `hundred`, then the following statement produces the value `fortunefivehundred` for the variable D:

  ```
  d=a||b||c;
  ```

- This example concatenates the value of a variable with a character constant.

  ```
  newname='Mr. or Ms. '||oldname;
  ```

  If the value of OLDNAME is `Jones`, then NEWNAME will have the value `Mr. or Ms. Jones`.

- Because the concatenation operation does not trim blanks, the following expression produces the value `JOHNbbbSMITH`:

  ```
  name='JOHN    '||'SMITH';
  ```

SAS Date and Time Values

The following sections discuss SAS date, time, and datetime values; using these values in programming; and the difference between a duration and a SAS date value.

Understanding SAS Date and Time Values

SAS date values are used in mathematical calculations and other programming techniques. The SAS System processes calendar date values by converting dates to integers representing the number of days between January 1, 1960, and a specified date. For example, the following calendar date values represent the date July 26, 1989:

```
072689   26JUL89    892607
7/26/89  26JUL1989  26 July 1989
```

The SAS date value representing July 26, 1989, is 10799.

Valid SAS date values may be positive or negative numbers representing dates ranging from 1582 A.D. to 20,000 A.D. Dates before January 1, 1960, are negative numbers; dates after are positive numbers.

Figure 4.1 shows some dates written in calendar form and as SAS date values. For additional information, refer to Chapter 13, "Working with Dates in the SAS System," in *SAS Language and Procedures: Usage, Version 6, First Edition.*

Figure 4.1 *SAS Dates*

Calendar Date

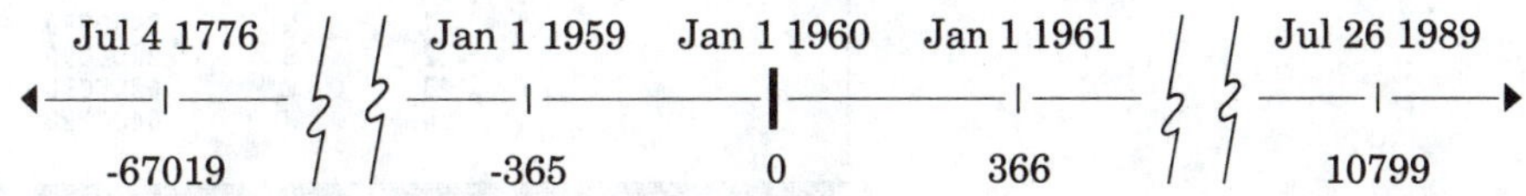

SAS Date Value

Note: The SAS System accepts two-digit or four-digit year values. Two-digit years are attributed to the century specified by the YEARCUTOFF= system option. The YEARCUTOFF= system default is 1900, allowing the years 1900 through 1999 to be specified as two-digit year values. You can also override the system default and specify a beginning date of your choice.

The SAS System processes time data in a manner similar to dates, converting a specific time to an integer representing the number of seconds since midnight of the current day. Therefore, *SAS time values* are independent of the date. For example, the time value for 9:30 a.m. is 34200.

SAS datetime values are integers representing the number of seconds between midnight, January 1, 1960, and a specified date. For example, the datetime value for 9:30 a.m., June 5, 1989, is 928661400.

Using SAS Date Values

The SAS System reads and displays date, time, and datetime values with directions called *informats* and *formats*. An informat reads fields according to a specified width and form. A format writes, or displays, data values according to a specified width and form.

The following example illustrates the correct use of informats, SAS date values, and formats in a calculation. The program reads four regional meeting dates and calculates the dates on which announcements should be mailed. The results are shown in Output 4.1.

```
data meeting;
   input region $ mtg : mmddyy8.;
   sendmail=mtg-45;
   cards;
N  11-24-90
S  12-28-90
E  12-03-90
W  10-04-90
;

proc print data=meeting;
   format mtg sendmail date.;
run;
```

Output 4.1 *Output from the PRINT Procedure*

```
                         The SAS System                          1

            OBS    REGION      MTG        SENDMAIL

             1       N       24NOV90      10OCT90
             2       S       28DEC90      13NOV90
             3       E       03DEC90      19OCT90
             4       W       04OCT90      20AUG90
```

Duration versus Date

When working with dates, it is important to remember the difference between a duration and a SAS date value. A *duration* is an integer representing the difference, or number of days, between *any* two dates. A SAS date value is an integer representing the number of days between January 1, 1960, and the date you enter. SAS date values represent the number of days in a date range that begins or ends with January 1, 1960.

For example, suppose you want to calculate the ages of employees from their birth dates. The following DATA step reads the birth date with the DATE7. informat and uses the function TODAY to assign today's date to a variable. To find an employee's age in days, subtract BIRTHDTE from TODAY to obtain the number of days between the employee's birth date and today (variable AGEDAYS). To convert that figure to years, divide the value of AGEDAYS by the number of days in a year. Therefore, the variable AGEYEARS contains the number of years since the employee's birth date.

```
data emplage;
   input id birthdte date7.;
   today=today();
   agedays=today-birthdte;
   ageyears=agedays/365.25;
   cards;
2145 01dec69
;
```

In this example, the employee's birth date is December 1, 1969. The SAS date value for December 1, 1969, is 3622, representing 3,622 days after January 1, 1960. Subtract 3622 from the SAS date value representing today's date to obtain the number of days between today and December 1, 1969. The value of AGEDAYS is the number of days between the birth date and today. It is not a SAS date value because it represents the number of days between two individual dates rather than the number of days relative to January 1, 1960. Divide the value of AGEDAYS by 365.25 to obtain the value of AGEYEARS, the number of years since December 1, 1969. The same principle applies to calculating time and datetime values.

BY-Group Processing

The SAS System provides a means for processing observations that are ordered or grouped according to the values of one or more variables. This method is referred to as *BY-group processing*, and it is available only for observations read from existing SAS data sets. You use the BY statement to invoke it in DATA and PROC steps. The following discussion describes BY-group processing for the DATA step. For a discussion of BY-group processing in SAS procedures, refer to the *SAS Procedures Guide, Version 6, Third Edition*.

Preparing the Data Sets

Before you process one or more SAS data sets using grouped or ordered data, you must ensure that the observations in all of the data sets occur in some predictable and corresponding pattern, such as the following:

- □ ascending or descending numeric order
- □ ascending or descending character order
- □ grouped, but not ordered, such as calendar order.

The SAS System detects the pattern by tracking the values of one or more temporary variables called the FIRST.*variable* and the LAST.*variable*.

If the observations are in the order you want, the SAS data set does not require any preprocessing. If the observations are not in the order you want, you can order observations one of two ways: sorting the data set or creating an index for the data set.

Note: If you are processing SAS/ACCESS views, refer to the documentation for your SAS/ACCESS interface product before you include a BY statement in your SAS programs. For PROC SQL views, refer to *SAS Guide to the SQL Procedure: Usage and Reference, Version 6, First Edition*.

Sorting

You can use the SORT procedure to change the physical order of the observations in the data set. Refer to Chapter 31, "The SORT Procedure," in the *SAS Procedures Guide* for a detailed description of the default sorting orders for numeric and character variables and for a list of options that allow you to choose other collating sequences. The chapter also contains a discussion of how to use the procedure BY statement efficiently so you can reduce the number of SORT procedures in an application. As a general rule, when you use PROC SORT, specify the variables in the procedure BY statement in the same order you plan to specify them in the DATA step BY statement.

Indexing

With Release 6.06 of base SAS software, you can also ensure that observations are processed in ascending numeric or character order by creating an index based on one or more variables in the SAS data set. If you specify a BY statement in a DATA step, the SAS System looks for an appropriate index. If one exists, the SAS System automatically retrieves the observations from the data set in indexed order. Refer to "Release 6.06: SAS Indexes" in Chapter 6 for a description of appropriate indexes for various BY statements and a list of the criteria the SAS System uses for selecting indexes.

Note: Because indexes require additional resources to create and maintain, you should determine if their use significantly improves performance. Depending on the nature of the data in your SAS data set, using PROC SORT to order data values can be more advantageous than indexing. Read "Release 6.06: SAS Indexes" in Chapter 6, "SAS Files," before you choose to create an index.

Understanding BY Groups

The descriptions of how the SAS System processes grouped data are based on an understanding of three concepts: BY variable, BY value, and BY group.

BY variable
: is a variable named in a BY statement. A BY statement can name one or more variables, and the SAS System expects the data sets to be ordered by the values of the variables named in this statement. When combining data sets, each data set must include the BY variable or variables.

BY value
: is the value or formatted value of a BY variable.

BY group
: is all observations with the same BY value. If you use more than one variable in a BY statement, a BY group is a group of observations with the same combination of values for these variables.

BY Groups with a Single BY Variable

In the following example, a SAS data set contains street names, cities, states, and ZIP codes arranged in an order that can be used with the following BY statement:

```
by zip;
```

In Figure 4.2, each BY group is separated from the next BY group with a dotted line. The data set is shown with the BY variable ZIP printed on the left for easy reading, but the position of the BY variable in the observations does not matter.

Figure 4.2 *BY Groups for the Single BY Variable ZIP*

BY variable

ZIP	STATE	CITY	STREET
33133	FL	Miami	Rice St
33133	FL	Miami	Thomas Ave
33133	FL	Miami	Surrey Dr
33133	FL	Miami	Trade Ave
33146	FL	Miami	Nervia St
33146	FL	Miami	Corsica St
33801	FL	Lakeland	French Ave
33809	FL	Lakeland	Egret Dr
85730	AZ	Tucson	Domenic Ln
85730	AZ	Tucson	Gleeson Pl

BY groups

BY values

The first BY group is all observations with the smallest BY value, which is 33133; the second BY group is all observations with the next smallest BY value, which is 33146, and so on. Within each BY group, the observations are arranged in the order in which they physically occur in the SAS data set.

BY Groups with Multiple BY Variables

In this example, the same data set is arranged in an order that can be used with the following BY statement:

```
by state city;
```

In Figure 4.3, each BY group is separated by a dotted line. The data set is shown with the BY variables STATE and CITY printed on the left for easy reading, but the position of the BY variables in the observations does not matter.

Figure 4.3 *BY Groups for the BY Variables STATE and CITY*

BY variables

STATE	CITY	STREET	ZIP	
AZ	Tucson	Domenic Ln	85730	BY group
AZ	Tucson	Gleeson Pl	85730	
FL	Lakeland	French Ave	33801	
FL	Lakeland	Egret Dr	33809	
FL	Miami	Nervia St	33146	
FL	Miami	Rice St	33133	
FL	Miami	Corsica St	33146	
FL	Miami	Thomas Ave	33133	
FL	Miami	Surrey Dr	33133	
FL	Miami	Trade Ave	33133	

BY values

The observations are arranged so that the observations for Arizona occur first. The observations within each value of STATE are arranged in order of the value of CITY. Each BY group has a unique combination of values for the variables STATE and CITY. For example, the BY value of the first BY group is **`AZ Tucson`**, and the BY value of the second BY group is **`FL Lakeland`**. Within each BY group, the observations are arranged according to the order in which they appear in the data set.

How the DATA Step Identifies BY Groups

In the DATA step, the SAS System identifies the beginning and end of each BY group by creating two temporary variables for each BY variable: FIRST.*variable* and LAST.*variable*. These temporary variables are available for DATA step programming but are not added to the output data set.

When an observation is the first in a BY group, the value of the FIRST.*variable* is set to 1. For all other observations in the BY group, the value of the FIRST.*variable* is 0. Likewise, if an observation is the last in a BY group, the value of LAST.*variable* is set to 1. For all other observations in the BY group, the value of LAST.*variable* is 0. If the observations are sorted by more than one BY variable, the FIRST.*variable* for each variable is set to 1 at the first occurrence of a new value for the variable.

The following example illustrates how the SAS System uses the FIRST.*variable* and LAST.*variable* to flag the beginning and end of BY groups. Six temporary variables are created within the program data vector. They can be used during the DATA step but do not become variables in the new data set.

The observations in the SAS data set in Figure 4.4 are arranged in an order that can be used with the following BY statement:

```
by state city zip;
```

The temporary variables in Figure 4.4 are FIRST.STATE, LAST.STATE, FIRST.CITY, LAST.CITY, FIRST.ZIP, and LAST.ZIP.

Figure 4.4 *FIRST. and LAST. Values for Three BY Groups*

Observations in Three BY Groups				Corresponding FIRST. and LAST. Values					
STATE	CITY	ZIP	STREET	FIRST. STATE	LAST. STATE	FIRST. CITY	LAST. CITY	FIRST. ZIP	LAST. ZIP
AZ	Tucson	85730	Gleeson Pl	1	1	1	1	1	1
FL	Miami	33133	Rice St	1	0	1	0	1	0
FL	Miami	33133	Thomas Ave	0	0	0	0	0	0
FL	Miami	33133	Surrey Dr	0	0	0	0	0	1
FL	Miami	33146	Nervia St	0	0	0	0	1	0
FL	Miami	33146	Corsica St	0	1	0	1	0	1

BY-Group Processing in a DATA Step

You can use the BY statement in a DATA step to modify the action of the SET, MERGE, or UPDATE statement. The SAS System expects observations to be ordered or grouped by the value of the variables specified in the BY statement. Generally, the observations are ordered by sorting or indexing the data set. You can use BY-group processing with data that are arranged by other methods, such as entering the observations into the SAS data set in the desired groupings. The following sections describe how the BY statement modifies the action of the DATA step and provides examples of how to use the BY statement with grouped data.

Differences in DATA Step Action

The most frequent use of BY-group processing in the DATA step is to combine two or more SAS data sets. When processing SET, MERGE, and UPDATE statements, the SAS System reads one observation at a time into the program data vector. With BY-group processing, the SAS System selects the observations from the data sets according to the values of the BY variable or variables. After processing all the observations from one BY group, the SAS System expects the next observation to be from the next BY group.

The BY statement modifies the action of the SET, MERGE, or UPDATE statement by controlling when the values in the program data vector are set to missing. During BY-group processing, the SAS System retains the values of variables until it has copied the last observation it finds for that BY group in any of the data sets. Without the BY statement, the SET statement sets variables to missing when it reads the last observation from any data set, and the MERGE statement does not set variables to missing after the DATA step starts reading observations into the program data vector.

You can take advantage of the temporary variables set up during BY-group processing to process observations conditionally. The FIRST.*variable* and LAST.*variable* are available for the subsetting IF or IF-THEN statements. You can use them to perform calculations and output observations when the first or the last observation of a BY group has been read into the program data vector.

Unordered Data

Data that are arranged in calendar order or by category can be used in BY-group processing. The NOTSORTED option in the BY statement tells the SAS System that the data are not in alphabetic or numeric order, but that they are arranged in groups according to the values of the BY variable.

The following example assumes that the data are grouped in calendar order by the variable MONTH, whose values are **JAN**, **FEB**, and **MAR**. The SAS System sets up the temporary variables FIRST.MONTH and LAST.MONTH, and you use them to conditionally output observations.

```
data totsale(drop=sales);
   set region.sales;
   by month notsorted;
   total+sales;
   if last.month;
run;
```

Data Grouped by Formatted Values

You can use the GROUPFORMAT option in the BY statement to ensure that the FIRST.*variable* and LAST.*variable* are assigned according to the formatted values of the variable. The GROUPFORMAT option is valid only in the DATA step that creates the SAS data set. Using the GROUPFORMAT option sets a flag that tells the SAS System to use formatted values for grouping observations when a FORMAT statement and a BY statement are used together in a DATA or PROC step. This option is particularly useful if you have user-written formats for grouping the data.

The following example shows how you might use the FORMAT procedure, the GROUPFORMAT option, and the FORMAT statement to create and print a simple data set. The data set is arranged by the formatted values of the variable SCORE.

```
   /* Create a User-defined Format */
proc format;
   value range 1-2='LOW' 3-4='MEDIUM' 5-6='HIGH';
run;

   /* Create the SAS Data Set */
data newtest;
   set test;
   format score range.;
   by groupformat score;
   run;
```

```
/* Print Using Formatted Values */
proc print data=newtest;
   var name score;
   by score;
   format score range.;
run;
```

Combining SAS Data Sets

In the DATA step, you can use the SET, MERGE, and UPDATE statements to combine SAS data sets in one of six ways:

- □ concatenating
- □ interleaving
- □ one-to-one reading
- □ one-to-one merging
- □ match-merging
- □ updating.

To obtain the results you want, you should understand how each of these methods combines observations, how each method treats duplicate values of common variables, and how each method treats missing values or nonmatched values of common variables. Some of the methods also require that you preprocess your data sets by sorting them or by creating indexes.

If you do not instruct it to do otherwise, the SAS System includes all variables and all observations from the input data sets in the output data set. The statements and data set options summarized in Table 4.2 are available to control which variables and observations are processed or written out. In general, use the statements to control which variables and observations are written to the output data sets. The WHERE statement is an exception: it controls which variables are read into the program data vector from the input data sets. You can use data set options on input or output data sets, depending on their function and what you want to control. Refer to Chapter 9 and Chapter 15 for details on using these statements and options in your DATA step programs.

Table 4.2 *Statements and Options to Control Processing and Output of Variables and Observations*

Function	Data Set Options	Statements
Controls variables	DROP=	DROP
	KEEP=	KEEP
	RENAME=	RENAME
Controls observations	WHERE=	WHERE
	FIRSTOBS=	subsetting IF
	OBS=	DELETE

How to Prepare Your Data Sets

Before using any of the methods listed in the previous section to combine data sets, you should follow these guidelines to ensure that you get the results you want:

- □ Know the contents of your data sets.
- □ Look for problem areas.
- □ Ensure that observations are in the correct order.
- □ Test your program.

Knowing the contents Use the DATASETS or CONTENTS procedure or the VAR display manager window to look at the descriptor information of each data set. They provide useful information such as the number of observations in each data set, the name and attributes of each variable, and which variables are included in indexes. If SAS/FSP software is available, you can use it to browse the data. Otherwise, printing a few observations from each data set can provide further information about the nature of the variables in the data set.

Looking for problems When you are looking for problem areas, note the following:

- □ variables with the same name but representing different data.

  The SAS System includes only one variable of a given name in the new data set. If you are merging two data sets that have variables with the same names but different data, the values from the last data set read are written over values from other data sets. You can rename variables before you combine the data sets by using the RENAME= data set option in the SET, UPDATE, or MERGE statement, or you can use the DATASETS procedure.
- □ common variables with same data but different attributes. The SAS System handles differences according to the kind of attribute:
  - □ If the type attribute is different, the SAS System stops processing the DATA step and issues an error message that the variables are incompatible. To correct this problem, you must use a DATA step to re-create the variable. The SAS statements you use depend on the nature of the variable.
  - □ If the length attribute is different, the SAS System takes the length from the first data set that contains the variable. In the following example, all data sets listed in the MERGE statement contain the variable MILEAGE. In QTR1, the length of the variable MILEAGE is 4 bytes; in QTR2, it is 8 bytes; and in QTR3 and QTR4, it is 6 bytes. In the output data set YEARLY, the length of the variable MILEAGE is 4 bytes, or the length derived from QTR1.

    ```
    data yearly;
       merge qtr1 qtr2 qtr3 qtr4;
       by account;
    run;
    ```

    If the DATA step in which you are combining the data sets contains a LENGTH statement and the LENGTH statement precedes the SET, MERGE, or UPDATE statement, the explicitly defined length overrides other defaults.

- If the label, format, and informat attributes are different, the SAS System takes the label, format, or informat from the first data set that contains the variable. Any explicitly specified informat, format, or label overrides a default. If all data sets contain explicitly specified attributes, the informat, format, or label specified in the first data set overrides the others.

Ensuring correct order If you are using BY-group processing to combine data sets, ensure that the observations in the data sets are sorted in the order of the variables listed in the BY statement or that the data sets have an appropriate index. The BY variable or variables must be common to both data sets, and they should have the same attributes.

Testing your program As a final step in preparing your data sets, you should test your program. Construct small temporary SAS data sets that contain observations that test all of your program's logic.

Concatenating

Concatenating is combining two or more data sets one after the other into a single data set. The number of observations in the new data set is the sum of the number of observations in the original data sets, and the order is all the observations from the first data set followed by all observations from the second data set and so on.

In the simplest case, all the input data sets contain the same variables. If the input data sets contain different variables, observations from one data set have missing values for variables defined only in other data sets. In either case, the variables in the new data set are the same as those in the old data sets.

To concatenate data sets, use the following form of the SET statement:

SET *data-set-1 . . . data-set-n*;

Options are not shown here for simplicity. For a complete description of the SET statement, including all the options, see Chapter 9.

DATA Step Processing during Concatenation

The SAS System concatenates data sets as follows:

1. During the compilation phase of the DATA step, the SAS System reads the descriptor information of each data set named in the SET statement and creates a program data vector that contains all the variables from all data sets as well as variables created by the DATA step.
2. The SAS System reads the first observation from the first data set into the program data vector, processes the first observation and executes any other statements in the DATA step, and writes the contents of the program data vector to the new data set. The SET statement does not reset the values in the program data vector to missing, except for those variables whose value is calculated or assigned during the DATA step.
3. The SAS System continues to read one observation at a time from the first data set until it finds an end-of-file indicator. The values of the variables in the program data vector are then set to missing, and the SAS System begins reading observations from the second data set and so forth until it reads all observations from all data sets.

Example of Concatenation

Output 4.2 shows the contents of two simple SAS data sets, ANIMAL and PLANT. Each data set contains the variable COMMON, and the observations are arranged in order of the values of COMMON. Note that the data sets contain different variables to show the effects of combining data sets more clearly. Generally, you would concatenate SAS data sets that have the same variables.

Output 4.2 *Data Sets before Concatenation*

```
                    Data Set ANIMAL                         1

              OBS    COMMON    ANIMAL

               1       a       ant
               2       b       bird
               3       c       cat
               4       d       dog
               5       e       eagle
               6       f       frog
```

```
                    Data Set PLANT                          2

              OBS    COMMON    PLANT

               1       a       apple
               2       b       banana
               3       c       coconut
               4       d       dewberry
               5       e       eggplant
               6       f       fig
```

The following program uses a SET statement to concatenate the data sets and prints the results:

```
libname example 'SAS-data-library';

data example.concat;
   set example.animal example.plant;
run;

proc print data=example.concat;
   title 'Data Set CONCAT';
run;
```

The resulting data set CONCAT has 12 observations, which is the sum of the observations from the combined data sets. See Output 4.3. The program data vector contains all variables from all data sets. The values of variables found in one data set but not in another are set to missing.

Output 4.3 *Concatenated Data Sets*

```
                        Data Set CONCAT                          1

              OBS    COMMON    ANIMAL    PLANT

                1      a       ant
                2      b       bird
                3      c       cat
                4      d       dog
                5      e       eagle
                6      f       frog
                7      a                 apple
                8      b                 banana
                9      c                 coconut
               10      d                 dewberry
               11      e                 eggplant
               12      f                 fig
```

Concatenating: Comments and Comparisons

You can concatenate data sets using the APPEND procedure and the APPEND statement in the DATASETS procedure. Chapter 15, "Concatenating SAS Data Sets," in *SAS Language and Procedures: Usage* contains instructions for concatenating data sets and compares the use of the SET statement and the APPEND procedure.

Interleaving

Interleaving uses a SET statement and a BY statement to combine data sets into one new data set. The number of observations in the new data set is the sum of the number of observations from the original data sets; however, the observations in the new data set are arranged by the values of the BY variable or variables and, within each BY group, by the order of the data sets in which they occur.

Before you can interleave data sets, the observations must be sorted or grouped by the same variable or variables you use in the BY statement, or you must have an appropriate index for the data sets.

To interleave data sets, use the following form of the SET and BY statements:

SET *data-set-1 . . . data-set-n*;
BY *variable-1 . . . variable-n*;

Options are not shown here for simplicity. See Chapter 9 for complete descriptions, including available options, of the SET and BY statements.

DATA Step Processing during Interleaving

The SAS System interleaves data sets as follows:

1. During the compilation phase of the DATA step, the SAS System reads the descriptor information of each data set named in the SET statement and creates a program data vector that contains all the variables from all data sets as well as variables created by the DATA step. It also creates the FIRST.*variable* and LAST.*variable* for each variable listed in the BY statement.

2. The SAS System compares the first observation from each data set named in the SET statement to determine which BY group should appear first in the new data set. It reads all observations from the first BY group from the selected data set. If this BY group appears in more than one data set, it reads from the data sets in the same order as they appear in the SET statement. The values of the variables in the

program data vector are set to missing each time the SAS System starts to read a new data set and when the BY group changes.

3. Then, the SAS System compares the next available observations from each data set to determine the next BY group and starts reading observations from the selected data set in the SET statement that contains observations for this BY group. The SAS System continues in this manner until it has read all observations from all data sets.

Examples of Interleaving

Output 4.4 shows the contents of two simple SAS data sets, ANIMAL and PLANT. Each data set contains a BY variable COMMON, and the observations are arranged in order of the values of the BY variable.

Output 4.4 *Data Sets before Interleaving*

```
                         Data Set ANIMAL                              1

                   OBS    COMMON    ANIMAL

                    1       a       ant
                    2       b       bird
                    3       c       cat
                    4       d       dog
                    5       e       eagle
                    6       f       frog
```

```
                          Data Set PLANT                              2

                  OBS    COMMON    PLANT

                   1       a       apple
                   2       b       banana
                   3       c       coconut
                   4       d       dewberry
                   5       e       eggplant
                   6       f       fig
```

The following program uses SET and BY statements to interleave the data sets and prints the results:

```
data example.interlev;
   set example.animal example.plant;
   by common;
run;

proc print data=example.interlev;
   title 'Data Set INTERLEV';
run;
```

The resulting data set INTERLEV has 12 observations, which is the sum of the observations from the combined data sets. See Output 4.5. The new data set contains all variables from both data sets. The value of variables found in one data set but not in the other are set to missing, and the observations are arranged in order of the values of the BY variable.

Output 4.5 *Interleaved Data Sets*

```
                        Data Set INTERLEV                          1

               OBS    COMMON    ANIMAL    PLANT

                 1      a       ant
                 2      a                 apple
                 3      b       bird
                 4      b                 banana
                 5      c       cat
                 6      c                 coconut
                 7      d       dog
                 8      d                 dewberry
                 9      e       eagle
                10      e                 eggplant
                11      f       frog
                12      f                 fig
```

Duplicate values of the BY variable If the data sets contain duplicate values of the BY variables, the observations are written to the new data set in the order they occur in the original data sets. Output 4.6 shows the data sets ANIMAL1 and PLANT1, which contain duplicate values of the BY variable COMMON.

Output 4.6 *Data Sets with Duplicate Values of the BY Variable*

```
                        Data Set ANIMAL1                           1

                    OBS    COMMON    ANIMAL1

                     1       a       ant
                     2       a       ape
                     3       b       bird
                     4       c       cat
                     5       d       dog
                     6       e       eagle
```

```
                        Data Set PLANT1                            2

                    OBS    COMMON    PLANT1

                     1       a       apple
                     2       b       banana
                     3       c       coconut
                     4       c       celery
                     5       d       dewberry
                     6       e       eggplant
```

The following program uses SET and BY statements to interleave the data sets and prints the results:

```
data example.interlv1;
   set example.animal1 example.plant1;
   by common;
run;

proc print data=example.interlv1;
   title 'Data Set INTERLV1';
run;
```

The number of observations in the new data set is the sum of the observations in all the data sets. See Output 4.7. The observations are written to the new data set in the order they occur in the original data sets.

Output 4.7 *Results of Interleaving Data Sets with Duplicate Values of the BY Variable*

```
                        Data Set INTERLV1                          1

              OBS    COMMON    ANIMAL1    PLANT1

                1      a        ant
                2      a        ape
                3      a                  apple
                4      b        bird
                5      b                  banana
                6      c        cat
                7      c                  coconut
                8      c                  celery
                9      d        dog
               10      d                  dewberry
               11      e        eagle
               12      e                  eggplant
```

Different BY values in each data set Output 4.8 shows the data sets ANIMAL2 and PLANT2. Both ANIMAL2 and PLANT2 contain BY values that are present in one data set but not in the other.

Output 4.8 *Data Sets with Different BY Values*

```
                        Data Set ANIMAL2                           1

                   OBS    COMMON    ANIMAL2

                    1       a        ant
                    2       c        cat
                    3       d        dog
                    4       e        eagle
```

```
                        Data Set PLANT2                            2

                  OBS    COMMON    PLANT2

                   1       a       apple
                   2       b       banana
                   3       c       coconut
                   4       e       eggplant
                   5       f       fig
```

The following program uses SET and BY statements to interleave these data sets and prints the results:

```
data example.interlv2;
   set example.animal2 example.plant2;
   by common;
run;

proc print data=example.interlv2;
   title 'Data Set INTERLV2';
run;
```

The resulting data set has nine observations arranged in the order of the values of the BY variable as shown in Output 4.9.

Output 4.9 *Results of Interleaving Data Sets with Different BY Values*

```
                    Data Set INTERLV2                              1

           OBS    COMMON    ANIMAL2     PLANT2

            1       a        ant
            2       a                   apple
            3       b                   banana
            4       c        cat
            5       c                   coconut
            6       d        dog
            7       e        eagle
            8       e                   eggplant
            9       f                   fig
```

Interleaving: Comments and Comparisons

In other languages, the term *merge* is often used to mean *interleave*. The SAS System reserves the term *merge* for the operation in which observations from two or more data sets are combined into one observation. The observations in interleaved data sets are not combined, just copied from the original data sets in the order of the values of the BY variable.

Chapter 16, "Interleaving SAS Data Sets," in *SAS Language and Procedures: Usage* contains instructions and detailed examples for interleaving data sets.

One-to-One Reading

One-to-one reading is combining observations from two or more data sets into one observation using two or more SET statements to read observations independently from each data set. This process is also called *one-to-one matching*. The new data set contains all the variables from all the input data sets. The number of observations in the new data set is the number of observations in the smallest original data set. If the data sets contain common variables, the values read in from the last data set replace those read in from earlier ones.

▶ ***Caution:*** *Use care when combining data sets with multiple SET statements.*

Using multiple SET statements to combine observations can produce undesirable results. Test your program on representative samples of the data sets before using this method to combine them.

Use this general form to combine data sets using more than one SET statement:

SET *data-set-1*;
SET *data-set-2*;

Options are not shown here for simplicity. For a complete description of the SET statement, including all available options, see Chapter 9.

DATA Step Processing during One-to-One Reading

The SAS System reads and combines observations as follows:

1. During the compilation phase of the DATA step, the SAS System reads the descriptor information of each data set named in the SET statement and creates a program data vector that contains all the variables from all data sets as well as variables created by the DATA step.
2. When the first SET statement is executed, it reads the first observation from the first data set into the program data vector. The second SET

statement reads the first observation from the second data set into the program data vector. If both data sets contain the same variables, the values from the second data set replace those from the first data set even if the value is missing. After reading the first observation from the last data set and executing any other statements in the DATA step, the SAS System writes the contents of the program data vector to the new data set. The SET statement does not reset the values in the program data vector to missing, except for those variables created or assigned values during the DATA step.

3. The SAS System continues reading from one data set then the other until it detects an end-of-file indicator in one of the data sets. It stops processing with the last observation of the shortest data set and does not read the remaining observations from the longer data sets.

Example of One-to-One Reading

Output 4.10 shows the contents of two simple SAS data sets, ANIMAL and PLANT. Both data sets contain the variable COMMON, and they are arranged in order of the values of that variable.

Output 4.10 *Data Sets before One-to-One Reading*

```
                    Data Set ANIMAL                         1

              OBS    COMMON    ANIMAL

               1       a       ant
               2       b       bird
               3       c       cat
               4       d       dog
               5       e       eagle
               6       f       frog
```

```
                    Data Set PLANT                          2

             OBS    COMMON    PLANT

              1       a       apple
              2       b       banana
              3       c       coconut
              4       d       dewberry
              5       e       eggplant
              6       f       fig
```

The following program uses two SET statements to combine observations from ANIMAL and PLANT and prints the results:

```
data example.twosets;
   set example.animal;
   set example.plant;
run;

proc print data=example.twosets;
   title 'Data Set TWOSETS';
run;
```

The resulting data set has six observations. Each observation in the new data set contains all variables from all data sets. See Output 4.11

Output 4.11 *Data Sets Combined with Two SET Statements*

```
                      Data Set TWOSETS                          1

          OBS    COMMON    ANIMAL    PLANT

           1       a       ant       apple
           2       b       bird      banana
           3       c       cat       coconut
           4       d       dog       dewberry
           5       e       eagle     eggplant
           6       f       frog      fig
```

One-to-One Reading: Comments and Comparisons

The results obtained by reading observations using two or more SET statements are similar to those obtained using the MERGE statement with no BY statement. However, with one-to-one reading, the SAS System stops processing before all observations are read from all data sets if the number of observations is not equal. Using multiple SET statements with other DATA step statements makes the following applications possible:

- □ merging one observation with many
- □ conditionally merging observations
- □ reading from the same data set twice.

The discussion of the SET statement in Chapter 9 contains more information on using more than one SET statement in a DATA step.

One-to-One Merging

One-to-one merging combines observations from two or more SAS data sets into a single observation in a new data set. To perform a one-to-one merge, you use the MERGE statement without a BY statement. The SAS System combines the first observation from all data sets in the MERGE statement into the first observation in the new data set, the second observation from all data sets into the second observation in the new data set, and so on. In a one-to-one merge, the number of observations in the new data set is equal to the number of observations in the largest data set named in the MERGE statement.

▶ ***Caution:*** *Use care when combining data sets with one-to-one merging.*

Using a one-to-one merge to combine observations can produce undesirable results. Test your program on representative samples of the data sets before using this method.

To merge data sets, use the following form of the MERGE statement:

MERGE *data-set-1* . . . *data-set-n*;

Options are not shown here for simplicity. For a complete description of the MERGE statement, including all available options, see Chapter 9.

DATA Step Processing during One-to-One Merging

Without a BY statement, the SAS System merges data sets as follows:

1. During the compilation phase of the DATA step, the SAS System reads the descriptor information of each data set named in the MERGE statement and creates a program data vector that contains all the variables from all data sets as well as variables created by the DATA step.

2. The SAS System reads the first observation from each data set into the program data vector, reading the data sets in the same order that they appear in the MERGE statement. If two data sets contain the same variables, the values from the second data set replace those from the first. After reading the first observation from the last data set and executing any other statements in the DATA step, it writes the contents of the program data vector to the new data set. Only those variables that are created or assigned values during the DATA step are set to missing.
3. The SAS System continues in this manner until it has read all observations from all data sets.

Examples of One-to-One Merging

Output 4.12 shows the contents of two SAS data sets, ANIMAL and PLANT. Both data sets contain the variable COMMON, and the observations are arranged in order of the values of COMMON.

Output 4.12 Data Sets before One-to-One Merge

```
                    Data Set ANIMAL                              1

               OBS    COMMON    ANIMAL

                1       a       ant
                2       b       bird
                3       c       cat
                4       d       dog
                5       e       eagle
                6       f       frog
```

```
                    Data Set PLANT                               2

               OBS    COMMON    PLANT

                1       a       apple
                2       b       banana
                3       c       coconut
                4       d       dewberry
                5       e       eggplant
                6       f       fig
```

The following program merges these data sets and prints the results:

```
data example.merge;
   merge example.animal example.plant;
run;

proc print data=example.merge;
   title 'Data Set MERGE';
run;
```

The resulting data set has six observations. Each observation in the new data set contains all variables from all data sets. See Output 4.13.

Output 4.13 *Data Set after One-to-One Merging*

```
                    Data Set MERGE                          1

          OBS    COMMON    ANIMAL    PLANT

           1       a       ant       apple
           2       b       bird      banana
           3       c       cat       coconut
           4       d       dog       dewberry
           5       e       eagle     eggplant
           6       f       frog      fig
```

Duplicate values of common variables The following example shows the undesirable results you can obtain by using the one-to-one merge with data sets that contain duplicate values of common variables. If a variable exists in more than one data set, the value from the last data set read is the one that is written to the new data set. The variables are combined exactly as they are read from each data set. In Output 4.14, the data sets ANIMAL1 and PLANT1 contain the variable COMMON, and each data set contains observations with duplicate values of COMMON.

Output 4.14 *Data Sets with Duplicate Values of Common Variables*

```
                    Data Set ANIMAL1                        1

              OBS    COMMON    ANIMAL1

               1       a       ant
               2       a       ape
               3       b       bird
               4       c       cat
               5       d       dog
               6       e       eagle
```

```
                    Data Set PLANT1                         2

              OBS    COMMON    PLANT1

               1       a       apple
               2       b       banana
               3       c       coconut
               4       c       celery
               5       d       dewberry
               6       e       eggplant
```

The following program produces the data set MERGE1 and prints the results:

```
   /* Illustrates undesirable result  */
data example.merge1;
   merge example.animal1 example.plant1;
run;

proc print data=example.merge1;
   title 'Data Set MERGE1';
run;
```

The number of observations in the new data set is six. See Output 4.15. Note that observations 2 and 3 contain undesirable values. The SAS System read the second observation from the data set ANIMAL1. It then read the second observation from the data set PLANT1 and replaced the values for the variables COMMON and PLANT1. The third observation was created the same way.

Output 4.15 *Undesirable Results with Duplicate Values of Common Variables*

```
                         Data Set MERGE1                              1

            OBS    COMMON    ANIMAL1    PLANT1

             1       a       ant        apple
             2       b       ape        banana
             3       c       bird       coconut
             4       c       cat        celery
             5       d       dog        dewberry
             6       e       eagle      eggplant
```

Different values of common variables The following example shows the undesirable results obtained from using the one-to-one merge to combine data sets with different values of common variables. If a variable exists in more than one data set, the value from the last data set read is the one that is written to the new data set even if the value is missing. Once the SAS System has processed all observations in a data set, all subsequent observations in the new data set have missing values for the variables unique to that data set. In this example, the data sets ANIMAL2 and PLANT2 have different values of common variables, as shown in Output 4.16.

Output 4.16 *Data Sets with Different Values of Common Variables*

```
                         Data Set ANIMAL2                             1

                  OBS    COMMON    ANIMAL2

                   1       a       ant
                   2       c       cat
                   3       d       dog
                   4       e       eagle
```

```
                         Data Set PLANT2                              2

                 OBS    COMMON    PLANT2

                  1       a       apple
                  2       b       banana
                  3       c       coconut
                  4       e       eggplant
                  5       f       fig
```

The following program merges observations from the data sets ANIMAL2 and PLANT2 and prints the results:

```
   /*  Illustrates undesirable result  */
data example.merge2;
   merge example.animal2 example.plant2;
run;

proc print data=example.merge2;
   title 'Data Set MERGE2';
run;
```

The results are shown in Output 4.17. Note that observations 2 and 3 contain undesirable values and that one value of the variable COMMON is not represented in the new data set. The new data set contains five observations. The last observation has a missing value for the variable ANIMAL2 because the SAS System detected an end-of-file indicator after reading the fourth observation in the data set ANIMAL2.

Output 4.17 *Undesirable Results with Different Values of Common Variables*

```
                      Data Set MERGE2                          1

          OBS    COMMON    ANIMAL2    PLANT2

           1       a        ant       apple
           2       b        cat       banana
           3       c        dog       coconut
           4       e        eagle     eggplant
           5       f                  fig
```

One-to-One Merging: Comments and Comparisons

The results from a one-to-one merge are similar to those obtained from using two or more SET statements to combine observations; however, with the one-to-one merge, the SAS System continues processing all observations in all data sets named in the MERGE statement.

Chapter 17, "Merging SAS Data Sets," in *SAS Language and Procedures: Usage* contains instructions and detailed examples for merging data sets. See Chapter 9 in this book for options available in the MERGE statement.

Match-Merging

Match-merging is combining observations from two or more SAS data sets into a single observation in a new data set according to the values of a common variable. The number of observations in the new data set is the sum of the largest number of observations in each BY group in all data sets. To perform a match-merge, you use the MERGE statement with a BY statement. Before you can perform a match-merge, all data sets must be sorted by the variables you specify in the BY statement or they must have an appropriate index.

To match-merge data sets, use the following general form of the MERGE statement and BY statement:

MERGE *data-set-1 . . . data-set-n*;
BY *variable-1 . . . variable-n*;

Options are not shown here for simplicity. See Chapter 9 for complete descriptions, including available options, of the MERGE and BY statements.

DATA Step Processing during Match-Merging

With a BY statement, the SAS System merges data sets as follows:

1. During the compilation phase of the DATA step, the SAS System reads the descriptor information of each data set named in the MERGE statement and creates a program data vector that contains all the variables from all data sets as well as variables created by the DATA step. It also creates the FIRST.*variable* and LAST.*variable* for each variable listed in the BY statement.

2. The SAS System looks at the first BY group in each data set named in the MERGE statement to determine which BY group should appear first in the new data set.

3. Then, the DATA step reads into the program data vector the first observation in that BY group from each data set, reading the data sets in the same order they appear in the MERGE statement. If a data set does not have any observations in that BY group, the program data vector contains missing values for the variables unique to that data set.

4. After processing the first observation from the last data set and executing any other statements in the DATA step, the SAS System writes the contents of the program data vector to the new data set. It retains the values of all variables in the program data vector except those variables created by the DATA step, whose values it sets to missing.
5. The SAS System continues to merge observations until it has written all observations from the first BY group to the new data set. When it has read all the observations in a BY group from all data sets, it sets all values in the program data vector to missing. It looks at the next BY group in each data set to determine which BY group should appear next in the new data set.
6. The SAS System repeats these steps until it has read all observations from all BY groups in all data sets.

Examples of Match-Merging

Output 4.18 shows the contents of two SAS data sets, ANIMAL and PLANT. Each data set contains a common BY variable, and the observations are arranged in order of the values of the BY variable.

Output 4.18 *Data Sets before Match-Merging*

```
                     Data Set ANIMAL                        1

               OBS    COMMON    ANIMAL

                1       a       ant
                2       b       bird
                3       c       cat
                4       d       dog
                5       e       eagle
                6       f       frog
```

```
                     Data Set PLANT                         2

               OBS    COMMON    PLANT

                1       a       apple
                2       b       banana
                3       c       coconut
                4       d       dewberry
                5       e       eggplant
                6       f       fig
```

The following program merges the data sets according to the values of the BY variable COMMON and prints the results:

```
data example.match;
   merge example.animal example.plant;
   by common;
run;

proc print data=example.match;
   title 'Data Set MATCH';
run;
```

The resulting data set has six observations. See Output 4.19. Each observation in the new data set contains all variables from all data sets.

Output 4.19 *Data Sets Combined by Match-Merging*

```
                         Data Set MATCH                         1

          OBS    COMMON    ANIMAL    PLANT

           1       a       ant       apple
           2       b       bird      banana
           3       c       cat       coconut
           4       d       dog       dewberry
           5       e       eagle     eggplant
           6       f       frog      fig
```

Duplicate values of the BY variable When the last observation from a BY group in one data set has been read into the program data vector, the SAS System retains its values for all variables unique to that data set until all observations for that BY group have been read from all data sets. In this example, the data sets ANIMAL1 and PLANT1 contain duplicate values of the BY variable COMMON, as shown in Output 4.20.

Output 4.20 *Data Sets with Duplicate Values of the BY Variable*

```
                         Data Set ANIMAL1                       1

                  OBS    COMMON    ANIMAL1

                   1       a        ant
                   2       a        ape
                   3       b        bird
                   4       c        cat
                   5       d        dog
                   6       e        eagle
```

```
                         Data Set PLANT1                        2

                 OBS    COMMON    PLANT1

                  1       a       apple
                  2       b       banana
                  3       c       coconut
                  4       c       celery
                  5       d       dewberry
                  6       e       eggplant
```

The following program produces the merged data set MATCH1 and prints the results:

```
data example.match1;
   merge example.animal1 example.plant1;
   by common;
run;

proc print data=example.match1;
   title 'Data Set MATCH1';
run;
```

The resulting data set has seven observations. See Output 4.21. In observation 2, the value of the variable PLANT1 is retained until all observations in the BY group are written to the new data set. Match-merging also produced the duplicate values in observations 4 and 5.

Output 4.21 *Results of Match-Merging Duplicate Values of the BY Variable*

```
                         Data Set MATCH1                         1

             OBS    COMMON    ANIMAL1    PLANT1

              1       a        ant       apple
              2       a        ape       apple
              3       b        bird      banana
              4       c        cat       coconut
              5       c        cat       celery
              6       d        dog       dewberry
              7       e        eagle     eggplant
```

Nonmatched observations The SAS System retains the values of all variables in the program data vector even if the value is missing. The data sets ANIMAL2 and PLANT2 do not contain all values of the BY variable COMMON, as shown in Output 4.22.

Output 4.22 *Data Sets with Nonmatched Observations*

```
                         Data Set ANIMAL2                        1

                    OBS    COMMON    ANIMAL2

                     1       a        ant
                     2       c        cat
                     3       d        dog
                     4       e        eagle
```

```
                         Data Set PLANT2                         2

                   OBS    COMMON    PLANT2

                    1       a       apple
                    2       b       banana
                    3       c       coconut
                    4       e       eggplant
                    5       f       fig
```

The following program produces the merged data set MATCH2 and prints the results:

```
data example.match2;
   merge example.animal2 example.plant2;
   by common;
run;

proc print data=example.match2;
   title 'Data Set MATCH2';
run;
```

The resulting data set has six observations. See Output 4.23. All values of the variable COMMON are represented in the new data set. The new observations contain missing values for the variables that are in one data set but not in the other.

Output 4.23 *Results of Match-Merge with Nonmatched Observations*

```
                    Data Set MATCH2                           1

     OBS    COMMON    ANIMAL2    PLANT2

      1       a        ant       apple
      2       b                  banana
      3       c        cat       coconut
      4       d        dog
      5       e        eagle     eggplant
      6       f                  fig
```

Match-Merging: Comments and Comparisons

Under very specific circumstances you can combine data sets using one-to-one reading, one-to-one merging, and match-merging and produce the same results. In the very simplest examples in this section, the data sets had these characteristics:

- □ All observations contained unique values for all the variables.
- □ There were no missing values for any of the variables in any data set.
- □ The observations were arranged so that corresponding values were arranged in the same order in both data sets.

Normally, your data do not meet these criteria, and you must select the method that achieves the results you want. You can test the methods available on representative samples of the data and compare the results.

Chapter 17 in *SAS Language and Procedures: Usage* contains additional instructions and detailed examples for match-merging data sets.

Updating Data Sets

To update data sets, you work with two input data sets. The data set containing the original information is the *master data set*, and the data set containing the new information is the *transaction data set*. The UPDATE statement uses observations from the transaction data set to change the values of corresponding observations from the master data set. You must use a BY statement with the UPDATE statement because all observations in the transaction data set are keyed to observations in the master data set by values of the BY variable.

Both the master data set and the transaction data set must be sorted by the same variable or variables you specify in the BY statement that accompanies the UPDATE statement. The values of the BY variable must be unique for each observation in the master data set. If you use more than one BY variable, the combination of values of all BY variables should be unique for each observation in the master data set. The BY variable or variables should be ones that you never need to update.

The number of observations in the new data set is the sum of the number of observations in the master data set and the number of unmatched observations in the transaction data set.

The general form of the UPDATE statement and the BY statement is as follows:

> UPDATE *master-data-set transaction-data-set*;
> BY *variable-list*;

Options are not shown here for simplicity. See Chapter 9 for complete descriptions, including available options, of the UPDATE and BY statements.

DATA Step Processing to Update Data Sets

The SAS System updates data sets as follows:

1. During the compilation phase of the DATA step, the SAS System reads the descriptor information of each data set named in the UPDATE statement and creates a program data vector that contains all the variables from both data sets as well as variables created by the DATA step. It also creates the FIRST.*variable* and LAST.*variable* for each variable listed in the BY statement.
2. Then, the SAS System looks at the first observation in each data set named in the UPDATE statement to determine which BY group should appear first. If the transaction BY value precedes the master BY value, the SAS System reads from the transaction data set only and sets the variables from the master data set to missing. If the master BY value precedes the transaction BY value, the SAS System reads from the master data set only and sets the variables from the transaction data set to missing. If the BY values in the master and transaction data sets are equal, it applies the first transaction by copying the values into the program data vector.
3. After completing the first transaction, the SAS System looks at the next observation in the transaction data set. If it finds one with the same BY value, it applies that transaction too. The first observation then contains the new values from both transactions.
4. If no other transactions exist for that observation, the SAS System writes the observation to the new data set and sets the values in the program data vector to missing.
5. The SAS System repeats these steps until it has read all observations from all BY groups in both data sets.

Examples of Updating Data Sets

Output 4.24 shows a data set MASTER that contains original values of the variables ANIMAL and PLANT. The data set NEWPLANT, shown in Output 4.25, is a transaction data set with new values of the variable PLANT.

Output 4.24 *Master Data Set*

```
                    Data Set MASTER                          1

          OBS    COMMON    ANIMAL    PLANT

           1       a       ant       apple
           2       b       bird      banana
           3       c       cat       coconut
           4       d       dog       dewberry
           5       e       eagle     eggplant
           6       f       frog      fig
```

Output 4.25 *Transaction Data Set*

```
                    Data Set NEWPLANT                    1

              OBS    COMMON    PLANT

               1       a       apricot
               2       b       barley
               3       c       cactus
               4       d       date
               5       e       escarole
               6       f       fennel
```

The following program updates MASTER with the transactions in the data set NEWPLANT and prints the results:

```
data example.update;
   update example.master example.newplant;
   by common;
run;

proc print data=example.update;
   title 'Data Set UPDATE';
run;
```

The resulting data set has six observations. Each observation in the new data set contains a new value for the variable PLANT. See Output 4.26.

Output 4.26 *Master Data Set Updated by Transaction Data Set*

```
                    Data Set UPDATE                      1

              OBS    COMMON    ANIMAL    PLANT

               1       a       ant       apricot
               2       b       bird      barley
               3       c       cat       cactus
               4       d       dog       date
               5       e       eagle     escarole
               6       f       frog      fennel
```

Duplicate values of the BY variable If the master data set contains two observations with the same value of the BY variable, the first observation is updated and the second observation is ignored and an error message is issued. If the transaction data set contains duplicate values of the BY variable, the SAS System applies both transactions to the observation. The last values copied into the program data vector are written to the new data set.

The example data sets MASTER1 and DUPPLANT are shown in Output 4.27.

Output 4.27 *Master and Transaction Data Sets with Duplicate BY Values*

```
                    Data Set MASTER1                     1

              OBS    COMMON    ANIMAL1    PLANT1

               1       a       ant        apple
               2       b       bird       banana
               3       b       bird       banana
               4       c       cat        coconut
               5       d       dog        dewberry
               6       e       eagle      eggplant
               7       f       frog       fig
```

```
                    Data Set DUPPLANT                          2

              OBS    COMMON     PLANT1

               1       a        apricot
               2       b        barley
               3       c        cactus
               4       d        date
               5       d        dill
               6       e        escarole
               7       f        fennel
```

The following program applies the transactions in DUPPLANT to MASTER1 and prints the results:

```
data example.update1;
   update example.master1 example.dupplant;
   by common;
run;

proc print data=example.update1;
   title 'Data Set UPDATE1';
run;
```

Note: When this DATA step executes, you receive an error message stating that you have more than one observation for a BY group. However, the DATA step continues to process, and the data set EXAMPLE.UPDATE1 is created.

The resulting data set has seven observations. See Output 4.28. Note that observations 2 and 3 contain duplicate values of the BY variable COMMON; however, the value of the variable PLANT1 was not updated in the second occurrence of the duplicate BY value.

Output 4.28 *Results of Updating Data Sets with Duplicate BY Values*

```
                    Data Set UPDATE1                              1

         OBS    COMMON    ANIMAL1     PLANT1

          1       a        ant        apricot
          2       b        bird       barley
          3       b        bird       banana
          4       c        cat        cactus
          5       d        dog        dill
          6       e        eagle      escarole
          7       f        frog       fennel
```

Nonmatched observations, missing values, and new variables If an observation in the master data set does not have a corresponding observation in the transaction data set, the SAS System writes the observation to the new data set without modifying it. Any observation from the transaction data set that does not correspond to an observation in the master data set is written to the program data vector and becomes the basis for an observation in the new data set. It can be modified by other transactions before it is written to the new data set. If a master data set observation does not need updating, the corresponding observation can be omitted from the transaction data set.

The SAS System does not replace existing values in the master data set with missing values if those values are coded as periods (for numeric variables) or blanks (for character variables) in the transaction data set. To replace existing values with missing values, you must create a transaction data set in which missing values are coded with the special missing value characters. See the UPDATE statement in Chapter 9 for an example of how you can use missing values to update a data set. In the same chapter, see the MISSING statement for a general description of missing value characters and their uses.

The transaction data set can contain new variables to be added to all observations in the master data set.

The data set MASTER2, shown in Output 4.29, is a master data set. Note that MASTER2 has a missing value for the variable PLANT2 in the first observation and that all of the values of the BY variable common are not included.

Output 4.29 *Master Data Set with Missing Values*

```
                         Data Set MASTER2                              1

              OBS    COMMON    ANIMAL2    PLANT2

               1       a       ant
               2       c       cat        coconut
               3       d       dog        dewberry
               4       e       eagle      eggplant
               5       f       frog       fig
```

The transaction data set NONPLANT, shown in Output 4.30, contains a new variable MINERAL, a new value of the BY variable COMMON, and missing values for several observations.

Output 4.30 *Transaction Data Set with New Variables, Nonmatched Observations, and Missing Values*

```
                        Data Set NONPLANT                              1

              OBS    COMMON    PLANT2     MINERAL

               1       a       apricot    amethyst
               2       b       barley     beryl
               3       c       cactus
               4       e
               5       f       fennel
               6       g       grape      garnet
```

The following program updates the data set MASTER2 and prints the results:

```
data example.update2;
   update example.master2 example.nonplant;
   by common;
run;

proc print data=example.update2;
   title 'Data Set UPDATE2';
run;
```

The resulting data set has seven observations. See Output 4.31. All observations now include values for the variable MINERAL. Note that the value of MINERAL is set to missing for some observations. Observations 2 and 6 in the transaction data set did not have corresponding observations in MASTER2, and they have become new observations. Observation 3 from the master data set was written to the new data set without change, and the value for PLANT2 in observation 4 was not changed to missing. Three observations in the new data set have updated values for the variable PLANT2.

Output 4.31 *Results of Updating with New Variables, Nonmatched Observations, and Missing Values*

```
                         Data Set UPDATE2                               1

 OBS    COMMON    ANIMAL2    PLANT2      MINERAL

  1       a       ant        apricot     amethyst
  2       b                  barley      beryl
  3       c       cat        cactus
  4       d       dog        dewberry
  5       e       eagle      eggplant
  6       f       frog       fennel
  7       g                  grape       garnet
```

Updating Data Sets: Comments and Comparisons

Chapter 18, "Updating SAS Data Sets," in *SAS Language and Procedures: Usage* contains instructions and detailed examples for updating data sets. See also the UPDATE statement in Chapter 9 in this book.

Array Processing

You use arrays in the SAS System to group variables together in order to apply the same process to all the variables.* The following example shows a DATA step that can be made easier to read through the use of an array. The three variables in the INPUT statement are a group of variables that hold information about SAS documentation.

```
     /* same action for different variables */
  data changes;
     infile file-specification;
     input ref 1-4 usage 6-10 intro 12-16;
     if ref=. then ref=0;
     if usage=. then usage=0;
     if intro=. then intro=0;
     more SAS statements
  run;
```

The pattern of action is the same in the three IF-THEN statements: the SAS System changes the missing values in each variable to 0s. The only difference in each IF-THEN statement is the variable name. You can make the program easier to read by telling the SAS System to perform the same action several times, changing only the variable affected. The technique is called array processing, and it involves the following:

- grouping variables into arrays
- repeating the action
- selecting the current variable to be acted on.

* Note that arrays in the SAS System are different from those in many other programming languages. In the SAS System, an array is simply a convenient way of temporarily identifying a group of variables. It is not a data structure, and it exists only for the duration of the DATA step. The *array-name* identifies the array and distinguishes it from any other arrays in the same DATA step; it is not a variable.

Grouping Variables into Arrays

In DATA step programming, you can put variables into a temporary group called an *array*. To define an array, use an ARRAY statement. A simple ARRAY statement has the following form:

ARRAY *array-name*{*number-of-elements*} *list-of-variables*;

where *array-name* is a SAS name that you choose to identify the group of variables, *number-of-elements*, enclosed in braces, tells the SAS System how many variables you are grouping, and *list-of-variables* contains their names. You can also use square brackets and parentheses to surround *number-of-elements*.

The following ARRAY statement creates an array named BOOKS, containing three variables REF, USAGE, and INTRO:

```
array books{3} ref usage intro;
```

Whenever you define an array, the SAS System assigns each array element an *array reference* with the form *array-name*{*subscript*}, where *subscript* is the position of the variable in the list (in this case, 1, 2, or 3). The subscript can be a number, the name of a variable whose value is the number, or an expression. Later in the DATA step when you want to process the variables in the array, you can use the array reference.

For example, the previous ARRAY statement assigns the variable REF the array reference BOOKS{1}; USAGE, BOOKS{2}; and INTRO, BOOKS{3}. From that point in the DATA step, you can refer to the variable by either its name or by its array reference. For example, the names REF and BOOKS{1} are equivalent.

Repeating an Action

To tell the SAS System to perform the same action several times, use an iterative DO loop. The simplest iterative DO loop for array processing has the following form:

DO *index-variable*=1 TO *number-of-variables-in-array*;
  more SAS statements
END;

An iterative DO loop begins with an iterative DO statement, contains other SAS statements, and ends with an END statement. The loop is processed repeatedly (iterates) according to the directions in the iterative DO statement. The iterative DO statement contains an *index-variable* whose name you choose and whose value changes in each iteration of the loop.

In array processing, you usually want the loop to execute as many times as there are variables in the array; therefore, you specify that the values of *index-variable* are 1 TO *number-of-variables-in-array*. By default, the SAS System increases the value of *index-variable* by 1 before each new iteration of the loop. When the value becomes greater than *number-of-variables-in-array*, the SAS System stops processing the loop. The SAS System automatically adds *index-variable* to the data set being created.

An iterative DO loop that executes three times and has an index variable named COUNT looks as follows:

```
do count=1 to 3;
   more SAS statements
end;
```

The first time the loop is processed, the value of COUNT is 1; the second time, 2; and the third time, 3. At the beginning of the fourth execution, the value of COUNT is 4, which exceeds the specified range of 1 TO 3. The SAS System stops processing the loop.

See "Variations on Basic Array Processing" later in this chapter for a discussion of other forms of DO-group array processing.

Selecting the Current Variable

Once you have grouped the variables and know how many times the loop will be processed, you must tell the SAS System which variable in the array to use in each iteration of the loop. Recall that variables in an array can be identified by their array references and that the subscript of the reference can be a variable name, a number, or an expression. Therefore, you can write programming statements in which the index variable of the DO loop is the subscript of the array reference (for example, *array-name*{*index-variable*}). When the value of the index variable changes, the subscript of the array reference (and therefore the variable referenced) also changes.

Building on the same example used earlier in this section, the following statement uses COUNT as the subscript of array references:

```
if books{count}=. then books{count}=0;
```

You can place this statement inside an iterative DO loop. When the value of COUNT is 1, the SAS System reads the array reference as BOOKS{1} and processes the IF-THEN statement on BOOKS{1} which is the variable REF. When COUNT has the value 2, the SAS System processes the statement on BOOKS{2}, the variable USAGE. When COUNT is 3, it processes the statement on BOOKS{3}, the variable INTRO. The complete iterative DO loop with array references appears as follows:

```
do count=1 to 3;
   if books{count}=. then books{count}=0;
end;
```

These statements tell the SAS System to

- □ perform the actions in the loop three times
- □ replace the array subscript COUNT with the current value of COUNT for each iteration of the IF-THEN statement
- □ locate the variable with that array reference and process the IF-THEN statement on it.

Placing the ARRAY statement and iterative DO loop in the following DATA step produces the data set shown in Output 4.32. The DROP= data set option excludes COUNT from the data set.

```
data chgdrop(drop=count);
   input ref usage intro;
   array book{3} ref usage intro;
   do count=1 to 3;
      if book{count}=. then book{count}=0;
   end;
   cards;
45 63 113
.  75 150
62 .   98
;

proc print data=chgdrop;
   title 'Data Set Produced with Array Processing';
run;
```

Output 4.32 *Using an Array to Produce a Data Set*

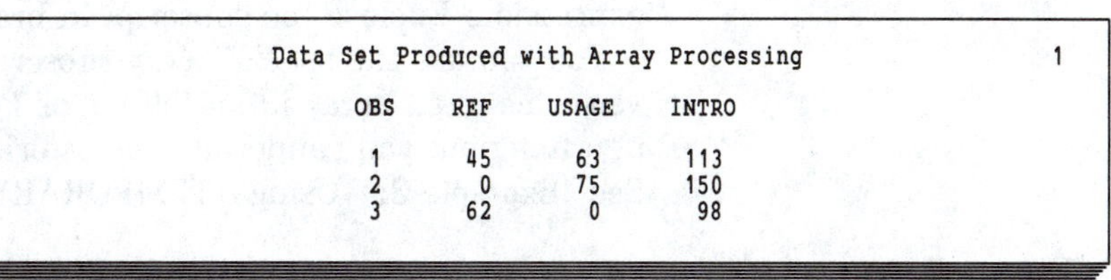

```
                Data Set Produced with Array Processing                1

                   OBS    REF    USAGE    INTRO

                    1      45      63      113
                    2       0      75      150
                    3      62       0       98
```

Referencing Arrays

You can use an array reference anywhere you can write a SAS expression, including the following SAS statements:

- □ assignment
- □ DO WHILE(*expression*)
- □ DO UNTIL(*expression*)
- □ IF
- □ INPUT
- □ PUT
- □ SELECT
- □ sum
- □ WINDOW.

You can also use array references in the arguments of SAS functions.

The ARRAY statement defining the array must appear in a DATA step before any references to that array. An array definition is only in effect for the duration of the DATA step. If you want to use the same array in several DATA steps, you must redefine the array in each step.

You can, however, redefine the array with the same variables in a later DATA step using a macro variable. A macro variable is useful for storing the variable names you need as shown here:

```
%let list=NC SC GA VA;

data one;
   array state{4} &list;
   more SAS statements
run;

data two;
   array state{4} &list;
   more SAS statements
run;
```

See Chapter 20, "SAS Macro Facility," for more information on macro variables.

A reference to an explicit array must contain the subscript. (See "Array Reference, Explicit" in Chapter 9.) The subscript can be any valid SAS expression. Enclose the subscript in braces, brackets, or parentheses.

You can use the special array subscript asterisk (*) to refer to all variables in an array in an INPUT or PUT statement or in the argument of a function; you cannot use the asterisk with _TEMPORARY_ arrays. See "Example 3: Using _TEMPORARY_ Arrays" later in this chapter.

Variations on Basic Array Processing

To process particular elements of an array, specify those elements as the range of the iterative DO statement as shown here.

```
array days{7} d1-d7;
```

You can process selected elements of this array with any of the following DO statements:

- `do i=2 to 4;`
- `do i=1 to 7 by 2;`
- `do i=3,5;`

The DIM Function

You can use the DIM function in the iterative DO statement to return the number of elements in a one-dimensional array or the number of elements in a specified dimension of a multidimensional array, when the lower bound of the dimension is 1. See "Multidimensional Arrays" later in this chapter for an example.

You can use the DIM function to change the number of elements in an array without respecifying the upper bound of all iterative DO groups that refer to that array. You can also use it when you have specified the number of elements in the array with an asterisk. Here are some examples:

- `do i=1 to dim(days);`
- `do i=1 to dim(days) by 2;`

See the DIM function in Chapter 11 for a complete discussion and examples.

DO WHILE and DO UNTIL Expressions

Arrays are often processed in iterative DO loops that use the array reference in a DO WHILE or DO UNTIL expression. In this DATA step, the iterative DO loop processes the elements of the array named TREND:

```
data test;
   array trend{5} x1-x5;
   input x1-x5 y;
   do i=1 to 5 while(trend{i}<y);
      more SAS statements
   end;
   cards;
data lines
;
```

Defining the Number of Elements in an Array

When defining the number of elements in an array, you can either specify the precise number of elements (as shown in previous examples), or you can simply use an asterisk enclosed in braces ({*}) to tell the SAS System to count the number of elements you list. You must list each array element if you use the asterisk to designate the number of elements.

If you specify the number of elements explicitly, you have the option of leaving off the names of the variables or array elements in the ARRAY statement. In this case, the SAS System creates variable names by concatenating the array name with the numbers 1, 2, 3, and so on. If a variable name in the series already exists, the SAS System uses that variable instead of creating a new one.

Multidimensional Arrays

Arrays are frequently used to group variables into a table-like format. These arrays are known as multidimensional arrays. They provide column and row arrangement of array variables, and they can include any number of dimensions.

To create a multidimensional array, place the number of elements in each dimension after the array name in the form {*n*, . . . }where *n* is required for each dimension of a multidimensional array.

Reading from right to left, the rightmost dimension represents columns; the next dimension represents rows; and each position farther left represents a higher dimension. In the following example, you create an array that contains ten variables—five temperature measures (T1 through T5) from two cities (C1 and C2):

```
array temprg{2,5} c1t1-c1t5 c2t1-c2t5;
```

This ARRAY statement defines a two-dimensional array with two rows and five columns. The SAS System places variables into a multidimensional array by filling all rows in order, beginning at the upper-left corner of the array (known as row-major order). You can think of the variables in the following arrangement:

```
c1t1 c1t2 c1t3 c1t4 c1t5
c2t1 c2t2 c2t3 c2t4 c2t5
```

When you want to refer to the elements of the array later with an array reference, you can use the array name and subscripts. Using the previous example, refer to variable C1T1 as TEMPRG{1,1}, C1T2 as TEMPRG{1,2}, C2T2 as TEMPRG{2,2}, and C2T5 as TEMPRG{2,5}.

Multidimensional arrays are usually processed inside nested DO loops. Nested DO loops for a two-dimensional array have the following form:

DO *index-variable-1*=1 TO *number-of-rows*;
    DO *index-variable-2*=1 TO *number-of-columns*;
        action to perform
    END;
END;

An array reference can use two or more index variables as the subscript in order to refer to two or more dimensions of an array. An array reference for a two-dimensional array has the following form:

array-name {*index-variable-1*,*index-variable-2*}

The following DATA step uses the TEMPRG array to process the ten variables grouped together in the array. The outer DO loop (DO I=1 TO 2) causes the SAS System to process the inner DO loop twice. The inner DO loop (DO J=1 TO 5) applies the ROUND function to all the variables in one row. For each execution of the loop, the SAS System substitutes the value of the array element corresponding to the current values of I and J. The output data set TEMPS contains the values of the variables rounded to the nearest whole number, as shown in Output 4.33.

```
data temps;
   array temprg{2,5} c1t1-c1t5 c2t1-c2t5;
   input c1t1-c1t5 /
         c2t1-c2t5;
   do i=1 to 2;
      do j=1 to 5;
         temprg{i,j}=round(temprg{i,j});
      end;
   end;
   cards;
89.5 65.4 75.3 77.7 89.3
73.7 87.3 89.9 98.2 35.6
75.8 82.1 98.2 93.5 67.7
101.3 86.5 59.2 35.6 75.7
;

proc print data=temps;
run;
```

Output 4.33 *Using a Multidimensional Array*

```
                              The SAS System                              1

OBS  C1T1  C1T2  C1T3  C1T4  C1T5  C2T1  C2T2  C2T3  C2T4  C2T5  I  J

 1    90    65    75    78    89     74   87    90    98    36   3  6
 2    76    82    98    94    68    101   87    59    36    76   3  6
```

You can rewrite the previous example using the DIM function to produce the same result:

```
do i=1 to dim(temprg);
   do j=1 to dim2(temprg);
      temprg{i,j}=round(temprg{i,j});
   end;
end;
```

The value of DIM(TEMPRG) is 2; the value of DIM2(TEMPRG) is 5. See the DIM function in Chapter 11.

Specifying Array Bounds

In the arrays shown so far, the subscript in each dimension of the array ranges from 1 to *n*, where *n* is the number of elements in that dimension. Thus, 1 is the lower bound and *n* is the upper bound of that dimension of the array. For example, in the following array the lower bound is 1 and the upper bound is 4:

```
array new{4} jackson poulenc andrew parson;
```

In the next statement, the bounds of the first dimension are 1 and 2 and those of the second dimension are 1 and 5:

```
array test{2,5} test1-test10;
```

Bounded array dimensions have the following form:

{<*lower-1* :>*upper-1*<,. . . <*lower-n* :>*upper-n*>}

Therefore, you can also write the previous ARRAY statements as follows:

```
array new{1:4} jackson poulenc andrew parson;
array test{1:2,1:5} test1-test10;
```

For most arrays, 1 is a convenient lower bound; thus, you do not need to specify the lower and upper bounds. However, specifying both bounds is useful when the array dimensions have a convenient beginning point other than 1.

For example, suppose you have ten variables named YEAR76 through YEAR85. The following ARRAY statements place the variables into two arrays named FIRST and SECOND:

```
array first{10} year76-year85;
array second{76:85} year76-year85;
```

With the first ARRAY statement, you must remember that element FIRST{4} is variable YEAR79, FIRST{7} is YEAR82, and so on. With the second ARRAY statement, element SECOND{79} is YEAR79 and SECOND{82} is YEAR82. The array references are easy to interpret.

To process the array named SECOND in a DO group, be sure that the range of the DO loop matches the range of the array as follows:

```
do i=76 to 85;
   if second{i}=9 then second{i}=.;
end;
```

Using the LBOUND and HBOUND Functions

You can also use the LBOUND and HBOUND functions to specify array bounds. The LBOUND function returns the lower bound of a one-dimensional array or the lower bound of a specified dimension of a multidimensional array. The HBOUND function returns the upper bound of a one-dimensional array or the upper bound of a specified dimension of a multidimensional array.

You can use the LBOUND and HBOUND functions to specify the starting and ending values of the iterative DO loop in order to process the elements of the array named SECOND:

```
do i=lbound(yrs) to hbound(yrs);
   if second{i}=9 then second{i}=.;
end;
```

In this example, the index variable in the iterative DO statement ranges from 76 to 85. See Chapter 11 for descriptions of the LBOUND and HBOUND functions.

Using the HBOUND Function Instead of the DIM Function

The following ARRAY statement defines an array with a total of five elements, a lower bound of 72, and an upper bound of 76; it represents the calendar years 1972 through 1976:

```
array years{72:76} first second third fourth fifth;
```

To process the array elements in an iterative DO loop, use the following statement:

```
do i=lbound(years) to hbound(years);
   more SAS statements
end;
```

The value of LBOUND(YEARS) is 72; the value of HBOUND(YEARS) is 76.

The DIM function, in this example, would return a value of 5, the total count of elements in array YEARS. Therefore, if you used the DIM function instead of the HBOUND function for the upper bound of the array, the statements inside the DO loop would not have executed.

Specifying Bounds in a Two-Dimensional Array

Suppose you have 40 variables named X60 through X99; they represent the years 1960 through 1999. You want to arrange them in an array by decades, as follows:

```
X60  X61  X62  X63  X64  X65  X66  X67  X68  X69
X70  X71  X72  X73  X74  X75  X76  X77  X78  X79
X80  X81  X82  X83  X84  X85  X86  X87  X88  X89
X90  X91  X92  X93  X94  X95  X96  X97  X98  X99
```

It is convenient to make the rows range from 6 through 9 and the columns range from 0 through 9. This ARRAY statement creates the array:

```
array x{6:9,0:9} x60-x99;
```

In array X, variable X63 is element X{6,3} and variable X89 is X{8,9}. You can remember these references easily. To process array X with iterative DO loops, use one of these methods:

□
```
do i=6 to 9;
   do j=0 to 9;
      if x{i,j}=0 then x{i,j}=.;
   end;
end;
```

□
```
do i=lbound1(x) to hbound1(x);
   do j=lbound2(x) to hbound2(x);
      if x{i,j}=0 then x{i,j}=.;
   end;
end;
```

Both examples change all values of 0 in variables X60 through X99 to missing. The first example sets the range of the DO groups explicitly, and the second example uses the LBOUND and HBOUND functions to return the bounds of each dimension of the array.

Examples of Array Processing

Example 1: Using Character Variables in an Array

You can specify character variables and their lengths in ARRAY statements. In the following example, you group variables into two arrays, NAMES and CAPS. Use the dollar sign ($) as you would in an INPUT statement to tell the SAS System to read in character values. If the variables have already been declared as character variables, you do not need to specify that in the array. The INPUT statement reads in all the variables in array NAMES.

The statement inside the DO loop uses the UPCASE function to change the values of the variables in array NAMES to uppercase and then store the uppercase values in the variables in the CAPS array. Output 4.34 shows the output data set TEXT.

```
data text;
   array names{*} $ n1-n9;
   array caps{*} $ c1-c9;
   input names{*};
   do i=1 to 9;
      caps{i}=upcase(names{i});
   end;
   cards;
smithers michaels gonzalez hurth frank bleigh rounder joseph peters
;

proc print data=text;
run;
```

Output 4.34 *Using Character Variables in an Array*

```
                              The SAS System                              1
OBS    N1        N2        N3       N4    N5    N6     N7      N8     N9
  1 smithers michaels gonzalez hurth frank bleigh rounder joseph peters
OBS    C1        C2        C3       C4    C5    C6     C7      C8     C9   I
  1 SMITHERS MICHAELS GONZALEZ HURTH FRANK BLEIGH ROUNDER JOSEPH PETERS 10
```

Example 2: Assigning Initial Values to the Elements of an Array

In this example, you create variables in an explicit array named TEST and assign them the initial values 90, 80, and 70. Then you read values into another array named SCORE and compare each element of SCORE to the corresponding element of TEST. If the value of the element in SCORE is greater than the value of the element in TEST, the variable NEWSCORE is assigned the value of SCORE and the OUTPUT statement writes the observation to the SAS data set.

The INPUT statement reads in a value for the variable named ID, then reads in values for all the variables in the SCORE array. Data set SCORE1 is shown in Output 4.35.

```
data score1(drop=i);
   array test{3} t1-t3 (90 80 70);
   array score{3} s1-s3;
   input id score{*};
   do i=1 to 3;
      if score{i}>=test{i} then
         do;
            newscore=score{i};
            output;
         end;
   end;
   cards;
1234  99 60 82
5678  80 85 75
;

proc print noobs;
   title 'Data Set Score1';
run;
```

Output 4.35 *Assigning Initial Values to the Elements of an Array*

```
                           Data Set Score1                         1
         T1    T2    T3    S1    S2    S3     ID     NEWSCORE
         90    80    70    99    60    82    1234       99
         90    80    70    99    60    82    1234       82
         90    80    70    80    85    75    5678       85
         90    80    70    80    85    75    5678       75
```

Example 3: Using _TEMPORARY_ Arrays

In the previous example, the elements of the array TEST are constants needed only for the duration of DATA step execution. You can use _TEMPORARY_ instead of specifying variable names and assign initial values to the temporary array elements. The following statements produce Output 4.36:

```
data score2(drop=i);
   array test{3} _temporary_ (90 80 70);
   array score{3} s1-s3;
   input id score{*};
      do i=1 to 3;
         if score{i}>=test{i} then
            do;
               newscore=score{i};
               output;
            end;
      end;
   cards;
1234  99 60 82
5678  80 85 75
;
proc print noobs;
   title 'Data Set Score2';
run;
```

Output 4.36 *Using _TEMPORARY_ Arrays*

```
                          Data Set Score2                              1

                   S1    S2    S3     ID     NEWSCORE

                   99    60    82    1234       99
                   99    60    82    1234       82
                   80    85    75    5678       85
                   80    85    75    5678       75
```

Dropping, Keeping, and Renaming Variables

The DROP, KEEP, and RENAME statements or the DROP=, KEEP=, and RENAME= data set options control which variables are processed or output during the DATA step. You can use one or a combination of these statements and data set options to achieve the results you want. The action taken by the SAS System depends largely on whether you

- □ use a statement or data set option or both
- □ specify the data set options on an input or an output data set.

See Chapter 9 for details about these statements and Chapter 15 for details about these data set options. The following sections provide some general rules you need to consider when determining the most efficient way to drop, keep, or rename variables.

Statements or Data Set Options

When dropping, keeping, and renaming variables, one of the first choices you need to make is whether to use a statement or a data set option. Table 4.3 summarizes the general differences between the DROP, KEEP, and RENAME statements and the DROP=, KEEP=, and RENAME= data set options.

Table 4.3 *Statements versus Data Set Options for Dropping, Keeping, and Renaming Variables*

Statements	Data Set Options
apply only to output data sets	apply to output or input data sets
apply to all output data sets	apply to individual data sets
are valid in DATA steps only	are valid in DATA steps and PROC steps
can appear anywhere in DATA steps	must immediately follow the name of each data set to which they apply

Input or Output Data Set

You must also consider whether you want to drop, keep, or rename the variable before it is read into the program data vector or as it is written to the new SAS data set. If you use the DROP, KEEP, or RENAME statement, the action always occurs as the variables are written to the output data set. With SAS data set options, where you use the option determines when the action occurs. If the option is used on an input data set, the variable is dropped, kept, or renamed before it is read into the program data vector. If used on an output data set, the data set option is applied as the variable is written to the new SAS data set. (In the DATA step, an input data set is one that is specified in a SET, MERGE, or UPDATE statement. An output data set is one that is specified in the DATA statement.) Consider the following facts when you make your decision:

- □ If variables are not written to the output data set and they do not require any processing, using an input data set option to exclude them from the DATA step is more efficient.
- □ If you want to rename a variable before processing it in a DATA step, you must use the RENAME= data set option in the input data set.
- □ If the action applies to output data sets, you can use either a statement or a data set option in the output data set.

Table 4.4 summarizes the action of data set options and statements when they are specified for input and output data sets. The last column of the table tells whether the variable is available for processing in the DATA step. If you want to rename the variable, use the information in the last column.

Table 4.4 *Status of Variables and Variable Names When Dropping, Keeping, and Renaming*

Where Specified	Data Set Option or Statement	Purpose	Status of Variable or Variable Name
input data set	DROP= KEEP=	includes or excludes variables from processing	if excluded, variables are not available for use in DATA step
	RENAME=	changes name of variable before processing	use new name in program statements and output data set options; use old name in other input data set options
output data set	DROP, KEEP	specifies which variables are written to all output data sets	all variables available for processing
	RENAME	changes name of variables in all output data sets	use old name in program statements; use new name in output data set options
	DROP= KEEP=	specifies which variables are written to individual output data sets	all variables are available for processing
	RENAME=	changes name of variables in individual output data sets	use old name in program statements and other output data set options

Order of Application

If your program requires that you use more than one data set option or a combination of data set options and statements, Figure 4.5 can help you determine in which order the SAS System drops, keeps, or renames variables. Within this order of application, the SAS System always applies a request to drop or keep a variable before it applies the request to rename a variable.

Figure 4.5 *Order of Application for Data Set Options and Statements*

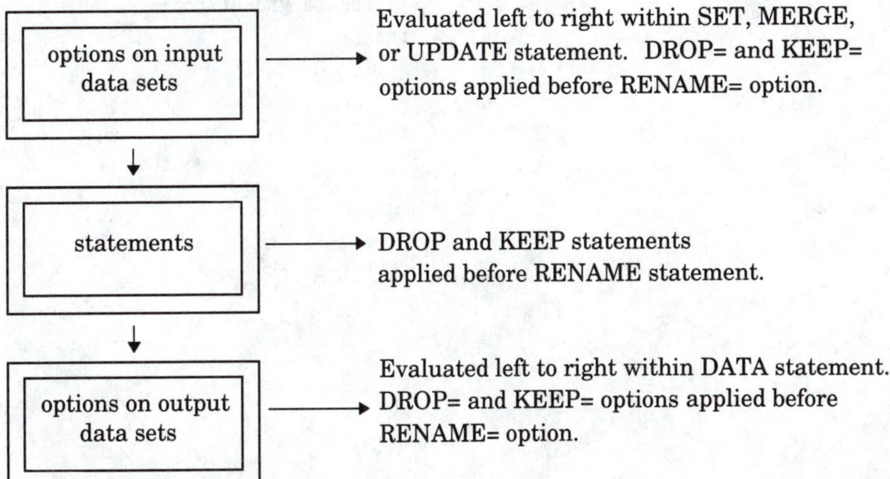
options on input data sets
Evaluated left to right within SET, MERGE, or UPDATE statement. DROP= and KEEP= options applied before RENAME= option.
statements
DROP and KEEP statements applied before RENAME statement.
options on output data sets
Evaluated left to right within DATA statement. DROP= and KEEP= options applied before RENAME= option.

Examples of Dropping, Keeping, and Renaming Variables

The following examples show specific ways to handle dropping, keeping, and renaming variables:

□ This example uses the DROP= and RENAME= data set options and the INPUT function to convert the variable POPRANK from character to numeric. The name POPRANK is changed to TEMPVAR before processing so that a new variable POPRANK can be written to the output data set. Note that the variable TEMPVAR is dropped from the output data set and that the new name TEMPVAR is used in the program statements.

```
data newstate(drop=tempvar);
   length poprank 8;
   set state(rename=(poprank=tempvar));
   poprank=input(tempvar,8.);
run;
```

□ This example uses the DROP statement and the DROP= data set option to control the output of variables to two new SAS data sets. The DROP statement applies to both data sets, CORN and BEAN. You must use the RENAME= data set option to rename the output variables BEANWT and CORNWT in each data set.

```
data corn(rename=(cornwt=yield) drop=beanwt)
     bean(rename=(beanwt=yield) drop=cornwt);
   set harvest;
   if crop='corn' then output corn;
   else if crop='bean' then output bean;
   drop crop;
run;
```

□ This example shows how to use data set options in the DATA statement and the RENAME statement together. Note that the new name QTRTOT is used in the DROP= data set option.

```
data qtr1 qtr2 ytd(drop=qtrtot);
   set ytdsales;
   if qtr=1 then output qtr1;
   else if qtr=2 then output qtr2;
   else output ytd;
   rename ytd=qtrtot;
run;
```

CHAPTER 5 SAS® Output

Introduction

SAS output is the result of executing SAS programs. Most SAS procedures and some DATA step applications produce output.

Base SAS software produces two forms of printed output:

- □ the SAS log, which contains a description of the SAS session and lists lines of source code executed
- □ the results of most SAS procedures and some DATA step applications, either routed to a file or printed on an output device.

This chapter discusses forms of SAS output, methods of tailoring output, understanding SAS errors and error messages, and changing the destination of output.

Note: The SAS Display Manager System provides another method of displaying and saving the SAS log and output. See Chapter 17, "SAS Display Manager Windows," and Chapter 18, "SAS Display Manager Commands," for details.

SAS Log

The SAS log includes information about how your SAS program was processed. Depending on the setting of SAS system options, the method of running the SAS System, and the program statements you specify, the log can include the following types of information:

- □ program statements
- □ any data sets created by the program

□ any warnings or error messages encountered during program execution

□ how many variables and observations each data set contains

□ how much time each step in the program required

□ messages or a listing of data lines.

You can write specific information to the SAS log (such as variable values or text strings) using the SAS statements described in "Writing to the Log" later in this chapter.

Because the SAS log provides a journal of program processing, it is an essential debugging tool. However, certain system options must be in effect to make the log effective for debugging your SAS programs. For a list of the SAS system options that can affect your log and output, see "Options That Affect the Appearance of Output" at the end of this chapter. For details about all SAS system options, see Chapter 16, "SAS System Options."

The log is also used by some of the SAS procedures that perform utility functions, for example the DATASETS and OPTIONS procedures. See the *SAS Procedures Guide, Version 6, Third Edition* for details.

Routing the Log

The destination of your log depends on the

□ host system

□ setting of SAS system options

□ method of running the SAS System.

There are several ways to route the SAS log to a destination other than that set up as a default. You can route the log to your terminal, to an external file, or directly to a printer. See "Changing the Destination of the Log and Output" later in this chapter for more information. Chapter 28, "The PRINTTO Procedure" in the *SAS Procedures Guide* also discusses redirecting the SAS log.

Table 5.1 shows the default destination of the SAS log for each method of operation.

Table 5.1 *Default Destinations for the SAS Log*

Method of Running the SAS System	Destination of SAS Log
display manager mode	the LOG window
interactive line mode	the terminal display (as statements are entered)
noninteractive mode	depends on the host system
batch mode	depends on the host system

■ **Host Information** ....

The default destination for the SAS log is host specific. See the SAS documentation for your host system for the default destination of the SAS log.

.... ■

See "Running the System" in Chapter 1, "Essential Concepts," for a discussion of methods of running the SAS System. For details about the display manager LOG window, see Chapter 17, or see Chapter 43, *"Using the SAS Display Manager System—the Basics,"* in *SAS Language and Procedures: Usage, Version 6, First Edition.*

Structure of the Log

Each line in your SAS program containing SAS statements is printed and numbered in the log. For example, the number 1 printed to the left of the DATA statement in Output 5.1 means that it is the first line in the program.

Interspersed with your SAS statements are messages from the SAS System. These messages sometimes begin with the word NOTE, the word WARNING, the word ERROR, or an error number, and they may refer to a SAS statement by its line number in the log.

■ **Host Information** .... The SAS log appears differently depending on your host system. See the SAS documentation for your host system.

.... ■

Output 5.1 represents a typical SAS log.

Output 5.1 *Sample SAS Log*

```
                ❶
NOTE: Copyright(c) 1985,1986,1987,1988 SAS Institute Inc., Cary, NC USA.
NOTE: SAS (r) Proprietary Software Release 6.xx  ❷
      Licensed to SAS Institute Inc., Site xxxxxxxx.  ❸
                                                      ❹
1      data logsamp;
2         infile file-specification;
3         input test $ 1-8 sex $ 18 year 20-23 score 25-27;
4         run;

NOTE: The infile DATA is:
      file-specification          ❺

NOTE: 44 records were read from the infile file-specification.
NOTE: The data set WORK.LOGSAMP has 44 observations and 4 variables.
                                                              ❻
5         proc sort data=logsamp;        ❹
6            by test;
7         run;

NOTE: SAS sort was used.
NOTE: The data set WORK.LOGSAMP has 44 observations and 4 variables.

8         proc print data=logsamp;
9            by test;                    ❹
10        run;
                                                           ❼
NOTE: SAS Institute Inc., SAS Circle, PO Box 8000, Cary, NC 27512-8000
```

The following list corresponds to the circled numbers in Output 5.1:

❶ copyright information

❷ the SAS System release used to run this program

❸ the name and site number of the computer installation where the program was run

❹ SAS statements that make up the program (if the SAS system options SOURCE and SOURCE2 are enabled)

❺ notes or warning messages about the raw data and where they were obtained (if the SAS system option NOTES is enabled)

❻ notes that contain the number of observations and variables for each data set created (if the SAS system option NOTES is enabled)

❼ the name and address of SAS Institute Inc. (appears when you end a SAS session).

Writing to the Log

You can instruct the SAS System to write additional information to the log by using the following statements:

PUT statement
: instructs the system to write selected lines generated by the DATA step (including text strings and variable values) to the log by default. Use the PUT statement in a DATA step.

%PUT statement
: enables you to write a message to the SAS log. It is a SAS macro program statement that is independent of the DATA step.

LIST statement
: instructs the system to list in the log the input data records for the observation being processed. The LIST statement operates only on data read with the INPUT statement; it has no effect on data read with SET, MERGE, or UPDATE statements. Use the LIST statement in a DATA step.

ERROR statement
: sets the automatic _ERROR_ variable to 1 and optionally writes a message you specify to the log. Use the ERROR statement in a DATA step.

Use the PUT, LIST, and ERROR statements in combination with conditional processing to debug DATA steps by writing selected information to the log. For more information, see the PUT, LIST, and ERROR statements in Chapter 9, "SAS Language Statements," and the %PUT statement in Chapter 20, "SAS Macro Facility."

Suppressing All or Part of the Log

When you have large SAS production programs or an application that you run on a regular basis without changes, you may want to suppress listing parts of the SAS log. SAS system options enable you to suppress SAS statements, system messages, and error messages. Note that all SAS system options remain in effect for the duration of your session or until you change them. You should not suppress log messages until you have successfully executed the program without errors.

The following list describes the SAS system options you can use to suppress all or parts of the log:

ERRORS=*n*
: specifies the maximum number of observations for which data error messages are printed. The default value is ERRORS=20.

NEWS
: controls whether news information maintained at your site is written to the SAS log.

NOTES
: controls whether notes (messages beginning with NOTE) are written to the SAS log. Because the notes are required for debugging, use this option until your program is error free.

SOURCE
: controls whether SAS source statements are written to the SAS log.

SOURCE2
: controls whether secondary source statements and notes about secondary source statements from files included by %INCLUDE statements are written to the SAS log.

For more information about how to use these and other system options, see Chapter 16.

Customizing the Log

The following SAS statements and system options enable you to customize the log. This is helpful when you use the log for report writing or for creating a permanent record.

PAGE statement
: causes the SAS System to skip to a new page of the SAS log and continue printing from there.

SKIP statement
: skips a specified number of lines in the log.

FILE statement
: enables you to identify the SAS log as the output file. When you do, you can use two options in the FILE statement to customize the log for that report.

LINESIZE=*value* option	specifies the maximum number of columns per line for the report specified and the maximum record length for data files.
PAGESIZE=*value* option	specifies the maximum number of lines to print on each page of output.

Note: FILE statement options apply only to the output specified in the FILE statement, whereas the LINESIZE= and PAGESIZE= SAS system options apply to all subsequent output.

LINESIZE=*value* system option
: specifies the line size (printer line width) for the SAS log and the SAS procedure output file used by the DATA step and procedures.

PAGESIZE=*value* system option
: specifies the number of lines that can be printed per page of SAS output.

■ **Host Information** .... The range of values is host dependent. See the SAS documentation for your host system. ■

For more information about customizing the log, see the PAGE, SKIP, and FILE statements in Chapter 9. See Chapter 16 for descriptions of the LINESIZE= and PAGESIZE= system options. For more information about the SAS log, see Chapter 22, "Directing the SAS Log and Output," in *SAS Language and Procedures: Usage*.

Printed Results of SAS Programs

Many SAS procedures process or analyze data and can produce output as one result. Output can also be generated by the DATA step, using a combination of the FILE and PUT statements.

Consult the procedure descriptions in the *SAS Procedures Guide* for examples of output from SAS procedures. For a discussion and examples of DATA step output, see the FILE and PUT statements in Chapter 9. This section describes how to tailor SAS output using certain SAS statements and system options.

Routing Procedure Output

Like the log destination, the destination of SAS procedure output and some DATA step applications depends on the

- □ host system
- □ setting of SAS system options
- □ method of running the SAS System.

There are several ways to route SAS output to a destination other than the default. You can route output to your terminal, to an external file, or directly to a printer. See "Changing the Destination of the Log and Output" later in this chapter, and Chapter 28 in the *SAS Procedures Guide* for details.

Table 5.2 shows the default destination of the SAS log for each method of operation.

Table 5.2 *Default Destinations for SAS Output*

Method of Running the SAS System	Destination of Procedure Output
display manager mode	the OUTPUT window
interactive line mode	the terminal display (as each step executes)
noninteractive mode	depends on the host system
batch mode	depends on the host system

■ **Host Information** . . . . . . The default destination of SAS output is host specific. See the SAS documentation for your host system for the default destination of SAS output.

. . . . ■

For details about the display manager OUTPUT window, see Chapter 17, or see Chapter 43 in *SAS Language and Procedures: Usage*.

Making Output Descriptive

There are several ways to customize SAS procedure output and DATA step output directed to the same place as procedure output. You can change the look of output by adding informative titles, footnotes, and labels, and by changing the way the information is formatted on the page. This section describes some SAS statements and system options that enable you to change the default output format.

TITLE statements
: print titles at the top of each output page. By default, the SAS System prints the following title:

```
The SAS System
```

You can use the TITLE statement or TITLES window to replace the default title or specify other descriptive titles for SAS programs. See the TITLE statement in Chapter 9 and the TITLES window in Chapter 17 for details and examples.

FOOTNOTE statements
: print footnotes at the bottom of each output page. You can also use the FOOTNOTES window for this purpose. See the FOOTNOTE statement in Chapter 9 and the FOOTNOTES window in Chapter 17 for details and examples.

LABEL statement
: associates descriptive labels with variables. With most procedure output, the SAS System writes the label rather than the variable name. See the LABEL statement in Chapter 9 for more information.

The LABEL statement also provides descriptive labels when used with certain SAS procedures. See the *SAS Procedures Guide* for information on using the LABEL statement with a specific procedure (for example, the PRINT procedure).

LINESIZE= and PAGESIZE= system options
: can change the default number of lines per page (page size) and characters per line (line size) for printed output. The default depends on the method of running the SAS System and the settings of certain SAS system options. Specify new page and line sizes in the OPTIONS statement or OPTIONS window. You can also specify line and page size for DATA step output in the FILE statement. See the FILE statement in Chapter 9 for details.

The values you use for the LINESIZE= and PAGESIZE= system options can significantly affect the appearance of the output produced by some SAS procedures. See the *SAS Procedures Guide* for details on a particular procedure.

NUMBER and PAGENO= system options
: control page numbering. The NUMBER system option controls whether the page number prints on the first title line of each page of printed output. You can also specify a beginning page number for the next page of output produced by the SAS System by using the PAGENO= system option.

DATE system option
: controls printing of date and time values. When this option is enabled, the SAS System prints on the top of each page of output the date and time the SAS job started. When you are running the SAS System in interactive mode, the time the job started is the time you started your SAS session.

CENTER system option
: controls whether output is centered. By default, the SAS System centers titles and procedure output on the page and on the terminal display.

See Chapter 16 for more information about using the SAS system options discussed in this section.

Reformatting Values

Certain SAS statements, procedures, and options enable you to print values using specified formats. You can apply or change formats with the FORMAT and ATTRIB statements, or with the VAR window in display manager. The SAS formats available are described in Chapter 14, "SAS Formats." See Chapter 9 for complete descriptions of the FORMAT and ATTRIB statements and Chapter 17 for details on the VAR window.

The FORMAT procedure enables you to design your own formats and informats, giving you added flexibility in displaying values. See Chapter 18, "The FORMAT Procedure," in the *SAS Procedures Guide* for more information.

Printing Missing Values

The SAS System represents ordinary missing numeric values on SAS output as a single period, and missing character values as a blank space. If you have specified special missing values for numeric variables, the SAS System writes the letter or the underscore. For character variables, the SAS System writes a series of blanks equal to the length of the variable.

The MISSING= system option enables you to specify a character to print in place of the period for ordinary missing numeric values. See Chapter 16 for a discussion of the MISSING= system option.

Changing the Destination of the Log and Output

You can redirect both the SAS log and procedure output to your terminal display, to a printer, or to an external file. You can redirect output using the following methods:

PRINTTO procedure
: routes DATA step, log, or procedure output from the system default destinations to the destination you choose. See Chapter 28 in the *SAS Procedures Guide* for more information.

FILENAME statement
: associates a fileref with an external file or output device and enables you to specify file and device attributes. To route PUT statement output, the FILENAME statement must be used with either the PRINTTO procedure, the FILE statement, or the display manager FILE command. See the FILENAME statement in Chapter 9 for a detailed discussion.

FILE command
: stores the contents of the LOG or OUTPUT windows in files you specify, when the command is issued from within display manager. See the FILE command in Chapter 18 for details.

system options
: redefine the destination of log and output for an entire SAS session or program. System options are specified when you invoke the SAS System. The system options used to route output are the ALTOG=, ALTPRINT=, LOG=, and PRINT= system options.

■ **Host Information** .... The way you specify output destinations when using the system options is dependent on the host system. See the SAS documentation for your host system for details. ■

Table 5.3 summarizes the methods available for changing the destination of the SAS log and output. The information is organized around the following methods that you can use to specify the destination:

- □ using statements or procedures in a SAS program or display manager session
- □ using display manager commands from a window command line
- □ specifying system options when you invoke the SAS System.

The table then gives the procedure, statement, command, or option you use and the result of the action.

Table 5.3 *Changing the Destination of the Log and Output*

Method of Specifying Destination	Action	Result
SAS statements	PROC PRINTTO	routes log or output to a file you specify when used with an argument; returns routing of log or output to the system default when used without an argument.
	FILENAME	routes PUT statement output to an external file or output device when used with a FILE statement, FILE display manager command, or PROC PRINTTO.
SAS Display Manager commands	FILE	stores a copy of the SAS log or output in a file you specify when used with an argument; sends a copy of the file to the last file specified when used without an argument.
Options at SAS invocation	ALTLOG=	routes a copy of the SAS log to an additional file.
	ALTPRINT=	routes a copy of the output to an additional file.
	LOG=	routes the SAS log to a file.
	PRINT=	routes the output to a file.

For more information on routing the log and output, see Chapter 22, "Directing the SAS Log and Output," in *SAS Language and Procedures: Usage*.

Errors

The SAS System can detect four kinds of errors:

- □ syntax errors
- □ semantic errors
- □ execution-time errors
- □ data errors.

The system finds syntax and semantic errors as it compiles each SAS step before the statements are executed. Data errors and execution-time errors are discovered during program execution. Each type of error is described in the following sections.

Syntax Errors

Syntax errors occur when program statements do not conform to the rules of the SAS language. Examples of syntax errors include misspelling a SAS keyword or forgetting a semicolon. When the SAS System encounters a syntax error, it first attempts to correct the error using a method called error recovery (see "Error Recovery" later in this section). If it cannot correct the error, the SAS System prints the word ERROR on the log, followed by an error message. Some errors are explained fully by the message that the SAS System prints; other error messages are not as easy to interpret. For example, because SAS statements are free-format (they can begin and end anywhere), when you fail to end a SAS statement with a semicolon, the SAS System does not always detect the error at the point where it occurs.

When the SAS System finds a syntax error, it does not execute the step where the error occurred. To warn you, it prints the following message:

```
NOTE: The SAS System stopped processing this step because of errors.
```

Whether subsequent steps are executed depends on which method of running the SAS System you use, as well as on the host. See the SAS documentation for your host system for details.

Semantic Errors

A semantic error occurs when the form of the elements in a SAS statement is correct, but the elements are not valid for that usage. Semantic errors are detected at compile time and do not cause the SAS System to enter syntax check mode. Examples of semantic errors include misspellings of variable names or erroneous references.

For example, in the following statement, the form of the DO OVER statement is accurate: it consists of the key words DO OVER and a SAS name, followed by a semicolon. However, if `educate` refers to something other than an implicit array, a semantic error results and the DATA step that contains the following statement does not execute:

```
do over educate;
```

Execution-Time Errors

Errors that occur when the SAS System executes the program on data values are called execution-time errors. Most execution-time errors produce warning messages, but allow the program to continue executing.* The location of an execution-time error is usually given as line and column numbers in a note or error message.

Common execution-time errors include the following:

- □ INPUT statements that do not match the data lines (for example, an INPUT statement in which you list the wrong columns for a variable or fail to indicate that the variable is a character variable)
- □ illegal mathematical operations (for example, division by 0)
- □ observations in the wrong order for BY-group processing
- □ reference to a nonexistent member of an array (occurs when the array's subscript is out of range)

---

* When running the SAS System in noninteractive mode, more serious errors may cause the system to enter syntax check mode and stop processing the program.

□ open and close errors on SAS data sets and other files in INFILE and FILE statements

□ illegal arguments to functions.

Another less common execution-time error can occur when you encounter an out-of-resources condition, such as a full disk or not enough memory for a SAS procedure to complete. When an out-of-resources condition occurs, a requestor panel is displayed that enables you to choose how to resolve the error. For details, see the CLEANUP system option in Chapter 16.

In the next example, an execution-time error occurs when the SAS System uses data values from the second observation to perform the division operation in the assignment statement. Division by 0 is an illegal mathematical operation and causes the execution-time error. The SAS System executes the entire step and prints a missing value for the variable COST in the output. The log contains

□ an error message

□ the values stored in the input buffer

□ the contents of the program data vector at the time the error occurred

□ a note, beginning with the word NOTE, explaining the error.

Note that the values listed in the program data vector include the _N_ and _ERROR_ automatic variables. These automatic variables are assigned temporarily to each observation and are not stored with the data set.

See Output 5.2 for the resulting SAS log and output.

```
data b;
   input item $ 1-14 amount 15-20 units 21-23;
   cost=amount/units;
   cards;
hammers       487   55
nylon cord    35    0
ceiling fans  1142  30
;

proc print;
run;
```

Output 5.2 *Execution-time Error: Log and Output*

```
5          data b;
              input item $ 1-14 amount 15-20 units 21-23;
7             cost=amount/units;
8             cards;

ERROR: Division by zero detected at line 7 column 15.
RULE:      ----+----1----+----2----+----3----+----4----+----5----+----6----+
10         nylon cord     35   0
ITEM=nylon cord AMOUNT=35 UNITS=0 COST=. _ERROR_=1 _N_=2
NOTE: Mathematical operations could not be performed at the following
      places. The results of the operations have been set to missing values.
      Each place is given by: (Number of times) at (Line):(Column).
      1 at 7:15
NOTE: The data set WORK.B has 3 observations and 4 variables.

12         ;
13
14         proc print;
15         run;

NOTE: The PROCEDURE PRINT printed page 1.
```

```
                              The SAS System                               1

               OBS    ITEM              AMOUNT    UNITS      COST

                1     hammers             487       55      8.8545
                2     nylon cord           35        0        .
                3     ceiling fans       1142       30     38.0667
```

Data Errors

Data errors occur when some data values are not appropriate for the SAS statements you have specified in the program. The SAS System detects data errors during execution of the INPUT statement and continues program execution. The location of a data error is usually given as line and column numbers in a note or error message. The log contains

- □ a note describing the error
- □ the values stored in the input buffer
- □ the values stored in the program data vector.

In this example, a character value in the NUMBER variable results in a data error during program execution. See Output 5.3 for the resulting SAS log and output.

```
data c;
   input name $ number;
   cards;
sue 35
joe xx
steve 22
;

proc print;
run;
```

Output 5.3 *Data Error: Log and Output*

```
5          data c;
6             input name $ number;
7             cards;

NOTE: Invalid data for NUMBER in line 9 5-6.
RULE:      ----+----1----+----2----+----3----+----4----+----5----+----6----+
9          joe xx
NAME=joe NUMBER=. _ERROR_=1 _N_=2
NOTE: The data set WORK.C has 3 observations and 2 variables.

11         ;
12
13         proc print;
14         run;

NOTE: The PROCEDURE PRINT printed page 1.
```

```
                              The SAS System                              1

                         OBS    NAME     NUMBER

                          1     sue        35
                          2     joe         .
                          3     steve      22
```

Error Processing

When it encounters most syntax or semantic errors, the SAS System underlines the point where it detects the error and identifies the error by number. If you are running noninteractive SAS programs or batch jobs and the SAS System encounters a syntax error, it enters syntax check mode and remains in this mode until the program finishes executing.

In syntax check mode, the SAS System reads the remaining statements, checks their validity as SAS statements, and identifies any other errors it finds. The SAS System does not execute subsequent DATA steps or procedures in the program, but it does create the descriptor portion of any output data sets specified in program statements. Any data sets created this way do not replace existing data sets with the same name, and they do not contain any observations.

When running the SAS System in interactive line mode or in display manager mode, syntax check mode is only in effect during the step where the SAS System encountered the error. When the system detects an error, it stops executing the current step and continues processing the next step.

Depending on the type and severity of the error, the method you use to run the SAS System, and your host system, the SAS System either stops program processing or it flags errors and continues processing.

You can force the SAS System to abend after an error by specifying the ERRORABEND system option. This option is useful mainly in debugged production programs that are unlikely to encounter errors.

Error Recovery

When it encounters certain syntax errors, the SAS System attempts to interpret what you meant, then continues processing your SAS program based on its assumption. This process is known as error recovery.

The SAS System locates the syntax error and attempts to repair it either by deleting, inserting, or replacing tokens (that is, words in the SAS language). The system underlines the place where it detects the syntax error, identifies the error with a number, and prints a corresponding message on the log. It then continues to read from that point forward for the remainder of that DATA step or procedure and subsequent DATA steps or procedures. In previous versions of SAS software, syntax errors always caused the SAS System to stop processing the step where the error occurred. Error recovery now provides the SAS System with the ability to correct some misspellings of keywords and to continue processing the step where the error occurred. For syntax errors that are left uncorrected, the SAS System does not execute the step where it finds the error.

This example includes a misspelling (corrected through error recovery) and other syntax errors that cannot be corrected. See Output 5.4 for the resulting SAS log.

```
daat a;
   x=2;
run;

data b;
   x=2;
   x=x(a b c d);
run;
```

Output 5.4 *Error Recovery*

```
5          daat a;
           14
6            x=2;
7          run;

WARNING 14-169: Assuming the symbol DATA was misspelled as DAAT.

NOTE: The data set WORK.A has 1 observations and 1 variables.

8
9          data b;
10           x=2;
11           x=x(a b c d);
               68  388
12         run;

ERROR 68-185: The function X is unknown.

ERROR 388-185: Expecting an arithmetic operator.

NOTE: The SAS System stopped processing this step because of errors.
NOTE: SAS set option OBS=0 and will continue to check statements.
      This may cause NOTE: No observations in data set.
WARNING: The data set WORK.B may be incomplete.  When this step was stopped
         there were 0 observations and 1 variables.


ERROR: Errors printed on page 1.

NOTE: SAS Institute Inc., SAS Circle, PO Box 8000, Cary, NC 27512-8000
```

Return Codes

■ **Host Information** ...... On some host systems, the SAS System passes a return code to the host system. Accessing the return code is host specific. See the SAS documentation for your host system for information. ■

For a discussion and examples of errors in SAS output, see Chapter 23, "Diagnosing and Avoiding Errors," in *SAS Language and Procedures: Usage.*

Options That Affect the Appearance of Output

You can control the appearance of both the SAS log and output with several SAS system options. Specify the options in an OPTIONS statement or in the display manager OPTIONS window. Once invoked, each SAS system option remains in effect for the duration of the session, or until you change the option. Default option settings vary among sites. See "Determining What Settings Are in Effect," in Chapter 3, "Components of the SAS Language."

The following list includes system options that can change the SAS log and SAS procedure output:

CENTER
: controls whether SAS procedure output is centered.

DATE
: controls whether the date and time that the SAS job began are printed at the top of each page of the SAS log and any print file created by the SAS System.

ERRORS=
: controls the maximum number of observations for which complete error messages are printed.

FORMCHAR=
: specifies the default formatting characters used to construct tabular outlines and dividers for various procedures, for example, the CALENDAR, FREQ, and TABULATE procedures.

FORMDLIM=
: specifies a character that is used to delimit page breaks in SAS output.

FULLSTIMER
: specifies whether all the performance statistics of your computer system that are available to the SAS System are written to the SAS log. You cannot specify the FULLSTIMER system option in the OPTIONS window.

LABEL
: permits SAS procedures to use labels with variables.

LINESIZE=
: specifies the line size (printer line width) for the SAS log and the SAS procedure output file used by the DATA step and procedures.

MISSING=
: specifies the character to be printed for missing numeric variable values.

NEWS
: specifies a file that contains messages to be written to the SAS log. Typically, the file contains information for users, for example, news items about the system.

NOTES
: controls whether notes are written to the SAS log.

NUMBER
: controls whether the page number prints on the first title line of each each page of printed output.

OVP
: controls whether output lines printed by the SAS System are overprinted.

PAGENO=
: specifies a beginning page number for the next page of printed output.

PAGESIZE=	specifies the number of lines that can be printed per page of SAS output.
SOURCE	controls whether SAS source statements are written to the SAS log.
SOURCE2	controls whether secondary source statements from files included by %INCLUDE statements are written to the SAS log.
SPOOL	controls whether SAS statements are written to a utility data set in the WORK data library for later use by a %INCLUDE or %LIST statement.
STIMER	specifies whether performance statistics of your computer system are written to the SAS log.

CHAPTER 6 SAS® Files

(continued on next page)

(continued from previous page)

Introduction

SAS files store information that is recognized and processed by the SAS System. SAS files are grouped into larger units called SAS data libraries. The most common type of file processed by the SAS System is the SAS data set.

With Release 6.06 of the SAS System, SAS Institute introduces new concepts in the way the SAS System stores and accesses data in SAS files. These new concepts have been incorporated into the SAS System in such a way that they expand its capabilities dramatically, but with little impact on the day-to-day use of the SAS language. The greatest impact is on the definition and nature of SAS files.

This chapter has three parts. The first part, called "New Concepts," acquaints you with new concepts. Some important changes with which you should be familiar include

□ the ability to access data in different formats through engines

□ the use of logical data models to define SAS data sets and SAS data libraries

□ the introduction of three new member types: VIEW, ACCESS, and PROGRAM

□ the consolidation of SAS catalogs into a single member type (CATALOG) that supports many entry types.

The second part of this chapter, called "Release 6.06," provides the detailed information you need to manage Release 6.06 SAS data libraries and files. This detailed information includes an explanation of naming conventions, an introduction to special SAS System files, and a list of SAS utilities for each member type.

The third part of this chapter, called "V606 Engine," describes the characteristics of SAS data sets created by the default engine for Release 6.06 and introduces the performance features available through the default engine.

New Concepts: Multiple Engine Architecture

This section introduces the concepts that are the foundation for the *Multiple Engine Architecture*. These concepts include the use of engines to read from or write to files and the use of data models as a framework for defining SAS data sets and SAS data libraries.

Different Methods for Accessing Data

To process data using SAS procedures or statements, your data must be in the form of a SAS data set. For Version 5, you put your data into the correct form by reading them from external files through a DATA step. The DATA step required an INFILE or CARDS statement to identify the source of the data values and an INPUT statement to describe the data. The data values and resulting descriptor information were stored in a physical format that could be processed by the SAS System. Once the data were in the correct form, you could access them by specifying the name of the file in a SET, MERGE, or UPDATE statement in the DATA step or in the DATA= option of a SAS procedure.

You can continue to use this method for many applications, but for data stored in certain formats, the SAS System provides additional methods of accessing the data directly for SAS processing. These additional methods are called engines, and they enable the SAS System to access data in ways not possible in earlier releases. With engines, you can

□ process your existing Version 5 data sets without copying them to Version 6 format

□ process data stored in files created by database management systems such as DB2,™ ORACLE,® Rdb/VMS,™ and SQL/DS™

□ process data created by BMDP,® SPSS,® and OSIRIS* statistical software products

□ create SAS data sets that have compressed observations, indexes, and other features

□ create logical SAS data sets from variables stored in more than one file or SAS data set.

Because Release 6.06 uses more than one engine to read from and write to files in different formats, its input/output architecture is referred to as the Multiple Engine Architecture (MEA).

How the SAS System Uses Data Models

A data model is a framework into which engines fit information for SAS processing. It is a logical representation of data or files, not a physical structure. Figure 6.1 illustrates how the SAS System uses the principle of data models to provide more flexibility in accessing data.

Figure 6.1 *Relationship of Engines and the SAS Data Set Model*

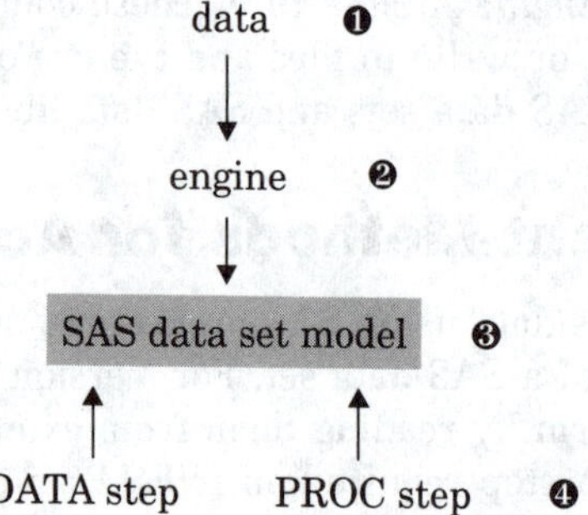

❶ Your data can be stored in files that were created by the SAS System, or they can be stored in files for which the SAS System provides an engine. When you specify a SAS data set name, the engine locates the appropriate file or files on your host system.

DB2 is a trademark of International Business Machines Corporation.
ORACLE is a registered trademark of Oracle Corporation.
Rdb/VMS is a trademark of Digital Equipment Corporation.
SQL/DS is a trademark of International Business Machines Corporation
BMDP is a registered trademark of BMDP Statistical Software, Inc.
SPSS is a registered trademark of SPSS, Inc.
* OSIRIS was produced by the Institute for Social Research, Ann Arbor, Michigan

❷ The engine opens the file and obtains the descriptive information required by the SAS System, for example, which variables are available and what attributes they have, whether the file has special processing characteristics such as indexes or compressed observations, and whether other engines are required for processing. The engine uses this information to organize the data in the correct logical form for SAS processing.

❸ This correct form is called the *SAS data set*, which consists of the descriptor information and the data values organized into columns and rows.

❹ SAS procedures and DATA step statements access and process the data only in its logical form. During processing, the engine executes whatever instructions are necessary to open and close physical files and to read and write data in appropriate formats.

Just as data accessed by an engine are organized into the SAS data set model, groups of files accessed by an engine are organized in the correct logical form for SAS processing. Once files are accessed as a *SAS data library*, you can use SAS utility windows and procedures to list their contents and to manage them. Figure 6.2 illustrates this relationship.

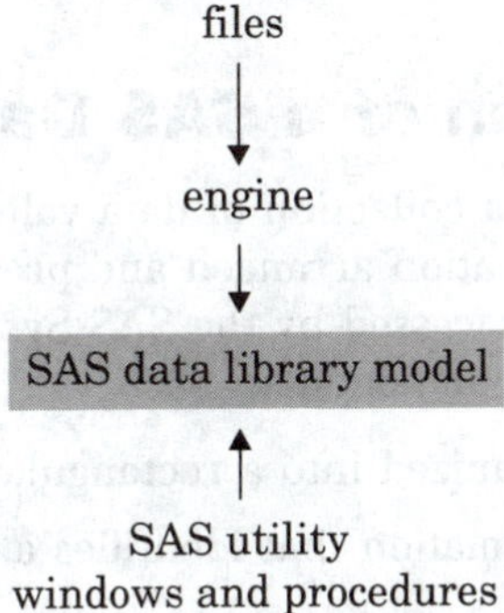

Figure 6.2 *Relationship of Engines and the SAS Data Library Model*

To understand fully how the SAS data models work, you must understand more about engines because each engine implements these models in a different way.

Basic Facts about Engines

Engines are sets of internal instructions the SAS System uses to read from and write to files. Engines open files, direct input/output operations, and gather descriptive information about files and their contents. The following list describes important features of engines:

- □ Every SAS data set and SAS data library is accessed through an engine.
- □ The SAS System provides a default engine, called the V606 engine, that it uses to write to newly created SAS data libraries if no other engine is specified.
- □ Engines determine certain processing characteristics of SAS data sets. For example, some engines are read-only, while other engines limit whether you can locate records by observation number. The SAS data

sets created and accessed by the default V606 engine have many features not available for other SAS data sets.

- The SAS System, by default, generally selects the appropriate engine to use when accessing a file. However, for certain purposes, you must specify the engine you want the SAS System to use.
- The SAS System can use one or more engines to process a DATA step or procedure. For example, the SAS System may use one engine to read from an input data set and another engine to write observations to the output data set.

New Concepts: SAS Data Set Model

The SAS data set model is the logical structure into which engines fit data for processing by the SAS System. In discussions of the SAS language, the term *SAS data set* is used to refer to data values that are organized and presented to the SAS System in this logical structure. As a logical data model, the SAS data set is independent of the format of the file that stores the data values or the engine used to retrieve them.

The next section describes the characteristics of the full SAS data set model.

Organization of a SAS Data Set

A *SAS data set* is a collection of data values and their associated descriptive information arranged and presented in a form that can be recognized and processed by the SAS System. All SAS data sets contain these two logical components:

- data values organized into a rectangular structure of columns and rows
- descriptor information that identifies attributes of both the data set and the data values.

A third logical component of the SAS data set is one or more indexes. For Release 6.06, only the SAS data sets created and accessed by the V606 engine contain this component of the SAS data set model.

Data Values

The columns, or data elements, are called variables in SAS data sets. The rows, or records, are called observations. Each observation is a collection of values for the variables. The diagram in Figure 6.3 illustrates the components of the full SAS data set model. Note that the data values are arranged in a rectangular structure and that the descriptor information and index can be separate elements.

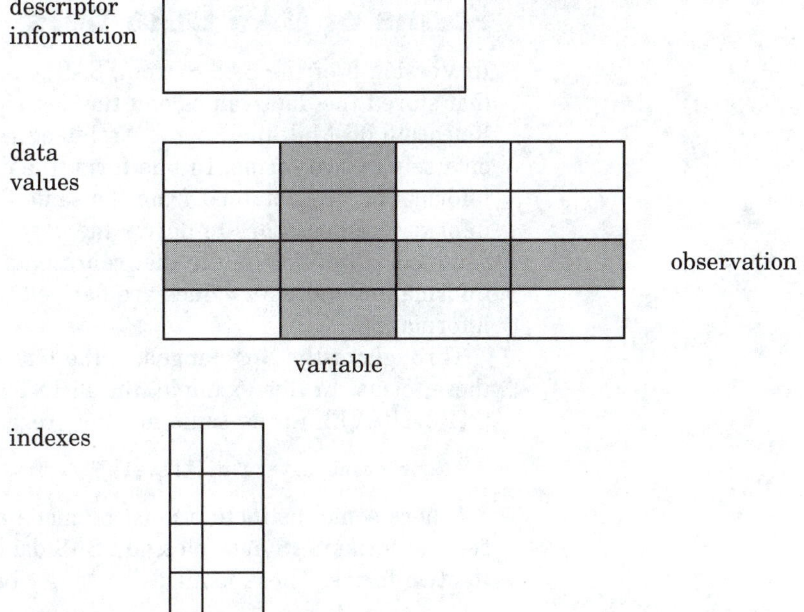

Figure 6.3 *Logical Components of the SAS Data Set Model*

Descriptor Information

The descriptor information for a SAS data set makes the data set self-documenting; that is, each SAS data set can supply the attributes of the data set and of its variables. Once the data are in the form of the SAS data set, you do not have to specify the attributes of the data set or the variables in your program statements. The SAS System obtains the information directly from the SAS data set.

The data set description includes the number of observations, the observation length, the date that the data set was last modified, and other facts. The variable descriptions include attributes such as name, type, length, format, label, and whether the variable is included in an index.

Indexes

The logical SAS data set model includes *indexes*. A SAS index contains the data values of the key variable or variables paired with a location identifier for the observation containing the value. The value/identifier pairs are ordered in a B-tree structure that enables the engine to search by value. Therefore, by using an index, the SAS System can quickly locate the observations associated with a data value or range of data values.

SAS data sets can be indexed by one or more variables, known as *key variables*. SAS indexes are classified as *simple* or *composite*, according to the number of key variables whose values make up the index.

For a detailed discussion of indexes and guidelines for creating and managing them, refer to the section "SAS Indexes" later in this chapter.*

* For more information on the data structure of indexes, refer to "Version 6 SAS Data Base System Architecture: Current and Future Features" by Steve Beatrous and William Clifford in *SUGI 13 Proceedings*.

Forms of SAS Data Sets

In Version 5 of the SAS System, SAS data sets were physical structures that stored the data values and the descriptor information in the same file. Release 6.06 Multiple Engine Architecture makes it possible to use SAS data sets in two forms. In one form, the data values and descriptor information are obtained from the same file. In the other form, only the information necessary to derive the descriptor information and data values is stored in the file that represents the SAS data set. The descriptor information and data values are derived from other sources using this information.

Throughout the SAS language, the term *SAS data set* refers to either of these forms. In this example, the PRINT procedure processes the data set QTR3.TRAVEL in the same manner, regardless of its form.

```
proc print data=qtr3.travel;
```

Where some distinction must be made about the structure of a SAS data set, the terms SAS data files and SAS data views are used to distinguish the two forms. These features are described in the next two sections.

SAS Data Files

A SAS data set is called a *SAS data file* if it is implemented in a form that contains both the data values and the descriptor information. When you obtain a list of files in a SAS data library, SAS data files have the type DATA.

Native SAS data files store the data values and descriptor information in a file formatted by the SAS System. In previous releases of the SAS System, all SAS data sets were native SAS data files. In Release 6.06, there is more than one type of native SAS data file. The SAS data sets accessed by the V606 engine and the Version 5 compatibility engines are the most common examples.

The SAS data set is implemented as an interface SAS data file if the data are stored in a file formatted by other software. Release 6.06 provides engines for reading data values stored in files formatted by BMDP, SPSS, or OSIRIS software. These files are interface SAS data files, and when their data values are accessed through an engine, the SAS System recognizes them as SAS data sets.

SAS Data Views

A SAS data set is a *SAS data view* if it is implemented in a form that obtains the descriptor information or data values, or both, from other files. Only the information necessary to derive the descriptor information or data values is stored in the file of member type VIEW, which represents the SAS data set. The sources of the data values are other SAS data sets or external files, depending on how the view is created. SAS data views are created and read by the engines provided for the SQL procedure and SAS/ACCESS software products.

PROC SQL views are native SAS data views. Using the SQL procedure, you can create views whose data values are obtained from one or more SAS data files, SAS/ACCESS views, or other PROC SQL views. PROC SQL views use the SQL language to identify which variables to obtain and how to obtain them. For detailed information, refer to the *SAS Guide to the SQL Procedure: Usage and Reference, Version 6, First Edition.*

SAS/ACCESS views are interface SAS data views. SAS/ACCESS software is designed to establish an interface to the data formatted by other software products. For example, SAS/ACCESS engines are available for SYSTEM 2000, DB2, ORACLE, Rdb/VMS, and SQL/DS database management system products. When you process a SAS/ACCESS view, the data remain stored in the appropriate format. The view tells where to find the data values and how to read them. See the documentation for your SAS/ACCESS interface for details.

The diagram in Figure 6.4 shows the forms in which SAS data sets are implemented.

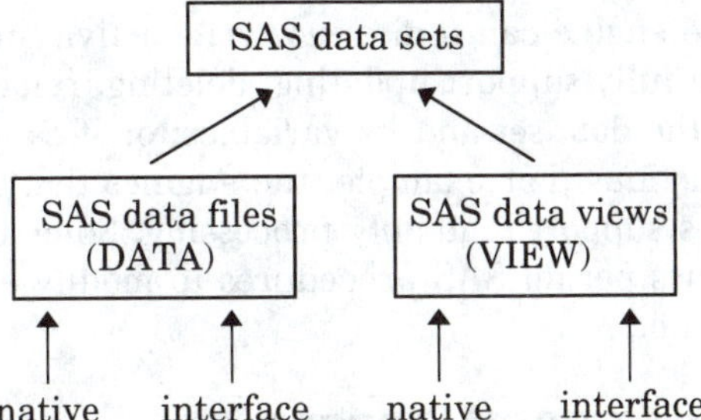

Figure 6.4 *Forms of SAS Data Sets*

Processing Characteristics of SAS Data Sets

SAS statements and procedures require that SAS data sets have certain characteristics in order to process the data correctly. Different statements and procedures require different processing characteristics. For example, the FSEDIT procedure requires the ability to update selected data values, and the POINT= option in the SET statement requires random access to observations and the ability to calculate observation numbers from record identifiers within the file.

The engine used to access a SAS data set determines its processing characteristics. The V606 engine supports all processing characteristics required by the SAS language. Other engines may limit certain functions. For example, access by observation number is not available for some SAS data views, and update level read/write activity is available for some SAS data views but not for others. Because these features depend on the engine, you can refer to the documentation for your SAS/ACCESS interface or the SQL procedure for details. Figure 6.5 and the explanations that follow provide an overview of the processing characteristics available in the full SAS data set model.

Figure 6.5 Processing Characteristics for the SAS Data Set Model

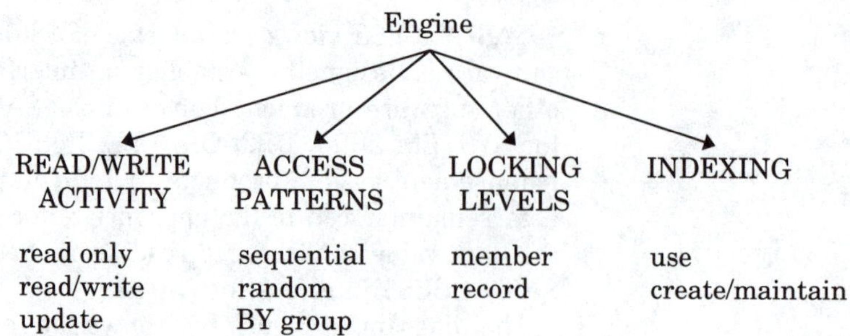

Read/Write Activity

The engine can limit read/write activity for a SAS data set to read-only; it can fully support updating, deleting, renaming, or redefining the attributes of the data set and its variables; or it can support only some of these functions. For example, the engines that access BMDP, OSIRIS, or SPSS files support read-only processing. Some engines that access SAS data views permit SAS procedures to modify existing observations while others do not.

Patterns of Access

SAS procedures and statements can read observations in SAS data sets in one of three general patterns.

sequential access
: processes observations one after the other, starting at the beginning of the file and continuing in sequence to the end of the file.

random access
: processes observations according to the value of some indicator variable without processing previous observations.

BY-group access
: groups and processes observations in order of the values of the variables specified in a BY statement.

In addition, SAS statements and procedures can require two or more passes of the data in the chosen pattern, or they can require that an observation number be calculated as part of the processing. If a SAS statement or procedure tries to access a SAS data set whose engine does not support the required access pattern, the SAS System prints an appropriate error message in the SAS log.

Levels of Locking

Some features of the SAS System require that SAS data sets support different levels at which update access is allowed. When a SAS data set can be opened concurrently by more than one SAS session or by more than one statement or procedure within a single session, the level of locking determines how many sessions, procedures, or statements can read and write to the file at the same time. For example, with the FSEDIT procedure, you can request two windows on the same SAS data set in one session. Some engines support this capability; others do not.

The levels supported are record level and member (data set) level. Member-level locking allows read access to many sessions, statements, or procedures, but restricts all other access to the SAS data set when a session, statement, or procedure acquires update access. Record-level locking allows concurrent read access and update access to the SAS data set by more than one session, statement, or procedure, but prevents concurrent update access to the same observation. Not all engines support both levels.

Indexes

One major new processing feature of the SAS data model is the ability to access observations by the values of key variables with indexes. For Release 6.06, only the V606 engine can create and maintain indexed SAS data sets.

New Concepts: SAS Data Library Model

The SAS data library model is the logical structure of files accessed by an engine for processing by the SAS System. In discussions of the SAS language, the term *SAS data library* is used as a blanket term to refer to files that are organized and presented to the SAS System in this logical structure. As a logical data model, the SAS data library is independent of the software used to format the files or their organization on your host system.

The SAS file system is arranged in a hierarchy and SAS data libraries are the highest level of organization. SAS data libraries contain SAS files. Each SAS file, in turn, stores information in smaller units that are characteristic of the type of SAS file. For example, SAS data sets store information as variables and observations, while SAS catalogs store information in units called entries.

The next section describes the characteristics of the full SAS data library model.

Organization of a SAS Data Library

A *SAS data library* is a collection of SAS files that are accessed by the same library engine and recognized as a logical unit by the SAS System. SAS files are named, stored, and retrieved according to the SAS data library to which they belong. SAS data libraries can contain files that you create, or they can be one of several special libraries that the SAS System provides for convenience, support, and customization capability. The SAS System does not limit the number of SAS files you can store in a SAS data library.

Members and Member Types

Each file in a SAS data library is a *member* of the library, and each member has a *member type* that identifies what kind of information is stored in the file. The member types that appear in a SAS data library depend on the SAS library engine used to access the library.

The diagram in Figure 6.6 shows the member types in the full model of the SAS data library, arranged by function. For Release 6.06, only the default engine supports the full SAS data library model. Other engines only support parts of this model. Each member type is described in detail elsewhere in this chapter.

Figure 6.6 *Member Types in the Full SAS Data Library Model*

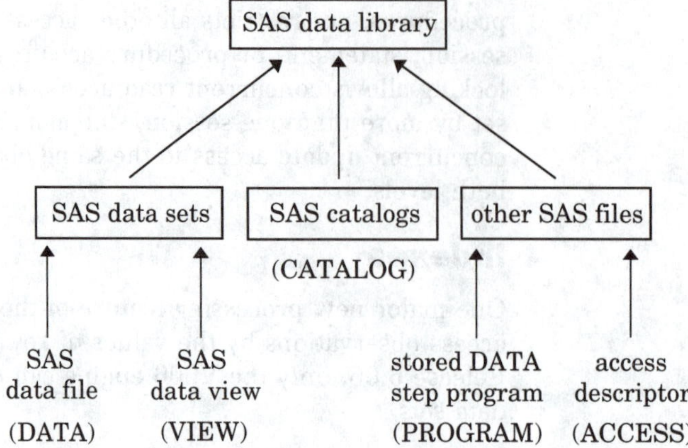

The SAS System determines the member type of a file from the context of the SAS program in which the file is created or specified; therefore, a library can contain files with the same name but different member types.

Note: Because they are used in the same context, SAS data files and SAS data views in the same library cannot have the same name.

Library Directories

SAS System utility windows and procedures enable you to obtain a list, or *directory*, of the members in a SAS data library. Each directory contains the name of each member and its member type. For the member type DATA, the directory indicates whether an index is associated with the data set. The directory also describes some attributes of the library, but the amount and nature of this information vary greatly with the host system.

Note: SAS data libraries can also contain various SAS utility files. These files are not listed in the library directory and are generally not available except during processing.

Implementation on Host Systems

As a structure for organizing, locating, and managing SAS files, the SAS data library is a logical concept that remains constant, regardless of the medium or host system in which it is stored. At the host system level, a SAS data library has different physical implementations, depending on the computer on which the SAS System is installed. For most SAS data libraries, the implementation roughly corresponds to the level of organization the host system uses to store and access files.

For instance, in directory-based host systems, a SAS data library is a group of SAS files stored in the same directory and accessed by the same engine. Other files can be stored in the directory, but only the files with file extensions assigned by the SAS System are recognized as part of the SAS data library. Under CMS, a SAS data library is a group of SAS files with the same filetype. Under MVS and VSE, SAS data libraries are implemented as specially formatted host system data sets that contain only SAS files.

Characteristics of SAS Data Libraries

The processing characteristics of SAS data libraries are determined by the engine used to access them. Other characteristics are determined by the fact that SAS data libraries have both a physical and a logical implementation. The next three sections describe some of these characteristics.

Processing Characteristics

The engine determines the basic level of read/write activity allowed for SAS data libraries. Depending on the engine, the SAS data library can be limited to read-only access, or it can allow files to be updated and created as well. For example, the access to sequential SAS files stored on tape or disk is limited to reading existing files or creating new ones. You cannot update selected observations in SAS data libraries stored in sequential format.

The engine also determines whether a particular access pattern can be used to retrieve information from files within the library. A pattern of access is the order in which the SAS procedure or statement locates and reads records within the file. The engine can restrict the access pattern for the library to sequential access, or it can allow random access.

Names

SAS data libraries are associated with one name within the host system, but you cannot use the host system names for SAS data libraries in SAS program statements. As a result, SAS data libraries have two names: a physical name and a logical name, or *libref*.

The *physical name* of the SAS data library identifies your SAS files to the host system and must, therefore, conform to the rules for naming files within your host system. The physical name fully identifies the directory, filetype or minidisk, or host system data set that contains the SAS data library. A libref is the way you identify those files as a unit to the SAS System. It is a temporary name you associate with the SAS data library during each SAS job or session.

Permanent and Temporary Libraries

SAS data libraries are generally stored as permanent data libraries; however, the SAS System provides a temporary, or scratch library, where you can store files for the duration of a SAS session or job.

A *permanent SAS data library* is one that resides on the external storage medium of your computer and is not deleted when the SAS session terminates. The library is available for processing in subsequent SAS sessions. When working with files in a permanent SAS data library, you generally specify a libref as the first part of a two-level SAS file name. The libref tells the SAS System where to find or store the file. Permanent SAS data libraries are stored until you delete them.

A *temporary SAS data library* is one that endures only for the current SAS session or job. SAS files created during the session or job are held in a special work space that may or may not be an external storage medium. This work space is generally assigned the default libref WORK. Once created, files in the temporary WORK library can be used in any DATA step or SAS procedure during the session, but they are not available for subsequent sessions. Normally, you specify that data sets be stored in or retrieved from this library by specifying a one-level name. Files held in the WORK library are deleted at the end of the SAS session if it ends normally.

There are a number of SAS system options that enable you to customize the way you name and work with your permanent and temporary SAS data libraries. See the USER=, WORK=, WORKINIT, and WORKTERM system options in Chapter 16, "SAS System Options."

Other Files in the Data Library Model

The next three sections describe catalogs, access descriptors, and stored program files and explain their function and structure.

SAS Catalogs

SAS catalogs are special files that can store many kinds of data structures as separate units in one SAS file, which has the member type CATALOG. Each separate unit is called an *entry*, and each entry has an *entry type* that identifies its structure to the SAS System. Each entry stores data as records whose attributes vary according to its entry type. Catalog entry types differ widely in content and purpose. Some entry types store SAS System information, for example, function key definitions and help window text. Others contain application information, for example, graphics templates, macros, statistical models, and screen definitions. Figure 6.7 shows the relationship between catalogs and entry types.

Figure 6.7 *Components of SAS Catalogs*

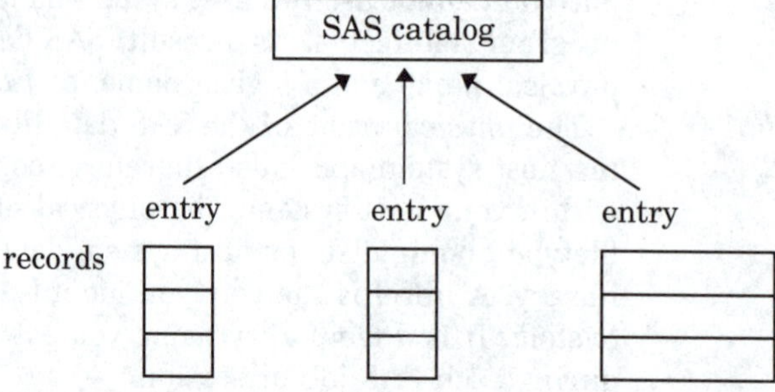

Each SAS catalog contains a directory of its contents. The catalog directory lists the entries, their entry types, and a brief description of each entry's contents.

Note: Files that were separate member types in Version 5 SAS software, (for example, SAS/IML work spaces, SAS/ETS models, and formats written with the FORMAT procedure) are now stored as entries within SAS catalogs.

Stored Compiled Programs

The Stored Program Facility of base SAS software produces files of the member type PROGRAM that contain compiled DATA step code. Refer to Appendix 3, "Stored Program Facility," for information about creating and using stored SAS programs.

Access Descriptors

SAS access descriptors are tools that enable you to create SAS/ACCESS views. Access descriptors are files of the member type ACCESS. You create them with the ACCESS procedure in SAS/ACCESS software. Access descriptors describe data stored in other vendors' database management systems (DBMS) or other interface products in a format that the SAS System can understand.

Each access descriptor holds essential information about the DBMS file you want to access, for example, its name, the column names, and the column types. It also contains corresponding information that describes the file in terms the SAS System can use, including librefs and variable attributes. Typically, you have only one access descriptor for a file, although it is possible to have more than one, and you can create many SAS/ACCESS views from one access descriptor.

Once you have created one or more SAS/ACCESS views based on an access descriptor, you can delete or make that access descriptor unavailable to the users of the view. The SAS System does not require the information stored in the access descriptor to use the SAS/ACCESS view in a DATA step or SAS procedure. See the SAS/ACCESS documentation for your Version 6 interface product for information on the creation and use of access descriptors and SAS/ACCESS views.

New Concepts: Engines

Some engines are limited in their purpose and capabilities. Others support a broader range of functions. The most convenient way to talk about engines is to describe the level at which they function and the way you use them. The following sections present the two basic types of engines, library engines and view engines, and provide an overview of the engines available for Release 6.06 software.

Library Engines

SAS *library engines* support the SAS data library model. They perform the following functions:

- determine certain fundamental processing characteristics, for example, the file formats, the patterns by which records are located and read, the type of read/write activity that can occur, and so on.
- present a list of SAS files for the library directory. All engines derive descriptor information for individual SAS data sets, but only the library engine can generate descriptor information for the SAS data library.
- support other engines that have a more specialized function, for example, reading SAS data views.

Library engines can be classified as native or interface.

Native Library Engines

Native library engines are engines that read from or write to files formatted by the SAS System only. You can select native library engines by specifying an engine name in a LIBNAME statement. If you do not specify an engine name, the SAS System automatically selects an appropriate engine.

■ **Host Information** ....

The rules for specifying native library engines can vary with the host system. Refer to the SAS documentation for your host system for details.
.... ■

The purpose and function of native library engines common to all host systems are described as follows:

default engine (V606)
: is the only engine that supports the full SAS data set model and the full SAS data library model. The V606 engine can read from and write to data sets that have compressed observations and index files, support view engines, and provide additional performance features.

compatibility engines
: enable you to access SAS data sets created by older versions of the SAS System without converting them to Release 6.06 format files. The SAS System determines whether the library is stored in disk or tape format, and automatically reads from and writes to the library in the correct format.

■ **Host Information** .... On some host systems, one compatibility engine reads both disk and tape. Other host systems have two separate compatibility engines—one for each storage medium. See the SAS documentation for your host system for the engine names and examples for using them. ■

sequential engine (TAPE)
: uses a simpler format to access Release 6.06 files on storage media that do not allow random access methods, for example, tape or sequential format on disk. The sequential engine for Release 6.06 is named TAPE.

transport engine (XPORT)
: makes moving your SAS data sets from one host system to another much easier, especially if you have data communication links available. See SAS Technical Report P-195, *Transporting SAS Files between Host Systems*, for examples of using the XPORT engine.

Interface Library Engines

Interface library engines read from or write to files formatted by other software. Release 6.06 provides three read-only, sequential engines for file formats that are accessed by the CONVERT procedure in Version 5. You must specify the name of these interface library engines in a LIBNAME statement.

SPSS
: reads SPSS Release 9 files and SPSS-X® files in either compressed or uncompressed format. The engine can also read the SPSS Portable File Format, which is analogous to the transport format for SAS data sets.

OSIRIS
: reads OSIRIS data and dictionary files in EBCDIC format.

BMDP
: reads BMDP save files.

SPSS-X is a registered trademark of SPSS, Inc.

■ **Host Information** .... The capabilities of these engines vary from one host system to another. See the SAS documentation for your host system for more complete information. ■

View Engines

SAS *view engines* support the SAS data set model only. They are characterized by functions that

- □ enable the SAS System to read SAS data views described by the SQL procedure or SAS/ACCESS software.
- □ modify or enhance the processing characteristics set by the library engine.
- □ perform in a transparent manner. For Release 6.06, the SAS System determines which view engine to use by reading the name stored in the file of member type VIEW. You cannot specify view engine names in the LIBNAME statement.

View engines are also classified as native and interface.

Native View Engines

Release 6.06 has one native view engine that accesses data sets described by the SQL procedure. PROC SQL views always retrieve data values from other SAS data files or SAS data views.

Interface View Engines

Interface view engines include engines supported by SAS/ACCESS software. These engines retrieve data directly from files formatted by other software. Interface engines enable you to use SAS procedures and program statements to process data values stored in these files without the cost of converting and storing them in files formatted by the SAS System. Contact your SAS Software Representative for a list of the SAS/ACCESS interfaces available at your site.

Release 6.06: SAS Data Libraries

This section provides information about names for SAS data libraries and describes special SAS System libraries. The information in this section applies to all SAS data libraries accessed by Release 6.06 of the SAS System. For general information about the structure and contents of SAS data libraries, refer to the earlier section "SAS Data Library Model."

Library Names

SAS data libraries have two names: a physical name and a logical name, or libref. The physical name of the SAS data library fully identifies the directory, filetype or minidisk, or host system data set that contains the SAS data library, and it must, therefore, conform to the rules for naming files within your host system.

The logical name, or libref, is the way you identify a group of files to the SAS System. It is a temporary name you associate with the physical name of the SAS data library during each SAS job or session. Under host systems, once the libref is assigned, you can read, create, or update files in a data library. A libref is valid only for the current SAS job or session and can be referenced repeatedly within that job or session. The SAS System does not limit the number of librefs you can assign during a session; however, your host system or site may place some limitations.

■ **Host Information** .... The rules for assigning and using librefs differ across host systems. See the SAS documentation for your host system for more specific information. ■

Methods for Associating and Clearing Librefs

You can associate a physical name with a libref using the LIBNAME statement, which is described in Chapter 9, "SAS Language Statements."

■ **Host Information** .... For some host systems, you can use host system commands or the LIBNAME statement to associate the libref with the SAS data library. Others require that you use host system commands to associate the libref but allow the use of the LIBNAME statement for other purposes. For host systems that do not provide any host system commands for associating librefs, you must use the LIBNAME statement. See the SAS documentation for your host system for more information on assigning librefs. ■

The most common form of the LIBNAME statement is used in this example to associate the libref ANNUAL with the physical name of the SAS data library.

```
libname annual 'SAS-data-library';
```

If you use the LIBNAME statement to assign the libref, the SAS System clears the libref automatically at the end of each job or session. If you want to clear the libref ANNUAL before the end of the session, you can issue the following form of the LIBNAME statement:

```
libname annual clear;
```

Librefs in Program Statements

Once defined, the libref is most commonly used as the first element in two-level SAS file names to identify where the SAS System can find or store the file. The following statement tells the SAS System to create the data set TRAVEL and store it in a permanent SAS data library with the libref ANNUAL:

```
data annual.travel;
```

Some SAS utility procedures enable you to copy, delete, or perform other file management tasks for entire libraries. For example, the libref is used as the argument in statements that contain the LIBRARY= option or equivalent options. The following example illustrates the use of the libref ANNUAL as the argument in the LIBRARY= option of the DATASETS procedures:

```
proc datasets library=annual;
```

The libref can also be used in a LIBNAME statement to associate a SAS library engine with a SAS data library.

■ **Host Information** .... See the SAS documentation for your host system for valid engine names and examples for using them.

.... ■

The following statement assigns a compatibility engine named V5 and the libref REGIONS to a SAS data library:

```
libname regions v5 'SAS-data-library';
```

Reserved Librefs

The SAS System reserves a number of names for special uses. You should not use the following names as librefs, except as intended. The purpose and content of these libraries are discussed later in this chapter.

LIBRARY
SASHELP
SASUSER
USER
WORK

■ **Host Information** .... There are other librefs reserved for the SAS System under some host systems. In addition, your host system may have reserved certain words that cannot be used as librefs.

.... ■

Sequential Data Libraries

The SAS System provides a number of features and procedures for reading from and writing to files stored on sequential format devices, either disk or tape. Before you store SAS data libraries in sequential format, you should consider the following restrictions:

- You cannot use random access methods with sequential SAS data sets.
- You can access only one of the SAS files in a sequential library or only one of the SAS files on a tape at any point in a SAS job. For example, you cannot read two or more SAS data sets in the same library or on the same tape in a single DATA step. However, you can access two or more SAS files in different sequential libraries or on different tapes at the same time if there are enough tape drives available. You can also access a SAS file during one DATA or PROC step, then access another SAS file in the same sequential library or on the same tape during a later DATA or PROC step.
- SAS data sets are the only SAS files on tape that you can read from or write to during a DATA or PROC step for some environments. However, you can always use the COPY procedure to transfer all members of a SAS data library to tape for storage and backup purposes.
- Considerations specific to your site can affect your use of tape. Consult your operations staff if you are not familiar with using tape storage at your location.

The SAS System can also access Version 5 SAS data libraries stored on tape by using compatibility engines.

■ **Host Information** .... The details for storing and accessing Release 6.06 and Version 5 SAS files in sequential format vary with the host system. See the SAS documentation for your host system for further information. ■

SAS System Libraries

Four special SAS System libraries provide convenience, support, and customization capability: WORK, USER, SASHELP, and SASUSER.

WORK Library

The WORK library is the temporary, or scratch, library automatically defined by the SAS System at the beginning of each SAS session or job. The WORK library stores two types of temporary files: those you create and those created internally by the SAS System as part of normal processing. Typically, the WORK library is deleted at the end of each SAS job or session if the session terminates normally.

To store or retrieve SAS files in the WORK library, specify a one-level name in your SAS program statements. The libref WORK is automatically assigned to these files as a system default unless you have assigned the USER libref. The following examples contain valid names for SAS data sets stored in the WORK library:

- □ `data test2;`
- □ `data work.test2;`
- □ `proc contents data=testdata;`
- □ `proc contents data=work.testdata;`

There are a number of SAS system options that enable you to customize the way you name and work with your permanent and temporary SAS data libraries. See the USER=, WORK=, WORKINIT, and WORKTERM system options in Chapter 16, "SAS System Options."

■ **Host Information** .... The WORK library is implemented differently on various host systems. See the SAS documentation for your host system for more information. ■

USER Library

The USER library allows you to read, create, and write files in a SAS data library other than WORK without specifying a libref as part of the SAS file name. Once you associate the libref USER with a SAS data library, the SAS System stores any file with a one-level name in that library.

Relation to WORK Library The USER libref overrides the default libref WORK for one-level names. When you refer to a file by a one-level name, the SAS System looks first for the libref USER. If USER is assigned to a SAS data library, files with one-level names are stored there. If you have not assigned the libref USER to a library, the files with one-level names are stored in the temporary library WORK. To refer to SAS files in the WORK library while the USER libref is assigned, you must specify a two-level name with WORK as the libref.

Ways to Assign You can assign the USER libref using the LIBNAME statement, a host system command, or the USER= system option. The form of the LIBNAME statement is shown in the following example. Here, the data set REGION is stored in a SAS data library.

```
libname user 'SAS-data-library';
data region;
```

With the USER= system option, you first assign a libref to a SAS data library; then you use the USER= option to specify that library as the default for one-level names. In this example, the data set PROCHLOR is stored in the SAS data library TESTLIB.

```
libname testlib 'SAS-data-library';
options user=testlib;
data prochlor;
```

■ **Host Information** ...... The methods and results of assigning the USER libref vary slightly from one host system to another. See the SAS documentation for your host system for more information. ■

SASHELP Library

Each SAS site receives the SASHELP library, which contains a group of catalogs with information used to control various aspects of your SAS session. The defaults stored in this library are for everyone using the SAS System at your installation. Your personal settings are stored in the SASUSER library, which is discussed later in this section. The SASHELP library for base SAS software contains the following catalogs:

BASE	stores help text windows and default form for printing the contents of display manager windows.
CORE	stores display manager function key definitions, PMENU entries, and engine names.
COPYRTE	stores copyright information.
DBI	stores catalogs for SAS/ACCESS products.
FSP	stores default windows for display manager and interactive windowing procedures.
HOST	stores host-specific features.
PDEVICE	contains forms default window.

If other SAS products are installed at your site, the SASHELP library contains catalogs used by those products. In many instances, the defaults in this library are tailored to your site by your SAS Software Representative. You can list the catalogs stored at your site by using one of the file management utilities discussed later in this section.

SASUSER Library

The SASUSER library contains SAS catalogs that enable you to tailor features of the SAS System for your needs. If the defaults in the SASHELP library are not suitable for your applications, you can modify them and store your personalized defaults in your SASUSER library. For example, in base SAS software, you can store your own defaults for function key settings or window attributes in a personal profile catalog named SASUSER.PROFILE.

The SAS System assigns the SASUSER library during system initialization, according to the information supplied by the SASUSER system option.

■ **Host Information** ....

On most host systems, the SASUSER data library is created if it does not already exist. However, the SASUSER library is implemented differently on various host systems. See the SAS documentation for your host system for more information.

Tools for Managing Libraries

Storing SAS files in data libraries facilitates file management and provides an efficient means of organizing related files. This section describes the tools you can use to manage SAS data libraries.

Host System Commands

You can use host system commands to copy, rename, and delete the host system file or files that make up a SAS data library. However, to maintain the integrity of your files, you must know how the SAS data library model is implemented on your host system. For example, on some host systems, SAS data sets and their associated indexes can be copied, deleted, or renamed as separate files. If you rename the file containing the SAS data set, but not its index, the index becomes unusable.

▶ ***Caution:*** *Using host system commands can damage files.*

You can avoid problems by always using SAS utilities to manage SAS files.

SAS Utilities

The SAS utilities available for SAS file management are designed to enable you to work with more than one SAS file at a time, as long as the files belong to the same library. One advantage of learning and using SAS utility windows and procedures is that they work on any host system at any level. Once you learn SAS utilities, you can handle any file management task for your SAS data libraries without knowing the host system commands. A second advantage is that SAS utility procedures automatically copy, rename, or delete any index files associated with your SAS data sets.

There are several SAS System windows and procedures available for performing file management tasks. You can use the following features alone or in combination, depending on what works best for you. See the *SAS Procedures Guide* for detailed information on SAS utility procedures. Using the SAS Display Manager System windows for managing SAS files is discussed in Chapter 17, "SAS Display Manager Windows."

CATALOG procedure
: provides all catalog management functions.

CONTENTS procedure
: lists the contents of libraries and data sets and provides general information about their size and characteristics.

COPY procedure
: provides statements for copying all the members of a library or individual files within the library.

DATASETS procedure
: provides all library management functions for all member types except catalogs. If your site does not use display manager, or if the SAS System executes in batch or interactive line mode, using this procedure can save you time and resources.

display manager windows
: include LIBNAME, DIR, VAR, and CATALOG windows that enable you to perform most file management tasks without submitting SAS program statements.

Release 6.06: SAS Data Sets

This section provides information about names for SAS data sets and describes special SAS System data set names. The information in this section applies to all SAS data sets accessed by Release 6.06 of the SAS System. For general information about the structure and contents of SAS data sets, refer to the earlier section "SAS Data Set Model."

Data Set Names

You can use any implementation of the SAS data set model as input for DATA or PROC steps by specifying its name in a SET, MERGE, or UPDATE statement or in the DATA= option of a SAS procedure. The information in the next four sections applies to all SAS data sets.

How and When Names Are Assigned

You name SAS data sets when you create them. Output SAS data sets created in a DATA step are named in the DATA statement. SAS data sets created in a procedure step are usually given a name in the procedure statement or an OUTPUT statement. If you do not specify a name for an output data set, the SAS System assigns a default name.

In Version 5, only SAS data sets created and named in a DATA or PROC step could be processed by the SAS System. With Release 6.06, there are other methods for accessing and naming SAS data sets used as input. If you are creating SAS data views, you assign the data set name using the SQL procedure or a SAS/ACCESS window. If you are using an interface library engine to access the data, the rules for assigning data set names vary according to the engine.

▶ ***Caution:*** *SAS data files and SAS data views in the same library cannot have the same name.*

The SAS System prevents you from giving the same name to SAS data views and SAS data files in the same library. Because you can specify them both as SAS data sets in the same program statements but cannot specify the member type, the SAS System cannot determine from the program statement which data set you want to process.

Parts of a Data Set Name

The complete name of every SAS data set has three elements. You assign the first two; the SAS System supplies the third. The form for SAS data set names is as follows:

libref.data-set-name.membertype

The elements of a SAS data set name include the following:

libref
: is the logical name of a SAS data library.

data-set-name
: is the data set name.

membertype
: is assigned by the SAS System. The member type is DATA for SAS data files and VIEW for SAS data views.

When you refer to SAS data sets in your program statements, use a one-level or two-level name, depending on the nature of the SAS data library where you store the data set.

Two-level Names

The form most commonly used to create, read, or write to SAS data sets in permanent SAS data libraries is the two-level name as shown here:

libref.data-set-name

When you create a new SAS data set, the libref indicates where it is to be stored. When you reference an existing SAS data set, the libref tells the SAS System where to find the file. The following examples show the use of two-level names in SAS program statements:

□ `data xechlor.peanut;`

□ `proc sort data=revenue.sales;`

One-level Names

You can omit the libref, and refer to SAS data sets with a one-level name in the following form:

data-set-name

Data sets with one-level names are automatically assigned to one of two special SAS System libraries: WORK or USER. Most commonly, they are assigned to the temporary library WORK and are deleted at the end of a SAS job or session. If you have associated the libref USER with a SAS data library, data sets with one-level names are stored in that library. The following examples show how one-level names are used in SAS program statements:

□ `data test3;`

□ `set sample;`

SAS System Data Sets

Special SAS System data set names provide a means for creating null SAS data sets and for naming and using default SAS data sets.

Null Data Sets

If you want to execute a DATA step but do not want to create a SAS data set, you can specify the keyword _NULL_ as the data set name. The following statement begins a DATA step that does not create a SAS data set:

```
data _null_;
```

Using _NULL_ causes the SAS System to execute the DATA step as if it were creating a new SAS data set, but no observations and no variables are written to an output data set. This process can be a more efficient use of computer resources if you are using the DATA step for some function, such as report writing, for which the output of the DATA step does not need to be stored as a SAS data set.

Default Data Sets

The SAS System keeps track of the most recently created SAS data set through the reserved name _LAST_. When you execute a DATA or PROC step without specifying an input SAS data set, by default, the SAS System uses the _LAST_ data set.

The _LAST_= system option enables you to designate a data set as the _LAST_ data set. The name you specify is used as the default data set until you create a new SAS data set. You can use the _LAST_= system option when you want to execute a SAS job that contains a number of procedure steps using an existing permanent SAS data set. Issuing the _LAST_= system option enables you to avoid specifying the SAS data set name in each procedure statement. The following OPTIONS statement specifies a default SAS data set:

```
options _last_=schedule.jan;
```

Automatic Naming Convention

If you do not specify a SAS data set name or the reserved name _NULL_ in a DATA statement, the SAS System automatically creates data sets with the names DATA1, DATA2, and so on, to successive data sets in the WORK or USER library. This feature is referred to as the DATA*n* naming convention. The following statement produces a SAS data set using the DATA*n* naming convention:

```
data;
```

Tools for Managing Data Sets

You can use the windows and procedures listed in the section "Tools for Managing Libraries" to copy, rename, delete, or obtain information about the contents of your SAS data sets.

Release 6.06: SAS Indexes

The ability to index SAS data sets is one of the new features available in Release 6.06 software. The SAS System can create, maintain, and use indexes to process SAS data sets created and accessed by the V606 engine. Creating indexes for V606 SAS data sets provides two major benefits. The first benefit is fast access to a subset of the observations, for example, when selecting observations by WHERE-expression processing. The second benefit is that data can be retrieved in the appropriate order for BY-group processing without first using the SORT procedure.

Note: You cannot index Version 5 SAS data sets without first converting them to V606 SAS data sets.

The material that follows describes the types of indexes for SAS data sets, outlines the criteria the SAS System uses when selecting an index, suggests guidelines for creating indexes, and provides information you need for managing indexes.

Overview of Indexes and Indexing

An *index* stores the values of SAS data set variables and a system of pointers that enable the SAS System, under some circumstances, to locate observations in the SAS data set more quickly and efficiently. Once you create an index for a data set, the SAS System determines when to use it.

When processing applications that include WHERE expressions, the SAS System verifies that the variables specified in the WHERE expression are included in an appropriate index and then uses the index only if it meets certain performance criteria. When processing programs that contain a BY statement, the SAS System always uses the index, if an appropriate one is available. In addition, the SQL procedure may use indexes to optimize joining SAS data sets by key variable values. For base SAS software, you cannot tell the SAS System to use an index during processing.

You can create and manage indexes for SAS data sets using the following features:

□ DATASETS procedure

□ some display manager windows

□ SQL procedure

□ SAS/IML software

□ Screen Control Language available in SAS/AF and SAS/FSP software.

Once the index exists, the SAS System treats it as part of the SAS data set. For example, if you add or delete observations, the index is updated automatically. If you copy a SAS data set with the COPY or DATASETS procedures, the SAS System recreates the index for you after the data set is copied.

Indexes require computer resources to store, use, and maintain, so you should create them only if their use significantly improves the performance of your SAS applications.

Types of Indexes

SAS data sets can be indexed by one or more variables, known as *key variables*. SAS indexes are classified as simple or composite, according to the number of key variables whose values make up the index. You can also limit indexes to unique values of key variables and exclude missing values from indexes.

Simple Indexes

A *simple index* locates observations by the values of one key variable. The key variable can be numeric or character. When you create a simple index, the SAS System automatically gives the index the same name as its key variable.

You can create more than one simple index for a SAS data set, but for Release 6.06, all the indexes associated with the data set are stored in one index file that has the same name as the SAS data set. You do not see the index listed as a separate file in a SAS library directory; however, on some host systems, you can see it if you use host system utilities to list the files.

The following example shows the PROC DATASETS statements you can use to create two simple indexes and then print the contents information for the SAS data set, showing which variables are included in indexes. The SAS data set COLLEGE.SURVEY contains two variables, CLASS and MAJOR, that are specified as key variables.

```
libname college 'SAS-data-library';

proc datasets library=college;
   modify survey;
      index create class;
      index create major;
   contents data=survey;
run;
```

In the contents listing in Output 6.1, the data set SURVEY has two indexes named CLASS and MAJOR.

Output 6.1 *Contents Listing Showing Simple Indexes*

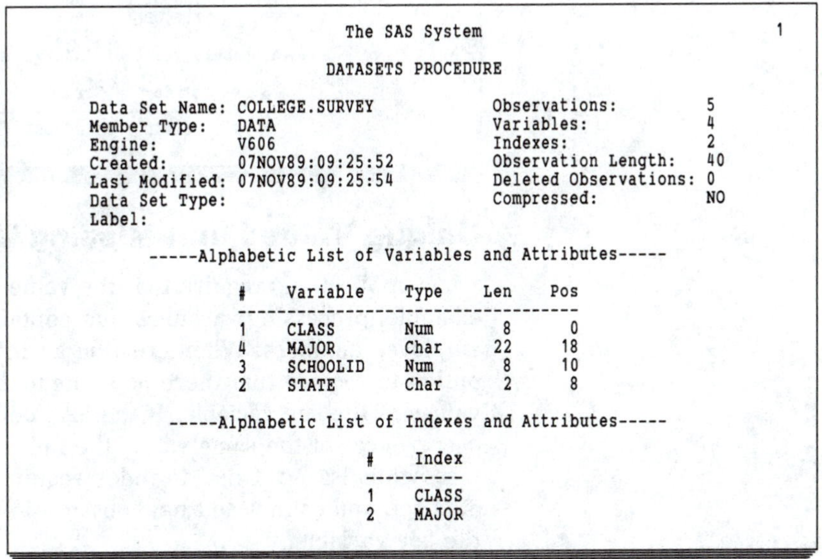

```
                              The SAS System                                1

                           DATASETS PROCEDURE

Data Set Name: COLLEGE.SURVEY                  Observations:          5
Member Type:   DATA                            Variables:             4
Engine:        V606                            Indexes:               2
Created:       07NOV89:09:25:52                Observation Length:    40
Last Modified: 07NOV89:09:25:54                Deleted Observations:  0
Data Set Type:                                 Compressed:            NO
Label:

             -----Alphabetic List of Variables and Attributes-----

                       #   Variable    Type    Len    Pos
                       ---------------------------------
                       1   CLASS       Num       8      0
                       4   MAJOR       Char     22     18
                       3   SCHOOLID    Num       8     10
                       2   STATE       Char      2      8

              -----Alphabetic List of Indexes and Attributes-----

                              #    Index
                              ----------
                              1    CLASS
                              2    MAJOR
```

Composite Indexes

A *composite index* locates observations by the values of two or more key variables. The variables used in the composite index can be numeric or character or a mixture. For a composite index, you must specify a unique index name when you create the index. You can create more than one composite index for a SAS data set.

You do not specify a composite index name in SAS program statements, except in certain SAS utility procedures. If you are using a BY statement to process a SAS data set with a composite index, specify the variable names in the BY statement.

This example shows the PROC DATASETS statements that create a composite index for the data set MAILLIST. The SAS data set contains two variables, ZIPCODE and SCHOOLID, that are specified as key variables.

```
proc datasets library=college;
   modify maillist;
      index create zipid=(zipcode schoolid);
   contents data=maillist;
run;
```

The contents listing in Output 6.2 shows one index ZIPID for the data set and indicates that it is composed of the values for ZIPCODE and SCHOOLID.

Output 6.2 *Contents Listing Showing Composite Index*

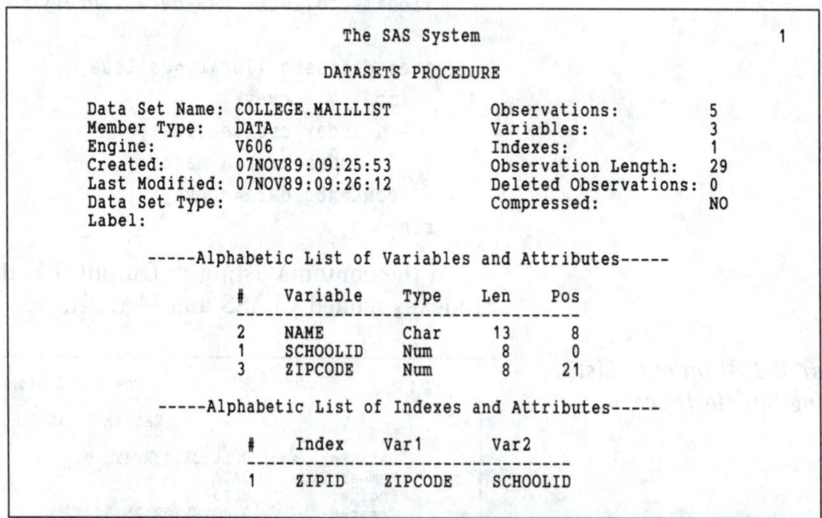

```
                                The SAS System                                1

                              DATASETS PROCEDURE

Data Set Name: COLLEGE.MAILLIST            Observations:          5
Member Type:   DATA                        Variables:             3
Engine:        V606                        Indexes:               1
Created:       07NOV89:09:25:53            Observation Length:    29
Last Modified: 07NOV89:09:26:12            Deleted Observations:  0
Data Set Type:                             Compressed:            NO
Label:

             -----Alphabetic List of Variables and Attributes-----

                     #    Variable    Type    Len    Pos
                     ---------------------------------
                     2    NAME        Char     13      8
                     1    SCHOOLID    Num       8      0
                     3    ZIPCODE     Num       8     21

              -----Alphabetic List of Indexes and Attributes-----

                      #    Index    Var1       Var2
                      -----------------------------
                      1    ZIPID    ZIPCODE    SCHOOLID
```

Unique Values and Missing Values

Some applications require that the values of key variables be unique, for example, processing variables that contain social security numbers or employee numbers. When creating an index, you can specify the UNIQUE option to require that there be a one-to-one match of observations to values of the key variable. If the SAS data set already contains multiple occurrences of the same value, the index is not created and an error message is issued. Once an index requiring unique values exists for a SAS data set, you cannot add new observations that contain duplicate values of the key variable.

```
proc datasets library=college;
   modify student;
   index create idnum / unique;
run;
```

If a key variable has missing values, you can omit them from the index. Omitting missing values with the NOMISS option is another feature available when creating an index. Using the NOMISS option does not prevent your adding new observations that contain missing values.

```
proc datasets library=college;
   modify student;
   index create religion / nomiss;
run;
```

▶ ***Caution:** Use the NOMISS option carefully.*

The SAS System does not select indexes created with the NOMISS option for BY-group processing. In addition, it does not select a NOMISS index for WHERE-expression processing if the WHERE expression is written so that missing values can satisfy the condition.

Criteria for Appropriate Indexes

The following sections tell you what criteria must be satisfied before the SAS System uses an existing index and provide some examples of appropriate indexes.

WHERE-Expression Processing

For Release 6.06, the SAS System uses an index to select observations that meet the conditions of the WHERE expression if all of the following statements are true:

- □ One or more of the variables in the WHERE expression has a simple index or is the first variable in a composite index. If an existing index does not select all observations that satisfy all the conditions specified in the WHERE expression, the SAS System does not select the index.
- □ The estimated computer resources required to locate observations by an index are fewer than those required to read the observations sequentially from the data set. As a general rule, the SAS System uses an index for WHERE processing if it predicts that the WHERE expression will select approximately one-third or fewer of the total number of observations in the data set.
- □ If the data set has more than one index that meets the conditions of the WHERE expression, the SAS System uses the index that selects the fewest observations.

If the SAS System selects and uses an index, the observations are retrieved in indexed order. If it does not use an index, the WHERE expression retrieves the observations in the physical order in which they occur in the SAS data set.

Simple Index An earlier example showed the statements for creating a simple index MAJOR for the SAS data set COLLEGE.SURVEY. The index MAJOR is an appropriate index for the following WHERE expressions that include the variable MAJOR:

- □ `where class=90 and major in ('BIOLOGY', 'AGRICULTURE');`
- □ `where major in ('BIOLOGY', 'CHEMISTRY', 'AGRICULTURE');`

If the index MAJOR is used, the observations are retrieved in indexed order of the variable MAJOR. The observations containing `AGRICULTURE` appear before the observations for `BIOLOGY`, and so on.

The index MAJOR is not appropriate because it does not select all observations that meet the conditions of the WHERE expression. The index MAJOR can retrieve all observations for which the value of the variable MAJOR is **BIOLOGY** or **AGRICULTURE**, but these observations may not include all observations for which the value of CLASS is 90.

```
where class=90 or major in ('BIOLOGY','AGRICULTURE');
```

Composite Index The composite index ZIPID for the SAS data set COLLEGE.MAILLIST can be used to select observations for the following WHERE expressions:

□ `where zipcode between 27600 and 27999 and schoolid not missing;`

□ `where zipcode between 33000 and 33999;`

The composite index ZIPID would not be selected to retrieve observations for the following WHERE expression because the variable SCHOOLID is not the first variable in the composite index:

```
where schoolid gt 10000;
```

BY-Group Processing

The SAS System always uses an index to retrieve observations for BY-group processing if an appropriate index exists. Observations are always retrieved in ascending order. Indexes created with the NOMISS option are ignored for BY-group processing. If you specify the DESCENDING or NOTSORTED options in the BY statement, indexes are not used to retrieve observations. The following criteria determine which index is used:

□ If the BY statement contains a single variable, the variable must appear in a simple index or be the first variable in a composite index.

□ If the BY statement contains more than one variable, the data set must have an index whose variables match the first one or more variables in the BY statement. If more than one index meets this criteria, the SAS System selects the index with the most variables. It uses a simple index if its variable matches the first variable of the BY statement and there are no appropriate composite indexes.

If the index fails to retrieve the observations in the correct order, the DATA or PROC step stops processing. The error message indicates that the data were not in ascending order.

Simple Index The SAS System always successfully uses the index MAJOR when processing the following BY statement. The index MAJOR was created in an earlier example.

```
by major;
```

The SAS System attempts to use the index MAJOR when processing this BY statement because there is a simple index for the first variable MAJOR:

```
by major state;
```

If the values of STATE are arranged in alphabetical order or in alphabetical order within values of MAJOR, the SAS System successfully processes the data as if they were sorted into BY groups. If the values of STATE are not in alphabetical order, the SAS System stops processing with the first incorrect value and issues an error message, just as it would if no index had been available.

Composite Index The index ZIPID, which includes the variables ZIPCODE and SCHOOLID, is appropriate for the following BY statements:

□ `by zipcode schoolid;`

□ `by zipcode;`

The SAS System attempts to use the index ZIPID when processing this BY statement because there is a composite index for the first two variables, ZIPCODE and SCHOOLID:

```
by zipcode schoolid name;
```

If the values of NAME are not in the correct order for processing, the SAS System stops processing with the first incorrect value and issues an error message.

The index ZIPID is not selected for these BY statements:

□ `by schoolid;`

□ `by schoolid zipcode;`

BY-Group and WHERE-Expression Processing

If you specify a BY statement and a WHERE expression in the same DATA or PROC step, the SAS System looks for one index that meets the conditions of both statements. If one index meets the conditions for the BY statement and another meets the conditions for the WHERE statement, the SAS System selects the index that satisfies the criteria for the BY statement. If existing indexes meet only the criteria for the WHERE statement, the SAS System does not use the index in processing either statement.

Guidelines for Creating an Index

Indexes require computer resources to create and maintain. For Release 6.06, indexes are stored in a separate file, and each time you change or delete values or observations in the SAS data set, the SAS System updates the corresponding values in the index. Using an index to retrieve all observations requires more computer resources than using sequential methods. The index saves resources when used to select a small subset of the observations. Before you create an index, you should decide if the improvement in performance is great enough to justify the extra resources required to create, store, and maintain it.

Use the following guidelines to determine whether an index might provide the optimum benefits for your application. These are guidelines only and exceptions are possible. The way to determine whether an index optimizes performance is to create the index, examine its impact on performance, and delete the index if performance does not significantly improve. Using an index may improve some phases of application performance while degrading others.

- Do not index a data set for WHERE-expression processing if you expect to retrieve more than one-third of the observations in the data set. An index performs best when the WHERE expression selects a small number of observations in the data set. Using an index to retrieve more than this number for BY-group processing, however, may be cost effective.
- Do not create an index unless the data set requires at least three pages of memory. If the data set is less than three pages, the SAS System can access the data set faster by reading the observations sequentially. The DATASETS procedure and the CONTENTS procedure report the number of memory pages for SAS data sets created by the V606 engine.
- Keep the number of indexes for one data set to a minimum for data that are updated frequently because the maintenance costs can be significant.
- Do not index variables that have widely skewed data values or whose data values are unevenly distributed. The formulas the SAS System uses to select an index for WHERE-expression processing are most effective if the values of the indexed variable are uniformly distributed. You can test the data to determine if an index significantly improves performance.
- Do not use the NOMISS option if you expect to use a BY statement or WHERE expressions that select missing values.

Tools for Managing Indexes

Although indexes are stored separately for Release 6.06, they are treated by the SAS System as extensions of a SAS data set. The index file has the same name as the SAS data set with which it is associated, and the file contains all the indexes available for the data set. Index files do not appear in a SAS library directory listing as separate member types. There is a column in the directory listing that indicates whether the SAS data set has an index file associated with it. To determine which variables are included in indexes, use the CONTENTS or DATASETS procedure to list the attributes of the data set.

The SAS System maintains the indexes so that they are efficient, even if you add many observations with the same or similar values of the key variable. If you perform file management tasks using SAS utilities, the SAS System also ensures that the indexes remain in a usable form. Table 6.1 indicates the action the SAS System takes when you use SAS procedures to perform certain file management tasks on indexed data sets.

Table 6.1 *How the SAS System Maintains Indexes*

Data Set Activity	Results for Index
Copy, move data set	A new index file is created.
Delete data set	The index file is deleted.
Rename data set	The index file is renamed to the new data set name.
Rename key variable	Simple indexes are renamed. For composite indexes, the variable is renamed, but the name of the composite index is not changed.
Add, delete observations	Value/identifier pairs are added or deleted.
Update observations	Old value/identifier pairs are deleted and new pairs are inserted.

You can sort a SAS data set containing indexes only if you direct the output of the SORT procedure to a new SAS data set so that the original SAS data set remains unchanged. The new SAS data set is not indexed.

Release 6.06: SAS Catalogs

In previous releases of SAS software, there was more than one kind of catalog. For example, Version 5 SAS software had full-screen catalogs and graphics catalogs. Files such as SAS/IML workspaces, SAS/ETS models, macros, and user-written formats were stored as separate member types. For Release 6.06, the SAS System stores all of these units as entries in catalogs, and all catalogs have the member type CATALOG. You can store a mixture of entry types in a SAS catalog. Which types you store and how many entries you store depend on your applications.

This section describes catalog names, lists the possible entry types, and describes special SAS System catalogs.

Catalog Names

In base SAS software, SAS catalog entries are generally accessed automatically by the SAS System when the information stored in them is required for processing. In other SAS software products, you must specify the catalog entry in various procedures. Because the requirements differ with the SAS procedure or software product, refer to the appropriate procedure or product documentation for details.

Parts of a Catalog Name

SAS catalog entries are fully identified by a four-level name in the following form:

```
libref.catalog.entry-name.entry-type
```

You commonly specify the two-level name for an entire catalog, as follows:

```
libref.catalog
```

The parts of a two-level catalog name are as follows:

libref
: is the logical name of the SAS data library to which the catalog belongs.

catalog
: is a valid SAS name for the file.

The entry name and entry type are required by some SAS procedures. If the entry type has been specified elsewhere or can be determined from context, you can use the entry name only. To specify entry names and entry types, use this form:

```
entry-name.entry-type
```

The parts of an entry name are as follows:

entry-name
: is a valid SAS name for the catalog entry.

entry-type
: is assigned by the SAS System when the entry is created. Entry types are listed in Table 6.2.

Entry Types

This table lists entry types, briefly describes the information stored in each type, and tells which SAS procedure or software products create it and which ones use it. Note that the SAS System creates some additional entry types for internal purposes. These specialized entries include the types AFCBT, AFGO, AFPGM, MACRO, and MSYMTAB. Although you may notice these entry types in a catalog directory, you cannot view or edit them.

Table 6.2 *Catalog Entry Types for SAS Software Products*

Entry Type	Contents	Created By	Used By
AFCBT	Status of in-progress CBT entries (internal only)	SAS/AF software	SAS/AF software, Base SAS software
AFGO	Information about the entry used in the last session (internal only)	SAS/AF software	SAS/AF software, Base SAS software
AFMACRO	Macros defined with a ### macro block in a Version 5 PROGRAM entry. Created when a Version 5 SAS/AF PROGRAM entry is converted to Version 6 format.	PROC CIMPORT	Base SAS software
AFPGM	PROGRAM entry values (internal only)	SAS/AF software	SAS/AF software, Base SAS software

(continued)

Table 6.2 *(continued)*

Entry Type	Contents	Created By	Used By
CBT	Text, including questions and possible responses, of a CBT application	PROC BUILD	SAS/AF software
CMAP	Color mapping	PROC GREPLAY	SAS/GRAPH software
DEV	Graphics or interactive windowing device information	PROC GDEVICE, Display manager	SAS/GRAPH software, Base SAS software
DEVMAP	Graphics device map for converting the internal standard character encoding to a device's character encoding	PROC GKEYMAP	SAS/GRAPH software
DICTNARY	Contains words used by the spelling checker	PROC SPELL, SPELL window	Base SAS software
EDPARMS	Attributes of editing environment	PROC BUILD, PROC FSLETTER	SAS/AF software, SAS/FSP software
FONT	Software font	PROC GFONT	SAS/GRAPH software
FORM	Printer information	FORM window	SAS/AF software, SAS/FSP software, Base SAS software
FORMAT	User-written numeric format	PROC FORMAT	Base SAS software
FORMATC	User-written character format	PROC FORMAT	Base SAS software
FORMULA	Formulas and window definitions	PROC FSVIEW	SAS/FSP software
GLOBAL	One of these graphics global statements: AXIS, LEGEND, PATTERN, or SYMBOL. The first three letters of the name of the entry are the first three letters of the statement name.	Global statements or equivalent windows	SAS/GRAPH software
GOPTIONS	Current graphics options	GOPTIONS statement	SAS/GRAPH software
GRSEG	Graphics output	Graphics procedures	SAS/GRAPH software, SAS/IML software, SAS/OR software, SAS/QC software
HELP	Help information for applications	PROC BUILD	SAS/AF software
IMOD	Module or subroutine	PROC IML	SAS/IML software
INFMT	User-written numeric informat	PROC FORMAT	Base SAS software
INFMTC	User-written character informat	PROC FORMAT	Base SAS software

(continued)

Table 6.2 *(continued)*

Entry Type	Contents	Created By	Used By
KEYMAP	Graphics key map for converting keyboard characters to the internal standard character encoding	PROC GKEYMAP	SAS/GRAPH software
KEYS	Function key settings	Interactive windowing procedures and windows	All products
LETTER	Text of letter	PROC FSLETTER	SAS/FSP software
LIST	Values used by an application	PROC BUILD	SAS/AF software
LOG	Text from LOG window	Display manager	Base SAS software
MACRO	Intermediate code for a SAS macro (internal only)	%MACRO statement	Base SAS software
MATRIX	Matrix	PROC IML	SAS/IML software
MENU	MENU windows	PROC BUILD	SAS/AF software
MODEL	Model files from the CMP compiler	PROC MODEL	SAS/ETS software
MSYMTAB	Information about a SAS macro variable (internal only)	%MACRO statement	Base SAS software
OUTPUT	Text from OUTPUT window	Display manager	Base SAS software
PMENU	Pull-down menus	PROC PMENU	Base SAS software
PROGRAM	Program window	PROC BUILD	SAS/AF software
SCREEN	Screen definition	PROC FSEDIT	SAS/FSP software
SOURCE	Text from NOTEPAD and PGM windows	Display manager	Base SAS software
TEMPLATE	Template for replay	PROC GREPLAY	SAS/GRAPH software
TITLE	Contains a TITLE, FOOTNOTE, or NOTE statement. The first three letters of the name are TTL for titles, FTN for footnotes, and NOT for notes.	TITLE, FOOTNOTE, or NOTE statements or TITLE or FOOTNOTE windows	All products
WSAVE	Window definitions and attributes	Display manager windows, PROC BUILD, PROC FSLIST, PROC FSLETTER	Base SAS software

SAS System Catalogs

The following sections describe two catalogs for base SAS software that contain specific SAS System information. Refer to the documentation for other SAS software products for a discussion of special SAS catalogs available.

User Profile Catalog

A user profile catalog (SASUSER.PROFILE) is available for customizing the way you work with the SAS System. The SAS System uses this catalog to store function key definitions, fonts for graphics applications, window attributes, and other information from display manager sessions or interactive windowing procedures.

The information in the user profile catalog is accessed automatically by the SAS System when you need it for processing. For example, each time you enter the KEYS window and change the settings, the SAS System stores the new settings with the KEYS entry type. Similarly, if you change and save the attributes for display manager windows, the changes are stored under the appropriate entry name and type. When you use the window or procedure, the SAS System then looks for information in the user profile catalog.

The SAS System searches in the following order to find catalog entries:

1. current catalog (if you are using SAS/FSP or SAS/AF software)
2. user profile catalog (SASUSER.PROFILE)
3. appropriate SASHELP catalog.

How Created The SAS System creates the user profile catalog the first time it needs to refer to it and discovers that it does not exist. If you are using display manager, this occurs during system initialization in your first SAS session. If you use one of the other modes of execution, the user profile catalog is created the first time you execute a SAS/FSP or SAS/AF software procedure that requires it.

■ **Host Information** .... The SASUSER library is implemented differently on various host systems. See the SAS documentation for your host system for more information on how and when it is created.
.... ■

Default Settings The default settings originally provided with the SAS System are stored in several catalogs in the SASHELP installation library. If you do not make any changes to key settings or other options, the SAS System uses the default settings. If you make changes, the new information is stored in your user profile catalog. To restore the original default settings, use the CATALOG procedure or CATALOG window to delete the appropriate entries from your user profile catalog. By default, the SAS System then uses the corresponding entry from the SASHELP library.

Format Catalogs

You can create and store user-written formats and informats using the FORMAT procedure. The procedure places each format or informat in an individual entry in a catalog named FORMATS. You specify the libref of the SAS data library where the catalog is to be stored in the PROC FORMAT statement, and the SAS System assigns the name FORMATS to the catalog. The name of each entry is the name you assign to the format or informat. The SAS System assigns the entry types FORMAT or FORMATC to numeric or character formats, respectively. The entry types INFMT or INFMTC are assigned to informats.

To use the formats or informats in your program statements, you must first associate the reserved libref LIBRARY with the SAS data library where they are stored. The SAS System looks for entries in the catalog LIBRARY.FORMATS that match the formats or informats specified in your SAS programs. You can store other types of entries in the FORMATS catalog, but you may prefer to reserve this catalog for formats and informats. Refer to *SAS Procedures Guide* for details on using PROC FORMAT.

Tools for Managing Catalogs

There are several SAS System features to help you manage the entries in catalogs. One feature is the CATALOG procedure, a part of base SAS software. Another is the CATALOG window in display manager and some full-screen procedures. There is also a catalog directory window for managing entries that is included in a number of interactive windowing procedures in SAS/AF, SAS/FSP, and SAS/GRAPH software. The following list summarizes the tools available for managing catalogs:

CATALOG procedure
: is similar to the DATASETS procedure. Use the CATALOG procedure to copy, delete, list, and rename entries in catalogs.

CATALOG window
: is a window you can bring up at any time in a display manager session or interactive windowing procedure. It displays the name, type, description, and date of last update for each entry in the specified catalog. CATALOG window commands enable you to rename, delete, and copy entries.

Catalog directory windows
: are available in some procedures in SAS/AF, SAS/FSP, and SAS/GRAPH software. A catalog directory window lists the same kind of information that the CATALOG window provides: entry name, type, description, and date of last update. See the description of each interactive windowing procedure for details on the catalog directory window for that procedure.

Release 6.06: Moving and Converting SAS Files

Moving SAS files from one host system to another depends greatly on your host systems, the member type and version of the SAS files you want to move, and the methods you have available for moving the files. You must also consider these factors if you want to convert some of your Version 5 SAS files to take advantage of Release 6.06 features.

Because there are so many alternatives for accomplishing these tasks, the subject cannot be covered adequately in this book. The purpose of this section is to provide terminology and to outline the tools and methods available under Release 6.06 of the SAS System. You should see one or all of the following sources for a complete discussion of moving and converting SAS files.

- *SAS Procedures Guide, Version 6, Third Edition*
- Technical Report P-195, *Transporting SAS Files between Host Systems*
- the SAS documentation for your host system.

Terminology

In SAS documentation, the following terms are used in specific ways. You should be familiar with them.

converting
: specifies to change a SAS file from a Version 5 format to a Release 6.06 or later version running on the same host system.

transport file
: specifies a sequential file containing a SAS data library, SAS catalogs, or SAS data sets in transport format.

transport format
: specifies a machine-independent file format that can be created by the XCOPY procedure, the COPY procedure with the EXPORT option, and the TRANSPORT= data set option of Version 5, or by the XPORT engine available in Release 6.06.

Moving Files

The methods you use for moving files depend on whether you are moving data sets or catalogs. You cannot move indexes, views, access descriptors, or stored programs. These files must be created again after their associated data sets are installed on the new host system.

General Steps

In general, the steps required to move SAS files from Release 6.06 on one host system to Release 6.06 on another host system are as follows:

1. Copy the SAS library, catalog, or data set into transport format.
2. Move the transport file to the new machine using either data communications software or magnetic medium.
3. Restore the SAS library, catalog, or data set in a format appropriate for the new host.

These steps outline the simplest possible situation that can occur. If you want to move a SAS data library, catalog, or data set and convert it to a different version of the SAS System, there are other factors you must consider.

Creating and Restoring Transport Files

Release 6.06 has three methods of creating and restoring a file in transport format. These methods include

□ the XPORT engine and the COPY procedure

□ the CPORT and CIMPORT procedures

□ the UPLOAD and DOWNLOAD procedures.

XPORT engine and PROC COPY Specify the XPORT engine in a LIBNAME statement and use PROC COPY to move SAS data sets into a transport file from the sending host system. On the receiving host system, use the same method to copy from the transport file into a new SAS data library.

```
   /* Writing a Transport File */
libname old file-specification-1;
libname trans xport file-specification-2;

proc copy in=old out=trans;
run;

   /* Restoring a Transport File */
libname new file-specification-1;
libname trans xport file-specification-2;

proc copy in=trans out=new;
run;
```

PROC CPORT and PROC CIMPORT Use the CPORT procedure on the old host system to copy SAS catalogs into a transport file. On the new host system, use the CIMPORT procedure to restore the SAS files. The *SAS Procedures Guide* contains detailed instructions for using PROC CPORT and PROC CIMPORT.

PROC UPLOAD and PROC DOWNLOAD Use the UPLOAD and DOWNLOAD procedures of SAS/CONNECT software to move SAS data sets and catalogs from one host system to another.

Converting SAS Files

You must consider the member type of SAS files when determining whether you can convert older files to Release 6.06. You can continue using Version 5 SAS data sets with Release 6.06 of the SAS System. If you want to use new features such as indexing, the SAS System provides a number of procedures and features to convert data sets.

To use Version 5 catalogs in Release 6.06 applications, you must convert them. A new SAS procedure, the V5TOV6 procedure, can convert all Version 5 data sets, catalogs, IML work spaces, ETS models, and user-written formats to a format compatible with Release 6.06 SAS software. Other methods are available for some Version 5 files, depending on your host system and the versions of the SAS System you have installed.

The following example lists some of the methods you can use for converting SAS data sets. Not all procedures are available for all host systems.

PROC V5TOV6	DATA step
PROC COPY	PROC CPORT/CIMPORT

The following example lists some of the methods you can use for converting SAS catalogs. Not all procedures are available for all host systems.

PROC V5TOV6
PROC CPORT/CIMPORT

Note: The CPORT and CIMPORT procedures are primarily intended for moving SAS files between host systems, but you can use them to convert catalogs and data sets.

V606 Engine: Features of the V606 Engine

The V606 engine is the default engine for writing SAS data libraries to disk format. If you do not specify an engine name on the LIBNAME statement when creating new SAS data libraries, the SAS System automatically selects this engine. The V606 engine is also automatically selected if you are accessing existing V606 SAS data sets on disk.

Note: If an engine name is not specified on the LIBNAME statement, you can use the ENGINE= system option to indicate that the SAS System is to use another default value.

The following section lists the processing characteristics of V606 SAS data sets and gives an overview of the performance features available only through the V606 engine.

Processing Characteristics

Although you can use a variety of methods to access your data, converting existing files to V606 SAS data sets offers some performance advantages. The V606 engine performs the following functions that are not available through other engines:

- □ supports all member types of the full SAS data library model, including DATA, VIEW, CATALOG, ACCESS, and PROGRAM.
- □ meets all the processing characteristics required by SAS statements and procedures. See Figure 6.5 in "SAS Data Set Model."
- □ creates, maintains, and uses indexes.
- □ reads and writes compressed (variable-length) observations. SAS data sets created by other engines have fixed-length observations. See also the COMPRESS= system option or COMPRESS= data set option for more information.
- □ assigns a permanent buffer size to V606 data sets and temporarily assigns the number of buffers to be used when processing them . See also the BUFNO= and BUFSIZE= system options and the corresponding data set options.
- □ repairs damaged SAS data sets, indexes, and catalogs.

■ **Host Information** .... The V606 engine has performance options that are host system-dependent. See the SAS documentation for your host system for a list of available options and specific information about using the features introduced in this section.
.... ■

Tools for Tuning Data Set Performance

This section describes the tools you can use to obtain performance data and defines how certain parameters control the use of memory and other computer resources. It also provides guidelines for using the new features of V606 SAS data sets.

Most SAS applications can run effectively on your host system without using these features. However, if you develop applications under the following circumstances, you may want to experiment with tuning their performance:

- □ You work with large data sets.
- □ You create production jobs that run repeatedly.
- □ You are responsible for establishing performance guidelines for a data center.
- □ You do interactive queries on large SAS data sets using SAS/FSP software.

The guidelines presented here are general because the data requirements of the application and the computing environment in which it runs vary greatly. You can achieve the best performance by experimenting with some of the performance tools available to you.

Where to Gather Performance Information

Computer performance can be measured in a number of ways because improving performance depends on the nature of your computer resources. If your computer system is limited in the amount of memory it can make available for processing your application, then improving performance means using less memory. On the other hand, if you must minimize external storage requirements or execution time, improving performance requires that you take a number of steps to reduce the size of the data set or the amount of overhead in reading and writing the data.

There are facilities within the SAS System that you can use to collect the data on which to base your tuning. PROC CONTENTS and PROC DATASETS provide information about the physical characteristics of your data sets. The STIMER and FULLSTIMER system options report the time required to run your application. Much of the information of interest to you is available only for V606 data sets. In addition, the amount and kind of performance information you obtain from these facilities depends largely on your host system.

You should consult a systems programmer at your site for other tools for measuring performance and for help in determining the best use of SAS performance options.

Data Set Characteristics The CONTENTS and DATASETS procedures provide information about the physical characteristics of V606 data sets. These characteristics help you determine the page size, or buffer size, that is optimal for your SAS application.

The *page size* of a SAS data set is the number of bytes of data that the SAS System moves between external storage and memory in one logical input/output operation. Each portion of the data set that can occupy that number of bytes is referred to as a *page* of the data set. The page size, or buffer size, is a permanent attribute of a V606 data set. For the V606 engine, the page size and the buffer size are analogous.

A *buffer* is a temporary storage area reserved for holding data after it has been read from or before it is written to the storage disk or tape. A SAS application or procedure processes the data in the buffer before it requests another page of data from the storage disk or tape.

You can obtain the following information about the characteristics of your input data sets by running PROC CONTENTS or PROC DATASETS.

These items are available for all host systems; other data may be available on your host system.

Observations
: are the number of observations in the data set that have not been deleted or flagged for deletion.

Observation Length
: is the observation size in memory, expressed in bytes.

Compressed
: is NO if stored observations are fixed-length; YES if stored observations are compressed and variable length.

Reuse
: is NO if new observations are added to the end of the data set; YES if new observations are inserted in unused space within the data set.

Data Set Page Size
: is the page size in bytes.

Number of Data Set Pages
: is the number of pages in the data set.

First Data Page
: is the page number of the page containing the first observation for noncompressed files. Descriptor information is stored before the observations in the file.

Max Obs per Page
: is the maximum number of observations that a page can hold for noncompressed files.

Obs in First Page
: is the number of observations in the first page for noncompressed files.

Index File Page Size
: is the size of the index file pages, if there is an index.

Number of Index File Pages
: is the total number of pages in the index file, if one exists.

Computer Time Measuring the computer resources used by a SAS application is difficult and host-specific. You can record a number of performance statistics in your SAS log by specifying the STIMER or FULLSTIMER system options. The format and content of the messages vary according to your host system. See Chapter 16, “SAS System Options,” for a full discussion of how to use them.

Options for Tuning Performance

Using performance options changes the way computer resources are allocated and the rules the SAS System uses to process the data. In many cases, you must use a combination of more than one option to achieve optimal performance for a given application. Because applications vary greatly in their processing requirements, the values you specify for one application do not necessarily provide the same benefits for other applications.

You can specify the three options described in this section as system options or data set options. See Chapter 15, “SAS Data Set Options,” and Chapter 16 for more information about their syntax and use.

■ **Host Information** .... The results of using these options vary with your host system. See the SAS documentation for your host system for default values and more information.

Buffer Size Using the BUFSIZE= data set or system option when you create a V606 SAS data set specifies a permanent page size for the data set. During processing, the SAS System uses the value you specify as the minimum number of bytes for one buffer. If the value is too small for one observation, the SAS System chooses the next largest size available for your host system. Use the following guidelines for specifying page size:

- □ To reduce the number of input/output operations, increase the page size. The number of input/output operations is reduced by a factor inversely proportional to the increase in page size. For example, if you double the page size, the number of input/output operations is halved. Start your tuning by using some simple factor such as doubling or tripling the default page size.
- □ To reduce the amount of memory required to process the application, reduce the page size. The number of input/output operations will increase, but the memory should be freed up.
- □ To make more efficient use of buffers, you can reduce the page size if the default allows wasted space. This situation can occur, for example, if you have small data sets. Use a smaller page size so there is not much wasted space and observations are packed more efficiently into the page.
- □ If a particular page size is not efficient for your host system, consult your systems programmer to determine if you should change the page size to a different value.

Buffer Number The BUFNO= data set or system option specifies the number of page buffers to allocate when you open the SAS data set to read from it or write to it. This value is not a permanent characteristic of the data set, and you can change it for each run of the application. Use the following guidelines for specifying the number of buffers:

- □ If you have memory constraints, use fewer buffers.
- □ On some host systems, you can increase the number of buffers and reduce the number of input/output operations during sequential access. The number of input/output operations is reduced by a factor inversely proportional to the increase in the number of buffers.
- □ To reduce input/output operations on a small data set, you can allocate one buffer for each page of data to be processed. This technique is most effective if you read the same observations several times during processing, for example, using the POINT= option in the SET statement.

Compressing Data Sets The COMPRESS= data set or system option sets the observation type to compressed or uncompressed. The observation type is a permanent characteristic of the data set. Use these guidelines when deciding whether to compress data sets:

- Using the COMPRESS= option decreases the size of the data set, thus reducing the number of input/output operations required. If your data contain many contiguous occurrences of the same byte, such as blanks or 0s, compressing the observations can produce a substantially smaller data set. The effect this action has on CPU time can vary from one host system to another.
- You cannot use random access methods such as the POINT= option in the SET statement with compressed data sets.
- By default, new observations are appended to the end of compressed SAS data sets, leaving some unused space within the SAS data set. You can control whether the SAS System writes the observations to this unused space by specifying the REUSE=YES option when creating the compressed SAS data set.

Indexing

Creating an index for SAS data sets provides two major benefits. The first benefit is fast access to a subset of the observations, for example, when selecting observations for processing using the WHERE expression. The second benefit is that data can be retrieved in order of their indexed values without first using the SORT procedure.

See "SAS Indexes" earlier in this chapter for a discussion on how the SAS System uses indexes to enhance the performance of V606 data sets.

Repairing Damaged Files

The V606 engine detects possible damage to SAS data sets, indexes, and catalogs and provides a means for repairing some of the damage. If one of the following events occurs while you are creating or updating a SAS file, the SAS System can recover the file and repair some of the damage:

- a system failure occurs while the data set or catalog is being processed or updated.
- damage to the storage device where a data set resides. In this case, you can restore the damaged data set from a backup device, but the data set and index no longer match.
- the disk where the data set or catalog is stored becomes full before the file is completely written to it.
- an input/output error occurs while writing to the data set or catalog.

When the failure occurs, the observations or records that were not written to the data set or catalog are lost and some of the information about where values are stored is inconsistent. The next time the SAS System reads the file, it recognizes that the file's contents are damaged.

Recovering SAS Data Sets

There are two ways to recover a damaged SAS data set, depending on the method of execution you are using:

- If you are using display manager or interactive line mode when the damage is detected, the SAS System displays a requestor window that asks if you want to repair the damage. If you answer yes, the SAS System processes the data and repairs the data set. Any new observations or alterations to the data values that were not written to the data set before the failure occurred do not appear in the repaired data set. The SAS System continues processing program statements after repairing the data set.

  Note: If the SAS data set is large, the time to repair it can be long. If you choose not to repair the damage immediately, the SAS System stops processing the step. You must later use the REPAIR statement of PROC DATASETS to repair the damage.

- If you are using noninteractive or batch mode when the damage is detected, the SAS System stops processing the step and sends a message to the SAS log. To repair the damage, you must use the REPAIR statement in PROC DATASETS.

See the *SAS Procedures Guide* for details on using the REPAIR statement.

Recovering Indexes

In addition to the failures listed earlier, you can damage the indexes for V606 data sets by using a host system command to delete, copy, or rename a SAS data set, but not its associated index file. You can use the REPAIR statement in PROC DATASETS to restore simple indexes (but not composite indexes) that are damaged in this manner.

You cannot use the REPAIR statement to recover indexes that are deleted by taking one of the following actions:

- copying a SAS data set by some means other than PROC COPY or PROC DATASETS, for example, using a DATA step
- using the FORCE option in the SORT procedure to write over the original data set.

Recovering Catalogs

When a system failure occurs, the entire catalog can be damaged or only certain entries. The V606 engine checks the catalog to see which entries may be damaged and attempts to recover the entire catalog or only those entries open at the time of the failure. If you use the REPAIR statement of the DATASETS procedure to restore a catalog, you receive a warning for entries that have possible damage. Entries that have been restored may not include updates that were not written to disk before the damage occurred.

CHAPTER 7 SAS® Display Manager System

Introduction

The SAS Display Manager System is one of four methods of operating the SAS System. The other three methods are introduced in Chapter 1, "Essential Concepts." For more information on methods of operating the SAS System, see Chapter 36, "Starting, Running, and Exiting the

SAS System," of *SAS Language and Procedures: Usage, Version 6, First Edition*.

The SAS Display Manager System (display manager) is an interactive, full-screen facility that you view and operate through a series of windows. Because it is an *interactive facility*, within one session you can accomplish a series of tasks rather than just one task. Display manager can be used to prepare and submit a program, view the results, and, if necessary, debug, modify, and resubmit the program. As a *full-screen facility*, it can be used to view, alter, and execute not just one line of SAS statements at a time but more lines than your terminal displays at a time.

The SAS Display Manager System can also be called the *SAS windowing environment* because it consists of a series of windows through which you issue commands to perform a variety of tasks. Although many of the windows are interdependent, each has one or more primary functions and enables you to perform a particular set of tasks. For details about display manager windows, see Chapter 17, "SAS Display Manager Windows."

The SAS Display Manager System consists of numerous commands that must be issued in its windows to accomplish tasks. Some of the commands can be issued in any window, others work in several windows, and others are window-specific. See Table 7.2, "Display Manager Commands—Definitions," for a list of all display manager commands and Chapter 18, "SAS Display Manager Commands," for complete documentation of commands. See "Commands" later in this chapter for instructions on issuing commands.

Capabilities of Display Manager

The SAS Display Manager System can be used to accomplish tasks other than issuing and debugging programs and viewing output. In addition to invoking, managing, and scrolling windows, display manager can do the following:

- customize windows
- search for text
- color windows
- manage libraries
- manage files
- cut, paste, and store text
- perform calculations
- schedule appointments
- use forms
- get help
- allow you to view and change options.

For more information on the SAS Display Manager System, see Chapter 37, "Using the SAS Display Manager System—the Basics," Chapter 38, "Using Commands to Manipulate Your Full-Screen Environment," and Chapter 39, "Mastering Your Environment with Selected Windows," of *SAS Language and Procedures: Usage*.

Relationship to the SAS Text Editor

The SAS Text Editor is used in some display manager windows and by full-screen procedures in other SAS software products, even if display manager has not been invoked.

The commands specific to the text editor are called *text-editing commands*. In addition, the text editor uses many categories of display manager commands. For more information on the SAS Text Editor, see Chapter 8, "SAS Text Editor," and Chapter 19, "SAS Text Editor Commands." Also, see Chapter 38 of *SAS Language and Procedures: Usage*.

SAS Windowing Environment

Display manager is a windowing environment that contains the following windows:

- □ four primary windows (PROGRAM EDITOR, LOG, OUTPUT, and OUTPUT MANAGER)
- □ other display manager windows
- □ requestor windows
- □ the PMENU facility.

Two other features of base SAS software produce windows that can be used with display manager: WINDOW and DISPLAY statements in the DATA step and %WINDOW and %DISPLAY statements in the macro facility. For further information, see Chapter 9, "SAS Language Statements," and *SAS Guide to Macro Processing, Version 6, Second Edition*.

Other windows that are not part of base SAS software can be accessed through and used in display manager. Examples include SAS/FSP windows, such as FSBROWSE, FSEDIT, FSLETTER, FSLIST, FSPRINT, and FSVIEW. Other examples include SAS/GRAPH windows, such as GRAPH, LEGEND, PATTERN, and SYMBOL. For information about these windows, refer to the documentation for SAS/FSP and SAS/GRAPH software.

Definition and Terminology

A conventional display manager window is a resizable, movable object on the display with borders and a name. It is manipulated with the command line, the action bar of the PMENU facility, or the function keys. The command line, in the upper left-hand corner of the window, is where display manager commands are typed to be issued. The action bar of the PMENU facility is a horizontal string of items across the top of the window. Function keys are keys on the keyboard that have been assigned command settings.

Most display manager windows can be opened and closed. Typically, a window is opened with a window-call command and closed with the END command. A window can be open even if it is not visible on the display. Once a window is opened, it remains open until specifically closed, even if it is obscured by other windows.* Only one window can be active at a time. The active window is open and displayed and contains the cursor. When a window is invoked with a window-call command, it is open, displayed, and active. The PROGRAM EDITOR, LOG, and OUTPUT windows are open by default. However, either the OUTPUT or OUTPUT MANAGER window can be closed as long as the other is open.

Note that requestor windows are not conventional display manager windows and, thus, do not have all of the characteristics of conventional windows. See "Requestor Windows" later in this chapter for details.

Primary Display Manager Windows

Display manager contains four primary windows: the PROGRAM EDITOR window, the LOG window, the OUTPUT window, and the OUTPUT MANAGER window. They are considered primary for several reasons. Together, they form the core of display manager as a windowing environment. These windows are closely connected. For example, when a program is issued from the PROGRAM EDITOR window, its output is displayed in the OUTPUT window, and a listing of that output appears in the OUTPUT MANAGER window. Programming statements and SAS System messages are recorded in the LOG window. In addition, while other display manager windows must be opened with a window-call command, the PROGRAM EDITOR window, the LOG window, and the OUTPUT window are open by default. Multiple executions of the NEXT or PREVWIND command activate each of the three windows, starting over among the three windows if other windows are not open. Note that the PROGRAM EDITOR and LOG windows cannot be closed.

PROGRAM EDITOR and LOG Windows

When you invoke display manager, you see the PROGRAM EDITOR and LOG windows by default. In the PROGRAM EDITOR window, you can

- □ enter and edit text, including SAS statements
- □ submit SAS statements
- □ copy an external file into the PROGRAM EDITOR window or copy the contents of the window into an external file
- □ copy a catalog entry into the PROGRAM EDITOR window or copy the contents of the window into a catalog entry.

The LOG window contains the SAS log, which is a record of the current SAS session. A typical log displays

- □ SAS statements issued during the current session
- □ notes, warnings, and error messages
- □ results of DATA step applications
- □ results of some SAS procedures, such as the OPTIONS procedure.

* To determine which windows are open, you can issue the TILE or CASCADE command, which repositions all open windows to make them visible. The RESIZE command returns the display to the window configuration that existed prior to the tiled or cascaded configuration.

Display 7.1 shows an example of the PROGRAM EDITOR and LOG windows.

Display 7.1 *The PROGRAM EDITOR and LOG Windows*

```
LOG
Command ===>

6     data test;
7        input x;
8     cards;

NOTE: The data set WORK.TEST has 4 observations and 1 variables.

13    ;
14    proc print;run;
```

```
PROGRAM EDITOR
Command ===>

00001 data test;
00002    input x;
00003 cards;
00004 2
00005 4
00006 6
```

OUTPUT and OUTPUT MANAGER Windows

Display manager's other primary windows are the OUTPUT and OUTPUT MANAGER windows. The OUTPUT window, also known as the LISTING window, contains output generated by most SAS procedures. Output subsequently generated during a SAS session is appended to the contents of the OUTPUT window.

Each time you execute a procedure, information about the output is added to the OUTPUT MANAGER window, which acts as a directory for the session's output. For each piece of output, the window specifies

- □ the name of the procedure that created it
- □ the order in which it falls, compared to other output
- □ the beginning page number
- □ the output's length in pages
- □ a description using the first 40 characters of any titles specified
- □ an indication that the output has been modified, if it has been.

The OUTPUT and OUTPUT MANAGER windows work together. When new output is generated, it appears in the OUTPUT window and is listed in the OUTPUT MANAGER window. When the OUTPUT window is cleared, the OUTPUT MANAGER window is also cleared.

Either the OUTPUT window or the OUTPUT MANAGER window must be open; both windows can also be open simultaneously. Closing one of the two windows automatically opens the other window if it is not already open. And, if only one window is open, it is displayed when output is generated. By default, the OUTPUT window is open and automatically appears when a procedure that produces output executes; the OUTPUT MANAGER window is closed and must be invoked with a window-call command. To open the OUTPUT window, specify

```
listing on
```

To open the OUTPUT MANAGER window, specify

```
manager on
```

You can toggle the display of the two windows if both are open by specifying either of the following:

```
output

next output
```

To close the OUTPUT window, specify

```
listing off
```

To close the OUTPUT MANAGER window, specify

```
manager off
```

In addition, from the OUTPUT MANAGER window, you can use selection-field commands to view and edit a given piece of output, as well as to file, print, delete, or rename output. Multiple selections can be executed simultaneously on separate pieces of output.

Display 7.2 shows an example of the OUTPUT MANAGER window.

***Display** 7.2* *The OUTPUT MANAGER Window*

```
OUTPUT MANAGER
Command ===>

     Procedure  Page#   Pages       Description

   _ PRINT          1       1       Printing A Column with No Heading
   _ PRINT          2       3       Using PROC PRINT with a BY Statement
   _ PRINT          5       1       Using PROC PRINT with SPLIT= Option
   _ CONTENTS       6       2       Using the CONTENTS Procedure
   _ CONTENTS       8       3       PROC CONTENTS with MEMTYPE= Option
```

Other Display Manager Windows

In addition to the four primary windows already discussed, display manager includes numerous other windows. Along with the four primary windows, these windows are listed alphabetically in Table 7.1. Brief descriptions of the windows, their invocations, and their window-call commands are included.

Table 7.1 *Display Manager Windows*

Window	Description	Invocation
AF	displays windowing applications created by SAS/AF software	AF <*arguments*>
APPOINTMENT	enters, updates, and displays daily calendar appointments	APPOINTMENT <*libref.SAS-data-set* <*start-weekday*> <B>>
CALCULATOR	performs mathematical operations	CALCULATOR
CATALOG	displays a directory of SAS catalog entries and enables you to manage entries	CATALOG <*libref.catalog*>
DIR	displays information about SAS files	DIR <*libref.type*>
FILENAME	displays assigned filerefs with their filenames	FILENAME
FOOTNOTES	enables you to enter, browse, and modify footnotes for output	FOOTNOTES
FORM	specifies printer, text format, and destination for output	FSFORM <*catalog-name.*>*form-name*
HELP	displays help information about the SAS System	HELP <*component-name*>
KEYS	enables you to browse, alter, and save function key settings	KEYS
LIBNAME	displays assigned librefs and their SAS data libraries and engines	LIBNAME
LOG	displays messages and SAS statements for the current SAS session	LOG
NOTEPAD	creates and stores notepads of text	NOTEPAD <*catalog-entry*>
OPTIONS	enables you to view and change some SAS system options	OPTIONS
OUTPUT	displays procedure output	LISTING
OUTPUT MANAGER	provides a directory of current output	MANAGER | MGR
PROGRAM EDITOR	enables you to enter, edit, and submit SAS statements and save source files	PROGRAM | PGM
SETINIT	displays licensed SAS software and expiration dates	SETINIT
SITEINFO	contains site-specific information	SITEINFO
TITLES	enables you to browse, enter, and modify titles for output	TITLES
VAR	displays information about SAS data set variables and their attributes	VAR <*libref.SAS-data-set*>

■ **Host Information** .... For information about host windows, see your SAS Software Consultant or refer to the SAS documentation for your host system. ■

Windows with Global Effect

Although all display manager windows have important functions, the following windows deserve special mention because of their potential to globally affect display manager:

- □ HELP window
- □ KEYS window
- □ OPTIONS window.

The HELP window provides help information about all parts of the SAS System. The KEYS window enables you to browse, alter, and save function key settings. The OPTIONS window enables you to view and change some SAS system options. Later in this chapter, the HELP, KEYS, and OPTIONS windows are discussed in terms of the tasks they perform.

Special Relationships among Display Manager Windows

In addition to the four primary windows, other display manager windows are closely linked because of the kind of information they contain and the functions they serve. The LIBNAME, DIR, CATALOG, and VAR windows are closely linked because a selection you make in one window can trigger the display of information in another, starting with the LIBNAME window and ending with either the VAR or CATALOG window.* The LIBNAME window contains information about all SAS data libraries and their librefs that are defined to the SAS System. The LIBNAME window lists the librefs, engine names, and SAS data library names. Selecting a SAS data library in the LIBNAME window opens the DIR window. The DIR window lists all SAS files contained in the SAS data library selected, their types, and index information. Selecting a SAS file in the DIR window opens the CATALOG window if the file is a catalog and the VAR window if the file is a SAS data set. The CATALOG window shows the entry name, type, and description for each catalog, as well as when the catalog was last updated. The VAR window displays information about the variables of the SAS data set selected, including length, format, informat, key information, and label.

Once these windows are opened in this sequence, continuing to issue the END command, starting from the VAR or CATALOG window, displays first the DIR window and then the LIBNAME window.

See Chapter 17 for complete information about these windows.

Requestor Windows

Requestor windows are windows that the SAS System displays so you can confirm, cancel, or modify an action. They often act as safeguards, for example by preventing you from overwriting the contents of a file. Although you cannot specifically invoke them, requestor windows appear

---

* Note that this approach is not the only way in which to open these windows. You can also use window-call commands to open each window separately.

in response to your actions. You must respond to the request before you can continue your current SAS session.

Display 7.3 shows an example of a requestor window that appears if you attempt to use the FILE command to store the contents of a window in an existing external file.

Display 7.3 *Sample Requestor Window*

```
LOG
Command ===>

    ------------------------------------------------------------
    | WARNING: The file already exists.  Enter R to replace it, |
    | enter A to append to it or C to cancel FILE command.      |
    | _                                                         |
    ------------------------------------------------------------

PROGRAM EDITOR
Command ===>

00001 data a;
00002    input x y z;
00003 2 4 6
00004 ;
00005
00006
```

In this case, you can replace the contents of the external file, append its contents, or cancel the operation. Then, the requestor window is removed, and the SAS System continues as you directed it.

Requestor windows may also appear when

- you issue the attention sequence
- the SAS System has insufficient computer resources to execute a given task
- you receive broadcast messages from your host system
- you attempt to access a nonexistent catalog as you invoke the CATALOG window
- you use the INCLUDE command to bring a file with special characters into a window
- you attempt to access a Version 5 catalog.

PMENU Facility

The *PMENU facility* is a menuing system that replaces the command line as a way to issue commands. The PMENU facility is the default for some windowing environments and an option for others. When it is optional, you can issue the PMENU command to activate the facility across windows in any full-screen environment. Once the PMENU facility is activated, an *action bar* appears containing several *items*. Depending on the host system and terminal, you can manipulate the action bar by placing the cursor on the item you want and pressing ENTER or RETURN, or by using a mouse to point and click. On an action bar that has not been customized, selecting an item displays a *pull-down menu*. The pull-down menu contains a list of choices called menu items. You can select the menu item you want in the same way you can manipulate the action bar.

You can use the PMENU procedure to customize the items on the action bar of the AF and DATA step windows. Items can be customized so they can not only display a pull-down menu but also execute commands or display dialog boxes. For more information about the PMENU procedure, see Chapter 26, "The PMENU Procedure," in *SAS Procedures Guide, Version 6, Third Edition.*

Once you have initially displayed the action bar, you can issue the COMMAND command to return to the command line but only in the active window. You can do this either by pressing a function key or by selecting menu items. Then the COMMAND command can be issued from the command line to reinstate the action bar in that window. Thus, the COMMAND command is a toggle.

■ **Host Information** .... Note that both the implementation and the appearance of the PMENU facility vary by host system and terminal. See your SAS Software Consultant or refer to the SAS documentation for your host system for details.

.... ■

Display 7.4 shows an action bar after an item has been selected.

Display 7.4 *PMENU Facility*

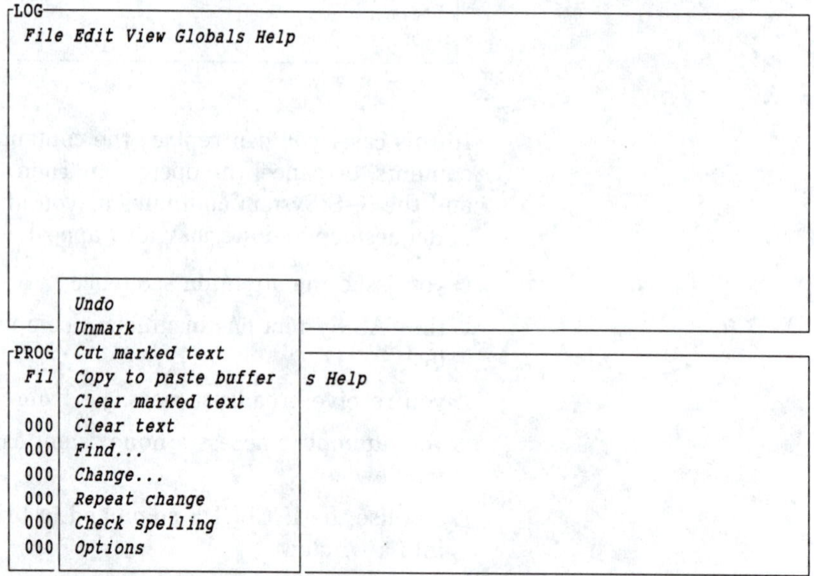

PMENU Action Bar Items

You typically find the following items on the PMENU action bar:

□ The File item enables you to copy and save catalogs and to file and include external files. It also enables you to exit your current window or SAS session.

□ The Edit item enables you to perform editing tasks, as well as to find and change and to cut and paste text.

□ The View item enables you to alter the appearance of the display.

□ The Locals item enables you to submit and recall text in the PROGRAM EDITOR window.

- The Globals item accesses windows and allows you to reinstate the command line.
- The Help item accesses the HELP and KEYS windows.

Dialog Boxes

Dialog boxes are another feature of the PMENU facility that appear in response to selecting a menu item from the pull-down menu. They obtain information, which you supply by filling in a field or by choosing a selection from a group of fields.

Dialog boxes are unique. Unlike requestor windows, you can use the CANCEL command to exit them voluntarily without supplying the information requested. A dialog box requests information in one of the following ways:

- You may be asked to fill in a field. For example, you may need to provide a filename. Fields that accept this type of information are called text fields.
- You may have to select one choice from a list of mutually exclusive choices. For example, you can choose a single color for the background of a window. A group of selections of this type is called a radio box, and each individual selection is called a radio button.
- You may be asked to indicate whether you want to select other choices. For example, you can choose various options by selecting any or all of the listed selections. A selection of this type is called a check box.

Note: The descriptor radio is used because you must turn off one selection as you turn on another much the same as you would a radio.

An example of a dialog box is shown in Display 7.5.

Display 7.5 *Sample Dialog Box*

```
LOG
File Edit View Globals Help

Signon...
    Enter script file name:

    NOTE: Leave blank to use the current setting.

    If you entered a script file name above,
    enter remote= value:

    NOTE: Leave blank to use the current setting.

                       <OK>                        <Cancel>
```

The name of the item associated with a dialog box appears in its upper left-hand corner with an ellipsis appended to it. In addition, dialog boxes have the two push buttons OK and CANCEL automatically built into them. A push button causes an action to occur. In a dialog box, selecting the OK push button causes the actions defined in the dialog box to be completed, and selecting the CANCEL push button cancels the actions in the dialog box.

Commands

In addition to being a windowing environment, display manager includes numerous commands you can issue to perform a variety of tasks. Some display manager commands work in all or most display manager and full-screen windows, and others are window-specific. In addition, text-editing commands that are part of the text editor can be used throughout many of the display manager and full-screen windows.

Types of Commands

In contrast to some text-editing commands that are traditionally issued from the numbered part of the display (and that are, therefore, categorized as line commands), display manager commands are traditionally issued from the command line. Display manager commands are complete words or abbreviations. Some take arguments that modify or complete the command; others do not take arguments.

Commands by Functional Categories

Display manager commands are best remembered by category.

- □ Window-call commands display a window and move the cursor to it, opening and activating it.
- □ Window-management commands help you use windows efficiently.
- □ Window size and position commands alter the size and position of windows on the display.
- □ Scrolling commands set the default vertical and horizontal scroll amounts and allow you to scroll the window's contents.
- □ Color commands change the color and highlighting attributes of selected portions of the window.
- □ Search commands search for and find text strings; some commands change text string contents.
- □ File-management commands control the storage, retrieval, printing, and deletion of files.
- □ Text-store commands mark and store text for cutting and pasting.
- □ Text cut-and-paste commands move or copy marked text into a special storage area called a *paste buffer* or move stored text from a paste buffer into a window.

□ The remaining categories of commands are window-specific, enabling each window to function:

- □ Appointment (APPOINTMENT window only)
- □ Calculator (CALCULATOR window only)
- □ Forms (FORM window only)
- □ Help (HELP window only)
- □ Notepad (NOTEPAD window only)
- □ Output (LOG and OUTPUT windows only)
- □ Program (PROGRAM EDITOR window only).

Table 7.2 defines and categorizes all of the display manager commands.

Table 7.2 *Display Manager Commands—Definitions*

Category	Command	Definition
Appointment	ADD	Adds a new line to the Time and Appointments fields
	PRINT ALL	Prints the days in the current month
Calculator	DECIMAL	Specifies the number of decimal places
	HEX	Turns hex mode on or off
	MEMCLEAR	Clears the memory register
	MEMMINUS	Subtracts register amount from the memory register
	MEMPLUS	Adds register amount to the memory register
	MEMRECALL	Puts memory contents into the primary operand area
	TAPE	Turns the tape display on and off
Color	COLOR	Changes the color and highlighting of selected portions of a window
File management	COPY	Copies a catalog entry into a window
	DELETE	Deletes a catalog entry
	FILE	Writes the contents of a window to an external file
	FORMNAME	Sets the default form name
	FREE	Frees the print file
	INCLUDE	Copies the contents of an external file into a window
	PRINT	Prints a file using the FORM subsystem
	PRTFILE	Sets the default print file
	SAVE	Writes the contents of a window to a catalog entry

(continued)

Table 7.2 *(continued)*

Category	Command	Definition
Forms	DES	Displays or changes the form's description
	=*n*	Displays a FORM window by numeric designation
	NEXTSCR	Scrolls to the next FORM window
	PREVSCR	Scrolls to the previous FORM window
Help	=X	Exits the HELP window
Notepad	DESCRIPTION	Assigns a description to be saved with the notepad
	NTITLE	Changes the displayed title of the NOTEPAD window
Output	AUTOSCROLL	Controls the display of lines in the LOG and OUTPUT windows
	LINESIZE	Sets or displays the line size of the active window
	PAGE	Specifies whether page breaks are honored
	PAGESIZE	Sets or displays the page size of the active window
Program	RECALL	Recalls submitted SAS statements
	SUBMIT	Submits SAS statements for execution
	SUBTOP	Submits the top *n* lines for execution
Scrolling	BACKWARD	Scrolls backward
	BOTTOM	Scrolls to the bottom line
	FORWARD	Scrolls forward
	HSCROLL	Specifies the default horizontal scroll amount
	LEFT	Scrolls left
	n	Scrolls to a designated line
	RIGHT	Scrolls right
	TOP	Scrolls to the top line
	VSCROLL	Specifies the default scroll amount forward or backward
Search	BFIND	Searches for the previous occurrence of a character string
	CHANGE	Finds and changes one character string to another
	FIND	Searches for a specified character string
	RCHANGE	Repeats the previous CHANGE command
	RFIND	Continues the search initiated with a FIND or BFIND command

(continued)

Table 7.2 *(continued)*

Category	Command	Definition
Text cut-and-paste	CUT	Removes marked text from the current window and stores it in a paste buffer
	PASTE	Inserts text stored in a paste buffer at the cursor location
Text-store	MARK	Identifies text you want to manipulate
	PCLEAR	Clears a paste buffer
	PLIST	Displays a list of current paste buffers in the LOG window
	SMARK	Identifies an area to be copied with the STORE command
	STORE	Copies marked text in a window and stores it in a paste buffer
	UNMARK	Returns marked text to normal status
Window-call	AF	Invokes the AF window
	APPOINTMENT	Invokes the APPOINTMENT window
	CALCULATOR	Invokes the CALCULATOR window
	CATALOG	Invokes the CATALOG window
	DIR	Invokes the DIR window
	FILENAME	Invokes the FILENAME window
	FOOTNOTES	Invokes the FOOTNOTES window
	FSFORM	Invokes the FORM window
	HELP	Invokes the HELP window
	KEYS	Invokes the KEYS window
	LIBNAME	Invokes the LIBNAME window
	LISTING	Invokes the OUTPUT window
	LOG	Invokes the LOG window
	MANAGER	Invokes the OUTPUT MANAGER window
	NOTEPAD	Invokes the NOTEPAD window
	OPTIONS	Invokes the OPTIONS window
	OUTPUT	Invokes either the OUTPUT window or the OUTPUT MANAGER window
	PROGRAM	Invokes the PROGRAM EDITOR window
	SETINIT	Invokes the SETINIT window
	SITEINFO	Invokes the SITEINFO window
	TITLES	Invokes the TITLES window
	VAR	Invokes the VAR window
Window-management	AUTOPOP	Determines whether a window is displayed when lines are written to it
	BYE	Ends a SAS session
	CANCEL	Cancels changes in a window and removes it from the display
	CLEAR	Clears the window's contents or the display of settings

(continued)

Table 7.2 *(continued)*

Category	Command	Definition
	COMMAND	Reactivates or deactivates the PMENU facility in the active window
	END	Closes a window and removes it from the display
	ENDSAS	Ends a SAS session
	HOME	Moves the cursor to the command line
	ICON	Makes the active window a smaller version of itself
	KEYDEF	Redefines or identifies a function key setting outside the KEYS window
	NEXT	Moves the cursor to the next window, activating it
	PMENU	Activates or deactivates the PMENU facility for all windows
	PREVCMD	Recalls the last command issued
	PREVWIND	Moves the cursor to the previous window, activating it
	PURGE	Removes nonshared function key settings among different terminals
	RESHOW	Rebuilds the windows displayed
	SCROLLBAR	Activates or deactivates scroll bars
	X	Enters host system mode and enables a command to be issued
	ZOOM	Causes the active window to fill the display
Window size and position	CASCADE	Creates a layered display of all open windows
	RESIZE	Returns to the configuration prior to the tiled or cascaded pattern
	TILE	Creates a mosaic of all open windows
	WDEF	Redefines the active window
	WSAVE	Saves command settings in the window(s)

Table 7.3 is a grid that shows the display manager commands and the windows in which they work.

Table 7.3
Display Manager Commands—Valid Windows

Windows ▶ ▼ Commands	AF	APPOINTMENT	CALCULATOR	CATALOG	DIR	FILENAME	FOOTNOTES	FORM	HELP	KEYS	LIBNAME	LOG	NOTEPAD	OPTIONS	OUTPUT	OUTPUT MANAGER	PROGRAM EDITOR	SETINIT	SITEINFO	TITLES	VAR	BROWSE MODE	EDIT MODE
ADD		■																					
AF	■	■	■	■	■	■	■	■	■	■	■	■	■	■	■	■	■	■	■	■	■	■	■
APPOINTMENT	■	■	■	■	■	■	■	■	■	■	■	■	■	■	■	■	■	■	■	■	■	■	■
AUTOSCROLL												■			■								
AUTOPOP									■			■			■	■	■						
BACKWARD	■	■		■	■	■	■	■	■	■	■	■	■	■	■	■	■	■	■	■	■	■	■
BFIND	■			■	■	■	■	■		■	■	■	■	■	■	■	■			■	■	■	■
BOTTOM	■			■	■	■	■	■		■	■	■	■	■	■	■	■	■	■	■	■	■	■
BYE	■	■	■	■	■	■	■	■	■	■	■	■	■	■	■	■	■	■	■	■	■	■	■
CALCULATOR	■	■	■	■	■	■	■	■	■	■	■	■	■	■	■	■	■	■	■	■	■	■	■
CANCEL	■	■	■	■	■	■	■	■	■	■	■		■	■	■					■	■	■	■
CASCADE	■	■	■	■	■	■	■	■		■	■	■	■	■	■	■	■	■	■	■	■	■	■
CATALOG	■	■	■	■	■	■	■	■	■	■	■	■	■	■	■	■	■	■	■	■	■	■	■
CHANGE										■			■				■						■
CLEAR	■	■	■	■	■	■	■	■	■	■	■	■	■	■	■	■	■			■	■		■
CLEAR LOG	■	■	■	■	■	■	■	■	■	■	■	■	■	■	■	■	■			■	■	■	■
CLEAR MASK	■	■	■					■	■								■					■	
CLEAR OUTPUT	■	■	■	■	■	■	■	■	■	■	■	■	■	■	■	■	■			■	■	■	■
CLEAR PGM	■	■	■	■	■	■	■	■	■	■	■	■	■	■	■	■	■			■	■	■	■
CLEAR RECALL	■	■	■	■	■	■	■	■	■	■	■	■	■	■	■	■	■			■	■	■	■
CLEAR TEXT	■	■	■					■	■			■	■		■		■						
COLOR	■	■	■	■	■	■	■	■	■	■	■	■	■	■	■	■	■	■	■	■	■	■	■
COLOR BACKGROUND	■	■	■	■	■	■	■	■	■	■	■	■	■	■	■	■	■	■	■	■	■	■	■
COLOR BANNER	■	■	■	■	■	■	■	■	■	■	■	■	■	■	■	■	■	■	■	■	■	■	■

(continued)

Table 7.3
(continued)

Windows ▶ / ▼ Commands	AF	APPOINTMENT	CALCULATOR	CATALOG	DIR	FILENAME	FOOTNOTES	FORM	HELP	KEYS	LIBNAME	LOG	NOTEPAD	OPTIONS	OUTPUT	OUTPUT MANAGER	PROGRAM EDITOR	SETINIT	SITEINFO	TITLES	VAR	BROWSE MODE	EDIT MODE
COLOR BORDER	■	■	■	■	■	■	■	■	■	■	■	■	■	■	■	■	■	■	■	■	■	■	■
COLOR BYLINE															■								
COLOR COMMAND	■	■	■	■	■	■	■	■	■	■	■	■	■	■	■	■	■	■	■	■	■	■	■
COLOR DATA												■			■								
COLOR ERROR												■			■								
COLOR FOOTNOTE															■								
COLOR HEADER															■								
COLOR MENU	■	■	■	■	■	■	■	■	■	■	■	■	■	■	■	■	■	■	■	■	■	■	■
COLOR MENUBORDER	■	■	■	■	■	■	■	■	■	■	■	■	■	■	■	■	■	■	■	■	■	■	■
COLOR MESSAGE	■	■	■	■	■	■	■	■	■	■	■	■	■	■	■	■	■	■	■	■	■	■	■
COLOR MTEXT													■										■
COLOR NOTES												■											
COLOR NUMS								■									■						
COLOR SCROLLBAR	■	■	■	■	■	■	■	■	■	■	■	■	■	■	■	■	■	■	■	■	■	■	■
COLOR SOURCE												■											
COLOR TEXT				■	■	■	■	■		■	■		■	■		■	■	■	■	■	■	■	■
COLOR TITLE															■								
COLOR WARNING												■											
COMMAND	■	■	■	■	■	■	■	■	■	■	■	■	■	■	■	■	■	■	■	■	■	■	■
COPY				■						■		■					■						■
CUT													■				■						■
DECIMAL			■																				
DELETE		■		■									■										

(continued)

Table 7.3
(continued)

Windows ▶ / ▼ Commands	AF	APPOINTMENT	CALCULATOR	CATALOG	DIR	FILENAME	FOOTNOTES	FORM	HELP	KEYS	LIBNAME	LOG	NOTEPAD	OPTIONS	OUTPUT	OUTPUT MANAGER	PROGRAM EDITOR	SETINIT	SITEINFO	TITLES	VAR	BROWSE MODE	EDIT MODE
DES								■															
DESCRIPTION													■										
DIR	■	■	■	■	■	■	■	■	■	■	■	■	■	■	■	■	■	■	■	■	■	■	■
END	■	■	■	■	■	■	■	■	■	■	■	■	■	■	■	■	■	■	■	■	■	■	■
ENDSAS	■	■	■	■	■	■	■	■	■	■	■	■	■	■	■	■	■	■	■	■	■	■	■
=n								■															
=X									■														
FILE												■	■		■		■					■	■
FILENAME	■	■	■	■	■	■	■	■	■	■	■	■	■	■	■	■	■	■	■	■	■	■	■
FIND	■			■	■	■	■	■		■	■	■	■	■	■	■	■			■	■	■	■
FOOTNOTES	■	■	■	■	■	■	■	■	■	■	■	■	■	■	■	■	■	■	■	■	■	■	■
FORMNAME	■							■	■			■	■		■		■					■	■
FORWARD	■	■		■	■	■	■	■	■	■	■	■	■	■	■	■	■	■	■	■	■	■	■
FREE		■	■					■				■	■		■	■	■					■	■
FSFORM	■	■	■	■	■	■	■	■	■	■	■	■	■	■	■	■	■	■	■	■	■	■	■
HELP	■	■	■	■	■	■	■	■	■	■	■	■	■	■	■	■	■	■	■	■	■	■	■
HEX			■																				
HOME	■	■	■	■	■	■	■	■	■	■	■	■	■	■	■	■	■	■	■	■	■	■	■
HSCROLL	■			■	■	■	■	■		■	■	■	■	■	■	■	■	■	■	■	■	■	■
ICON	■	■	■	■	■	■	■	■	■	■	■	■	■	■	■	■	■	■	■	■	■	■	■
INCLUDE													■				■						
KEYDEF	■	■	■	■	■	■	■	■	■	■	■	■	■	■	■	■	■	■	■	■	■	■	■
KEYS	■	■	■	■	■	■	■	■	■	■	■	■	■	■	■	■	■	■	■	■	■	■	■
LEFT	■	■		■	■	■	■	■	■	■	■	■	■	■	■	■	■	■	■	■	■	■	■
LIBNAME	■	■	■	■	■	■	■	■	■	■	■	■	■	■	■	■	■	■	■	■	■	■	■
LINESIZE												■			■								
LISTING	■	■	■	■	■	■	■	■	■	■	■	■	■	■	■	■	■	■	■	■	■	■	■
LOG	■	■	■	■	■	■	■	■	■	■	■	■	■	■	■	■	■	■	■	■	■	■	■
MANAGER	■	■	■	■	■	■	■	■	■	■	■	■	■	■	■	■	■	■	■	■	■	■	■
MARK		■	■	■	■	■	■		■	■	■	■	■	■	■	■	■	■	■	■	■	■	■
MEMCLEAR			■																				
MEMMINUS			■																				

(continued)

Table 7.3
(continued)

Windows ▶ / ▼ Commands	AF	APPOINTMENT	CALCULATOR	CATALOG	DIR	FILENAME	FOOTNOTES	FORM	HELP	KEYS	LIBNAME	LOG	NOTEPAD	OPTIONS	OUTPUT	OUTPUT MANAGER	PROGRAM EDITOR	SETINIT	SITEINFO	TITLES	VAR	BROWSE MODE	EDIT MODE
MEMPLUS			■																				
MEMRECALL			■																				
n	■			■	■	■	■	■	■	■	■	■	■	■	■	■	■			■	■	■	■
NEXT	■	■	■	■	■	■	■	■	■	■	■	■	■	■	■	■	■	■	■	■	■	■	■
NEXTSCR								■															
NOTEPAD	■	■	■	■	■	■	■	■	■	■	■	■	■	■	■	■	■	■	■	■	■	■	■
NTITLE													■										
OPTIONS	■	■	■	■	■	■	■	■	■	■	■	■	■	■	■	■	■	■	■	■	■	■	■
OUTPUT	■	■	■	■	■	■	■	■	■	■	■	■	■	■	■	■	■	■	■	■	■	■	■
PAGE															■								
PAGESIZE															■								
PASTE													■				■						■
PCLEAR				■	■	■	■		■	■	■	■	■	■	■	■	■	■	■	■	■	■	■
PROGRAM	■	■	■	■	■	■	■	■	■	■	■	■	■	■	■	■	■	■	■	■	■	■	■
PLIST				■	■	■	■		■	■	■	■	■	■	■	■	■	■	■	■	■	■	■
PMENU	■	■	■	■	■	■	■	■	■	■	■	■	■	■	■	■	■	■	■	■	■	■	■
PREVCMD	■	■	■	■	■	■	■	■	■	■	■	■	■	■	■	■	■	■	■	■	■	■	■
PREVSCR								■															
PREVWIND	■	■	■	■	■	■	■	■	■	■	■	■	■	■	■	■	■	■	■	■	■	■	■
PRINT		■	■									■	■		■		■					■	■
PRINT ALL		■																					
PRTFILE	■	■	■					■	■			■	■		■		■					■	■
PURGE										■													
RCHANGE										■			■				■						■
RECALL	■																■						
RESHOW	■	■	■	■	■	■	■	■	■	■	■	■	■	■	■	■	■	■	■	■	■	■	■
RESIZE	■	■	■	■	■	■	■	■		■	■	■	■	■	■	■	■	■	■	■	■	■	■
RFIND	■			■	■	■	■	■		■	■	■	■	■	■	■	■			■	■	■	■
RIGHT	■	■		■	■	■	■	■	■	■	■	■	■	■	■	■	■	■	■	■	■	■	■
SAVE	■									■		■	■		■		■	■				■	■

(continued)

Table 7.3
(continued)

Windows ▶ / ▼ Commands	AF	APPOINTMENT	CALCULATOR	CATALOG	DIR	FILENAME	FOOTNOTES	FORM	HELP	KEYS	LIBNAME	LOG	NOTEPAD	OPTIONS	OUTPUT	OUTPUT MANAGER	PROGRAM EDITOR	SETINIT	SITEINFO	TITLES	VAR	BROWSE MODE	EDIT MODE
SCROLLBAR	■	■	■	■	■	■	■	■	■	■	■	■	■	■	■	■	■	■	■	■	■	■	■
SETINIT	■	■	■	■	■	■	■	■	■	■	■	■	■	■	■	■	■	■	■	■	■	■	■
SITEINFO	■	■	■	■	■	■	■	■	■	■	■	■	■	■	■	■	■	■	■	■	■	■	■
SMARK			■	■	■	■	■	■		■	■	■	■	■	■	■	■	■	■	■	■	■	■
STORE			■	■	■	■	■	■	■	■	■	■	■	■	■	■	■	■	■	■	■	■	■
SUBMIT																	■						
SUBTOP																	■						
TAPE			■																				
TILE	■	■	■	■	■	■	■	■		■	■	■	■	■	■	■	■	■	■	■	■	■	■
TITLES	■	■	■	■	■	■	■	■	■	■	■	■	■	■	■	■	■	■	■	■	■	■	■
TOP	■			■	■	■	■	■		■	■	■	■	■	■	■	■	■	■	■	■	■	■
UNMARK			■	■	■	■	■	■	■	■	■	■	■	■	■	■	■	■	■	■	■	■	■
VAR	■	■	■	■	■	■	■	■	■	■	■	■	■	■	■	■	■	■	■	■	■	■	■
VSCROLL	■			■	■	■	■	■		■	■	■	■	■	■	■	■	■	■	■	■	■	■
WDEF	■			■	■	■	■			■	■	■	■	■	■	■	■	■	■	■	■	■	■
WSAVE				■	■	■	■			■	■	■	■	■	■	■	■	■	■	■	■	■	■
X	■	■	■	■	■	■	■	■	■	■	■	■	■	■	■	■	■	■	■	■	■	■	■
ZOOM	■	■	■	■	■	■	■	■	■	■	■	■	■	■	■	■	■	■	■	■	■	■	■

Selection-Field Commands

In addition to the commands listed in Tables 7.2 and 7.3, many display manager windows include selection-field commands. These commands are one-letter commands, which vary among windows in availability and functionality. However, selection-field commands enable you to

- □ invoke an EDIT window
- □ browse entries or observations
- □ rename or delete entries, observations, files, or descriptions
- □ cancel or verify the rename or delete process
- □ select an entry
- □ save or print output.

Selection-field commands are documented by window in Chapter 17.

Behavior of Commands in Different Windows

A few commands behave differently, depending on the window in which they are used. These differences are documented by window in Chapter 17.

Command Execution

Display manager commands can be executed in one of three ways:

□ from the command line

□ with function keys

□ through the PMENU facility.

Whether you use the command line or the PMENU facility may depend on which is the default at your site, whether you can change the default, and your preference. Function keys offer a convenient way to issue commands. Note that some commands can be interrupted with the attention sequence.

■ **Host Information** ....

Whether the PMENU facility or the command line is the default depends on your site and host system. See your SAS Software Consultant for information specific to your site or refer to the SAS documentation for your host system.

.... ■

Executing Commands from the Command Line

All display manager commands can be executed from the command line by typing the command on the command line and pressing ENTER or RETURN. As mentioned, some commands take arguments that modify or complete the command. Some arguments are optional and others are required. Other commands take no arguments. Complete syntax information is provided for each display manager command in Chapter 18.

Many commands function like on/off switches and take ON and OFF arguments. For example, you can issue the ZOOM command by specifying

```
zoom on
```

The window enlarges to fill the display. You return the window to its previous size by specifying

```
zoom off
```

You can achieve the same effect by issuing the command with no argument. The first time you issue the command, it reverses the current setting. The second time you issue the command, it returns to the previous setting. This on/off switch effect is known as a *toggle*. When you issue a command as a toggle, the SAS System generates a note telling you the current setting.

Executing Commands with Function Keys

All display manager commands can also be executed with function keys, whether the command line or the PMENU facility is active. The KEYS window lists the current definitions for all function keys; the current definitions remain in effect until you change them.

Function keys are convenient for issuing the most commonly used commands and for commands whose effects hinge on cursor position. Examples of the latter include entire command categories, such as the text cut-and-paste commands and the text-store commands. You can also use function keys to

□ issue multiple commands

□ insert text strings

□ insert comments in programs.

Display 7.6 shows the KEYS window with the first three function key settings altered accordingly. With one keystroke, the setting of the first function key issues three commands. The setting of the second function key inserts a text string, and the setting of the third function key inserts a comment in the program.

Display 7.6 *Customized Function Key Settings*

```
LOG                              KEYS <DMKEYS>
Command ===>                     Command ===>

                                 Key    Definition

                                 F1     pgm; zoom on; find print
                                 F2     ~MORE INFORMATION NEEDED
                                 F3     ~/* RAWDATA IN APPENDIX A */
                                 F4     cut
                                 F5     paste
                                 F6     store
                                 F7     prevwind
                                 F8     next
                                 F9     pmenu
PROGRAM EDITOR                   F10    scrollbar
Command ===>                     F11    keys
                                 F12    undo
00001                            F13    help
00002                            F14    zoom
00003                            F15    zoom off; submit
00004                            F16    pgm; recall
00005                            F17    rfind
00006                            F18    rchange
```

Suppose you press a function key defined to issue a command other than a line command, and the command line already contains text. The key's definition is inserted before the text on the command line, which can be an advantage. For example, if you want to continue to change the background color of your display, you can define a function key as COLOR BACK and type the color on the command line. For example, by typing RED on the command line, you are actually specifying COLOR BACK RED.

You can change any key setting by typing over the definition for a key in the KEYS window; the new definition takes effect immediately.

Issue the CANCEL command to cancel changes you made in that session of the KEYS window since the most recent execution of the END command. All changes are canceled, the window is closed, and the previously invoked window is displayed. Issue the SAVE or END command to save all changes. In the KEYS window, type over a definition and issue the END or SAVE command with no argument to store the settings in your default catalog.

You can create another set of customized key settings by specifying any valid SAS name as an argument to the SAVE command. The key settings are stored under the specified name. A message indicates that the function key settings are saved. See the KEYS window in Chapter 17 for more information about saving key settings.

For added efficiency, issue the KEYDEF command to change a function key setting outside the KEYS window for the duration of your current SAS session. The new setting takes effect immediately. For example, specify the following to change function key 24 to the AUTOPOP command:

```
keydef f24 autopop
```

To determine the setting of a function key, issue the KEYDEF command with the *key-name* argument only. The SAS System issues a message identifying the definition of the function key you specified.

■ **Host Information** .... The names of function keys vary by terminal. For details, see your SAS Software Consultant or refer to your host documentation. ■

Executing Commands with the PMENU Facility

You can use the PMENU facility to execute commands in addition to using function keys and instead of using the command line. The PMENU facility is the default for some windowing environments and an option for others. As the default, the PMENU facility's action bar appears automatically. When the PMENU facility is optional, issuing the PMENU command replaces the command line with an action bar across all windows in any full-screen environment. Commands are issued in one of the following ways:

□ by moving the cursor to an item on the action bar or a menu item on the pull-down menu and pressing ENTER or RETURN

□ by using a mouse to point at an item on the action bar or a menu item on the pull-down menu and click.

Once you have displayed the action bar, you can issue the COMMAND command to reinstate the command line in the active window only. Do this either by pressing a function key or by selecting a menu item. The COMMAND command is then executed from the command line to reinstate the action bar; thus, the COMMAND command is a toggle.

For more information on the PMENU facility, see "PMENU Facility" earlier in this chapter and Chapter 26 in *SAS Procedures Guide.*

Special Features

The SAS System has special features that enable you to

□ interrupt the execution of some commands

□ issue host system commands during a SAS session.

Interrupting Execution of Commands

You can use the attention sequence to interrupt execution of the following display manager commands:*

COPY	RECALL
FILE	SAVE
INCLUDE	SUBMIT
PRINT	SUBTOP

After the attention sequence executes, a requestor window appears to instruct you how to proceed. For example, interrupting the SUBMIT command can generate the following message:

```
Press Y to cancel submitted statements, N to continue.
```

■ **Host Information** .... The attention sequence varies by host system and terminal. It may be one key press, two keys pressed simultaneously, or a sequence of two or more key presses. See your SAS Software Consultant or refer to the SAS documentation for your host system for details. ■

Executing Host System Commands from a SAS Session

Use the X command to execute host system commands during a SAS session. The X command enables you to return to your host environment without ending your SAS session. Issuing the X command with the appropriate host system command returns you directly to your host environment. Issuing it without specifying an argument puts you into a host system submode. In this submode, you can issue host system commands or return to your SAS session. A message appears immediately after you issue the X command telling you how to return to your SAS session.

■ **Host Information** .... The commands used with the X command, both the host commands and the commands to return to a SAS session, vary by host system. See your SAS Software Consultant or refer to the SAS documentation for your host system for details. ■

SAS Display Manager System Tasks

Display manager is a diverse windowing environment in which you can accomplish a variety of tasks. Some of these tasks are discussed in this section; note that they are not necessarily organized by command category or separated by windows. For complete reference information, see the documentation for individual windows in Chapter 17 and the documentation for individual display manager commands in Chapter 18, "SAS Display Manager Commands."

* Except for the FILE command, the attention sequence cannot be used to interrupt these commands in the full-screen windows of SAS/AF, SAS/FSP, and SAS/GRAPH software.

Invoking Windows

Windows are invoked and activated through window-call commands, which are either the names or aliases of windows. They are also invoked by

- □ using the PMENU facility
- □ issuing the NEXT or PREVWIND command (for windows that have already been opened)
- □ in some cases, issuing a selection-field command in another window.

Managing Windows

A number of commands are used to manage windows. Commands such as END, BYE, and ENDSAS close a window or exit a SAS session. In some windows, the CANCEL command cancels an action and closes the window. The NEXT command activates the next open window, and the PREVWIND command activates the previous open window. The ZOOM command either enlarges a window to fill the display or returns it to its previous size. The AUTOPOP command, which is used as a toggle, determines whether a window is displayed when lines are written to it.

The KEYDEF command changes a function key setting for the duration of a SAS session. The PURGE command, which is executed in the KEYS window only, removes all nonshared function key names from different terminals.

The SCROLLBAR command activates scroll bars, which are tools to control vertical and horizontal scrolling. The ICON command makes the active window a smaller version of itself but does not display the window's contents.

Scrolling

The scrolling commands enable you either to set the default vertical or horizontal scroll amount or to implement scrolling. The HSCROLL and VSCROLL commands set the horizontal and vertical scrolling defaults. The BACKWARD, FORWARD, LEFT, and RIGHT commands move the contents of the window vertically or horizontally. With these four commands, you can scroll the default amount set by the HSCROLL or VSCROLL command, or you can override the default by specifying an argument. The *n*, TOP, and BOTTOM commands move the cursor to a specific location in the window rather than in a general direction. The *n* command moves the cursor to the line specified, the TOP command scrolls to the top line in the window, and the BOTTOM command scrolls to the bottom line in the window.

Customizing Windows

Several commands enable you to customize a window. The WSAVE command saves the current configuration of a window beyond the current SAS session. The WDEF command resizes the active window by specifying a new starting row and column and the number of rows and columns in the window. The CASCADE command creates a layered display of all open windows, and the TILE command creates a mosaic of all open windows. The RESIZE command returns the display to the window configuration that existed before you issued the CASCADE or TILE command.

■ **Host Information** .... All host systems have commands that enable you to move, shrink, and enlarge windows. See your SAS Software Consultant or refer to the SAS documentation for your host system for details on these commands. ■

Searching for Text

You can search for, find, and change text strings in most windows by using the following group of commands, known as search commands:

BFIND	RCHANGE
CHANGE	RFIND
FIND	

If the search process reaches the last occurrence of the text string in the window, the SAS System issues a message indicating that there are no more occurrences of the text string.

For greatest efficiency, the search commands can be used together. The CHANGE and RCHANGE commands are often used together because the RCHANGE command continues to change the character string specified in the previous CHANGE command. The CHANGE command can also be used with the RFIND and RCHANGE commands.

Cutting, Pasting, and Storing Text

With display manager, SAS/AF software, and SAS/FSP software, you can cut, paste, and store text in windows and from one window to another. By marking text (parts of lines, entire lines, or blocks of text), you can copy information from one window to another.

■ **Host Information** .... In addition, on some host systems you can cut and paste text across window boundaries using the SMARK command. See the SMARK command in Chapter 18. ■

A paste buffer is a temporary storage location that holds the contents of text stored with the STORE or CUT command. There is one default paste buffer, named DEFAULT, but you can specify other buffers by naming them in the CUT and STORE commands using the BUFFER= option. The number of paste buffers you can have in one session depends on the limitations of your host. The contents of a paste buffer remain in effect only for the current working SAS session.

Note: The CUT command is used only in windows that permit editing, such as the PROGRAM EDITOR and NOTEPAD windows in display manager and the SAS procedure windows that use the edit feature of the text editor.

Basic Commands

The commands listed below form the core of the text cut-and-paste and text-store features.

CUT	PLIST
MARK	SMARK
PASTE	STORE
PCLEAR	UNMARK

See Chapter 18 for detailed descriptions of these commands.

The MARK command enables you to mark text inside scrollable areas of the display in order to find and change text or to cut or store text in a paste buffer. The UNMARK command returns marked text to normal status, removing any highlighting that resulted when you marked the text. The SMARK command, a host-specific command, enables you to mark text across window boundaries in nonscrollable portions of the display. Text marked with the SMARK command cannot be cut with the CUT command but can be stored in a paste buffer using the STORE command.

The STORE and CUT commands are similar. The STORE command copies the marked text into the paste buffer but leaves the original text intact and unmarked. You can use the MARK and STORE commands in all windows. However, in some windows you cannot mark an area larger than the current display. If you need to mark and store more than one display's worth of text, use the APPEND argument in consecutive STORE commands. The CUT command deletes marked text from the window and copies it into the paste buffer.

The PASTE command inserts text that you stored in a paste buffer with the CUT or STORE command. When you paste text into windows that use the text editor, all the text stored in the paste buffer is inserted. The PASTE command is also used to paste stored text into input fields in SAS windows that do not use the text editor but that contain input fields. These include windows such as the KEYS and TITLE windows as well as many SAS/FSP windows. In this case, only the first line of the paste buffer is inserted.

You can view the names of paste buffers in the SAS log by using the PLIST command. Remember that the contents of paste buffers used during a single SAS session are cleared when you end the session. You can clear the contents of paste buffers by issuing the PCLEAR command.

Using the Cut-and-Paste and Text-Store Commands

Many of the cut-and-paste and text-store commands include arguments with which you specify the way you want to store text, where you want to store text, and how you want to paste text. See the individual descriptions of the display manager cut-and-paste and text-store commands in Chapter 18 for details.

You can issue cut-and-paste and text-store commands from the command line or by using function keys. It is often effective to use a combination of function keys and command-line specifications. See "Executing Commands with Function Keys" earlier in this chapter for details.

Obtaining Help Information

Information about the SAS System is available through the HELP window, which is an online menu-driven facility that contains help information about all products within the SAS System. Its primary window includes a menu for you to identify the part of the SAS System for which you want information. You can use the following approaches to access the HELP window:

□ Access the primary menu for the HELP window by issuing the HELP command from one of the three primary display manager windows open by default: PROGRAM EDITOR, LOG, and OUTPUT. From that menu, you can request information for SAS software procedures, windows, and other components of SAS software.*

□ Access a specific HELP window that contains information about a particular component of SAS software by issuing the HELP command followed by the name of the component.

□ Directly access a specific HELP window that contains information about a window, other than about the PROGRAM EDITOR, LOG, and OUTPUT windows, by issuing the HELP command from that window.

The primary window contains the following categories of help information from which you can select specific information:

□ data management

□ report writing

□ graphics

□ tutorial

□ modeling and analysis tools

□ utilities

□ SAS language

□ SAS global commands

□ SAS windows

□ host information.

In addition, an index is provided for your convenience. To select an item, move the cursor to the category you want and press ENTER or RETURN, or use a mouse to point and click.

Viewing and Changing Options

Although SAS system options can be set as you invoke the SAS System, you can change the settings of many system options within display manager in one of the following ways:**

□ submit an OPTIONS statement from the PROGRAM EDITOR window

□ use the OPTIONS window to change option settings.

The OPTIONS window displays the current settings for system options. Type over the value in the Value column of the window. The new settings take effect as soon as you press ENTER or RETURN. Note that the form of the values in the OPTIONS window differs from the form of the values

---

* Components of SAS software for which you can obtain help information include procedures, windows, product names, statements, CALL routines, data set options, and SAS system options. For information on obtaining help for a specific component, see the header block for that component in the appropriate chapter in this book.

** Note that only portable options are displayed and can be changed in the OPTIONS window. You must use the OPTIONS statement to set host options and the OPTIONS procedure to view the settings.

in OPTIONS statements. For example, in the OPTIONS window, DATE is listed as either on or off. In an OPTIONS statement, DATE takes the forms shown in the following statements:

□ `options date;`

□ `options nodate;`

Settings remain in effect for the duration of the SAS session or until you change them again, either in the OPTIONS window or in an OPTIONS statement. You can issue the CANCEL command to cancel changes made while the window is still open.

For more information about options, see Chapter 3, "Components of the SAS Language," and Chapter 16, "SAS System Options."

Programming with Commands

The programming commands work only in the PROGRAM EDITOR window. The SUBMIT command submits all SAS statements in the PROGRAM EDITOR window.

▶ ***Caution:*** *The SAS System always attempts to execute text submitted by the SUBMIT command.*

If you inadvertently issue the SUBMIT command when the PROGRAM EDITOR window contains text other than SAS statements, the SAS System attempts to execute whatever is submitted, which may generate numerous error messages.

By default, the SUBTOP command submits the top line of statements, and the RECALL command returns the most recently submitted statements to the PROGRAM EDITOR window. Both the SUBTOP and RECALL commands take numeric arguments.

Managing Files

Display manager provides two mechanisms for managing files:

□ file-management commands

□ windows.

Using Commands

The FILE command enables you to copy the contents of a window into an external file; conversely, the INCLUDE command enables you to copy the contents of an external file into a window. Both commands have arguments that enable you to replace either the window or file contents. Additionally, the FILE command has an argument that appends the window contents to the end of the file. The FILE command generates a requestor window that prevents you from inadvertently overwriting the contents of a file.

Similar to the FILE and INCLUDE commands are the SAVE and COPY commands, which function in the same way but handle catalog entries instead of external files. The COPY command copies a catalog entry into a window, and the SAVE command saves a window's contents to a catalog entry.

Other file-management commands include the PRTFILE command, which sets the default print file; the PRINT command, which prints a file using the FORM subsystem; and the FORMNAME command, which sets the default names of forms.

Using Windows

The LIBNAME window displays information about SAS data libraries, their librefs, and their engines. From the LIBNAME window, you can select a libref, which activates the DIR window. The DIR window not only includes a listing of SAS files, their types, and their index status, but also enables you to browse observations and rename or delete files. From the DIR window, you can also browse the VAR window.

The VAR window displays information about a data set's variables and enables you to change their names, formats, informats, and labels. The CATALOG window includes a listing of catalog entries, their types, and their descriptions. You can browse this listing, as well as copy, rename, and delete entries. The NOTEPAD window enables you to view and edit catalog entries. The FILENAME window displays information about external files and their filerefs that are defined to the SAS System.

For more information about SAS files, see Chapter 6, "SAS Files."

Using Forms

You can create or edit a form by issuing the FSFORM command; note that a form name must be specified during invocation. The FSFORM command opens the FORM window, which enables you to customize output, including the printer name, text format, and destination. The FORM window actually consists of six windows, which have the following functions:*

- □ selecting a printer
- □ specifying page formats
- □ specifying carriage control
- □ specifying print file parameters
- □ defining printer control information
- □ composing printer control language.

The NEXTSCR and PREVSCR commands scroll the windows, and the PRINT command prints output using a form.

Using Personal Business Tools

The CALCULATOR window enables you to perform mathematical operations, including addition, subtraction, multiplication, division, factoring, and hex conversion. The operations are performed primarily through keystrokes. For example, to add 2 and 2, type the number 2 and press ENTER or RETURN; type the number 2 again and press the plus sign.

The APPOINTMENT window appears as a monthly calendar with a daily log to its right that includes a column for time. The calendar is labeled with the current month and year, and the free-format data field is labeled with the current date. The APPOINTMENT window enables you to enter, update, and display daily calendar appointments. You can display times and descriptors for the appointments, which are stored automatically in a SAS data set. If the Time field contains a to-do

---

* The Print File Parameters window is optional.

indication, the to-do item is brought forward automatically to the current date when the appointment calendar is initialized until you indicate that the task is done.

Issuing the LEFT and RIGHT commands displays other appointments for other days in the current month; issuing the FORWARD and BACKWARD commands displays other months. Overtyping the year with another year displays the overtyped year. Then, you can enter, update, or browse information for the new year.

Changing Colors

If you have a color monitor, you can change both the color and highlighting of selected portions, or *field types*, of a window by using the COLOR command. If you have a monochrome monitor, you can change the highlighting attributes.* You can issue the COLOR command in one of the following ways:

- □ Specify the COLOR command with the field type and color only to change the color and eliminate highlighting.
- □ Specify the COLOR command with the field type, color, and highlighting to change the color and highlighting.

Instead of specifying a color, you can specify the NEXT argument to change the color of a field. Then, the field is displayed in a different color each time you use the NEXT argument.**

On many terminals, available colors and their letter designations are

B	blue	W	white
R	red	K	black
G	green	M	magenta
C	cyan	A	grey | gray
P	pink	N	brown
Y	yellow	O	orange

Available highlighting attributes and their letter designations are

H	highlight
U	underline
R	reverse video
B	blinking

See Table 7.3 for a list of color commands and the windows in which they work.

* Color and highlighting support varies among video devices. Where some but not all colors are available, a color is matched to its closest available counterpart.

** Along with the availability of colors, the order of colors also varies.

CHAPTER 8 SAS® Text Editor

Introduction

Definition

The *SAS Text Editor* is a full-screen editing facility available in certain windows of the SAS Display Manager System, as well as in windows of SAS/AF, SAS/FSP, and SAS/GRAPH software. You can use the text editor to

- □ edit text
- □ rearrange and reformat lines or blocks of text
- □ automatically flow, split, or wrap text
- □ check spelling and flag errors
- □ create and use a dictionary.

Relationship to the SAS Display Manager System

The text editor is used in certain display manager windows. It is also used in certain windows of SAS/AF, SAS/FSP, and SAS/GRAPH software. In all windows that use the text editor, in addition to the text editing commands, display manager commands from the following categories are also available:

- □ color
- □ scrolling

□ text cut-and-paste

□ text-store

□ search

□ file-management.

For more information about display manager, see Chapter 7, "SAS Display Manager System." For more information about display manager commands, see Chapter 18, "SAS Display Manager Commands."

Requestor Windows

Although windows are discussed in detail in Chapter 7, requestor windows deserve special mention here because they affect all parts of display manager. Requestor windows are windows that the SAS System displays so you can confirm, cancel, or modify an action. They often act as safeguards, for example, by preventing you from overwriting the contents of a file. The text editor uses requestor windows to verify commands. Although you cannot specifically invoke requestor windows, they appear in response to your actions. You must respond to the request before you can continue your current SAS session.

SAS Text Editor Commands

Types of Commands

Commands specific to the text editor are called text-editing commands because they perform editing functions in windows. These text editing commands fall into one of two subcategories:

□ command-line commands

□ line commands.

The two subcategories are differentiated by the number and type of characters used and by the area of the window from which they are traditionally executed. Command-line commands are complete words or abbreviations. Some take arguments that modify or complete the command; others do not take arguments. Some arguments are optional, and others are required. Except for the MASK command, line commands are not complete words. Some are single-letter commands typed in the numeric field of one line to affect only that line. Others are double-letter or block commands typed in the numeric fields of the beginning and ending lines to be affected.

Some line commands take a numeric argument. Some require a target command, such as the B (before) or A (after) command. See Chapter 19, "SAS Text Editor Commands," for complete syntax information on the commands.

The two command subcategories are also differentiated by the types of functions they perform. Most line commands rearrange or reformat text. Among other things, they move, delete, copy, and align lines or blocks of text. They also insert blank lines. Command-line commands have more diverse capabilities. In addition to rearranging and reformatting text, their functionality ranges from reversing the effects of commands to changing the default case of text.

Table 8.1 briefly describes all of the text editor commands.

Table 8.1 *Categories and Descriptions of SAS Text Editor Commands*

Category	**Command**	**Description**
Command-line Commands	AUTOADD	controls automatic line addition
	AUTOFLOW	controls whether text is flowed when included, copied, or pasted
	AUTOSPLIT	determines whether text is split at carriage return or after ENTER or RETURN is pressed
	AUTOWRAP	controls whether text is wrapped when it is included, copied, or filed
	BOUNDS	sets left and right boundaries when text is flowed
	CAPS	changes the default case of text
	CURSOR	moves the cursor to the command line
	DICT	creates, maintains, and invokes an auxiliary dictionary
	FILL	places fill characters beginning at the current cursor position
	INDENT	retains left-margin indention when text is flowed
	NUMBERS	adds or removes line numbers
	RESET	removes any pending line commands
	SPELL	checks text for correct spelling and flags errors
	UNDO	reverses the effects of actions
Line Commands	C and CC	copy one or more lines
	CL and CCL	lowercase all characters in one or more designated lines of text
	COLS	displays a line ruler that marks horizontal columns
	CU and CCU	uppercase all characters in one or more designated lines of text
	D and DD	delete one or more lines
	I	inserts one or more new lines
	JC and JJC	center one or more designated lines of text
	JL and JJL	left align one or more designated lines of text
	JR and JJR	right align one or more designated lines of text
	M and MM	move one or more lines of text
	MASK	defines the initial contents of a new line
	R and RR	repeat one or more designated lines of text
	TC	connects two lines of text
	TF	flows text to a blank line or to the end of text
	TS	splits text at the cursor
	) and))	shift right one or more designated lines of text
	(and ((	shift left one or more designated lines of text
	> and >>	shift right one or more designated lines of text
	< and <<	shift left one or more designated lines of text

Table 8.2 lists the text editor commands and the windows in which they work.

Table 8.2 *SAS Text Editor Commands—Valid Windows*

Windows ▶ / ▼ Commands	BROWSE MODE	EDIT MODE	LOG	NOTEPAD	OUTPUT	PROGRAM EDITOR
AUTOADD		■		■		■
AUTOFLOW		■		■		■
AUTOSPLIT		■		■		■
AUTOWRAP	■	■	■	■	■	■
BOUNDS	■	■	■	■	■	■
C and CC		■		■		■
CAPS	■	■	■	■	■	■
CL and CCL		■		■		■
COLS		■		■		■
CU and CCU		■		■		■
CURSOR	■	■	■	■	■	■
D and DD		■		■		■
DICT	■	■	■	■	■	■
(and ((		■		■		■
) and))		■		■		■
FILL		■		■		■
I		■		■		■
INDENT		■		■		■
JC and JJC		■		■		■
JL and JJL		■		■		■
JR and JJR		■		■		■
M and MM		■		■		■
MASK		■		■		■

(continued)

Table 8.2 *(continued)*

Commands ▼ / Windows ▶	BROWSE MODE	EDIT MODE	LOG	NOTEPAD	OUTPUT	PROGRAM EDITOR
NUMBERS	■	■		■		■
R and RR		■		■		■
RESET		■		■		■
< and <<		■		■		■
> and >>		■		■		■
SPELL	■	■	■	■	■	■
TC		■		■		■
TF		■		■		■
TS		■		■		■
UNDO		■		■		■

Behavior of Commands in Different Windows

Some commands behave differently depending on the window in which they are used. These differences are documented by window in Chapter 17, "SAS Display Manager Windows."

Command Execution

Text-editing commands have already been categorized as either command-line commands or line commands. You can issue these commands in one of four ways:

- □ from the command line
- □ from the numbered field of the display
- □ through the PMENU facility
- □ with function keys.

Command-line commands can be executed in all ways except from the numbered field of the display. Line commands can be executed in all ways except through the PMENU facility. Whether you use the command line or the PMENU facility may depend on which is the default at your site, whether you can change the default, and your own preference. Function keys offer a convenient way to execute both types of text-editing commands.

You can reverse, or undo, the results of most text-editing commands that modify text with the UNDO command. In addition, some of the display manager commands available in the text editor can be interrupted with the attention sequence.

■ **Host Information** ......

Whether the PMENU facility or the command line is the default depends on your site and host system. Refer to the SAS documentation for your host system or see your SAS Software Consultant for information specific to your site. ■

Executing Commands from the Command Line

All text-editing command-line commands can be executed from the command line by typing the command on the command line and pressing ENTER or RETURN. As mentioned, some commands take arguments. Some commands function like on/off switches and in fact take ON and OFF arguments. For example, issuing the following command executes the CAPS command:

```
caps on
```

The default type becomes uppercase. You can then return the default type to lowercase by specifying

```
caps off
```

The same effect is achieved by issuing the CAPS command with no argument specified. The first time you issue the command, it reverses the current setting; the second time you execute the command, it returns to the previous setting. This on/off switch effect is known as a toggle. When you issue a command as a toggle, the SAS System generates a note that indicates the current setting.

Line commands can also be issued from the command line. Type the line command on the command line, preceded by a colon; then move your cursor to the line you want altered. Press ENTER or RETURN to issue the command. For example, suppose you want to issue the COLS command. From the command line, specify

```
:cols
```

Then, to execute the command, move the cursor to a scrollable area and press ENTER or RETURN.

Executing Commands from the Numbered Display

Line commands can be typed in the numbered part of the display and executed by pressing ENTER or RETURN. Follow line commands that have a numeric argument with a space before issuing them. The example in Display 8.1 shows how to use the MM (move, block) command with the A (after) command to specify a target. The commands have been typed but not issued. To issue them, press ENTER or RETURN.

Display 8.1 *Issuing the MM Line Command*

```
LOG
Command ===>
```

```
PROGRAM EDITOR
Command ===>

00001 data test1;
00002    input a b;
mm003 1 2
mm004 3 4
a0005 cards;
00006 ;
```

Executing Commands with Function Keys

Whether the command line or the PMENU facility is active, you can execute both command-line and line commands with function keys; simply press the key that corresponds to the command you want to execute. The KEYS window lists the current definitions for all function keys; the current definitions remain in effect unless you change them.

Function keys are convenient for issuing the most commonly used commands and commands whose effects depend on cursor position. Text-editing examples include the SPELL and DICT command-line commands and the D (delete) and I (insert) line commands. You can also use function keys to

□ issue multiple commands

□ insert text strings

□ insert comments in code.

To issue line commands, type over the setting of a function key with the line command setting you want, preceded by a colon. Then, use the function key to issue the command as you would any other command.

Display 8.2 shows the KEYS window with the first function key (f1) defined to execute the I (insert) line command. In this example, one keystroke inserts a line in the PROGRAM EDITOR window. Display 8.2 also shows

□ f2 defined to issue multiple commands

□ f3 defined to insert a text string

□ f4 defined to insert comments in code.

Display 8.2 *Customized Function Key Settings*

```
LOG
 Command ===>

PROGRAM EDITOR
 Command ===>

 00001
 00002
 00003
 00004
 00005
 00006
```

```
KEYS <DMKEYS>
 Command ===>

 Key      Definition

 F1       :i
 F2       pgm;zoom;change paint print
 F3       ~MORE INFORMATION NEEDED
 F4       ~/* ADD FIRST DATA SET */
 F5       paste
 F6       store
 F7       prevwind
 F8       next
 F9       pmenu
 F10      command
 F11      keys
 F12      undo
 F13      help
 F14      zoom
 F15      zoom off; submit
 F16      pgm; recall
 F17      rfind
 F18      rchange
```

You can change any key setting by typing over the definition for a key in the KEYS window. The new definition takes effect immediately. Issuing the CANCEL command cancels changes you made in that session of the KEYS window since the most recent execution of the END command. All changes are canceled, the window is closed, and the previously invoked window is displayed. Issue the SAVE or END command to save all changes. After you type over a definition, issue the SAVE or END command with no operand to store the settings in your default catalog. You can create another set of customized key settings by specifying any valid SAS name as an argument to the SAVE command. A message appears indicating the function key settings are saved. See the KEYS window in Chapter 17 for more information about saving key settings.

For added efficiency, issue the KEYDEF command to change a function key setting outside the KEYS window. The new setting is in effect immediately for the duration of the SAS session. For example, specify the following command to change function key 10 to the SPELL command:

```
keydef f10 spell
```

To determine the setting of a function key, issue the KEYDEF command with the *key-name* argument only. The SAS System generates a note indicating the current setting.

Executing Commands with the PMENU Facility

You can use the PMENU facility to execute commands. The PMENU facility offers the same functions as executing commands on the command line and using function keys. At some sites, the PMENU facility's action bar appears automatically, by default. At other sites, the command line is the default, and the PMENU facility is optional. When the PMENU facility is optional, issuing the PMENU command replaces the command line with an action bar across all windows in any full-screen environment.

Depending on your host system and terminal, commands are issued in one of the following ways:

- □ by moving the cursor to an item on the action bar, or to a menu item on the pull-down menu, and pressing ENTER or RETURN
- □ by using a mouse to point to an item on the action bar, or to a menu item on the pull-down menu, and click.

For a more complete discussion of the PMENU facility, see Chapter 7. Also, see the PMENU command in Chapter 18, and see Chapter 26, "The PMENU Procedure," in *SAS Procedures Guide, Version 6, Third Edition.*

Display 8.3 shows the PROGRAM EDITOR window after the PMENU command has been executed.

Display 8.3 *PMENU Facility*

```
LOG
 File Edit View Globals Help
```

```
PROGRAM EDITOR
 File Edit View Locals Globals Help

 00001
 00002
 00003
 00004
 00005
 00006
```

Special Features

The SAS System has special features that enable you to

- □ reverse the effects of some commands
- □ interrupt execution of some commands
- □ execute host system commands during a SAS session.

Reversing the Effects of Commands

The UNDO command reverses the effects of text-editing commands that modify text. It cannot reverse the effects of a previous execution of the UNDO command. Continuing to issue the UNDO command reverses a series of commands, starting with the most recently issued and moving backward. The UNDO command does not take arguments.

■ **Host Information** . . . .

How the UNDO command handles text entry varies by host system. On some host systems, one execution of the UNDO command undoes all text entry changes made between function key and ENTER or RETURN presses. On other host systems, one execution of the UNDO command undoes text entry for only one line of text. Refer to the SAS documentation for your host system for details or see your SAS Software Consultant.

. . . . ■

Interrupting Execution of Commands

You can use the attention sequence to interrupt execution of the following display manager commands that can be used by the text editor:*

FILE	COPY
PRINT	SUBMIT
SAVE	SUBTOP
INCLUDE	RECALL

After the attention sequence executes, a requestor window appears to instruct you how to proceed.

■ **Host Information** . . . .

The attention sequence varies by host system and terminal. It may be one key press, two keys pressed simultaneously, or a sequence of two or more key presses. Refer to the SAS documentation for your host system for details or see your SAS Software Consultant.

. . . . ■

Executing Host System Commands from a SAS Session

Use the X command to execute host system commands during a SAS session. The X command enables you to return to your host environment without ending your SAS session. Issuing the X command with the appropriate host system command returns you directly to your host environment. Issuing it without specifying an argument puts you into a host system submode. In this submode, you can execute host system commands or return to your SAS session. A message appears immediately after you issue the X command telling you how to return to your SAS session.

■ **Host Information** . . . .

The commands issued with the X command, both the host commands and the commands to return to a SAS session, vary by host system. Refer to the SAS documentation for your host system for details or see your SAS Software Consultant.

. . . . ■

* Except for the FILE command, the attention sequence cannot be used to interrupt these commands in the full-screen windows of SAS/AF, SAS/FSP, and SAS/GRAPH software.

SAS Text Editor Tasks

Text-editing tasks include editing text; rearranging and reformatting text; wrapping, flowing, and splitting text automatically; checking spelling and flagging errors; and creating and using dictionaries. For comprehensive information on text-editing commands, see Chapter 19.

Editing Text

Several commands enable you to edit text in a window:

- □ The CL and CU commands lowercase and uppercase existing text; the CCL and CCU commands produce the same results for blocks of text.
- □ The CAPS command changes the default, so whatever you subsequently type or modify is automatically lowercased or uppercased.
- □ The MASK command displays and allows editing of the initial contents of new lines created with the I (insert) line command. Although the default is a blank line, you can change the default to any text string you want and insert the string with the I command.
- □ The UNDO command reverses the effects of all text-editing commands that modify text.

The COLS line command makes text entry easier when you are typing a program with column input. Display 8.4 shows the COLS command executed and a program with column input entered.

Display 8.4 *Executing the COLS Command*

```
LOG
 Command ===>




PROGRAM EDITOR
 Command ===>

 00001 data test;
 00002 input @4 name @10 age;
 *COLS ----|----10---|----20---|----30---|----40---|----50---|----60---|---
 00004    sue    12
 00005    bob    14
 00006 ;
```

Rearranging and Reformatting Text

Numerous commands enable you to rearrange and reformat text. For example, the following line commands shift, add, or remove text. Except for the I command, block commands are available to perform the same functions for blocks of text.

- □ The D command deletes a line.
- □ The M command moves a line to the destination specified.
- □ The R command repeats a line.

- The C command copies a line to the destination specified.
- The I command inserts a blank line.

A group of line commands rearranges text horizontally on the display. The JR, JL, and JC commands right align, left align, and center text. Block commands perform the same functions for blocks of text. The < (less than) and > (greater than) and the ((left parenthesis) and) (right parenthesis) commands move text left or right the number of spaces specified. Block commands perform the same functions for blocks of text.

Wrapping, Flowing, and Splitting Text

Several line commands and command-line commands determine whether text is wrapped, flowed, and split. Others actually implement the wrap, flow, and split. The AUTOSPLIT command determines whether text is split at the cursor position when you press ENTER or RETURN. The TS line command then implements the split at the cursor and also moves the text down the number of lines designated. The AUTOFLOW command determines whether text is flowed automatically as it is brought into a window with the INCLUDE, PASTE, and COPY commands. Both the TF and TC line commands rearrange text already in the window. The TF command flows text within a paragraph, and the TC command connects two lines of text.

Both the INDENT and BOUNDS commands affect the TF and TS commands. The BOUNDS command sets left and right boundaries for text already in a window that is flowed with the TF command. The BOUNDS command also resets the left and right boundaries for text brought into the window with the INCLUDE, COPY, and PASTE commands when the AUTOFLOW command is on. With the AUTOFLOW command on, the left boundary setting is honored when text is split with the TS command. The INDENT command specifies that the current indention at the left margin is used when text already in the window is flowed with the TF command or split with the TS command. The INDENT command also specifies that the current indention at the left margin is used when text is brought into the window with the INCLUDE, COPY, and PASTE commands when the AUTOFLOW command is on.

The AUTOWRAP command controls whether text that cannot fit on one line is wrapped automatically to the next line when it is brought into a window with the INCLUDE or COPY command or sent to an external file with the FILE command. Finally, the AUTOADD command controls whether blank lines are added at the end of the window as you scroll forward past existing text.

Checking Spelling and Flagging Errors

The text editor's SPELL and DICT commands, in conjunction with the SPELL windows, enable you to find and correct spelling errors and to maintain dictionaries.

Using the SPELL Command

Through the SPELL command, the text editor offers a spelling checker that

- □ flags unrecognized words
- □ displays suggestions for unrecognized words
- □ adds unrecognized words to an auxiliary dictionary
- □ replaces unrecognized words with other selections.

This spelling checker can be used to check all words or a specific subset, such as the previously unrecognized word or the next unrecognized word. Because cursor position is significant, the SPELL command works most efficiently when issued with a function key.

The SPELL command checks words against a dictionary, either a master dictionary created with the SPELL procedure or an auxiliary dictionary you name. When you create a dictionary, its contents are saved in your SASUSER.PROFILE catalog. If you do not create or specify an auxiliary dictionary, new words are stored in a temporary dictionary in effect only for the duration of your current full-screen task.

Using the SPELL Windows

In some cases, the SPELL command displays a window. When you specify SPELL ALL to check all words and unrecognized words are found, the SPELL: Unrecognized Words window appears listing all unrecognized words. You can use this window to add the unrecognized words to a dictionary by issuing the REMEMBER command.

Executing the SUGGEST command from the SPELL: Unrecognized Words window displays the SPELL: Suggestions window, which displays the last unrecognized word as well as suggestions for its correct spelling. You can issue the REMEMBER command to add the unrecognized word to a dictionary or to select a replacement by positioning the cursor on a word and pressing ENTER or RETURN.

Note that for efficiency you can combine some arguments, such as the ALL and SUGGEST arguments. For example, specifying the following command checks the spelling of all words and bypasses the SPELL: Unrecognized Words window:

```
spell all suggest
```

Display 8.5 shows the results of executing this command.

Display 8.5 *SPELL: Suggestions Window*

```
┌LOG──────────────────────────────────────────────────────────────────
│ Command ===>
│
│                        ┌SPELL: Suggestions────────────────────────────
│                        │ Command ===>
│                        │
│                        │    Unrecognized word: spel
│                        │                at line: 1
│                        │    Dictionary: ________    ALL OCCURRENCES
│                        │
│                        │       Suggestions listed below
│                        │
│                        │
└────────────────────────│       sped
                         │       spew
┌PROGRAM EDITOR──────────│       spell
│ Command ===>           │
│                        │
│ 00001 The spel command │
│ 00002                  │
│ 00003                  │
│ 00004                  │
│ 00005                  │
│ 00006                  │
│                        └──────────────────────────────────────────────
└─────────────────────────────────────────────────────────────────────
```

For complete information about the SPELL command, see Chapter 19.

Creating and Using Dictionaries

The DICT command maintains, uses, and creates auxiliary dictionaries.

▶ ***Caution:*** *Use the SPELL procedure to create permanent auxiliary dictionaries.*

Use the SPELL procedure, not the SPELL or DICT command, to create permanent auxiliary dictionaries. The SPELL and DICT commands exist for the convenience of the full-screen task.

Use the INCLUDE argument with the DICT command to include the auxiliary dictionary you specify. If no name is specified, the SAS System checks the SASUSER.PROFILE catalog first and the SASHELP.BASE catalog second. Use the FREE argument to release the dictionary and the CREATE command to create an auxiliary dictionary. If no name is specified, the dictionary is stored in the SASUSER.PROFILE catalog.

For complete information about the DICT command, see Chapter 19. For more information about the spelling checker and dictionary, see Chapter 33, "The SPELL Procedure," in *SAS Procedures Guide*.

Reference

PART 2

CHAPTER 9 SAS® Language Statements

(continued on next page)

(continued from previous page)

Background information on SAS language statements, including a table listing all statements, appears in Chapter 3, "Components of the SAS Language." See Table 3.1, "Executable and Declarative Statements in the DATA Step," Table 3.2, "Categories and Descriptions of DATA Step Statements," and Table 3.3, "Categories and Descriptions of Global Statements."

ABORT

Stops executing the current DATA step, SAS job, or SAS session

DATA step

HELP ABORT

Syntax

ABORT <ABEND |RETURN> <*n*>;

Description

The ABORT statement causes the SAS System to stop processing the current DATA step. What happens next depends on the method of operation you are using to submit your SAS statements, the arguments you use with the ABORT statement, and your host system. The ABORT statement usually appears as part of an IF-THEN statement clause or a SELECT statement clause designed to stop processing when an error condition occurs.

Note: When you execute an ABORT statement in a DATA step, the SAS System does not use data sets created in the step to replace existing data sets with the same name.

You can use the following arguments with the ABORT statement:

no argument
: produces these results under the following methods of operation:

  batch mode and noninteractive mode

  □ stops processing the current DATA step and writes an error message to the SAS log. Data sets may contain an incomplete number of observations, or no observations, depending on when the SAS System encountered the ABORT statement.

  □ sets the OBS= system option to 0.

  □ continues limited processing of the remainder of the SAS job, including executing macro statements, executing system options statements, and syntax checking of program statements.

  □ creates output data sets for subsequent DATA and PROC steps with no observations.

  display manager mode

  □ stops processing the current DATA step

  □ creates a data set containing the observations processed before encountering the ABORT statement

  □ prints a message to the log that an ABORT statement terminated the DATA step

  □ continues processing any DATA or PROC steps that follow the ABORT statement.

  interactive line mode

  stops processing the current DATA step. Any further DATA steps or procedures execute normally.

■ **Host Information** ...... The following ABORT statement options can produce different results depending on your host system. See your site documentation for complete information about how your host system handles jobs that end abnormally and how it returns user-specified condition codes.

.... ■

ABORT

continued

ABEND

causes abnormal termination of the current SAS job or session. Results depend on the method of operation:

batch mode and noninteractive mode

- □ stops processing immediately
- □ sends an error message to the SAS log stating that execution was terminated by the ABEND option of the ABORT statement
- □ does not execute any subsequent statements or check syntax
- □ returns control to the host system; further action is based on how your host system and your site treat jobs that end abnormally.

display manager mode and interactive line mode

stops processing immediately and returns you to the host system.

RETURN

causes the immediate normal termination of the current SAS job or session. Results depend on the method of operation:

batch mode and noninteractive mode

- □ stops processing immediately
- □ sends an error message to the SAS log stating that execution was terminated by the RETURN option of the ABORT statement
- □ does not execute any subsequent statements or check syntax
- □ returns control to the host system with a condition code indicating an error.

display manager mode and interactive line mode

stops processing immediately and returns you to the host system.

n

enables you to specify a condition code that the SAS System returns to the host system when it stops executing. The range of values you can use depends on your host system. The value of *n* must be an integer as illustrated in the following examples:

□ `abort abend 255;`

□ `abort return 255;`

Comparisons

When you are using display manager or interactive line mode, the ABORT statement and the STOP statement both stop processing, but the ABORT statement sets the value of the automatic variable _ERROR_ to 1, and the STOP statement does not.

In batch or noninteractive mode, the ABORT and STOP statements also have different effects. Use the STOP statement in batch or noninteractive mode to continue processing with the next DATA or PROC step.

In Release 6.03 SAS software, the RETURN and ABEND options are equivalent. In Release 6.06 SAS software, they produce different results, depending on your host system.

Example

The following example uses the ABORT statement as part of an IF-THEN statement to stop execution of the SAS System when it encounters a data value that would otherwise cause a division-by-zero error.

```
if volume=0 then abort;
density=mass/volume;
```

See Also

STOP statement

SAS documentation for your host system

Vendor documentation for your host system

ARRAY, Explicit

Defines elements of an explicit array

DATA step

HELP ARRAY

Syntax

ARRAY *array-name{subscript}*<$> <*length*>
<<*array-elements*> <(*initial-values*)>>;

Description

The ARRAY statement defines a set of variables (either all numeric or all character) as elements of an array. Array processing is used to apply the same process to a group of items. When defining an explicit array, the ARRAY statement must contain

- □ an array name
- □ a subscript that indicates the number of elements in the array
- □ a description of the elements.

Other items, such as initial values for the elements, can also appear in the statement.

You refer to elements of the array by the array name and subscript. Because you usually want to process more than one element in an array, arrays are often referenced within iterative DO, DO WHILE, or DO UNTIL groups. For a discussion of referencing arrays, see "Array Reference, Explicit" later in this chapter. To learn how to process the arrays you create with ARRAY statements, refer to "Array Processing" in Chapter 4, "Rules of the SAS Language."

Note: Implicit arrays are supported primarily for compatibility with previous releases of the SAS System. Using explicit arrays is recommended.

You can use the following arguments with the explicit ARRAY statement:

array-name

names the array. *Array-name* must be a valid SAS name that is not the name of a SAS variable in the same DATA step.

▶ ***Caution:*** *Using the name of a SAS function as an array name can cause unpredictable results.*

If you inadvertently use a function name as the name of the array, the SAS System treats parenthetical references involving the name as array references, not function references, for the duration of the DATA step. A warning message is written to the SAS log.

{subscript}

is either an asterisk, a number, or a range of numbers used to describe the number and arrangement of elements in the array. In this book, the subscript is enclosed in braces ({ }). Brackets ([ ]) and parentheses (( )) are also allowed. *{Subscript}* has one of the following forms:

{dimension-size-1 < , . . . *dimension-size-n* >*}*

indicates the number of elements in each dimension of the array. *Dimension-size* is a numeric representation of either the number of elements in a one-dimensional array, or the number of elements in each dimension of a multidimensional array.

An array with one dimension can be defined as follows:

```
array simple{3} red green yellow;
```

This ARRAY statement defines an array named SIMPLE that groups together three variables named RED, GREEN, and YELLOW.

An array with more than one dimension is known as a multidimensional array. Specify the number of elements in each dimension after the array name. You can have any number of dimensions in a multidimensional array.

For example, a two-dimensional array provides row and column arrangement of array elements. Reading from left to right, the leftmost dimension represents rows and the next dimension represents columns. Thus, the following statement defines a two-dimensional array with five rows and three columns:

```
array x{5,3} score1-score15;
```

The SAS System places variables into a two-dimensional array by filling all rows in order, beginning at the upper-left corner of the array (known as row-major order).

You can also specify the bounds of each dimension of an array using the following form:

{<*lower*:> *upper* <, . . . <*lower*:> *upper*>}

where *lower* is the lower bound of that dimension and *upper* is the upper bound.

In most explicit arrays, the subscript in each dimension of the array ranges from 1 to *n*, where *n* is the number of elements in that dimension. Thus, 1 is the *lower* bound and *n* is the *upper* bound of that dimension of the array.

Note that in the preceding example, the value of each dimension is by default the upper bound of that dimension. To illustrate the point, the following ARRAY statement is a longhand version of that example:

```
array x{1:5,1:3} score1-score15;
```

For most arrays, 1 is a convenient lower bound; thus, you do not need to specify the lower and upper bounds. However, specifying both bounds is useful when the array dimensions have a convenient beginning point other than 1.

Note: Processing time can be enhanced if a lower bound of 0 is used because it reduces the computational time for subscript evaluation.

{*}

indicates that the SAS System is to determine the subscript by counting the variables in the array. When you specify the asterisk, you must also include *array-elements*. You cannot use the asterisk with _TEMPORARY_ arrays or when defining a multidimensional array.

$

indicates that the elements in the array are character. The dollar sign is not necessary if the elements have been previously defined as character.

length

specifies the length of elements in the array that have not been previously assigned a length.

ARRAY, Explicit

continued

array-elements

names the elements that make up the array. *Array-elements* must be either all numeric or all character and they can be listed in any order. The elements can be one of the following:

variables

lists variable names. The names must be variables you define in the ARRAY statement, or variables the SAS System creates by concatenating the array name and a number. For instance, when the subscript is a number (not the asterisk), you do not need to name each variable in the array. Instead, the SAS System creates variable names by concatenating the array name and the numbers 1, 2, 3, . . . *n*.

For example, the following ARRAY statement creates an array named MEAL, with three elements named MEAL1, MEAL2, and MEAL3.

```
array meal{3};
```

The following SAS variables enable you to reference variables that have been previously defined in the same DATA step:

- □ _NUMERIC_ indicates all numeric variables.
- □ _CHARACTER_ indicates all character variables.
- □ _ALL_ indicates all variables. In this case, all the previously defined variables must be of the same type.

TEMPORARY

creates a list of temporary data elements. Temporary data elements can be numeric or character. They behave like DATA step variables with the following exceptions:

- □ They do not have names. You must refer to temporary data elements by the array name and dimension.
- □ They do not appear in the output data set.
- □ You cannot use the special subscript asterisk (*) to refer to all the elements.
- □ Temporary data element values are always automatically retained, rather than being reset to missing at the beginning of the next iteration of the DATA step.

Arrays of temporary elements are useful when the only purpose for creating an array is to perform a calculation. To preserve the result of the calculation, assign it to a variable. You can improve performance time by using temporary data elements.

(initial-values)

gives initial values for the corresponding elements in the array. Initial values can be assigned to both *variables* and temporary data elements. Specify one or more initial values as follows:

(*initial-value-1*< , . . . *initial-value-n*>)

Elements and values are matched by position. If there are more array elements than initial values, the remaining array elements receive missing values and the SAS System issues a warning.

Follow *array-elements* with initial values enclosed in parentheses; separate the initial values with blanks or commas. The following statement assigns an initial value of 90 to variable T1, 80 to T2, and 70 to T3:

```
array test{3} t1 t2 t3 (90 80 70);
```

To assign initial values to character variables, enclose each value in quotes, and separate the values with commas or blanks, as follows:

```
array test2{*} a1 a2 a3 ('a','b','c');
```

If you have not previously specified the attributes of the array elements (such as length or type), the attributes of any initial values you specify are automatically assigned to the corresponding array element. Initial values are retained until a new value is assigned to the array element.

Comparisons

The primary distinction between explicit and implicit arrays is that explicit arrays contain an explicit specification of the number of elements in the array; implicit arrays do not. In addition, explicit arrays allow you to specify bounds on a multidimensional array other than 1 and *n*, where *n* is the number of elements in that dimension. Therefore, explicit arrays are more powerful and more flexible than implicit arrays. Implicit arrays are provided primarily for compatibility with previous releases of the SAS System. Using explicit arrays is recommended.

An ARRAY statement defines an array. To use an array element in a program statement, put an array reference in the statement. Explicit array elements are referenced explicitly by the array name and subscript. Implicit array elements are referenced by evaluating the current value of an index variable associated with the array.

If you have worked with arrays in other programming languages, note that arrays in the SAS System are different from those in many other languages. In the SAS System, an array is simply a convenient way of temporarily identifying a group of variables. It is not a data structure, and it exists only for the duration of the DATA step. *Array-name* identifies the array and distinguishes it from any other arrays in the same DATA step; it is not a variable.

Examples

The following ARRAY statements define valid arrays:

□ `array rain{5} janr febr marr aprr mayr;`

□ `array month{*} jan feb jul oct nov;`

□ `array x{*} _NUMERIC_;`

□ `array test{3} _TEMPORARY_ (90 80 70);`

□ `array days{7} d1-d7;`

□ `array x{5,3} score1-score15;`

□ `array new{2:5} green jacobs denato fetzer;`

□ `array test{3:4,3:7} test1-test10;`

□ `array qbx{10}; /* defines variables qbx1-qbx10 */`

ARRAY, Explicit

continued

See Also

Implicit ARRAY statement and explicit and implicit array references

"Array Processing" in Chapter 4, "Rules of the SAS Language"

ARRAY, Implicit

Defines elements of an implicit array

DATA step

HELP ARRAY

Syntax

ARRAY *array-name*<(*index-variable*)> <$> <*length*>
array-elements<(*initial-values*)>;

Description

The implicit ARRAY statement consists of an array name, an index variable (either one you supply or a default), and a list of names (either variable names or names of other implicit arrays). Implicit arrays do not contain an explicit reference to the number of elements in the array.

Note: Implicit arrays are supported for compatibility with previous releases of the SAS System. Using explicit arrays is recommended.

Refer to an element of the array by setting the index variable to the number of the element you want to process and using the array name in a subsequent statement. Because you usually want to process more than one element of an array, implicit arrays are often referenced within iterative DO, DO OVER, DO WHILE, or DO UNTIL groups. For a discussion of referencing implicit arrays, see "Array Reference, Implicit" later in this chapter.

You can use the following arguments with the implicit ARRAY statement:

array-name

names the array. *Array-name* must be a valid SAS name that is not the name of a SAS variable in the same DATA step. When the array name appears in a subsequent SAS statement in the same DATA step, the SAS System substitutes one of the array elements for the array name based on the value of the index variable.

▶ ***Caution:*** *Using the name of a SAS function as an array name can cause unpredictable results.*

If you inadvertently use a function name as the name of the array, the SAS System treats parenthetical references involving the name as array references, not function references, for the duration of the DATA step. A warning message is written to the SAS log.

(*index-variable*)

gives the name of a variable whose value defines the current element of the array. The index-variable must be enclosed in parentheses; braces and brackets are not allowed.

All implicit arrays use an index variable even if you do not specify one in the ARRAY statement. If you do not include an index variable, the SAS System automatically creates the variable _I_ to hold the index value. The automatic index variable can range in value from 1 to the number of elements of the array.

An index variable you specify is included in the SAS data set unless it is excluded by a DROP or KEEP statement or a DROP= or KEEP= data set option. The automatic index variable _I_ is not included in the data set unless you explicitly specify _I_ in the ARRAY statement.

ARRAY, Implicit

(index-variable continued)

If the index variable's value is not an integer, it is truncated to an integer using the rules of the INT function.

$

indicates that the elements in the array are character. The dollar sign is not necessary if the elements have been previously defined as character.

length

specifies the length of elements in the array that have not been previously assigned a length.

array-elements

names the elements that make up the array. *Array-elements* must be either all numeric or all character and they can be listed in any order. Valid elements include

- □ variable names
- □ other implicit arrays
- □ numbered variable lists
- □ _NUMERIC_
- □ _CHARACTER_
- □ _ALL_ (when the variables in the data set are all numeric or all character).

For example, the following INPUT statement reads in variables X1 through X3 as character variables using the $8. informat and variables X4 through X5 as numeric variables. The ARRAY statement uses the special variable _CHARACTER_ to include only the character variables in the array.

```
input (x1-x3) ($8.) x4-x5;
array item _character_;
```

A variable or an implicit array can be an element in more than one implicit array. You must refer to implicit array elements with implicit references; you cannot use explicit references.

Comparisons

The primary distinction between implicit and explicit arrays is that implicit arrays do not contain an explicit specification of the number of elements in the array; explicit arrays do. In addition, explicit arrays enable you to specify bounds on a multidimensional array other than 1 and *n*, where *n* is the number of elements in that dimension. Therefore, explicit arrays are more powerful and more flexible than implicit arrays. Implicit arrays are provided primarily for compatibility with previous releases of the SAS System. Using explicit arrays is recommended.

An implicit ARRAY statement defines an implicit array. To process an implicit array, you must use an implicit array reference in a subsequent program statement. Implicit array elements are referenced by the current value of the index variable associated with the array. Explicit array elements are referenced explicitly by the array name and subscript.

If you have worked with arrays in other programming languages, note that arrays in the SAS System are different from those in many other languages. In the SAS System, an array is simply a convenient way of temporarily identifying a group of variables. It is not a data structure, and it exists only for the duration of the DATA step. *Array-name* identifies the array and distinguishes it from any other arrays in the same DATA step; it is not a variable.

Examples

Example 1: Assigning Variable Types and Lengths

The following statements define an implicit array named ITEM. The INPUT statement reads in the character variables X1 and X2, each having a length of 3. The dollar sign and length designation of 12 in the ARRAY statement define the rest of the array elements as 12-byte character variables.

```
input x1 $3. x2 $3.;
array item(j) $ 12 x1-x10;
```

Example 2: Omitting the Index Variable

In this example, the statement defines an array QUESTION with 20 elements Q1 through Q20.

```
array question q1-q20;
```

The SAS System assigns the automatic index variable _I_ to the array. To reference the array in a subsequent SAS statement, you must set the automatic index variable to a certain value, then reference the array name.

```
_I_=13;
put question;
```

These statements write the value of the 13th array element (Q13) to the SAS log.

See Also

Explicit ARRAY statement and explicit and implicit array references

"Array Processing" in Chapter 4, "Rules of the SAS Language"

INT function in Chapter 11, "SAS Functions"

Array Reference, Explicit

Describes the elements in an explicit array to be processed

DATA step

HELP ARRAY

Syntax

array-name{*subscript*}

Description

To refer to an explicit array in a program statement, use an array reference. An explicit array reference consists of the array name and subscript. The ARRAY statement defining the array must appear in a DATA step before any references to that array. An array definition is only in effect for the duration of the DATA step. If you want to use the same array in several DATA steps, you must redefine the array in each step.

You can use an explicit array reference anywhere that you can write a SAS expression, including SAS functions and the following SAS statements:

- □ assignment statement
- □ sum statement
- □ DO UNTIL(*expression*)
- □ DO WHILE(*expression*)
- □ IF
- □ INPUT
- □ PUT
- □ SELECT
- □ WINDOW.

You can use the following arguments when referencing an explicit array:

array-name
: is the name of an explicit array previously defined with an ARRAY statement in the same DATA step.

{*subscript*}
: specifies the subscript. It can be a single variable or a list of variables separated by commas, a single asterisk, a SAS expression, or an integer with a value between the lower and upper bounds of the array, inclusive. Any of the following forms may be used:

{*variable-1*< , . . . *variable-n*>}
: indicates a variable, or variable list that is usually used with DO-loop processing. For each execution of the DO loop, the current value of this variable becomes the subscript of the array element being processed.

For example, the following statements process each element of the array, using the value of variable I as the subscript on the array references for each iteration of the DO loop. If an array element has a value of 99, the IF-THEN statement changes that value to 100.

```
array days{7} d1-d7;
do i=1 to 7;
   if days{i}=99 then days{i}=100;
end;
```

{*}
forces the SAS System to treat the elements in the array as a variable list. The asterisk can be used with the INPUT and PUT statements, and with some SAS functions.

When you define an array that contains temporary array elements, you cannot reference the array elements with an asterisk. See "ARRAY, Explicit" earlier in this chapter.

The following are examples of valid uses of the asterisk in explicit array references:

- □ `totcost=sum(of array-name{*});`
- □ `input array-name{*};`
- □ `put array-name{*};`

{*expression-1*< , . . . *expression-n*>}
indicates a SAS expression. The expression must evaluate to a valid subscript value when the statement containing the array reference executes.

When reading an array, specify the subscript following the array name. In the following example, the INPUT statement reads in variables A1, A2, and the third element (A3) of the array named ARR1:

```
array arr1{*} a1-a3;
x=1;
input a1 a2 arr1{x+2};
```

Using the DIM Function

The DIM function is often used in the iterative DO statement to return the number of elements in a dimension of an array, when the lower bound of the dimension is 1. This function saves you from having to change the upper bound of the DO statement if you change the number of array elements. For example, because the function DIM(NEW) returns a value of 4, the following statements process all the elements in the array:

```
array new{*} score1-score4;
do i=1 to dim(new);
   new{i}=new{i}+10;
end;
```

For more discussion, see the DIM function in Chapter 11, "SAS Functions."

Array Reference, Explicit

continued

Comparisons

An explicit ARRAY statement defines an array, whereas an explicit array reference processes members of the array. An implicit array reference does not include a reference to specific elements. Instead, it uses an index variable associated with the implicit array.

Examples

Example 1: Referencing Many Arrays in One Statement

You can refer to more than one array in a single SAS statement. In this example, you create two arrays, DAYS and HOURS. The statements inside the DO loop substitute the current value of variable I to reference each array element in both arrays.

```
array days{7} d1-d7;
array hours{7} h1-h7;
do i=1 to 7;
   if days{i}=99 then days{i}=100;
   hours{i}=days{i}*24;
end;
```

Example 2: Treating an Array as a Variable List

In this example, the ARRAY statement creates an array of 100 variables automatically named X1 through X100. To read in these variables, use the asterisk array reference to treat the elements as a variable list. The 2. informat applies to each array element.

```
data hundred;
   array x{100};
   input x{*} 2.;
   do i=1 to dim(x);
      put x{i};
   end;
   cards;
data lines
;
```

For additional examples of using explicit arrays in SAS programs, see "Array Processing" in Chapter 4.

See Also

Explicit ARRAY and implicit ARRAY statements and implicit array reference

"Array Processing" in Chapter 4, "Rules of the SAS Language"

DIM function in Chapter 11, "SAS Functions"

Array Reference, Implicit

Describes the elements in an implicit array to be processed

DATA step

HELP ARRAY

Syntax

array-name

Description

To refer to the elements in an implicit array use an array reference. An implicit array reference consists of the array name. The SAS System evaluates the value of the index variable associated with the array name to locate the individual elements.

The ARRAY statement defining the array must appear in a DATA step before any references to that array. An array definition is only in effect for the duration of the DATA step. If you want to use the same array in several DATA steps, you must redefine the array in each step.

You can use an implicit array reference in the following DATA step statements:

- assignment statement
- sum statement
- iterative DO
- DO OVER *array-name*
- DO UNTIL(*expression*)
- DO WHILE(*expression*)
- IF
- IF-THEN/ELSE
- INPUT
- PUT
- SELECT.

You can also use implicit array names in the arguments of SAS functions. However, an implicit array name in a function is not a substitute for a variable list because only one element of the array is processed in any given execution of the function.

You use the following argument when referencing an implicit array:

array-name

is the name of an implicit array defined previously in the same DATA step. To refer to an implicit array element, set the index variable to the index of the element you want, and then use the array name in a SAS statement.

For example, the ARRAY statement defines an implicit array named BIG with 20 elements. The assignment statement sets the index variable to 11. Then, the PUT statement writes the value of Y1, the 11th element of array BIG, to the SAS log.

```
array big (i) x1-x10 y1-y10;
i=11;
put big;
```

Array Reference, Implicit

(array-name continued)

If the index variable is out of range (less than 1 or greater than the number of elements in the array) when the array name is used, the DATA step stops processing and the SAS System prints an error message in the log.

Comparisons

An implicit ARRAY statement defines an implicit array, whereas an implicit array reference processes members of the array. The SAS System references implicit array elements by evaluating the current value of an index variable associated with *array-name*. An explicit array reference processes members of an explicit array.

Examples

Example 1: Iterative DO-Loop Processing

In this example, an index variable is not specified in the ARRAY statement. Therefore, the SAS System substitutes the automatic index variable _I_.

```
data test;
   input score1-score5;
   array s score1-score5;
   do _i_=1 to 5;
      s=s*100;
   end;
   cards;
data lines
;
```

The index variable of the array must also be the index variable of the iterative DO statement. If you do not specify an index variable in the ARRAY statement, use _I_ as the index variable in iterative DO loops that process the array. You can process more than one array in an iterative DO loop.

Example 2: DO OVER Processing

The DO OVER statement is often used to process the elements of an implicit array. The statement tells the SAS System to repeat the statements inside the DO loop for all the elements in the array. In this example, the IF-THEN statement inside the DO loop changes all missing values in the array elements to 0:

```
data two;
   input id x1-x10 y1-y10;
   array big (i) x1-x10 y1-y10;
   do over big;
      if big=. then big=0;
   end;
   cards;
data lines
;
```

You can process more than one array in a DO OVER group if the arrays have the same number of elements and the same index variable, as in the following example:

```
data ftoc;
   input f1-f100;
   array f f1-f100;    /* both arrays use _I_ index variable */
   array c c1-c100;
   do over f;          /* repeats DO loop 100 times */
      c=(f-32)*5/9;
   end;
   cards;
data lines
;
```

Example 3: Multidimensional Implicit Subscripting

Because an implicit array can be an element of another implicit array, double and higher-level implicit subscripting is possible. The ARRAY statements in the following DATA step change missing values to 0s for 10 test answers on each of three tests (a total of 30 answers):

```
data three;
   array test1 (j) t1q1-t1q10;
   array test2 (j) t2q1-t2q10;
   array test3 (j) t3q1-t3q10;
   array answer (k) test1-test3;
   input t1q1-t1q10 t2q1-t2q10 t3q1-t3q10;
   do k=1 to 3;
      do j=1 to 10;
         if answer=. then answer=0;
      end;
   end;
   cards;
data lines
;
```

In this example, the DO OVER statement can be used in place of the iterative DO statements. You can nest DO OVER statements only if a different index variable is defined for each array referenced by the nested

Array Reference, Implicit

continued

DO OVER statements. The following is an example of nested DO OVER statements:

```
do over answer;
   do over test1;
      if answer=. then answer=0;
   end;
end;
```

Because TEST1, TEST2, and TEST3 have the same number of elements, it makes no difference which of the three array names is specified in the inner DO OVER statement.

See Also

Explicit ARRAY, implicit ARRAY, DO, iterative DO, DO OVER, and DO WHILE statements and explicit array reference

"Array Processing" in Chapter 4, "Rules of the SAS Language"

Assignment

Evaluates an expression and stores the result in a variable

DATA step

HELP ASSIGNMENT

Syntax

variable=*expression*;

Description

Assignment statements evaluate an expression and store the result in a variable.

You use the following arguments to compose an assignment statement:

variable
: names a new or existing variable. *Variable* can be the variable name, array reference, or SUBSTR function.

expression
: is any valid SAS expression. The expression can contain the variable used on the left side of the equal sign. When a variable appears on both sides of a statement, the original value on the right side is used to evaluate the expression, and the result is stored in the variable on the left side of the equal sign.

Examples

The following are examples of assignment statements with different kinds of expressions:

□ `name='Amanda Jones';`

□ `wholname='Ms. '||name;`

□ `a=a+b;`

See Also

"SAS Expressions" in Chapter 4, "Rules of the SAS Language"

ATTRIB

Associates a format, informat, label, and/or length with one or more variables

DATA step

HELP ATTRIB

Syntax

ATTRIB *variable-list-1 attribute-list-1*
< . . . *variable-list-n attribute-list-n*>;

Description

The ATTRIB statement can associate a format, informat, label, length, or any combination of these items with one or more variables in a single statement within a DATA step.

Using the ATTRIB statement in the DATA step permanently associates attributes with variables by changing the descriptor information of the SAS data set containing the variables.

You can use the following arguments with an ATTRIB statement:

variable-list
names the variables you want to associate with the attributes.

attribute-list
specifies one or more attributes to assign to *variable-list*. You can specify one or more of the following attributes in the ATTRIB statement:

FORMAT=*format*
associates a format with variables in *variable-list*. The format can be either a standard SAS format or a format defined with the FORMAT procedure.

INFORMAT=*informat*
associates an informat with variables in *variable-list*. The informat can be either a standard SAS informat or an informat defined with the FORMAT procedure.

LABEL=*'label'*
associates a label with variables in *variable-list*.

LENGTH=<$>*length*
specifies the length of variables in *variable-list*. Put a dollar sign ($) in front of the length of character variables. Use the ATTRIB statement before the SET statement to change the length of variables in an output data set when using an existing data set as input.

■ **Host Information** .... For numeric variables, the minimum length you can specify with the LENGTH= specification is 2 on some host systems, and 3 on others.

.... ■

You can use an ATTRIB statement in a PROC step, but the rules are different.

Comparisons

You can also assign single attributes to variables with FORMAT, INFORMAT, LABEL, and LENGTH statements. Either an ATTRIB statement or an individual attribute statement can change an attribute associated with a variable.

Examples

Here are examples of valid ATTRIB statements containing

□ single variable and single attribute:

```
attrib cost length=4;
```

□ single variable with multiple attributes:

```
attrib saleday informat=mmddyy. format=worddate.;
```

□ multiple variables with the same multiple attributes:

```
attrib x y length=$4 label='TEST VARIABLE';
```

□ multiple variables with different multiple attributes:

```
attrib x length=$4 label='TEST VARIABLE'
       y length=$2 label='RESPONSE';
```

□ variable list with single attribute:

```
attrib month1-month12 label='MONTHLY SALES';
```

See Also

FORMAT, INFORMAT, LABEL, and LENGTH statements

Chapter 3, "Components of the SAS Language"

Chapter 4, "Rules of the SAS Language"

Chapter 13, "SAS Informats"

Chapter 14, "SAS Formats"

BY

Controls the operation of a SET, MERGE, or UPDATE statement in the DATA step and sets up special grouping variables

DATA step and PROC step

HELP BY

Syntax

BY <DESCENDING> <GROUPFORMAT> *variable-1*
< . . . <DESCENDING> <GROUPFORMAT> *variable-n*>
<NOTSORTED>;

Description

A BY statement is used in a DATA step to control the operation of a SET, MERGE, or UPDATE statement and to set up special grouping variables. The BY statement applies only to the SET, MERGE, or UPDATE statement that immediately precedes it in the DATA step, and only one BY statement can accompany each SET, MERGE, or UPDATE statement in a DATA step.

The data sets listed in the SET, MERGE, or UPDATE statements must be sorted by the values of the variables listed in the BY statement or have an appropriate index, unless you use the NOTSORTED option with the BY statement. As a default, the SAS System expects the data sets to be arranged in ascending numeric order or in alphabetical order. The observations can be arranged by sorting the data set, by creating an index for the variables, or by inputting the observations in order. Refer to "BY-Group Processing" in Chapter 4 for information on how to prepare your SAS data sets before using the BY statement. If you are using SAS data views, refer to the appropriate SAS documentation for your database management system before using the BY statement. Refer to the *SAS Procedures Guide* for information on using the BY statement with SAS procedures.

You can use the following arguments with the BY statement:

variable
: names each variable by which the data set is sorted or indexed. The data set can be sorted or indexed by more than one variable. The variables in the BY statement define the BY variables the SAS System uses during processing. The following statement indicates that the data set or data sets are sorted in alphabetical order by the character variable CITY:

```
by city;
```

The following statement indicates that the data set or data sets are sorted or indexed in alphabetical order by the character variable CITY, and within each value of CITY, in ascending order by the numeric variable ZIPCODE:

```
by city zipcode;
```

DESCENDING
: indicates that the data sets are sorted in descending order by that variable. For example, the following statement specifies that the data set is sorted in descending order of the values of X and, within each X value, in ascending order of Y:

```
by descending x y;
```

The following statement specifies that the data set is sorted in descending order of the values of both X and Y:

```
by descending x descending y;
```

Note: You cannot use the DESCENDING option with indexed data sets because indexes are always stored in ascending order.

GROUPFORMAT
tells the SAS System to use the formatted values of the variable when assigning FIRST.*variable* and LAST.*variable* in a DATA step. If you omit the GROUPFORMAT option, the SAS System assigns FIRST.*variable* and LAST.*variable* using unformatted values of the BY variable.

The GROUPFORMAT option is useful when you define your own formats to display grouped data. Using the GROUPFORMAT option in the DATA step ensures that BY groups you use to create a data set match those in PROC steps which report grouped, formatted data. BY-group processing in the DATA step using the GROUPFORMAT option is the same as BY-group processing with formatted values in SAS procedures. Use either a FORMAT or ATTRIB statement to associate formats with variables in a DATA step.

You must sort the observations in a data set based on the value of the BY variables before using the GROUPFORMAT option in the BY statement. If you also use the NOTSORTED option, you can group the observations in a data set by the formatted value of the BY variables instead of sorting them.

Refer to "BY-Group Processing" in Chapter 4 for an example of using the GROUPFORMAT option. The following example shows the correct placement of the GROUPFORMAT option in the BY statement:

```
by groupformat range;
```

Note: You cannot use the GROUPFORMAT option in a BY statement in a PROC step.

NOTSORTED
specifies that observations with the same BY value are grouped together, but are not necessarily sorted in alphabetical or numeric order. The NOTSORTED option can appear anywhere in the BY statement.

The NOTSORTED option is useful if you have data that fall into other logical groupings such as chronological order or categories. In the following example, if the data in the data set TRAVEL are arranged by the name of the month in which the expenses were accrued, you can process the data by the variable MONTH using these statements:

```
set travel;
by month nonsorted;
```

The FIRST.MONTH and LAST.MONTH variables are reset at the beginning and end of each new month.

Comparisons

The following sections describe the differences in the way the SAS System handles the BY statement when it is used with the SET, MERGE, or UPDATE statements.

BY

continued

SET Statement

Using a SET statement with a BY statement in a DATA step to read only one data set creates FIRST. variables and LAST. variables, and produces an error message if the data set is not sorted based on the values of the BY variables (and you do not use the NOTSORTED option). You can use FIRST. variables and LAST. variables in conditions in program statements.

Using a SET statement with a BY statement to read two or more data sets interleaves the data sets. The SAS System reads all the observations in the first BY group from one data set, then all the observations in the first BY group from the next data set, and so on. The output data set contains all the observations in the input data sets sorted according to the variables in the BY statement. The values of the variables in the program data vector are set to missing when the value of a BY group changes. You can use both the NOTSORTED and DESCENDING options.

MERGE Statement

Using a MERGE statement with a BY statement joins the data sets listed in the MERGE statement by matching values of the variables listed in the BY statement. FIRST. variables and LAST. variables are created for each variable listed in the BY statement. The values of the variables in the program data vector are set to missing when the value of a BY group changes.

You cannot use the NOTSORTED option with the MERGE statement. You can use the DESCENDING option, but only if all data sets being merged contain observations sorted in descending order of the variables in the BY statement.

UPDATE Statement

You must always use the BY statement with the UPDATE statement to identify the matching variable or variables to use in the update. The values of the variables in the program data vector are set to missing when the value of a BY group changes. The SAS System creates FIRST. variables and LAST. variables. The DESCENDING option is valid with the UPDATE statement, but you cannot use the NOTSORTED option.

BY Statement with SAS Procedures

You can specify the BY statement with some SAS procedures to modify their action. Refer to the individual procedure in the *SAS Procedures Guide* for a discussion of how the BY statement affects processing for SAS procedures.

See Also

MERGE, SET, and UPDATE statements

"BY-Group Processing" and "Combining SAS Data Sets" in Chapter 4, "Rules of the SAS Language"

"SAS Indexes" in Chapter 6, "SAS Files"

SAS Procedures Guide, Version 6, Third Edition

CALL

Invokes or calls a SAS CALL routine

DATA step

HELP CALL

Syntax

CALL *routine* (*parameter-1*<, . . . *parameter-n*>);

Description

The CALL statement invokes a SAS CALL routine. SAS CALL routines can assign variable values and perform other system functions.

You can use the following arguments with the CALL statement:

routine names the SAS CALL routine you want to invoke.

(parameter) is a piece of information to be passed to or returned from the routine. This information, which depends on the specific routine, should be enclosed in parentheses.

Note: The CALL routines in base SAS software are described in Chapter 12, "SAS CALL Routines." Other SAS System products provide additional CALL routines.

See Also

"CALL Routines" in Chapter 3, "Components of the SAS Language"

Chapter 12, "SAS CALL Routines"

CARDS

Indicates that data lines follow

DATA step

HELP CARDS

Syntax

CARDS;

Description

The CARDS statement indicates that data lines follow the statement. Use the CARDS statement when you are reading data in your SAS program with the INPUT statement. Always place the CARDS statement directly before the first data line.

The SAS System recognizes the end of the data lines when it sees a semicolon. Therefore, use the CARDS statement only when the data do not contain semicolons. The first line after the last data line should be either a null statement (a line containing a single semicolon) or another SAS statement (such as RUN, DATA, PROC, or TITLE) ending with a semicolon on the same line:

□
```
   cards;
data lines
;
```

□
```
   cards;
data lines
run;
```

The CARDS statement must be the last statement in your DATA step (unless you use the RUN statement), and it must be followed immediately by data lines. The SAS System handles data line length with the system option CARDIMAGE. If you use CARDIMAGE, the system treats data lines as if they were punched card images, exactly 80 bytes long and padded with blanks. If you use NOCARDIMAGE, data lines longer than 80 columns are read in their entirety. Refer to Chapter 16, "SAS System Options," for details.

The CARDS statement does not provide input options for reading data. However, you can access some options by using the CARDS statement in conjunction with an INFILE statement. See the INFILE statement in this chapter for more information.

Only one CARDS statement can be used in a DATA step. To enter two sets of data when using the INPUT and CARDS statements, use two separate DATA steps.

Comparisons

The CARDS statement is used whenever data do not contain semicolons. If your data contain semicolons, use the CARDS4 statement.

The following SAS statements read raw data lines or observations stored in other files or data sets:

- □ The INFILE statement reads raw data lines stored in another file.
- □ The %INCLUDE statement reads SAS program statements or data lines stored in SAS files or external files.
- □ The SET, MERGE, and UPDATE statements read observations from existing SAS data sets.

CARDS

continued

Example

In the following example, the SAS System reads in two character variables, NAME and DEPT, for each observation in the DATA step:

```
data person;
   input name $ dept $;
   cards;
John Sales
Mary Acctng
;
```

See Also

CARDS4 and INFILE statements

CARDIMAGE system option in Chapter 16, "SAS System Options"

CARDS4

Indicates that data lines containing semicolons follow

DATA step

HELP CARDS4

Syntax

CARDS4;

Description

The CARDS4 statement indicates that data lines containing semicolons follow the statement. This statement prevents the SAS System from treating a semicolon in the data as a signal of the end of the data lines. After the last data line, a line consisting of four semicolons in columns 1 through 4 signals the end of the data.

Comparisons

You use the CARDS4 statement when your data contain semicolons. When data do not contain semicolons, use the CARDS statement.

Example

In this example, the SAS System reads data lines, including the internal semicolons, until it encounters the line of four semicolons. Execution continues with the rest of the program.

```
data _null_;
   input number citation & $50.;
   file file-specification;
   put number @3 citation;
   cards4;
1  SMITH, 1982
2  ALLEN ET AL., 1975; BRADY, 1983
3  BROWN, 1990; LEWIS, 1984; WILLIAMS, 1982
;;;;
```

See Also

CARDS statement

INFILE statement

Comment

Documents the purpose of the job

Global

HELP COMMENT

Syntax

******message*;

or

/**message**/

Description

The comment statement can be used anywhere in a SAS job to document the purpose of the job, explain unusual segments of the program, or describe steps in a complex program or calculation. The SAS System ignores text in comment statements during processing.

You use the following argument with the comment statement:

message explains or documents the job. The message can be any length.

The SAS System allows two types of comments. Comments of the form **message*; must be written as separate statements and cannot contain internal semicolons.

Comments of the form /**message**/ may be written within statements or anywhere a single blank may appear. These comments can contain semicolons.

▶ ***Caution:*** *Avoid placing the /* comment symbols in columns 1 and 2.*

On some host systems, the SAS System may interpret a /* in columns 1 and 2 as a request to end the SAS job or session. Refer to the documentation for your host system for more information.

Note: The SAS System will not support nested comments.

Examples

The two types of comments are illustrated in the following examples:

□
```
*Test run;
```

□
```
*This code finds the number in the BY group;
```

□
```
*-----------------------------------------------------*
|        This uses one comment statement              |
|               to draw a box.                        |
*-----------------------------------------------------* ;
```

□
```
input @1 name $20.  /* last name    */
      @50 age 3.    /* customer age */
      @200 test 8.; /* score test   */
```

DATA

Begins a DATA step and provides names for any output SAS data sets

DATA step

HELP DATA

Syntax

DATA <*data-set-name-1* <(*data-set-options-1*)>>
< . . . *data-set-name-n*<(*data-set-options-n*)>>;

Description

The DATA statement begins a DATA step and provides names for any SAS data sets being created. It also enables you to specify data set options that control certain features of each new data set. The DATA statement is most commonly written with at least one data set name following it, although the SAS System can provide a default name.

You can use the following arguments with the DATA statement:

no argument
: automatically assigns the names DATA1, DATA2, and so forth to each successive data set you create. This feature is referred to as the DATA*n* naming convention.

data-set-name
: is the name you assign to the new data set. It must conform to the rules for SAS names, and there may be additional restrictions imposed by your host system. The data set name can be a one-level name (for example, FITNESS), a two-level name (for example, OUT.FITNESS), or one of the special SAS data set names. See "Data Set Names" in Chapter 6, "SAS Files," for a description of the types of SAS data set names and when to use each type.

A DATA statement can name one data set:

- `data fitness;`
- `data out.fitness;`

It can also name more than one data set:

- `data year1 year2 year3;`
- `data males females;`
- `data library.total errors;`

(*data-set-options*)
: are optional arguments appearing in parentheses after a SAS data set name. They specify one or more actions the SAS System is to take when writing observations to the output data set. The form of SAS data set options is as follows:

(*option-1*=*value-1* <. . . *option-n*=*value-n*>)

The following example shows the form of the LABEL= and RENAME= data set options when used in the DATA statement:

```
data fitness(label='HEALTH CLUB' rename=(weight=pounds));
```

For a list of data set options that you can use for output data sets, refer to Table 3.11, "SAS Data Set Options," in Chapter 3.

DATA

continued

Example

For a detailed description of the DATA step and a step-by-step explanation of how the SAS System builds a SAS data set, refer to Chapter 2, "The DATA Step."

See Also

"SAS Data Set Options" in Chapter 3, "Components of the SAS Language"

"SAS Names" in Chapter 4, "Rules of the SAS Language"

"SAS Data Sets" in Chapter 6, "SAS Files"

DELETE

Stops processing of the current observation

DATA step

HELP DELETE

Syntax

DELETE;

Description

The DELETE statement tells the SAS System to stop processing the current observation. The observation is not written to any data set, and the SAS System returns immediately to the beginning of the DATA step for another iteration.

The DELETE statement is often used as the THEN clause in an IF-THEN statement or as part of a conditionally executed DO group. If a DELETE statement is executed for every observation, the new data set has no observations.

Comparisons

In general, use the DELETE statement when it is easier to specify a condition for excluding observations from the data set, and there is no need to continue processing the DATA step statements for the current observation. Use the subsetting IF statement when it is easier to specify a condition for including observations.

Do not confuse the DROP statement with the DELETE statement. The DROP statement excludes variables from an output data set; the DELETE statement excludes observations.

Examples

You can use the DELETE statement as shown in the following examples:

□
```
delete;                                  /* by itself         */
```

□
```
if leafwt=. then delete;                 /* as part of if-then */
```

□
```
data topsales;
   infile file-specification;
   input region office product yrsales;
   if yrsales<100000 then delete;        /* to subset raw data */
run;
```

See Also

DO, DROP, subsetting IF, and IF-THEN statements

Chapter 9, "Creating Subsets of Observations," in *SAS Language and Procedures: Usage, Version 6, First Edition*

DISPLAY

Displays a window created with the WINDOW statement

DATA step

HELP DISPLAY

Syntax

DISPLAY *window*<*.group*> <NOINPUT> <BLANK> <BELL>;

Description

The DISPLAY statement displays a window created with the WINDOW statement. Once you display a window, the window remains visible until you display another window over it or until the end of the DATA step. When you display a window containing fields where you can enter values, you must either enter a value or press ENTER at *each* unprotected field to cause the SAS System to proceed to the next display. You cannot skip any fields. While a window is being displayed, you can use commands and function keys to view other windows, change the size of the current window, and so on. SAS execution proceeds to the next display only after you have pressed ENTER at all unprotected fields.

A DATA step containing a DISPLAY statement continues execution until the last observation read by a SET, MERGE, UPDATE, or INPUT statement has been processed or until a STOP or ABORT statement is executed. (You can also issue the END command on the command line of the window to stop the execution of the DATA step.)

You must create a window before you can display it. See the WINDOW statement later in this chapter for a description of how to create windows. A window displayed with the DISPLAY statement does not become part of the SAS log or output file.

You can use the following arguments with the DISPLAY statement:

window<*.group*>
: names the window and group of fields to be displayed. If the window has more than one group of fields, give the complete *window.group* specification; if a window contains a single unnamed group, use only *window*.

NOINPUT
: specifies that you cannot input values into fields displayed in the window. If you do not use NOINPUT, you can input values into unprotected fields displayed in the window. If you use NOINPUT in all DISPLAY statements in a DATA step, you *must* include a STOP statement to stop processing the DATA step.

  The NOINPUT option is useful when you want to allow values to be entered into a window at some times but not others. For example, you can display a window once for entering values and a second time for verifying them.

BLANK
: clears the window. Use the BLANK option when you want to display different groups of fields in a window and you do not want text from the previous group to appear in the current display.

BELL
: produces an audible alarm, beep, or bell sound when the window is displayed, if your terminal is equipped with a speaker device that provides sound.

Example

The following DATA step creates and displays a window named START. The START window fills the entire screen. Both lines of text are centered.

```
data _null_;
   window start
         #5 @28 'WELCOME TO THE SAS SYSTEM'
         #12 @30 'PRESS ENTER TO CONTINUE';
   display start;
   stop;
run;
```

Although the START window in this example does not require you to input any values, you must press ENTER to cause SAS execution to proceed to the STOP statement. If you omit the STOP statement, the DATA step executes endlessly unless you enter END on the command line of the window. (Because this DATA step does not read any observations, the SAS System cannot detect an end-of-file to cause DATA step execution to cease.) If you add the NOINPUT option to the DISPLAY statement, the window displays quickly and is removed.

See Also

WINDOW statement

Chapter 7, "SAS Display Manager System"

DM

Submits SAS display manager or text editor commands as SAS statements

Global

HELP DM

Syntax

DM<*window*> '*command-1*<; . . . *command-n*>' <*window*>;

Description

The DM statement enables you to submit SAS display manager or text editor commands as SAS statements. Execution occurs when the statement is submitted to the SAS System. This statement is useful for

- □ changing display manager features during a SAS session
- □ changing display manager features at the beginning of each SAS session by placing the DM statement in an autoexec file
- □ performing utility functions in full-screen applications, such as saving a file with the FILE command or clearing a window with the CLEAR command.

You can use the following arguments with the DM statement:

window

specifies the active window. This is an optional argument that can appear in the DM statement either preceding or following the command or series of commands. Its placement affects the outcome of the statement as follows:

- □ If you name a window before the commands, those commands apply to that window.
- □ If you name a window after the commands, the SAS System executes the commands, then makes that window the active window. The active window is opened and contains the cursor.

In either case, if you omit the window name, the SAS System uses the PROGRAM EDITOR window as the default.

'command'

can be any valid display manager command or text editor command and must be enclosed in single quotes. If you want to issue several commands, separate them with semicolons.

If you specify CATALOG as the active window, for instance, and have other SAS statements following the DM statement (for example, in an autoexec file), those statements are not submitted to the SAS System until control returns to display manager. Statements following the DM statement are executed before statements submitted from the CATALOG window.

Examples

You can use the DM statement as shown in this section.

□ If you are using a color monitor, use the DM statement to change the color of your PROGRAM EDITOR window display. The following statement changes text color in the PROGRAM EDITOR window to cyan and command line text to red. Because no window is specified either before or after the command string, the action applies to the PROGRAM EDITOR window, and after execution, the cursor returns to the window.

```
dm 'color text cyan; color command red';
```

□ The following statement clears the log, changes the color of the sequence numbers in the PROGRAM EDITOR window to green, and makes the OUTPUT window the active window:

```
dm log 'clear; pgm; color numbers green' output;
```

□ You can also issue text editor commands with the DM statement. For example, you can instruct the SAS System to capitalize all the text you enter in the PROGRAM EDITOR window by first submitting the following DM statement:

```
dm 'caps on';
```

□ The following statement clears the log and makes the OUTPUT window the active window:

```
dm log 'clear' output;
```

See Also

"Running the System" in Chapter 1, "Essential Concepts"

Chapter 17, "SAS Display Manager Windows"

Chapter 18, "SAS Display Manager Commands"

Chapter 19, "SAS Text Editor Commands"

DO

Designates a group of statements to be executed as a unit

DATA step

HELP DO

Syntax

DO;
more SAS statements
END;

Description

The DO statement designates a group of statements to be executed as a unit until a matching END statement is encountered. The statements between the DO and END statements are called a DO group. DO statements can be nested within DO groups.*

A simple DO statement is often used within IF-THEN/ELSE statements to designate a group of statements to be executed depending on whether an IF condition is true or false.

The DO statement takes no arguments.

Comparisons

The DO statement is the simplest form of DO-group processing. There are four other forms of the DO statement.

- □ The iterative DO statement executes statements between DO and END statements repetitively based on the value of an index variable. The iterative DO statement can contain a WHILE or UNTIL clause.
- □ The DO OVER statement executes the statements in a DO loop for the elements in an implicit array.
- □ The DO UNTIL statement executes statements in a DO loop repetitively until a condition is true, checking the condition after each execution of the DO loop.
- □ The DO WHILE statement executes statements in a DO loop repetitively while a condition is true, checking the condition before each execution of the DO loop.

Example

The following statements show an example of a simple DO group:

```
if years>5 then
   do;
      months=years*12;
      put years= months=;
   end;
else yrsleft=5-years;
```

The statements between DO and END are performed only when the value of YEARS is greater than 5. If YEARS is less than or equal to 5, statements in the DO group are skipped and the program continues with the last assignment statement.

* Limitations on the number of nested DO statements you can use depend on the memory capabilities of your system. See your hardware documentation for more information.

See Also

Iterative DO statement

DO OVER statement

DO UNTIL statement

DO WHILE statement

DO, Iterative

Executes statements between DO and END repetitively based on the value of an index variable

DATA step

HELP DO

Syntax

DO *index-variable=specification-1*<, . . . *specification-n*>;
  more SAS statements
END;

Description

The iterative DO statement causes the statements between DO and END statements to be executed repetitively based on the value of the index variable.

You can use the following arguments with the iterative DO statement:

index-variable

names a variable whose value governs execution of the DO group. Unless dropped, the index variable is included in the data set being created.

▶ ***Caution:*** *Avoid changing the index variable within the DO group.*

If you modify the index variable within the iterative DO group, you may cause infinite looping.

specification

denotes an expression or series of expressions in the following form:

start <TO *stop*> <BY *increment*> <WHILE | UNTIL(*expression*)>

The order of the optional TO and BY clauses can be reversed. When you use more than one *specification*, each is evaluated prior to its execution. The elements of the syntax are described here:

start

specifies the initial value of the index variable. When used with TO *stop* or BY *increment*, *start* must be a number or an expression that yields a number. The DO group is executed first with *index-variable* equal to *start*. The value of *start* is evaluated before the first execution of the loop.

When used without TO *stop* or BY *increment*, the value of *start* can be a series of items expressed in the following form:

item-1<, . . . *item-n*>;

The items may be either all numeric or all character constants, or they may be variables. Enclose character constants in quotes. The DO group is executed once for each value in the list. Here are some examples:

- `do month='JAN','FEB','MAR';`
- `do count=2,3,5,7,11,13,17;`
- `do i=5;`

TO *stop*

specifies the ending value of the index variable. *Stop* can be a number or an expression that yields a number.

When both *start* and *stop* are present, execution continues (based on the value of *increment*) until the value of *index-variable* passes the value of *stop*. When only *start* and *increment* are present, execution continues (based on the value of *increment*) until a statement directs execution out of the loop, or until a WHILE or UNTIL expression specified in the DO statement is satisfied. If neither *stop* nor *increment* is specified, the group executes according to the value of *start*. The value of *stop* is evaluated before the first execution of the loop.

Any changes to *stop* made within the DO group do not affect the number of iterations. To stop iteration of a loop before it finishes processing, change the value of *index-variable* to pass the value of *stop*, or use a GO TO statement to jump to a statement outside the loop.

The following iterative DO statements use the *start* TO *stop* syntax:

- `do i=1 to 10;`
- `do i=1 to exit;`
- `do i=1 to x-5;`

BY *increment*

specifies a number (or an expression that yields a number) to control incrementing of *index-variable*. The value of *increment* is evaluated prior to the execution of the loop. Any changes to the increment made within the DO group do not affect the number of iterations. The following statement executes the DO group when the value of COUNT is 2, 4, 6, and 8:

```
do count=2 to 8 by 2;
```

The value of COUNT after the final execution of the DO group is 10.

If no increment is specified, the index variable is increased by 1. When *increment* is positive, *start* must be the lower bound and *stop*, if present, must be the upper bound for the loop. If *increment* is negative, *start* must be the upper bound and *stop*, if present, must be the lower bound for the loop.

WHILE(*expression*)
UNTIL(*expression*)

evaluates, either before or after execution of the DO group, any SAS expression you specify enclosed in parentheses. A WHILE or UNTIL specification affects only the clause in which it is located.

A WHILE expression is evaluated before each execution of the loop, so that the statements inside the group are executed repetitively while the expression is true. An UNTIL expression is evaluated after each execution of the loop, so that the statements inside the group are executed repetitively until the expression is true. See the DO WHILE and DO UNTIL statements later in this chapter for more information.

DO, Iterative

(WHILE continued)

The following statements are examples of using WHILE and UNTIL clauses:

- □ `do i=1 to 10 while(x<y);`
- □ `do i=2 to 20 by 2 until((x/3)>y);`
- □ `do i=10 to 0 by -1 while(month='JAN');`

Comparisons

There are four other forms of the DO statement.

- □ The DO statement, the simplest form of DO-group processing, designates a group of statements to be executed as a unit, usually as a part of IF-THEN/ELSE statements.
- □ The DO OVER statement executes the statements in a DO group for the elements in an implicit array.
- □ The DO UNTIL statement executes statements in a DO loop repetitively until a condition is true, checking the condition after each execution of the DO loop.
- □ The DO WHILE statement executes statements in a DO loop repetitively while a condition is true, checking the condition before each execution of the DO loop.

Examples

Example 1: Using the Iterative DO Statement

In each of the following examples, the DO group is executed ten times. The first example uses the preferred approach. In the second example, without specifying a WHILE or UNTIL clause in the DO statement, infinite looping can occur. The third example demonstrates using an UNTIL clause to set a flag, then checking the flag during each iteration of the loop.

□
```
do i=1 to 10;
   SAS statements
end;
```

□
```
do i=1 by 1;
   SAS statements
   if i=10 then go to f;
end;
f:put 'FINISHED';
```

□
```
do i=1 to 10 until(flag);
   SAS statements
   if expression then flag=1;
   SAS statements
end;
```

Example 2: Stopping Execution of the DO Loop

In this example, setting the value of the index variable to the current value of EXIT causes the loop to terminate.

```
data iterate1;
   input x;
   exit=10;
   do i=1 to exit;
      y=x*normal(0);
         /* if y>25, changing i's value stops execution */
      if y>25 then i=exit;
      output;
   end;
   cards;
5
1000
2500
;
```

You can also use a GO TO statement to jump to a statement outside the loop, as follows:

```
if y>25 then goto out;
```

In this example, OUT is a label on a statement located outside the DO loop.

Example 3: Using Other Forms of the Iterative DO Statement

The following are examples of valid iterative DO statements:

- `do i=1 to n;`
- `do i=n to 1 by -1;`
- `do i=k+1 to n-1;`
- `do i=1 to k-1, k+1 to n;`
- `do i=.1 to .9 by .1, 1 to 10 by 1, 20 to 100 by 10;`
- `do i='SATURDAY','SUNDAY';`
- `do i='01JAN90'd,'25FEB90'd,'18APR90'd;`
- `do i='01JAN90'd to '01JAN91'd by 1;`

See Also

Explicit ARRAY statement

Explicit array reference

DO statement

DO OVER statement

DO UNTIL statement

DO WHILE statement

DO OVER

Executes the statements in a DO loop for the elements in an implicit array

DATA step

HELP DO

Syntax

DO OVER *array-name;*
more SAS statements
END;

Description

The DO OVER statement executes the statements in a DO loop for all the elements in an implicit array. The DO OVER statement can be used only with implicit arrays.

You use the following argument with the DO OVER statement:

array-name specifies an array that has been previously defined in an implicit ARRAY statement.

The DO OVER statement automatically executes the statements in the DO loop for each element of the array, unless you specify otherwise. It is equivalent to the following statement:

```
do i=1 to k;
```

In this statement, I is the index variable of the array, and K is the number of elements in the array.

Note: While implicit arrays are still supported in this version of the SAS System, using explicit arrays is recommended because of their power and flexibility. See "Array Processing" in Chapter 4 for background information on arrays.

Comparisons

There are four other forms of the DO statement.

- □ The DO statement, the simplest form of DO-group processing, designates a group of statements to be executed as a unit, usually as a part of IF-THEN/ELSE statements.
- □ The iterative DO statement executes statements between DO and END statements repetitively based on the value of an index variable.
- □ The DO UNTIL statement executes statements in a DO loop repetitively until a condition is true, checking the condition after each execution of the DO loop.
- □ The DO WHILE statement executes statements in a DO loop repetitively while a condition is true, checking the condition before each execution of the DO loop.

Example

In the following example, the DO OVER statement causes each variable in the implicit array to be multiplied by 100:

```
data test;
   input score1-score5;
   array s score1-score5;
   do over s;
      s=s*100;
   end;
   cards;
 .95 .88 .57 .90 .65
 ;
```

See Also

Implicit ARRAY statement

Implicit array reference

DO statement

Iterative DO statement

DO UNTIL statement

DO WHILE statement

DO UNTIL

Executes statements in a DO loop repetitively until a condition is true

DATA step

HELP DO

Syntax

DO UNTIL(*expression*);

Description

The DO UNTIL statement executes the statements in a DO loop repetitively until a certain condition is true.

You use the following argument with the DO UNTIL statement:

(expression) is any valid SAS expression, enclosed in parentheses. The expression is evaluated at the bottom of the loop after the statements in the DO loop have been executed. If the expression is true, the DO loop is not executed again. The DO loop is always executed at least once.

Comparisons

There are four other forms of the DO statement.

- □ The DO statement, the simplest form of DO-group processing, designates a group of statements to be executed as a unit, usually as a part of IF-THEN/ELSE statements.
- □ The iterative DO statement executes statements between DO and END statements repetitively based on the value of an index variable.
- □ The DO OVER statement executes the statements in a DO loop for the elements in an implicit array.
- □ The DO WHILE statement executes statements in a DO loop repetitively while a condition is true, checking the condition before each execution of the DO loop. The DO UNTIL statement evaluates the condition at the bottom of the loop; the DO WHILE statement evaluates the condition at the top of the loop.

  Note: The statements in a DO UNTIL loop are always executed at least one time, whereas if the condition is false, a DO WHILE loop does not execute even once.

Example

These statements repeat the loop until N is greater than or equal to 5. The expression N>=5 is evaluated at the bottom of the loop. There are five iterations in all (0, 1, 2, 3, 4).

```
n=0;
do until(n>=5);
   put n=;
   n+1;
end;
```

See Also

DO, iterative DO, DO OVER, and DO WHILE statements

"SAS Expressions" in Chapter 4, "Rules of the SAS Language"

DO WHILE

Executes statements repetitively while a condition is true

DATA step

HELP DO

Syntax

DO WHILE(*expression*);

Description

The DO WHILE statement executes the statements in a DO loop repetitively while a condition is true.

You use the following argument with the DO WHILE statement:

(*expression*) is any valid SAS expression, enclosed in parentheses. The expression is evaluated at the top of the loop before the statements in the DO loop are executed. If the expression is true, the DO loop is executed. If the expression is false the first time it is evaluated, the DO loop is not executed at all.

Comparisons

There are four other forms of the DO statement.

- □ The DO statement, the simplest form of DO-group processing, designates a group of statements to be executed as a unit, usually as a part of IF-THEN/ELSE statements.
- □ The iterative DO statement executes statements between DO and END statements repetitively based on the value of an index variable.
- □ The DO OVER statement executes the statements in a DO loop for the elements in an implicit array.
- □ The DO UNTIL statement executes statements in a DO loop repetitively until a condition is true, checking the condition after each execution of the DO loop. The DO WHILE statement evaluates the condition at the top of the loop; the DO UNTIL statement evaluates the condition at the bottom of the loop.

  Note: If the expression is false, the statements in a DO WHILE loop do not execute. However, because the DO UNTIL expression is evaluated at the bottom of the loop, the statements in the DO UNTIL loop always execute at least once.

Example

These statements repeat the loop while the value of N is less than 5. The expression N LT 5 is evaluated at the top of the loop. There are five iterations in all (0, 1, 2, 3, 4).

```
n=0;
do while(n lt 5);
   put n=;
   n+1;
end;
```

DO WHILE

continued

See Also

DO, iterative DO, DO OVER, and DO UNTIL statements

"SAS Expressions" in Chapter 4, "Rules of the SAS Language"

DROP

Excludes variables from output SAS data sets

DATA step

HELP DROP

Syntax

DROP *variable-list;*

Description

The DROP statement omits variables you specify from one or more SAS data sets created by a DATA step. The SAS System includes any variables you do not list. The DROP statement applies to all the SAS data sets created within the same DATA step and can appear anywhere in the step. The variables in the DROP statement are available for processing in the DATA step. If no DROP or KEEP statement appears, all data sets created in the DATA step contain all variables. Do not use both DROP and KEEP statements within the same DATA step.

You use the following argument with the DROP statement:

variable-list specifies the names of the variables to omit from the output data set. You can list the variables in any form allowed by the SAS System, such as

- `drop time shift batchnum;`
- `drop grade1-grade20;`

Comparisons

The DROP statement differs from the DROP= data set option in the following ways:

- You cannot use the DROP statement in SAS PROC steps.
- The DROP statement applies to all output data sets named in the DATA statement. To exclude variables from some data sets but not from others, use the DROP= data set option in the DATA statement.

The KEEP statement is a parallel statement that specifies a list of variables to write to output data sets. Use the KEEP statement instead of the DROP statement if the number of variables to include is significantly smaller than the number to omit.

Do not confuse the DROP statement with the DELETE statement. The DROP statement excludes variables from output data sets; the DELETE statement excludes observations.

Example

In the following example, the variables PURCHASE and REPAIR are used in processing but are not written to the output data set INVENTRY:

```
data inventry;
   infile file-specification;
   input unit part purchase repair;
   totcost=sum(purchase,repair);
   drop purchase repair;
run;
```

DROP

continued

See Also

DELETE and KEEP statements

DROP= data set option in Chapter 15, "SAS Data Set Options"

END

Ends a DO group or a SELECT group

DATA step

HELP END

Syntax

END;

Description

The END statement is the last of the SAS statements that make up a DO group or a SELECT group. The END statement must end every DO group and SELECT group in your SAS job.

Examples

A simple DO group and a simple SELECT group are shown here:

□
```
do;
  more SAS statements
end;
```

□
```
select(expression);
   when(expression) SAS statement;
   otherwise SAS statement;
end;
```

See Also

DO statement

SELECT statement

ENDSAS

Terminates a SAS job or session after execution of the current DATA or PROC step

Global

HELP ENDSAS

Syntax

ENDSAS;

Description

The ENDSAS statement terminates a SAS job or session after execution of the current DATA or PROC step. The statement is most useful in interactive or display manager sessions. The SAS System requires ENDSAS statements to occur at statement boundaries (that is, after a semicolon). ENDSAS statements cannot be part of other statements such as IF-THEN statements.

Comparisons

The SAS System also provides BYE and ENDSAS commands, which can be issued on any display manager command line.

See Also

BYE and ENDSAS commands in Chapter 18, "SAS Display Manager Commands"

ERROR

Sets _ERROR_ to 1 and, optionally, writes a message to the SAS log

DATA step

HELP ERROR

Syntax

ERROR <*message*>;

Description

The ERROR statement sets the automatic variable _ERROR_ to 1 and, optionally, writes a message you specify to the SAS log. When the value of _ERROR_ is 1, the SAS System writes the data lines corresponding to the current observation in the SAS log.

You can use the following arguments with the ERROR statement:

no argument
: sets the automatic variable _ERROR_ to 1 without printing any message in the log.

message
: writes a message to the log. *Message* can include character literals (enclosed in quotes), variable names, formats, and pointer controls.

Comparisons

The ERROR statement is equivalent to the following series of statements: an assignment statement setting _ERROR_ to 1, a FILE LOG statement, a PUT statement (if you specify a message), and another FILE statement resetting FILE to any previously specified setting.

Examples

In the following examples, the SAS System writes the error message and the variable name and value to the log for each observation that satisfies the condition in the IF-THEN statement. In the first example, the ERROR statement automatically resets the FILE statement specification to the previously specified setting. The second example uses a series of statements to produce the same results.

□
```
file file-specification;
if type='teen' & age>19 then
   error 'type and age don"t match ' age=;
```

□
```
file file-specification;
if type='teen' & age>19 then
   do;
      file log;
      put 'type and age don"t match ' age=;
      _error_=1;
      file file-specification;
   end;
```

See Also

PUT statement

"Automatic Variables" in Chapter 2, "The DATA Step"

FILE

Specifies the current output file for PUT statements

DATA step

HELP FILE

Syntax

FILE *file-specification*<*options*> <*host-options*>;

Description

The FILE statement specifies the output file for PUT statements in the current DATA step. By default, PUT statement output is written to the SAS log. You can use the FILE statement to route this output to either the same file to which procedure output is written or to a different file. You can indicate whether or not carriage control characters should be added to the file. Note that the FILE statement specifies an external file, not a SAS data set.

More than one FILE statement can be used in a DATA step. Because the FILE statement is executable, it can be used in conditional (IF-THEN) processing.

You can use the FILE statement with the INFILE and PUT statements to update an external file in place. You can update an entire record or update only selected fields within a record. When you use the FILE and INFILE statements this way, use the following guidelines:

- □ Always place the INFILE statement first.
- □ Specify the same fileref or physical filename in the INFILE and FILE statements.
- □ Use options that are common to both the FILE and INFILE statements in the INFILE statement. (Any such options used in the FILE statement are ignored.)
- □ Use the SHAREBUFFERS option in the INFILE statement to allow the FILE and INFILE statements to use the same buffer, which saves CPU time and enables you to update individual fields instead of entire records.

See "Example 1: Updating an External File" later in this section.

■ **Host Information** .... Using the FILE statement requires host-specific information. See the SAS documentation for your host system before using this statement.
.... ■

You can use the following arguments with the FILE statement:

file-specification
: identifies an external file to which you want to write output with a PUT statement. It is required. *File-specification* can have the following forms:

'*external-file*'
: specifies the physical name of an external file and must be enclosed in quotes. The physical name is the name by which the host system recognizes the file.

fileref
: gives the fileref of an external file. The fileref must have previously been associated with an external file in a FILENAME statement or in an appropriate host command. See the FILENAME statement later in this chapter.

fileref(file)

gives a fileref previously assigned to an external file that is an aggregate storage location. Follow the fileref with the name of a file or member, enclosed in parentheses, that resides in that location. The fileref must have previously been associated with an external file in a FILENAME statement or in an appropriate host command. See the FILENAME statement in this chapter.

■ **Host Information** .... Different host systems call an aggregate grouping of files by different names, such as a directory, a MACLIB, or a partitioned data set. For details on specifying external files, see the SAS documentation for your host system.

.... ■

LOG

directs the lines produced by PUT statements to the SAS log. Since output lines are by default written to the SAS log, a FILE LOG statement is needed only to restore the default action or to specify additional FILE statement options.

At the beginning of each execution of a DATA step, the fileref that indicates where the PUT statements write is automatically set to LOG. Therefore, the first PUT statement in a DATA step always writes to the SAS log, unless preceded by a FILE statement that specifies otherwise.

PRINT

directs the lines produced by PUT statements to the same print file as the output produced by SAS procedures. When PRINT is the fileref, the SAS System uses carriage control characters and writes the lines with the characteristics of a print file. Note that when writing to a print file, the value of the N= option (discussed later in "Options") must be either 1 or PAGESIZE. For a complete discussion of print files, see Chapter 5, "SAS Output."

■ **Host Information** .... The carriage control characters that are written to a file can be host-specific. See the SAS documentation for your host system.

.... ■

options

allow you to control how the output file is written and, among other things, to specify what action will be taken if the pointer attempts to write past the end of the line in the output file. See "Options" for option definitions.

host-options

are host-specific options.

■ **Host Information** .... See the SAS documentation for your host system for descriptions of host-specific options.

.... ■

FILE
continued

Options

You can use the following options with the FILE statement:

BLKSIZE=*block-size*
: specifies the block size of the output file.

■ **Host Information** .... The default value of the block size is host-dependent. For more details about the implementation of this option on your host, see the SAS documentation for your host system. ■

COLUMN=*variable*
COL=*variable*
: defines a variable that the SAS System sets to the current column location of the pointer. You supply the variable name; the SAS System then automatically assigns the value of the current column location to the COLUMN= variable. Like automatic variables, the COLUMN= variable is not written to the data set.

DROPOVER
: discards data items that exceed the output line length (as specified by the LINESIZE= option in the FILE statement). Use the DROPOVER option when you want the DATA step to continue execution if the PUT statement attempts to write past the current line length, *but* you do not want the data item that exceeds the line length to be written on a new line.

By default, data that exceed the current line length are written on a new line. When you specify DROPOVER, the SAS System drops (or ignores) an entire item when there is not enough space in the current line to write it. When this occurs, the column pointer remains positioned after the last value written in the current line. Thus, the PUT statement may write other items in the current output line if they fit in the space remaining or if the column pointer is repositioned. When a data item is dropped, the DATA step continues normal execution (_ERROR_=0). At the end of the DATA step, a message is printed for each file from which data were lost.

See the FLOWOVER and STOPOVER options later in this section.

FILENAME=*variable*
: defines a character variable, whose name you supply, that the SAS System sets to the value of the physical name of the file currently open for PUT statement output. By default, this variable has a length of eight characters. If the physical filename is longer, you can use a LENGTH statement to assign this variable a longer length, as shown in the following example. Like automatic variables, the FILENAME= variable is not written to the SAS data set.

For example, the following DATA step causes a file identification message to print in the log and assigns the value of the current output file to the variable MYOUT. The PUT statement, demonstrating the assignment of the proper value to MYOUT, writes the value of that variable to the output file.

```
data _null_;
   length myout $ 200;
   file file-specification filename=myout;
   put myout=;
   stop;
run;
```

The PUT statement writes a line to the current output file in the form

```
MYOUT=your-output-file
```

Note that the line contains the physical name of the current output file. See also the FILEVAR= option.

FILEVAR=*variable*
defines a variable whose change in value causes the FILE statement to close the current output file and open a new one. The next PUT statement that executes writes to the new file specified as the value of the FILEVAR= variable. The value of a FILEVAR= variable is expressed as a character string that contains a physical filename. The variable has a default length of eight characters. Use another statement, such as a LENGTH statement or an INPUT statement, to assign it a longer length if necessary. Like automatic variables, the FILEVAR= variable is not written to the data set.

The following DATA step uses the FILEVAR= option to dynamically change the currently opened output file to a new physical file:

```
data _null_;
   length name $ 200;

      /* Read instream data lines for value to assign to the */
      /* NAME variable.                                      */
   input name $;

      /* Close the current output file and open a new one    */
      /* when the NAME variable changes.                     */
   file file-specification filevar=name mod;
   date = date();

      /* Append a log record to currently open output file.  */
   put 'records updated ' date date.;
   cards;
external-file-1
external-file-2
external-file-3
;
```

FLOWOVER
causes data that exceed the current line length to be written on a new line. This action is the default. When a PUT statement attempts to write beyond the maximum allowed line length (as specified by the LINESIZE= option in the FILE statement), the current output line is

FILE

(FLOWOVER continued)

written to the file and the data item that exceeds the current line length is written to a new line.

If the PUT statement contains a trailing @, the pointer is positioned after the data item on the new line, and the next PUT statement writes to that line. This process continues until the end of the input data is reached or until a PUT statement without a trailing @ causes the current line to be written to the file.

See the DROPOVER and STOPOVER options in this section.

HEADER=*label*

defines a statement label that identifies a group of SAS statements that you want to execute each time SAS begins a new output page. The first statement after the label must be an executable statement; otherwise, you can use any SAS statement in the group of statements labeled for execution with the HEADER= option.

To prevent the statements in this group from executing with each iteration of the DATA step, use two RETURN statements: one precedes the label and the other appears as the last statement in the group. Use the HEADER= option only when writing to print files. See "Example 2: Executing Statements when a New Page is Begun" later in this section.

LINE=*variable*

defines a variable whose value is the current relative line number within the group of lines available to the output pointer. You supply the variable name; the SAS System then automatically assigns the value. The LINE= variable is set at the end of PUT statement execution to the number of the next available line.

The LINE= variable can have a value from 1 up to the value specified by the N= option or with the #*n* line pointer control. If neither is specified, the LINE= variable has a value of 1. Like automatic variables, the value of the LINE= variable is not written to the data set.

LINESIZE=*line-size*
LS=*line-size*

sets the maximum number of columns per line for reports and the maximum record length for data files.

■ **Host Information** ....

The range of values allowed is host-dependent. The lowest value available is 64 on all hosts; the highest value is dependent on the maximum logical record length allowed for a specific file. See the SAS documentation for your host system.

.... ■

If a PUT statement tries to write a line that is longer than the value specified by the LINESIZE= option, the SAS System writes the line as two or more separate records by default. (The FLOWOVER option is the default; the DROPOVER and STOPOVER options request that a different action be taken.)

For example, the following PUT statement writes three separate records:

```
file file-specification linesize=80;
put name $ 1-50 city $ 71-90 state $ 91-104;
```

The value of NAME appears in the first record, CITY begins in the first column of the second record, and STATE in the first column of the third record.

The default LINESIZE= value is determined by one of two options:

- □ the LINESIZE= system option when you write to a print file (a file that contains carriage control characters) or to the SAS log.
- □ the LRECL= option in the FILE statement when you write to a nonprint file. See the LRECL= option.

Compare the LINESIZE= and LRECL= options: the LINESIZE= option tells the SAS System how much of the line to use; the LRECL= option specifies the physical line length of the file.

LINESLEFT=*variable*
LL=*variable*

defines a variable whose value is the number of lines left on the current page. You supply the variable name; the SAS System assigns that variable the value of the number of lines left on the current page. The LINESLEFT= variable is set at the end of PUT statement execution. Like automatic variables, the LINESLEFT= variable is not written to the data set. See "Example 3: Determining New Page by Lines Left on Current Page." Compare the LINESLEFT= option with the PAGESIZE= option later in this section.

LRECL=*logical-record-length*

specifies the logical record length of the output file. If you do not use the LRECL= option, the SAS System chooses a value based on the host system file characteristics. Compare with the LINESIZE= option: the LRECL= option specifies the physical line length of the file; the LINESIZE= option tells the SAS System how much of the line to use.

■ **Host Information** ....

For more details about the LRECL= option, see the SAS documentation for your host system.

.... ■

MOD

writes the output lines after any existing lines in the file. See the OLD option.

N=*available-lines*

specifies the number of lines you want available to the output pointer in the current iteration of the DATA step. *Available-lines* can be expressed as a number (*n*) or as the keyword PAGESIZE or PS.

n

specifies the number of lines available to the output pointer. For example, if N=4, four lines at a time are available to the pointer, and the system can move back and forth between the four lines while composing them before moving on to the next set of four.

FILE

continued

PAGESIZE
PS

specifies that the entire page is available to the output pointer. For example, setting N=PAGESIZE allows you to compose a page of multiple columns one column at a time. N=PAGESIZE is valid only when sending output to a print file. See "Example 4: Arranging the Contents of an Entire Page."

If the current output file is a print file, *available-lines* must have a value of either 1 or PAGESIZE.

There are two ways to control the number of lines available to the output pointer:

- the N= option
- the #*n* line pointer control in a PUT statement.

If the N= option is not specified and no # pointer controls are used, one line is available; that is, by default, N=1. If N= is not used but there are # pointer controls, N= has the highest value specified for a # pointer control in any PUT statement in the current DATA step. See the PUT statement later in this chapter for a complete discussion of the # pointer control.

NOTITLES
NOTITLE

suppresses printing of the current title lines on the pages of print files. When NOTITLES is omitted, the SAS System prints any titles currently defined.

OLD

replaces the previous contents of the file. OLD is the default setting. See the MOD option.

PAD
NOPAD

controls whether records written to an external file are padded with blanks to the length specified in the LRECL= option. The PAD option provides a quick way to create fixed-length records in a variable-length file. NOPAD is the default when writing to a variable-length file; PAD is the default when writing to a fixed-length file.

PAGESIZE=*value*
PS=*value*

sets the number of lines per page for your reports. After the value of the PAGESIZE= option is reached, the output pointer advances to line 1 of a new page.

The value may range from 20 to 500. If no value is specified, the value of the PAGESIZE= system option is used. See Chapter 16 for more information on the PAGESIZE= system option.

If any TITLE statements are currently defined, the lines they occupy are included in counting the number of lines for each page.

PRINT
NOPRINT

controls whether carriage control characters are placed in the output lines. The PRINT option is not necessary if you are using fileref PRINT. When writing to a print file, the value of the N= option must be either 1 or PAGESIZE.

■ **Host Information** .... The carriage control characters that are written to a file can be host-specific. See the SAS documentation for your host system. ■

RECFM=*record-format*

specifies the record format of the output file.

■ **Host Information** .... Values for *record-format* are host-dependent. For more details, see the SAS documentation for your host system. ■

STOPOVER

stops processing the DATA step immediately if a PUT statement attempts to write a data item that exceeds the current line length. In such a case, the SAS System discards the data item that exceeds the current line length, writes the portion of the line built before the error occurred, and issues an error message.

See the FLOWOVER and DROPOVER options earlier in this section.

Comparisons

Contrast the FILE statement with the INFILE statement and the FILE command.

□ The FILE statement specifies the output file for PUT statements in the DATA step, just as the INFILE statement specifies the input file for INPUT statements in the DATA step. Both allow you to use options that provide the SAS System with additional information about the external file being used.

□ The FILE statement specifies the external file to which PUT statement output is written. The FILE command, which can be executed from any window in display manager, specifies an external file and writes the contents of the window to the file.

FILE
continued

Examples

Example 1: Updating an External File

The following example shows use of the INFILE statement with the SHAREBUFFERS option and the INPUT, FILE, and PUT statements to update an external file in place:

```
data _null_;

      /* The INFILE and FILE statements specify the same file. */
   infile file-specification-1 sharebuffers n=3;
   file file-specification-1;
   input name $ 1-34 phone $ 35-46 #2 company $ 1-34 addr1 $ 35-72
         #3 addr2 $ 1-34 addr3 $ 35-72;
   if company= 'SAS Institute Inc.' then addr3='Cary, NC 27512-8000';
   if phone='919-467-8000' then phone='919-677-8000';
   put #1 phone 35-46 #3 addr3 35-72;
run;
```

Example 2: Executing Statements When a New Page Is Begun

The following DATA step illustrates use of the HEADER= option:

```
data _null_;
   set sprint;
   by dept;
   file print header=newpage;
   if first.dept then put _page_;
   put @22 salesrep @34 salesamt;

      /* RETURN statement is necessary before the label     */
      /* to prevent the header from executing for each      */
      /* iteration of the DATA step.                        */
   return;
   newpage:
      put @20 'Sales for 1989' /
          @20 dept=;

         /* RETURN statement is necessary as final          */
         /* statement in labeled group.                     */
      return;
run;
```

The SAS System executes the statements after the NEWPAGE label when it begins printing a new page.

Example 3: Determining New Page by Lines Left on Current Page

The following DATA step demonstrates using the LINESLEFT= option to determine where the page break should occur, according to the number of lines left on the current page:

```
data _null_;
   set info;
   file print linesleft=remain pagesize=20;
   put @5 name @30 phone @35 bldg @37 room;

      /* When there are fewer than seven lines left on   */
      /* the page, the PUT _PAGE_ statement begins a new */
      /* page and positions the pointer at line 1.  */
   if remain<7 then put _page_ ;
run;
```

Example 4: Arranging the Contents of an Entire Page

This example shows use of the N=PAGESIZE option in a DATA step to produce a two-column telephone book listing, each column containing a name and a phone number:

```
data _null_;
   file print n=pagesize;
   do col=1, 40;
      do line=1 to 20;
         set info;
         put #line @col name $20. +1 phone 4.;
      end;
   end;
   put _page_;
run;
```

The N=PAGESIZE option makes all lines on the page available to the pointer, enabling you to compose a complete column. The variables LINE and COL mark the current line and column of the pointer. The SET statement reads a SAS data set containing the names and telephone numbers. The PUT statement writes the NAME and PHONE values on the current line (the LINE value) at the current column (the COL value). The value of LINE is increased by 1 until 20 names are written.

When the inner DO loop is satisfied, the first column is complete; COL is increased to 40 to move the pointer over to the second column; and 20 more names are written in that column. When the outer DO loop is satisfied, the report includes two columns of 20 names each.

When the last value in the last column has been written, the PUT _PAGE_ statement writes the entire page. In the next execution of the DATA step, the COL and LINE values begin at 1 again.

FILE

continued

See Also

FILENAME, LABEL, PUT, RETURN, and TITLE statements

"Printed Results of SAS Programs" in Chapter 5, "SAS Output"

PAGESIZE= and LINESIZE= system options in Chapter 16, "SAS System Options"

SAS documentation for your host system for host-specific options

FILENAME

Associates a SAS fileref with an external file or an output device; disassociates a fileref and external file; lists attributes of external files

Global

HELP FILENAME

Syntax

FILENAME *fileref* <*device-type*> '*external-file*' <*host-options*>;
FILENAME *fileref* | _ALL_ CLEAR;
FILENAME *fileref* *device-type* <*host-options*>;
FILENAME *fileref* | _ALL_ LIST;

Description

The FILENAME statement temporarily associates a valid SAS name with an external file or an output device. An external file is a file created and maintained on the host operating system from which you need to read data, SAS programming statements, or autocall macros or to which you want to write output. Once a fileref (file reference name) is associated with an external file, it can then be used as a shorthand reference for that file in the SAS programming statements (INFILE, FILE, and %INCLUDE) and display manager commands (FILE and INCLUDE) that access external files. Note that you can associate a fileref with a single external file or with an aggregate storage location that contains many individual external files.

■ **Host Information** .... Different host systems call an aggregate grouping of files by different names, such as a directory, a MACLIB, or a partitioned data set. For details on specifying external files, see the SAS documentation for your host system.
■

The association between a fileref and an external file lasts only for the duration of the SAS session or until you change it or discontinue it with another FILENAME statement. You can change the fileref for a file as often as you want.

To disassociate a fileref from a file, use a FILENAME statement, specifying the fileref and the CLEAR option.

You can also use a FILENAME statement to write the attributes of one or more external files to the SAS log.

■ **Host Information** .... Using the FILENAME statement requires host-specific information. See the SAS documentation for your host system before using this statement. Note also that host commands are available on some hosts that associate a fileref with a file and break that association.
■

Associating a Fileref with an External File

You can use the following form of the FILENAME statement to associate a fileref with an external file on disk:

FILENAME *fileref* '*external-file*'<*host-options*>;

FILENAME

continued

To assign a fileref to a file other than a disk file, you may need to specify a device type, depending on your host system, as shown in the following form:

FILENAME *fileref* <*device-type*> '*external-file*' <*host-options*>;

You can use the following arguments in a FILENAME statement to associate a fileref with an external file:

fileref
: is any valid SAS name.

'*external-file*'
: is the physical name of an external file. The physical name is the name recognized by the host system. You can associate a fileref with a single file or with an aggregate file storage location.

■ **Host Information** .... For details on specifying the physical names of external files, see the SAS documentation for your host system. ■

device-type
: specifies the type of device. Valid values include the following: *

DISK
: specifies that the device is a disk drive. When assigning a fileref to a file on disk, you are not required to specify DISK.

TAPE
: specifies that the device is a tape drive.

DUMMY
: specifies a bit bucket or null device. Specifying DUMMY can be useful for testing.

■ **Host Information** .... Additional specifications may be required when you specify some devices. See the SAS documentation for your host system before specifying a value other than DISK. Values in addition to the ones listed here may be available on some hosts. ■

host-options
: specify host-specific details such as file attributes and processing attributes.

■ **Host Information** .... See the SAS documentation for your host system for descriptions of host-specific options. ■

* For additional device types, see "Associating a Fileref with a Terminal, Printer, or Plotter."

Disassociating a Fileref from an External File

Use the following form of the FILENAME statement to break the association between a fileref and an external file:

FILENAME *fileref* | _ALL_ CLEAR;

You use the following arguments in a FILENAME statement to disassociate a fileref from an external file:

fileref
: is a valid SAS name that has been associated previously with an external file in a FILENAME statement or in a host command.

ALL
: is a SAS keyword. By specifying it rather than a fileref, you can clear all of the filerefs you have assigned during the current session.

CLEAR
: breaks the association of a fileref with an external file.

Associating a Fileref with a Terminal, Printer, or Plotter

Use the following form of the FILENAME statement to associate a fileref with an output device:

FILENAME *fileref* *device-type* <*host-options*>;

You can use the following arguments in a FILENAME statement when associating a fileref with an output device:

fileref
: is any valid SAS name.

device-type
: specifies the type of output device. Valid values are

TERMINAL
: associates a fileref with your monitor so that with a FILE statement you can route output to the display.

If you are using the SAS Display Manager System, routing output to the display monitor causes the display manager windows to be replaced with a blank display to which your directed output is written. The effect is like viewing output in a line mode SAS session. When the SAS System once again needs to write to a display manager window, you are prompted to press a key to return to display manager mode. Output written to the monitor this way is not saved when you return to the SAS System.

PRINTER | PLOTTER
: adds special control characters to output. See *host-options*.

■ **Host Information** .... The carriage control characters that are written to a file can be host-specific. Also note that when you specify PRINTER or PLOTTER, additional specifications may be required on some hosts. See the SAS documentation for your host system.

.... ■

FILENAME

continued

DUMMY
: specifies a bit bucket or null device. Specifying DUMMY can be useful for testing.

■ **Host Information:** .... Note that additional values for *device-type* are available on some hosts. See the SAS documentation for your host system.

host-options
: specify host-specific details such as file attributes and processing attributes. Host options can also be used to specify a destination when you are assigning a fileref to an output device. When you do not specify a destination, output may be routed to a default device.

■ **Host Information** .... See the SAS documentation for your host system for descriptions of host-specific options. .... ■

Listing External File Attributes

Use the following form of the FILENAME statement to list the attributes of external files in the SAS log:

FILENAME *fileref* | _ALL_ LIST;

You can use the following arguments in a FILENAME statement when listing file attributes:

fileref
: is any valid SAS name.

ALL
: is a SAS keyword. Specify _ALL_ to list the attributes of all external files to which you have assigned filerefs during the current session.

LIST
: prints to the SAS log a list of the attributes for the external files specified.

Comparisons

Contrast using the FILENAME and LIBNAME statements with using an INFILE statement with and without a fileref.

□ The FILENAME statement associates a fileref with an external file. The fileref can then be specified in a SAS INFILE, FILE, or %INCLUDE statement. You can read raw data or SAS source statements from an external file, or you can write SAS source statements or PUT statement output to an external file. The LIBNAME statement, on the other hand, associates a libref with a SAS data library so that in your SAS job you can read or write permanent SAS files, such as SAS data sets. See "Example 1: Using a FILENAME and a LIBNAME Statement."

□ If you do not use a FILENAME statement or an appropriate host command to associate a fileref with an external file, you must specify the physical filename in the SAS statement that refers to the file. The following example shows the input data file specified with a fileref in the INFILE statement:

```
filename sales 'your-input-file';

data jansales;
   infile sales;
   input salesrep $20. +6 jansales febsales marsales;
run;
```

This example shows an input data file specified with the physical filename, in quotes, in the INFILE statement:

```
data jansales;
   infile 'your-input-file';
   input salesrep $20. +6 jansales febsales marsales;
run;
```

■ **Host Information** .... For details on specifying physical filenames, see the SAS documentation for your host system. ■

Examples

Example 1: Using a FILENAME and a LIBNAME Statement

This example reads data from a file that has been associated with the fileref GREEN and creates a permanent SAS data set stored in a SAS data library that has been associated with the libref SAVE.

```
filename green 'your-input-file';
libname save 'SAS-data-library';

data save.vegetabl;
   infile green;
   input lettuce cabbage broccoli;
run;
```

Example 2: Associating a Fileref with an Aggregate Storage Location

If you associate a fileref with an aggregate storage location, you can then use the fileref, followed in parentheses by an individual filename, to read from or write to any of the individual external files stored there.

■ **Host Information** .... Some hosts allow you to read from but not write to members of aggregate storage locations. See the SAS documentation for your host system. ■

FILENAME

continued

In the following example, the FILENAME statement assigns a fileref to an aggregate storage location. Both INFILE statements use the same fileref, but each specifies a different individual file.

```
filename sales 'aggregate-storage-location';

data total1;
   infile sales(region1);
   input machine $ jansales febsales marsales;
   totsale=jansales+febsales+marsales;
run;

data total2;
   infile sales(region2);
   input machine $ jansales febsales marsales;
   totsale=jansales+febsales+marsales;
run;
```

Example 3: Routing PUT Statement Output

In this example, the FILENAME statement associates the fileref OUT with a printer specified with a host-dependent option, and the FILE statement directs PUT statement output to that printer.

```
filename out printer host-options;

data sales;
   file out print;
   input salesrep $20. +6 jansales febsales marsales;
   put _infile_;
   cards;
Jones, E. A.                124357 155321 167895
Lee, C. R.                  111245 127564 143255
Desmond, R. T.               97631 101345 117865
;
```

Note that you can use the FILENAME and FILE statements to route PUT statement output to several different devices during the same session.

To route PUT statement output to your display monitor, use the TERMINAL option in the FILENAME statement, as shown in the following DATA step:

```
filename show terminal;

data sales;
   file show;
   input salesrep $20. +6 jansales febsales marsales;
   put _infile_;
   cards;
Jones, E. A.                124357 155321 167895
Lee, C. R.                  111245 127564 143255
Desmond, R. T.               97631 101345 117865
;
```

See Also

FILE, %INCLUDE, INFILE, and LIBNAME statements

"External Files" in Chapter 2, "The DATA Step"

FILE and INCLUDE commands in Chapter 18, "SAS Display Manager Commands"

SAS documentation for your host system for details on specifying files and associating filerefs with files in host commands

FOOTNOTE

Prints up to ten lines of text at the bottom of the procedure output

Global

HELP FOOTNOTE

Syntax

FOOTNOTE<*n*> <'*text*' | "*text*">;

Description

The FOOTNOTE statement prints lines of text at the bottom of the procedure output. You can use the following arguments with the FOOTNOTE statement:

no argument — cancels all existing footnotes.

n — specifies the relative line to be occupied by the footnote. For footnotes, lines are pushed up from the bottom. The FOOTNOTE statement with the highest number appears on the bottom line. *N* can range from 1 to 10. If you omit *n*, the SAS System assumes a value of 1.

'*text*'
"*text*" — specifies the text of the footnote in single or double quotes. For compatibility with previous releases, the SAS System accepts some text without quotes. When you are writing new programs or updating existing programs, *always* surround text with quotes. Refer to "Using Quotes" in Chapter 3.

■ **Host Information** ....

The maximum footnote length allowed depends on the host system and the value of the LINESIZE= system option. Refer to the SAS documentation for your host system for more information.

.... ■

A FOOTNOTE statement takes effect when the step or RUN group with which it is associated executes. Once you specify a footnote for a line, the SAS System repeats the same footnote on all pages until you cancel or redefine the footnote for that line. When a FOOTNOTE statement is specified for a given line, it cancels the previous FOOTNOTE statement for that line and for all footnote lines with higher numbers.

Comparisons

The SAS System also allows you to create footnotes with the display manager FOOTNOTES window.

Examples

The following examples of a FOOTNOTE statement result in the same footnote:

□ `footnote8 "Managers' Meeting";`

□ `footnote8 'Managers'' Meeting';`

See Also

TITLE statement

"Step Boundary" in Chapter 2, "The DATA Step"

"Using Quotes" in Chapter 3, "Components of the SAS Language"

"Options That Affect the Appearance of Output" in Chapter 5, "SAS Output"

FOOTNOTES window in Chapter 17, "SAS Display Manager Windows"

FORMAT

Associates formats with variables in a DATA step

DATA step

HELP FORMAT

Syntax

FORMAT *variables* <*format*> <DEFAULT=*default-format*>;

Description

The FORMAT statement associates formats with variables in a DATA step. When the SAS System writes the values of variables, it uses any format associated with a variable to print the values. A single FORMAT statement can associate the same format with several variables or different formats with different variables. The FORMAT statement can use standard SAS formats or formats defined using the FORMAT procedure.

Using a FORMAT statement in the DATA step permanently associates a format with a variable by changing the descriptor information of the SAS data set containing the variable.

If a variable appears in more than one FORMAT statement, the SAS System uses the format most recently assigned.

You can use the following arguments with the FORMAT statement:

variables

names the variables you want to associate with a format. To disassociate a format from a variable, use the variable's name in a FORMAT statement with no format. Make sure the null FORMAT statement follows the SET statement.

format

specifies the format for writing the values of the variables.

DEFAULT=*default-format*

specifies a temporary default format for displaying values of variables during the current DATA step. A DEFAULT= format specification applies to the following variables:

- □ those not named in a FORMAT or ATTRIB statement
- □ those not permanently associated with a format within a SAS data set
- □ those not written with the explicit use of a format.

A DEFAULT= specification in a FORMAT statement is only valid within a DATA step. A DEFAULT= specification can occur in any position within a FORMAT statement and can contain either a numeric default, a character default, or both. A FORMAT statement can contain a DEFAULT= specification alone, a DEFAULT= specification along with other format specifications, or just one or more format specifications.

Default formats are not permanently associated with variables in a data set but apply only during the current DATA step. If you do not specify a default format, the SAS System uses the BEST*w*. format as the numeric default and the $*w*. format as the character default.

You can use a FORMAT statement in some PROC steps, but the rules are different. See the *SAS Procedures Guide* for more information.

Comparisons

The ATTRIB statement can also associate formats with variables. Either an ATTRIB or a FORMAT statement can change a format associated with a variable. You can associate, change, or disassociate formats and variables in existing SAS data sets with the DIR display manager window.

Examples

Example 1: Assigning Formats and Defaults

The following program illustrates using a FORMAT statement to establish formats and default formats for numeric and character variables. Note that the default formats are not associated with variables in the data set but affect the way the PUT statement writes them in the current DATA step.

```
data tfmt;
   format y 10.3
          w $char3.
          default=8.2
          default=$char8.;
   w='Good morning.';
   x=12.1;             /* Note that the default formats apply */
   y=13.2;             /* to x and z and the assigned formats */
   z='Howdy-doody';    /* to y and w in this example.         */
   put w/x/y/z;
run;

proc contents data=tfmt;
run;

proc print data=tfmt;
run;
```

Selected results of this DATA step are as follows:

□ from the PUT statement

```
----+----1----+----2
Goo
   12.10
13.200
Howdy-do
```

□ from PROC CONTENTS

```
-----Alphabetic List of Variables and Attributes-----

    #    Variable    Type    Len    Pos    Format
    ---------------------------------------------
    2    W           Char      3      8    $CHAR3.
    3    X           Num       8     11
    1    Y           Num       8      0    10.3
    4    Z           Char     11     19
```

FORMAT

continued

□ from PROC PRINT

```
OBS       Y      W     X          Z

 1     13.200   Goo   12.1   Howdy-doody
```

Example 2: Removing a Format

The following code illustrates how to remove an existing format. The order of the FORMAT and the SET statements is important.

```
data rtest;
   set rtest;
   format x;
run;
```

See Also

ATTRIB statement

Chapter 14, "SAS Formats"

DIR window in Chapter 17, "SAS Display Manager Windows"

GO TO

Moves execution immediately to the statement label indicated

DATA step

HELP GOTO

Syntax

GO TO *label*;

Description

The GO TO statement tells the SAS System to jump immediately to the statement label indicated in the GO TO statement and begin executing statements from that point.

The destination of the GO TO is identified by the statement label in the GO TO statement. The GO TO statement and destination must be in the same DATA step. The alias for GO TO is GOTO.

You must use the following argument with the GO TO statement:

label specifies a statement label that identifies the GO TO destination, which must be within the same DATA step.

Comparisons

The GO TO statement and the LINK statement are similar. However, a GO TO statement is often used without a RETURN statement, whereas a LINK statement is usually used with an explicit RETURN statement. Another difference is in the action of a subsequent RETURN statement. A RETURN after a LINK statement returns execution to the statement following the LINK statement. A RETURN after a GO TO statement returns execution to the beginning of the DATA step (unless a LINK statement precedes the GO TO statement, in which case execution continues with the first statement after the LINK statement).

GO TO statements can often be replaced by DO-END and IF-THEN/ELSE programming logic.

Examples

You can use the GO TO statement as shown here.

□ In this example, if the condition is true, the GO TO statement instructs the SAS System to jump to a label called ADD and to continue execution from there. If the condition is false, the SAS System executes the PUT statement and then the statement associated with the GO TO label:

```
data info;
   input x;
   if 1<=x<=5 then goto add;
   put x=;
   add: sumx+x;
   cards;
7
16
323
;
```

GO TO

continued

Because every DATA step contains an implied RETURN at the end of the step, program execution returns to the top of the step after the sum statement is executed. Therefore, an explicit RETURN statement at the bottom of the DATA step is not necessary.

□ If you do not want the sum statement to execute for observations that do not meet the condition, rewrite the code as follows:

```
data info;
   input x;
   if 1<=x<=5 then goto add;
   put x=;
   return;     /* SUM statement not executed if x<1 or x>5 */
   add: sumx+x;
   cards;
7
16
323
;
```

See Also

DO statement
LINK statement
RETURN statement
Statement labels

IF, Subsetting

Continues processing only those observations that meet the condition

DATA step

HELP IF

Syntax

IF *expression*;

Description

The subsetting IF statement causes the DATA step to continue processing only those raw data records or those observations from a SAS data set that meet the condition of the expression specified in the IF statement. Therefore, the resulting SAS data set or data sets contain a subset of the original external file or SAS data set.

The subsetting IF statement does not require additional statements to stop processing observations. If the expression is false, no further statements are processed for that observation or record, and the SAS System returns to the top of the DATA step. The subsetting IF statement is equivalent to the following IF-THEN statement:

```
if not (expression) then delete;
```

You use the following argument with the subsetting IF statement:

expression
: is any valid SAS expression. If the expression is true for the observation or record (its value is neither 0 nor missing), the SAS System continues executing statements in the DATA step, and includes the current observation in the data set. If the expression is false (its value is 0 or missing), the SAS System immediately returns to the beginning of the DATA step, does not include the current observation in the data set, and does not execute the remaining program statements in the DATA step.

Comparisons

When you are creating SAS data sets, use the subsetting IF statement when it is easier to specify a condition for including observations. When it is easier to specify a condition for excluding observations, use the DELETE statement.

The subsetting IF and the WHERE statements are not equivalent. The two statements work differently and produce different output data sets in some cases. The most important differences are summarized as follows:

- The subsetting IF statement selects observations that have been read into the program data vector. The WHERE statement selects observations before they are brought into the program data vector. The subsetting IF is less efficient than the WHERE statement because it must read each observation from the input data set into the program data vector.
- The subsetting IF statement and WHERE statement can produce different results in DATA steps that interleave, merge, or update SAS data sets.

IF, Subsetting

continued

□ When the subsetting IF statement is used with the MERGE statement, the SAS System selects observations after the current observations are combined. When the WHERE statement is used with the MERGE statement, the SAS System applies the selection criteria to each input data set before combining the current observations.

□ The subsetting IF statement can select observations from an existing SAS data set or from raw data read with the INPUT statement. The WHERE statement can select observations only from existing SAS data sets.

□ The subsetting IF statement is executable; the WHERE statement is not.

□ The subsetting IF statement used within a DATA step can include SAS functions; the WHERE statement cannot.

Examples

You can use the subsetting IF statement as shown here.

□ The following statement results in a data set containing only those observations with the value F for the variable SEX:

```
if sex='F';
```

□ This statement results in a data set containing all observations for which the value of the variable AGE is not missing or 0:

```
if age;
```

See Also

DELETE, IF-THEN/ELSE, and WHERE statements

Chapter 4, "Rules of the SAS Language"

WHERE= data set option in Chapter 15, "SAS Data Set Options"

Chapter 9, "Creating Subsets of Observations," in *SAS Language and Procedures: Usage, Version 6, First Edition*

IF-THEN/ELSE

Executes a SAS statement for observations meeting specific conditions

DATA step

HELP IF

Syntax

IF *expression* **THEN** *statement*;
<**ELSE** *statement*;>

Description

The IF-THEN statement executes a SAS statement for observations read from a SAS data set, records in an external file, or computed values that meet conditions specified in the IF clause. An optional ELSE statement gives an alternative action if the THEN clause is not executed. The ELSE statement, if used, must immediately follow the IF-THEN statement.

You use the following arguments with the IF-THEN statement:

expression
: is any valid SAS expression. The SAS System evaluates the expression in an IF statement to produce a result that is either nonzero, zero, or missing. A nonzero and nonmissing result causes the expression to be true; a result of zero or missing causes the expression to be false.

statement
: can be any executable SAS statement or DO group. Refer to Table 3.1 in Chapter 3 for a list of executable SAS statements.

Comparisons

Use a SELECT group rather than a series of IF-THEN statements when you have a long series of mutually exclusive conditions. Use subsetting IF statements, without a THEN clause, to continue processing only those observations or records that meet the condition specified in the IF clause.

Examples

The following examples show valid IF-THEN/ELSE statements:

□ `if x then delete;`

□ `if status='OK' and type=3 then count+1;`

□ `if age ne agecheck then delete;`

□
```
if x=0 then
   if y ne 0 then put 'X ZERO, Y NONZERO';
   else put 'X ZERO, Y ZERO';
else put 'X NONZERO';
```

IF-THEN/ELSE

continued

□
```
if answer=9 then
   do;
      answer=.;
      put 'INVALID ANSWER FOR ' id=;
   end;
else
   do;
      answer=answer10;
      valid+1;
   end;
```

□
```
data region;
   input city $ 1-30;
   if city='New York City' or city='Miami' then
      region='ATLANTIC COAST';
   else if city='San Francisco' or city='Los Angeles' then
        region='PACIFIC COAST';
   cards;
data lines
;
```

See Also

DO statement

Subsetting IF statement

SELECT statement

%INCLUDE

Includes SAS statements and data lines

DATA step

HELP INCLUDE

Syntax

%INCLUDE *source-1* < . . . *source-n*>
</< SOURCE2 > <S2=*length*> <*host-options*>>;

Description

The %INCLUDE statement accesses SAS statements and data lines from three possible sources:

□ external files

□ lines entered earlier in the same job or session

□ lines you enter from the keyboard.

The alias for %INCLUDE is %INC.

■ **Host Information** ....

The %INCLUDE statement is host-dependent. As a supplement to this documentation, see your host documentation for additional software features, for methods of referring to and accessing host files, and before you run the examples in this documentation. ■

The %INCLUDE statement is most often used when running the SAS System in interactive line mode, noninteractive mode, or batch mode. Although you can use the %INCLUDE statement when running the SAS System in display manager mode, it may be more practical to use the INCLUDE and RECALL display manager commands to access data lines and program statements, and submit these lines again. See Chapter 18, "SAS Display Manager Commands," for details about each command, and Chapter 7, "SAS Display Manager System," for general information.

When you execute a program that contains the %INCLUDE statement, the SAS System executes your code, including any statements or data lines you bring into the program with the %INCLUDE statement. You can specify any number of sources in a %INCLUDE statement, and you can mix the types of included sources. Note, however, that although it is possible to include information from multiple sources in one %INCLUDE statement, it may be easier to understand a program that uses separately coded %INCLUDE statements for each source.

The %INCLUDE statement must begin at a statement boundary. That is, it must be the first statement in a SAS job or immediately follow a semicolon ending another statement. A %INCLUDE statement cannot immediately follow a CARDS or CARDS4 statement (or PARMCARDS or PARMCARDS4, in procedures that use those statements); however, you can include data lines with the %INCLUDE statement using one of these methods:

□ Make the CARDS or CARDS4 statement the first line in the file containing the data.

□ Place the CARDS or CARDS4 statement in one file, and the data lines in another file. Then use both sources in a single %INCLUDE statement.

The %INCLUDE statement can be nested within a file that has been accessed with %INCLUDE. The maximum number of nested %INCLUDE statements you can use depends on system-specific limitations of your host

%INCLUDE

continued

(such as available memory or the number of files you can have open concurrently).

You can use the following arguments with the %INCLUDE statement:

source

describes the location of the information you want to access with the %INCLUDE statement. The three possible sources are

□ *file-specification*, in which you access an external file

□ *internal-lines*, in which you access lines entered earlier in the same SAS job or session

□ *keyboard-entry*, in which you enter the statements or data lines directly from the terminal.

You must specify at least one *source* in the %INCLUDE statement. Each source is described here in detail.

file-specification

identifies an external file that you want to bring into your program. You must include an entire external file; you cannot selectively include lines.

Including external sources is useful in all types of SAS processing: batch, display manager, interactive line, and noninteractive.

■ **Host Information** .... For complete details on specifying the physical names of external files, see the SAS documentation for your host system. ■

File-specification can have the following forms:

'external-file'

specifies the physical name of an external file. The physical name is the name by which the host system recognizes the file. It must be enclosed in quotes.

For example, to include an external file called MY-FILE, place the physical name of the file in quotes after the %INCLUDE statement, according to your host specifications:

```
%include 'my-file';
```

fileref

gives the fileref of an external file. The fileref must have been associated previously with an external file in a FILENAME statement or in an appropriate host command.

For example, using the FILENAME statement, assign the fileref IN1 to MY-FILE as follows:

```
filename in1 'my-file';
```

Then, you can later access MY-FILE with IN1 as follows:

```
%inc in1;
```

See the FILENAME statement earlier in this chapter for more details.

fileref(file-1 <,... file-n>)
gives a fileref of an aggregate storage location. The fileref must have been associated previously with an aggregate storage location in a FILENAME statement or in an appropriate host command.

■ **Host Information** .... Different host systems call an aggregate grouping of files by different names, such as a directory, a MACLIB, a text library, or a partitioned data set. For complete details on specifying external files, see the SAS documentation for your host system.

.... ■

Follow the fileref with the name of a file or member, enclosed in parentheses, that resides in that location. For example, using the FILENAME statement, assign the fileref STORAGE to an aggregate storage location:

```
filename storage 'aggregate-storage-location';
```

Then, you can later include a file using the following statement:

```
%inc storage(filename);
```

You can also access several files or members from this storage location by listing them in parentheses after the fileref in a single %INCLUDE statement. Separate filenames with a comma or a blank space. The following %INCLUDE statement demonstrates this method:

```
%inc storage(file-1,file-2,file-3);
```

You can optionally place quotes around the filename inside the parentheses when accessing files from an aggregate storage location.

■ **Host Information** .... The character length allowed for filenames is host-specific. See your host documentation for information on accessing files from a storage location containing several files.

.... ■

internal-lines
includes lines entered earlier in the same SAS job or session. Use a %LIST statement to determine the line numbers you want to include. Including internal lines is most useful in interactive line mode processing. Although you can use the %INCLUDE statement to access previously submitted lines when running the SAS System in display manager mode, it may be more practical to recall lines with the display manager RECALL command, then submit the lines with the SUBMIT command.

Note: The SPOOL system option controls internal access to previously submitted lines when running the SAS System in interactive line mode, noninteractive mode, and batch mode. Use the OPTIONS procedure to determine the default setting of the SPOOL system option on your system.

%INCLUDE

(internal-lines continued)

Internal lines can be included by using any of the following:

n includes line *n*.

n-m
n:m includes lines *n* through *m*.

Here is an example:

```
%include 1 5 9-12 13:16;
```

This statement causes the SAS System to process lines 1, 5, 9 through 12, and 13 through 16 as though you had entered them once more at the terminal.

keyboard-entry

is a method for preparing a program so that you can interrupt the current program's execution, enter statements or data lines from the keyboard, then resume program processing. Use this method when running the SAS System in noninteractive or interactive line mode. The SAS System pauses during processing and prompts you to enter statements from the terminal.

Use the following argument to include source from the keyboard:

* prompts you to enter data from the terminal. Place an asterisk (*) after the %INCLUDE statement in your code, as in the following example:

```
proc print;
   %include *;
run;
```

To resume processing the original source program, you must enter a %RUN statement from the terminal.

You can use a %INCLUDE * statement in a batch job by creating a file with the fileref SASTERM that contains the statements you would otherwise enter from the terminal. The %INCLUDE * statement causes the SAS System to read from the file referenced by SASTERM. Insert a %RUN statement into the file referenced by SASTERM where you want the SAS System to resume reading from the original source.

Note: The fileref SASTERM must have been previously associated with an external file in a FILENAME statement or an appropriate host command.

SOURCE2

causes the SAS log to show the source statements that are being included in your SAS program. The SAS log also displays the fileref and the filename of the source and the level of nesting (1, 2, 3, and so on). The SAS system option SOURCE2 produces the same results. However, the SOURCE2 statement option is effective only for the execution or duration of the %INCLUDE statement. In addition, when you specify the option in a %INCLUDE statement, it overrides the setting of the same system option for the duration of the include operation.

S2=*length*

specifies the length of the record to be used for input.

Text input from the %INCLUDE statement can be either fixed or variable length. Fixed-length records are either unsequenced or sequenced at the end of each record. For fixed-length records, the value given in the S2= option is the ending column of the data.

Variable-length records are either unsequenced or sequenced at the beginning of each record. For variable-length records, the value given in the S2= option is the starting column of the data.

The S2= system option also specifies the length of secondary source statements accessed by the %INCLUDE statement, but it is effective for the duration of your SAS session, whereas the S2= option in the %INCLUDE statement affects only the current include operation. If you use the option in the %INCLUDE statement, it overrides the system option setting for the duration of the include operation. For a detailed discussion of fixed- and variable-length input records, see the S= and the S2= system options in Chapter 16.

Length can have the following values:

S
: sets S2 equal to the current setting of the S= SAS system option.

0
: tells the SAS System to use the setting of the SEQ= system option to determine whether the line contains a sequence field. If the line does contain a sequence field, the SAS System determines line length by excluding the sequence field from the total length.

n
: specifies a number greater than zero that corresponds to the length of the line to be read, when the file contains fixed-length records. When the file contains variable-length records, *n* specifies the column in which to begin reading data.

host-options

are host-specific options. Host systems may implement various options for the %INCLUDE statement. See your host documentation for a list of options and their functions.

Comparisons

The difference between the %INCLUDE statement and the display manager INCLUDE command is that the %INCLUDE statement executes the statements immediately, while the INCLUDE command brings the included lines into the PROGRAM EDITOR window. You must issue the display manager SUBMIT command to execute those lines.

Examples

Example 1: Including an External File

Suppose you want to store a portion of a program in a file and include it in a program you will write later. First, create a file named MY-FILE containing the following program:

```
data monthly;
   input x y month $;
   cards;
```

%INCLUDE

continued

```
1 1 January
2 2 February
3 3 March
4 4 April
;
```

You can include the program later by using the physical filename, or by pointing to the file with a fileref. Depending on your host system requirements for specifying external files, you determine the precise value of *file-specification* in this example:

```
%include file-specification;

proc print;
run;
```

The SAS System executes the DATA step and then the PROC step.

Example 2: Including Input from the Terminal

▶ ***Caution:*** *The method shown in this example is valid only when running the SAS System in noninteractive or interactive line mode.*

Suppose your program contains a PROC PRINT statement and you want to add a customized TITLE or WHERE statement during processing. Here is the original program:

```
data report;
   infile file-specification;
   input month $ salesamt $;
proc print;
   %include *;
run;
```

When you execute the DATA step, the SAS System prompts you to enter statements at the terminal. You can then enter statements such as

```
where month='January';
title 'Data for month of January';
```

When you are finished entering statements for the title and you want to resume processing, use the %RUN statement, as follows:

```
   /* data entry complete; resume processing */
%run;
```

The %RUN statement signals to the SAS System to leave keyboard-entry mode and resume reading and executing remaining SAS statements from the original program.

See Also

%LIST and %RUN statements

SOURCE2 and S2= SAS system options in Chapter 16, "SAS System Options"

INCLUDE command in Chapter 18, "SAS Display Manager Commands"

INFILE

Identifies an external file to read with an INPUT statement

DATA step

HELP INFILE

Syntax

INFILE *file-specification* <*options*> <*host-options*>;

Description

An INFILE statement identifies an external file that you want to read with an INPUT statement. Because the INFILE statement identifies the file to be read, it must execute before the INPUT statement that reads the data lines. You can use it in conditional processing (in an IF-THEN statement, for example) because it is executable.

You can read from several external files within one DATA step. To read from multiple input files in a single iteration of the DATA step, you can use multiple INFILE and INPUT statements. To read from one file, then close it and open another, you can use the FILEVAR= option. (FILEVAR= enables you to dynamically change the current input file within your SAS job. See "Example 1: Reading from More Than One Input File.")

When you use more than one INFILE statement for the same fileref and you use options in each INFILE statement, the effect is additive. That is, the options specified in each INFILE statement are added to the options specified in any previous INFILE statements for that file. To avoid confusion, use all options in the first INFILE statement for a given file.

You can use the INFILE statement in combination with the FILE statement to update records in an external file. To do so, follow these steps:

1. Specify the INFILE statement before the FILE statement.
2. Specify the same fileref or physical filename in each statement.
3. Use options that are common to both the INFILE and FILE statements in the INFILE statement instead of the FILE statement. (Any such options used in the FILE statement are ignored.)

See "Example 4: Updating an External File." To update individual fields within a record instead of the entire record, use the SHAREBUFFERS option.

■ **Host Information** ...... The INFILE statement contains host-specific material. See the SAS documentation for your host system before using this statement. ■

You can use the following arguments with the INFILE statement:

file-specification
: identifies the source of input data records, either an external file or in-stream data, and is required. *File-specification* can have the following forms:

  'external-file'
  : specifies the physical name of an external file. The physical name is the name by which the host system recognizes the file. It must be enclosed in quotes.

INFILE

continued

fileref

gives the fileref of an external file. The fileref must have been associated previously with an external file in a FILENAME statement or in an appropriate host command.

fileref(file)

gives a fileref of an aggregate storage location. Follow the fileref with the name of a file or member, enclosed in parentheses, that resides in that location. The fileref must have been associated previously with an aggregate storage location in a FILENAME statement or in an appropriate host command.

■ **Host Information** .... Different host systems call an aggregate grouping of files by different names, such as a directory, a MACLIB, or a partitioned data set. For details on specifying external files, see the SAS documentation for your host system.

.... ■

CARDS

specifies that the input data immediately follow the CARDS or CARDS4 statement in your SAS job. Normally, the INFILE statement is used only when the DATA step reads input data from a file rather than in-stream data. Because the INFILE statement has many options that affect how the INPUT statement reads data, you may want to use it even when reading in-stream data to take advantage of its options. The DATA step, therefore, would contain both an INFILE statement and a CARDS or CARDS4 statement.

```
data exam;
   infile cards options;
   input...;
   more SAS statements
   cards;
data lines
   ;
```

options

specifies one or more INFILE statement options. These options describe the input file's characteristics and specify how it is to be read with the INPUT statement. See descriptions under "Options."

host-options

are host-specific options.

■ **Host Information** .... See the SAS documentation for your host system for descriptions of host-specific options.

.... ■

Options

You can use the following options with the INFILE statement:

BLKSIZE=*block-size*
: specifies the block size of the input file.

■ **Host Information** ....

The default value of the BLKSIZE= option is host-dependent. For more details about the implementation of this option on your host, see the SAS documentation for your host system.
.... ■

COLUMN=*variable*
COL=*variable*
: defines a variable that the SAS System sets to the column location of the input pointer. You supply the variable name; the SAS System then automatically assigns the value of the current column location of the input pointer to the COLUMN= variable. Like automatic variables, the COLUMN= variable is not written to the data set. For example, these statements produce lines in the log:

```
data one;
   infile cards column=c;
   input @5 x 3. @;
   put c=;
   input @12 y 3.;
   put c=;
   cards;
    111    222
;
```

The lines produced are

```
C=8
C=15
```

See the LINE= option.

DELIMITER=*delimiters*
DLM=*delimiters*
: specifies a delimiter other than a blank (the default) for list input. *Delimiters* can be expressed as a list of delimiting characters or as a character variable.

'list-of-delimiting-characters'
: specifies one or more (up to 200) characters to be read as delimiters. The list of characters must be enclosed in quotes. For example, if the input data fields are separated by commas, set the DELIMITER= option to a comma. This strategy allows the input data in the following example to be read with list input:

```
data new;
   infile cards delimiter=',';
   input x y z;
   cards;
1,2,3
4,5,6
7,8,9
;
```

INFILE

(DELIMITER= continued)

If you want more than one character to be treated as a delimiter, simply specify them with the DELIMITER= option. In the following example, the characters a, b, ab, ba, aa, and bb function as delimiters:

```
data new3;
   infile cards delimiter='ab';
   input x y z;
   cards;
1aa2ab3
4bb5ba6
7a8b9
;
```

character-variable

specifies a character variable whose value is to be used as the delimiter. The following example uses a character variable to set the value of the DELIMITER= option:

```
data new;
   z=',';
   infile cards delimiter=z;
   input a b c;
   cards;
1,2,3
4,5,6
7,8,9
;
```

END=*variable*

defines a variable, whose name you supply, that the SAS System sets to 1 when the current line is the last in the input file. The value of the END= variable is 0 until the last line is processed. Like automatic variables, the END= variable is not written to the data set.

You cannot use the END= option when you use the UNBUFFERED option or when you read in-stream data (using the CARDS statement). END= is also invalid when an INPUT statement reads more than one data line at a time. For these cases, use the EOF= option.

EOF=*label*

specifies a statement label as the object of an implicit GO TO statement when the INFILE statement reaches end-of-file. The SAS System jumps to the labeled statement when an INPUT statement attempts to read from a file that has no more records. The EOF= option is often used when reading from multiple input files sequentially.

Use the EOF= option instead of the END= option when the DATA step uses

- □ INPUT statements that read more than one data line at a time.
- □ the CARDS statement.
- □ the UNBUFFERED option in an INFILE statement. (See the UNBUFFERED option.)

EOV=*variable*

defines a variable, whose name you supply, that the SAS System sets to 1 when the first record in a file in a series of concatenated files is read. The variable is set only when the next file is encountered. You must reset the EOV= variable back to 0 after the SAS System encounters each boundary. Like automatic variables, the EOV= variable is not written to the data set.

EXPANDTABS
NOEXPANDTABS

specifies whether to expand tab characters to the standard tab setting, which is set at 8-column intervals starting at column 9. NOEXPANDTABS is the default. EXPANDTABS is useful if you are reading data that contain the tab character native to your host system.

FILENAME=*variable*

defines a variable, whose name you supply, that the SAS System sets to the value of the physical name of the currently open input file. Like automatic variables, the FILENAME= variable is not written to the data set. For example, the following DATA step prints the name of the currently open input file to the log:

```
data _null_;
   length myinfile $ 200;
   infile file-specification filename=myinfile;
   put myinfile=;
   stop;
run;
```

Note that you can use the LENGTH statement, as shown here, to give the FILENAME= variable a length long enough to contain the value of the filename. A line in the following form is written to the log:

```
MYINFILE=your-input-file
```

Note that the physical name of the current output file is written to the log. See also the FILEVAR= option.

FILEVAR=*variable*

defines a variable whose name you supply and whose change in value causes the INFILE statement to close the current input file and open a new one. The next INPUT statement that executes reads from the new file specified by the FILEVAR= variable. The value of a FILEVAR= variable is expressed as a character string that contains a physical filename.

```
data _null_;
   length name $ 200;

      /* Reads a value for NAME from the data lines below.   */
   input name $;

      /* The FILEVAR= option specifies that the current infile*/
      /* be closed and a new one be opened if the value of the*/
      /* NAME variable has changed when INFILE executes.      */
   infile file-specification filevar=name end=end;
   do until(end);
```

INFILE

(FILEVAR= continued)

```
         /* Reads value for X from the current record in the  */
         /* currently open input file.                         */
      input x $ 1-30;

         /* Writes the name of the currently open input file  */
         /* and the current value of X to the log.             */
      put name= x=;
   end;
   cards;
external-file-1
external-file-2
external-file-3
;
```

The FILEVAR= option enables you to dynamically change the currently opened input file to a new physical file. See "Example 1: Reading from More Than One Input File." Like automatic variables, the FILEVAR= variable is not written to the data set.

FIRSTOBS=*record-number*
: indicates that you want to begin reading the input file at the record number specified, rather than beginning with the first record. For example, the following INFILE statement specifies that reading begin at record 100:

```
infile file-specification firstobs=100;
```

FLOWOVER
: specifies that if the INPUT statement uses list input and reads past the end of the current record, then it is to continue reading data from the next record. FLOWOVER is the default.

LENGTH=*variable*
: defines a variable, whose name you supply, that the SAS System sets to the length of the current input line. This option is useful in conjunction with the $VARYING. informat.

You can reset the value of the LENGTH= variable in program statements. Note that the LENGTH= variable is specified in an INFILE statement but that it is not assigned a value until an INPUT statement is executed.

LINE=*variable*
: defines a variable, whose name you supply, that the SAS System sets to the line location of the pointer in the input buffer. The value of the LINE= variable is the current relative line number within the group of lines specified by the N= option or by the #*n* line pointer control

in the INPUT statement. Thus, the value of the LINE= variable ranges from 1 up to the value of the N= variable. For example, consider the following statements:

```
data test;
   infile cards n=2 line=x;
   input name $ 1-15 #2 id 3-6;
   put x=;
   cards;
J. Brooks
  4097
T. R. Ansen
  4032
;
```

These statements produce the following line for each execution of the DATA step, because the pointer is on the second line in the input buffer when the PUT statement executes:

```
x=2
```

See also the COLUMN= option.

LINESIZE=*line-size*
LS=*line-size*

limits the record length available to the INPUT statement when you do not want to read the entire record.

For example, suppose your data lines contain a sequence number in columns 73 through 80. You can use the following INFILE statement to restrict the INPUT statement to the first 72 columns of the lines and prevent inadvertently reading a sequence number as data:

```
infile file-specification linesize=72;
```

If an INPUT statement attempts to read past the column specified by the LINESIZE= option, the action taken depends on whether the FLOWOVER, MISSOVER, or STOPOVER option is in effect. FLOWOVER is in effect unless another option is specified.

LRECL=*logical-record-length*

specifies the logical record length. If you do not use the LRECL= option, the SAS System chooses a value based on the host system's file characteristics. Compare LRECL= with the LINESIZE= option:

□ LRECL= specifies the physical line length of the file.

□ LINESIZE= tells the SAS System how much of the line it is to use.

■ **Host Information** .... Values for *logical-record-length* are host-dependent. For more details, see the SAS documentation for your host system. ■

MISSOVER

prevents a SAS program from going to a new input line if, when using list input, it does not find values in the current line for all the INPUT statement variables. When an INPUT statement reaches the end of the current record, values that are expected but not found are set to missing.

INFILE

(MISSOVER continued)

For example, suppose you are reading temperature data. Each input line in the following example contains from one to five temperatures:

```
data weather;
   infile cards missover;
   input temp1-temp5;
   cards;
97.9 98.1 98.3
98.6 99.2 99.1 98.5 97.5
96.2 97.3 98.3 97.6 96.5
;
```

The SAS System reads the three values on the first data line as values of TEMP1, TEMP2, and TEMP3. The MISSOVER option causes the SAS System to set the values of TEMP4 and TEMP5 to missing for that observation because there are no values for those variables in the current input line.

When the MISSOVER option is *not* used, the SAS System goes to the second data line for the TEMP4 and TEMP5 values and prints the message

```
NOTE: SAS went to a new line when INPUT
      statement reached past the end of a line.
```

In this case, the SAS System reads data line 3 the next time it executes the INPUT statement.

N=*available-lines*

specifies the number of lines you want available to the input pointer. When the N= option is not used, the number of lines available to the pointer is the highest value following a # pointer control in any INPUT statement in the DATA step. When you do not use a # pointer control, N= has a default value of 1. The N= value affects only the number of lines that the pointer can access at a time; it has no effect on the number of lines an INPUT statement reads.

OBS=*record-number*

specifies the record number of the last record that you want to read from an input file that is being read sequentially. For example, the following statement processes only the first 100 records in the file:

```
infile file-specification obs=100;
```

You can use the OBS= and the FIRSTOBS= options together to read a range of records from the middle of your file:

```
infile file-specification firstobs=100 obs=200;
```

This INFILE statement results in 101 records being read, record 100 through record 200.

PAD
NOPAD
: controls whether records read from an external file are padded with blanks to the length specified in the LRECL= option. NOPAD is the default.

PRINT
NOPRINT
: specifies whether the input file contains carriage control characters. Using the PRINT option allows you to use a print file as input to a DATA step without removing the carriage control characters.

RECFM=*record-format*
: specifies the record format of the input file.

■ **Host Information** ....

Values for *record-format* are host-dependent. For more details, see the SAS documentation for your host system.

SHAREBUFFERS
SHAREBUFS
: specifies that the FILE statement and the INFILE statements share the same buffer. When using the INFILE, FILE, and PUT statements to update an external file in place, the SHAREBUFFERS option saves CPU time by preventing what is being written with the PUT statement from being copied to an output buffer. Instead, the PUT statement output is written straight from the INPUT buffer. SHAREBUFFERS is useful when you want to update specific fields, not an entire record. See "Example 4: Updating an External File."

START=*variable*
: defines a variable whose name you supply and whose value is used as the first column number of the record that the PUT _INFILE_ statement is to write.

For example, you can use the START= option when you want to make a copy of a file but do not want to copy the first 10 columns of each record. The following statements copy from column 11 to the end of each record in the input buffer:

```
data _null_;
   infile file-specification start=s;
   input;
   s=11;
   file out;
   put _infile_;
run;
```

STOPOVER
: stops processing the DATA step when an INPUT statement using list input reaches the end of the current record without finding values for all variables in the statement.

When the STOPOVER option is used and an input line does not contain the expected number of values, the SAS System sets _ERROR_ to 1, stops building the data set as though a STOP

INFILE

(STOPOVER continued)

statement had executed, and prints the incomplete data line. Here is an example:

```
data y;
   infile cards stopover;
   input x1-x4;
   cards;
1 2 3
5 6 7 8
9 4 0
;
```

When the SAS System reads the first data line, it does not find an X4 value. Because STOPOVER is used in the INFILE statement, the SAS System sets _ERROR_ to 1, stops building the data set, and prints data line 1.

Without the STOPOVER option, the SAS System would print the message

```
NOTE: SAS went to a new line when INPUT
      statement reached past the end of a line.
```

Then, it would continue to line 2 and read 5 as the value for X4. The next time the DATA step executes, the SAS System would read a new line, in this case, line 3. An error message reporting a lost-card condition would also be printed in the log when the system tried to go to another line to find a value for variable X4.

UNBUFFERED
UNBUF

tells the SAS System not to perform a buffered read. When the UNBUFFERED option is used, the SAS System never sets the END= variable to 1. Note that when you read in-stream data (using the CARDS statement), the UNBUFFERED option is in effect.

Comparisons

The INFILE statement specifies the input file for INPUT statements in the DATA step. The FILE statement specifies the output file for PUT statements in the DATA step.

An INFILE statement is usually used when data must be read from an external file. A CARDS statement is used when data are read from the job stream. To take advantage of certain data-reading options available only in the INFILE statement, however, you can use an INFILE statement with the reserved fileref CARDS and a CARDS statement in the same DATA step.

Examples

Example 1: Reading from More Than One Input File

If your program reads from two files, you can use one of two methods for specifying which file an INPUT statement is to read: multiple INFILE statements or the FILEVAR= option in an INFILE statement. Use multiple INFILE statements when you want multiple files to remain open and change which file is being read. Use the FILEVAR= option when you want to close one file and open another.

The following DATA step reads from two input files during each iteration of the DATA step. As the system switches from one file to the other, each file remains open. The pointer remains in place to begin reading from that location the next time an INPUT statement reads from that file.

```
data qtrtot;
   infile file-specification-1;              /* first file         */
   input name $ jansales febsales marsales;/* read from 1st file */
   qtr1tot=jansales+febsales+marsales;
   infile file-specification-2;              /* second file        */
   input @7 aprsales maysales junsales;      /* read from 2nd file */
   qtr2tot=aprsales+maysales+junsales;
   drop jansales febsales marsales aprsales maysales junsales;
run;
```

This DATA step shows using the FILEVAR= option to read from a different file during each iteration of the DATA step:

```
data allsales;
   length nowread $ 200;

      /* This INPUT statement reads a value from the instream */
      /* data lines and assigns it to NOWREAD.                */
   input nowread $ ;

      /* This INFILE statement closes the current file and    */
      /* opens a new one if the value of NOWREAD has changed  */
      /* when the INFILE statement executes.                  */
   infile file-specification filevar=nowread end=done;
   do until(done);

         /* This INPUT statement reads from the currently     */
         /* open input file.                                  */
      input region $ name $ 9-21 jansales febsales marsales;
      output;
   end;
   cards;
external-file-1
external-file-2
external-file-3
;
```

INFILE

continued

Example 2: Truncating Copied Records

The LENGTH= option is useful when copying the input file to another file with the PUT _INFILE_ statement. You can use LENGTH= to truncate the copied records. For example, the following statements truncate the last 20 columns from the input lines before they are copied to the output file:

```
data _null_;
   infile file-specification-1 length=a;
   input;
   a=a-20;
   file file-specification-2;
   put _infile_;
run;
```

Example 3: Reading Files Containing Variable-Length Records

This example shows how to use the LENGTH= option, in combination with the $VARYING. informat, to read a file containing variable-length records:

```
data a;
   infile file-specification length=linelen;    /* LINELEN created*/
   input firstvar 1-10 @;                        /* LINELEN assigned a value    */
   varlen=linelen-10;                            /* VARLEN's value  calculated  */
   input @11 secondvr $varying200. varlen;
run;
```

The following occurs in this DATA step:

1. The INFILE statement creates the variable LINELEN but does not assign it a value.
2. When the first INPUT statement executes, the SAS System is able to determine the line length of the record and assigns that value to the variable LINELEN. The single trailing @ holds the record in the input buffer for the next INPUT statement.
3. Then the assignment statement uses the two known lengths (the length of FIRSTVAR and the length of the entire record) to determine the length of VARLEN.
4. The second INPUT statement can then use the value of VARLEN in combination with the informat $VARYING200. to read the variable SECONDVR.

Example 4: Updating an External File

The following example shows how to use the INFILE statement with the SHAREBUFFERS option and the INPUT, FILE, and PUT statements to update an external file in place:

```
data _null_;

   /* The INFILE and FILE statements specify the same file. */
   infile file-specification-1 sharebuffers n=3;
   file file-specification-1 ;
   input name $ 1-34 phone $ 35-46 #2 company $ 1-34 addr1 $ 35-72
         #3 addr2 $ 1-34 addr3 $ 35-72;
   if company= 'SAS Institute Inc.' then addr3='Cary, NC 27512-8000';
   if phone='919-467-8000' then phone='919-677-8000';
   put #1 phone 35-46 #3 addr3 35-72;
run;
```

See Also

FILENAME, INPUT, and PUT statements

"Reading Raw Data" in Chapter 2, "The DATA Step"

"SAS System Options" in Chapter 3, "Components of the SAS Language"

SAS documentation for your host system for host-specific INFILE statement options

INFORMAT

Associates informats with variables

DATA step

HELP INFORMAT

Syntax

INFORMAT *variables* <*informat*> <DEFAULT=*default-informat*>;

Description

The INFORMAT statement associates informats with variables. In a DATA step, the INFORMAT statement can specify a default informat for variables listed in an INPUT statement. A single INFORMAT statement can associate the same informat with several variables or different informats with different variables. The INFORMAT statement can use standard SAS informats or informats defined using the FORMAT procedure.

Using an INFORMAT statement in the DATA step permanently associates an informat with a variable by changing the descriptor information of the SAS data set containing the variable. If a variable appears in more than one INFORMAT statement, the SAS System uses the informat most recently assigned.

Because an INFORMAT statement defines the length of previously undefined character variables, you can truncate the values of character variables in a DATA step if an INFORMAT statement precedes a SET statement.

You can use the following arguments with the INFORMAT statement:

variables

names the variables to associate with an informat. To disassociate an informat from a variable, use the variable's name in an INFORMAT statement with no informat. Make sure the null INFORMAT statement follows the SET statement.

informat

specifies the informat for reading the values of the variables. Informats associated with variables using an INFORMAT statement behave like informats used with a colon modifier. The SAS System reads the variables using list input, but with an informat. In modified list input, the SAS System

- does not use the value of *w* in an informat to specify column positions or input field widths in an external file
- uses the value of *w* in an informat to specify the length of previously undefined character variables
- ignores the value of *w* in numeric informats
- uses the value of *d* in an informat in the same way it usually does for numeric informats
- treats blanks embedded an input data as delimiters unless you change their status with a DELIMITER= option specification in an INFILE statement.

DEFAULT= *default-informat*
: specifies a temporary default informat for reading values during the current DATA step. A DEFAULT= informat specification applies to any of the following variables:

- □ those not named in an INFORMAT or ATTRIB statement
- □ those not permanently associated with an informat within a SAS data set
- □ those not read with an explicit informat in the current DATA step.

A DEFAULT= specification in an INFORMAT statement applies only during the current DATA step, so that default informats are not permanently associated with variables in a data set. A DEFAULT= specification can occur in any position within the INFORMAT statement and can contain either a numeric default, a character default, or both. An INFORMAT statement can contain a DEFAULT= specification alone, a DEFAULT= specification along with other informat specifications, or one or more informat specifications.

If no default is specified, the SAS System uses the *w.d* informat as the default for numeric variables and the *$w.* informat as the default for character variables.

You can use an INFORMAT statement in some PROC steps, but the rules are different. See the *SAS Procedures Guide* for more information.

Comparisons

The ATTRIB statement can also associate informats with variables. Either an ATTRIB or an INFORMAT statement can change an informat associated with a variable. You can associate, change, or disassociate informats and variables in existing SAS data sets with the DIR display manager window.

Examples

Example 1: Specifying Defaults

The following program illustrates how to use an INFORMAT statement to establish a default numeric informat and a default character informat:

```
data infex;
   informat default=3.1 default=$char4.;
   input x1-x10 name $;
   put x1-x10 name;
   cards;
11 22 33 44 55 66 77 88 99 100Johnny
;
```

Here are the results of this DATA step:

```
----+----1----+----2----+----3----+----4----+----5
1.1 2.2 3.3 4.4 5.5 6.6 7.7 8.8 9.9 10 John
```

INFORMAT

continued

Example 2: Specifying Numeric and Character Informats

The following program illustrates how a single INFORMAT statement can associate a character informat and a numeric informat with SAS variables. Note that although the character variables do not fully occupy 15 column positions, the INPUT statement reads them correctly, demonstrating the successful use of modified list input.

```
data name;
   informat fname lname $15. n1 6.2 n2 7.3;
   input fname lname n1 n2;
   cards;
Tom Smith 35 11
;

proc print data=name;
run;

proc contents data=name;
run;
```

Selected results from this program are as follows:

□ from PROC PRINT

```
OBS     FNAME      LNAME      N1       N2

  1      Tom       Smith     0.35    0.011
```

□ from PROC CONTENTS

```
-----Alphabetic List of Variables and Attributes-----

    #    Variable     Type    Len    Pos    Informat
    --------------------------------------------------
    1    FNAME        Char     15      0    $15.
    2    LNAME        Char     15     15    $15.
    3    N1           Num       8     30    6.2
    4    N2           Num       8     38    7.3
```

Example 3: Removing an Informat

The following code illustrates how to remove an existing informat. The order of the INFORMAT and SET statements is important.

```
data rtest;
   set rtest;
   informat x;
run;
```

See Also

ATTRIB and INPUT statements

Chapter 13, "SAS Informats"

DIR window in Chapter 17, "SAS Display Manager Windows"

INPUT

Describes the arrangement of values in an input record and assigns input values to corresponding SAS variables

DATA step

HELP INPUT

Syntax

INPUT <*specification-1*> < . . . *specification-n*> <@ | @@>;

Description

The INPUT statement describes the arrangement of values in an input record and assigns input values to corresponding SAS variables. Use the INPUT statement only for reading data records stored in an external file or for data records following a CARDS statement in the job stream. If the data are already in a SAS data set, use a SET, MERGE, or UPDATE statement instead. A DATA step that reads raw data, whether from an external file or in-stream data, can include multiple INPUT statements.

There are four ways to describe a record's values in the INPUT statement:

- □ column
- □ list (simple and modified)
- □ formatted
- □ named.

Each variable value is read with one of these input styles. An INPUT statement may contain any or all of the available input styles, depending on the arrangement of data values in the input records. See "Examples" later in this section.

The following INPUT statements, reading the character variable NAME and the numeric variable AGE, illustrate column, list, formatted, and named input.*

With *column input,* the variable name is followed in the INPUT statement by the column numbers which indicate where the variable values are found in the data records:

```
input name $ 1-8 age 11-12;
```

This INPUT statement can read the following data records:

```
----+----1----+----2----+
Peterson  21
Morgan    17
```

Note that if the variable is character instead of numeric, a $ appears between the variable name and column numbers.

With *list input,* the variable names are simply listed in the INPUT statement, with a $ following the name of each character variable:

```
input name $ age;
```

* Character and numeric data are defined in "Kinds of Data" in Chapter 2.

INPUT

continued

This INPUT statement can read data values separated by blanks or aligned in columns (with at least one blank between):

```
----+----1----+----2----+
Peterson 21
Morgan 17
```

With *formatted input*, you specify an informat after the variable name in the INPUT statement. The informat indicates the variable's data type and field width.

```
input name $char8. +2 age 2.;
```

This INPUT statement reads the following data records correctly:

```
----+----1----+----2----+
Peterson  21
Morgan    17
```

Note the use of the pointer control +2 to move the input pointer to the field containing the variable value for the variable AGE.

With *named input*, you specify the name of the variable followed by an equal sign, and the SAS System looks for a variable name and equal sign in your input data:

```
input name= $ age=;
```

This INPUT statement reads the following data records correctly:

```
----+----1----+----2----+
name=Peterson age=21
name=Morgan age=17
```

See "Examples" later in this section showing multiple input styles in a single INPUT statement. See detailed descriptions of each style of input in "INPUT, Column," "INPUT, List," "INPUT, Formatted," and "INPUT, Named" later in this chapter.

You can use the following arguments with the INPUT statement:

no argument

has several uses. It can

- □ bring an input data line into the input buffer without creating any SAS variables
- □ read an input record into the input buffer so that it can be copied to an output file
- □ release an input line held by a trailing @ or a double trailing @.

An INPUT statement without variable names is called a null INPUT statement.

specification
can include the following:

variable
names the variable whose value is to be read.

(*variable-list*)
is any valid variable list enclosed in parentheses. Note that (*variable-list*) must be followed by (*informat-list*). See "Grouping Variables and Informats" in "INPUT, Formatted" later in this chapter.

$
indicates that the variable has character, rather than numeric, values. If the variable has been previously defined as character, the $ sign is not required.

pointer-control
moves the input pointer to a specified line or column in the input buffer. See "Pointer Controls and Line-Hold Specifiers" later in this section.

column-specifications
specify columns in data lines where variable values are to be read. See "INPUT, Column" later in this chapter.

format-modifiers
allow list input to be used to read data that cannot be read with simple list input. See "INPUT, List" later in this chapter.

informat.
specifies an informat to be used to read a variable value. See "INPUT, Formatted" for a discussion of reading data values with informats. You can also use list input, enhanced with format modifiers, to read data with informats. See "INPUT, List."

(*informat-list*)
lists the informats to be used to read the preceding list of variables. Note that (*informat-list*) must follow (*variable-list*). See "Grouping Variables and Informats" in "INPUT, Formatted."

@
(trailing @) holds the input record for the execution of the next INPUT statement. The trailing @ line-hold specifier must appear at the end of the INPUT statement when used. For a complete description of the trailing @, see "Pointer Controls and Line-Hold Specifiers."

@@
(double trailing @) holds the input record for the execution of the next INPUT statement, even across iterations of the DATA step. The double trailing @ line-hold specifier must appear at the end of the INPUT statement when used. For a complete description of the double trailing @, see "Pointer Controls and Line-Hold Specifiers."

Pointer Controls and Line-Hold Specifiers

As the SAS System reads values from data records in the input buffer, it keeps track of its position with a pointer. You can determine the pointer's current column and line location with the COLUMN= and LINE= options in the INFILE statement. Pointer controls are provided in the

INPUT

continued

INPUT statement so that you can reset the pointer's column and line position when instructing the INPUT statement where to read the data value in the data records. Line-hold specifiers allow you to hold a data record in the input buffer to be processed by another INPUT statement.

Using column and line pointer controls, you can specify the absolute number of the line or column to which you want to move the pointer or you can specify a column or line location relative to the current one. Table 9.1 lists all pointer controls and line-hold specifiers that you can use with the INPUT statement. Complete descriptions are given later in this section.

Table 9.1 *Pointer Controls Available in the INPUT Statement*

Pointer Controls	Relative	Absolute
column pointer controls	+*n* +*numeric-variable* +(*expression*)	@*n* @*numeric-variable* @(*expression*) @'*character-string*' @*character-variable* @(*character-expression*)
line pointer controls	/	#*n* #*numeric-variable* #(*expression*)
line-hold specifiers	@ (trailing @) @@ (double trailing @)	(not applicable) (not applicable)

Specify pointer controls before the variable to which they apply. Line pointer controls at the end of the INPUT statement can be used to move to the next input line or define the number of input lines per observation.

Column pointer controls Column pointer controls indicate the column in which an input value starts.

@*n*
: moves the pointer to column *n*. Note that *n* must be a positive integer. If not an integer, the decimal portion is truncated and only the integer value is used. If zero is associated with the @ pointer control, the pointer moves to column 1.

  For example, the following statement moves the pointer to column 15:

```
input @15 sales 5.;
```

@*numeric-variable*
: moves the pointer to the column given by the value of *numeric-variable,* which must be a positive integer. If not an integer, the decimal portion is truncated and only the integer value is used. If zero or a negative number is associated with the @ pointer control, the pointer moves to column 1.

The following INPUT statement moves the pointer to column 25 to read a value for variable NAME:

```
a=25;
input @a name $10.;
```

@(*expression*)
moves the pointer to the column given by the value of *expression*. *Expression* must result in a positive integer. If not an integer, the decimal portion is truncated and only the integer value is used. If zero or a negative number is associated with the @ pointer control, the pointer moves to column 1.

The following INPUT statement uses an expression to move the pointer to column 30:

```
b=10;
input @(b*3) grade 2.;
```

@'*character-string*'
locates the specified series of characters in the input line and moves the pointer to the first column after *character-string*.

@*character-variable*
locates the series of characters in the input line given by the value of *character-variable* and moves the pointer to the first column after that series of characters.

For example, the following statement reads in the WEEKDAY character variable. The second @1 moves the pointer to the beginning of the input line. It then scans for the value of WEEKDAY and reads the value for SALES from the next nonblank column after the value of WEEKDAY:

```
input @1 day 1. @5 weekday $10. @1 @weekday sales 8.2;
```

@(*character-expression*)
locates the series of characters identified by *character-expression* and moves the pointer to the first column after the series. See "Example 5: Positioning the Pointer."

+*n*
moves the pointer *n* columns. Note that *n* must be a positive integer or zero. If not an integer, the decimal portion is truncated and only the integer value is used.

For example, the following statement moves the pointer to column 23, reads a value for LENGTH from the next four columns (23, 24, 25, and 26), and then advances the pointer five columns to read a WIDTH value in columns 32 through 35:

```
input @23 length 4. +5 width 4.;
```

INPUT

continued

+*numeric-variable*

moves the pointer the number of columns given by the value of *numeric-variable*, which can be a positive or negative integer or zero. If not an integer, the decimal portion is truncated and only the integer value is used. If the current column position becomes less than 1, the pointer is set in column 1. If the value is greater than the length of the input buffer, the next record is read and the pointer is positioned in column 1.

+(*expression*)

moves the pointer the number of columns given by *expression*. The expression can result in a positive or negative integer or zero. If not an integer, the decimal portion is truncated and only the integer value is used. If a negative integer or zero, the pointer is set in column 1. If the value is greater than the length of the input buffer, the next record is read and the pointer is positioned in column 1.

Line pointer controls Line pointer controls specify the input line from which the INPUT statement is to read a value. When reading more than one record at a time into the input buffer, you should use the N= option in the INFILE statement to specify the number of lines to be read. If you do not use the N= option, you need to take special precautions. See "Reading More Than One Record per Observation" later in this section.

The following four line pointer controls are used when more than one input line is read to construct a single observation:

#*n*

moves the pointer to line *n*, which must be a positive integer. For example, the following INPUT statement indicates that the value for ID be read from columns 3 and 4 of the second line in the input buffer:

```
input @12 name $10. #2 id 3-4;
```

#*numeric-variable*

moves the pointer to the line given by the value of *numeric-variable*, which must be a positive integer. If not an integer, the decimal portion is truncated and only the integer value is used.

#(*expression*)

moves the pointer to the line given by the value of *expression*. *Expression* must result in a positive integer. If not an integer, the decimal portion is truncated and only the integer value is used.

/

advances the pointer to column 1 of the next input line. For example, the following statement reads values for AGE and GRADE from one input line and then skips to the next line to read values for SCORE1 through SCORE5:

```
input age grade / score1-score5;
```

Line-hold specifiers Line-hold specifiers keep the pointer on the current input line when

□ a data line is read by more than one INPUT statement (trailing @)

□ one input line has values for more than one observation (double trailing @).

Use a single trailing @ to allow the next INPUT statement to read from the same record. Use a double trailing @ to allow a record to be held for the next INPUT statement even across iterations of the DATA step.

@

(trailing @) holds a data line for the next INPUT statement in the step. The trailing @ prevents the next INPUT statement from automatically releasing the current input record and reading the next one into the input buffer. The @ is called a *trailing at sign* because it must be the last item in the INPUT statement.

Normally, each INPUT statement in a DATA step reads a new data line into the input buffer. When you use a trailing @, the following occurs:

□ The pointer position remains the same.

□ No new record is read into the input buffer.

□ The next INPUT statement for the same iteration of the DATA step continues reading the same record rather than a new one.

A line held with a trailing @ is released automatically when

□ a null INPUT statement executes:

```
input;
```

□ the system returns to the top of the DATA step to begin the next iteration.

See "Example 3: Holding a Record in the Input Buffer."

@@

(double trailing @) holds an input line for further iterations of the DATA step. The @@ symbol (called a *double trailing at sign*) is useful when each input line contains values for several observations.

The SAS System releases a line held by a double trailing @

□ immediately if the pointer moves past the end of the line

□ immediately if a null INPUT statement executes:

```
input;
```

□ when the next iteration of the DATA step begins if an INPUT statement with a single trailing @ executes later in the DATA step:

```
input @;
```

See "Example 4: Holding a Record across Iterations of the DATA Step."

Pointer Location after Reading

To combine styles of input in a single INPUT statement, it is important to understand the location of the input pointer after a value is read. With column and formatted input, the pointer reads the columns indicated in the INPUT statement and stops in the next column. With list input,

INPUT

continued

however, the pointer scans data lines to locate data values and reads a blank as the indication that a value has ended. After reading a value with list input, the pointer stops in the second column after the value.

For example, the following data lines can be read with list, column, and formatted input:

```
----+----1----+----2----+----3
REGION1     49670
REGION2      97540
REGION3     86342
```

The following INPUT statement uses list input to read this data:

```
input region $ jansales;
```

After reading a value for REGION, the pointer stops in column 9.

The following INPUT statements use column and formatted input to read the data lines:

□ `input region $ 1-7 jansales 12-16;`

□ `input region $7. +4 jansales 5.;`

To read a value for the variable REGION, both of these INPUT statements instruct the pointer to read 7 columns and then stop in column 8.

```
----+----1----+----2----+----3
REGION1     49670
```

Reading More than One Record per Observation

The highest number following the # pointer control in the INPUT statement determines how many records are read into the input buffer. You can override this number by using the N= option in the INFILE statement. For example, in this statement, the highest value after the # is 3:

```
input @31 age 3. #3 id 3-4 #2 @6 name $20.;
```

Thus, the INPUT statement reads three input lines each time it executes unless the N= option has been used in the associated INFILE statement.

When each observation has multiple input lines, but values are not read from the last line, a # pointer control in the INPUT statement must specify the last line unless the N= option has been used in the INFILE statement. For example, if there are four lines per observation, but values are read only from the first two lines, the INPUT statement may look as follows:

```
input name $ 1-10 #2 age 13-14 #4;
```

When you have advanced to the next line with the / pointer control, you must use the #*n* pointer control in the INPUT statement or the N=

option in the INFILE statement to define the number of records read into the input buffer and move the pointer back to an earlier line. The following statement requires the #2 pointer control unless the INFILE statement uses the N= option:

```
input a / b #1 @52 c #2;
```

This statement reads a value for A from the first line, for B from the second, and then returns to column 1 of the first line and moves to column 52 to read a value for C. The #2 pointer control identifies two input lines for each observation, so the pointer can return to the first line for the value of C.

If the number of input lines per observation varies, use the N= option in the INFILE statement to give the maximum number of lines per observation. The N= option overrides any specification implied by pointer controls.

Reading Past the End of a Line

When @ or + pointer controls are used with a value that moves the pointer to or past the end of the current line and the next value is to be read from the current column, the SAS System goes to column 1 of the next line to read it. It also writes this message to the SAS log:

```
NOTE: SAS went to a new line when INPUT statement reached
      past the end of a line.
```

Use the STOPOVER option in the INFILE statement if you want to treat this condition as an error and stop building the data set.

You can also use the MISSOVER option in the INFILE statement to set the remaining INPUT statement variables to missing values if the pointer reaches the end of a line.

Positioning the Pointer before the Record

When a column pointer control tries to move the pointer to a position before the beginning of the record, the pointer is positioned in column 1. For example, the following DATA step specifies that the pointer be located in column −5:

```
data test(drop=x);
   x=-5;
   input a @x b;
   cards;
1 2
;
```

After reading a value for variable A, the pointer is positioned in column 1.

INPUT

continued

SAS Format Modifiers for Error Reporting

SAS format modifiers for error reporting define the amount of information printed in the log when the SAS System encounters an error in an input value.

? suppresses the invalid data message that the SAS System prints when it encounters an invalid data value. Here are two examples:

- ```
  input x ? 10-12;
  ```
- ```
  input (x1-x10) (? 3.1);
  ```

When the SAS System encounters an invalid character in a value for the variable indicated, it takes the actions described in "Invalid Data and How They Are Handled" in Chapter 2, except that it does *not* print the invalid data message. Note that _ERROR_ is set to 1.

?? suppresses the printing of both the error messages and the input lines when invalid data values are read. The ? and ?? message modifiers both suppress the invalid data message. The ?? modifier also prevents the automatic variable _ERROR_ from being set to 1 when invalid data are read. Thus, the following two sets of statements are equivalent:

- ```
  input x ?? 10-12;
  ```
- ```
  input x ? 10-12;
  _error_=0;
  ```

Invalid X values are still set to missing values.

End-of-File

End-of-file occurs when an INPUT statement reaches the end of the data. When a DATA step tries to read another record after end-of-file has been reached, the DATA step execution stops. Using the END= or EOF= option in the INFILE statement, you can detect end-of-file and stop executing INPUT statements for that input file if you want to continue executing the DATA step. See the INFILE statement earlier in this chapter for more details.

Arrays

The INPUT statement can use array references to read input data values. An array reference can be used in a pointer control if enclosed in parentheses.

You can use the array subscript asterisk (*) to input all elements of a previously defined explicit array. The array can be single- or multidimensional, and the subscript can be enclosed in braces, brackets, or parentheses. The form of this statement is

INPUT *array-name*{*};

You can use list, column, or formatted input; you cannot input values to an array defined with _TEMPORARY_ using the asterisk subscript. For example, the following statements create variables X1 through X100 and read data values into the variables using the 2. informat:

```
array x{100};
input x{*} 2.;
```

Comparisons

Use the INPUT statement to read data in external files or data entered instream (following the CARDS statement) that need to be described to the SAS System. Use the SET, MERGE, or UPDATE statement to read a SAS data set, which already contains descriptive information about data values.

Examples

Example 1: Using Multiple Styles of Input in One INPUT Statement

The INPUT statement in the following DATA step demonstrates that different input styles may be used in a single INPUT statement:

```
data club1;
   input idno name $18. team $ 25-30 strtwght endwght;
   cards;
1023 David Shaw         red    189 165
1049 Amelia Serrano     yellow 189 165
more data lines
;
```

The value for IDNO is read with list input. The value for NAME is read with formatted input, the value for TEAM with column input, and the values for STRTWGHT and ENDWGHT with list input.

Example 2: Using a Null INPUT Statement

The following DATA step copies records from the input file to the output file without creating any SAS variables:

```
data _null_;
   infile file-specification-1;
   file file-specification-2;
   input;
   put _infile_;
run;
```

INPUT

continued

Example 3: Holding a Record in the Input Buffer

This example reads a file that contains two kinds of input data lines. One type of data line gives information about a particular college course; the other contains information about the students taking that course. Two INPUT statements are needed to read the two lines because they have different variables and different formats. Lines containing class information have a C in column 1; lines containing student information have an S in column 1, as shown here:

```
----+----1----+----2----+
C HIST101 Watson
S Williams 0459
```

You need to check each line as it is read to know which INPUT statement to use. You need an INPUT statement that reads only the variable telling whether the line is a student or class record.

```
data schedule;
   infile file-specification;
   input type $ 1 @;
   if type='C' then input course $ prof $;
   else if type='S' then input name $ id;
run;
```

The first INPUT statement reads the TYPE value from column 1 of every line. Since this INPUT statement ends with a trailing @, the next INPUT statement in the DATA step reads the same line. The IF-THEN statements that follow check whether the line is a class or student line, and each gives an INPUT statement to read the rest of the line. Note that the INPUT statements without a trailing @ release the held line.

Example 4: Holding a Record across Iterations of the DATA Step

For this example, suppose you have input with each line containing several NAME and AGE values. You want to read first a NAME value and an AGE value, then output the observation, then read another set of NAME and AGE values to output, and so on until you have read and output all the input values in the line. Use a double trailing @ in your INPUT statement.

```
data three;
   input name $ age @@;
   cards;
JOHN 13 MARY 12 SUE 15 TOM 10
;
```

Example 5: Positioning the Pointer

The following examples illustrate different ways to position the pointer:

□ The @ *numeric-variable* pointer control is often combined with a trailing @. In this example, the SAS System obtains the value of X for the current observation in the first INPUT statement and uses that value to determine the column to move to in the second INPUT statement:

```
data one;
   input x @;
   if 1<=x<=10 then input @x city $12.;
   else input @50 county $10.;
   more SAS statements
   cards;
data lines
;
```

□ This example uses the absolute column pointer @ and a character variable to position the pointer. The raw data contain records that look like the following:

```
values NEW YORK 2
values RALEIGH 1
values CARY 3
values CHAPEL HILL 2
```

A permanent SAS data set named IN.SURVEY has already been created from this file. IN.SURVEY contains a character variable CITY whose values are the city names given here. Suppose you discover that you need to add the numeric values following the city names in the file as a numeric variable named GROUP. You can use this DATA step:

```
data out.survey2;
   set in.survey;
   infile file-specification;
   input @(trim(city)) group : 8.;
run;
```

The INPUT statement scans each data line for the series of characters in the value of CITY for that observation and reads the value of GROUP beginning in the next nonblank column. Note that the TRIM function is used to trim trailing blanks from the character value so that an exact match is found between the character string in the input data and the stored value of the variable CITY in the data set IN.SURVEY.

Note: This example assumes that the observations in IN.SURVEY are still in the order of the original data lines and that you have not deleted or added any observations.

□ This example uses the @ pointer control and a character expression to position the pointer. The data records in the file look as follows:

```
85 values JAN values JAN85 6.2 values
84 values OCT values OCT84 11.3 values
85 values JUL values JUL85 1.6 values
85 values AUG values AUG85 1.4 values
```

INPUT

continued

□ To read a value for variable RAIN beginning at the first nonblank column following the month and year, you can use the following DATA step:

```
data rainfall;
   infile file-specification;
   input @1 year $2. @11 month $3. @;
   input @(month||year) rain : 4.1;
run;
```

The first INPUT statement reads values for YEAR and MONTH. The second INPUT statement concatenates those values to determine the location of variable RAIN in the data lines.

Example 6: Moving the Pointer Backward

You can use the @ pointer control to move the pointer backward. The following INPUT statement first reads a value for BOOK starting at column 26 and then moves back to column 1 on the same line to read a value for COMPANY:

```
input @26 book $ @1 company;
```

To move backward, you can also use +*numeric-variable* or +(*expression*). Both of the following INPUT statements move the pointer backward one column:

□
```
m=-1;
input x 1-10 +m y 2.;
```

□
```
input x 1-10 +(-1) y 2.;
```

See Also

INPUT statement, column; INPUT statement, formatted; INPUT statement, list; INPUT statement, named; and explicit array reference

"Reading Raw Data" and "External Files" in Chapter 2, "The DATA Step"

INPUT, Column

Reads input values from specified columns and assigns to corresponding SAS variables

DATA step

HELP INPUT

Syntax

INPUT *variable* <$> *start-column* <*−end-column*> <*.decimals*>
<@ | @@>;

Description

With column input, the column numbers containing the value follow a variable name in the INPUT statement. To be read with column input, data values must be in

- the same columns on all the input lines
- standard numeric or character form.*

Features of column input include the following:

- Character values can contain embedded blanks.
- Character values can be from 1 to 200 characters long.
- No placeholder is required for missing data. A blank field is interpreted as missing and does not cause other values to be read incorrectly.
- If a field contains a single period, the variable value is set to missing whether numeric or character.
- Input values can be read in any order, regardless of their position in the record.
- Values or parts of values can be reread. For example, the following INPUT statement reads an ID value in columns 10 through 15 and then reads a value from column 13 as a value for the variable GROUP:

```
input id 10-15 group 13;
```

- Both leading and trailing blanks within the field are ignored. Therefore, if numeric values contain blanks that represent zeros or if you want to retain leading and trailing blanks in character values, you must read the value with an informat. See "INPUT, Formatted" later in this chapter for more information.
- Data records following the CARDS statement (instream data) are always padded to a fixed length in multiples of 80. The setting of the CARDIMAGE system option determines whether data past column 80 are read or truncated.
- When using column input to read a file that contains varying-length records, you may need to use the PAD option in the INFILE statement to pad the records to a fixed length. See the INFILE statement earlier in this chapter.

* Standard and nonstandard data values are defined in "Kinds of Data" in Chapter 2.

INPUT, Column

continued

You can use the following arguments with an INPUT statement that specifies column input:

variable
: names the variable whose value the INPUT statement is to read.

$
: indicates that the variable has character, rather than numeric, values. If the variable has been previously defined as character, the $ sign is not required.

start-column
: is the first column of the input record that contains the variable's value.

−*end-column*
: is the last column of the input record that contains the variable value. If the variable value occupies only one column, omit *end-column*. For example, in the following INPUT statement, values for the character variable GENDER occupy only column 16:

```
input name $ 1-10 pulse 11-13 waist 14-15 gender $ 16;
```

.decimals
: gives the number of digits to the right of the decimal if the input value does not contain an explicit decimal point. An explicit decimal point in the input value overrides a decimal specification in the INPUT statement. For example, this statement reads the value of NUMBER with two decimal places:

```
input number 10-15 .2;
```

When this INPUT statement is used to read input data for the variable NUMBER, the resulting values are as follows:

Input Data	SAS Statement	Result
`----+----1----+----2`	`input number 10-15 .2;`	
2314		23.14
2		.02
400		4.00
-140		-1.40
12.234		12.234 *
12.2		12.2 *

* The decimal specification in the INPUT statement is overridden by the input data value.

@
: (trailing @) holds the input record for the execution of the next INPUT statement. The trailing @ line-hold specifier, if used, must appear at the end of the INPUT statement. For a complete description of the trailing @, see "Pointer Controls and Line-Hold Specifiers" under the INPUT statement earlier in this chapter.

@@
: (double trailing @) holds the input record for the execution of the next INPUT statement, even across iterations of the DATA step. The double trailing @ line-hold specifier, if used, must appear at the end of the INPUT statement. For a complete description of the double trailing @, see "Pointer Controls and Line-Hold Specifiers" under the INPUT statement earlier in this chapter.

Example

The following DATA step demonstrates reading data records with column input:

```
data scores;
   input name $ 1-18 score1 25-27 score2 30-32 score3 35-37;
   cards;
Joe                     11  32  76
Mitchel                 13  29  82
Susan                   14  27  74
;
```

See Also

INPUT statement

INPUT, Formatted

Reads input values with specified informats and assigns them to corresponding SAS variables

DATA step

HELP INPUT

Syntax

INPUT <*pointer-control*> *variable informat.*<@ | @@>;
INPUT <*pointer-control*> (*variable-list*) (*informat-list*) <@ | @@>;
INPUT <*pointer-control*> (*variable-list*) (<*n**> *informat.*) <@ | @@>;

Description

With formatted input, an informat follows a variable name and defines how values of that variable are to be read. An informat gives the data type and field width of an input value. Informats allow you to read data stored in nonstandard form, such as packed decimal, or numbers that contain invalid characters such as commas.* See Chapter 3 for background information on SAS informats and Chapter 13 for descriptions of SAS informats.

Missing values in formatted input are generally represented by a single period for a numeric value and by blanks for a character value. The informat used with formatted input determines the way blanks are interpreted. For example, the $CHAR. informat reads blanks as part of the value, whereas the BZ. informat turns blanks into zeros. See Chapter 13 for more information on how a particular informat handles data.

Simple formatted input requires that the variables be in the same order as their corresponding values in the input data. You can read variables in any order by using pointer controls, described in the INPUT statement earlier in this chapter. See "Examples" later in this section.

You can use the following arguments with an INPUT statement that specifies formatted input:

pointer-control
: moves the input to a specified line or column in the input buffer. For complete descriptions of pointer controls, see "Pointer Controls and Line-Hold Specifiers" under the INPUT statement earlier in this chapter.

variable
: is the variable that the INPUT statement is to read.

(*variable-list*)
: is any valid variable list enclosed in parentheses. Note that (*variable-list*) must be followed by (*informat-list*). See "Grouping Variables and Informats" later in this section.

informat.
: specifies a SAS informat to use when reading the data values. Decimal points included in the actual input values always override decimal specifications in a numeric informat. See Chapter 13 for complete descriptions of all SAS informats.

(*informat-list*)
: lists the informats to be used to read the input values for the preceding list of variables. Note that (*informat-list*) must be preceded by (*variable-list*). See

* Standard and nonstandard data values are defined in "Kinds of Data" in Chapter 2.

the next section, "Grouping Variables and Informats." In the INPUT statement, (*informat-list*) can include the following:

informat.
: specifies the informat to be used to write the variable values.

pointer-control
: specifies one of the following pointer controls to be used to position a value: @, #, /, or +.

*n**
: specifies that the next informat in an informat list is to be repeated *n* times. For example, the following INPUT statement reads GRADES1, GRADES2, and GRADES3 with the 7.2 informat and reads GRADES4 and GRADES5 with the 5.2 informat:

```
input (grades1-grades5) (3 * 7.2, 2 * 5.2);
```

See "Grouping Variables and Informats."

@
: (trailing @) holds the input record for the execution of the next INPUT statement. The trailing @ line-hold specifier, if used, must appear at the end of the INPUT statement. For a complete description of the trailing @, see "Pointer Controls and Line-Hold Specifiers" under the INPUT statement earlier in this chapter.

@@
: (double trailing @) holds the input record for the execution of the next INPUT statement, even across iterations of the DATA step. The double trailing @ line-hold specifier, if used, must appear at the end of the INPUT statement. For a complete description of the double trailing @, see "Pointer Controls and Line-Hold Specifiers" under the INPUT statement earlier in this chapter.

Grouping Variables and Informats

When input values are arranged in a pattern, they can be described with a grouped informat list. A grouped informat list consists of two lists:

- the names of the variables to be read
- their corresponding informats separated by either blanks or commas.

Each list must be enclosed in parentheses. You can write shorter INPUT statements with informat lists because

- the informat list is recycled until all variables have been read
- numbered variable names can be used in abbreviated form to avoid listing all the individual variables.

INPUT, Formatted

continued

You can use as many informat lists as necessary in an INPUT statement, but informat lists cannot be nested. For example, if the values for the five variables SCORE1 through SCORE5 are arranged four columns per value without intervening blanks, the following INPUT statement reads their values:

```
input (score1-score5) (4. 4. 4. 4. 4.);
```

However, if you specify more variables than informats, the informat list is reused to read the remaining variables. Therefore, this shorter informat list accomplishes the same thing:

```
input (score1-score5) (4.);
```

When all the values in the variable list have been read, the INPUT statement ignores any directions remaining in the informat list. The following DATA step illustrates this point:

```
data test;
   input (x y z) (2.,+1);
   cards;
12 24 36
10 20 30
;
```

The value of X is read using the 2. informat and the +1 column pointer control moves the pointer forward one column. The value of Y is read using the 2. informat and, again, the +1 column pointer moves the pointer forward one column. Then, the value of Z is read using the 2. informat. The +1 pointer control remaining in the third cycle of the informat list is not used.

The *n** modifier in informat lists specifies that the next informat is to be repeated *n* times, as in the following INPUT statement:

```
input (name score1-score5) ($10. 5*4.);
```

See "Example 2: Using Informat Lists."

Storing informats

Informats specified in the INPUT statement are not stored with the SAS data set. Informats specified with the INFORMAT or ATTRIB statement are stored, allowing you to read a data value with an informat in a later DATA step without specifying the informat or to input data using the FSEDIT procedure in SAS/FSP software.

Comparisons

When a variable is read with formatted input, the pointer movement is like that of column input, not list input. The pointer moves the length specified in the informat and stops at the next column. If you need to use informats to read data not aligned in columns, you may need to use modified list input instead of formatted input, to take advantage of the scanning feature of list input. See "INPUT, List" later in this chapter.

Examples

Example 1: Formatted Input with Pointer Controls

The following INPUT statement uses informats and pointer controls:

```
data jansales;
   infile file-specification;
   input item $10. +5 jan comma5. +5 feb comma5. +5 mar comma5.;
run;
```

It can read these data records:

```
----+----1----+----2----+----3----+----4----+----5
trucks         1,382      2,789      3,556
jeeps          1,235      2,543      3,987
landrovers     2,391      3,011      3,658
```

When reading the variable ITEM, the SAS System reads the value from the first 10 columns in the data line. The pointer stops in column 11. The trailing blanks are discarded, and the value of ITEM is written to the program data vector. The pointer then moves 5 columns to the right before it begins reading the value of the variable JAN with the COMMA5. informat, which allows numeric values containing a comma to be read. The pointer moves again before reading the variables FEB and MAR, also with the COMMA5. informat.

Example 2: Using Informat Lists

The following DATA step uses the character informat $10. to read the variable NAME and uses the numeric informat 4. to read the five variables SCORE1 through SCORE5:

```
data scores;
   input (name score1-score5) ($10. 5*4.);
   cards;
Whittaker 121 114 137 156 142
Smythe    111 97  122 143 127
;
```

See Also

INPUT statement and INPUT statement, list

"Informats" in Chapter 3, "Components of the SAS Language"

Chapter 13, "SAS Informats"

INPUT, List

Scans data lines for input values and assigns them to corresponding SAS variables

DATA step

HELP INPUT

Syntax

INPUT <*pointer-control*> *variable* <$> <&> <@ | @@>;
INPUT <*pointer-control*> *variable* <: | &> <*informat.*> <@ | @@>;

Description

List input requires you to list the variable names in the INPUT statement in the order in which the fields appear in the data records. With list input, the SAS System scans the data line to locate the next value, ignoring additional intervening blanks. Data read with list input are not required to be in specific columns, but by default each value must be separated from the next by at least one blank. Though with list input you cannot skip any data values to read subsequent ones, you can ignore all values after a given point in the data record.

Simple list input (without the enhancements provided by format modifiers) places several restrictions on the type of data that can be read:

- □ By default, input values must be separated by at least one blank.*
- □ Each missing value must be represented by a period, not a blank.
- □ Character input values cannot be longer than 8 bytes unless given a longer length in an earlier LENGTH, ATTRIB, or INFORMAT statement.
- □ Character values cannot contain embedded blanks.
- □ Fields must be read in order.
- □ Data must be in standard numeric or character format.**

You can make list input more versatile by using one of two *format modifiers* to overcome several of the restrictions of simple list input. The & (ampersand) format modifier allows you to use list input to read character values that contain embedded blanks. The : (colon) format modifier allows you to read data values that need the additional instructions that informats can provide but that are not aligned in columns.*** For example, you can use it to read character values longer than 8 bytes or numeric values that contain nonstandard values. Pointer controls allow you to read data values out of order.

Because list input interprets a blank as a delimiter for data values, you must use additional features to read values that contain blanks. For example, you can use the & format modifier to read character values containing single embedded blanks, but your data values must be separated by two or more blanks. To read values that contain leading, trailing, or embedded blanks with list input, you can use the DELIMITER= option in the INFILE statement to specify another character to be used as a delimiter. If your input data use blanks as delimiters and contain leading, trailing, or embedded blanks, you must use either column or formatted input.

---

* Using the DELIMITER= option in the INFILE statement, you can define a delimiter other than a blank to be used with list input.

** Standard and nonstandard data values are defined in "Kinds of Data" in Chapter 2.

*** Data values aligned in columns can be easily read with formatted input and pointer controls.

You can use the following arguments with an INPUT statement that specifies simple or modified list input:

pointer-control
: moves the input pointer to a specified line or column. See "Pointer Controls and Line-Hold Specifiers" under the INPUT statement earlier in this chapter.

variable
: names the variable whose value the INPUT statement is to read.

$
: indicates that the preceding variable contains character, rather than numeric, values. If the variable has been previously defined as character, the $ sign is not required.

&
: indicates that a character value may have one or more single embedded blanks and is to be read from the next nonblank column until the pointer reaches two consecutive blanks or the end of the input line, whichever comes first.

  The & (ampersand) format modifier follows the variable name and $ sign that it affects. See "Example 2: Reading Character Data Containing Embedded Blanks."

  The & modifier, like the : modifier, can also be used to precede a specified informat. The terminating condition for the & modifier is two blanks, whether or not an informat is specified. See "Example 3: Using Informats with List Input."

:
: allows an informat to be specified for reading a data value. The : (colon) format modifier indicates that the value is to be read from the next nonblank column until the pointer reaches the next blank column or the end of the data line, whichever comes first. Though the pointer continues reading until it reaches the next blank column, it truncates the value of a character variable if the field is longer that its formatted length. If the length of the variable has not been previously defined, its value is read and stored with the informat length.

  For example, examine the following INPUT statement:

```
input lastname :$15.;
```

  It uses list input to read the first data value correctly in the following data lines:

```
Smith 123 Highway
Longlastname 527 Avenue
```

INPUT, List

continued

informat.
: specifies an informat to use when reading the data values. Note that decimal points included in the actual input values always override decimal specifications in a numeric informat. See Chapter 13 for complete descriptions of all SAS informats.

@
: (trailing @) holds the input record for the execution of the next INPUT statement. The trailing @ line-hold specifier, if used, must appear at the end of the INPUT statement. For a complete description of the trailing @, see "Pointer Controls and Line-Hold Specifiers" under the INPUT statement earlier in this chapter.

@@
: (double trailing @) holds the input record for the execution of the next INPUT statement, even across iterations of the DATA step. The double trailing @ line-hold specifier, if used, must appear at the end of the INPUT statement. For a complete description of the double trailing @, see "Pointer Controls and Line-Hold Specifiers" under the INPUT statement earlier in this chapter.

Comparisons

Because list input and formatted input use different methods for determining how far to read, modified list input (which uses informats) and formatted input cannot be used to read the same data configurations. The following DATA step uses modified list input to read the first data value and formatted input to read the second:

```
data jansales;
   input item : $10. amount comma5.;
   cards;
trucks 1,382
jeeps 1,235
landrovers 2,391
;
```

The first value in these data lines can be read with modified list input because the list input stops reading at the first blank space and then moves the pointer to the second column after the end of the field. The pointer is then in the correct position to begin reading the AMOUNT value with formatted input.

Formatted input, on the other hand, continues reading the entire formatted length. The following INPUT statement uses formatted input to read both data values:

```
input item $10. +1 amount comma5.;
```

To read this data correctly with formatted input requires that the second data value not fall within the 10-column range of the informatted length of the first value, as shown here:

```
----+----1----+----2----+
trucks     1,382
jeeps      1,235
landrovers 2,391
```

Note also that when the first variable is read with formatted input, the pointer control +1 must be used to move the pointer to the column where the value of the variable AMOUNT begins.

Examples

Example 1: Using Simple List Input

The INPUT statement in the following DATA step uses simple list input to read data values:

```
data scores;
   input name $ score1 score2 score3 team $;
   cards;
Joe 11 32 76 red
Mitchel 13 29 82 blue
Susan 14 27 74 green
;
```

The next INPUT statement reads only the first four fields in the previous data lines, demonstrating that you are not required to read all the fields in the record:

```
input name $ score1 score2 score3;
```

INPUT, List

continued

Example 2: Reading Character Data Containing Embedded Blanks

The following DATA step shows use of the & format modifier to read character values containing embedded blanks with list input:

```
data one;
   infile file-specification;
   input name $ & age;
run;
```

Here are sample data lines from the file being read:

```
----+----1----+----2----+
T. Jones  20
J. Rede  31
```

Note that the & format modifier follows the variable it affects in the INPUT statement. Note also that two blanks separate the NAME field from the AGE field in the data records.

You can also specify an informat when using the & format modifier, as shown here:

```
data one;
   input lastname & $15. name1 $;
   cards;
Longlastname1 John
Mc Allister  Mike
Longlastname3  Jim
;
```

Note that the values for the variable LASTNAME are terminated with two blanks.

Example 3: Using Informats with List Input

The following DATA step uses modified list input to read data values with an informat:

```
data jansales;
   input item : $10. number;
   cards;
trucks 32
jeeps 15
landrovers 4
;
```

The $10. informat allows a character variable of up to ten characters to be read.

Example 4: Reading Data with Commas as Delimiters

The following DATA step uses the DELIMITER= option in the INFILE statement to read data values separated by commas, instead of blanks, with list input:

```
data a;
   infile cards delimiter=',';
   input name $ score1-score5;
   cards;
John,100,95,90,97,85
Mary,88,100,98,92,99
;
```

See Also

INFILE statement

INPUT statement

INPUT, Named

Reads data values that contain variable names followed by an equal sign and a value for the variable and assigns values to corresponding SAS variables

DATA step

HELP INPUT

Syntax

INPUT <*pointer-control*> *variable*= <$> <@ | @@>;
INPUT *variable*= <$> *start-column* <−*end-column*> <.*decimals*>
    <@ | @@>;
INPUT <*pointer-control*> *variable*= *informat.*<@ | @@>;

Description

Named input can be used when your data lines contain variable names followed by an equal sign and a value for the variable. The form of the INPUT statement for reading variables with named input is distinguished by the equal sign following a variable name. For example, use named input to read an input line containing AGE=21, rather than just the value 21 for the numeric variable AGE.

The INPUT statement begins reading named input at the current location of the input pointer. Thus, if the input lines include some data values at the beginning of the line that cannot be read with named input, you can use another input style to read them. See "Example 1: Using Named Input." Once the INPUT statement starts reading named input, however, the SAS System expects all remaining values in the input line to be in this form.

Note that you do not have to specify the variables in the INPUT statement in the same order in which they occur in the data records. You are also not required to specify a variable for each field in the record.

When you use named input to read character values that contain embedded blanks, put two blanks before and after the data value, as when you use list input to read character values that contain embedded blanks.

You can use the following arguments with an INPUT statement that specifies named input:

pointer-control
: moves the input pointer to a specified line or column in the input buffer. For complete descriptions of pointer controls, see "Pointer Controls and Line-Hold Specifiers" under the INPUT statement earlier in this chapter.

variable=
: names the variable whose value the INPUT statement is to read. In the input data, the field has the form

    variable=*value*

$
: indicates that the preceding variable contains character, rather than numeric, values. If the variable has been previously defined as character, the $ sign is not required.

informat.
: specifies a SAS informat to use when reading the data values. Note that decimal points included in the actual input values always override decimal specifications in a numeric informat. See Chapter 13 for complete descriptions of all SAS informats.

@
: (trailing @) holds the input record for the execution of the next INPUT statement. The trailing @ line-hold specifier must appear at the end of the INPUT

statement when used. For a complete description of the trailing @, see "Pointer Controls and Line-Hold Specifiers" under the INPUT statement earlier in this chapter.

@@ (double trailing @) holds the input record for the execution of the next INPUT statement, even across iterations of the DATA step. The double trailing @ line-hold specifier must appear at the end of the INPUT statement when used. For a complete description of the double trailing @, see "Pointer Controls and Line-Hold Specifiers" under the INPUT statement earlier in this chapter.

Restrictions

The following restrictions apply to reading data with named input:

- You cannot switch to another input style for a particular input line once you start reading it with named input. All of the remaining values on the input line must be in the form *variable=value*. If any of the values are not in named input form, the SAS System handles them as invalid data. You can, however, read input data in other forms with corresponding input styles before starting to use named input.
- If named input values continue after the end of the current input line, a slash (/) at the end of the input line tells the SAS System to go to the next line and continue reading with named input. For example, the following INPUT statement uses named input:

  ```
  input name=$ age=;
  ```

  It can read the following data lines:

  ```
  name=John      /
  age=34
  ```

- If you do not define a variable for all named input data values, _ERROR_ is set to 1 and a note is written to the log. Here is an example:

  ```
  data a;
     input x= y=;
     cards;
  x=1 y=3 z=10
  ;
  ```

  A note is written to the log stating that variable Z is not defined and _ERROR_ is set to 1.
- If you have used a variable that appears in a line of named input in any other statement (for example, a LENGTH, ATTRIB, FORMAT, or INFORMAT statement), the value is automatically read from the input, whether or not it is explicitly specified in the INPUT statement. Even if you explicitly read only one named input value with the INPUT statement, all of the remaining named input values in the current record are read, and the values are assigned to the corresponding variables.
- You cannot reference an array with an asterisk or expression subscript.

INPUT, Named

continued

Examples

Example 1: Using Named Input

The following INPUT statement uses named input to read values for the variables NAME and SEX. Note that the first variable ID, is read with list input. Note also that the variables read with named input are not read in order and the field containing AGE=*value* in the data line is skipped altogether.

```
data test;
   input id name=$20. sex=$;
   cards;
4798 age=23 sex=m name=JOHN SMITH
;
```

This DATA step builds the data set TEST, writes a note to the log reporting that the variable AGE is not defined, and sets _ERROR_ to 1.

Example 2: Reading Character Variables with Embedded Blanks

The following DATA step reads character variables containing embedded blanks with named input. Note that two spaces both precede and follow the value of the variable HEADER, which is **AGE=60 AND UP.** Note too that the field itself contains an equal sign.

```
data test2;
   informat header $30. name $15.;
   input header= name=;
   cards;
HEADER=  AGE=60 AND UP  NAME=JOHN DOE
;
```

See Also

INPUT statement

KEEP

Includes variables in output SAS data sets

DATA step

HELP KEEP

Syntax

KEEP *variable-list*;

Description

The KEEP statement writes variables you specify to one or more SAS data sets created by a DATA step. The SAS System omits any variables you do not list. The KEEP statement applies to all SAS data sets created within the same DATA step and can appear anywhere in the step. If no KEEP or DROP statement appears, all data sets created in the DATA step contain all variables. Do not use both the KEEP and DROP statements within the same DATA step.

You can use the following argument with the KEEP statement:

variable-list
: specifies the names of the variables to write to the output data set. You can list the variables in any form allowed by the SAS System, such as the following:

- `keep name address city state zip phone;`
- `keep rep1-rep5;`

Comparisons

The KEEP statement differs from the KEEP= data set option in the following ways:

- You cannot use the KEEP statement in SAS PROC steps.
- The KEEP statement applies to all output data sets named in the DATA statement. To write different variables to different data sets, you must use the KEEP= data set option.

The DROP statement is a parallel statement that specifies variables to omit from the output data set. Use the DROP statement instead of the KEEP statement if the number of variables to omit is significantly smaller than the number of variables to include.

The KEEP and DROP statements select variables to include in output data sets. The subsetting IF statement selects observations.

Do not confuse the KEEP statement with the RETAIN statement. The RETAIN statement causes the SAS System to hold the value of a variable from one iteration of the DATA step to the next iteration. The KEEP statement does not affect the value of variables, but only specifies which variables to include in any output data sets.

KEEP

continued

Example

The following example uses the KEEP statement to include only the variables NAME and AVG in the output data set. The variables SCORE1 through SCORE20 from which AVG is calculated are not written to the data set AVERAGE.

```
data average;
   infile file-specification;
   input name $ score1-score20;
   avg=mean(of score1-score20);
   keep name avg;
run;
```

See Also

DROP, subsetting IF, and RETAIN statements

KEEP= data set option in Chapter 15, "SAS Data Set Options"

LABEL

Assigns labels to variables

DATA step

HELP LABEL

Syntax

LABEL *variable-1='label-1'* . . . *<variable-n='label-n'>*;

Description

The LABEL statement associates descriptive labels with variables. Using a LABEL statement in a DATA step permanently associates labels with variables by affecting the descriptor information of the SAS data set containing the variables. You can associate any number of variables with labels in a single LABEL statement.

You can use the following arguments with a LABEL statement:

variable
: names the variable you want to label.

'label'
: specifies a label of up to 40 characters, including blanks. You must enclose the label in either single or double quotes. To include quotes as part of the label, follow the rules in "Using Quotes" in Chapter 3.

  To remove a label from a variable with a LABEL statement, assign a label equal to a blank enclosed in quotes. Make sure the null LABEL statement follows the SET statement. Once you remove a label from a variable this way, the SAS System uses the name of the variable, rather than a blank space, in output where the label would have otherwise appeared.

You can use a LABEL statement in a PROC step, but the rules are different. See the *SAS Procedures Guide* for more information.

Comparisons

The ATTRIB statement can also associate labels with variables. Both the ATTRIB and the LABEL statements can change a label associated with a variable.

Examples

Example 1: Specifying Labels

Here are several valid LABEL statements.

□
```
label compound='Type of Drug';
```

□
```
label score1="Grade on April 1 Test"
      score2="Grade on May 1 Test";
```

□
```
label date="Today's Date ";
```

□
```
label n='Mark''s Experiment Number';
```

LABEL

continued

Example 2: Removing a Label

The following code illustrates how to remove an existing label. The order of the LABEL and SET statements is important.

```
data rtest;
   set rtest;
   label x=' ';
run;
```

See Also

ATTRIB statement

Labels, Statement

Identifies a statement referred to by another statement

DATA step

HELP LABELS

Syntax

label: *statement*;

Description

The statement label identifies the destination of a GO TO statement, LINK statement, the HEADER= option in a FILE statement, or the EOF= option in the INFILE statement.

You can use the following arguments in a statement label:

label
: specifies any valid SAS name. Follow the label with a colon (:).

statement
: specifies any executable statement in the same DATA step as the statement or option that references it. The following list identifies executable SAS statements:

ABORT	IF-THEN	PUT
assignment	INFILE	sum
CALL	INPUT	RETURN
DELETE	LINK	SELECT
DISPLAY	LIST	SET
DO	LOSTCARD	STOP
ERROR	MERGE	subsetting IF
FILE	null	UPDATE
GO TO	OUTPUT	

A null statement can have a label:

```
ABC:;
```

No two statements in a DATA step may have the same label. If a statement in a DATA step is labeled, it should be referenced by a statement or option in the step.

Comparisons

The LABEL statement assigns a descriptive label to a variable. A statement label identifies a statement or group of statements referred to in the same DATA step by another statement, such as a GO TO statement.

Labels, Statement

continued

Example

In the following example, if the value of variable STOCK is 0, the GO TO statement causes the SAS System to jump to the statement labeled REORDR. When STOCK is not 0, execution continues to the RETURN statement and then returns to the beginning of the DATA step for the next observation.

```
data inventry order;
   input item $ stock @;
   if stock=0 then go to reordr;  /* go to label reordr: */
   output inventry;
   return;
   reordr: input supplier $;      /* destination of GOTO statement */
   put 'ORDER ITEM ' item 'FROM ' supplier;
   output order;
   cards;
```

See Also

HEADER= option in the FILE statement

GO TO statement

EOF= option in the INFILE statement

LINK statement

LENGTH

Specifies the number of bytes for storing variables

DATA step

HELP LENGTH

Syntax

LENGTH <*variable-specification-1* < . . . *variable-specification-n*>>
<DEFAULT=*n*>;

Description

The LENGTH statement specifies the number of bytes the SAS System is to use for storing values of variables in each data set being created. It occurs within a DATA step and is not an executable statement.

■ **Host Information** .... Valid variable lengths depend on your host system. For details, refer to the SAS documentation for your host system. ■

You can use the following arguments with the LENGTH statement:

variable-specification
has the following form:

variable-1 < . . . *variable-n*> <$> *length*

where

variable
names the variable to be assigned a length. If the variable is a character variable, the length applies to the program data vector and the output data set. If the variable is a numeric variable, the length applies only to the output data set. The variables named can include any variables in the DATA step, including ones to be dropped from the output data set. Array references are not allowed.

$
indicates that the preceding variable or variables are character variables.

length
is a numeric constant that specifies a number of bytes. The length is not a format; it does not contain a period. For numeric variables, *length* can range from 2 to 8 or 3 to 8, depending on your host system. For character variables, *length* can range from 1 to 200 on all host systems.

DEFAULT=*n*
changes the default number of bytes used for storing the values of newly created numeric variables from 8 to the value of *n*. The value of *n* can range from 2 to 8 or 3 to 8, depending on your host system.

In general, the length of a variable depends on the following:

- □ whether the variable is numeric or character
- □ how the variable was created
- □ whether a LENGTH or ATTRIB statement is present.

LENGTH

continued

Subject to the rules for assigning lengths in general, lengths assigned with the LENGTH statement can be changed in the ATTRIB statement and vice versa. "Numeric Values" and "Character Values" in Chapter 3 discuss assigning lengths to variables.

▶ ***Caution:*** *Avoid shortening numeric variables containing fractions.*

The precision of a numeric variable is closely tied to its length, especially when the variable contains fractional values. You can safely shorten variables containing integers according to the rules given in the SAS documentation for your host system, but shortening variables containing fractions may eliminate important precision. For more information, see "Numeric Values" in Chapter 3.

Comparisons

The ATTRIB statement can assign the length as well as many other attributes of variables.

Example

The following LENGTH statement sets the length of the character variable NAME to 20 and changes the default number of bytes used for storing the values of newly created numeric values from 8 to 4:

```
length name $ 20 default=4;
```

See Also

ATTRIB statement

"Numeric Values" and "Character Values" in Chapter 3, "Components of the SAS Language"

SAS Procedures Guide, Version 6, Third Edition for information on the LENGTH statement in PROC steps

LIBNAME

Associates a SAS libref with a SAS data library

Global

HELP LIBNAME

Syntax

LIBNAME *libref* <*engine*> <'*SAS-data-library*'>
<*engine/host-options*>;
LIBNAME *libref* | _ALL_ CLEAR;
LIBNAME *libref* | _ALL_ LIST;

Description

The LIBNAME statement associates a SAS library reference, or *libref,* with the physical name of a permanent SAS data library. The physical name is the name recognized by your host system. A SAS data library is a collection of SAS files and is the highest level of organization for information within the SAS System. As a unit of organization, a SAS data library is a logical concept that is constant regardless of the media or host on which it is stored.

This logical concept has different implementations depending on your computer, but it roughly corresponds to the level of organization your host system uses to access and store files. For example, on directory-based systems, a SAS data library is a group of SAS files stored in the same directory. Other files can be stored in the directory, but only the files with SAS file extensions are recognized as part of the SAS data library. Under the CMS environment, it is a group of SAS files with the same filetype. Under the MVS and VSE environments, SAS data libraries are implemented as specially formatted host data sets in which only SAS files are stored.

The LIBNAME statement has three uses:

□ associating a libref, an engine, or engine/host-specific options with a SAS data library

□ disassociating, or clearing, a libref

□ listing the characteristics of your SAS data libraries.

Associating Librefs, Engines, and Engine/Host Options

Use the following form of the LIBNAME statement to associate a libref, an engine, or engine/host options with a SAS data library:

LIBNAME *libref* <*engine*> <'*SAS-data-library*'> <*engine/host-options*>;

You can use the following arguments with this form of the LIBNAME statement:

libref
: is any valid SAS name. Refer to "SAS Names" in Chapter 4 for a definition of valid SAS names.

engine
: is a valid engine name.

LIBNAME

(engine continued)

■ **Host Information** ....

Some engines, such as the compatibility engines that read Version 5 SAS data sets, are implemented differently on different host systems. Refer to the SAS documentation for your host system for a list of valid engine names. For a general discussion of the uses and functions of engines, refer to "Engines" in Chapter 6.

.... ■

A SAS engine is a set of internal instructions that the SAS System uses for writing to and reading from files in a SAS data library. Generally, the SAS System automatically determines the appropriate engine to use for accessing the files in the library. If you want to create a new library with an engine other than the default engine, you can override the automatic selection. For example, to store the library YEARLY in Release 6.06 sequential format on disk, you must specify the engine name TAPE in the LIBNAME statement.

```
libname yearly tape 'SAS-data-library';
```

You can use the LIBNAME statement to associate a SAS engine even if you used a host command to assign a libref.

```
libname yearly tape;
```

'SAS-data-library'

must be a valid physical name for the SAS data library on your host system. The physical name must be enclosed in single or double quotes.

■ **Host Information** ....

Refer to the SAS documentation for your host system and to the documentation provided by the vendor for your host system for the rules on specifying the physical name of the SAS data library.

.... ■

■ **Host Information** ....

For some hosts, you have the option of using host commands or the LIBNAME statement to associate the libref with the SAS data library. Other hosts require that you use host commands only. For hosts that do not provide any commands for this function, you must use the LIBNAME statement. See the SAS documentation for your host system for more information on assigning librefs.

.... ■

Associating a libref with the physical name of a SAS data library allows you to refer to the SAS data library in your program statements. When reading, updating, or creating files that belong to a permanent SAS library, you can first use the LIBNAME statement to specify a libref and then include the libref as the first part of a two-level SAS filename in your program statements. The association between the libref and the directory or file remains in effect until you end the SAS session or until you clear the libref. Refer to Chapter 6 for information on how to use the libref when referring to SAS data libraries and SAS files.

Note: If you specify the reserved libref USER or issue the USER= system option to associate the name USER with an existing libref, you can use a one-level name when you create, read, or update permanent SAS files. The libref and USER= system option are in effect for the current SAS session only.

The most common form of the LIBNAME statement contains only the libref and physical name for your SAS data library:

LIBNAME *libref* '*SAS-data-library*';

In the following example, the libref FINANCE is associated with the physical name of a permanent SAS data library:

```
libname finance 'SAS-data-library';
```

This example illustrates how to associate the libref USER with a permanent SAS data library. After issuing this statement, you can access files stored in the library with a one-level name.

```
libname user 'SAS-data-library';
```

engine/host-options
: are one or more options listed in the general form *keyword=value*. You can use as many of these options as required.

■ **Host Information** .... Refer to the SAS documentation for your host system for information on the availability and use of engine/host-specific options. ■

Disassociating a Libref

The SAS System automatically removes the association, or clears, a libref at the end of your job or session. If you want to associate the libref with a different SAS data library, you do not have to end the current session or clear the libref. The SAS System automatically reassigns the libref when you issue a LIBNAME statement for the new SAS data library.

If, however, you want to remove the current libref, you can do so by using the following form of the LIBNAME statement:

LIBNAME *libref* | _ALL_ CLEAR;

When this statement is submitted, the SAS System prints a message to the log stating that the libref has been removed.

You can use the following arguments with this form of the LIBNAME statement:

libref
: is any valid SAS name. Refer to Chapter 4 for a definition of valid SAS names.

ALL
: is a SAS keyword. By specifying it rather than a libref, you can clear all of the librefs you have assigned during the current session.

CLEAR
: specifies that you want to remove the association between the current libref and the SAS data library.

LIBNAME
continued

Listing Data Library Attributes

In Release 6.06 of SAS software, you can use the following form of the LIBNAME statement to list the attributes of SAS data libraries:

LIBNAME *libref* | _ALL_ LIST;

You can use the following arguments with this form of the LIBNAME statement:

libref is any valid SAS name. Refer to Chapter 4 for a definition of valid SAS names.

ALL is a SAS keyword. By specifying it rather than a libref, you can list the attributes of all the SAS data libraries to which you have assigned librefs during the current session as well as the WORK, SASUSER, and SASHELP libraries.

LIST prints to the SAS log a list of the attributes for SAS data libraries. The items appearing in the list vary according to your host system.

Here are two examples of this type of LIBNAME statement:

□ `libname prochlor list;`

□ `libname _all_ list;`

Comparisons

Use the FILENAME statement to associate a fileref with an external file or group of files so you can

□ read from the files using the INFILE or the %INCLUDE statement

□ write to the files using the FILE statement

□ identify a library of SAS autocall macros.

Use the LIBNAME statement for SAS data libraries only.

See Also

FILENAME statement

"SAS Names" in Chapter 4, "Rules of the SAS Language"

Chapter 6, "SAS Files"

LINK

Jumps to a statement label

DATA step

HELP LINK

Syntax

LINK *label*;

Description

The LINK statement tells the SAS System to jump immediately to the statement label indicated in the LINK statement and to continue executing statements from that point until a RETURN statement is executed. The RETURN statement sends program control to the statement immediately following the LINK statement.

The LINK statement and the destination must be in the same DATA step. The destination is identified by a statement label in the LINK statement.

The LINK statement may branch to a group of statements that contains another LINK statement. This arrangement is known as nesting. To avoid infinite looping, the SAS System has set a maximum on the number of nested LINK statements. Therefore, you may have up to ten LINK statements with no intervening RETURN statements. When more than one LINK statement has been executed, a RETURN statement tells the SAS System to return to the statement following the last LINK statement executed.

You must use the following argument with the LINK statement:

label specifies a statement label that identifies the LINK destination.

Comparisons

The difference between the LINK and GO TO statements is in the action of a subsequent RETURN statement. A RETURN statement after a LINK statement returns execution to the statement following LINK. A RETURN statement after a GO TO statement returns execution to the beginning of the DATA step, unless a LINK statement precedes GO TO, in which case execution continues with the first statement after LINK. In addition, a LINK statement is usually used with an explicit RETURN statement whereas a GO TO statement is often used without a RETURN statement.

When your program executes a group of statements at several points in the program, using the LINK statement simplifies coding and makes program logic easier to follow. If your program executes a group of statements at only one point in the program, using DO-group logic rather than LINK-RETURN logic is simpler.

Example

In this example, when the value of variable TYPE is `aluv`, the LINK statement diverts program execution to the statements associated with the label CALCU. Program execution continues until it encounters the RETURN statement which sends program execution back to the first statement following LINK. The SAS System executes the assignment statement, outputs the observation, then returns to the top of the DATA step to read the next observation. When the value of TYPE is not `aluv`,

LINK

continued

the SAS System executes the assignment statement, outputs the observation, and returns to the top of the DATA step.

```
data hydro;
   input type $ depth station $;
   if type ='aluv' then link calcu;  /* link to label calcu: */
   date=today();
   return;                           /* return to top of step */
   calcu: if station='site_1' then elevatn=6650-depth;
   else if station='site_2' then elevatn=5500-depth;
   return;                           /* return to date=today(); */
   cards;
aluv 523 site_1
uppa 234 site_2
aluv 666 site_2
more data lines
;
```

See Also

DO statement

GO TO statement

RETURN statement

Statement labels

LIST

Writes to the SAS log the input data records for the observation being processed

DATA step

HELP LIST

Syntax

LIST;

Description

The LIST statement causes the input data records for the observation being processed to be listed in the SAS log. When the LIST statement is executed, the SAS System causes the current input record to be printed at the end of the current iteration of the DATA step. Unprintable characters are printed in hexadecimal form. A ruler indicating columns appears before the first record listed.

Note that the LIST statement operates only on data read with an INPUT statement; it has no effect on data read with a SET, MERGE, or UPDATE statement.

Comparisons

Contrast the LIST statement with the PUT statement.

- The LIST statement writes at the end of each iteration of the DATA step while the PUT statement writes immediately.
- The LIST statement writes the input data records exactly as they appear. The PUT statement writes the variables or literals specified.
- The LIST statement automatically prints a hexadecimal value if it encounters an unprintable character. The PUT statement represents characters in hexadecimal only when a hex format is given.
- The LIST statement writes only to the SAS log. The PUT statement can write to any file.
- The LIST statement has an effect only when your data are read with an INPUT statement. The PUT statement can be used regardless of which statement is used to read data in the DATA step.

Example

The LIST statement is useful for printing suspicious input records read by an INPUT statement. Here is an example:

```
data employee;
   input ssn 1-9 #3 w2amt 1-6;
   if w2amt=. then list;
   cards;
123456789
JAMES SMITH
356.79
345671234
JEFFREY THOMAS
.
;
```

LIST

continued

The LIST statement causes the three current input data records to be printed in the SAS log each time a value for W2AMT is missing:

```
----+----1----+----2----+----3----+----4----+----5----+----6
11   345671234
12   JEFFREY THOMAS
13   .
```

Note that the numbers 11, 12, and 13 represent line numbers in the SAS log.

See Also

PUT statement

%LIST

Lists lines entered in the current session

Global

HELP %LIST

Syntax

%LIST <*n*<:*m* | −*m*>>;

Description

The %LIST statement lists lines entered earlier in the current session. The %LIST statement without arguments displays all program lines; when you type in a line number or range of line numbers, the SAS System displays those lines of code. When the SAS System is in interactive line mode, and when the SPOOL system option is in effect, all SAS statements and data lines are saved automatically when submitted and can be displayed with the %LIST statement.*

▶ ***Caution:** The SPOOL system option controls whether SAS statements are saved.*

In interactive line mode processing, if NOSPOOL is in effect, you cannot list previous lines with the %LIST statement.

Note: The SPOOL system option has no effect in display manager sessions.

The %LIST statement can be used anywhere in a SAS job except between a CARDS or CARDS4 statement and the matching semicolon (;) or semicolons (;;;;). This statement is useful mainly in interactive line mode sessions to display SAS program code on the monitor. It is also useful to determine lines to include when using the %INCLUDE statement.

You can use the following arguments with the %LIST statement:

no argument	displays all program lines.
n	lists line *n*.
n–m *n:m*	lists lines *n* through *m*.

Example

The following %LIST statement lists lines 10 through 20:

```
%list 10-20;
```

See Also

%INCLUDE statement

SPOOL option in Chapter 16, "SAS System Options"

Chapter 18, "SAS Display Manager Commands"

* It is not necessary to use %LIST in display manager sessions because program lines are automatically displayed in the SAS log after you submit a program. In batch mode, lines are not spooled, therefore do not use %LIST.

LOSTCARD

Resynchronizes the input data when the SAS System encounters a missing record in data with multiple records per observation

DATA step

HELP LOSTCARD

Syntax

LOSTCARD;

Description

The LOSTCARD statement resynchronizes the input data when the SAS System encounters a missing record in data in which multiple records must be read to create a single observation. The LOSTCARD statement prevents the SAS System from reading a record from the next group, when the current group has fewer records than expected. Without specific instructions such as the LOSTCARD statement, the SAS System does not discover that a record is missing until it reaches the end of the data. The values for the observations in the SAS data set after the missing record was encountered may be incorrect.

The LOSTCARD statement is most useful when input data have a fixed number of records per observation and when each record for an observation contains an identification variable with the same value. This statement usually appears in conditional processing, for example, in the THEN clause of an IF-THEN statement or in a statement in a SELECT group.

When the LOSTCARD statement is executed, the SAS System takes the following steps:

1. Three things are written to the SAS log: a lost card message, a ruler, and all the records read in the attempt to build the current observation.
2. The first record in the group of records being read is discarded, no observation is output, and the SAS System returns to the beginning of the DATA step.
3. The value of the automatic variable _N_ is not incremented by 1. (Normally, _N_ is incremented by 1 at the top of each iteration of the DATA step.)
4. The SAS System attempts to build an observation by beginning with the second record in the group and reading the number of records specified in the INPUT statement.
5. If the IF condition for a lost card is still true, steps 1 through 4 are repeated. To make the log easier to read, the SAS System prints the message and ruler only once for a given group of records. In addition, each record is printed only once; a record is not printed repeatedly when it is used in successive attempts to build an observation.
6. When the SAS System encounters a group of records for which the IF condition is not true, it builds an observation and outputs it to the SAS data set.

Example

The following example illustrates how to use the LOSTCARD statement in a conditional construct:

```
data inspect;
   input id 1-3 reject 8-9 #2 idcheck 1-3 pass;
   if id ne idcheck then
      do;
         put 'ERROR IN DATA RECORDS ' id= idcheck=;
         lostcard;
      end;
   cards;
301    32
301    61432
302    53
302    83171
400    92845
411    46
411    99551
;
```

In this example, two input records are used to construct each observation. When the identification number in record 1 (variable ID) does not match the identification number in the second record (IDCHECK), you know that a record has been misplaced or left out. The IF-THEN DO statement specifies that if a record is missing, the SAS System should print the message given in the PUT statement and execute the LOSTCARD statement. Note that the first record for the third observation (IDCHECK=400) is missing. The resulting data set has three observations with ID values 301, 302, and 411. There is no observation for ID=400.

The PUT and LOSTCARD statements cause the following statements to be written to the SAS log when the DATA step executes:

```
ERROR IN DATA RECORDS ID=400 IDCHECK=411
NOTE: LOST CARD.
RULE:----+---1----+----2----+----3----+----4----+----5----+----6
 15   400    92845
 16   411    46
```

Note that the numbers 15 and 16 represent line numbers in the SAS log.

See Also

IF-THEN statement

MERGE

Joins observations from two or more SAS data sets into single observations

DATA step

HELP MERGE

Syntax

MERGE *data-set-name-1* <(*data-set-options*)>
data-set-name-2 <(*data-set-options*)>
<. . . *data-set-name-n*<(*data-set-options*)>>
<END=*variable-name*>;

Description

The MERGE statement joins corresponding observations from two or more SAS data sets into single observations in a new SAS data set. The way the SAS System joins the observations depends on whether a BY statement accompanies the MERGE statement.

You can use the following arguments with the MERGE statement:

data-set-name

names two or more existing SAS data sets from which observations are read. The names can be a one-level name (for example, FITNESS), a two-level name (for example, IN.FITNESS), or one of the special SAS data set names. See "SAS Data Sets" in Chapter 6 for a description of the types of names for SAS data sets and when to use each type.

The following MERGE statements give examples of various types of data set names:

- `merge males females;`
- `merge in.fitness lib.health;`
- `merge year1 year2 year3;`
- `merge track save.field swim;`

(*data-set-options*)

appear in parentheses after a SAS data set name. When used with the MERGE statement, they specify actions the SAS System is to take when reading observations into the DATA step for processing. The form of (*data-set-options*) is

(*option-1*=*value-1* < . . . *option-n*=*value-n*>)

The following example shows the form of the DROP= and RENAME= data set options when used with the MERGE statement:

```
merge weight fitness(drop=name rename=(weight=pounds));
```

For a list of data set options that you can use for input data sets, refer to Table 3.11, "SAS Data Set Options," in Chapter 3.

END=*variable-name*

names and creates a temporary variable that contains an end-of-file indicator. The variable, which is initialized to 0, is set to 1 when the MERGE statement is processing the last observation. If the input data sets have different numbers of observations, the END= variable is set to 1 when the last observation from all data sets is processed. The END= variable is not added to any SAS data set being created.

The MERGE statement is flexible and has a variety of uses in SAS programming. The examples in this description illustrate basic uses of the

MERGE statement. Other applications include using more than one BY variable, merging more than two data sets, and merging a few observations with all observations in another data set.

One-to-One Merging

In one-to-one merging of data sets, the MERGE statement is not accompanied with a BY statement. The discussion in "Combining SAS Data Sets" in Chapter 4 tells how the SAS System builds observations using a one-to-one merge and explains the precautions you should take when using this method.

The following code gives an example of one-to-one merging:

```
data benefits.qtr1;
   merge benefits.jan benefits.feb;
run;
```

Match-Merging

If you want to match observations from two or more SAS data sets based on the values of some variables, use a BY statement after the MERGE statement. To perform match-merging, the variables in the BY statement must be common to all data sets as in the following example:

```
data inventry;
   merge stock orders;
   by partnum;
run;
```

Only one BY statement can accompany each MERGE statement in a DATA step. The BY statement should immediately follow the MERGE statement to which it applies. The data sets listed in the MERGE statement must be in order of the values of the variables listed in the BY statement, or they must have an appropriate index.

The SAS System processes observations in the same BY group according to steps described in "Combining SAS Data Sets" in Chapter 4.

Comparisons

The UPDATE statement also combines observations from two SAS data sets, but UPDATE performs the special function of changing or updating the values of selected observations in a master file. You can also add observations using the UPDATE statement.

Examples

Refer to "Combining SAS Data Sets" in Chapter 4 for detailed examples of one-to-one merging and match-merging with data sets that have duplicate or missing observations.

See Also

BY, SET, and UPDATE statements

"Rules for Combining SAS Data Sets" in Chapter 4, "Rules of the SAS Language"

MISSING

Assigns characters in your input data to represent special missing values for numeric data

Global

HELP MISSING

Syntax

MISSING *character-1* < . . . *character-n*>;

Description

The MISSING statement declares that certain values in your input data represent special missing values for numeric data. It usually appears within a DATA step, but it is global in scope.

You use the following argument with the MISSING statement:

character is the value in your input data that represents a special missing value. Special missing values may be any of the 26 letters of the alphabet (uppercase or lowercase) or the underscore (_).

Comparisons

The MISSING= system option allows you to specify a character to be printed when numeric variables contain ordinary missing values (.). If your data contain characters representing special missing values, such as a or z, do not use the MISSING= option to define them; simply define these values in a MISSING statement.

Example

With survey data, you want to identify certain kinds of missing data. When coding the data, place an A in the ANSWER field when the respondent is not at home at the time of the survey; place an R in the ANSWER field when the respondent refuses to answer. Then, when you write your SAS program, use the MISSING statement to identify to the SAS System that the values A and R in the input data lines are to be considered special missing values rather than invalid numeric data values.

```
data surv;
   missing a r;
   input id answer;
   cards;
1001 2
1002 R
1003 1
1004 A
1005 2
;
```

The data set contains exactly those values you coded in your input data.

See Also

UPDATE statement

"Missing Values in Input Data" in Chapter 2, "The DATA Step"

"Missing Values" in Chapter 4, "Rules of the SAS Language"

Null

Acts as a placeholder

Global

HELP NULL

Syntax

;

or

;;;;

Description

The null statement is a single semicolon that serves as a placeholder. Although no action is performed by the statement, it is an executable statement. Thus, in a DATA step, a label can precede the null statement.

The SAS System accepts null statements with one or four semicolons. Use a single semicolon to signal the end of data lines following the CARDS statement. Use four semicolons to indicate the end of data lines following the CARDS4 statement. A null statement following data lines represents a step boundary.

Examples

The following examples contain null statements:

□
```
   cards;
data lines
;

proc print
   data=comm(keep=x rename=(x=visiti1));
run;
```

□
```
   cards4;
   data lines containing semicolons
   ;;;;

proc print
   data=comm(keep=x rename=(x=visiti1));
run;
```

□
```
   if x=1 then
      if y=2 then
         z=3;
      else;            /* this goes with y=2 */
   else z=0;           /* this goes with x=1 */
```

See Also

CARDS, CARDS4, GO TO, and LABEL statements

"Step Boundary" in Chapter 2, "The DATA Step"

OPTIONS

Changes the value of one or more SAS system options

Global

HELP OPTIONS

Syntax

OPTIONS *option-1* < . . . *option-n*>;

Description

The OPTIONS statement changes the value of one or more SAS system options. The change remains in effect for the rest of the job or session or until changed again. (If you want a particular group of options to be in effect for all your SAS jobs or sessions, store an OPTIONS statement in an autoexec file or list the system options in a configuration file.)

■ **Host Information** .... The system options available depend on your host system. For details, see the SAS documentation for your host system. ■

Use the following argument with the OPTIONS statement:

option specifies a SAS system option to be changed.

An OPTIONS statement can appear at any place in a SAS program, except within data lines or parameter card lines.

An OPTIONS statement entered within a DATA or PROC step takes effect for that step. An OPTIONS statement entered outside of a step takes effect with the following step.

■ **Host Information** .... Depending on your host system, the syntax used to specify a system option in the OPTIONS statement may be different from the syntax used at SAS invocation. For details, see the SAS documentation for your host system. ■

Comparisons

The OPTIONS statement requires you to enter the complete statement including the OPTIONS keyword, the system option name and value, if necessary. However, in the OPTIONS display manager window, the options' names and settings are displayed in columns. To change a setting, simply type over the value displayed and press ENTER or RETURN.

Example

The following example suppresses the date normally printed in SAS output and sets a line size of 72:

```
options nodate linesize=72;
```

See Also

"SAS System Options" in Chapter 3, "Components of the SAS Language"

Chapter 16, "SAS System Options"

OUTPUT

Writes the current observation to a SAS data set

DATA step

HELP OUTPUT

Syntax

OUTPUT <*data-set-name-1*> <. . . *data-set-name-n*>;

Description

The OUTPUT statement tells the SAS System to write the current observation to a SAS data set immediately, not at the end of the DATA step. The OUTPUT statement can be used alone or conditionally as part of an IF-THEN or SELECT statement or in DO-loop processing. If no data set name is specified in the OUTPUT statement, the observation is written to the data set or data sets listed in the DATA statement.

By default, every DATA step contains an implicit OUTPUT statement at the end of the step that tells the SAS System to write observations to the data set or data sets being created. Placing an explicit OUTPUT statement in a DATA step overrides the automatic output, and the SAS System adds an observation to a data set only when an explicit OUTPUT statement is executed. Once you use an explicit OUTPUT statement to write an observation to any one data set, there is no longer an implicit OUTPUT statement at the end of the DATA step. Thus, you must use an explicit OUTPUT statement to write observations to any other data set created in that DATA step.

You can use the following arguments with the OUTPUT statement:

no argument
: causes the current observation to be written to all data sets named in the DATA statement.

data-set-name
: specifies the name of a data set to which the SAS System writes the observation. You can specify up to as many data sets in the OUTPUT statement as you specified in the DATA statement for that DATA step. All names specified in the OUTPUT statement must also appear in the DATA statement.

The following examples show how an OUTPUT statement may be used:

□ `output;`

□ `if deptcode gt 2000 then output;`

□ `if phone=. then output markup;`

Comparisons

The OUTPUT statement writes observations to a SAS data set. The PUT statement writes variable values or text to a SAS output file or to an external file. The results of the PUT statement are raw data, not SAS data set observations.

OUTPUT

continued

Example 1: Creating Multiple Observations from Each Line of Input

Use the OUTPUT statement if you want to create two or more observations from each line of input data. The following SAS code creates three observations in the data set RESPONSE for each observation in the data set SULFA:

```
data response;
   set sulfa;
   drop time1-time3;
   time=time1;
   output;
   time=time2;
   output;
   time=time3;
   output;
run;
```

Example 2: Creating Multiple Data Sets from a Single Input File

Use the OUTPUT statement if you want to create more than one SAS data set from one input file. In the following example, the OUTPUT statement writes observations to two data sets, OZONE and OXIDES:

```
data ozone oxides;
   infile file-specification;
   input city $ 1-15 date date7. chemical $ 26-27 ppm 29-30;
   if chemical='O3' then output ozone;
   else output oxides;
run;
```

Example 3: Creating One Observation from Several Lines of Input

Use the OUTPUT statement if you want to combine several input observations into one observation. In this example, the OUTPUT statement creates one observation that totals the values of DEFECTS in the first ten observations of the input data set:

```
data discards;
   set gadgets;
   reps+1;
   if reps=1 then total=0;
   total+defects;
   drop defects;
   if reps=10 then output;
run;
```

See Also

DATA and PUT statements

Chapter 8, "Acting on Selected Observations," in *SAS Language and Procedures: Usage, Version 6, First Edition*

PAGE

Skips to a new page in the log

Global

HELP PAGE

Syntax

PAGE;

Description

The PAGE statement is used to skip to a new page in the log, when running the SAS System in display manager, batch, or noninteractive mode. The PAGE statement itself does not appear in the log. When running the SAS System in interactive line mode, the PAGE statement may print blank lines to the terminal (or altlog file).

See Also

LIST statement

Chapter 5, "SAS Output"

LINESIZE= and PAGESIZE= options in Chapter 16, "SAS System Options"

PUT

Writes lines to the SAS log, to the SAS procedure output file, or to the external file specified in the most recent FILE statement

DATA step

HELP PUT

Syntax

PUT <*specification-1* < . . . *specification-n*>> <@ | @@>;

Description

The PUT statement writes lines to the SAS log, to the SAS procedure output file, or to the external file specified in the most recently executed FILE statement. If no FILE statement executes before a PUT statement in the current iteration of a DATA step, the lines are written to the SAS log.

The PUT statement can write lines containing variable values, character strings, or both. With specifications in the PUT statement, you can list items to be written, indicate their position, and specify how they are to be formatted.

You can write variable values in one of four basic output styles: column, list, formatted, or named. These styles are described briefly here but documented fully under "PUT, Column," "PUT, List," "PUT, Formatted," and "PUT, Named" later in this chapter.

With *column output,* enter a range of numbers after the variable name; these numbers specify a range of columns into which values are written.

```
put name 6-15 weight 17-19;
```

With *list output,* simply list the variables in the PUT statement in the order you want to write them.

```
put name weight sex;
```

With *formatted output,* specify a format after the variable name.

```
put date mmddyy8. time hhmm5.;
```

You can specify a SAS format or a user-written format.

With *named output,* list the variable name followed by an equal sign.

```
put name= weight= sex=;
```

A single PUT statement can combine any or all types of output as well as use features that give you even more control over where values are written, such as column pointer controls, line pointer controls, and line-hold specifiers.

When you combine different output styles, it is important to understand where the output pointer is located after each value is written. See "Pointer Location after an Item Is Written" later in this section for complete details on pointer location.

You can use the following arguments with the PUT statement:

no argument
: causes the current output line to be written immediately to the current file, even if the current output line is blank. (The current output line consists of the contents of the output buffer for the PUT statement.) A PUT statement without arguments is called a null PUT statement. The null PUT statement releases an output line being held by a previous PUT statement with a trailing @. See "Line-hold specifiers" later in this section for more information on the trailing @.

specification
can include what is to be written, how it is to be written, and where it is to be written. The following forms are valid for *specification:*

variable
names the variable whose value is to be written.

(*variable-list*)
is any valid variable list enclosed in parentheses. Note that (*variable-list*) must be followed by (*format-list*). See "Grouping Variables and Formats" under "PUT, Formatted" later in this chapter.

'*character-string*'
specifies a string of text to be written by the PUT statement. The string must be enclosed in quotes. Only list output allows you to specify a character string; column and formatted output allow you to specify only variables. See "PUT, List" later in this chapter.

*n**
specifies that the subsequent character string is to be repeated *n* times, as in the following example:

```
put 132*'_';
```

This PUT statement writes a line of 132 underscores.

pointer-control
moves the output pointer to a specified line or column. See "Pointer Controls" later in this section.

format.
specifies a format to use when writing the variable values. See "PUT, Formatted" for more information.

(*format-list*)
lists the formats to be used to write the values of the preceding list of variables. Note that (*format-list*) must follow (*variable-list*). See "PUT, Formatted" for more information.

INFILE
writes the last record read from the file currently being used as input, either from the current input file or from data lines following a CARDS statement. If the most recent INPUT statement for the current input file reads more than one record, PUT _INFILE_ writes only the last record on which the input pointer was positioned.

With each iteration of the DATA step, the PUT _INFILE_ statement in the following example writes the most recently read line of data to the SAS log.

```
data _null_;
   input;
   put _infile_;
   cards;
data lines
;
```

PUT

continued

ALL
: writes the values of all variables, including automatic variables, defined in the current DATA step using named output. See "PUT, Named" later in this chapter.

@ | @@
: (trailing or double trailing @) holds the output record for the execution of the next PUT statement even across iterations of the DATA step. The trailing @ or double trailing @ line-hold specifier, if used, must appear at the end of the PUT statement. For complete descriptions, see "Line-hold specifiers" later in this section.

Pointer Controls

As the SAS System writes values with the PUT statement, it keeps track of its position with a pointer. Pointer controls are provided in the PUT statement so that you can reset the pointer's column and line position when instructing the PUT statement where to write the variables and character strings in the output lines. Line-hold specifiers enable you to hold a data record in the output buffer so another PUT statement can write to it.

Using column and line pointer controls, you can specify the absolute number of the line or column to which you want to move the pointer or you can specify a column or line location relative to the current one. Table 9.2 lists all pointer controls and line-hold specifiers that you can use with the PUT statement. Complete descriptions follow the table.

Table 9.2 *Pointer Controls Available in the PUT Statement*

Pointer Controls	Relative	Absolute
column pointer controls	+*n*	@*n*
	+*numeric-variable*	@*numeric-variable*
	+*(expression)*	@*(expression)*
line pointer controls	/	#*n*
	PAGE	#*numeric-variable*
	OVERPRINT	#*(expression)*
line-hold specifiers	@ (trailing @)	(not applicable)
	@@ (double trailing @)	(not applicable)

Column pointer controls Column pointer controls indicate the column in which an output value starts.

@*n*
: moves the pointer to column *n*. Note that *n* must be a positive integer. If *n* is not an integer, the decimal portion is truncated and only the integer value is used. If *n* is zero or negative, the pointer moves to column 1.

For example, the following statement moves the pointer to column 15:

```
put @15 sales 5.;
```

@numeric-variable

moves the pointer to the column given by the value of *numeric-variable*, which must be a positive integer. If the value is not an integer, the decimal portion is truncated and only the integer value is used. If the value is zero or negative, the pointer moves to column 1.

The following PUT statement moves the pointer to column 25 to write a value for variable NAME:

```
a=25;
put @a name $10.;
```

@(expression)

moves the pointer to the column given by the value of *expression*. *Expression* must result in a positive integer. If the result is not an integer, the decimal portion is truncated and only the integer value is used. If the result is zero or negative, the pointer moves to column 1.

The following PUT statement uses an expression to move the pointer to column 30:

```
b=10;
put @(b*3) grade 2.;
```

+*n*

moves the pointer *n* columns. Note that *n* must be a positive integer or zero. If *n* is not an integer, the decimal portion is truncated and only the integer value is used.

For example, the following statement moves the pointer to column 23, writes a value for LENGTH in the next four columns (23, 24, 25, and 26), and then advances the pointer five columns to write a WIDTH value in columns 32 through 35:

```
put @23 length 4. +5 width 4.;
```

+*numeric-variable*

moves the pointer the number of columns given by the value of *numeric-variable*, which can be any integer. If the value is not an integer, the decimal portion is truncated and only the integer value is used.

If the value results in a pointer position prior to the current line, the pointer is set in column 1. If the value results in a pointer position past the end of the current line, then the current record is written and the pointer is set in column 1 on the next line.

+*(expression)*

moves the pointer the number of columns given by *expression*. The expression can result in any integer. If the result is not an integer, the decimal portion is truncated and only the integer value is used.

If the result is a pointer position prior to the current line, the pointer is set in column 1. If the result is a pointer position past the end of the current line, then the current record is written and the pointer is set in column 1 on the next line.

PUT

continued

Line pointer controls Line pointer controls specify the output line where the PUT statement is to write a value.

#n

moves the pointer to line *n*, which must be a positive integer. For example, the following PUT statement writes the value for ID in columns 3 and 4 of the second line in the output buffer:

```
put @12 name $10. #2 id 3-4;
```

#numeric-variable

moves the pointer to the line given by the value of *numeric-variable*, which must be a positive integer. If the value is not an integer, the decimal portion is truncated and only the integer value is used.

#(expression)

moves the pointer to the line given by the value of *expression*. *Expression* must result in a positive integer. If the result is not an integer, the decimal portion is truncated and only the integer value is used.

/

moves the pointer to column 1 of the next line. For example, the following statement first writes values of AGE and GRADE on one line and then skips to the next line to write values of SCORE1 through SCORE5 beginning in column 1:

```
put age grade / score1-score5;
```

OVERPRINT

causes whatever follows the keyword OVERPRINT to be printed on the output line most recently written to by a PUT statement. You can use the OVERPRINT option when your PUT statements are directed to a print file and when the N= option in the FILE statement has a value of 1. The OVERPRINT option in the PUT statement has no effect when you write lines to the display.

You can use OVERPRINT in combination with both column pointer controls and other line pointer controls. See "Example 4: Using the OVERPRINT Option."

PAGE

advances the pointer to the first line of a new page. The SAS System automatically begins a new page when a line exceeds the current PAGESIZE= value. You can use the _PAGE_ option in the PUT statement along with variables, strings of text, and other PUT statement features.

If the current output file is a print file, _PAGE_ produces an output line containing the appropriate carriage control character. _PAGE_ has no effect on a nonprint file.

Line-hold specifiers Line-hold specifiers keep the pointer on the current output line.

@ | @@

(trailing or double trailing @) holds a data line for another PUT statement, even across iterations of the DATA step. The @ and @@ are called *trailing* because if either is used, it must follow all other items in the PUT statement. Note that in the PUT statement, unlike the INPUT statement, trailing @ and double trailing @ produce the same effect.*

Usually, each PUT statement in a DATA step writes a new data line. When you want to use more than one PUT statement to write values on the same output line, you can use an @ or @@ as the last item in your PUT statement to hold the pointer at its current location. The next PUT statement executed, whether in the same or the next iteration of the DATA step, writes to the same line rather than to a new line.

A trailing @ or double trailing @ holds the current output line until one of the following is encountered:

- a PUT statement without a trailing @
- a PUT statement specifying _PAGE_
- the end of the current line (determined by the current value of the LRECL= or LINESIZE= option in the FILE statement, if specified, or of the LINESIZE= system option)
- the end of the last iteration of the DATA step.

Using a trailing @ or double trailing @ can cause the SAS System to attempt to write past the current line length since the pointer value is unchanged when the next PUT statement executes. See "When the Pointer Goes Past the End of a Line" later in this section for more information.

Pointer Location after an Item Is Written

The pointer location after an item is written depends on which output style is used and whether a character string or a variable is specified. When a PUT statement uses column or formatted output, the pointer is set to the first column after the end of the field specified in the PUT statement. Only variable values can be written with these two styles.

When list or named output is used to write a variable value, the pointer is positioned in the second column after the value since the PUT statement automatically skips a column after writing each value. When list output is used to write a character string, however, the pointer is located in the first column after the string.

After an _INFILE_ specification, the pointer is located in the first column after the record written from the current input file.

You can find the pointer's current location using the COLUMN= and LINE= options in the FILE statement.

When the Pointer Goes Past the End of a Line

The SAS System does not write an output line that is longer than the current output line length. The line length of the current output file is determined by the value of the LINESIZE= option in the current FILE statement, if specified, or by the value of the LINESIZE= system option (for print files) or the LRECL= option in the FILE statement (for nonprint

---

* In the INPUT statement, a line held by a trailing @ is released automatically when the DATA step begins a new iteration.

PUT

continued

files). You may inadvertently send the pointer beyond the current line length with one or more of the following specifications:

□ an @ sign to hold the current line for a value that does not fit in the remaining space

□ a + pointer control with a value that moves the pointer to a column beyond the current line length

□ a column range that exceeds the current line length (for example, PUT X 90–100 when the current line length is 80)

□ a variable value or character string that does not fit in the space remaining on the current output line.

By default, when a PUT statement attempts to write past the end of the current line, the SAS System withholds the entire item that overflows the current line, writes the current line, then writes the overflow item on a new line, starting in column 1. See the FLOWOVER, DROPOVER, and STOPOVER options in the FILE statement earlier in this chapter.

Arrays

You can write an array element with the PUT statement. The subscript can be any SAS expression that results in a valid subscript when the PUT statement executes. You can use an array reference in a *numeric-variable* construction with a pointer control if you enclose the reference in parentheses, as shown here:

□ @(*array-name*{i})

□ +(*array-name*{i})

□ #(*array-name*{i})

You can use the array subscript asterisk (*) to write all elements of a previously defined explicit or implicit array to a file. The array can be single- or multidimensional, but it cannot be a _TEMPORARY_ array. You can enclose the subscript in braces, brackets, or parentheses, and you can print the array using list, column, formatted, or named output. You can use an array reference with list output as shown here:

```
put array-name{*};
```

To use an array reference with formatted output, follow the array reference with a format in parentheses, as follows:

```
put (array-name{*}) (4.);
```

Comparisons

Both the INPUT and PUT statements use the trailing @ and double trailing @ line-hold specifiers to hold the current line in the input or output buffer, respectively. In an INPUT statement, a double trailing @ is required to hold a line in the input buffer from one iteration of the DATA step to the next. In a PUT statement, however, a trailing @ has the same effect as a double trailing @; both hold a line across iterations of the DATA step.

Both the PUT and OUTPUT statements create output in a DATA step. The PUT statement uses an output buffer and writes output lines to a file, the SAS log, or your display. The OUTPUT statement uses the program data vector and writes observations to a SAS data set.

Examples

Example 1: Using Multiple Output Styles in One PUT Statement

The following PUT statement uses pointer controls and list, column, formatted, and named output, and specifies both character strings and variable names:

```
data one;
   input name $25. weight date date7. id $;
   put name 'on ' date date7. ' weighs ' weight +(-1) '.'
       id= 45-51;
   cards;
Winston Blank                   176 25nov89 0459
Georgia Austin                  118 25nov89 0365
;
```

This program writes the following lines to the SAS log:*

```
----+----1----+----2----+----3----+----4----+----5----+----6
Winston Blank on 25NOV89 weighs 176.        ID=0459
Georgia Austin on 25NOV89 weighs 118.       ID=0365
```

Note the insertion of spaces within character strings, use of a pointer control to move the pointer backward, and use of named input for the last variable in the PUT statement.

Example 2: Moving the Pointer within a Page

The following examples show how to use column and line pointer controls to position the output pointer.

□ To move the pointer to a specific column, use the @ followed by the column number, variable, or expression whose value is that column number. For example, the following statement moves the pointer to column 15 and writes the value of SALES using list output:

```
put @15 sales;
```

The PUT statement in this example moves the pointer to the column indicated by the value of SPACE and writes the value of X using the 5.2 format:

```
data one;
   input space x;
   put @space x 5.2;
```

* The ruled line is for illustrative purposes only; it is not produced by the PUT statement.

PUT

continued

□ To move the pointer backward, you can use one of two methods shown in the following DATA step:

```
data one;
   infile sales;
   input year total;

      /* Use an expression to move the pointer backward.  */
   put 'The profit for ' year 'is ' total +(-1) '.';

      /* Use numeric variable with negative value to move */
      /* pointer backward.                                */
   x=-1;
   put 'The profit for ' year 'is ' total +x '.';
run;
```

Since the TOTAL value is written using list output, a blank is inserted after each TOTAL value. Moving the pointer backward by one space removes the unwanted blank that occurs between the value and the period.

□ The following PUT statement uses the / line pointer control:

```
put @12 name $10. / id 3-4;
```

It writes the value for NAME beginning in column 12 of one output line and then writes a value for ID in columns 3 and 4 of the next line.

Example 3: Moving the Pointer to a New Page

This example demonstrates moving the output pointer to the first line of a new page after printing information for the last observation in a county:

```
data _null_;
   set states;
   by county;
   file print;
   put name 1-10 @15 pop comma9.;
   if last.county then put _page_;
run;
```

PUT _PAGE_ advances the pointer to line 1 of the new page when the value of LAST.COUNTY is 1.* This example prints a footer message before exiting from the page:

```
put name 1-10 @15 pop comma9.;
if last.county then put // 'THIS IS THE LAST OF '
   county $10. _page_;
```

When an observation is the last for a county, the PUT statement skips two lines and prints the message `THIS IS THE LAST OF` followed by the current value of COUNTY before skipping to the next page.

* For a discussion of the FIRST. and LAST. variables, see "BY-Group Processing" in Chapter 4.

Example 4: Using the OVERPRINT Option

The following PUT statement underlines a title by overprinting with underscores at the column specified:

```
put @15 'TITLE OF PAGE' overprint @15 '_____________';
```

The following example shows the OVERPRINT option used to underscore a value written by a previous PUT statement:

```
data _null_;
   set class;
   file print;
   put name 1-10 @15 grade 2.;
   if grade > 96 then put overprint @15 '__';
run;
```

It underlines grades above 96 on the output line printed by the first PUT statement.

The following example shows OVERPRINT used with both a column pointer control and another line pointer control:

```
put @5 name $8. overprint @5 '________'/ @20 address;
```

This PUT statement writes a value for NAME, underlines it by overprinting underscores, and then goes to the next line to write an ADDRESS value.

Example 5: Holding and Releasing Output Lines

The following DATA step demonstrates holding and releasing an output line with a PUT statement:

```
data _null_;
   input name $ weight;
   put name @;
   if weight ne . then put @15 weight;
   else put;
run;
```

This example demonstrates the following:

- □ The trailing @ in the first PUT statement holds the current output line after the value of the variable NAME is written.
- □ If the condition is met in the IF-THEN statement, the second PUT writes the value of the variable WEIGHT and releases the current output line. If the condition is not met, the second PUT never executes and no value for WEIGHT is written.
- □ When the condition is not met, the ELSE PUT statement executes, releasing the output line and positioning the output pointer at column 1 in the output buffer.

See Also

FILE statement

PUT statement, column; PUT statement, formatted; PUT statement, list; and PUT statement, named

PUT, Column

Writes variable values in the specified columns in the output line

DATA step

HELP PUT

Syntax

PUT *variable* <$> *start-column*<*−end-column*> <*.decimal-places*>
<@ | @@>;

Description

Column output indicates the position of each variable in the output lines by specifying in a PUT statement each variable name and the columns its value will occupy. The PUT statement writes the values of the variable in the specified columns of the output line. If a value requires fewer columns than specified, a character variable is left-aligned in the specified columns, and a numeric variable is right-aligned in the specified columns. See "Examples."

There is no limit to the number of column specifications you can make in a single PUT statement. You can write anywhere in the output line, even if a value overwrites columns written earlier in the same statement. Column output can be combined with any of the other output styles in a single PUT statement.

You can use the following arguments with a PUT statement using column output:

variable
: names the variable whose value is to be written.

$
: indicates that the variable contains character values rather than numeric values. If the variable has already been defined as a character variable, a $ is not necessary in the PUT statement. For example, a $ is not required in the following PUT statement since the variable NAME is defined as character in the INPUT statement:

```
input name $ 1-15;
put name 1-15;
```

start-column
: is the first column of the field where the value is to be written in the output line.

−end-column
: is the last column of the field for the value. If the value is to occupy only one column in the output line, omit the *−end-column* specification.

.decimal-places
: is a period followed by a positive integer that specifies the number of digits you want on the right side of the decimal point. See "Examples."

@
@@
: (trailing or double trailing @) holds the output record for the execution of the next PUT statement even across iterations of the DATA step. The trailing @ or double trailing @ line-hold specifier, if used, must appear at the end of the PUT statement. For complete descriptions, see "Pointer Controls" under the PUT statement earlier in this chapter.

Examples

You can use column output in the PUT statement as shown here.

□ The following PUT statement uses column output:

```
put name $ 1-20 score1 23-25 score2 28-30  score3 33-35;
```

It produces the following output lines:*

```
----+----1----+----2----+----3----+----4----+----5
Mitchell Singer       89   78   93
Rachel Hope           89   78  113
```

Note that the values for the character variable NAME begin in column 1, the left boundary of the specified field (columns 1 through 20). The values for the numeric variables SCORE1 through SCORE3 appear flush with the right boundary of their field.

□ The following statement produces the same output lines, but writes the SCORE1 value first and the NAME value last:

```
put score1 23-25 score2 28-30  score3 33-35 name $ 1-20;
```

□ The following DATA step specifies decimal points with column output:

```
data _null_;
   x=11;
   y=15;
   put x 10-18 .1 y 20-28 .1;
run;
```

It produces the following line in the SAS log:

```
----+----1----+----2----+----3----+----4----+----5
              11.0      15.0
```

See Also

PUT statement

* The ruled line is for illustrative purposes only; it is not produced by the PUT statement.

PUT, Formatted

Writes variable values in the specified format in the output line

DATA step

HELP PUT

Syntax

PUT <*pointer-control*> *variable format.* <@ | @@>;
PUT <*pointer-control*> (*variable-list*) (*format-list*) <@ | @@>;

Description

Formatted output describes the output lines by listing variable names and formats for writing the values. With formatted output, the PUT statement writes each value using the format that follows the variable name. No blanks are automatically added between values. If the value uses fewer columns than specified, character values are left-aligned and numeric values are right-aligned in the field specified by the format width. Formatted output, combined with pointer controls, makes it possible to specify the exact line and column location to write each variable.

You can use the following arguments with a PUT statement using formatted output:

pointer-control
: moves the output pointer to a specified line or column. See "Pointer Controls" under the PUT statement earlier in this chapter.

variable
: names the variable you want to write.

(*variable-list*)
: is any valid variable list enclosed in parentheses. Note that (*variable-list*) must be followed by (*format-list*). See the next section "Grouping Variables and Formats."

format.
: specifies a format to use when writing the variable values.

The width you specify for the format must provide enough space to write the value and any commas, dollar signs, decimal points, or other special characters that the format includes. For example, if the value of X is 100, the following PUT statement writes the formatted value, which takes seven columns:

```
put x dollar7.2;
```

X is written as follows:

```
$100.00
```

You can specify either a SAS format (see Chapter 14, "SAS Formats") or a format you define. See Chapter 18, "The FORMAT Procedure," in the *SAS Procedures Guide*.

Note that in the PUT statement you can add an alignment specification to a format to override the default alignment:

-L   left aligns the value.

-C   centers the value.

-R   right aligns the value.

This alignment specification can be added to numeric or character values. For example, the following PUT statement centers the value of X in the specified field:

```
put x dollar7.2-c;
```

See "Example 3: Overriding Default Alignment of Formatted Values."

(format-list)
lists the formats to be used to write the preceding list of variables. Note that (*format-list*) must follow (*variable-list*). See the next section "Grouping Variables and Formats." In a PUT statement, a *format-list* can include the following:

format.
specifies the format to be used to write the variable values. You can specify either a SAS format or a format you define with the FORMAT procedure.

pointer-control
specifies one of the following pointer controls to be used to position a value: @, #, /, +, and OVERPRINT. See "Example 1: Using Format Lists."

'character-string'
specifies one or more characters to be placed between formatted values. For example, the following PUT statement places a hyphen between formatted values:

```
put bldg $ (code1 code2 code3) (3. '-');
```

A hyphen is printed between the values of CODE1, CODE2, and CODE3 as shown here:

```
A 113-246-391
B 504-651-395
```

See "Example 2: Specifying a Character in a Format List."

*n**
specifies that the next format in a format list is to be repeated *n* times. In this example, the PUT statement writes GRADES1, GRADES2, and GRADES3 with the 7.2 format and writes GRADES4 and GRADES5 with the 5.2 format:

```
put (grades1-grades5) (3 * 7.2, 2 * 5.2);
```

For more information, see "Grouping Variables and Formats."

@
@@
(trailing or double trailing @) holds the output record for the execution of the next PUT statement even across iterations of the DATA step. The trailing @ or double trailing @ line-hold specifier, if used, must appear at the end of the PUT statement. For complete descriptions, see "Pointer Controls" under the PUT statement earlier in this chapter.

PUT, Formatted

continued

Grouping Variables and Formats

When you want to write values in a pattern on the output lines, using format lists can shorten your coding time. A format list consists of a list of variable names, enclosed in parentheses, followed by a corresponding list of formats, also enclosed in parentheses. You can also specify a reference to all elements in an array as (*array-name*{*}), followed by a list of formats. You cannot, however, specify the elements in a _TEMPORARY_ array in this way.

You must separate items in a format list either by blanks or by commas. You can include any of the pointer controls (@, #, /, +, and OVERPRINT) in the list of formats, as well as *n**, and a character string. You can use as many format lists as necessary in a PUT statement; however, format lists cannot be nested.

When there are more variables than format items, the SAS System uses the same format list repeatedly until all the variables have been written. When the format list includes more formats and pointer controls than are needed, the PUT statement ignores any remaining specifications in the format list after all the variable values have been written. See "Example 1: Using Format Lists" and "Example 2: Specifying a Character in a Format List."

Examples

Example 1: Using Format Lists

You can use format lists with the PUT statement as shown here.

- The following example uses a format list to write the five variables SCORE1 through SCORE5, one after another, using four columns for each value with no blanks in between:

```
put (score1-score5) (4. 4. 4. 4. 4.);
```

- Here is a simpler way to write the previous PUT statement:

```
put (score1-score5) (4.);
```

- The following PUT statement specifies an array name and a format list:

```
put (array1{*}) (4.);
```

- This example shows a format list that includes more specifications than are necessary when the PUT statement writes the last variable:

```
put (x y z) (2.,+1);
```

  This PUT statement writes the value of X using the 2. format, moves the pointer forward one column, writes the value of Y using the 2. format, moves the pointer forward one column, and writes the value of Z using the 2. format. The +1 pointer control remaining in the third cycle of the format list is not used.

Example 2: Specifying a Character in a Format List

This example formats some values and writes a - (hyphen) between the values of variables BLDG and ROOM:

```
data mail;
  input name & $15. bldg $ room;
  put name @20 (bldg room) ($1. "-", 3.);
  cards;
Bill Perkins  J 126
Sydney Riley  C 219
;
```

The following lines are written to the log:

```
Bill Perkins       J-126
Sydney Riley       C-219
```

Example 3: Overriding Default Alignment of Formatted Values

This example uses an alignment specification as part of a format:

```
data scores;
   input name $ score1 score2;
   put name $12.-r +3 score1 5. score2 5.;
   cards;
Roger 102 115
Ted 87 91
;
```

The following lines are written to the log:*

```
----+----1----+----2----+----3----+----4
       Roger     102  115
         Ted      87   91
```

The value of the character variable NAME is right-aligned in the formatted field. (Left alignment is the default for character variables.)

See Also

PUT statement

* The ruled line is for illustrative purposes only; it is not produced by the PUT statement.

PUT, List

Writes the specified character strings or variable values in the output line

DATA step

HELP PUT

Syntax

PUT <*pointer-control*> *variable* <$> <@ | @@>;
PUT <*pointer-control*> <*n**>'*character-string*' <@ | @@>;
PUT <*pointer-control*> *variable* : *format.* <@ | @@>;

Description

With list output, you simply list the names of the variables whose values you want written or specify a character string in quotes. The PUT statement writes a variable value, leaves a blank, and then writes the next value. See "Example 1: Writing Values with List Input."

You can specify variable values and character strings in a single PUT statement. When a variable is written with list output, a blank space is automatically inserted following it, so the output pointer stops at the second column following the variable value. When a character string is written, however, no blank space is automatically inserted, so the output pointer stops at the column immediately following the last character in the string. See "Example 2: Writing Character Strings and Variable Values."

With list output, missing values for numeric variables are written as a single period. Character values are left-aligned in the field; leading and trailing blanks are removed. To include blanks (in addition to the blank inserted after each value), use formatted or column output instead of list output.

You can use the following arguments with a PUT statement using list output:

pointer-control
: moves the output pointer to a specified line or column. See "Pointer Controls" under the PUT statement earlier in this chapter.

variable
: names the variable whose value you want written.

'*character-string*'
: specifies a string of text, enclosed in quotes, to be written by the PUT statement. To avoid misinterpretation, always put a space after a closing quote in a PUT statement. If a quote is followed immediately by T, D, or DT, the SAS System considers it a SAS time, date, or datetime value. If followed by X, a quoted string is interpreted as a hex constant.

  When insufficient space remains on the current line to write the entire text of a character string, the SAS System withholds the entire string and takes the action described in "When the Pointer Goes Past the End of a Line" under the PUT statement earlier in this chapter. See "Example 2: Writing Character Strings and Variable Values."

$
: specifies that the variable contains character rather than numeric values. If the variable has already been defined as character, the $ sign is not necessary in the PUT statement. For example, a $ sign is

not required in the following PUT statement since the variables NAME and SEX are defined as character in the INPUT statement:

```
input name $ 1-10 sex $ 12 age 14-15;
put name sex age;
```

*n**

specifies that the subsequent character string is to be repeated *n* times, as in the following example:

```
put 132*'_';
```

This PUT statement writes a line of 132 underscores.

:

precedes a format, causing the PUT statement to write the variable's value using the format, but otherwise treating the value as is expected with list output. All leading and trailing blanks are deleted, and each value is followed by a single blank. See "Comparisons."

format.

specifies a format to use when writing the data values. The format can be either a SAS format (see Chapter 14) or a format you define (see the FORMAT procedure in the *SAS Procedures Guide).*

@ | @@

(trailing or double trailing @) holds the output record for the execution of the next PUT statement even across iterations of the DATA step. The trailing @ or double trailing @ line-hold specifier, if used, must appear at the end of the PUT statement. For complete descriptions, see "Pointer Controls" under the PUT statement earlier in this chapter.

Comparisons

Because list output and formatted output use different methods for determining how far to move the pointer after a variable value is written, modified list output (which uses formats) and formatted output produce different results in the output lines. The following DATA step uses modified list output to write each output line:

```
data a;
   input x y;
   put x : comma10.2 y : 7.2;
   cards;
12353.20 7.10
6231 121
;
```

The following lines are written to the SAS log:*

```
----+----1----+----2----+
12,353.20 7.10
6,231.00 121.00
```

* The ruled line is for illustrative purposes only; it is not produced by the PUT statement.

PUT, List

continued

In comparison, the following example uses formatted output:

```
put x comma10.2 y 7.2;
```

It writes these lines to the SAS log, aligning the values in columns:

```
----+----1----+----2----+
 12,353.20   7.10
  6,231.00 121.00
```

Examples

Example 1: Writing Values with List Output

The following DATA step uses a PUT statement with list output to write the variable values specified to the SAS log:

```
data class;
   input name $ 1-10 sex $ 12 age 15-16;
   put name sex age;
   cards;
HENRY      M  13
JOE        M  14
HENRIETTA  F  11
;
```

These lines appear in the SAS log:*

```
----+----1----+----2----+
HENRY M 13
JOE M 14
HENRIETTA F 11
```

Example 2: Writing Character Strings and Variable Values

When using a PUT statement to write both character strings and variable values, you may want to place a blank space as the last character in a character string to avoid spacing problems. When a character string that provides punctuation follows a variable value, you need to move the output pointer backward to prevent an unwanted space from appearing in the output line.

In the following PUT statement, note the spacing within quotes and the use of pointer controls:

```
data _null_;
   input errortot day $;
   put errortot 'errors were reported on ' day +(-1) '.';
   cards;
56 Monday
42 Tuesday
;
```

* The ruled line is for illustrative purposes only; it is not produced by the PUT statement.

This DATA step writes the following lines to the SAS log:

```
56 errors were reported on Monday.
42 errors were reported on Tuesday.
```

Example 3: Writing Values with Modified List Output

The following DATA step uses modified list output to write several variable values in the output line:

```
data _null_;
   input salesrep : $10. tot : comma6. date : date7.;
   put 'Sales for ' salesrep : $12.'totalled '
       tot : dollar9. 'for week of ' date : worddate20. + (-1) '.';
   cards;
Wilson 15,300 12OCT89
Hoffman 9,600 12OCT89
;
```

These lines appear in the SAS log:

```
Sales for Wilson totalled $15,300 for week of October 12, 1989.
Sales for Hoffman totalled $9,600 for week of October 12, 1989.
```

See Also

PUT statement

PUT, Named

Writes variable values preceded by the variable name and an equal sign

DATA step

HELP PUT

Syntax

PUT <*pointer-control*> *variable*= <@ | @@>;
PUT <*pointer-control*> *variable*=<*format.*> <@ | @@>;
PUT *variable*=<$> *start-column*<−*end-column*>
<*.decimal-places*> <@ | @@>;

Description

With named output, the PUT statement writes variable values preceded by the variable name and an equal sign. To indicate named output, follow the variable name with an equal sign in the PUT statement, and use either list, column, or formatted output specifications to indicate how to position the variable name and values.

You can use list output to insert a blank space between each variable value automatically, or you can use pointer controls or column specifications to align the output in columns. You can also specify a format following the equal sign to be used to print the variable value.

You can use the following arguments with a PUT statement that uses named output:

pointer-control
: moves the output pointer to a specified line or column. See "Pointer Controls" under the PUT statement earlier in this chapter.

variable=
: names the variable whose value the PUT statement is to write in the form *variable*=*value*.

format.
: specifies a format to use when writing the data values.

The width you specify for the format must provide enough space to write the value and any commas, dollar signs, decimal points, or other special characters that the format includes. For example, look at the following PUT statement:

```
put x=dollar7.2;
```

When X=100, the formatted value takes seven columns:

```
X=$100.00
```

Note that the formatted width does *not* include the columns required by the variable name and equal sign. Note also the alignment of the formatted numeric value. Leading blanks are deleted. The value immediately follows the equal sign; it is not aligned on the right side of the formatted length, as in unnamed formatted output.

You can specify either a SAS format (see Chapter 14) or a format you define (see the FORMAT procedure in the *SAS Procedures Guide*).

start-column
: is the first column of the field where the variable name, equal sign, and value are to be written in the output line.

–end-column
is the last column of the field for the value. If the variable value, variable name, and equal sign require more space than the columns specified, the PUT statement will write past the end column rather than truncate the value. Be sure that you leave enough space before beginning the next item.

@ | @@
(trailing or double trailing @) holds the output record for the execution of the next PUT statement even across iterations of the DATA step. The trailing @ or double trailing @ line-hold specifier, if used, must appear at the end of the PUT statement. For complete descriptions, see "Pointer Controls" under the PUT statement earlier in this chapter.

Examples

Named output can be used in the PUT statement as shown here.

□ The following PUT statement combines named output with column pointer controls to align the output:

```
put name= @12 height= weight=;
```

Thus, if the current record contains the values **Ann**, 63.3, and 95.1, the PUT statement writes the following line:*

```
----+----1----+----2----+----3----+----4----+----5
NAME=Ann   HEIGHT=63.3 WEIGHT=95.1
```

□ The following example specifies an output format for the variable AMOUNT:

```
put item= @25 amount=dollar12.2;
```

When the value of ITEM is **binders** and the value of AMOUNT is 153.25, the following output line is produced:

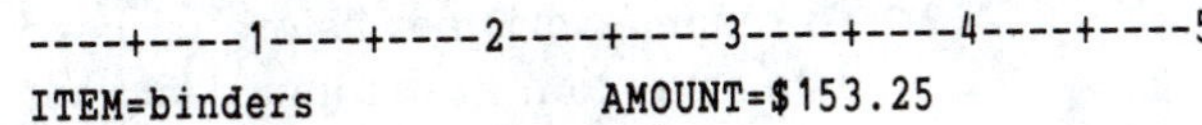

```
----+----1----+----2----+----3----+----4----+----5
ITEM=binders            AMOUNT=$153.25
```

See Also

PUT statement

* The ruled line is for illustrative purposes only; it is not produced by the PUT statement.

RENAME

Specifies new names for variables in output SAS data sets

DATA step

HELP RENAME

Syntax

RENAME *old-name-1=new-name-1* . . . *<old-name-n=new-name-n>*;

Description

You can use the RENAME statement in a DATA step to rename one or more variables in all output data sets in which the variables occur.

You can use the following arguments with the RENAME statement:

old-name is the name of the variable as it appears in the input data set.

new-name is the name to be used in the output data set.

The following statements show some examples:

□
```
rename street=address;
```

□
```
rename time1=temp1 time2=temp2 time3=temp3;
```

The RENAME statement changes the name of a variable in the output data set only. Use the new names of renamed variables in SAS data set options for output data sets containing renamed variables. Use the original names of renamed variables in DATA step program statements.

Comparisons

The RENAME statement differs from the RENAME= data set option in the following ways:

- □ You cannot use the RENAME statement in SAS PROC steps.
- □ The RENAME statement applies to all output data sets. If you want to rename different variables in different data sets, you must use the RENAME= data set option.
- □ To rename variables before processing, you must use the RENAME= data set option in the input data set or data sets.

Use the RENAME statement when renaming variables is required by your program logic. To rename variables as a file management task, use the DATASETS procedure or the VAR display manager window. These methods are simpler and do not require DATA step processing.

Examples

You can use the RENAME statement as shown here.

□ This example illustrates using the old name of the variable in program statements. The variable OLDDEPT is named NEWDEPT in the output data set, and the variable OLDACCNT is named NEWACCNT.

```
rename olddept=newdept oldaccnt=newaccnt;
if oldaccnt>5000;
keep olddept oldaccnt items volume;
```

□ In the following example, the old name OLDACCNT is used in the program statements. However, the new name NEWACCNT is used in the DATA statement because the SAS System applies the RENAME statement before it applies the KEEP= data set option.

```
data market(keep=newdept newaccnt items volume);
   set sales;
   rename olddept=newdept oldaccnt=newaccnt;
   if oldaccnt>5000;
run;
```

See Also

RENAME= data set option in Chapter 15, "SAS Data Set Options"

VAR window in Chapter 17, "SAS Display Manager Windows"

Chapter 34, "Modifying Data Set Names and Attributes," in *SAS Language and Procedures: Usage, Version 6, First Edition*

Chapter 17, "DATASETS Procedure," in the *SAS Procedures Guide, Version 6, Third Edition*

RETAIN

Causes a variable created by an INPUT or assignment statement to retain its value from one iteration of the DATA step to the next

DATA step

HELP RETAIN

Syntax

RETAIN <*element-list-1* <*initial-value-1* | (*initial-value-1*) | (*initial-value-list-1*)>
< . . . *element-list-n* <*initial-value-n* | (*initial-value-n*) | (*initial-value-list-n*)>>>;

Description

The RETAIN statement causes a variable whose value is assigned by an INPUT or assignment statement to retain its value from the current iteration of the DATA step to the next. Without a RETAIN statement, the SAS System automatically sets variables assigned values by an INPUT or assignment statement to missing before each iteration of the DATA step.

You can use a RETAIN statement to specify initial values for individual variables, a list of variables, or members of an array. If a value appears in a RETAIN statement, variables appearing before it in the list are set to that value initially. (If you assign different initial values to the same variable by naming it more than once in a RETAIN statement, the last value is used.) You can also use a RETAIN statement to assign an initial value other than the default value of 0 to a variable whose value is assigned by a sum statement.

The RETAIN statement is not an executable statement; therefore, it can appear anywhere in the DATA step.

It is redundant to name any of the following items in a RETAIN statement, since their values are automatically retained from one iteration of the DATA step to the next:

- □ variables read with a SET, MERGE or UPDATE statement
- □ a variable whose value is assigned in a sum statement
- □ the automatic variables _N_, _ERROR_, _I_, _CMD_, and _MSG_
- □ variables created by the END= or IN= option in the SET, MERGE, or UPDATE statement or by options that create variables in the FILE and INFILE statements
- □ data elements specified in a temporary array.

You can, however, use a RETAIN statement to assign an initial value to any of the previous items, with the exception of _N_ and _ERROR_.

You can use the following arguments with a RETAIN statement:

no argument
: causes the values of all variables created with INPUT or assignment statements to be retained from one iteration of the DATA step to the next.

element-list
: specifies variable names, variable lists, or array names whose values you want retained.

  Note that if you specify _ALL_, _CHAR_, or _NUMERIC_, only the variables defined before the RETAIN statement are affected. For example, the following statement does not retain the values of variables defined later in the DATA step:

```
retain _all_;
```

initial-value

specifies an initial value, numeric or character, for one or more of the preceding elements. If you omit *initial-value*, the initial value is missing. *Initial-value* is assigned to all the elements that precede it in the list. All members of a variable list, therefore, are given the same initial value. See (*initial-value*) and (*initial-value-list*).

For example, the following RETAIN statement sets the values of variables MONTH1 through MONTH5 initially to 1:

```
retain month1-month5 1 year 0 a b c 'XYZ';
```

YEAR is set initially to 0; variables A, B, and C are each set to a value of **XYZ**.

(*initial-value*)

specifies an initial value, numeric or character, for a single preceding element or for the first in a list of preceding elements. For example, the following RETAIN statement assigns the initial value 1 to only the variable MONTH1:

```
retain month1-month5 (1);
```

Variables MONTH2 through MONTH5 are set to missing initially.

(*initial-value-list*)

specifies an initial value, numeric or character, for individual elements in the preceding list. In this case, the SAS System matches the first value in the list with the first variable in the list of elements, the second value with the second variable, and so on. Initial values can be separated by blank spaces or commas. For example, both of the following statements are correct:

- `retain var1-var4 (1 2 3 4);`
- `retain var1-var4 (1,2,3,4);`

If there are more variables than initial values, the remaining variables are assigned an initial value of missing and the SAS System issues a warning message.

Comparisons

The RETAIN statement specifies variables whose values are *not set to missing* at the beginning of each iteration of the DATA step. The KEEP statement specifies variables that are to be included in any data set that is being created.

RETAIN

continued

Examples

Example 1: Overview of the RETAIN Operation

The following example shows how to use variable names and array names as elements in the RETAIN statement and shows assignment of initial values with and without parentheses:

```
data _null_;
   array city{3} $ city1-city3;
   array cp{3} citypop1-citypop3;
   retain year taxyear 1988 city ' ' cp (10000,50000,100000);
   file file-specification print;
   put 'Values at beginning of DATA step:' / @3 _all_ /;
   input gain;
   do i=1 to 3;
      cp{i}=cp{i}+gain;
      end;
   put 'Values after adding GAIN to city populations:' / @3 _all_;
   cards;
5000
10000
;
```

The initial values assigned by the RETAIN statement are as follows:

- □ YEAR and TAXYEAR are assigned the initial value 1988.
- □ CITY1, CITY2, and CITY3 are assigned missing values.
- □ CITYPOP1 is assigned the value 10000.
- □ CITYPOP2 is assigned 50000.
- □ CITYPOP3 is assigned 100000.

The following text shows the lines written by the PUT statements:

```
Values at beginning of DATA step:
  CITY1=  CITY2=  CITY3=  CITYPOP1=10000 CITYPOP2=50000 CITYPOP3=100000
YEAR=1988 TAXYEAR=1988 GAIN=. I=. _ERROR_=0 _N_=1

Values after adding GAIN to city populations:
  CITY1=  CITY2=  CITY3=  CITYPOP1=15000 CITYPOP2=55000 CITYPOP3=105000
YEAR=1988 TAXYEAR=1988 GAIN=5000 I=4 _ERROR_=0 _N_=1
Values at beginning of DATA step:
  CITY1=  CITY2=  CITY3=  CITYPOP1=15000 CITYPOP2=55000 CITYPOP3=105000
YEAR=1988 TAXYEAR=1988 GAIN=. I=. _ERROR_=0 _N_=2

Values after adding GAIN to city populations:
  CITY1=  CITY2=  CITY3=  CITYPOP1=25000 CITYPOP2=65000 CITYPOP3=115000
YEAR=1988 TAXYEAR=1988 GAIN=10000 I=4 _ERROR_=0 _N_=2
Values at beginning of DATA step:
  CITY1=  CITY2=  CITY3=  CITYPOP1=25000 CITYPOP2=65000 CITYPOP3=115000
YEAR=1988 TAXYEAR=1988 GAIN=. I=. _ERROR_=0 _N_=3
```

Note that the first PUT statement is executed three times, while the second PUT statement is executed only twice. The DATA step ceases execution when the INPUT statement executes for the third time and reaches the end of the file.

Example 2: Selecting One Value from a Series of Observations

In this example, the data set ALLSCOR contains several observations for each identification number, variable ID. Different observations for a particular ID value may have different values of the variable GRADE. You want to create a new data set, STUDENTS, containing one observation for each ID value. The observation must have the highest GRADE value of all observations for that ID in BESTSCOR.

```
libname class 'SAS-data-library';

proc sort data=class.allscor;
   by id;
run;

data class.bestscor;
   set class.allscor;
   by id;
   retain highest;             /* Prevents HIGHEST from being reset*/
                               /* to missing for each iteration.   */
   if first.id then highest=.; /* Sets HIGHEST to missing for each */
                               /* different ID value.              */
   highest=max(highest,grade); /* Compares HIGHEST to GRADE in     */
                               /* current iteration and resets     */
                               /* value if GRADE is higher.        */
   drop grade;
   if last.id then output;
run;
```

See Also

Assignment statement

BY statement

INPUT statement

MERGE statement

SET statement

Sum statement

UPDATE statement

RETURN

Stops executing statements at the current point in the DATA step and returns to a predetermined point

DATA step

HELP RETURN

Syntax

RETURN;

Description

The RETURN statement tells the SAS System to stop executing statements at the current point in the DATA step and to return to a predetermined point before continuing execution. The point to which the SAS System returns depends on the order in which statements are executed in the DATA step.

The RETURN statement is often used with the LINK statement, the GO TO statement, and the HEADER= option in the FILE statement. For a discussion of the specific action the RETURN statement takes in each of these cases, see the GO TO, LINK, and FILE statements in this chapter.

When a RETURN statement causes a return to the beginning of the DATA step, an implicit OUTPUT statement writes the current observation to any new data sets (unless explicit OUTPUT statements are used in the step). Every DATA step has an implied RETURN statement as its last executable statement.

Example

In the following example, when the values of X and Y are the same, the SAS System executes the RETURN statement and adds the observation to the data set. When the values of X and Y are not equal, the SAS System executes the remaining statements and adds the observation to the data set.

```
data survey;
   input x y;
   if x=y then return;
   put x= y=;
   cards;
21 25
20 20
17 17
;
```

See Also

FILE statement

GO TO statement

LINK statement

RUN

Executes the previously entered SAS statements

Global

HELP RUN

Syntax

RUN <CANCEL>;

Description

The RUN statement executes the previously entered SAS statements. You can use the following argument with the RUN statement:

CANCEL
: terminates the current step without executing it. The SAS System prints a message indicating that the step was not executed. The CANCEL option does not prevent execution of a DATA step containing a CARDS or CARDS4 statement.

Examples

The following examples use valid RUN statements:

□
```
proc print data=report;
   title 'Status Report';
run;
```

□
```
data circle;
   infile file-specification;
   input radius;
   c=2*4.13*radius;
   /* Incorrect value for PI */
run cancel;
```

See Also

"Step Boundary" in Chapter 2, "The DATA Step"

Appendix 3, "SAS Stored Program Facility"

%RUN

Ends source statements following a %INCLUDE * statement

Global

HELP %RUN

Syntax

%RUN;

Description

The %RUN statement ends the prompting for source statements from the terminal begun by a %INCLUDE statement followed by an asterisk. This form of the %INCLUDE statement specifies that you must enter source lines from the keyboard. The %RUN statement causes the SAS System to stop reading input from the terminal (including subsequent SAS statements on the same line as %RUN) and resume reading from the previous input source.

Comparisons

The %RUN statement ends the prompting for source statements and returns program control to the original source program, when using the %INCLUDE statement. The RUN statement simply executes previously entered DATA or PROC steps.

Example

To request keyboard-entry source on a %INCLUDE statement, follow the statement with an asterisk, as follows:

```
%include *;
```

When it executes this statement, the SAS System prompts you to enter source lines from the keyboard. When you finish entering code from the keyboard, type

```
%run;
```

This statement returns processing to the program that contains the %INCLUDE statement.

The type of prompt depends on how you are running the SAS session. The include operation is most useful in interactive line and noninteractive modes but can also be used in display manager and batch modes. When you are running the SAS System in batch mode, you must include the %RUN statement in the external file referenced by the SASTERM fileref.

See Also

%INCLUDE and RUN statements

SELECT

Executes one of several statements or groups of statements

DATA step

HELP SELECT

Syntax

SELECT <(*select-expression*)>;
  WHEN-*1* (*when-expression-1*<, . . . *when-expression-n*>) *statement*;
  < . . . **WHEN**-*n* (*when-expression-1*<, . . . *when-expression-n*>) *statement*;>
  <**OTHERWISE** *statement*;>
END;

Description

The SELECT statement in the DATA step allows the SAS System to execute one of several statements or groups of statements.

The SELECT statement begins a SELECT group; SELECT groups contain WHEN statements that identify SAS statements to be executed when a particular condition is true. You must use at least one WHEN statement in a SELECT group. An optional OTHERWISE statement specifies a statement to be executed if no WHEN condition is met. An END statement ends a SELECT group.

You can use the following arguments with the SELECT statement:

(select-expression)
: specifies any valid SAS expression that evaluates to a single value. If used, *select-expression* must be placed in parentheses.

(when-expression)
: specifies any valid SAS expression. The way a *when-expression* is used depends on whether a *select-expression* is present.

If the *select-expression* is present, the SAS System evaluates the *select-expression* and *when-expression*. The SAS System then compares the two for equality and returns a value of true or false. If the comparison is true, *statement* is executed. When the comparison is false, execution proceeds to the next *when-expression* in the current WHEN statement, or to the next WHEN statement if no more expressions are present. If no WHEN statements remain, execution proceeds to the OTHERWISE statement, if one is present. If the result of all SELECT-WHEN comparisons is false and no OTHERWISE statement is present, the SAS System issues an error message and stops executing the DATA step.

If no *select-expression* is present, the *when-expression* is evaluated to produce a result of true or false. If the result is true, *statement* is executed. If the result is false, the SAS System proceeds to the next *when-expression* in the current WHEN statement, or to the next WHEN statement if no more expressions are present, or to the OTHERWISE statement, if one is present. (That is, the SAS System performs the action indicated in the first true WHEN statement.) If the result of all *when-expressions* is false and no OTHERWISE statement is present, the SAS System issues an error message. If more than one WHEN statement has a true *when-expression*, only the first WHEN statement is used. Once a *when-expression* is true, no other *when-expressions* are evaluated.

SELECT

continued

statement
: can be any executable SAS statement, including DO, SELECT, and null statements.

Null statements used in WHEN statements cause the SAS System to recognize a condition as true without taking further action. Null statements used in OTHERWISE statements prevent the SAS System from issuing an error message when all WHEN conditions are false.

Comparisons

Use a SELECT group rather than a series of IF-THEN statements when you have a long series of mutually exclusive conditions. Large numbers of conditions make a SELECT group more efficient than IF-THEN/ELSE statements. SELECT groups also make the program easier to read and debug.

Use IF-THEN/ELSE statements for programs with few statements. Subsetting IF statements should be used without a THEN clause to continue processing only those observations or records that meet the condition specified in the IF clause.

Examples

The following examples use SELECT statements:

□
```
select (a);
   when (1) x=x*10;
   when (2);
   when (3,4,5) x=x*100;
   otherwise;
end;
```

□
```
select (payclass);
   when ('monthly') amt=salary;
   when ('hourly')
     do;
        amt=hrlywage*min(hrs,40);
        if hrs>40 then put 'CHECK TIMECARD';
     end;           /* end of do      */
   otherwise put 'PROBLEM OBSERVATION';
end;                /* end of select */
```

□
```
select;
   when (mon in ('JUN', 'JUL', 'AUG', 'SEPT')) put 'SUMMER ' mon=;
   when (mon in ('MAR', 'APR', 'MAY')) put 'SPRING ' mon=;
   otherwise put 'FALL OR WINTER ' mon=;
end;
```

□
```
   /* incorrect usage to select value of 2 */
select (x);
   when (x=2) put 'two';         /* evaluates T/F and compares */
end;                             /* for equality with x        */


   /* correct usage */
select(x);
   when (2) put 'two';   /* compares 2 to x for equality */
end;


   /* correct usage */
select;
   when (x=2) put 'two';
end;
```

See Also

DO statement

Subsetting IF statement

IF-THEN/ELSE statement

SET

Reads observations from one or more SAS data sets

DATA step

HELP SET

Syntax

SET <*data-set-name-1*<(*data-set-options-1*)>>
< . . . *data-set-name-n*<(*data-set-options-n*)>>
<POINT=*variable-name*>
<NOBS=*variable-name*> <END=*variable-name*>;

Description

The SET statement reads observations from one or more existing SAS data sets. You can include any number of SET statements in a DATA step, and each SET statement can read any number of SAS data sets. Each time the SET statement is executed, the SAS System reads one observation into the program data vector. The SET statement reads all variables and all observations from the input data sets unless you tell the SAS System to do otherwise.

The following statements read each observation from the existing data set ONE, and write each observation to the new data set TWO:

```
data two;
   set one;
run;
```

The SET statement is flexible and has a variety of uses in SAS programming. These uses are determined by the options and statements you use with the SET statement. They include the following tasks:

- □ reading observations and variables from existing SAS data sets for further processing in the DATA step
- □ concatenating and interleaving data sets
- □ reading SAS data sets using direct access methods.

You can use the following arguments with the SET statement:

no argument
: reads the most recently created data set.

data-set-name
: specifies a one-level name (for example, FITNESS), a two-level name (for example, IN.FITNESS), or one of the special SAS data set names. See Chapter 6 for a description of the levels of SAS data set names and when to use each level.

(*data-set-options*)
: specifies actions the SAS System is to take when reading variables or observations into the program data vector for processing. The syntax of SAS data set options is as follows:

  (*option-1*=*value-1* < . . . *option-n*=*value-n*>)

  The following example shows the form of the DROP= and RENAME= data set options when used with the SET statement:

```
set fitness(drop=name rename=(weight=pounds));
```

Refer to "SAS Data Set Options" in Chapter 3 for a list of the data set options you can use with input data sets.

POINT=*variable-name*

reads SAS data sets using random (direct) access by observation number. With the POINT= option, you name a temporary variable whose value is the number of the observation you want the SET statement to read. You must supply the values of the POINT= variable (for example, by using the POINT= variable as the index variable in some form of the DO statement). The POINT= variable is available anywhere in the DATA step, but it is not added to any new SAS data set. The POINT= option cannot be used with a BY statement, a WHERE statement, or a WHERE= data set option. In addition, it cannot be used with transport format data sets, compressed data sets, data sets in sequential format on tape or disk, and SAS/ACCESS views or the SQL procedure views that read data from external files.

The following statements select a subset of 50 observations from the data set DRUGTEST:

```
data sample;
   do obsnum=1 to 100 by 2;
      set drugtest point=obsnum;
      if _error_ then abort;
      output;
   end;
   stop;
run;
```

▶ *Caution:* *Continuous loops can occur when you use the POINT= option.*

When using the POINT= option, you must include a STOP statement to stop processing the DATA step, programming logic that checks for an invalid value of the POINT= variable, or both. Because the POINT= option reads only those observations specified in the DO statement, the SAS System cannot read an end-of-file indicator as it would if the file were being read sequentially. Since reading an end-of-file indicator ends a DATA step automatically, failure to substitute another means of ending the DATA step when using the POINT= option can cause the DATA step to go into a continuous loop. If the SAS System reads an invalid value of the POINT= variable, it sets the automatic variable _ERROR_ to 1. You can use this information to check for conditions that cause continuous DO-loop processing, or you can include a STOP statement at the end of the DATA step, or both.

NOBS=*variable-name*

creates and names a temporary variable whose value is usually the total number of observations in the input data set or data sets. If more than one data set is listed in the SET statement, the value of the NOBS= variable is the total number of observations in the data sets listed. At compilation time, the SAS System reads the descriptor portion of each data set and assigns the value of the NOBS= variable automatically. Thus, you can refer to the NOBS= variable before the SET statement. The variable is available in the DATA step but is not added to the new data set. The NOBS= and POINT= options are independent of each other.

For certain SAS views, the SAS System cannot determine the number of observations. In these cases, the SAS System sets the value of the NOBS= variable to the largest positive integer value available on the host system.

SET

(NOBS= continued)

In this example, the NOBS= option is used to set the termination value for DO-loop processing. The value of the temporary variable LAST is the sum of the observations in SURVEY1 and SURVEY2.

```
do obsnum=1 to last by 100;
   set survey1 survey2 point=obsnum nobs=last;
   output;
end;
stop;
```

END=*variable-name*

creates and names a temporary variable that contains an end-of-file indicator. The variable, which is initialized to zero, is set to 1 when the SET statement reads the last observation of the last data set listed. This variable is not added to any new data set.

This example uses the END= variable LAST to tell the SAS System to output the variable REVENUE only after the last observation of the data set RENTAL has been read:

```
set rental end=last;
   totdays+days;
   if last then revenue=totdays*65.78;
```

Comparisons

The SET statement reads existing SAS data sets only. Use the INPUT statement to read records from a raw data file and create SAS variables and observations.

Examples

Example 1: Concatenating SAS Data Sets

If more than one data set name appears in the SET statement, the resulting output data set is a concatenation of all the data sets listed. The SAS System reads all observations from the first data set, then all from the second data set, and so on until all observations from all the data sets have been read.

The following example concatenates the three SAS data sets HEALTH, EXERCISE, and WELL into one output data set named FITNESS:

```
data fitness;
   set health exercise well;
run;
```

Example 2: Interleaving SAS Data Sets

To interleave two or more SAS data sets, use a BY statement after the SET statement as follows:

```
data april;
   set payable recvable;
   by account;
run;
```

Only one BY statement can accompany each SET statement in a DATA step. The BY statement should immediately follow the SET statement to which it applies. The data sets listed in the SET statement must be sorted by the values of the variables listed in the BY statement, or they must have an appropriate index.

Example 3: Reading a SAS Data Set

In the following DATA step, all observations in the data set NC.MEMBERS are read into the program data vector. Only those observations whose value of CITY is `Raleigh` are output to the new data set RALEIGH.MEMBERS.

```
data raleigh.members;
   set nc.members;
   if city='Raleigh';
run;
```

Example 4: Merging a Single Observation with All Observations in a SAS Data Set

An observation to be merged into an exisitng data set can be one created by a SAS procedure or another DATA step. In this example, the data set AVGSALES has only one observation.

```
data national;
   if _n_=1 then set avgsales;
   set totsales;
run;
```

Example 5: Reading from the Same Data Set More Than Once

In the following example, the SAS System treats each SET statement independently; that is, it reads from one data set as if it were reading from two separate data sets:

```
data drugxyz;
   set trial5(keep=sample);
   if sample>2;
   set trial5;
run;
```

For each iteration of the DATA step, the first SET statement reads one observation. The next time the first SET statement is executed, it reads the next observation. Each SET statement can read different observations with the same iteration of the DATA step.

SET
continued

Example 6: Combining One Observation with Many

You can subset observations from one data set and combine them with observations from another data set using direct access methods, as follows:

```
data south;
   set revenue;
   if region=4;
   set expense point=_n_;
run;
```

See Also

BY, DO, INPUT, MERGE, STOP, and UPDATE statements

"Automatic Variables" in Chapter 2, "The DATA Step"

SKIP

Skips lines in the SAS log

Global

HELP SKIP

Syntax

SKIP <*n*>;

Description

The SKIP statement skips a specified number of lines in the SAS log. The SKIP statement itself does not appear in the log. This statement can be used when running the SAS System in all methods of operation.

You can use the following arguments with the SKIP statement:

no argument — causes the SAS System to skip one line in the log.

n — is a positive integer that specifies the number of lines you want to skip in the log. If the number specified is greater than the number of lines remaining on the page, the SAS System skips to the top of the next page.

See Also

PAGE statement

Chapter 5, "SAS Output"

LINESIZE= and PAGESIZE= options in Chapter 16, "SAS System Options"

STOP

Stops execution of the current DATA step

DATA step

HELP STOP

Syntax

STOP;

Description

The STOP statement causes the SAS System to stop processing the current DATA step immediately and resume processing statements after the end of the current DATA step. The SAS System outputs a data set for the current DATA step; however, the observation being processed when the STOP statement executes is not added. The STOP statement can be used alone or in an IF-THEN or SELECT statement. Here are some examples:

- `stop;`
- `if idcode=9999 then stop;`
- ```
  select (a);
  when (0) output;
  otherwise stop;
  ```

You should use the STOP statement with any features that read SAS data sets using random access methods, such as the POINT= option in the SET statement. The SAS System does not detect an end-of-file with this access method, and you must include program statements to prevent continuous processing of the DATA step.

Comparisons

When you are using display manager mode or other interactive methods of operation, the STOP statement and the ABORT statement both stop processing, but the ABORT statement sets the value of the automatic variable _ERROR_ to 1, and the STOP statement does not.

In batch or noninteractive mode, the two statements also have different effects. Use the STOP statement in batch or noninteractive mode to continue processing with the next DATA or PROC step.

Example

The following example shows how to use the STOP statement to avoid an infinite loop within a DATA step when you are using random access methods:

```
data sample;
   do sampobs=10 to 1000 by 10;
      set master.research point=sampobs;
      output;
   end;
   stop;
run;
```

See Also

ABORT statement

POINT= option in the SET statement
```

Sum

Adds the result of an expression to an accumulator variable

DATA step

HELP SUM

Syntax

variable+expression;

Description

Sum statements add the result of an expression to an accumulator variable. The sum statement contains the following arguments:

variable
: specifies the name of the accumulator variable. *Variable* must be numeric; any valid SAS variable name can be used. The variable is automatically set to 0 before the first observation is read. The variable's value is retained from one execution to the next, just as if it had appeared in a RETAIN statement. To initialize a sum variable to a value other than 0, include it in a RETAIN statement with an initial value.

expression
: is any valid SAS expression. The expression is evaluated and the result added to the accumulator variable. The SAS System treats an expression that produces a missing value as zero.

Comparisons

The sum statement is equivalent to using the SUM function and the RETAIN statement, as shown here:

```
retain variable 0;
variable=sum(variable,expression);
```

Examples

The following are examples of valid sum statements that illustrate various expressions:

- `balance+(-debit);`
- `sumxsq+x*x;`
- `nx+(x ne .);`
- `if status='ready' then OK+1;`

See Also

RETAIN statement

SUM function in Chapter 11, "SAS Functions"

TITLE

Specifies title lines for SAS output

Global

HELP TITLE

Syntax

TITLE<*n*> <'*text*' | "*text*">;

Description

TITLE statements specify title lines to be printed on SAS print files and other SAS output. Each TITLE statement specifies one title line. You can use the following arguments with the TITLE statement:

no argument
: cancels all existing titles.

n
: specifies the relative line containing the title line. *N* can range from 1 to 10. The title line with the highest number appears on the bottom line. If you omit *n*, the SAS System assumes a value of 1. Therefore, TITLE or TITLE1 may be specified for the first title line. Skipping some values of *n* in a series of TITLE statements causes the corresponding lines to be blank.

'*text*'
"*text*"
: specifies text enclosed in single or double quotes. For compatibility with previous releases, the SAS System accepts some text without quotes. When writing new programs or updating existing programs, you should *always* surround text with quotes.

  To include quotes as part of the title, follow the rules in "Using Quotes" in Chapter 3.

■ **Host Information** ....

The maximum title length allowed depends on your host system and the value of the LINESIZE= system option. Refer to the SAS documentation for your host system for more information.

.... ■

A TITLE statement takes effect when the step or RUN group with which it is associated executes. Once you specify a title for a line, it is used for all subsequent output until you cancel the title or define another title for that line. A TITLE statement for a given line cancels the previous TITLE statement for that line and for all lines with larger *n* numbers. For example, if a TITLE5 statement is followed by a TITLE2 statement, the SAS System prints only the line specified in the TITLE2 statement.
The following statement suppresses a title on line *n* and all lines after it:

```
titlen;
```

Comparisons

The SAS System also allows you to create titles with the display manager TITLES window.

Examples

The following are examples of valid TITLE statements:

□ `title 'First Draft';`

□ `title2 "Year's End Report";`

□ `title2 'Year''s End Report';`

See Also

FOOTNOTE statement

"Step Boundary" in Chapter 2, "The DATA Step"

"Using Quotes" in Chapter 3, "Components of the SAS Language"

"Options That Affect the Appearance of Output" in Chapter 5, "SAS Output"

LINESIZE= system option in Chapter 16, "SAS System Options"

TITLES window in Chapter 17, "SAS Display Manager Windows"

UPDATE

Updates a master file by applying transactions

DATA step

HELP UPDATE

Syntax

UPDATE *master-data-set*<(*data-set-options*)>
transaction-data-set<(*data-set-options*)>
<END=*variable-name*>;

Description

The UPDATE statement combines observations from two SAS data sets in a manner similar to the MERGE statement, but the UPDATE statement performs the special function of updating master file information by applying transactions. The transaction data set contains observations that are matched to observations in the master data set by at least one variable. During the update process, the SAS System replaces existing values with new values from the transaction data set. The UPDATE statement can also be used to add new observations.

The UPDATE statement must be accompanied by a BY statement giving the name of one or more identifying variables by which observations are matched. Only one BY statement can accompany each UPDATE statement in a DATA step. The BY statement should immediately follow the UPDATE statement to which it applies. The data sets listed in the UPDATE statement must be sorted by the values of the variables listed in the BY statement, or they must have an appropriate index.

Each observation in the master data set should have a unique value of the BY variable or BY variables. The transaction data set can contain more than one observation with the same BY value. Multiple transaction observations are all applied to the master observation before it is written to the output file.

You can use the following arguments with the UPDATE statement:

master-data-set
: names the SAS data set used as the master file. The name can be a one-level name (for example, FITNESS), a two-level name (for example, IN.FITNESS), or one of the special SAS data set names.

(data-set-options)
: specifies actions the SAS System is to take when reading variables into the DATA step for processing. *Data-set-options* must appear within parentheses and follow a SAS data set name. The form of SAS data set options is as follows:

  (*option-1*=*value-1*< . . . *option-n*=*value-n*>)

  The following example shows the form of the DROP= and RENAME= data set options when used with the UPDATE statement:

```
update health fitness(drop=name rename=(weight=pounds));
```

  For a list of data set options that you can use for input data sets, refer to Table 3.11, “SAS Data Set Options,” in Chapter 3.

transaction-data-set
: names the SAS data set containing changes to be applied to the master data set. The name can be a one-level name (for example, HEALTH), a two-level name (for example, IN.HEALTH), or one of the special SAS

data set names. The following UPDATE statements give examples of various types of data set names:

□ `update ledger january;`

□ `update corn.yield corn.harvest2;`

See Chapter 6 for a description of the levels of names for SAS data sets and when to use each level.

END=*variable-name*
creates and names a temporary variable that contains an end-of-file indicator. The variable, which is initialized to 0, is set to 1 when the UPDATE statement processes the last observation. This variable is not added to any data set.

Transaction Data Sets

Usually, the master data set and the transaction data set contain the same variables. However, to reduce processing time, you can create a transaction data set that contains only those variables that are being updated. The transaction data set can also contain new variables to be added to the output data set.

The output data set contains one observation for each observation in the master data set. If any transaction observations are not matched with master observations, they become new observations in the output data set. Observations that are not to be updated can be omitted from the transaction data set. Refer to "Combining SAS Data Sets" in Chapter 4.

Missing Values

If you want to update some but not all variables and if the variables you want to update differ from one observation to the next, you must set to missing those variables that are not changing. Regular missing value characters in the transaction data set do not replace existing values in the master data set, so they are not replaced in the output observation.

If, however, you intend to replace existing values with missing values, you must use special missing value characters in the transaction data set. To create the transaction data set, use the MISSING statement in the DATA step. If you define one of the special missing values **A** through **Z** for the transaction data set, the SAS System updates numeric variables in the master data set to that value. For example, if you use the character **M** to represent missing values, the character **M** replaces the existing values in the master data set. Using a single underscore (_) to represent missing values in the transaction data set changes the numeric variables in the master data set to a regular missing value, period (.); character values are changed to the regular missing value, blank.

Refer to the MISSING statement earlier in this chapter for more information about defining and using special missing value characters.

Comparisons

The MERGE statement can be used to update observations in a file. However, the MERGE statement replaces existing values in the master data set with missing values from the transaction data set and writes duplicate values of the BY variable as two observations in the output data set.

UPDATE

continued

Examples

You can use the UPDATE statement as shown here.

- The following program statements create an output data set OHIO.QTR1 by applying transactions to the master data set OHIO.JAN. The BY variable STORE must appear in both OHIO.JAN and OHIO.WEEK4, and its values in the master data set should be unique.

```
data ohio.qtr1;
   update ohio.jan ohio.week4;
   by store;
run;
```

- This example illustrates the DATA steps used to create a master data set PAYROLL and a transaction data set INCREASE that contains regular and special missing value characters.

```
   /* Create the Master Data Set */
data payroll;
   input id salary;
   cards;
1011 245
1026 269
1028 374
1034 333
1057 582
;

   /* Create the Transaction Data Set */
data increase;
   input id salary;
   missing A _;
   cards;
1011 376
1026 .
1028 374
1034 A
1057 _
;

   /* Update Master with Transaction */
data newpay;
   update payroll increase;
   by id;
run;

proc print data=newpay;
run;
```

The output from the PRINT procedure shows the following:

```
OBS      ID      SALARY

 1      1011      376
 2      1026      269
 3      1028      374
 4      1034        A
 5      1057        .
```

In the data set NEWPAY, the salary for 1034 is the special missing value character A; the salary for 1057 is represented by the regular missing value character, period (.); and the salary for 1026 remains 269.

See Also

BY, MERGE, MISSING, and SET statements

"Combining SAS Data Sets" in Chapter 4, "Rules of the SAS Language"

MISSING= system option in Chapter 16, "SAS System Options"

WHERE

Selects observations from SAS data sets that meet a particular condition

DATA step and PROC steps

HELP WHERE

Syntax

WHERE *where-expression*;

Description

The WHERE statement enables you to specify a condition that the data must satisfy before the SAS System brings observations from existing SAS data sets into the program data vector. Using the WHERE statement improves the efficiency of your SAS programs because the SAS System is not required to read all observations from the input data set.

■ **Performance Note** .... Using indexed SAS data sets can significantly improve performance when you are using WHERE expressions to access a subset of the observations in a SAS data set. Refer to "SAS Indexes" in Chapter 6 for a complete discussion of WHERE-expression processing with indexed data sets and a list of guidelines you should consider before indexing your SAS data sets. ■

Note: You can use the WHERE statement with any SAS procedure that reads a SAS data set. The WHERE statement is useful for subsetting the original data set for processing by the procedure. The *SAS Procedures Guide* documents the action of the WHERE statement only in those procedures for which you can specify more than one data set. In all other cases, the WHERE statement performs as documented here.

You can specify one WHERE statement for each SET, MERGE, or UPDATE statement in a DATA step. The WHERE statement applies to all data sets in the preceding SET, MERGE, or UPDATE statement, and variables used in the WHERE statement must appear in all those data sets. You cannot use the WHERE statement with programming statements that select observations by observation number, such as the OBS= data set option and the POINT= option in the SET statement. When you use the WHERE statement, the FIRSTOBS= data set option must be 1. You cannot use the WHERE statement to select records from an external file containing raw data.

For each iteration of the DATA step, the first operation the SAS System performs in each execution of a SET, MERGE, or UPDATE statement is to determine whether the observation in the input data set meets the condition of the WHERE statement. The WHERE statement takes effect immediately after the input data set options are applied and before any other statement in the DATA step is executed. If a DATA step combines observations using a WHERE statement with a MERGE or UPDATE statement, the SAS System selects observations from each input data set before it combines them.

If a DATA step contains both a WHERE statement and a BY statement, the WHERE statement is executed before BY groups are created. When creating BY groups, the SAS System assigns a FIRST.*variable* or LAST.*variable* value of 1 to the first or last observation selected by the WHERE statement, regardless of whether that observation was the first or last observation for that BY group in the input data set.

The WHERE statement cannot be executed conditionally; that is, you cannot use it as part of an IF-THEN statement.

You can use the following argument with the WHERE statement:

where-expression
: is a valid arithmetic or logical expression that generally consists of a sequence of operands and operators. The operands and operators described in the next several sections are also valid for the WHERE= data set option and the WHERE command in SAS/FSP software.

Operands Used in WHERE Expressions

Operands include constants, time and date values, values of variables obtained from the SAS data sets, and values created within the WHERE expression itself. You cannot use variables created within the DATA step (for example, FIRST.*variable*, LAST.*variable*, _N_, or variables created in assignment statements) in a WHERE expression because the WHERE statement is executed before the SAS System brings observations into the DATA or PROC step. Also, WHERE expressions make comparisons using unformatted values of variables.

You can use operands in WHERE statements as follows:

□ `where score>50;`

□ `where date>='01jan87'd and time>='9:00't;`

□ `where state='Mississippi';`

As in other SAS expressions, the names of numeric variables can stand alone. The SAS System treats values of 0 or missing as false; other values are true. The following examples are valid WHERE expressions containing the numeric variables EMPNUM and SSN:

□ `where empnum;`

□ `where empnum and ssn;`

The names of character variables can also stand alone in WHERE expressions. If you use the name of a character variable by itself as a WHERE expression, the SAS System selects observations where the value of the character variable is not blank.

Operators Used in the WHERE Expression

You can include both SAS operators and special WHERE expression operators in the WHERE statement. **You cannot use SAS functions in WHERE expressions.**

SAS Operators

Table 9.3 lists the SAS operators that are available for the WHERE expression. For the rules the SAS System follows when evaluating WHERE expressions, refer to Chapter 4.

WHERE

continued

Table 9.3 *SAS Operators Available in the WHERE Statement*

<table>
<tr><th>Operator Type</th><th>Symbol or Mnemonic</th><th>Description</th></tr>
<tr><td>Arithmetic</td><td>*</td><td>multiplication</td></tr>
<tr><td></td><td>/</td><td>division</td></tr>
<tr><td></td><td>+</td><td>addition</td></tr>
<tr><td></td><td>−</td><td>subtraction</td></tr>
<tr><td></td><td>**</td><td>exponentiation</td></tr>
<tr><td>Comparison</td><td>= or EQ</td><td>equal to</td></tr>
<tr><td></td><td>^= or NE *</td><td>not equal to</td></tr>
<tr><td></td><td>> or GT</td><td>greater than</td></tr>
<tr><td></td><td>< or LT</td><td>less than</td></tr>
<tr><td></td><td>>= or GE</td><td>greater than or equal to</td></tr>
<tr><td></td><td><= or LE</td><td>less than or equal to</td></tr>
<tr><td></td><td>IN</td><td>equal to one of a list</td></tr>
<tr><td>Logical (Boolean)</td><td>& or AND</td><td>logical and</td></tr>
<tr><td></td><td>| or OR **</td><td>logical or</td></tr>
<tr><td></td><td>~ ^, ¬, or NOT *</td><td>logical not</td></tr>
<tr><td>Other</td><td>><</td><td>minimum</td></tr>
<tr><td></td><td><></td><td>maximum</td></tr>
<tr><td></td><td>|| ***</td><td>concatenation of character variables</td></tr>
<tr><td></td><td>( )</td><td>indicate order of evaluation</td></tr>
<tr><td></td><td>+ prefix</td><td>positive number</td></tr>
<tr><td></td><td>− prefix</td><td>negative number</td></tr>
</table>

* The caret (^), tilde (~), and the not sign (¬) all indicate a logical not. Use the character available on your keyboard, or use the mnemonic equivalent.

** The OR symbol (|), broken vertical bar (¦), and exclamation point (!) all indicate a logical or. Use the character available on your keyboard, or use the mnemonic equivalent.

*** Two OR symbols (||), two broken vertical bars (¦¦), or two exclamation points (!!) indicate concatenation. Use the character available on your keyboard.

You can use the colon modifier (:) with any of the comparison operators. See Chapter 10, "SAS Operators," for a description of the colon modifier.

Operators for WHERE Expression Only

The operators that follow are only valid in WHERE expressions.

BETWEEN-AND operator The BETWEEN-AND operator selects observations in which the values of the variables fall within a range of values. You can specify the limits of the range as constants or expressions. Any range you specify with the BETWEEN-AND operator is an inclusive range, so that a value equal to one of the limits of the range is within the range. The BETWEEN-AND operator has the following form:

WHERE *variable* BETWEEN *value* AND *value*;

Here are two examples:

□ `where empnum between 500 and 1000;`

□ `where taxes between salary*0.30 and salary*0.50;`

You can combine the NOT operator with the BETWEEN-AND operator to select values that fall outside the range.

```
where empnum not between 500 and 1000;
```

CONTAINS operator The CONTAINS or question mark (?) operator selects observations that include the string specified in the WHERE expression. This operator is available for character variables only. The position of the string in the variable does not matter; however, the operator distinguishes between uppercase and lowercase characters when making comparisons. The following examples select observations containing the values **Mobay** and **Brisbayne** for the variable COMPANY, but they do not select the observation containing **Bayview**:

□ `where company ? 'bay';`

□ `where company contains 'bay';`

IS NULL or IS MISSING operator The IS NULL or IS MISSING operator selects all observations in which the value of a variable is missing. This operator selects observations with both regular or special missing value characters and can be used for both character and numeric data. The operator has the following form:

□ `where idnum is missing;`

□ `where name is null;`

This operator is equivalent to these expressions:

□ `where` *`variable`*`<=.Z;`

□ `where` *`variable`*`=' ';`

You can combine the NOT operator with the IS MISSING or IS NULL operators to select nonmissing values, as follows:

```
where salary is not missing;
```

LIKE operator By using a LIKE condition, you can select observations by comparing the values of character variables to patterns specified in the WHERE expression. The LIKE operator distinguishes between uppercase and lowercase characters when making comparisons.

There are two special characters available for specifying patterns: the percent sign (%) and the underscore (_). Using the percent sign in a pattern tells the SAS System that any number of characters can occupy that position. The following WHERE statement selects all employees with a name that starts with the letter **N**. The names can be of any length.

```
where lastname like 'N%';
```

WHERE

continued

Using an underscore in a pattern matches just one character in the value for each underscore character. You can specify more than one consecutive underscore character in a pattern, and you can specify a percent sign and an underscore in the same pattern. For example, you can use different forms of the LIKE operator to select character values from this list of first names:

```
Diana
Diane
Dianna
Dianthus
Dyan
```

The following table shows which of these names is selected by various forms of the WHERE expression used with the LIKE operator:

Pattern	Name Selected
`like 'D_an'`	Dyan
`like 'D_an_'`	Diana, Diane
`like 'D_an__'`	Dianna
`like 'D_an%'`	all names from list

You can combine the NOT operator with the LIKE operator to select values that do not have the specified pattern, as follows:

```
where frstname not like 'D_an%';
```

You can use a SAS character expression to specify a pattern, but you cannot use a SAS character expression which uses a SAS function.

Sounds-like operator Use the sounds-like operator (=*) with character variables to select observations that contain a spelling variation of the word or words specified in the WHERE expression. The sounds-like operator uses the Soundex algorithm to compare the variable value and the operand, and although it is useful, it does not always select all possible variations. For example, if you want to select observations from this list that contain names that sound like `Smith`:

```
Schmitt
Smith
Smithson
Smitt
Smythe
```

The following expression selects all the names on this list except `Schmitt` and `Smithson`:

```
where lastname=*'Smith';
```

SAME-AND operator Use the SAME-AND operator to add more clauses to an existing WHERE statement later in the program without retyping the original clauses. This is useful with

- □ interactive SAS procedures
- □ full-screen SAS procedures that allow you to type WHERE clauses on the command line
- □ any kind of RUN-group processing.

Use the SAME-AND operator when you already have a WHERE condition defined, and you want to insert additional conditions. The SAME-AND operator has the following form:

WHERE *condition-1*;
more SAS statements
WHERE SAME AND *condition-2*;
more SAS statements
WHERE SAME AND *condition-n*;

The SAS System selects observations that satisfy the conditions after the SAME-AND operator in addition to any previously defined conditions. The SAS System treats all of the existing conditions as though they were clauses separated by AND operators in a single WHERE statement.

The following example shows how to use the SAME-AND operator within RUN groups in PROC GPLOT. The SAS data set YEARS has three variables, and contains quarterly data for the 1980-1987 period.

```
proc gplot data=years;
   plot unit*quar=year;
run;

   where year>1981;
run;

   where same and year<1986;
run;

quit;
```

In this example, the second WHERE statement is equivalent to the following statement.

```
where year>1981 and year<1986;
```

Comparisons

You can use the WHERE command in SAS/FSP software to subset data for editing and browsing. You can use both the WHERE statement and WHERE= data set option in full-screen procedures and in conjunction with the WHERE command.

To select observations from individual data sets when a SET, MERGE, or UPDATE statement specifies more than one data set, apply a WHERE= data set option to each data set. In the DATA step, if a WHERE statement and a WHERE= data set option apply to the same data set, the SAS System uses the data set option and ignores the statement.

WHERE

continued

The most important differences between the WHERE statement in the DATA step and the subsetting IF statement are as follows:

- □ The WHERE statement selects observations before they are brought into the program data vector, making it a more efficient programming technique. The subsetting IF statement works on observations that are already in the program data vector.
- □ The WHERE statement can produce a different data set from the subsetting IF when a BY statement accompanies a SET, MERGE, or UPDATE statement, since the SAS System assigns values to the FIRST.*variable* and LAST.*variable* before the subsetting IF statement selects, but after the WHERE statement selects.
- □ The WHERE statement cannot be executed conditionally as part of an IF statement, but the subsetting IF statement can.
- □ The WHERE statement selects observations in SAS data sets only, whereas the subsetting IF statement selects observations from an existing SAS data set or from observations created with an INPUT statement.
- □ The subsetting IF statement cannot be used in SAS full-screen procedures to subset observations for browsing or editing.

Do not confuse the WHERE statement with the DROP or KEEP statement. Use the DROP and KEEP statements to select variables for processing. The WHERE statement selects observations.

See Also

Subsetting IF statement

"SAS Expressions" and "SAS Operators" in Chapter 4, "Rules of the SAS Language"

WHERE= data set option in Chapter 15, "SAS Data Set Options"

SAS/FSP Software: Usage and Reference, Version 6, First Edition

SAS Guide to the SQL Procedure: Usage and Reference, Version 6, First Edition

SAS/IML Software: Usage and Reference, Version 6, First Edition

WINDOW

Creates customized windows for your applications

DATA step

HELP WINDOW

Syntax

WINDOW *window* <*window-options*> *field-definition-1*
< . . . *field-definition-n*>;
WINDOW *window* <*window-options*> *group-definition-1*
< . . . *group-definition-n*>;

Description

You can use the WINDOW statement in display manager, interactive line, or noninteractive mode to create customized windows for your applications.* Windows you create can display text and accept input; they have command and message lines, and the window name appears at the top of the window. You can use commands and function keys with windows you create. A window definition remains in effect only for the DATA step containing the WINDOW statement.

You must define a window before you display it. Use the DISPLAY statement to display windows created with the WINDOW statement. See the description of the DISPLAY statement earlier in this chapter. See "Examples" later in this section for several examples of DATA steps that define and display windows.

You can use the following arguments with the WINDOW statement:

window
names the window. Window names must conform to SAS naming conventions.

window-options
specifies characteristics of the window as a whole. Specify all *window-options* before any field or GROUP= specifications. *Window-options* can include the following:

COLOR=*color*
specifies the color of the window background for host systems that have this capability. On other hosts, this option affects the color of the window border. If you do not specify a color, the SAS System uses black. *Color* can be one of the following:

WHITE	BLUE	YELLOW
GREEN	PINK	GRAY
RED	BLACK	BROWN
CYAN	MAGENTA	ORANGE

The representation of colors may vary, depending on the monitor being used. The COLOR= option has no effect on monochrome monitors.

COLUMNS=*columns*
specifies the number of columns in the window, excluding borders. If you do not specify a number, the window fills all remaining columns in the display; the number of columns available depends on the type of monitor being used.

* You cannot use the WINDOW statement in batch mode because no terminal is connected to a batch executing process.

WINDOW

continued

ICOLUMN=*column*
: specifies the initial column within the display at which the window is displayed. If you do not specify a number, the SAS System displays the window at column 1.

IROW=*row*
: specifies the initial row (or line) within the display at which the window is displayed. If you do not specify a number, the SAS System displays the window at row 1.

KEYS=<<*libref.*>*catalog.*>*keys-entry*
: specifies the name of a KEYS entry that contains the function key definitions for the window. If you specify just an entry name, the SAS System looks in the SASUSER.PROFILE catalog for a KEYS entry of the name specified. You can also specify the three-level name of a KEYS entry, in the form

```
libref.catalog.keys-entry
```

If you omit the KEYS= option, the SAS System uses the current function key settings defined in the KEYS window.

To create a set of function key definitions for a window, use the KEYS display manager window. Define the keys as you want, and then use the SAVE command to save the definitions in the SASUSER.PROFILE catalog or in a SAS data library and catalog that you specify. For more information, see the KEYS window in Chapter 17.

MENU=<<*libref.*>*catalog.*>*pmenu-entry*
: specifies the name of a pull-down menu (pmenu) you have built with the PMENU procedure. If you specify just an entry name, the SAS System looks in the SASUSER.PROFILE catalog for a PMENU entry of the name specified. You can also specify the three-level name of a PMENU entry, in the form

```
libref.catalog.pmenu-entry
```

ROWS=*rows*
: specifies the number of rows (or lines) in the window, excluding borders. If you do not specify a number, the window fills all remaining rows in the display; the number of rows available depends on the type of monitor being used.

field-definition
: identifies and describes a variable or character string to be displayed in a window or within a group of related fields. A window or group can contain any number of fields, and you can define the same field in several groups or windows. The form of *field-definition* is given in "Field Definitions" later in this section.

group-definition
: names a group and defines all fields within a group. A group definition consists of two parts: the GROUP= option and one or more field definitions.

GROUP=*group*

names a group of related fields. The GROUP= name must be a valid SAS name. When you refer to a group in a DISPLAY statement, write the name as *window.group*.

A group contains all fields in a window that you want to display at the same time. You can display various groups of fields within the same window at different times by naming each group. Choose the group to appear by specifying *window.group* in the DISPLAY statement. If you omit the GROUP= specification, the window contains one unnamed group of fields.

Specifying several groups within a window prevents repetition of window options that do not change and helps you to keep track of related displays. For example, if you are defining a window to check data values, you can arrange the display of variables and messages for most data values in the data set in a group named STANDARD; you can arrange the display of different messages in a group named CHECKIT that appears when data values meet the conditions you want to check.

field-definition

identifies and describes a variable or character string to be displayed in a window or within a group of related fields. A window or group can contain any number of fields, and you can define the same field in several groups or windows. The form of a *field-definition* is given in "Field Definitions."

Field Definitions

Use a field definition to identify a variable or character string to be displayed, its position, and its attributes. Enclose character strings in quotes. The position of an item is its beginning row (or line) and column. Attributes include color, whether you can enter a value into the field, and characteristics such as highlighting.

You can define a field to contain a variable value or a character string, but not both. The form of a field definition for a variable value is

<row column> variable <format> options

The form for a character string is

<row column> 'character-string' options

The elements of a field definition are described here.

row column

identifies the position of the variable or character string. If you omit *row* in the first field of a window or group, the SAS System uses the first row of the window; if you omit *row* in a later field specification, the SAS System continues on the row containing the previous field. If you omit *column*, the SAS System uses column 1 (the left border of the window). Although you can specify either *row* or *column* first, the examples in this book show the row first.

The SAS System keeps track of its position in the window with a pointer. For example, when you tell it to write a variable's value in the third column of the second row of a window, the pointer moves to row 2, column 3 to write the value. Use the pointer controls listed here to move the pointer to the appropriate position for a field.

WINDOW

(row column continued)

In a field definition, *row* can be one of the following row pointer controls:

#n
: specifies row *n* within the window; *n* must be a positive integer.

#numeric-variable
: specifies the row within the window given by the value of *numeric-variable,* which must be a positive integer. If not an integer, the decimal portion is truncated and only the integer is used.

#(expression)
: specifies the row within the window given by the value of *expression. Expression* can contain both explicit and implicit array references and must evaluate to a positive integer. Enclose *expression* in parentheses.

/
: moves the pointer to column 1 of the next row.

In a field definition, *column* can be one of the following column pointer controls:

@n
: specifies column *n* within the window; *n* must be a positive integer.

@numeric-variable
: specifies the column within the window given by the value of *numeric-variable,* which must be a positive integer. If not an integer, the decimal portion is truncated and only the integer is used.

@(expression)
: specifies the column within the window given by the value of *expression. Expression* can contain both explicit and implicit array references and must evaluate to a positive integer. Enclose *expression* in parentheses.

+n
: moves the pointer *n* columns; *n* must be a positive integer.

+numeric-variable
: moves the pointer the number of columns given by the *numeric-variable,* which must be a positive or negative integer. If not an integer, the decimal portion is truncated and only the integer is used.

variable

names a variable to be displayed or to be assigned the value you enter at that position when the window is displayed. *Variable* can also be an explicit or implicit array reference.

To allow a variable value in a field to be displayed but not changed by the user, use the PROTECT= option (described later in this section). You can also protect an entire window or group for the current execution of the DISPLAY statement by specifying the NOINPUT option in the DISPLAY statement.

If a field definition contains the name of a new variable, that variable is added to the data set being created (unless you use a KEEP or DROP specification).

format

gives the format for the variable. If a field displays a variable but does not allow it to be changed (that is, you use the PROTECT=YES option), *format* can be any SAS format or a format you define with the FORMAT procedure. If a field can both display a variable and accept input, you must either specify the informat in an INFORMAT or ATTRIB statement or use a SAS format such as $CHAR. or TIME. that has a corresponding informat. If a format is specified, the corresponding informat is assigned automatically to fields that can accept input.

If you do not specify *format*, the SAS System uses an informat and format specified elsewhere (for example, in an ATTRIB, INFORMAT, or FORMAT statement or permanently stored with the data set) or a SAS default informat and format. A format and informat in a WINDOW statement override an informat and format specified elsewhere.

'character-string'

contains the text of a character string to be displayed. The character string must be enclosed in quotes. Note that you cannot enter a value in a field containing a character string.

options

include any of the following:

ATTR=*highlighting-attribute*
A=*highlighting-attribute*

controls the following highlighting attributes of the field:

BLINK	causes the field to blink.
HIGHLIGHT	displays the field at high intensity.
REV_VIDEO	displays the field in reverse video.
UNDERLINE	underlines the field.

To specify more than one highlighting attribute, use the form

ATTR=(*highlighting-attribute-1*, . . .)

The highlighting attributes available depend on the type of monitor you use.

AUTOSKIP=YES | NO
AUTO=YES | NO

controls whether the cursor moves to the next unprotected field of the current window or group when you have entered data in all positions of a field. If you use AUTOSKIP=YES, the cursor moves automatically to the next unprotected field; if you use AUTOSKIP=NO, the cursor does not move automatically. By default, the value is NO.

WINDOW

continued

COLOR=*color*
C=*color*

specifies a color for the variable or character string. By default, the value is WHITE. *Color* can be one of the following:

WHITE	BLUE	YELLOW
GREEN	PINK	GRAY
RED	BLACK	BROWN
CYAN	MAGENTA	ORANGE

The representation of colors may vary, depending on the monitor you use. The COLOR= option has no effect on monochrome monitors.

DISPLAY=YES | NO

controls whether the contents of a field are displayed. If you use DISPLAY=YES, the SAS System displays characters in a field as you type them in. If you use DISPLAY=NO, the entered characters are not displayed. By default, the value is YES.

PERSIST=YES | NO

controls whether a field is displayed by all executions of a DISPLAY statement in the same iteration of the DATA step until the DISPLAY statement contains the BLANK option. If you use PERSIST=NO, each execution of a DISPLAY statement displays only the current contents of the field. If you use PERSIST=YES, each execution of the DISPLAY statement displays all previously displayed contents of the field as well as those scheduled for display by the current DISPLAY statement. If the new contents overlap persisting contents, the persisting contents are no longer displayed. By default, the value is NO. The PERSIST= option is most useful when the position of a field changes in each execution of a DISPLAY statement. See "Example 3: Persisting and Nonpersisting Fields" later in this section.

PROTECT=YES | NO
P=YES | NO

controls whether information can be entered into a field. If you use PROTECT=YES, you cannot enter information into a field. PROTECT=NO allows you to enter information. NO is the default. Use the PROTECT= option only for fields containing variables; fields containing text are automatically protected.

REQUIRED=YES | NO

controls whether a field can be left blank. If you use REQUIRED=NO, you can leave a field blank. NO is the default. If you try to leave a field blank that was defined with REQUIRED=YES, the SAS System does not allow you to input values in any subsequent fields in the window.

Automatic Variables

The WINDOW statement creates two automatic SAS variables: _CMD_ and _MSG_.

CMD contains the last command from the window's command line that was not recognized by display manager. _CMD_ is a character variable of length 80; its value is set to ' ' (blank) before each execution of a DISPLAY statement.

MSG contains a message you specify to be displayed in the message area of the window. _MSG_ is a character variable with length 80; its value is set to ' ' (blank) after each execution of a DISPLAY statement.

For example, you can use the _CMD_ and _MSG_ automatic variables to send a message when a user executes an erroneous display manager command in a window defined with the WINDOW statement:

```
if _cmd_ ne ' ' then _msg_='CAUTION: UNRECOGNIZED COMMAND '||_cmd_;
```

When a command containing an error is entered, the SAS System sets the value of _CMD_ to the text of the erroneous command. Because the value of _CMD_ is no longer blank, the IF statement is true. The THEN statement assigns _MSG_ the value created by concatenating 'CAUTION: UNRECOGNIZED COMMAND' and the value of _CMD_ (up to a total of 80 characters). The next time a DISPLAY statement displays that window, the message line of the window displays

```
CAUTION: UNRECOGNIZED COMMAND command
```

Command is the erroneous display manager command.

Displaying Windows

The DISPLAY statement enables you to display windows. Once you display a window, the window remains visible until you display another window over it or until the end of the DATA step. When you display a window containing fields into which you can enter values, you must either enter a value or press ENTER at *each* unprotected field to cause the SAS System to proceed to the next display. While a window is being displayed, you can use commands and function keys to view other windows, change the size of the current window, and so on. SAS execution proceeds to the next display only after you have pressed ENTER in all unprotected fields.

A DATA step containing a DISPLAY statement continues execution until the last observation read by a SET, MERGE, UPDATE, or INPUT statement has been processed or until a STOP or ABORT statement is executed. (You can also issue the END command to stop execution of the DATA step.)

Comparisons

The %WINDOW and %DISPLAY statements in the macro language create and display windows controlled by the macro facility.

WINDOW

continued

Examples

Example 1: Creating a Single Window

The following DATA step creates a window with a single group of fields. Display 9.1 shows the window.

```
data _null_;
   window start
          #5 @26 'WELCOME TO THE SAS SYSTEM' color=yellow
          #7 @19 'THIS PROGRAM CREATES TWO SAS DATA SETS'
          #8 @26 'AND USES THREE PROCEDURES'
          #12 @27 'PRESS ENTER TO CONTINUE';
   display start;
   stop;
run;
```

The START window fills the entire display. The first line of text is yellow; the other three lines are white. The text is centered on each line. The START window does not require you to input any values. However, to exit the window you must do one of two things:

- □ Press ENTER to cause DATA step execution to proceed to the STOP statement.
- □ Issue the END command.

If the STOP statement is omitted from the program, the DATA step executes endlessly until you execute END from the window, either with a function key or from the command line. (Since this DATA step does not read any observations, the SAS System cannot detect an end-of-file to cause DATA step execution to cease.)

Display 9.1 *Window with a Single Group of Fields*

```
START
 Command ===>


                         WELCOME TO THE SAS SYSTEM

                  THIS PROGRAM CREATES TWO SAS DATA SETS
                         AND USES THREE PROCEDURES



                          PRESS ENTER TO CONTINUE
```

Example 2: Displaying Two Windows Simultaneously

The following statements assign news articles to reporters. The list of article topics is stored as variable ART in SAS data set IN.ARTICLE. With this application, you can examine each topic, assign it to a writer, and create a new SAS data set named SAVE.ASSIGN containing the topics and reporters' names. You can also make certain you assign topics evenly among the reporters. The following SAS program displays two windows, shown in Display 9.2, that enable you to accomplish this task:

```
libname save 'SAS-data-library';
libname in 'SAS-data-library';

data save.assign;
   set in.article end=final;
   drop a b j s t;
   window assign irow=18 color=yellow
          #3 @10 'ARTICLE:' +1 art protect=yes 'NAME:' +1 name $14.;
   window showtot irow=1 rows=11 color=cyan
          group=subtot
          #1 @10 'Adams has' +1 a
          #2 @10 'Brown has' +1 b
          #3 @10 'Johnson has' +1 j
          #4 @10 'Smith has' +1 s
          #5 @10 'Thomas has' +1 t
          group=lastmsg
          #8 @10
          'ALL ARTICLES ASSIGNED. PRESS ENTER TO STOP PROCESSING';
   display assign blank;
   if name='Adams' then a+1;
   else if name='Brown' then b+1;
   else if name='Johnson' then j+1;
   else if name='Smith' then s+1;
   else if name='Thomas' then t+1;
   display showtot.subtot blank noinput;
   if final then display showtot.lastmsg;
run;
```

WINDOW

continued

Display 9.2 *Multiple Windows for Data Entry and Displaying Running Totals*

```
SHOWTOT
 Command ===>

           Adams has 3
           Brown has 2
           Johnson has 2
           Smith has 3
           Thomas has 3

ASSIGN
 Command ===>


           ARTICLE: Education Cost                    NAME: Brown

                                                                R
```

In the ASSIGN window (which fills the bottom half of the display), you see the name of the article and a field into which you enter a reporter's name. After you enter the first name, the SAS System displays group SHOWTOT.SUBTOT in the SHOWTOT window (which fills the top half of the display). SHOWTOT.SUBTOT shows you the number of articles assigned to each reporter (including the assignment you just made). As you continue to make assignments, SHOWTOT.SUBTOT contains the subtotal assigned to each reporter so far (because the group from the previous iteration of the DATA step is displayed until after you make the new assignment).

During the last iteration of the DATA step, the SAS System displays group SHOWTOT.LASTMSG, which tells you that you are finished and what you should do to end the DATA step. The text in SHOWTOT.LASTMSG is displayed at the bottom of the last group of totals so that you can examine the totals (because the DISPLAY statement does not contain the BLANK option).

Example 3: Persisting and Nonpersisting Fields

This example demonstrates the PERSIST= option and the simultaneous display of two windows.

```
data _null_;
   array row{3} r1-r3;
   array col{3} c1-c3;
   input row{*} col{*};
   window one
         rows=20 columns=36
         #1 @14 'PERSIST=YES' color=red
         #(row{i}) @(col{i}) 'Hello' color=red persist=yes;
```

```
      window two
             icolumn=43 rows=20 columns=36
             #1 @14 'PERSIST=NO' color=blue
             #(row(i)) @(col(i)) 'Hello' color=blue persist=no;
      do i=1 to 3;
         display one;
         display two;
      end;
      cards;
   5 10 15 5 10 15
   ;
```

Display 9.3 shows the results of this DATA step after its third iteration. Note that window ONE shows **Hello** in all three positions in which it was displayed. Window TWO shows only the third and final position in which **Hello** was displayed.

Display 9.3 *Using the PERSIST= Option and Simultaneous Display*

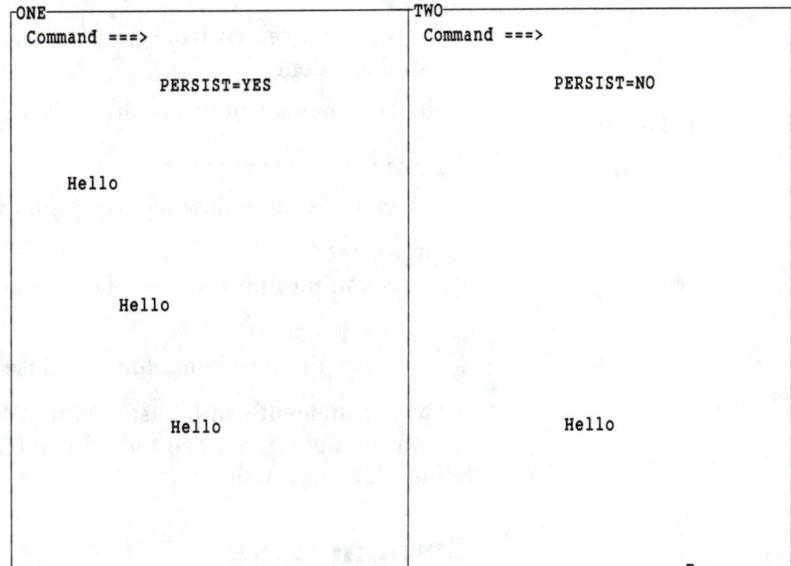

See Also

DISPLAY statement

"PMENU Facility" in Chapter 7, "SAS Display Manager System"

"Display Design Guidelines" in Chapter 2, "The SAS/AF Programming Environment," in *SAS/AF Software: Usage and Reference, Version 6, First Edition*

Chapter 3, "Macro Program Statements," in the *SAS Guide to Macro Processing, Version 6 Edition* for details on the %WINDOW statement

X

Issues a host command from within a SAS session

Global

HELP X

Syntax

X <'*command*'>;

Description

The X statement issues a host command from within a SAS session when you run SAS in display manager or interactive line mode. The SAS System executes the X statement immediately.

■ **Host Information** ....

The X statement is host-dependent. See the SAS documentation for your host system to determine whether it is a valid statement on your system. Keep in mind the following points:

- On some hosts, the X statement is not valid in batch or noninteractive mode.
- The way you return from host system mode to the SAS session is host-dependent.
- The commands you use with the X statement are host-specific.

.... ■

You can use the following arguments with the X statement:

no argument
: puts you into host system mode, where you can issue host commands.

'*command*'
: specifies the host command. Enclose the command in quotes.

The X statement can be used with SAS macros to write portable code to run on multiple hosts. See the *SAS Guide to Macro Processing, Version 6 Edition* for information.

Comparisons

The X command used in a display manager session functions exactly like the X statement, except you issue the command from a command line. You submit the X statement from the program editor.

See Also

X command in Chapter 18, "SAS Display Manager Commands"

CHAPTER 10 SAS® Operators

Introduction

SAS operators are symbols used in SAS expressions to request a comparison, logical operation, arithmetic calculation, or concatenation. SAS expressions that include several operators are called *compound expressions*. The SAS System follows certain rules that govern the order it evaluates each part of a compound expression.

For further information and examples of using SAS operators, see "SAS Operators" in Chapter 4, "Rules of the SAS Language."

Table of Operators

In the following table, SAS operators are grouped according to their priority of evaluation (first column). In compound expressions, the SAS System evaluates the part of the expression containing operators from Group I first; it evaluates Group II expressions next, and so on down to Group VII. Parentheses are often used in compound expressions to group operands; expressions within parentheses are evaluated before those outside. In addition, if a compound expression contains more than one operator from the same group, certain rules govern which part of the expression the SAS System evaluates first. These rules are listed in the table in the column named Order of Evaluation.

The other columns in the table are described here.

Symbols
: lists the actual symbols you use to request the comparisons, operations, and calculations.

Mnemonic Equivalent
: lists written-out, alternate forms of the symbol. In some cases, such as when your keyboard does not support special symbols, you should use the alternate form.

Definition
: defines the symbol.

Example
: provides brief examples of how to use the symbol or mnemonic equivalent in a SAS expression.

Table 10.1 *Summary of SAS Operators*

<table>
<tr><th>Priority</th><th>Order of Evaluation</th><th>Symbols</th><th>Mnemonic Equivalent</th><th>Definition</th><th>Example</th></tr>
<tr><td>Group I</td><td>right to left</td><td>**[1]</td><td></td><td>exponentiation</td><td><code>y=a**2;</code></td></tr>
<tr><td></td><td></td><td>+[2]</td><td></td><td>positive prefix</td><td><code>y=+(a*b);</code></td></tr>
<tr><td></td><td></td><td>−[2]</td><td></td><td>negative prefix</td><td><code>z=-(a+b);</code></td></tr>
<tr><td></td><td></td><td>^ ¬ ˜[3]</td><td>NOT</td><td>logical not</td><td><code>if not z then put x;</code></td></tr>
<tr><td></td><td></td><td>><</td><td>MIN</td><td>minimum</td><td><code>x=a><b;</code>[4]</td></tr>
<tr><td></td><td></td><td><></td><td>MAX</td><td>maximum</td><td><code>x=a<>b;</code></td></tr>
<tr><td>Group II</td><td>left to right</td><td>*</td><td></td><td>multiplication</td><td><code>c=a*b;</code></td></tr>
<tr><td></td><td></td><td>/</td><td></td><td>division</td><td><code>f=g/h;</code></td></tr>
<tr><td>Group III</td><td>left to right</td><td>+</td><td></td><td>addition</td><td><code>c=a+b;</code></td></tr>
<tr><td></td><td></td><td>−</td><td></td><td>subtraction</td><td><code>f=g-h;</code></td></tr>
<tr><td>Group IV</td><td>left to right</td><td>|| !! ¦¦[5]</td><td></td><td>concatenate character values</td><td><code>name='J'||'SMITH';</code></td></tr>
<tr><td>Group V[6]</td><td>left to right[7]</td><td><</td><td>LT</td><td>less than</td><td><code>if x<y then c=5;</code></td></tr>
<tr><td></td><td></td><td><=</td><td>LE</td><td>less than or equal to</td><td><code>if x le y then a=0;</code></td></tr>
<tr><td></td><td></td><td>=</td><td>EQ</td><td>equal to</td><td><code>if y eq (x+a) then output;</code></td></tr>
<tr><td></td><td></td><td>¬=</td><td>NE</td><td>not equal to</td><td><code>if x ne z then output;</code></td></tr>
<tr><td></td><td></td><td>>=</td><td>GE</td><td>greater than or equal to</td><td><code>if y>=a then output;</code></td></tr>
<tr><td></td><td></td><td>></td><td>GT</td><td>greater than</td><td><code>if z>a then output;</code></td></tr>
<tr><td></td><td></td><td></td><td>IN</td><td>equal to one of a list</td><td><code>if state in ('NY','NJ','PA') then region='NE';</code></td></tr>
<tr><td>Group VI</td><td>left to right</td><td>&</td><td>AND</td><td>logical and</td><td><code>if a=b & c=d then x=1;</code></td></tr>
<tr><td>Group VII</td><td>left to right</td><td>| ! ¦[8]</td><td>OR</td><td>logical or</td><td><code>if y=2 or x=3 then a=d;</code></td></tr>
</table>

1 Because Group I operators are evaluated from right to left, the expression x=2**3**4 is evaluated as x=(2**(3**4)).

2 The plus (+) and minus (−) signs can be either prefix or arithmetic operators. A plus or a minus sign is a prefix operator only when it appears at the beginning of an expression or when it is immediately preceded by a left parenthesis or another operator.

3 Depending on the characters available on your keyboard, the symbol can be the not sign (¬), tilde (~), or caret (^). The SAS system option CHARCODE allows various other substitutions for unavailable special characters.

4 In this example of the MIN operator, the SAS System evaluates −3><−3 as −(3><−3), which is equal to −(−3), which equals +3. This is because Group I operators are evaluated from right to left.

5 Depending on the characters available on your keyboard, the symbol you use as the concatenation operator can be a single vertical bar (|), broken vertical bar (¦), or exclamation mark (!).

6 Group V operators are comparison operators. The result of a comparison operation is 1 if the comparison is true and 0 if it is false. Missing values are the lowest in any comparison operation.

The symbols =< (less than or equal to) and => (greater than or equal to) are also allowed for compatibility with previous versions of the SAS System.

When making character comparisons, you can use a colon (:) after any of the comparison operators to compare only the first character(s) of the value. The SAS System truncates the longer value to the length of the shorter value during the comparison. For example, if name=:'P' compares the value of the first character of NAME to the letter P. See "Character Comparisons" in Chapter 4 for details.

7 An exception to this rule occurs when two comparison operators surround a quantity. For example, the expression x<y<z is evaluated as (x<y) and (y<z).

8 Depending on the characters available on your keyboard, the symbol you use for the logical or can be a single vertical bar (|), broken vertical bar (¦), or exclamation mark (!). You can also use the mnemonic equivalent OR.

CHAPTER 11 SAS® Functions

(continued on next page)

(continued from previous page)

(continued on next page)

(continued from previous page)

Background information on SAS functions, including a table listing all functions, appears in Chapter 3, "Components of the SAS Language." See Table 3.5, "Categories and Descriptions of Functions."

ABS

Absolute value

Arithmetic

HELP FUNCTION

Syntax

ABS(*argument*)

Description

argument is numeric.

The ABS function returns a nonnegative number equal in magnitude to that of the argument.

Examples

```
□ x=abs(2.4);

□ x=abs(-3);
```

The values returned are 2.40000 and 3.00000, respectively.

ARCOS

Arccosine

Trigonometric and hyperbolic

HELP FUNCTION

Syntax

ARCOS(*argument*)

Description

argument is numeric and between −1 and 1.

The ARCOS function returns the arccosine (inverse cosine) of the argument. The value returned is in radians.

Examples

□ `x=arcos(1);`

□ `x=arcos(0);`

□ `x=arcos(-.5);`

The values returned are 0.00000, 1.57078, and 2.09440, respectively.

ARSIN

Arcsine

Trigonometric and hyperbolic

HELP FUNCTION

Syntax

ARSIN(*argument*)

Description

argument is numeric and between −1 and 1.

The ARSIN function returns the arcsine (inverse sine) of the argument. The value returned is in radians.

Examples

□ `x=arsin(0);`

□ `x=arsin(1);`

□ `x=arsin(-.5);`

The values returned are 0.00000, 1.57080, and −0.52360, respectively.

ATAN

Arctangent

Trigonometric and hyperbolic

HELP FUNCTION

Syntax

ATAN(*argument*)

Description

argument is numeric.

The ATAN function returns the arctangent (inverse tangent) of the argument. The value returned is in radians.

Examples

- `x=atan(1);`
- `x=atan(0);`
- `x=atan(-9);`

The values returned are 0.78540, 0.00000, and −1.46014, respectively.

BETAINV

Quantile from the beta distribution

Quantile

HELP FUNCTION

Syntax

BETAINV(*p*,*a*,*b*)

Description

p is a numeric probability, with $0<p<1$.

a is a numeric shape parameter, with $a>0$.

b is a numeric shape parameter, with $b>0$.

The BETAINV function returns the *p*th quantile from the beta distribution with shape parameters *a* and *b*. The probability that an observation from a beta distribution is less than or equal to the returned quantile is *p*.

The BETAINV function is the inverse of the PROBBETA function.

Example

```
x=betainv(.001,2,4);
```

The returned value is 0.01010. The beta distribution is related to many statistical distributions (for example, the *F* distribution). See Abramowitz and Stegun (1964).

BYTE

Returns one character in the ASCII or EBCDIC collating sequence

Character

HELP FUNCTION

Syntax

BYTE(*n*)

Description

The BYTE function returns the *n*th character in the ASCII or EBCDIC collating sequence, depending on the sequence your host system uses.

You can use the following argument with the BYTE function:

n is an integer representing a specific ASCII or EBCDIC character. The value of *n* must be between 0 and 255 for EBCDIC collating sequences. For ASCII collating sequences, the characters corresponding to values between 0 and 127 represent the standard character set. Other ASCII characters corresponding to values between 128 and 255 are available on certain ASCII systems, but the information represented by those characters varies from system to system.

Example

The following statements return a value of `P` on an ASCII system and a value of & on an EBCDIC system:

```
x=byte(80);
put x;
```

See Also

COLLATE function

RANK function

CEIL

Smallest integer that is greater than or equal to the argument

Truncation

HELP FUNCTION

Syntax

CEIL(*argument*)

Description

argument is numeric.

The CEIL function returns the smallest integer that is greater than or equal to the argument. If the argument is within 10^{-12} of an integer, the function returns that integer.

Examples

```
□ x=ceil(2.1);
□ x=ceil(3);
□ x=ceil(-2.4);
□ x=ceil(1+1.e-11);
□ x=ceil(-1+1.e-11);
□ x=ceil(1+1.e-13);
```

The values returned are 3, 3, −2, 2, 0, and 1, respectively.

CINV

Quantile from the chi-square distribution

Quantile

HELP FUNCTION

Syntax

CINV(*p*,*df*<,*nc*>)

Description

p is a numeric probability, with $0<p<1$.

df is a numeric degrees of freedom parameter, with $df>0$.

nc is an optional numeric noncentrality parameter, with $nc \geq 0$.

The CINV function returns the *p*th quantile from the chi-square distribution with degrees of freedom *df* and a noncentrality parameter *nc*. The probability that an observation from a chi-square distribution is less than or equal to the returned quantile is *p*. This function accepts a noninteger degrees of freedom parameter *df*.

The CINV function is the inverse of the PROBCHI function.

If the optional parameter *nc* is not specified or has the value 0, the quantile from the central chi-square distribution is returned. The noncentrality parameter *nc* is defined such that if X is a normal random variable with mean μ and variance 1., X^2 has a noncentral chi-square distribution with $df=1$ and $nc=\mu^2$. For large values of *nc*, the algorithm could fail; in that case, a missing value is returned.

Examples

```
□ q1=cinv(.95,3);
□ q2=cinv(.95,3.5,4.5);
```

The values returned are 7.81473 and 17.50458, respectively.

COLLATE

Returns an ASCII or EBCDIC collating sequence character string

Character

HELP FUNCTION

Syntax

COLLATE(*start-position*<,*end-position*>) | (*start-position*<,,*length*>)

Description

The COLLATE function returns a string of characters from the ASCII or EBCDIC collating sequence, depending on the sequence your host system uses.

You can use the following arguments with the COLLATE function:

start-position
: specifies the numeric position in the collating sequence of the first character to be returned. If you specify only *start-position*, COLLATE returns consecutive characters from that position to the end of the collating sequence or up to 200 characters, whichever comes first.

end-position
: specifies the numeric position in the collating sequence of the last character to be returned. If you specify *end-position*, COLLATE returns all character values in the collating sequence between *start-position* and *end-position*, inclusive. If you omit *end-position* in favor of *length*, mark the *end-position* place with a comma.

  The maximum *end-position* for the EBCDIC collating sequence is 255. For ASCII collating sequences, the characters corresponding to *end-position* values between 0 and 127 represent the standard character set. Other ASCII characters corresponding to *end-position* values between 128 and 255 are available on certain ASCII systems, but the information represented by those characters varies from system to system.

length
: specifies the number of characters you want. Specify *length* if you do not specify *end-position* (or do not specify *length* if you specify *end-position*) to explicitly specify the length of the result.

If you specify both *end-position* and *length*, COLLATE ignores *length*. If you request a string longer than the remainder of the sequence, COLLATE returns a string through the end of the sequence.

Examples

These statements return the same results on ASCII and EBCDIC systems, as shown in the output that follows:

On ASCII systems:

```
x=collate(48,,10);
y=collate(48,57);
put @1 x @20 y;
```

On EBCDIC systems:

```
x=collate(240,,10);
y=collate(240,249);
put @1 x @20 y;
```

```
----+----1----+----2----+----3----+----4
0123456789         0123456789
```

See Also

BYTE function
RANK function

COMPOUND

Compound interest parameters

Financial

HELP FUNCTION

Syntax

COMPOUND(*a*,*f*,*r*,*n*)

Description

a is numeric, the initial amount, with $a \geq 0$.

f is numeric, the future amount (at the end of *n* periods), with $f \geq 0$.

r is numeric, the periodic interest rate expressed as a fraction, with $r \geq 0$.

n is an integer, the number of compounding periods, with $n \geq 0$.

The COMPOUND function returns the missing argument in the list of four arguments from a compound interest calculation. The arguments are related by

$$f = a(1 + r)^n \quad .$$

One missing argument must be provided. It is then calculated from the remaining three. No adjustment is made to convert the results to round numbers.

Example

The accumulated value of an investment of $2000 at a nominal annual interest rate of 9 percent, compounded monthly after 30 months, can be expressed as

```
future=compound(2000,.,.09/12,30);
```

The value returned is 2502.54. The second argument has been set to missing, indicating that the future amount is to be calculated. The 9 percent nominal annual rate has been converted to a monthly rate of 0.09/12. The rate argument is the fractional (not the percentage) interest rate per compounding period.

COMPRESS

Removes specific characters from character expressions

Character

HELP FUNCTION

Syntax

COMPRESS(*source*<,*characters-to-remove*>)

Description

The COMPRESS function removes blanks or characters you specify from a character expression you also specify and returns the result.

You can use the following arguments with the COMPRESS function:

source
: specifies a SAS character expression containing characters you want to remove.

characters-to-remove
: specifies the character or characters you want to remove from a SAS character expression. If you specify a literal string of characters, you must enclose the string in quotes. If you use an expression or variable, you need not enclose it in quotes. If you specify nothing, the SAS System removes blanks from *source* and returns that value.

Examples

Example 1: Compressing Blanks

These statements return the output that follows:

```
a='AB C D ';
b=compress(a);
put b;
```

```
----+----1----+----2
ABCD
```

Example 2: Compressing Special Characters

These statements return the output that follows:

```
x='A.B (C=D);';
y=compress(x,'.;()');
put y;
```

```
----+----1----+----2
AB C=D
```

See Also

LEFT function

TRIM function

COS

Trigonometric cosine

Trigonometric and hyperbolic

HELP FUNCTION

Syntax

COS(*argument*)

Description

argument is numeric and specified in radians.

The COS function returns the cosine of the argument.

Examples

□ `x=cos(.5);`

□ `x=cos(0);`

□ `x=cos(3.14159/3);`

The values returned are 0.87758, 1.00000, and 0.50000, respectively.

COSH

Hyperbolic cosine

Trigonometric and hyperbolic

HELP FUNCTION

Syntax

COSH(*argument*)

Description

argument is numeric.

The COSH function returns the hyperbolic cosine of the argument, given by

(exp(*argument*) + exp(−*argument*)) / 2 .

Examples

□ `x=cosh(0);`

□ `x=cosh(-5);`

□ `x=cosh(.5);`

The values returned are 1.00000, 74.20995, and 1.12763, respectively.

CSS

Corrected sum of squares

Sample statistics

HELP FUNCTION

Syntax

CSS(*argument,argument*, . . .)

Description

argument is numeric. At least two arguments are required. The argument list may consist of a variable list, preceded by OF. See "Using Function Arguments" in Chapter 3, "Components of the SAS Language."

The CSS function returns the corrected sum of squares of the nonmissing arguments.

Examples

- □ `x1=css(5,9,3,6);`
- □ `x2=css(5,8,9,6,.);`
- □ `x3=css(8,9,6,.);`
- □ `x4=css(of x1-x3);`

The values returned are 18.75000, 10.00000, 4.66667, and 101.11574, respectively.

CV

Coefficient of variation

Sample statistics

HELP FUNCTION

Syntax

CV(*argument,argument*, . . .)

Description

argument is numeric. At least two arguments are required. The argument list may consist of a variable list, preceded by OF. See "Using Function Arguments" in Chapter 3.

The CV function returns the coefficient of variation of the nonmissing arguments.

Examples

- □ `x1=cv(5,9,3,6);`
- □ `x2=cv(5,8,9,6,.);`
- □ `x3=cv(8,9,6,.);`
- □ `x4=cv(of x1-x3);`

The values returned are 43.47826, 26.08203, 19.92424, and 40.95354, respectively.

DACCDB

Accumulated declining balance depreciation

Financial

HELP FUNCTION

Syntax

DACCDB(*p*,*v*,*y*,*r*)

Description

p is numeric, the period for which the calculation is to be done. For noninteger *p* arguments, the depreciation is prorated between the two consecutive time periods preceding and following the fractional period.

v is numeric, the depreciable initial value of the asset.

y is numeric, the lifetime of the asset, with $y>0$.

r is numeric, the rate of depreciation expressed as a decimal, with $r>0$.

The DACCDB function returns the accumulated depreciation using a declining balance method, defined by

$$\text{DACCDB}(p,v,y,r) = \begin{cases} 0 & p \le 0 \\ v\left(1 - (1 - \frac{r}{y})^{int(p)}\right)\left(1 - (p - int(p))\frac{r}{y}\right) & p > 0 \end{cases}$$

where int(*p*) is the integer part of *p*. The *p* and *y* arguments must be expressed using the same units of time. A double declining balance is obtained by setting *r* equal to 2.

Example

An asset has a depreciable initial value of $1000 and a fifteen-year lifetime. Using a 200 percent declining balance, the depreciation throughout the first 10 years can be expressed as

```
a=daccdb(10,1000,15,2);
```

The value returned is 760.93. The first and the third arguments are expressed in years.

DACCDBSL

Accumulated declining balance converting to a straight-line depreciation

Financial

HELP FUNCTION

Syntax

DACCDBSL(*p*,*v*,*y*,*r*)

Description

p is numeric, the period for which the calculation is to be done.

v is numeric, the depreciable initial value of the asset.

y is an integer, the lifetime of the asset, with $y>0$.

r is numeric, the rate of depreciation expressed as a fraction, with $r>0$.

The DACCDBSL function returns the accumulated depreciation using a declining balance method, with conversion to a straight-line depreciation function defined by

$$\text{DACCDBSL}(p,v,y,r) = \text{DEPDBSL}(1,v,y,r) + \text{DEPDBSL}(2,v,y,r) + \ldots + \text{DEPDBSL}(p,v,y,r) \quad .$$

The declining balance with conversion to a straight-line depreciation chooses for each time period the method of depreciation (declining balance or straight-line on the remaining balance) that gives the larger depreciation. The *p* and *y* arguments must be expressed using the same units of time.

Example

An asset has a depreciable initial value of $1000 and a ten-year lifetime. Using a declining balance rate of 150 percent the accumulated depreciation of that asset in its fifth year can be expressed as

```
y5=daccdbsl(5,1000,10,1.5);
```

The value returned is 564.99. The first and the third arguments are expressed in years.

DACCSL

Accumulated straight-line depreciation

Financial

HELP FUNCTION

Syntax

DACCSL(*p*,*v*,*y*)

Description

p is numeric, the period for which the calculation is to be done. For fractional *p*, the depreciation is prorated between the two consecutive time periods preceding and following the fractional period.

v is numeric, the depreciable initial value of the asset.

y is numeric, the lifetime of the asset, with $y>0$.

The DACCSL function returns the accumulated depreciation using the straight-line method, given by

$$\text{DACCSL}(p,v,y) = \begin{cases} 0 & p < 0 \\ v\dfrac{p}{y} & 0 \le p \le y \\ v & p > y \end{cases} \quad .$$

The *p* and *y* arguments must be expressed using the same units of time.

Example

An asset, acquired on 01APR86, has a depreciable initial value of $1000 and a ten-year lifetime. The accumulated depreciation in the value of the asset through 31DEC87 can be expressed as

```
a=daccsl(1.75,1000,10);
```

The value returned is 175.00. The first and the third arguments are expressed in years.

DACCSYD

Accumulated sum-of-years-digits depreciation

Financial

HELP FUNCTION

Syntax

DACCSYD(*p*,*v*,*y*)

Description

p is numeric, the period for which the calculation is to be done. For noninteger *p* arguments, the depreciation is prorated between the two consecutive time periods preceding and following the fractional period.

v is numeric, the depreciable initial value of the asset.

y is numeric, the lifetime of the asset, with $y>0$.

The DACCSYD function returns the accumulated depreciation using the sum-of-years-digits method, given by

$$\text{DACCSYD}(p,v,y) = \begin{cases} 0 & p<0 \\ v\dfrac{\text{int}(p)\left(y-\frac{\text{int}(p)-1}{2}\right)+\left(p-\text{int}(p)\right)\left(y-\text{int}(p)\right)}{\text{int}(y)\left(y-\frac{\text{int}(y)-1}{2}\right)+\left(y-\text{int}(y)\right)^2} & 0\le p\le y \\ v & p>y \end{cases}$$

where int(*y*) indicates the integer part of *y*. The *p* and *y* arguments must be expressed using the same units of time.

Example

An asset, acquired on 01OCT86, has a depreciable initial value of $1000 and a five-year lifetime. The accumulated depreciation of the asset throughout 01JAN88 can be expressed as

```
y2=DACCSYD(15/12,1000,5);
```

The value returned is 400.00. The first and the third arguments are expressed in years.

DACCTAB

Accumulated depreciation from specified tables

Financial

HELP FUNCTION

Syntax

DACCTAB(*p,v,t1, . . . ,tn*)

Description

p — is numeric, the period for which the calculation is to be done. For noninteger *p* arguments, the depreciation is prorated between the two consecutive time periods preceding and following the fractional period.

v — is numeric, the depreciable initial value of the asset.

t1, . . . ,tn — are numeric, the fractions of depreciation for each time period.

The DACCTAB function returns the accumulated depreciation using user-specified tables, given by

$$\text{DACCTAB}(p,v,t_1, \ldots ,t_n) = \begin{cases} 0 & p \leq 0 \\ v\left(t_1 + t_2 + \ldots + t_{\text{int}(p)} + (p - \text{int}(p))\, t_{\text{int}(p)+1}\right) & 0 < p < n \\ v & p \geq n\ . \end{cases}$$

For a given *p*, only the arguments *t1, . . . ,tk* need to be specified with k=ceil(p).

Example

An asset has a depreciable initial value of $1000 and a five-year lifetime. Using a table of the annual depreciation rates of .15, .22, .21, .21, and .20 during the first, second, third, fourth, and fifth years, respectively, the accumulated depreciation throughout the third year can be expressed as

```
y3=DACCTAB(3,1000,.15,.22,.21,.24,.20);
```

The value returned is 580.00. The fourth rate, .24, and the fifth rate, .20, can be omitted since they are not needed in the calculation.

DATE

Returns the current date as a SAS date value

Date and time

HELP FUNCTION

Syntax

DATE()

Description

The DATE function produces the current date as a SAS date value representing the number of days between January 1, 1960 and the current date. The alias for the DATE function is TODAY.

Example

The following statements illustrate the DATE function:

```
tday=date();
if (tday-datedue)> 15 then
   do;
      put 'As of ' tday date7. 'Account #'
           account 'is more than 15 days overdue.';
   end;
```

See Also

TODAY function

"SAS Date and Time Values" in Chapter 4, "Rules of the SAS Language."

DATEJUL

Converts a Julian date to a SAS date value

Date and time

HELP FUNCTION

Syntax

DATEJUL(*julian-date*)

Description

The DATEJUL function converts a Julian date to a SAS date value.

You can use the following argument with the DATEJUL function:

julian-date specifies any valid SAS numeric expression representing a Julian date in the form *yyddd* or *yyyyddd*, where *yy* or *yyyy* represents the year and *ddd* the day of the year. Two-digit year values are based on the YEARCUTOFF= system option. The value of *ddd* must be between 1 and 365 (or 366 for a leap year).

Examples

The following statements return values of 10957 and 14976:

- `start=datejul(89365);`
- `end=datejul(2001001);`

See Also

JULDATE function

"SAS Date and Time Values" in Chapter 4, "Rules of the SAS Language."

DATEPART

Extracts the date from a SAS datetime value

Date and time

HELP FUNCTION

Syntax

DATEPART(*datetime*)

Description

The DATEPART function returns a SAS date value corresponding to the date portion of a SAS datetime value.

You can use the following argument with the DATEPART function:

datetime specifies a SAS expression representing a SAS datetime value.

Example

The following example of the DATEPART function returns a value equivalent to February 1, 1989. The PUT statement writes the resulting value as `February 1, 1989`:

```
   /* CONN shows when the computer session began */
conn='01feb89:8:45'dt;
servdate=datepart(conn);
put servdate worddate.;
```

See Also

DATETIME and TIMEPART functions

"SAS Date and Time Values" in Chapter 4, "Rules of the SAS Language."

DATETIME

Returns the current date and time of day

Date and time

HELP FUNCTION

Syntax

DATETIME()

Description

The DATETIME function returns the current date and time of day as a SAS datetime value.

Example

The following example returns a SAS value representing the number of seconds between January 1, 1960 and the current date:

```
when=datetime();
put when=;
```

See Also

DATE and TIME functions

"SAS Date and Time Values" in Chapter 4, "Rules of the SAS Language."

DAY

Returns the day of the month from a SAS date value

Date and time

HELP FUNCTION

Syntax

DAY(*date*)

Description

The DAY function produces an integer representing the day of the month from a SAS date value. Integers can range from 1 through 31.

You can use the following argument with the DAY function:

date specifies a SAS expression representing a SAS date value.

Example

The following statements assign a value of 5 to D:

```
now='05may89'd;
d=day(now);
```

See Also

MONTH and YEAR functions

"SAS Date and Time Values" in Chapter 4, "Rules of the SAS Language."

DEPDB

Declining balance depreciation

Financial

HELP FUNCTION

Syntax

DEPDB(*p,v,y,r*)

Description

p is numeric, the period for which the calculation is to be done. For noninteger *p* arguments, the depreciation is prorated between the two consecutive time periods preceding and following the fractional period.

v is numeric, the depreciable initial value of the asset.

y is numeric, the lifetime of the asset, with $y>0$.

r is numeric, the rate of depreciation expressed as a fraction, with $r \geq 0$.

The DEPDB function returns the depreciation using the declining balance method, given by

$$\mathrm{DEPDB}(p,v,y,r) = \mathrm{DACCDB}(p,v,y,r) - \mathrm{DACCDB}(p-1,v,y,r) \quad .$$

The *p* and *y* arguments must be expressed using the same units of time. A double declining balance is obtained by setting *r* equal to 2.

Example

An asset has an initial value of $1000 and a fifteen-year lifetime. Using a declining balance rate of 200 percent, the depreciation of the value of the asset for the tenth year can be expressed as

```
y10=DEPDB(10,1000,15,2);
```

The value returned is 36.78. The first and the third arguments are expressed in years.

DEPDBSL

Declining balance converting to a straight-line depreciation

Financial

HELP FUNCTION

Syntax

DEPDBSL(*p,v,y,r*)

Description

p is an integer, the period for which the calculation is to be done.

v is numeric, the depreciable initial value of the asset.

y is an integer, the lifetime of the asset, with $y>0$.

r is numeric, the rate of depreciation expressed as a fraction, with $r \geq 0$.

The DEPDBSL function returns the depreciation using the declining balance method with conversion to a straight-line depreciation, given by

$$\mathrm{DEPDBSL}(p,v,y,r) = \begin{cases} 0 & p < 0 \\ v\dfrac{r}{y}\left(1 - \dfrac{r}{y}\right)^{p-1} & p < t \\ v\left(1 - \dfrac{r}{y}\right)^{\frac{t-1}{y-t+1}} & p \geq t \\ 0 & p > y \end{cases}$$

where

$$t = int(y - \frac{y}{r} + 1)$$

where $t = int(y - y/r + 1)$ and *int*( ) denotes the integer part of a numeric argument. The *p* and *y* arguments must be expressed using the same units of time. The declining balance changing to a straight-line depreciation chooses for each time period the method of depreciation (declining balance or straight-line on the remaining balance) that gives the larger depreciation.

Example

An asset has a depreciable initial value of $1000 and a ten-year lifetime. Using a declining balance rate of 150 percent, the depreciation of the value of the asset in the fifth year can be expressed as

```
y5=DEPDBSL(5,1000,10,1.5);
```

The value returned is 87.00. The first and the third arguments are expressed in years.

DEPSL

Straight-line depreciation

Financial

HELP FUNCTION

Syntax

DEPSL(*p*,*v*,*y*)

Description

p is numeric, the period for which the calculation is to be done. For fractional *p*, the depreciation is prorated between the two consecutive time periods preceding and following the fractional period.

v is numeric, the depreciable initial value of the asset.

y is numeric, the lifetime of the asset, with $y>0$.

The DEPSL function returns the straight-line depreciation, given by

$$\text{DEPSL}(p,v,y) = \text{DACCSL}(p,v,y) - \text{DACCSL}(p-1,v,y) \quad .$$

The *p* and *y* arguments must be expressed using the same units of time.

Example

An asset, acquired on 01APR86, has a depreciable initial value of $1000 and a ten-year lifetime. The depreciation in the value of the asset for the year 1986 can be expressed as

```
d=DEPSL(9/12,1000,10);
```

The value returned is 75.00. The first and the third arguments are expressed in years.

DEPSYD

Sum-of-years-digits depreciation

Financial

HELP FUNCTION

Syntax

DEPSYD(*p*,*v*,*y*)

Description

p is numeric, the period for which the calculation is to be done. For noninteger *p* arguments, the depreciation is prorated between the two consecutive time periods preceding and following the fractional period.

v is numeric, the depreciable initial value of the asset.

y is numeric, the lifetime of the asset in number of depreciation periods, with $y>0$.

The DEPSYD function returns the sum-of-years-digits depreciation, given by

$$DEPSYD(p,v,y) = DACCSYD(p,v,y) - DACCSYD(p-1,v,y) \quad .$$

The *p* and *y* arguments must be expressed using the same units of time.

Examples

An asset, acquired on 01OCT86, has a depreciable initial value of $1000 and a five-year lifetime. The depreciations in the value of the asset for the years 1986 and 1987 can be expressed as

```
y1=DEPSYD(3/12,1000,5);
y2=DEPSYD(15/12,1000,5);
```

The values returned are 83.33 and 316.67, respectively. The first and the third arguments are expressed in years.

DEPTAB

Depreciation from specified tables

Financial

HELP FUNCTION

Syntax

DEPTAB(*p,v,t1, . . . ,tn*)

Description

p is numeric, the period for which the calculation is to be done. For noninteger *p* arguments, the depreciation is prorated between the two consecutive time periods preceding and following the fractional period.

v is numeric, the depreciable initial value of the asset.

t1, . . . ,tn are numeric, the fractions of depreciation for each time period.

The DEPTAB function returns the depreciation using specified tables, given by

$$DEPTAB(p,v,t_1, \ldots, t_n) = DACCTAB(p,v,t_1, \ldots, t_n) - DACCTAB(p-1,v,t_1, \ldots, t_n)$$

For a given *p*, only the arguments *t1, . . . ,tk* need to be specified with k=ceil(*p*).

Example

An asset has a depreciable initial value of $1000 and a five-year lifetime. Using a table of the annual depreciation rates of .15, .22, .21, .21, and .21 during the first, second, third, fourth, and fifth years, respectively, the depreciation in the third year can be expressed as

```
y3=deptab(3,1000,.15,.22,.21,.21,.21);
```

The value returned is 210.00.

DHMS

Returns a SAS datetime value from date, hour, minute, and second

Date and time

HELP FUNCTION

Syntax

DHMS(*date,hour,minute,second*)

Description

The DHMS function produces a SAS datetime value from numeric values that represent the date, hour, minute, and second.

You can use the following arguments with the DHMS function:

date specifies a SAS expression representing a SAS date value.

hour specifies a SAS expression representing an integer from 0 through 23.

minute specifies a SAS expression representing an integer from 0 through 59.

second specifies a SAS expression representing an integer from 0 through 59.

Example

The following statement illustrates how to use the DHMS function:

```
dtid=dhms('01jan89'd,15,30,15);
```

See Also

HMS function

"SAS Date and Time Values" in Chapter 4, "Rules of the SAS Language."

DIF

Difference with the *n*th lag

Special

HELP FUNCTION

Syntax

DIF<*n*>(*argument*)

Description

n specifies the number of lags.

argument is numeric.

The DIF functions, DIF1, DIF2, . . . , DIF100, return the first differences between the argument and its *n*th lag. DIF1 can also be written as DIF. DIF*n* is defined as

difn(x)=x-lagn(x) .

See the description of the LAG*n* family of functions for details on storing and returning values from the LAG*n* queue. The function DIF2(X) is not equivalent to the second difference DIF(DIF(X)).

Example

Consider this DATA step and the output that follows:

```
data two;
   input x @@;
   z=lag(x);
   d=dif(x);
   cards;
1 2 6 4 7
;

proc print;
run;
```

```
OBS     X          Z          D
 1      1          .          .
 2      2          1          1
 3      6          2          4
 4      4          6         -2
 5      7          4          3
```

DIGAMMA

Digamma function

Mathematical

HELP FUNCTION

Syntax

DIGAMMA(*argument*)

Description

argument is numeric. Nonpositive integers are invalid.

The DIGAMMA function returns the ratio, given by

$$\Psi(x) = \Gamma'(x) / \Gamma(x) \quad .$$

where $\Gamma(.)$ and $\Gamma'(.)$ denote the GAMMA function and its derivative, respectively. For *argument*>0, the DIGAMMA function is the derivative of the LGAMMA function.

Example

```
x=digamma(1);
```

The value returned is −0.57722, which is the negative of Euler's constant.

DIM

Returns the number of elements in an array

Arithmetic

HELP FUNCTION

Syntax

DIM<*n*>(*array-name*) | (*array-name, bound-n*)

Description

The DIM function returns the number of elements in a one-dimensional array or the number of elements in a specified dimension of a multidimensional array when the lower bound of the dimension is 1. Use the DIM function in array processing to avoid changing the upper bound of an iterative DO group each time you change the number of array elements.

You can use the following arguments with the DIM function:

n
: specifies the dimension, in a multidimensional array, for which you want to know the number of elements. For example, the following statement returns the number of elements in the second dimension of a multidimensional array called NAMES:

```
dim2(names)
```

If no *n* value is specified, the DIM function returns the number of elements in the first dimension of the array.

array-name
: specifies the name of an array previously defined in the same DATA step.

bound-n
: specifies the dimension, in a multidimensional array, for which you want to know the number of elements. Use *bound-n* only when *n* is not specified. For example, the following statement returns the number of elements in the second dimension of a multidimensional array called NAMES:

```
dim(names,2)
```

Comparisons

The DIM function always returns a total count of the number of elements in an array dimension, whereas the HBOUND function returns the literal value of the upper bound of an array dimension. This distinction is important when the lower bound of an array dimension has a value other than 1 and the upper bound has a value other than the total number of elements in the array dimension.

Examples

Example 1: One-dimensional Array

In the following statements, the DIM function returns a value of 5. Therefore, the SAS System repeats the statements in the DO loop five times.

```
array big{5} weight sex height state city;
do i=1 to dim(big);
   SAS statement;
end;
```

Example 2: Multidimensional Array

In the following example, the value of DIM(MULT) is 5, while DIM2(MULT) is 10, and DIM3(MULT) is 2. Using the alternate form produces the same results. The value of DIM(MULT,1) is 5, DIM(MULT,2) is 10, and DIM(MULT,3) is 2.

```
array mult{5,10,2} mult1-mult100;
```

See Also

HBOUND and LBOUND functions

"Array Processing" in Chapter 4, "Rules of the SAS Language"

Explicit ARRAY and explicit array reference in Chapter 9, "SAS Language Statements"

ERF

Error function

Mathematical

HELP FUNCTION

Syntax

ERF(*argument*)

Description

argument is numeric.

The ERF function returns the integral, given by

$$ERF(x) = 2/\sqrt{\pi}\int_0^x e^{-z^2}dz \; .$$

Examples

The ERF function can be used to find the probability (p) that a normally distributed random variable with mean 0 and standard deviation 1 will take on a value less than X. For example, the quantity given by

```
p=.5+.5*erf(x/sqrt(2));
```

is equivalent to PROBNORM(X). Consider the following examples:

- □ `y=erf(1);`
- □ `y=erf(-1);`

The values returned are 0.84270 and −0.84270, respectively.

ERFC

Complementary error function

Mathematical

HELP FUNCTION

Syntax

ERFC(*argument*)

Description

argument is numeric.

The ERFC function returns the complement to the ERF function (that is, 1−ERF(*argument*)).

EXP

Exponential function

Mathematical

HELP FUNCTION

Syntax

EXP(*argument*)

Description

argument is numeric.

The EXP function raises the constant *e*, approximately given by 2.71828, to the power supplied by the argument. The result is limited by the maximum value of a floating-point decimal value on the computer.

Examples

□ `y=exp(1);`

□ `y=exp(0);`

The values returned are 2.71828 and 1.00000, respectively.

FINV

Quantile from the *F* distribution

Quantile

HELP FUNCTION

Syntax

FINV(*p,ndf,ddf*<*,nc*>)

Description

p is a numeric probability, with $0<p<1$.

ndf is a numeric numerator degrees of freedom parameter, with $ndf>0$.

ddf is a numeric denominator degrees of freedom parameter, with $ddf>0$.

nc is an optional numeric noncentrality parameter, with $nc\geq 0$.

The FINV function returns the *p*th quantile from the *F* distribution with numerator degrees of freedom *ndf*, denominator degrees of freedom *ddf*, and noncentrality parameter *nc*. The probability that an observation from the *F* distribution is less than the quantile is *p*. This function accepts noninteger degrees of freedom parameters *ndf* and *ddf*. The FINV function is the inverse of the PROBF function.

If the optional parameter *nc* is not specified or has the value 0, the quantile from the central *F* distribution is returned. The noncentrality parameter *nc* is defined such that if X and Y are normal random variables with means μ and *0*, respectively, and variance 1, then X^2/Y^2 has a noncentral *F* distribution with $nc=\mu^2$. For large values of *nc*, the algorithm could fail; in that case, a missing value is returned.

Examples

□ `q1=finv(.95,2,10);`

□ `q2=finv(.95,2,10.3,2);`

The values returned are 4.1028 and 7.5838, respectively.

FIPNAME

Converts FIPS codes to state names (uppercase)

State and ZIP code

HELP FUNCTION

Syntax

FIPNAME(*expression*)

Description

The FIPNAME function converts a U.S. Federal Information Processing Standards (FIPS) code to the corresponding state name in uppercase, returning a value of up to 20 characters.

You can use the following argument with the FIPNAME function:

expression specifies a numeric expression representing a U.S. FIPS code.

Example

The following statements return the value **NORTH CAROLINA**:

```
x=fipname(37);
put x;
```

See Also

FIPNAMEL function

FIPNAMEL

Converts FIPS codes to state names in upper- and lowercase

State and ZIP code

HELP FUNCTION

Syntax

FIPNAMEL(*expression*)

Description

The FIPNAMEL function converts a U.S. Federal Information Processing Standards (FIPS) code to the corresponding state name in upper- and lowercase, returning values of up to 20 characters.

You can use the following argument with the FIPNAMEL function:

expression specifies a numeric expression representing a U.S. FIPS code.

Example

The following statements return the value `North Carolina`:

```
x=fipnamel(37);
put x;
```

See Also

FIPNAME function

FIPSTATE

Converts FIPS codes to two-character postal codes

State and ZIP code

HELP FUNCTION

Syntax

FIPSTATE(*expression*)

Description

The FIPSTATE function converts a U.S. Federal Information Processing Standards (FIPS) code to a two-character postal state code in uppercase.

You can use the following argument with the FIPSTATE function:

expression specifies a numeric expression representing a U.S. FIPS code.

Example

The following statements return the value `NC`:

```
x=fipstate(37);
put x;
```

See Also

STFIPS function

FLOOR

Largest integer that is less than or equal to the argument

Truncation

HELP FUNCTION

Syntax

FLOOR(*argument*)

Description

argument is numeric.

The FLOOR function returns the largest integer that is less than or equal to the argument. If the argument is within 10^{-12} of an integer, the function returns that integer.

Examples

□ `x=floor(2.1);`

□ `x=floor(-2.4);`

□ `x=floor(3);`

□ `x=floor(-1.6);`

□ `x=floor(1. -1.e-13);`

The values returned are 2, −3, 3, −2, and 1, respectively.

FUZZ

Nearest integer if the argument is within 1E−12

Truncation

HELP FUNCTION

Syntax

FUZZ(*argument*)

Description

argument is numeric.

The FUZZ function returns the nearest integer value if the argument is within 1E−12 of the integer (that is, if the absolute difference between the integer and argument is less than 1E−12). Otherwise, the argument is returned.

Examples

□ `x=fuzz(5.9999999999999);`

□ `x=fuzz(5.99999999);`

The values returned are 6.000000000000000 and 5.999999990000000, respectively.

GAMINV

Quantile from the gamma distribution

Quantile

HELP FUNCTION

Syntax

GAMINV(*p*,*a*)

Description

p is a numeric probability with $0<p<1$.

a is a numeric shape parameter, with $a>0$.

The GAMINV function returns the *p*th quantile from the gamma distribution, with shape parameter *a*. The probability that an observation from a gamma distribution is less than or equal to the returned quantile is *p*. The GAMINV function is the inverse of the PROBGAM function.

Examples

□ `x=gaminv(.5,9);`

□ `x=gaminv(.1,2.1);`

The values returned are 8.66895 and 0.58419, respectively.

GAMMA

Gamma function

Mathematical

HELP FUNCTION

Syntax

GAMMA(*argument*)

Description

argument is numeric. Nonpositive integers are invalid.

The GAMMA function returns the integral, given by

$$\text{GAMMA}(x) = \int_0^\infty t^{x-1} e^{-t} \, dt \quad .$$

For positive integers GAMMA(x) is (x −1)!. This function is commonly denoted by $\Gamma(x)$.

Example

```
x=gamma(6);
```

The value returned is 120.00000.

HBOUND

Returns the upper bound of an array

Arithmetic

HELP FUNCTION

Syntax

HBOUND<*n*>(*array-name*) | (*array-name, bound-n*)

Description

The HBOUND function returns the upper bound of a one-dimensional array or the upper bound of a specified dimension of a multidimensional array. Use the HBOUND function in array processing to avoid changing the upper bound of an iterative DO group each time you change the bounds of the array. The HBOUND and LBOUND functions can be used together to return the values of the upper and lower bounds of an array dimension.

You can use the following arguments with the HBOUND function:

n

specifies the dimension for which you want to know the upper bound. For example, the following statement returns the upper bound of the second dimension of a multidimensional array called ADDRESS:

```
hbound2(address);
```

If no *n* value is specified, the HBOUND function returns the upper bound of the first dimension of the array.

array-name

specifies the name of an array previously defined in the same DATA step.

bound-n

specifies the dimension for which you want to know the upper bound. Use *bound-n* only if *n* is not specified. For example, the following statement returns the upper bound of the second dimension of a multidimensional array called ADDRESS:

```
hbound(address,2);
```

Comparisons

The HBOUND function returns the literal value of the upper bound of an array dimension, whereas the DIM function returns a total count of the number of elements in an array dimension. This distinction is important when the lower bound of an array dimension has a value other than 1 and the upper bound has a value other than the total number of elements in the array dimension.

Examples

Example 1: One-dimensional Array

In the following statements, the HBOUND function returns the upper bound of the dimension, a value of 5. Therefore, the SAS System repeats the statements in the DO loop five times.

```
array big{5} weight sex height state city;
do i=1 to hbound(big);
   SAS statement;
end;
```

Example 2: Multidimensional Array

In the following example, the value of HBOUND(MULT) is 6, while HBOUND2(MULT) is 13, and HBOUND3(MULT) is 2. Using the alternate form produces the same results. The value of HBOUND(MULT,1) is 6, HBOUND(MULT,2) is 13, and HBOUND(MULT,3) is 2.

```
array mult{2:6,4:13,2} mult1-mult100;
```

See Also

DIM and LBOUND functions

"Array Processing," in Chapter 4, "Rules of the SAS Language"

Explicit ARRAY and Explicit array reference in Chapter 9, "SAS Language Statements"

HMS

Returns a SAS time value from hour, minute, and second values

Date and time

HELP FUNCTION

Syntax

HMS(*hour,minute,second*)

Description

The HMS function produces a SAS time value from hour, minute, and second values.

You can use the following arguments with the HMS function:

hour
: specifies a SAS expression representing an integer from 0 through 23.

minute
: specifies a SAS expression representing an integer from 0 through 59.

second
: specifies a SAS expression representing an integer from 0 through 59.

Example

The following statement illustrates how to use the HMS function:

```
hrid=hms(12,45,10);
```

See Also

DHMS, HOUR, MINUTE, and SECOND functions

"SAS Date and Time Values" in Chapter 4, "Rules of the SAS Language."

HOUR

Returns the hour from a SAS time or datetime value

Data and time

HELP FUNCTION

Syntax

HOUR(<*time* | *datetime*>)

Description

The HOUR function returns a numeric value representing the hour from a SAS time or datetime value. Numeric values can range from 0 through 23. The HOUR function always returns a positive number.

You can use the following arguments with the HOUR function:

time specifies a SAS expression representing a SAS time value.

datetime specifies a SAS expression representing a SAS datetime value.

Example

The following statements return a value of 1:

```
now='1:30't;
h=hour(now);
```

See Also

MINUTE and SECOND functions

"SAS Date and Time Values" in Chapter 4, "Rules of the SAS Language."

INDEX

Searches the source for the character string specified by the excerpt

Character

HELP FUNCTION

Syntax

INDEX(*source*,*excerpt*)

Description

The INDEX function searches *source* for a specific character string and returns the position of its first character.

You can use the following arguments with the INDEX function:

source identifies the character expression to search.

excerpt identifies the character string to search for in a character expression.

The INDEX function searches *source*, from left to right, for the first occurrence of the string specified in *excerpt* and returns the position in *source* of the string's first character. If the string is not found in *source*, INDEX returns a value of 0.

Example

The following statements return the value 10:

```
a='ABC.DEF (X=Y)';
b='X=Y';
x=index(a,b);
put x;
```

See Also

INDEXC function

INDEXC

Locates the first occurrence in the source of characters present in any of the excerpts

Character

HELP FUNCTION

Syntax

INDEXC(*source,excerpt-1*<, . . . *excerpt-n*>)

Description

The INDEXC function searches *source*, from left to right, for the first occurrence of any character present in other specified arguments and returns an integer representing the position in *source* of the character found. INDEXC returns a value of 0 if it finds none of the characters in *excerpt-1* through *excerpt-n* in *source*.

You can use the following arguments with the INDEXC function:

source
: identifies the SAS character expression to search.

<*excerpt-1, . . . excerpt-n*>
: identifies characters for which to search.

Example

The following statements return the value 4:

```
a='ABC.DEP (X2=Y1)';
x=indexc(a,'0123456789',';()=. ');
put x;
```

See Also

INDEX function

INPUT

Returns the value produced when a SAS expression is read using a specified informat

Special

HELP FUNCTION

Syntax

INPUT(*source*, <? | ??> *informat*)

Description

The INPUT function enables you to read the value of *source* using a specified informat. The informat determines whether the result is numeric or character.

You can use the INPUT function to convert character values to numeric values. By specifying a character informat with a numeric value, you can also convert numeric values to character. However, you should not use the INPUT function to do this. Instead, use the PUT function to convert numeric values to character values.

You can use the following arguments with the INPUT function:

source
: contains the SAS expression to which you want to apply a specific informat. *Source* can be character or numeric.

?
??
: The optional question mark (?) and double question mark (??) format modifiers suppress the printing of both the error messages and the input lines when invalid data values are read. The ? modifier suppresses the invalid data message. The ?? modifier also supresses the invalid data message and, in addition, prevents the automatic variable _ERROR_ from being set to 1 when invalid data are read.

informat
: is the SAS informat you want to apply to the source.

Comparisons

The INPUT function is similar to reading in data using informats with the INPUT statement. The INPUT function returns the value produced when a SAS expression is read using a specified informat. You store the value in a variable using an assignment statement. With formatted input, you specify an informat after the variable name in the INPUT statement; then the SAS System reads the variable using the informat.

Examples

Example 1: Converting Character Values to Numeric Values

The following example uses the INPUT function to convert a character value to a numeric value and store it in another variable. The COMMA9. informat reads the value of the SALE variable, stripping the commas. The resulting value, 2115353, is stored in FMTSALE.

```
data testin;
   input sale $9.;
   fmtsale=input(sale,comma9.);
   cards;
2,115,353
;
```

Example 2: Using PUT and INPUT Functions

In this example, the PUT function returns a numeric value as a character string. The value 122591 is assigned to the CHARDATE variable. Then, the INPUT function returns the value of the character string as a SAS date value using a SAS data informat. The value 11681 is stored in the SASDATE variable.

```
numdate=122591;
chardate=put(numdate,z6.);
sasdate=input(chardate,mmddyy6.);
```

Example 3: Suppressing Error Messages

In the following example, the question mark (?) format modifier tells the SAS System not to print the invalid data error message if it finds data errors. The automatic variable _ERROR_ is set to 1 and input data lines are written to the SAS log.

```
y=input(x,? 3.1);
```

Because the double question mark (??) format modifier suppresses printing of error messages and input lines and prevents the automatic variable _ERROR_ from being set to 1 when invalid data are read, the following two examples produce the same result:

- `y=input(x,?? 2.);`
- `y=input(x,? 2.);`
  `_error_=0;`

See Also

PUT function

INPUT statement in Chapter 9, "SAS Language Statements"

Chapter 13, "SAS Informats"

INT

Integer value

Truncation

HELP FUNCTION

Syntax

INT(*argument*)

Description

argument is numeric.

The INT function returns the integer portion of the argument (truncates the decimal portion). If the argument's value is within 10^{-12} of an integer, the function results in that integer. If the value of *argument* is positive, INT(*argument*) has the same result as FLOOR(*argument*). If the value of *argument* is negative, INT(*argument*) has the same result as CEIL(*argument*).

Examples

```
□ x=int(2.1);
□ x=int(-2.4);
□ x=int(3);
□ x=int(-1.6);
```

The values returned are 2, −2, 3, and −1, respectively.

INTCK

Returns the number of time intervals in a given time span

Date and time

HELP FUNCTION

Syntax

INTCK(*interval,from,to*)

Description

The INTCK function returns an integer representing the number of time intervals that occur in a given time span.

You can use the following arguments with the INTCK function:

interval
: specifies a character constant or variable. *Interval* can appear in upper- or lowercase.

  The type of interval must match the type of value in *from* and *to*. For example, you use

  □ date intervals when *from* and *to* contain date values.

  □ datetime intervals when *from* and *to* contain datetime values.

  □ time intervals when *from* and *to* contain time values.

  The value of the character constant or variable must be one of those listed in the following table:

Date Intervals	Datetime Intervals	Time Intervals
DAY	DTDAY	HOUR
WEEK	DTWEEK	MINUTE
MONTH	DTMONTH	SECOND
QTR	DTQTR	
YEAR	DTYEAR	

from
: specifies a SAS expression representing a SAS date, time, or datetime value that identifies the beginning of a specified time span.

to
: specifies a SAS expression representing a SAS date, time, or datetime value that identifies the end of a specified time span.

The INTCK function counts intervals from fixed interval beginnings, not in multiples of an interval unit from the *from* value. Partial intervals are not counted. For example, WEEK intervals are counted by Sundays rather than seven-day multiples from the *from* argument. YEAR intervals are counted from 01JAN, not in 365-day multiples.

Examples

The following statements illustrate the INTCK function:

- □ `qtr=intck('qtr','10jan90'd,'01jul90'd);`
- □ `date=intck('year','31dec89'd,'1jan90'd);`
- □ `year=intck('year','1jan89'd,'31dec89'd);`

The SAS System returns a value of 2 in the first example. A value of 1 is returned in the second example, even though only one day has elapsed. An 01JAN date is counted between the *from* and *to* values, so a YEAR interval is added. In the third example, 01JAN is not counted between the *from* and *to* values, so an interval is not added. The third example returns a value of 0, even though 364 days have elapsed.

See Also

INTNX function

"SAS Date and Time Values" in Chapter 4, "Rules of the SAS Language."

INTNX

Advances a date, time, or datetime value by a given interval

Date and time

HELP FUNCTION

Syntax

INTNX(*interval,from,number*)

Description

The INTNX function generates a SAS date, time, or datetime value that is a given number of time intervals from a starting value, indicated by *from*.

You can use the following arguments with the INTNX function:

interval specifies a character constant or variable. *Interval* can appear in upper- or lowercase.

The type of interval must match the type of value in *from* and *number*. For example, you use

- □ date intervals when *from* contains date values.
- □ datetime intervals when *from* contains datetime values.
- □ time intervals when *from* contains time values.

(interval continued)

The value of the character constant or variable must be one of those listed in the following table:

Date Intervals	Datetime Intervals	Time Intervals
DAY	DTDAY	HOUR
WEEK	DTWEEK	MINUTE
MONTH	DTMONTH	SECOND
QTR	DTQTR	
YEAR	DTYEAR	

from specifies a SAS expression representing a SAS date, time, or datetime value identifying a starting point.

number specifies a negative or positive integer representing the specific number of time *intervals.*

The INTNX function counts intervals from fixed interval beginnings, not in multiples of an interval unit from the *from* value. Therefore, month intervals are counted from the beginning of the month, and year intervals are counted from 01JAN.

Examples

The following examples produce values equivalent to January 1, 1992 and January 1, 1990:

□ `yr=intnx('year','05feb89'd,3);`

□ `x=intnx('month','05jan90'd,0);`

See Also

INTCK function

"SAS Date and Time Values" in Chapter 4, "Rules of the SAS Language."

INTRR

The internal rate of return as a fraction

Financial

HELP FUNCTION

Syntax

INTRR(*freq,c0,c1, . . . ,cn*)

Description

freq

is numeric, the number of payments over a specified base period of time associated with the desired internal rate of return, with *freq*>0. The case *freq*=0 is a flag to allow continuous compounding.

c0,c1, . . . ,cn

are numeric, the optional cash payments.

The INTRR function returns the internal rate of return over a specified base period of time for the set of cash payments *c0,c1, . . . ,cn*. The time intervals between two consecutive payments are assumed to be equal. The argument *freq*>0 describes the number payments occurring over the specified base period of time.

The internal rate of return is the interest rate such that the sequence of payments has a 0 net present value (see the NETPV function). It is given by

$$r = \begin{cases} \dfrac{1}{x^{\text{freq}}} - 1 & \text{freq} > 0 \\ -\log_e x & \text{freq} = 0 \end{cases}$$

where x is the real root, nearest to 1, of the polynomial

$$\sum_{i=0}^{n} c_i x^i = 0 \quad .$$

The routine uses Newton's method to look for the internal rate of return nearest to 0. Depending on the value of payments, a root for the equation does not always exist; in that case, a missing value is returned.

Missing values in the payments are treated as 0 values. When *freq*>0, the computed rate of return is the effective rate over the specified base period. To compute a quarterly internal rate of return (the base period is three months) with monthly payments, set *freq* to 3.

If *freq* is 0, continuous compounding is assumed and the base period is the time interval between two consecutive payments. The computed internal rate of return is the nominal rate of return over the base period. To compute with continuous compounding and monthly payments, set *freq* to 0. The computed internal rate of return will be a monthly rate.

Example

For an initial outlay of $400 and expected payments of $100, $200, and $300 over the following three years, the annual internal rate of return can be expressed as

```
rate=intrr(1,-400,100,200,300);
```

The value returned is 0.19438.

IRR

The internal rate of return as a percentage

Financial

HELP FUNCTION

Syntax

IRR(*freq,c0,c1, . . . ,cn*)

Description

freq
: is numeric, the number of payments over a specified base period of time associated with the desired internal rate of return, with *freq*>0. The case *freq*=0 is a flag to allow continuous compounding.

c0,c1, . . . ,cn
: are numeric, the optional cash payments.

The IRR function is identical to INTRR, described earlier, except that the rate returned is a percentage.

JULDATE

Returns the Julian date from a SAS date value

Date and time

HELP FUNCTION

Syntax

JULDATE(*date*)

Description

The JULDATE function converts a SAS date value to a numeric value representing a Julian date.

You can use the following argument with the JULDATE function:

date
: specifies a SAS date value to be converted to a five- or seven-digit Julian date. If *date* falls within the 100-year span defined by the YEARCUTOFF= system option, the result has five digits; the first two are the year, and the next three are the day of the year. Otherwise, the SAS System returns seven digits; the first four are the year, and the next three are the day of the year. Thus, 1JAN89 is 89001 in Julian representation; 31DEC1878 is 1878365.

The YEARCUTOFF= system option defines the year value.

Examples

The following statements return values corresponding to December 31, 1988 and January 1, 2001:

□ `julian=juldate('31dec88'd);`

□ `julian=juldate(01jan2001'd);`

See Also

DATEJUL function

"SAS Date and Time Values" in Chapter 4, "Rules of the SAS Language"

YEARCUTOFF= system option in Chapter 16, "SAS System Options"

KURTOSIS

Kurtosis or 4th moment

Sample statistics

HELP FUNCTION

Syntax

KURTOSIS(*argument*,*argument*, . . .)

Description

argument is numeric. At least four arguments are required. The argument list may consist of a variable list, preceded by OF. See "Using Function Arguments" in Chapter 3, "Components of the SAS Language."

The KURTOSIS function returns the kurtosis statistic of the nonmissing arguments.

Examples

□ `x1=kurtosis(5,9,3,6);`

□ `x2=kurtosis(5,8,9,6,.);`

□ `x3=kurtosis(8,9,6,1);`

□ `x4=kurtosis(8,1,6,1);`

□ `x5=kurtosis(of x1-x4);`

The values returned are 0.92800, −3.30000, 1.50000, −4.48338, and −5.06569, respectively.

LAG

Lagged values from a queue

Special

HELP FUNCTION

Syntax

LAG<*n*>(*argument*)

Description

n
: specifies the number of lagged values.

argument
: is numeric or character.

The LAG functions, LAG1, LAG2, . . . , LAG100 return values from a queue. LAG1 can also be written as LAG. A LAG*n* function stores a value in a queue and returns a value stored previously in that queue. Each occurrence of a LAG*n* function in a program generates its own queue of values.

The queue for a LAG*n* function is initialized with *n* missing values, where *n* is the length of the queue (for example, a LAG2 queue is initialized with two missing values). When the LAG*n* function is executed, the value at the top of the queue is removed and returned, the remaining values are shifted upwards, and the new value of the argument is placed at the bottom of the queue. Hence, missing values are returned for the first *n* executions of a LAG*n* function, after which the lagged values of the argument begin to appear.

Storing values at the bottom of the queue and returning values from the top of the queue occurs only when the function is executed. A LAG*n* function that is executed conditionally will store and return only values from the observations for which the condition is satisfied.

If the argument of a LAG*n* function is an array name, a separate queue is maintained for each variable in the array.

Examples

Consider the following DATA and PROC steps:

```
data one;
   input x @@;
   y=lag1(x);
   z=lag2(x);
   cards;
1 2 3 4 5 6
;

proc print;
   title 'Lag Output';
run;
```

This data set contains the values for X, Y, and Z as shown below:

```
    Lag Output

OBS    X    Y    Z

 1     1    .    .
 2     2    1    .
 3     3    2    1
 4     4    3    2
 5     5    4    3
 6     6    5    4
```

The LAG1 function returns one missing value and the values of X (lagged once); the LAG2 function returns two missing values and then the values of X (lagged twice).

LBOUND

Returns the lower bound of an array

Arithmetic

HELP FUNCTION

Syntax

LBOUND<*n*>(*array-name*) | (*array-name*, *bound-n*)

Description

The LBOUND function returns the lower bound of a one-dimensional array or the lower bound of a specified dimension of a multidimensional array. Use the LBOUND function in array processing to avoid changing the lower bound of an iterative DO group each time you change the bounds of the array. The LBOUND and HBOUND functions can be used together to return the values of the lower and upper bounds of an array dimension.

You can use the following arguments with the LBOUND function:

n
: specifies the dimension for which you want to know the lower bound. For example, the following statement returns the lower bound of the second dimension of a multidimensional array named ADDRESS:

```
lbound2(address)
```

If no *n* value is specified, the LBOUND function returns the lower bound of the first dimension of the array.

array-name
: specifies the name of an array previously defined in the same DATA step.

bound-n
: specifies the dimension for which you want to know the lower bound. Use *bound-n* only if *n* is not specified. For example, the following statement returns the lower bound of the second dimension of a multidimensional array named ADDRESS:

```
lbound(address,2)
```

Examples

Example 1: One-dimensional Array

In the following statements, the LBOUND function returns the lower bound of the dimension, a value of 2. Therefore, the SAS System repeats the statements in the DO loop five times.

```
array big{2:6} weight sex height state city;
do i=lbound(big) to hbound(big);
   more SAS statements;
end;
```

Example 2: Multidimensional Array

In the following example, the value of LBOUND(MULT) is 2, while LBOUND2(MULT) is 4, and LBOUND3(MULT) is 1. Using the alternate form produces the same results. LBOUND(MULT,1) is 2, LBOUND(MULT,2) is 4, and LBOUND(MULT,3) is 1.

```
array mult{2:6,4:13,2} mult1-mult100;
```

See Also

DIM and HBOUND functions

"Array Processing" in Chapter 4, "Rules of the SAS Language"

Explicit ARRAY and explicit array reference in Chapter 9, "SAS Language Statements"

LEFT

Left aligns a SAS character expression

Character

HELP FUNCTION

Syntax

LEFT(*argument*)

Description

The LEFT function returns an argument with leading blanks moved to the end of the value. The argument's length does not change.

You can use the following argument with the LEFT function:

argument specifies any valid SAS character expression.

Example

The following statements produce a character string with `DUE DATE` shifted left three spaces, with trailing blanks instead of leading blanks.

```
a='   DUE DATE';
b=left(a);
```

See Also

COMPRESS function

RIGHT function

TRIM function

LENGTH

Returns the length of an argument

Character

HELP FUNCTION

Syntax

LENGTH(*argument*)

Description

The LENGTH function returns the length of an argument. The result is an integer representing the position of the right-most nonblank character in the argument. If the value of the argument is missing, LENGTH returns a value of 1. If the argument is an uninitialized numeric variable, LENGTH returns a value of 12.

You can use the following argument with the LENGTH function:

argument specifies any valid SAS character expression.

Example

The following statements return the value `6`:

```
len=length('ABCDEF');
put len;
```

LGAMMA

Natural logarithm of the GAMMA function

Mathematical

HELP FUNCTION

Syntax

LGAMMA(*argument*)

Description

argument is numeric and positive.

The LGAMMA function returns the natural logarithm of the GAMMA function of the argument (see the GAMMA function).

Examples

□ `x=lgamma(2);`

□ `x=lgamma(1.5);`

The values returned are 0.00000 and −0.12078, respectively.

LOG

Natural logarithm

Mathematical

HELP FUNCTION

Syntax

LOG(*argument*)

Description

argument is numeric and positive. The LOG function returns the natural (Naperian) logarithm of the argument.

The base *e* of the natural logarithm is approximately 2.71828.

Examples

□ `x=log(1);`

□ `x=log(10);`

The values returned are 0.00000 and 2.30259, respectively.

LOG10

Logarithm to the base 10

Mathematical

HELP FUNCTION

Syntax

LOG10(*argument*)

Description

argument is numeric and postive.

The LOG10 function returns the common logarithm (log to the base 10) of the argument.

Examples

```
□ x=log10(1);
□ x=log10(10);
□ x=log10(100);
```

The values returned are 0.00000, 1.00000, and 2.00000, respectively.

LOG2

Logarithm to the base 2

Mathematical

HELP FUNCTION

Syntax

LOG2(*argument*)

Description

argument is numeric and positive.

The LOG2 function returns the logarithm to the base 2 of the argument.

Examples

```
□ x=log2(2);
□ x=log2(.5);
```

The values returned are 1.00000 and −1.00000, respectively.

MAX

Largest value

Sample statistics

HELP FUNCTION

Syntax

MAX(*argument,argument, . . .*)

Description

argument is numeric. At least two arguments are required. The argument list may consist of a variable list, preceded by OF. See "Using Function Arguments" in Chapter 3.

The MAX function returns the largest of the nonmissing arguments.

Examples

```
□ x1=max(2,6,.);
□ x2=max(2,-3,1,-1);
□ x3=max(3,.,-3);
□ x4=max(of x1-x3);
```

The values returned are 6.00000, 2.00000, 3.00000, and 6.00000, respectively.

Note that the MAX function does not necessarily return the same value as the MAX operator described in Chapter 3.

MDY

Returns a SAS date value from month, day, and year values

Date and time

HELP FUNCTION

Syntax

MDY(*month,day,year*)

Description

The MDY function produces a SAS date value from numeric expressions that represent the month, day, and year.

You can use the following arguments with the MDY function:

month
: specifies a numeric expression representing an integer from 1 through 12.

day
: specifies a numeric expression representing an integer from 1 through 31.

year
: specifies a numeric expression representing an integer identifying a specific year. Use the YEARCUTOFF= system option to define the year range.

Example

The following statements produce a SAS date value corresponding to August 27, 1990 for BIRTHDAY:

```
m=8;
d=27;
y=90;
birthday=mdy(m,d,y);
put birthday=worddate.;
```

See Also

DAY, MONTH, and YEAR functions

"SAS Date and Time Values" in Chapter 4, "Rules of the SAS Language."

MEAN

Arithmetic mean or average

Sample statistics

HELP FUNCTION

Syntax

MEAN(*argument,argument*, . . .)

Description

argument
: is numeric. At least one argument is required. The argument list may consist of a variable list, preceded by OF. See "Using Function Arguments" in Chapter 3.

The MEAN function returns the average of the nonmissing arguments.

Examples

```
□ x1=mean(2,.,.,6);
□ x2=mean(1,2,3,2);
□ x3=mean(of x1-x2);
```

The values returned are 4.00000, 2.00000, and 3.00000, respectively.

MIN

Smallest value

Sample statistics

HELP FUNCTION

Syntax

MIN(*argument*,*argument*, . . .)

Description

argument is numeric. At least two arguments are required. The argument list may consist of a variable list, preceded by OF. See "Using Function Arguments" in Chapter 3.

The MIN function returns the smallest value of the nonmissing arguments.

Examples

```
□ x1=min(2,.,6);
□ x2=min(2,-3,1,-1);
□ x3=min(0,4);
□ x4=min(of x1-x3);
```

The values returned are 2.00000, −3.00000, 0.00000, and −3.00000, respectively.

Note that the MIN function does not necessarily return the same value as the MIN operator described in Chapter 3.

MINUTE

Returns the minute from a SAS time or datetime value

Date and time

HELP FUNCTION

Syntax

MINUTE(<*time* | *datetime*>)

Description

The MINUTE function returns an integer representing a specific minute of the hour. MINUTE always returns a positive number.

You can use the following arguments with the MINUTE function:

time specifies a SAS expression representing a SAS time value.

datetime specifies a SAS expression representing a SAS datetime value.

Example

The following statements produce a value of 19 for M:

```
time='3:19:24't;
m=minute(time);
```

See Also

HOUR and SECOND functions

"SAS Date and Time Values" in Chapter 4, "Rules of the SAS Language"

MOD

Remainder value

Arithmetic

HELP FUNCTION

Syntax

MOD(*argument-1,argument-2*)

Description

argument-1 is numeric.

argument-2 is numeric and cannot be 0.

The MOD function returns the remainder when the integer quotient of *argument-1* divided by *argument-2* is calculated.

Examples

□ `x=mod(6,3);`

□ `x=mod(10,3);`

□ `x=mod(11,3.5);`

□ `x=mod(10,-3);`

The values returned are 0.00000, 1.00000, 0.50000, and 1.00000, respectively.

MONTH

Returns the month from a SAS date value

Date and time

HELP FUNCTION

Syntax

MONTH(*date*)

Description

The MONTH function returns a numeric value representing the month from a SAS date value. Numeric values can range from 1 through 12.

You can use the following argument with the MONTH function:

date specifies a SAS expression representing a SAS date value.

Example

The following statements produce a value of 1 for M:

```
date='25jan89'd;
m=month(date);
```

See Also

DAY and YEAR functions

"SAS Date and Time Values" in Chapter 4, "Rules of the SAS Language."

MORT

Amortization parameters

Financial

HELP FUNCTION

Syntax

MORT(*a*,*p*,*r*,*n*)

Description

a is numeric, the initial amount.

p is numeric, the periodic payment.

r is numeric, the periodic interest rate expressed as a fraction.

n is an integer, the number of compounding periods, with $n \geq 0$.

The MORT function returns the missing argument in the list of four arguments from an amortization calculation with a fixed interest rate compounded each period. The arguments are related by

$$p = \frac{ar(1+r)^n}{(1+r)^n - 1} \quad .$$

One missing argument must be provided. It is then calculated from the remaining three. No adjustment is made to convert the results to round numbers.

Example

An amount of $50,000 is borrowed for 30 years at an annual interest rate of 10 percent compounded monthly. The monthly payment can be expressed as

```
payment=mort(50000, . ,.10/12,30*12);
```

The value returned is 438.79. The second argument has been set to missing, indicating that the future value is to be calculated. The 10 percent nominal annual rate has been converted to a monthly rate of 0.10/12. The rate is the fractional (not the precentage) interest rate per compounding period. The 30 years are converted into 30*12 months.

N

Number of nonmissing values

Sample statistics

HELP FUNCTION

Syntax

N(*argument*,*argument*, . . .)

Description

argument is numeric. At least one argument is required. The argument list may consist of a variable list, preceded by OF. See "Using Function Arguments" in Chapter 3.

The N function returns the number of nonmissing values in the list of arguments.

Examples

```
□ x1=n(1,0,.,2,5,.);
□ x2=n(1,2);
□ x3=n(of x1-x2);
```

The values returned are 4, 2, and 2, respectively.

NETPV

The net present value as a fraction

Financial

HELP FUNCTION

Syntax

NETPV(*r*,*freq*,*c0*,*c1*, . . . ,*cn*)

Description

r
: is numeric, the interest rate over a specifed base period of time expressed as a fraction.

freq
: is numeric, the number of payments during the base period of time specified with the rate *r*, with *freq*>0. The case *freq*=0 is a flag to allow continuous discounting.

c0,*c1*, . . . ,*cn*
: are optional numeric cash payments.

The NETPV function returns the net present value for the set of cash payments *c0*,*c1*, . . . ,*cn* with a rate *r* over a specified base period of time. The time intervals between two consecutive payments are assumed to be equal. The argument *freq*>0 describes the number of payments occurring over the specified base period of time.

The net present value is given by

$$\text{NETPV}\ (r,freq,c_0,c_1,\ldots,c_n) = \sum_{i=0}^{n} c_i x^i,$$

where

$$x = \begin{cases} 1/(1+r)^{(1/freq)} & freq > 0 \\ e^{-r} & freq = 0 \end{cases} .$$

Missing values in the payments are treated as 0 values. When *freq*>0, the rate *r* is the effective rate over the specified base period. To compute with a quarterly rate (the base period is three months) of 4 percent with monthly cash payments, set *freq* to 3 and set *r* to .04.

If *freq* is 0, continuous discounting is assumed. The base period is the time interval between two consecutive payments, and the rate *r* is a nominal rate.

To compute with a nominal annual interest rate of 11 percent discounted continuously with monthly payments, set *freq* to 0 and set *r* to .11/12.

Example

For an initial investment of $500 that returns biannual payments of $200, $300, and $400 over the succeeding 6 years and an annual discount rate of 10 percent, the net present value of the investment can be expressed as

```
value=netpv(.10,.5,-500,200,300,400);
```

The value returned is 95.98.

NMISS

Number of missing values

Sample statistics

HELP FUNCTION

Syntax

NMISS(*argument,argument, . . .*)

Description

argument is numeric. At least one argument is required. The argument list may consist of a variable list, preceded by OF. See "Using Function Arguments" in Chapter 3.

The NMISS function returns the number of missing values in the list of arguments.

Examples

□ `x1=nmiss(1,0,.,2,5,.);`

□ `x2=nmiss(1,0);`

□ `x3=nmiss(of x1-x2);`

The values returned are 2, 0, and 0, respectively.

NORMAL

Random variate from a normal distribution

Random number

HELP FUNCTION

Syntax

NORMAL(*seed*)

Description

seed is an integer $<2^{31}-1$. (See "Notes on Random Number Functions" in Chapter 3 for a complete discussion of *seed*.) If *seed*$\leq$0, the time of day is used to initialize the seed stream.

The NORMAL function returns a variate generated from a normal distribution with mean 0 and variance 1. The Box-Muller transformation of RANUNI uniform variates is used.

A *normal variate* X with mean MU and variance SIGMASQ can be generated as follows:

```
x=mu+sqrt(sigmasq)*normal(seed);
```

A *lognormal variate* X with mean

exp(MU + SIGMASQ / 2)

and variance

exp(2*MU + 2*SIGMASQ) − exp(2*MU + SIGMASQ)

can be generated as follows:

```
x=exp(mu+sqrt(sigmasq)*normal(seed));
```

The NORMAL function is identical to the RANNOR function.

NPV

Net present value with the rate expressed as a percentage

Financial

HELP FUNCTION

Syntax

NPV(*r,freq,c0,c1, . . . ,cn*)

Description

r
: is numeric, the interest rate over a specifed base period of time expressed as a percentage.

freq
: is numeric, the number of payments during the base period of time specified with the rate *r*, with *freq*>0. The case *freq*=0 is a flag to allow continuous discounting.

c0,c1, . . . ,cn
: are optional numeric cash payments.

The NPV function is identical to NETPV, described earlier, except that the *r* argument is provided as a percentage.

ORDINAL

Largest value of a part of a list

Sample statistics

HELP FUNCTION

Syntax

ORDINAL(*count,argument,argument*, . . .)

Description

count is an integer less than the number of elements in the list of arguments.

argument is numeric. At least two arguments are required. The argument list may consist of a variable list, preceded by OF. See "Using Function Arguments" in Chapter 3.

The ORDINAL function returns the count*th* largest of the arguments, beginning from the lowest value.

Example

```
x1=ordinal(4,1,2,3,-4,5,6,7);
```

The value returned is 3.

POISSON

Probability from the Poisson distribution

Probability

HELP FUNCTION

Syntax

POISSON(*m,n*)

Description

m is a numeric mean parameter, with $m \geq 0$.

n is an integer random variable, with $n \geq 0$.

The POISSON function returns the probability that an observation from a Poisson distribution, with mean *m*, is less than or equal to *n*. This function is given by

$$Q_p(m,n) = \sum_{j=0}^{n} e^{-m} \frac{m^j}{j!} \ .$$

To compute the probability that an observation is equal to a given value, *n*, compute the difference of two probabilities from the Poisson distribution, given by

$$Q_p(m,n) - Q_p(m,n-1) \ .$$

Example

```
p=poisson(1,2);
```

The value returned is 0.91970.

PROBBETA

Probability from the beta distribution

Probability

HELP FUNCTION

Syntax

PROBBETA(x,a,b)

Description

x is a numeric random variable, with $0 \le x \le 1$.

a is a numeric shape parameter, with $a > 0$.

b is a numeric shape parameter, with $b > 0$.

The PROBBETA function returns the probability that an observation from a beta distribution, with shape parameters a and b, is less than or equal to x. This function is given by

$$I_x(a,b) = \frac{1}{\frac{\Gamma(a)\Gamma(b)}{\Gamma(a+b)}} \int_0^x t^{a-1}(1-t)^{b-1}\,dt$$

where $\Gamma(.)$ is the GAMMA function.

The BETAINV function is the inverse of the PROBBETA function.

The PROBBETA function is related to many of the common distributions of statistics and also has applications in analyzing order statistics (see Michael and Schucany 1979).

Example

```
p=probbeta(.2,3,4);
```

The value returned is 0.09888.

PROBBNML

Probability from the binomial distribution

Probability

HELP FUNCTION

Syntax

PROBBNML(p,n,m)

Description

p is a numeric probability of success parameter, with $0 \le p \le 1$.

n is an integer number of independent Bernoulli trials parameter, with $n > 0$.

m is an integer number of successes random variable, with $0 \le m \le n$.

The PROBBNML function returns the probability that an observation from a binomial distribution, with probability of success p, number of trials n, and number of successes m, is less than or equal to m. This function is given by

$$Q_b(p,n,m) = \sum_{j=0}^{m} \binom{n}{j} p^j (1-p)^{n-j}$$

To compute the probability that an observation is equal to a given value *m*, compute the difference of two probabilities from the binomial distribution, given by

$$Q_b(p,n,m) - Q_b(p,n,m-1) \quad .$$

Example

```
p=probbnml(0.5,10,4);
```

The value returned is 0.37695.

PROBCHI

Probability from the chi-square distribution

Probability

HELP FUNCTION

Syntax

PROBCHI(*x*,*df*<,*nc*>)

Description

x is a numeric random variable, with $x \geq 0$.

df is a numeric degrees of freedom parameter, with $df > 0$.

nc is an optional numeric noncentrality parameter, with $nc \geq 0$.

The PROBCHI function returns the probability that an observation from a chi-square distribution, with degrees of freedom *df* and noncentrality parameter *nc*, is less than or equal to *x*. This function accepts a noninteger degrees of freedom parameter *df*. If the optional parameter *nc* is not specified or has the value 0, the value returned is from the central chi-square distribution. The function is given by

$$P_c(x \mid df,nc) = e^{\frac{-nc}{2}} \sum_{j=0}^{\infty} \frac{\left(\frac{nc}{2}\right)^j}{j!} P_c(x \mid df + 2j)$$

or

$$P_c(x \mid df,nc) = e^{\frac{-nc}{2}} \sum_{j=0}^{\infty} \frac{\left(\frac{nc}{2}\right)^j}{j!} P_g\left(\frac{x}{2} \middle| \frac{df}{2} + j\right)$$

where $P_c(.|.)$ denotes the central chi-square probability function, given by

$$P_c(x|a) = P_g(x/2 \;|a/2)$$

and $P_g(.|.)$ is the probability from the gamma distribution.

The CINV function is the inverse of the PROBCHI function. The significance level for a chi-square test statistic is given by

```
p=1-probchi(x,df);
```

Example

```
p=probchi(11.264,11);
```

The value returned is 0.57858.

PROBF

Probability from the F distribution

Probability

HELP FUNCTION

Syntax

PROBF(*x,ndf,ddf*<*,nc*>)

Description

x is a numeric random variable, with $x \geq 0$.

ndf is a numeric numerator degrees of freedom parameter, with $ndf > 0$.

ddf is a numeric denominator degrees of freedom parameter, with $ddf > 0$.

nc is an optional numeric noncentrality parameter, with $nc \geq 0$.

The PROBF function returns the probability that an observation from an *F* distribution, with numerator degrees of freedom *ndf*, denominator degrees of freedom *ddf*, and noncentrality parameter *nc*, is less than or equal to *x*. The function accepts noninteger degrees of freedom parameters *ndf* and *ddf*. If the optional parameter *nc* is not specified or has the value 0, the value returned is from the central *F* distribution. This function is given by

$$P_f(x \mid ndf,ddf,nc) = e^{\frac{-nc}{2}} \sum_{j=0}^{\infty} \frac{\left(\frac{nc}{2}\right)^j}{j!} I_{\frac{(ndf)x}{ddf+(ndf)x}} \left(\frac{ndf}{2} + j, \frac{ddf}{2} \right)$$

where $I_.(.,.)$ is the beta distribution function.

The FINV function is the inverse of the PROBF function. The significance level for an *F* test statistic is given by

```
p=1-probf(x,ndf,ddf);
```

Example

```
p=probf(3.32,2,3);
```

The value returned is 0.82639.

PROBGAM

Probability from the gamma distribution

Probability

HELP FUNCTION

Syntax

PROBGAM(*x*,*a*)

Description

x is a numeric random variable, with $x \geq 0$.

a is a numeric shape parameter, with $a > 0$.

The PROBGAM function returns the probability that an observation from a gamma distribution, with shape parameter a, is less than or equal to *x*. The function is given by

$$P_g(x \mid a) = \frac{1}{\Gamma(a)} \int_0^x t^{a-1} e^{-t}\, dt$$

where Γ(.) is the GAMMA function.

The GAMINV function is the inverse of the PROBGAM function.

Example

```
p=probgam(1,3);
```

The value returned is 0.08030.

PROBHYPR

Probability from the hypergeometric distribution

Probability

HELP FUNCTION

Syntax

PROBHYPR(*N*,*K*,*n*,*x*<,*r*>)

Description

N is an integer population size parameter, with $N \geq 1$.

K is an integer number of items in the category of interest parameter, with $0 \leq K \leq N$.

n is an integer sample size parameter, with $0 \leq n \leq N$.

x is an integer random variable, with $\max(0, K+n-N) \leq x \leq \min(K,n)$.

r is an optional numeric odds ratio parameter, with $r \geq 0$.

The PROBHYPR function returns the probability that an observation from an extended hypergeometric distribution, with population size *N*, number of items *K*, sample size *n*, and odds ratio *r*, is less than or equal to *x*. If the optional parameter *r* is not specified or is set to 1, the value returned is from the usual hypergeometric distribution. The extended hypergeometric distribution is given by

$$Q_h(N,K,n,x,r) = \sum_{j=0}^{x} Q_i$$

where

$$Q_i = \begin{cases} \dfrac{\binom{K}{i}\binom{N-K}{n-i} r^i}{\sum_{j=0}^{m} \binom{K}{j}\binom{N-K}{n-j} r^j} & \max(0,K+n-N) \le i \le \min(K,n) \\ 0 & \text{otherwise} \end{cases}$$

where

X_1 is binomially distributed with parameters K and p_1.

X_2 is binomially distributed with parameters N−K and p_2.

$q_1 = 1 - p_1$

$q_2 = 1 - p_2$

$r = (p_1 q_2) / (p_2 q_1)$.

When $p_1 = p_2$, r=1 (the default), and PROBHYPR returns the probability from the usual hypergeometric distribution, given by

$$Q_h(N,K,n,x,r) = \sum_{i=0}^{x} Q_i$$

where

$$Q_i = \begin{cases} \dfrac{\binom{K}{i}\binom{N-K}{n-i}}{\binom{N}{n}} & \max(0,K+n-N) \le i \le \min(K,n) \\ 0 & \text{otherwise} \end{cases} .$$

Example

```
p=probhypr(200,50,10,2);
```

The value returned is 0.52367.

PROBIT

Quantile from the standard normal distribution

Quantile

HELP FUNCTION

Syntax

PROBIT(p)

Description

p is a numeric probability, with $0<p<1$.

The PROBIT function returns the pth quantile from the standard normal distribution. The probability that an observation from the standard normal distribution is less than or equal to the returned quantile is p. The result could be truncated to lie between −8.222 and 7.941.

The PROBIT function is the inverse of the PROBNORM function.

Examples

```
□  x=probit(.025);
□  x=probit(1.e-7);
```

The values returned are −1.95996 and −5.19934, respectively.

PROBNEGB

Probability from the negative binomial distribution

Probability

HELP FUNCTION

Syntax

PROBNEGB(*p*,*n*,*m*)

Description

p is a numeric probability of success parameter, with $0 \leq p \leq 1$.

n is an integer number of successes parameter, with $n \geq 1$.

m is a positive integer random variable, the number of failures, with $m \geq 0$.

The PROBNEGB function returns the probability that an observation from a negative binomial distribution, with probability of success *p* and number of successes *n*, is less than or equal to *m*. This function is given by

$$Q_{nb}(p,n,m) = p^n \sum_{j=0}^{m} \binom{n+j-1}{j} (1-p)^j \quad .$$

To compute the probability that an observation is equal to a given value *m*, compute the difference of two probabilities from the negative binomial distribution, given by

$$Q_{nb}(p,n,m) - Q_{nb}(p,n,m-1) \quad .$$

Example

```
p=probnegb(.5,2,1);
```

The value returned is 0.50000.

PROBNORM

Probability from the standard normal distribution

Probability

HELP FUNCTION

Syntax

PROBNORM(*x*)

Description

x is a numeric random variable.

The PROBNORM function returns the probability that an observation from the standard normal distribution is less than or equal to x. The function is given by

$$P(x) = \frac{1}{\sqrt{2\pi}} \int_{-\infty}^{x} e^{\frac{-t^2}{2}} dt \quad .$$

The PROBIT function is the inverse of PROBNORM.

Example

```
p=probnorm(1.96);
```

The value returned is 0.97500.

PROBT

Probability from the *t* distribution

Probability

HELP FUNCTION

Syntax

PROBT(*x*,*df*<,*nc*>)

Description

x is a numeric random variable.

df is a numeric degrees of freedom parameter, with $df>0$.

nc is an optional numeric noncentrality parameter, with $nc \geq 0$.

The PROBT function returns the probability that an observation from a Student's *t* distribution, with degrees of freedom *df* and noncentrality parameter *nc*, is less than or equal to x. This function accepts a noninteger degree of freedom parameter *df*. If the optional parameter, *nc*, is not specified or has the value 0, the value returned is from the central Student's *t* distribution. The function is given by

$$P_t(x \mid df, nc) = e^{\frac{-nc^2}{2}} \sum_{j=0}^{\infty} \frac{\left(\frac{nc^2}{2}\right)^j}{j!} I_{\frac{df}{df+x^2}} \left(\frac{df}{2}, \frac{1}{2} + j \right)$$

where $I_{.}(.,.)$ denotes the beta distribution function.

The TINV function is the inverse of the PROBT function. The significance level of a two-tailed *t* test is given by

```
p=(1-probt(abs(x),df))*2;
```

Example

```
x=probt(.9,5);
```

The value returned is x=0.79531.

PUT

Returns a value using a specified format

Special

HELP FUNCTION

Syntax

PUT(*source*, <? | ??> *format*)

Description

The PUT function enables you to write the value of *source* with a specified format. The format must be the same type (numeric or character) as the value of *source*. The result of the PUT function is always a character string. If the source is numeric, the resulting string is right aligned. If the source is character, the result is left aligned.

You can use the PUT function to convert a numeric value to a character value. The PUT function writes (or produces a reformatted result) only while it is executing. To preserve the result, you must assign it to a variable.

You can use the following arguments with the PUT function:

source
: identifies the SAS variable or constant whose value you want to reformat. The *source* can be character or numeric.

?
??
: The optional question mark (?) and double question mark (??) format modifiers suppress printing both the error messages and the input lines when invalid data values are read. The ? modifier suppresses the invalid data message. The ?? modifier also suppresses the invalid data message and, in addition, prevents the automatic variable _ERROR_ from being set to 1 when invalid data are read.

format
: contains the SAS format you want applied to the variable or constant specified in the source. The *format* must be of the same type as the source, either character or numeric.

Comparisons

The PUT function and the PUT statement are similar. The PUT function returns a value using a specified format. Use an assignment statement to store the value in a variable. The PUT statement writes a value to an external destination (either the SAS log or a destination you specify).

Examples

Example 1: Converting Numeric Values to Character Values

In the following example, the first statement converts the values of CC, a numeric variable, into the four-character hexadecimal format, and the second writes the same value that the PUT function returns.

```
cchex=put(cc,hex4.);
put cc hex4.;
```

Example 2: Using PUT and INPUT Functions

In this example, the PUT function returns a numeric value as a character string. The value 122591 is assigned to the CHARDATE variable. Then, the INPUT function returns the value of the character string as a SAS date value using a SAS date informat. The value 11681 is stored in the SASDATE variable.

```
numdate=122591;
chardate=put(numdate,z6.);
sasdate=input(chardate,mmddyy6.);
```

Example 3: Suppressing Error Messages

In the following example, the question mark (?) format modifier tells the SAS System not to print the invalid data error message if it finds data errors. The automatic variable _ERROR_ is set to 1 and input data lines are written to the SAS log.

```
y=put(x,? 3.1);
```

Because the double question mark ?? format modifier suppresses the printing of error messages and input lines and prevents the automatic variable _ERROR_ from being set to 1 when invalid data are read, the following two examples produce the same result:

□ `y=put(x,?? 2.);`

□ `y=put(x,? 2.);`
`_error_=0;`

See Also

INPUT function

PUT statement in Chapter 9, "SAS Statements"

Chapter 14, "SAS Formats"

QTR

Returns the yearly quarter from a SAS date value

Date and time

HELP FUNCTION

Syntax

QTR(*date*)

Description

The QTR function returns a value of 1, 2, 3, or 4 from a SAS date value to indicate the quarter of the year during which a date value falls.

You can use the following argument with the QTR function:

date a SAS expression representing a SAS date value.

Example

Consider the following statements, which return values corresponding to 20JAN89 for X and 1 for Y:

```
x=10612;
y=qtr(x);
```

```
put y=;
put x=date7.;
```

See Also

YYQ function

"SAS Date and Time Values" in Chapter 4, "Rules of the SAS Language"

RANBIN

Random variate from a binomial distribution

Random number

HELP FUNCTION

Syntax

RANBIN(*seed,n,p*)

Description

seed is an integer $<2^{31}-1$. (See "Notes on Random Number Functions" in Chapter 3 for a complete discussion of *seed*.) If *seed*≤ 0, the time of day is used to initialize the seed stream.

p is a numeric probability of success parameter, with $0<p<1$.

n is an integer number of independent Bernoulli trials parameter, with $n>0$.

The RANBIN function returns a variate generated from a binomial distribution with mean *np* and variance $np(1-p)$. If $n\leq 50$, an inverse transform method applied to a RANUNI uniform variate is used. If $n>50$, the normal approximation to the binomial distribution is used. In that case, the Box-Muller transformation of RANUNI uniform variates is used.

The CALL RANBIN routine, an alternative to the RANBIN function, gives greater control of the seed and random number streams. For details, see the CALL RANBIN routine.

RANCAU

Random variate from a Cauchy distribution

Random number

HELP FUNCTION

Syntax

RANCAU(*seed*)

Description

seed is an integer $<2^{31}-1$. (See "Notes on Random Number Functions" in Chapter 3 for a complete discussion of *seed*.) If *seed*≤ 0, the time of day is used to initialize the seed stream.

The RANCAU function returns a variate generated from a Cauchy distribution with location parameter 0 and scale parameter 1. An acceptance-rejection procedure applied to RANUNI uniform variates is used. If *u* and *v* are independent uniform $(-1/2, 1/2)$ variables and $u^2+v^2\leq 1/4$, then u/v is a Cauchy variate. A Cauchy variate X with location parameter ALPHA and scale parameter BETA can be generated as follows:

```
x=alpha+beta*rancau(seed);
```

The CALL RANCAU routine, an alternative to the RANCAU function, gives greater control of the seed and random number streams. For details, see the CALL RANCAU routine.

RANEXP

Random variate from an exponential distribution

Random number

HELP FUNCTION

Syntax

RANEXP(*seed*)

Description

seed is an integer $<2^{31}-1$. (See "Notes of Random Number Functions" in Chapter 3 for a complete discussion of *seed*.) If *seed*≤ 0, the time of day is used to initialize the seed stream.

The RANEXP function returns a variate generated from an exponential distribution with parameter 1. An inverse transform method applied to a RANUNI uniform variate is used.

An exponential variate X with parameter LAMBDA can be generated as follows:

```
x=ranexp(seed)/lambda;
```

An extreme value variate X with location parameter ALPHA and scale parameter BETA can be generated as follows:

```
x=alpha-beta*log(ranexp(seed));
```

A geometric variate X with parameter P can be generated as follows:

```
x=floor(-ranexp(seed)/log(1-p));
```

The CALL RANEXP routine, an alternative to the RANEXP function, gives greater control of the seed and random number streams. For details, see the CALL RANEXP routine.

RANGAM

Random variate from a gamma distribution

Random number

HELP FUNCTION

Syntax

RANGAM(*seed,a*)

Description

seed is an integer $<2^{31}-1$. (See "Notes on Random Number Functions" in Chapter 3 for a complete discussion of *seed*.) If *seed*≤ 0, the time of day is used to initialize the seed stream.

a is a numeric shape parameter, with $a>0$.

The RANGAM function returns a variate generated from a gamma distribution with parameter *a*. For $a>1$, an acceptance-rejection method due to Cheng (1977) is used. For $a\leq 1$, an acceptance-rejection method due to Fishman is used (1978, Algorithm G2). To expedite execution, internal variables are calculated only on initial calls (that is, with each new *a*).

A gamma variate X with shape parameter ALPHA and scale BETA can be generated as follows:

```
x=beta*rangam(seed,alpha);
```

If 2*ALPHA is an integer, a chi-square variate X with 2*ALPHA degrees of freedom can be generated as follows:

```
x=2*rangam(seed,alpha);
```

If N is a positive integer, an Erlang variate X can be generated as follows:

```
x=beta*rangam(seed,N);
```

It has the distribution of the sum of N independent exponential variates whose means are BETA.

And finally, a beta variate X with parameters ALPHA and BETA can be generated as follows:

```
y1=rangam(seed,alpha);
y2=rangam(seed,beta);
x=y1/(y1+y2);
```

The CALL RANGAM routine, an alternative to the RANGAM function, gives greater control of the seed and random number streams. For details, see the CALL RANGAM routine.

RANGE

Range of values

Sample statistics

HELP FUNCTION

Syntax

RANGE(*argument,argument, . . .*)

Description

argument is numeric. At least two arguments are required. The argument list may consist of a variable list, preceded by OF. See "Using Function Arguments" in Chapter 3.

The RANGE function returns the difference between the largest and the smallest of the nonmissing arguments.

Examples

```
□ x0=range(.,.);
□ x1=range(-2,6,3);
□ x2=range(2,6,3,.);
□ x3=range(1,6,3,1);
□ x4= range(of x1-x3);
```

The values returned are ., 8.00000, 4.00000, 5.00000, and 4.00000, respectively.

RANK

Returns the position of a character in the ASCII or EBCDIC collating sequence

Character

HELP FUNCTION

Syntax

RANK(*x*)

Description

The RANK function returns an integer representing the position of a character in the ASCII or EBCDIC collating sequence, depending on the sequence your host system uses.

You can use the following argument with the RANK function:

x is a character in the ASCII or EBCDIC collating sequence.

Example

The following statements return the value 65 on ASCII systems and the value 193 on EBCDIC systems:

```
n=rank('A');
put n;
```

See Also

BYTE function

COLLATE function

RANNOR

Random variate from a normal distribution

Random number

HELP FUNCTION

Syntax

RANNOR(*seed*)

Description

seed is an integer $<2^{31}-1$. (See "Notes on Random Number Functions" in Chapter 3 for a complete dicussion of *seed*.) If *seed*≤ 0, the time of day is used to initialize the seed stream.

The RANNOR function returns a variate generated from a normal distribution with mean 0 and variance 1. The Box-Muller transformation of RANUNI uniform variates is used.

A normal variate X with mean MU and variance SIGMASQ can be generated as follows:

```
x=MU+sqrt(SIGMASQ)*rannor(seed);
```

A lognormal variate X with mean

exp(MU + SIGMASQ/2)

and variance

exp(2*MU + 2*SIGMASQ) − exp(2*MU + SIGMASQ)

can be generated as follows:

```
x=exp(MU+sqrt(SIGMASQ)*rannor(seed));
```

The RANNOR function is identical to the NORMAL function. The CALL RANNOR routine, an alternative to the RANNOR function, gives greater control of the seed and random number streams. For details, see the CALL RANNOR routine.

RANPOI

Random variate from a Poisson distribution

Random number

HELP FUNCTION

Syntax

RANPOI(*seed*,*m*)

Description

seed is an integer $<2^{31}-1$. (See "Notes on Random Number Functions" in Chapter 3 for a complete discussion of *seed*.) If *seed*≤ 0, the time of day is used to initialize the seed.

m is a numeric mean parameter, with $m \geq 0$.

The RANPOI function returns a variate generated from a Poisson distribution with mean *m*. For $m<100$, an inverse transform method applied to a RANUNI uniform variate is used. Two independent Poisson variates are generated: one with parameter INT(*m*), which is the integer part of *m*, and the other with parameter $m-$INT(*m*). The sum of the Poisson variates is returned (Fishman 1976). For integer $m<100$, only the first of these is generated. For $m \geq 100$, the normal approximation of a Poisson random variable is used. In that case, the Box-Muller transformation of RANUNI uniform variates is used. To expedite execution, internal variables are calculated only on initial calls (that is, with each new *m*).

The CALL RANPOI routine, an alternative to the RANPOI function, gives greater control of the seed and random number streams. For details, see the CALL RANPOI routine.

RANTBL

Random variate from a tabled probability

Random number

HELP FUNCTION

Syntax

RANTBL(*seed*,p_1, . . . p_i, . . . ,p_n)

Description

seed is an integer $<2^{31}-1$. (See "Notes on Random Number Functions" in Chapter 3 for a complete discussion of *seed*.) If *seed*≤ 0, the time of day is used to initialize the seed stream.

p_i is numeric with $0 \leq p_i \leq 1$ for $0<i \leq n$.

The RANTBL function returns a variate generated from the probability mass function defined by p_1 through p_n. An inverse transform method applied to a RANUNI uniform variate is used. RANTBL returns

1 with probability p_1
2 with probability p_2
.
.
.
n with probability p_n
$n+1$ with probability $1-\Sigma_{i=1}^{n} p_i$ if $\Sigma_{i=1}^{n} p_i \leq 1$.

If for some index $j<n$ $\Sigma_{i=1}^{j} p_i \geq 1$, RANTBL returns only the indices 1 through j with the probability of occurrence of the index j equal to $1-\Sigma_{i=1}^{j-1} p_i$.

Let n=3, P1, P2, and P3 be three probabilities with P1+P2+P3=1, and M1, M2, and M3 be three variables. The variable X in these statements

```
array m{3} m1-m3;
x=m{rantbl(seed, of p1-p3)};
```

will be assigned one of the values of M1, M2, or M3 with probabilities of occurrence P1, P2, and P3, respectively.

The CALL RANTBL routine, an alternative to the RANTBL function, gives greater control of the seed and random number streams. For details, see the CALL RANTBL routine.

RANTRI

Random variate from a triangular distribution

Random number

HELP FUNCTION

Syntax

RANTRI(*seed,h***)**

Description

seed is an integer $<2^{31}-1$. (See "Notes on Random Number Functions" in Chapter 3 for a complete discussion of *seed*.) If *seed* ≤ 0, the time of day is used to initialize the seed stream.

h is numeric with $0<h<1$.

The RANTRI function returns a variate generated from the triangular distribution with parameter *h*. An inverse transform method applied to a RANUNI uniform variate is used.

A triangular distribution X on the interval [A,B] with mode C ϵ (A,B) can be generated as follows:

```
x=(b-a)*rantri(seed,(c-a)/(b-a))+a;
```

The CALL RANTRI routine, an alternative to the RANTRI function, gives greater control of the seed and random number streams. For details, see the CALL RANTRI routine.

RANUNI

Random variate from a uniform distribution

Random number

HELP FUNCTION

Syntax

RANUNI(*seed*)

Description

seed is an integer $<2^{31}-1$. (See "Notes on Random Number Functions" in Chapter 3 for a complete discussion of *seed*.) If *seed* ≤ 0, the time of day is used to initialize the seed.

The RANUNI function returns a number generated from the uniform distribution on the interval (0,1) using a prime modulus multiplicative generator with modulus $2^{31}-1$ and multiplier 397204094 (see Fishman and Moore 1982).

The RANUNI function is identical to the UNIFORM function. The CALL RANUNI routine, an alternative to the RANUNI function, gives greater control of the seed and random number streams. For details, see the CALL RANUNI routine.

REPEAT

Repeats a character expression

Character

HELP FUNCTION

Syntax

REPEAT(*argument,n*)

Description

The REPEAT function returns a character value consisting of the first argument repeated *n* times. Thus, the first argument appears *n+1* times in the result.

You can use the following arguments with the REPEAT function:

argument
: specifies any valid SAS character expression.

n
: specifies the number of times you want to repeat *argument*. The value you specify for *n* must be greater than or equal to 0.

Example

The following statements return the value **ONEONEONE**:

```
x=repeat('ONE',2);
put x;
```

REVERSE

Reverses a character expression

Character

HELP FUNCTION

Syntax

REVERSE(*argument*)

Description

The REVERSE function returns the argument's characters in reverse order.

You can use the following argument with the REVERSE function:

argument specifies any valid SAS character expression.

Example

This statement returns the character string **zyx** preceded by three leading blanks:

```
backward=reverse('xyz   ');
```

RIGHT

Right aligns a character expression

Character

HELP FUNCTION

Syntax

RIGHT(*argument*)

Description

The RIGHT function returns an argument with trailing blanks moved to the beginning of the value. The argument's length does not change.

You can use the following argument with the RIGHT function:

argument specifies any valid character expression.

Example

The following SAS statements produce a character string with **DUE DATE** shifted right three spaces, with leading blanks instead of trailing blanks.

```
a='DUE DATE   ';
b=right(a);
```

See Also

COMPRESS function

LEFT function

TRIM function

ROUND

Rounds to the nearest round-off unit

Truncation

HELP FUNCTION

Syntax

ROUND(*argument,round-off-unit*)

Description

argument is numeric.

round-off-unit is numeric and nonnegative.

The ROUND function returns a value rounded to the nearest round-off unit. If *round-off-unit* is not provided, a default value of 1 is used and *argument* is rounded to the nearest integer.

Examples

□ `x=round(223.456,1);`

□ `x=round(223.456,.01);`

□ `x=round(223.456,100);`

□ `x=round(223.456);`

The values returned are 223.00000, 223.46000, 200.00000, and 223.00000, respectively.

SAVING

The future value of a periodic saving

Financial

HELP FUNCTION

Syntax

SAVING(*f,p,r,n*)

Description

f is numeric, the future amount (at the end of n periods), with $f \geq 0$.

p is numeric, the fixed periodic payment, with $p \geq 0$.

r is numeric, the periodic interest rate expressed as a decimal, with $r \geq 0$.

n is an integer, the number of compounding periods, with $n \geq 0$.

The SAVING function returns the missing argument in the list of four arguments from a periodic saving. The arguments are related by

$$f = \frac{p(1 + r)\left((1 + r)^n - 1\right)}{r}.$$

One missing argument must be provided. It is then calculated from the remaining three. No adjustment is made to convert the results to round numbers.

Example

A savings account pays a 5 percent nominal annual interest rate, compounded monthly. For a monthly deposit of $100, the number of payments needed to accumulate at least $12,000, can be expressed as

```
number=saving(12000,100,.05/12,.);
```

The value returned is 97.18 months. The fourth argument is set to missing, indicating that the number of payments is to be calculated. The 5 percent nominal annual rate is converted to a monthly rate of 0.05/12. The rate is the fractional (not the percentage) interest rate per compounding period.

SCAN

Returns a given word from a character expression

Character

HELP FUNCTION

Syntax

SCAN(*argument,n*<*,delimiters*>)

Description

The SCAN function separates a character expression into words and returns the *n*th word.

You can use the following arguments with the SCAN function:

argument specifies any valid SAS character expression.

n specifies a numeric expression that produces the number of the word in a string you want SCAN to return. SCAN returns a blank value if there are fewer than *n* words in an argument.

delimiters specifies a character expression that produces characters you want SCAN to use as word separators in a string. If you represent *delimiters* as a constant, you must enclose *delimiters* in quotes. Leading delimiters before the first word have no effect. If there are two or more contiguous delimiters, SCAN treats them as one. On ASCII systems, if you do not specify *delimiters*, the SAS System treats all of the following characters as *delimiters*:

blank . < (+ & ! $ *) ; ^ − / , % ¦

On ASCII systems without the ^ character, SCAN uses the ~ character instead.

On EBCDIC systems, if you do not specify *delimiters*, the SAS System treats all of the following characters as *delimiters*:

blank . < (+ | & ! $ *) ; ¬ − / , % ¦ ¢

Example

The following statements return the value `X=Y`:

```
arg='ABC.DEF(X=Y)';
word=scan(arg,3);
put word;
```

SECOND

Returns the second from a SAS time or datetime value

Date and time

HELP FUNCTION

Syntax

SECOND(<*time* | *datetime*>)

Description

The SECOND function produces a positive, numeric value representing a specific second. Numeric values can range from 0 through 59.

You can use the following arguments with the SECOND function:

time specifies a SAS expression representing a SAS time value.

datetime specifies a SAS expression representing a SAS datetime value.

Example

The following statements produce a value of 24 for S:

```
time='3:19:24't;
s=second(time);
```

See Also

HOUR and MINUTE functions

"SAS Date and Time Values" in Chapter 4, "Rules of the SAS Language."

SIGN

Sign of a value

Arithmetic

HELP FUNCTION

Syntax

SIGN(*argument*)

Description

argument is numeric.

The SIGN function returns a value of -1 if $x<0$; a value of 0 if $x=0$; and a value of 1 if $x>0$.

Examples

- `x=sign(-5);`
- `x=sign(5);`
- `x=sign(0);`

The values returned are -1, 1, and 0, respectively.

SIN

Trigonometric sine

Trigonometric and hyperbolic

HELP FUNCTION

Syntax

SIN(*argument*)

Description

argument is numeric and specified in radians.

The SIN function returns the sine of the argument.

Examples

□ `x=sin(.5);`

□ `x=sin(0);`

□ `x=sin(3.14159/4);`

The values returned are 0.47943, 0.00000, and 0.70711, respectively.

SINH

Hyperbolic sine

Trigonometric and hyperbolic

HELP FUNCTION

Syntax

SINH(*argument*)

Description

argument is numeric.

The SINH function returns the hyperbolic sine of the argument, given by

$$(\exp(argument) - \exp(-argument))/2 \quad .$$

Examples

□ `x=sinh(0);`

□ `x=sinh(1);`

□ `x=sinh(-1);`

The values returned are 0.00000, 1.17520, and -1.17520, respectively.

SKEWNESS

Skewness

Sample statistics

HELP FUNCTION

Syntax

SKEWNESS(*argument,argument,argument,* . . .)

Description

argument is numeric. At least three arguments are required. The argument list may consist of a variable list, preceded by OF. See "Using Function Arguments" in Chapter 3.

The SKEWNESS function returns the skewness statistic of the nonmissing arguments.

Examples

```
□ x1=skewness(0,1,1);

□ x2=skewness(2,4,6,3,1);

□ x3=skewness(2,0,0);

□ x4=skewness(of x1-x3);
```

The values returned are −1.73205, 0.59013, 1.73205, and −0.95310, respectively.

SQRT

Square root of a value

Arithmetic

HELP FUNCTION

Syntax

SQRT(*argument*)

Description

argument is numeric and nonnegative.

The SQRT function returns the square root of the argument.

Examples

```
□ x=sqrt(25);

□ x=sqrt(4);
```

The values returned are 5.00000 and 2.00000, respectively.

STD

Standard deviation

Sample statistics

HELP FUNCTION

Syntax

STD(*argument,argument*, . . .)

Description

argument is numeric. At least two arguments are required. The argument list may consist of a variable list, preceded by OF. See "Using Function Arguments" in Chapter 3.

The STD function returns the standard deviation of the nonmissing arguments.

Examples

```
□ x1=std(2,6);
□ x2=std(2,6,.);
□ x3=std(2,4,6,3,1);
□ x4=std(of x1-x3);
```

The values returned are 2.82843, 2.82843, 1.92354, and 0.52244, respectively.

STDERR

Standard error of the mean

Sample statistics

HELP FUNCTION

Syntax

STDERR(*argument,argument*, . . .)

Description

argument is numeric. At least two arguments are required. The argument list may consist of a variable list, preceded by OF. See "Using Function Arguments" in Chapter 3.

The STDERR function returns the standard error of the mean of the nonmissing arguments.

Examples

```
□ x1=stderr(2,6);
□ x2=stderr(2,6,.);
□ x3=stderr(2,4,6,3,1);
□ x4=stderr(of x1-x3);
```

The values returned are 2.00000, 2.00000, 0.86023, and 0.37992, respectively.

STFIPS

Converts state postal codes to FIPS state codes

State and ZIP code

HELP FUNCTION

Syntax

STFIPS(*postal-code*)

Description

The STFIPS function converts a two-character state postal code to the corresponding numeric U.S. Federal Information Processing Standards (FIPS) code.

You can use the following argument with the STFIPS function:

postal-code specifies a character expression containing the two-character standard state postal code. Characters can be in upper- or lowercase. STFIPS ignores trailing blanks, but generates an error if the expression contains leading blanks.

Example

The following statements return the value 37:

```
fips=stfips ('NC');
put fips;
```

See Also

FIPSTATE function

STNAME

Converts state postal codes to state names (all uppercase)

State and ZIP code

HELP FUNCTION

Syntax

STNAME(*postal-code*)

Description

The STNAME function converts a two-character state postal code to the corresponding state name in uppercase. Returned values can contain up to 20 characters.

You can use the following argument with the STNAME function:

postal-code specifies a character expression containing the two-character standard state postal code. Characters can be in upper- or lowercase. STNAME ignores trailing blanks, but generates an error if the expression contains leading blanks.

Example

The following statements return the value `NORTH CAROLINA`:

```
state=stname('NC');
put state;
```

See Also

STNAMEL function

STNAMEL

Converts state postal codes to state names in upper- and lowercase

State and ZIP code

HELP FUNCTION

Syntax

STNAMEL(*postal-code*)

Description

The STNAMEL function converts a two-character state postal code to the corresponding state name in upper- and lowercase. Return values can contain up to 20 characters.

You can use the following argument with the STNAMEL function:

postal-code specifies a character expression containing the two-character standard state postal code. Characters can be in upper- or lowercase. STFIPS ignores trailing blanks, but generates an error if the expression contains leading blanks.

Example

The following statements return the value `North Carolina`:

```
state=stnamel('NC');
put state;
```

See Also

STNAME function

SUBSTR

Extracts a substring from an argument or replaces character value contents

Character

HELP FUNCTION

Syntax

SUBSTR (*argument,position*<*,n*>)

Description

The SUBSTR function performs two distinct operations, depending on where you use it. If you use SUBSTR on the right side of an assignment statement, it returns a portion of an expression you specify in *argument*. The portion begins with the character specified by *position* and is the number of characters specified by *n*.

If you use SUBSTR on the left side of an assignment statement instead of a variable, the SAS System places the value of the expression on the right side of the assignment statement into the *argument* of SUBSTR, replacing *n* characters starting with the character you specify in *position*.

You can use the following arguments with the SUBSTR function:

argument
: specifies any valid SAS character expression. On the right side of an assignment statement, *argument* can be any character expression. On the left side of the assignment statement, *argument* must be a character variable.

position
: is a numeric expression specifying the beginning character position.

n
: is a numeric expression specifying the length of the substring to extract or replace, depending on which side of the assignment statement you use SUBSTR.

If you omit *n* on the right side of an assignment statement, the SAS System extracts the remainder of the expression. If you omit *n* on the left side of an assignment statement, the SAS System uses all of the characters on the right side of the assignment statement in replacing the values of *argument*.

If the value of *n* is larger than the length of the expression remaining in *argument* after *position*, the SAS System only extracts or replaces all remaining characters.

Examples

Example 1: Right Side of Assignment Statement

These statements return the output that follows:

```
date='06MAY89';
month=substr(date,3,3);
year=substr(date,6,2);
put @1 month @20 year;
```

```
----+----1----+----2----+----3
MAY                 89
```

Example 2: Left Side of Assignment Statement

The following statements return the values `CATNAP` and `CATTY`:

```
a='KIDNAP';
substr(a,1,3)='CAT';
put a;
b=a;
substr(b,4)='TY';
put b;
```

SUM

Sum

Sample statistics

HELP FUNCTION

Syntax

SUM(*argument*,*argument*, . . .)

Description

argument is numeric. At least two arguments are required. The argument list may consist of a variable list, preceded by OF. See "Using Function Arguments" in Chapter 3.

The SUM function returns the sum of the nonmissing arguments.

Examples

□ `x1=sum(4,9,3,8);`

□ `x2=sum(4,9,3,8,.);`

□ `x3=sum(of x1-x2);`

The values returned are 24.00000, 24.00000, and 48.00000, respectively.

SYMGET

Returns the value of a macro variable during DATA step execution

Special

HELP FUNCTION

Syntax

SYMGET(*argument*)

Description

The SYMGET function returns the value of a macro variable during DATA step execution. The SYMGET function is listed with macro facility features in Chapter 20, "SAS Macro Facility," and it is documented in the *SAS Guide to Macro Processing, Version 6, Second Edition.*

You can use the following specification with the SYMGET function:

argument is a character expression that identifies the macro variable whose value you want to retrieve.

See Also

"DATA Step Interfaces" in Chapter 20, "SAS Macro Facility"

SAS Guide to Macro Processing, Version 6, Second Edition

TAN

Trigonometric tangent

Trigonometric and hyperbolic

HELP FUNCTION

Syntax

TAN(*argument*)

Description

argument is numeric and specified in radians, and is not an odd multiple of $\pi/2$.

The TAN function returns the tangent of the argument.

Examples

```
□ x=tan(.5);
□ x=tan(0);
□ x=tan(3.14159/3);
```

The values returned are 0.54630, 0.00000, and 1.73205, respectively.

TANH

Hyperbolic tangent

Trigonometric and hyperbolic

HELP FUNCTION

Syntax

TANH(*argument*)

Description

argument is numeric.

The TANH function returns the hyperbolic tangent of the argument, given by

(exp(*argument*)−exp(−*argument*))/(exp(*argument*)+exp(−*argument*)) .

Examples

```
□ x=tanh(0);
□ x=tanh(.5);
□ x=tanh(-.5);
```

The values returned are 0.00000, 0.46212, and −0.46212, respectively.

TIME

Returns the current time of day

Date and time

HELP FUNCTION

Syntax

TIME()

Description

The TIME function returns the current time of day as a SAS time value.

Example

The SAS System assigns CURRENT a SAS time value corresponding to 14:32:00 if the following statements are executed exactly at 2:32 p.m.:

```
current=time();
put current=time.;
```

See Also

"SAS Date and Time Values" in Chapter 4, "Rules of the SAS Language."

TIMEPART

Extracts a time value from a SAS datetime value

Date and time

HELP FUNCTION

Syntax

TIMEPART(*datetime*)

Description

The TIMEPART function extracts a SAS time value from a datetime value.

You can use the following argument with the TIMEPART function:

datetime specifies a SAS expression representing a SAS datetime value.

Example

The SAS System assigns TIME a SAS value corresponding to 10:40:17 if the following statements are executed exactly at 10:40:17 on any date:

```
datim=datetime();
time=timepart(datim);
```

See Also

"SAS Date and Time Values" in Chapter 4, "Rules of the SAS Language."

TINV

Quantile from the *t* distribution

Quantile

HELP FUNCTION

Syntax

TINV(*p*,*df*<,*nc*>)

Description

p is a numeric probability, with $0<p<1$.

df is numeric degrees of freedom parameter, with $df>0$.

nc is an optional numeric noncentrality parameter, with $nc \geq 0$.

The TINV function returns the *p*th quantile from the Student's *t* distribution with degrees of freedom *df* and a noncentrality parameter *nc*. The probability that an observation from a *t* distribution is less than or equal to the returned quantile is *p*.

The TINV function is the inverse of the PROBT function. The TINV function accepts a noninteger degree of freedom parameter *df*. If the optional parameter *nc* is not specified or is 0, the quantile from the central *t* distribution is returned. For large values of *nc*, the algorithm could fail. In that case, a missing value is returned.

Examples

□ `x=tinv(.95,2);`

□ `x=tinv(.95,2.5,3);`

The values returned are 2.91999 and 11.03383, respectively.

TODAY

Returns the current date as a SAS date value

Date and time

HELP FUNCTION

Syntax

TODAY()

Description

The TODAY or DATE function produces the current date as a SAS date value representing the number of days between January 1, 1960 and the current date. The alias for the TODAY function is DATE.

Example

Executing the statements below on January 20, 1989 assigns CURRENT a value corresponding to January 20, 1989:

```
current=today();
put current=worddate.;
```

See Also

DATE and DATETIME functions

"SAS Date and Time Values" in Chapter 4, "Rules of the SAS Language."

TRANSLATE

Replaces specific characters in a character expression

Character

HELP FUNCTION

Syntax

TRANSLATE(*source,to-1,from-1*<, . . . *to-n,from-n*>)

Description

The TRANSLATE function copies a character value, substituting individual characters you specify for other individual characters already specified, returning the altered character value.

You can use the following arguments with the TRANSLATE function:

source
: specifies the SAS expression containing the original character value.

to
: specifies the characters you want TRANSLATE to use as substitutes.

from
: specifies the characters you want TRANSLATE to replace. Values of *to* and *from* correspond on a character-by-character basis; TRANSLATE changes character one of *from* to character one of *to*, and so on. If *to* has less characters than *from*, TRANSLATE changes the extra *from* characters to blanks. If *to* has more characters than *from*, TRANSLATE ignores the extra *to* characters.

The maximum number of pairs of *to* and *from* arguments the TRANSLATE function accepts depends on the computer system you use to run the SAS System. There is no functional difference between using several pairs of short arguments, or fewer pairs of longer arguments.

■ **Host Information** .... You must have pairs of *to* and *from* arguments on some host systems. On other host systems, a segment of the collating sequence replaces null *from* arguments. See the SAS documentation for your host system for more information.

.... ■

Example

The following statements return the value `XYZB`:

```
x=translate('XYZW','AB','VW');
put x;
```

TRIGAMMA

Trigamma function

Mathematical

HELP FUNCTION

Syntax

TRIGAMMA(*argument*)

Description

argument is numeric. Nonpositive integers are invalid.

The TRIGAMMA function returns the derivative of the DIGAMMA function. For *argument*>0, the TRIGAMMA function is the second derivative of the LGAMMA function.

Example

```
x=trigamma(3);
```

The value returned is 0.39493.

TRIM

Removes trailing blanks from character expressions

Character

HELP FUNCTION

Syntax

TRIM(*argument*)

Description

The TRIM function copies a character argument, removing any trailing blanks, and returns the trimmed argument as a result. TRIM is useful for concatenating because concatenation does not remove trailing blanks.

When you assign the result of the TRIM function to a variable, TRIM does not affect the length of the receiving variable. If the trimmed value is shorter than the length of the receiving variable, the SAS System pads the value with new blanks as it assigns it to the variable.

You can use the following argument with the TRIM function:

argument specifies any valid SAS character expression.

Example

These SAS statements return the values that follow:

```
data test;
   input part1 $ 1-10 part2 $ 11-20;
   hasblank=part1||part2;
   noblank=trim(part1)||part2;
   put hasblank= / noblank=;
   cards;
apple     sauce
;


HASBLANK=apple     sauce
NOBLANK=applesauce
```

See Also

COMPRESS function

LEFT function

RIGHT function

TRUNC

Truncates a numeric value to a specified length

Truncation

HELP FUNCTION

Syntax

TRUNC(*number,length*)

Description

number is numeric.

length is numeric and integer.

The TRUNC function truncates a full-length *number* (stored as a double) to a smaller number of bytes, as specified in *length,* and pads the truncated bytes with 0s. The truncation and subsequent expansion duplicate the effect of storing numbers in less than full length and then reading them.

Example

```
data x;
  length x 3;
  x=1/5;
run;

data y;
  set x;
  if x ne 1/5 then put 'x ne 1/5' ;
  if x eq trunc(1/5,3) then put 'x eq trunc(1/5,3)';
run;
```

The variable X is stored with a length of 3 and, therefore, each of the above comparisons is true.

UNIFORM

Random variate from a uniform distribution

Random number

HELP FUNCTION

Syntax

UNIFORM(*seed*)

Description

seed is numeric $<2^{31}-1$. (See "Notes on Random Number Functions" in Chapter 3 for a complete discussion of *seed.*) If *seed*≤ 0, the time of day is used to initialize the seed.

The UNIFORM function returns a number generated from the uniform distribution on the interval (0,1), using a prime modulus multiplicative generator with modulus $2^{31}-1$ and multiplier 397204094 (see Fishman and Moore 1982). The UNIFORM function is identical to the RANUNI function.

UPCASE

Converts all letters in an argument to uppercase

Character

HELP FUNCTION

Syntax

UPCASE(*argument*)

Description

The UPCASE function copies a character argument, converting all lowercase letters to uppercase letters, and returns the altered value as a result.

You can use the following argument with the UPCASE function:

argument specifies any valid SAS character expression.

Example

The following statements return the value `JOHN B. SMITH`:

```
name=upcase('John B. Smith');
put name;
```

USS

Uncorrected sum of squares

Sample statistics

HELP FUNCTION

Syntax

USS(*argument,argument,* . . .)

Description

argument is numeric. At least two arguments are required. The argument list may consist of a variable list, preceded by OF. See "Using Function Arguments" in Chapter 3.

The USS function returns the uncorrected sum of squares of the nonmissing arguments.

Examples

- `x1=uss(4,2,3.5,6);`
- `x2=uss(4,2,3.5,6,.);`
- `x3=uss(of x1-x2);`

The values returned are 68.25000, 68.25000, and 9316.12500, respectively.

VAR

Variance

Sample statistics

HELP FUNCTION

Syntax

VAR(*argument,argument* . . .)

Description

argument is numeric. At least two arguments are required. The argument list may consist of a variable list, preceded by OF. See "Using Function Arguments" in Chapter 3.

The VAR function returns the variance of the nonmissing arguments.

Examples

□ `x1=var(4,2,3.5,6);`

□ `x2=var(4,6,.);`

□ `x3=var(of x1-x2);`

The values returned are 2.72917, 2.00000, and 0.26584, respectively.

VERIFY

Returns the position of the first character unique to an expression

Character

HELP FUNCTION

Syntax

VERIFY(*source,excerpt-1*<, . . . *excerpt-n*>)

Description

The VERIFY function returns the position of the first character in *source* that is not present in any *excerpt*. If VERIFY finds every character in *source* in at least one *excerpt*, it returns a 0.

You can use the following arguments with the VERIFY function:

source
: specifies any valid SAS character expression.

<*excerpt-1*, . . . *excerpt-n*>
: specifies any valid SAS character expression.

Example

The following statements return the value **INVALID GRADE VALUE GRADE=q**:

```
data scores;
  input grade : $1. @@;
  check='abcdf';
  x=verify(grade,check);
  if x gt 0 then put 'INVALID GRADE VALUE ' grade=;
  cards;
a b c b c d f a a q a b d d b
;
```

WEEKDAY

Returns the day of the week from a SAS date value

Date and time

HELP FUNCTION

Syntax

WEEKDAY(*date*)

Description

The WEEKDAY function produces an integer representing the day of the week, where 1=Sunday, 2=Monday, . . . , 7=Saturday, from a SAS date value.

You can use the following argument with the WEEKDAY function:

date specifies a SAS expression representing a SAS date value.

Example

The following statement assigns X a value of 1:

```
x=weekday('12feb89'd);
```

See Also

"SAS Date and Time Values" in Chapter 4, "Rules of the SAS Language."

YEAR

Returns the year from a SAS date value

Date and time

HELP FUNCTION

Syntax

YEAR(*date*)

Description

The YEAR function produces a four-digit numeric value representing the year from a SAS date value.

You can use the following argument with the YEAR function:

date specifies a SAS expression representing a SAS numeric value.

Example

The following statements assign a value of 1989 to Y:

```
date='25dec89'd;
y=year(date);
```

See Also

DAY and MONTH functions

"SAS Date and Time Values" in Chapter 4, "Rules of the SAS Language."

YYQ

Returns a SAS date value from the year and quarter

Date and time

HELP FUNCTION

Syntax

YYQ(*year*,*quarter*)

Description

The YYQ function returns a SAS date value corresponding to the first day of the specified quarter.

You can use the following arguments with the YYQ function:

year specifies a two- or four-digit value representing a specific year. The YEARCUTOFF= system option defines the year value for two-digit dates.

quarter specifies either 1, 2, 3, or 4, representing a specific quarter of the year.

If either *year* or *quarter* is missing, or if the quarter value is not a valid number, the result is missing.

Example

The following statement assigns DV the SAS date value corresponding to July 1, 1990:

```
dv=yyq(90,3);
```

See Also

QTR and YEAR functions

"SAS Date and Time Values" in Chapter 4, "Rules of the SAS Language"

YEARCUTOFF= system option in Chapter 16, "SAS System Options"

ZIPFIPS

Converts ZIP codes to FIPS state codes

State and ZIP Code

HELP FUNCTION

Syntax

ZIPFIPS(*zip-code*)

Description

The ZIPFIPS function returns the two-digit numeric U.S. Federal Information Processing Standards (FIPS) code corresponding to its five-character ZIP code argument.

You can use the following argument with the ZIPFIPS function:

zip-code specifies any valid SAS character expression containing a five-digit ZIP code. The character expressions you use must have a length of five, or the ZIPFIPS function generates an error.

Example

The following statements return the value 37:

```
fips=zipfips('27511');
put fips;
```

See Also

ZIPNAME function

ZIPNAMEL function

ZIPSTATE function

ZIPNAME

Converts ZIP codes to state names (all uppercase)

State and ZIP Code

HELP FUNCTION

Syntax

ZIPNAME(*zip-code*)

Description

The ZIPNAME function returns the name of the state corresponding to its five-character ZIP code argument. ZIPNAME returns character values up to 20 characters long, all in uppercase.

You can use the following argument with the ZIPNAME function:

zip-code
: specifies any valid SAS character expression containing a five-digit ZIP code. The character expressions you use must have a length of five, or the ZIPNAME function generates an error.

Example

The following statements return the value **NORTH CAROLINA**:

```
state=zipname('27511');
put state;
```

See Also

ZIPFIPS function

ZIPNAMEL function

ZIPSTATE function

ZIPNAMEL

Converts ZIP codes to state names in upper- and lowercase

State and ZIP Code

HELP FUNCTION

Syntax

ZIPNAMEL(*zip-code*)

Description

The ZIPNAMEL function returns the name of the state corresponding to its five-character ZIP code argument. ZIPNAMEL returns character values up to 20 characters long in upper- and lowercase.

You can use the following argument with the ZIPNAMEL function:

zip-code specifies any valid SAS character expression containing a five-digit ZIP code. The character expressions you use must have a length of five, or the ZIPNAMEL function generates an error.

Example

The following statements return the value `North Carolina`:

```
state=zipnamel('27511');
put state;
```

See Also

ZIPFIPS function

ZIPNAME function

ZIPSTATE function

ZIPSTATE

Converts ZIP codes to state postal codes

State and ZIP Code

HELP FUNCTION

Syntax

ZIPSTATE(*zip-code*)

Description

The ZIPSTATE function returns the two-character state postal code corresponding to its five-character ZIP code argument. ZIPSTATE returns character values in uppercase.

You can use the following argument with the ZIPSTATE function:

zip-code specifies any valid SAS character expression containing a five-digit ZIP code. The character expressions you use must have a length of five, or the ZIPSTATE function generates an error.

Example

The following statements return the value `NC`:

```
st=zipstate('27511');
put st;
```

See Also

ZIPFIPS function
ZIPNAME function
ZIPNAMEL function

References

Abramowitz, M. and Stegun, I. (1964), *Handbook of Mathematical Functions with Formulas, Graphs, and Mathematical Tables*, National Bureau of Standards Applied Mathematics Series #55, Washington, D.C.: U.S. Government Printing Office.

Cheng, R.C.H. (1977), "The Generation of Gamma Variables," *Applied Statistics*, 26, 71–75.

Fishman, G.S. (1976), "Sampling from the Poisson Distribution on a Computer," *Computing*, 17, 145–156.

Fishman, G.S. (1978), *Principles of Discrete Event Simulation*, New York: John Wiley & Sons.

Fishman, G.S. and Moore, L.R. (1982), "A Statistical Evaluation of Multiplicative Congruential Generators with Modulus $(2^{31}-1)$," *Journal of the American Statistical Association*, 77, 129–136.

Michael, J. and Schucany, W. (1979), "A New Approach to Testing Goodness of Fit for Censored Data," *Technometrics*, 21, 435–441.

CHAPTER 12 SAS® CALL Routines

Background information on SAS CALL routines, including a table listing all CALL routines, appears in Chapter 3, "Components of the SAS Language." See Table 3.6, "Categories and Descriptions of CALL Routines."

LABEL

Variable label to specified character variable

Variable control

HELP CALL

Syntax

LABEL(*variable-1, variable-2***)**

Description

variable-1 specifies any valid SAS variable. Variable labels can be up to 40 characters in length. If *variable-1* does not have a label, the variable name is assigned as the value of *variable-2*.

variable-2 specifies any valid SAS character variable. Variable labels can be up to 40 characters long; therefore, the length of *variable-2* should be at least 40 characters to avoid truncating variable labels.

The CALL LABEL routine assigns the label of the variable specified as *variable-1* to the character variable specified as *variable-2*.

Example

The following example uses the CALL LABEL routine with array references to assign the labels of all variables in data set OLD as values of the variable LAB in data set NEW:

```
data new;
   set old;
   array abc{*} _character_;  /* all character variables in old  */
   array def{*} _numeric_;    /* all numeric variables in old    */
   length lab $40;            /* lab is not in either array      */
   do i=1 to dim(abc);
      call label(abc{i},lab); /* get label of character variable */
      output;                 /* write label to an observation   */
   end;
   do j=1 to dim(def);
      call label(def{j},lab); /* get label of numeric variable   */
      output;                 /* write label to an observation   */
   end;
   stop;
   keep lab;
run;
```

RANBIN

Random variate from a binomial distribution

Random number

HELP CALL

Syntax

RANBIN(*seed*,*n*,*p*,*x*)

Description

seed
: is an integer-valued numeric variable, with an absolute value $<2^{31}-1$. If $seed \leq 0$, the time of day is used to initialize the seed stream. A new value for *seed* is returned each time CALL RANBIN is executed.

n
: is an integer number of independent Bernoulli trials parameter, with $n>0$. If $n \leq 50$ or $np \leq 5$, an inverse transform method applied to a RANUNI uniform variate is used. If $n>50$ and $np>5$, the normal approximation to the binomial distribution is used. In that case, the Box-Muller transformation of RANUNI uniform variates is used.

p
: is a numeric probability of success parameter, with $0<p<1$.

x
: is a numeric SAS variable. A new value for the random variate *x* is returned each time CALL RANBIN is executed.

The CALL RANBIN routine updates *seed* and returns a variate *x* generated from a binomial distribution with mean *np* and variance $np\,(1-p)$. The seed must be initialized prior to the CALL statement.

With multiple CALL RANBIN statements, it is possible to control the generation of multivariates by adjusting the seeds. The CALL RANBIN statement produces a separate stream for each seed, while the RANBIN function produces only a single stream of random variates, even with multiple RANBIN function occurrences in the same DATA step.

By adjusting the seeds, streams of variates can be forced to agree or disagree for some or all of the observations in the same, or in subsequent, DATA steps. With nonpositive seeds, when the time of day is used to initialize the seed stream, it will not be possible to duplicate the stream of variates at a later time (unless the first CALL RANBIN is only used to return a positive seed that is to be saved).

Example

The following DATA step illustrates the use of the CALL RANBIN routine:

```
data case;
   retain seed1 seed2 seed3 45;
   n=2000;
   p=.2;
   do i=1 to 10;
      call ranbin(seed1,n,p,x1);
      call ranbin(seed2,n,p,x2);
      x3=ranbin(seed3,n,p);
      if i=5 then
         do;
            seed2=18;
            seed3=18;
         end;
      output;
   end;
run;

proc print;
   id i;
   var seed1-seed3 x1-x3;
run;
```

The output is shown here:

I	SEED1	SEED2	SEED3	X1	X2	X3
1	1404437564	1404437564	45	385	385	385
2	1445125588	1445125588	45	399	399	399
3	1326029789	1326029789	45	384	384	384
4	1988843719	1988843719	45	421	421	421
5	2137808851	18	18	430	430	430
6	1233028129	991271755	18	392	374	392
7	50049159	1437043694	18	424	384	424
8	802575599	959908645	18	371	383	371
9	100573943	1225034217	18	428	388	428
10	414117170	425626811	18	402	403	402

Changing SEED2 for the CALL RANBIN statement, when I=5, forced the stream of the variates for X2 to deviate from the stream of the variates for X1, while changing SEED3 on the RANBIN function had no effect.

RANCAU

Random variate from a Cauchy distribution

Random number

HELP CALL

Syntax

RANCAU(*seed*,*x*)

Description

seed is an integer-valued numeric variable, with an absolute value $<2^{31}-1$. If $seed \leq 0$, the time of day is used to initialize the seed stream. A new value for *seed* is returned each time CALL RANCAU is executed.

x is a numeric SAS variable. A new value for the random variate *x* is returned each time CALL RANCAU is executed.

The CALL RANCAU routine updates *seed* and returns a variate *x* generated from a Cauchy distribution with location parameter 0 and scale parameter 1. The seed must be initialized prior to the CALL statement.

With multiple CALL RANCAU statements, it is possible to control the generation of multivariates by adjusting the seeds. The CALL RANCAU statement produces a separate stream for each seed, while the RANCAU function produces only a single stream of random variates, even with multiple RANCAU function occurrences in the same DATA step. By adjusting the seeds, streams of variates can be forced to agree or disagree for some or all of the observations in the same, or in subsequent, DATA steps.

With nonpositive seeds, when the time of day is used to initialize the seed stream, it will not be possible to duplicate the stream of variates at a later time (unless the first CALL RANCAU is only used to return a positive seed that is to be saved).

An acceptance-rejection procedure applied to RANUNI uniform variates is used. If *u* and *v* are independent uniform $(-1/2, 1/2)$ variables and $u^2+v^2 \leq 1/4$, then u/v is a Cauchy variate.

Example

The following example illustrates the use of the CALL RANCAU routine:

```
data case;
   retain seed1 seed2 seed3 45;
   do i=1 to 10;
      call rancau(seed1,x1);
      call rancau(seed2,x2);
      x3=rancau(seed3);
      if i=5 then
         do;
            seed2=18;
            seed3=18;
         end;
      output;
   end;
run;

proc print;
   id i;
   var seed1-seed3 x1-x3;
run;
```

The output is shown here:

I	SEED1	SEED2	SEED3	X1	X2	X3
1	1404437564	1404437564	45	-1.14736	-1.14736	-1.14736
2	1326029789	1326029789	45	-0.23735	-0.23735	-0.23735
3	1988843719	1988843719	45	-0.15474	-0.15474	-0.15474
4	1233028129	1233028129	45	4.97935	4.97935	4.97935
5	50049159	18	18	0.20402	0.20402	0.20402
6	802575599	991271755	18	3.43645	4.44427	3.43645
7	1233458739	1437043694	18	6.32808	-1.79200	6.32808
8	52428589	959908645	18	0.18815	-1.67610	0.18815
9	1216356463	1225034217	18	0.80689	3.88391	0.80689
10	1711885541	425626811	18	0.92971	-1.31309	0.92971

Changing SEED2 for the CALL RANCAU statement, when I=5, forced the stream of the variates for X2 to deviate from the stream of the variates for X1, while changing SEED3 on the RANCAU function had no effect.

RANEXP

Random variate from an exponential distribution

Random number

HELP CALL

Syntax

RANEXP(*seed,x*)

Description

seed
: is an integer-valued numeric variable, with an absolute value $<2^{31}-1$. If *seed*≤ 0, the time of day is used to initialize the seed stream. A new value for *seed* is returned each time CALL RANEXP is executed.

x
: is a numeric variable. A new value for the random variate *x* is returned each time CALL RANEXP is executed.

The CALL RANEXP routine updates *seed* and returns a variate *x* generated from an exponential distribution with parameter 1. The seed must be initialized prior to the CALL statement.

With multiple CALL RANEXP statements, it is possible to control the generation of multivariates by adjusting the seeds. The CALL RANEXP statement produces a separate stream for each seed, while the RANEXP function produces only a single stream of random variates, even with multiple RANEXP function occurrences in the same DATA step. By adjusting the seeds, streams of variates can be forced to agree or disagree for some or all of the observations in the same, or in subsequent, DATA steps.

With nonpositive seeds, when the time of day is used to initialize the seed stream, it will not be possible to duplicate the stream of variates at a later time (unless the first CALL RANEXP is only used to return a positive seed that is to be saved).

An inverse transform method applied to a RANUNI uniform variate is used.

Example

The following example illustrates the CALL RANEXP routine:

```
data case;
   retain seed1 seed2 seed3 45;
   do i=1 to 10;
      call ranexp(seed1,x1);
      call ranexp(seed2,x2);
      x3=ranexp(seed3);
      if i=5 then
         do;
            seed2=18;
            seed3=18;
         end;
      output;
   end;
   run;

proc print;
   id i;
   var seed1-seed3 x1-x3;
run;
```

The output is shown here:

I	SEED1	SEED2	SEED3	X1	X2	X3
1	694315054	694315054	45	1.12913	1.12913	1.12913
2	1404437564	1404437564	45	0.42466	0.42466	0.42466
3	2130505156	2130505156	45	0.00794	0.00794	0.00794
4	1445125588	1445125588	45	0.39610	0.39610	0.39610
5	1013861398	18	18	0.75053	0.75053	0.75053
6	1326029789	707222751	18	0.48211	1.11071	0.48211
7	932142747	991271755	18	0.83457	0.77306	0.83457
8	1988843719	422705333	18	0.07674	1.62538	0.07674
9	516966271	1437043694	18	1.42407	0.40171	1.42407
10	2137808851	1264538018	18	0.00452	0.52959	0.00452

Changing SEED2 for the CALL RANEXP statement, when I=5, forced the stream of the variates for X2 to deviate from the stream of the variates for X1, while changing SEED3 on the RANEXP function had no effect.

RANGAM

Random variate from a gamma distribution

Random number

HELP CALL

Syntax

RANGAM(*seed*, *a*, *x*)

Description

seed is an integer-valued numeric variable, with an absolute value $<2^{31}-1$. If $seed \leq 0$, the time of day is used to initialize the seed stream. A new value for *seed* is returned each time CALL RANGAM is executed.

a is a numeric shape parameter, with $a>0$.

x is a numeric variable. A new value for the random variate *x* is returned each time CALL RANGAM is executed.

The CALL RANGAM routine updates *seed* and returns a variate *x* generated from a gamma distribution with parameter *a*. The seed must be initialized prior to the CALL statement.

With multiple CALL RANGAM statements, it is possible to control the generation of multivariates by adjusting the seeds. The CALL RANGAM statement produces a separate stream for each seed, while the RANGAM function produces only a single stream of random variates, even with multiple RANGAM function occurrences in the same DATA step. By adjusting the seeds, streams of variates can be forced to agree or disagree for some or all of the observations in the same, or in subsequent, DATA steps.

With nonpositive seeds, when the time of day is used to initialize the seed stream, it will not be possible to duplicate the stream of variates at a later time (unless the first CALL RANGAM is only used to return a positive seed that is to be saved).

For $a>1$, an acceptance-rejection method due to Cheng (1977) is used. For $a \leq 1$, an acceptance-rejection method due to Fishman (1978) is used. To expedite execution, internal variables are calculated only on initial calls (that is, with each new *a*).

Example

The following example illustrates the CALL RANGAM routine:

```
data case;
   retain seed1 seed2 seed3 45;
   a=2;
   do i=1 to 10;
      call rangam(seed1,a,x1);
      call rangam(seed2,a,x2);
      x3=rangam(seed3,a);
      if i=5 then
         do;
            seed2=18;
            seed3=18;
         end;
      output;
   end;
run;
```

```
proc print;
   id i;
   var seed1-seed3 x1-x3;
run;
```

The output is shown here:

I	SEED1	SEED2	SEED3	X1	X2	X3
1	1404437564	1404437564	45	1.30569	1.30569	1.30569
2	1326029789	1326029789	45	1.87514	1.87514	1.87514
3	1988843719	1988843719	45	1.71597	1.71597	1.71597
4	50049159	50049159	45	1.59304	1.59304	1.59304
5	802575599	18	18	0.43342	0.43342	0.43342
6	100573943	991271755	18	1.11812	1.32646	1.11812
7	1986749826	1437043694	18	0.68415	0.88806	0.68415
8	52428589	959908645	18	1.62296	2.46091	1.62296
9	1216356463	1225034217	18	2.26455	4.06596	2.26455
10	805366679	425626811	18	2.16723	6.94703	2.16723

Changing SEED2 for the CALL RANGAM statement, when I=5, forced the stream of the variates for X2 to deviate from the stream of the variates for X1, while changing SEED3 on the RANGAM function had no effect.

RANNOR

Random variate from a normal distribution

Random number

HELP CALL

Syntax

RANNOR(*seed*, *x*)

Description

seed is an integer-valued numeric variable, with an absolute value $<2^{31}-1$. If *seed*≤ 0, the time of day is used to initialize the seed stream. A new value for *seed* is returned each time CALL RANNOR is executed.

x is a numeric variable. A new value for the random variate *x* is returned each time CALL RANNOR is executed.

The CALL RANNOR routine updates *seed* and returns a variate *x* generated from a normal distribution, with mean 0 and variance 1. The seed must be initialized prior to the CALL statement.

With multiple CALL RANNOR statements, it is possible to control the generation of multivariates by adjusting the seeds. The CALL RANNOR statement produces a separate stream for each seed, while the RANNOR function produces only a single stream of random variates, even with multiple RANNOR function occurrences in the same DATA step. By adjusting the seeds, streams of variates can be forced to agree or disagree for some or all of the observations in the same, or in subsequent, DATA steps.

With nonpositive seeds, when the time of day is used to initialize the seed stream, it will not be possible to duplicate the stream of variates at a later time (unless the first CALL RANNOR is only used to return a positive seed that is to be saved).

The Box-Muller transformation of RANUNI uniform variates is used.

Example

The following example illustrates the use of the CALL RANNOR routine:

```
data case;
   retain seed1 seed2 seed3 45;
   do i=1 to 10;
      call rannor(seed1,x1);
      call rannor(seed2,x2);
      x3=rannor(seed3);
      if i=5 then
        do;
          seed2=18;
          seed3=18;
        end;
      output;
   end;
run;

proc print;
   id i;
   var seed1-seed3 x1-x3;
run;
```

The output is shown here:

I	SEED1	SEED2	SEED3	X1	X2	X3
1	1404437564	1404437564	45	-0.85252	-0.85252	-0.85252
2	1445125588	1445125588	45	-0.05865	-0.05865	-0.05865
3	1326029789	1326029789	45	-0.90628	-0.90628	-0.90628
4	1988843719	1988843719	45	1.15526	1.15526	1.15526
5	2137808851	18	18	1.68697	1.68697	1.68697
6	1233028129	991271755	18	-0.47276	-1.44726	-0.47276
7	50049159	1437043694	18	1.33423	-0.87677	1.33423
8	802575599	959908645	18	-1.63511	-0.97261	-1.63511
9	100573943	1225034217	18	1.55410	-0.64742	1.55410
10	414117170	425626811	18	0.10736	0.14963	0.10736

Changing SEED2 for the CALL RANNOR statement, when I=5, forced the stream of the variates for X2 to deviate from the stream of the variates for X1, while changing SEED3 on the RANNOR function had no effect.

RANPOI

Random variate from a Poisson distribution

Random number

HELP CALL

Syntax

RANPOI(*seed*,*m*,*x*)

Description

seed is an integer-valued numeric variable, with an absolute value $<2^{31}-1$. If *seed*≤ 0, the time of day is used to initialize the seed stream. A new value for *seed* is returned each time CALL RANPOI is executed.

m is a numeric mean parameter, with $m \geq 0$.

x is a numeric variable. A new value for the random variate *x* is returned each time CALL RANPOI is executed.

The CALL RANPOI routine updates *seed* and returns a variate *x* generated from a Poisson distribution, with mean *m*. The seed must be initialized prior to the CALL statement.

With multiple CALL RANPOI statements, it is possible to control the generation of multivariates by adjusting the seeds. The CALL RANPOI statement produces a separate stream for each seed, while the RANPOI function produces only a single stream of random variates, even with multiple RANPOI function occurrences in the same DATA step. By adjusting the seeds, streams of variates can be forced to agree or disagree for some or all of the observations in the same, or in subsequent, DATA steps.

With nonpositive seeds, when the time of day is used to initialize the seed stream, it will not be possible to duplicate the stream of variates at a later time (unless the first CALL RANPOI is only used to return a positive seed that is to be saved).

For $m<100$, an inverse transform method applied to a RANUNI uniform variate is used. Two independent Poisson variates are generated: one with parameter INT(*m*), which is the integer part of *m*, and the other with parameter *m*−INT(*m*). The sum of the Poisson variates is returned (Fishman 1976). For integer $m<100$, only the first of these is generated.

For $m \geq 100$, the normal approximation of a Poisson random variable is used. In that case, the Box-Muller transformation of RANUNI uniform variates is used. To expedite execution, internal variables are calculated only on initial calls (that is, with each new *m*).

Example

The following example illustrates the use of the CALL RANPOI routine:

```
data case;
   retain seed1 seed2 seed3 45;
   m=120;
   do i=1 to 10;
      call ranpoi(seed1,m,x1);
      call ranpoi(seed2,m,x2);
      x3=ranpoi(seed3,m);
      if i=5 then
         do;
            seed2=18;
            seed3=18;
         end;
      output;
   end;
run;

proc print;
   id i;
   var seed1-seed3 x1-x3;
run;
```

The output is shown here:

I	SEED1	SEED2	SEED3	X1	X2	X3
1	1404437564	1404437564	45	111	111	111
2	1445125588	1445125588	45	119	119	119
3	1326029789	1326029789	45	110	110	110
4	1988843719	1988843719	45	133	133	133
5	2137808851	18	18	138	138	138
6	1233028129	991271755	18	115	104	115
7	50049159	1437043694	18	135	110	135
8	802575599	959908645	18	102	109	102
9	100573943	1225034217	18	137	113	137
10	414117170	425626811	18	121	122	121

Changing SEED2 for the CALL RANPOI statement, when I=5, forced the stream of the variates for X2 to deviate from the stream of the variates for X1, while changing SEED3 on the RANPOI function had no effect.

RANTBL

Random variate from a tabled probability distribution

Random number

HELP CALL

Syntax

RANTBL(*seed*,p_1, . . . p_i, . . . , p_n,*x*)

Description

seed is an integer-valued numeric variable, with an absolute value $<2^{31}-1$. If $seed \leq 0$, the time of day is used to initialize the seed stream. A new value for *seed* is returned each time CALL RANTBL is executed.

p_i is a numeric SAS value, with $0 \leq p_i \leq 1$ for $0 < i \leq n$.

x is a numeric SAS variable. A new value for the random variate *x* is returned each time CALL RANTBL is executed.

The CALL RANTBL routine updates *seed* and returns a variate *x* generated from the probability mass function defined by p_1 through p_n. The seed must be initialized prior to the CALL statement.

With multiple CALL RANTBL statements, it is possible to control the generation of multivariates by adjusting the seeds. The CALL RANTBL statement produces a separate stream for each seed, while the RANTBL function produces only a single stream of random variates, even with multiple RANTBL function occurrences in the same DATA step. By adjusting the seeds, streams of variates can be forced to agree or disagree for some or all of the observations in the same, or in subsequent, DATA steps.

With nonpositive seeds, when the time of day is used to initialize the seed stream, it will not be possible to duplicate the stream of variates at a later time (unless the first CALL RANTBL is only used to return a positive seed that is to be saved).

An inverse transform method applied to a RANUNI uniform variate is used. RANTBL returns the following data:

1 with probability p_1
2 with probability p_2
.
.
.
n with probability p_n
$n+1$ with probability $1 - \Sigma_{i=1}^{n} p_i$ if $\Sigma_{i=1}^{n} p_i \leq 1$.

If for some index $j<n$ $\Sigma_{i=1}^{j} p_i \geq 1$, RANTBL returns only the indices 1 through j with the probability of occurrence of the index j equal to

$1 - \Sigma_{i=1}^{j-1} p_i$.

Example

The following example illustrates the use of the CALL RANTBL routine:

```
data case;
  retain seed1 seed2 seed3 45;
  input p1-p9;
  do i=1 to 10;
    call rantbl(seed1,of p1-p9,x1);
    call rantbl(seed2,of p1-p9,x2);
    x3=rantbl(seed3,of p1-p9);
    if i=5 then
      do;
        seed2=18;
        seed3=18;
      end;
    output;
  end;
  cards;
.02 .04 .06 .08 .1 .12 .14 .16 .18
;

proc print;
  id i;
  var seed1-seed3 x1-x3;
run;
```

The output is shown here:

I	SEED1	SEED2	SEED3	X1	X2	X3
1	694315054	694315054	45	6	6	6
2	1404437564	1404437564	45	8	8	8
3	2130505156	2130505156	45	10	10	10
4	1445125588	1445125588	45	8	8	8
5	1013861398	18	18	7	7	7
6	1326029789	707222751	18	8	6	8
7	932142747	991271755	18	7	7	7
8	1988843719	422705333	18	10	4	10
9	516966271	1437043694	18	5	8	5
10	2137808851	1264538018	18	10	8	10

Changing SEED2 for the CALL RANTBL statement, when I=5, forced the stream of variates for X2 to deviate from the stream of variates for X1, while changing SEED3 on the RANTBL function had no effect.

RANTRI

Random variate from a triangular distribution

Random number

HELP CALL

Syntax

RANTRI(*seed*,*h*,*x*)

Description

seed is an integer-valued numeric variable, with an absolute value $<2^{31}-1$. If $seed \leq 0$, the time of day is used to initialize the seed stream. A new value for *seed* is returned each time CALL RANTRI is executed.

h is a numeric SAS value, with $0<h<1$.

x is a numeric SAS variable. A new value for the random variate *x* is returned each time CALL RANTRI is executed.

The CALL RANTRI routine updates *seed* and returns a variate *x* generated from a triangular distribution with parameter *h*. The seed must be initialized prior to the CALL statement.

With multiple CALL RANTRI statements, it is possible, by adjusting the seeds, to control the generation of multivariates. The CALL RANTRI statement produces a separate stream for each seed, while the RANTRI function produces only a single stream of random variates, even with multiple RANTRI function occurrences in the same DATA step. By adjusting the seeds, streams of variates can be forced to agree or disagree for some or all of the observations in the same, or in subsequent, DATA steps.

With nonpositive seeds, when the time of day is used to initialize the seed stream, it will not be possible to duplicate the stream of variates at a later time (unless the first CALL RANTRI is only used to return a positive seed that is to be saved).

An inverse transform method applied to a RANUNI uniform variate is used.

Example

The following example illustrates the use of the CALL RANTRI routine:

```
data case;
   retain seed1 seed2 seed3 45;
   h=.2;
   do i=1 to 10;
      call rantri(seed1,h,x1);
      call rantri(seed2,h,x2);
      x3=rantri(seed3,h);
      if i=5 then
         do;
            seed2=18;
            seed3=18;
         end;
      output;
   end;
run;
```

```
proc print;
   id i;
   var seed1-seed3 x1-x3;
run;
```

The output is shown here:

I	SEED1	SEED2	SEED3	X1	X2	X3
1	694315054	694315054	45	0.26424	0.26424	0.26424
2	1404437564	1404437564	45	0.47388	0.47388	0.47388
3	2130505156	2130505156	45	0.92047	0.92047	0.92047
4	1445125588	1445125588	45	0.48848	0.48848	0.48848
5	1013861398	18	18	0.35015	0.35015	0.35015
6	1326029789	707222751	18	0.44681	0.26751	0.44681
7	932142747	991271755	18	0.32713	0.34371	0.32713
8	1988843719	422705333	18	0.75690	0.19841	0.75690
9	516966271	1437043694	18	0.22063	0.48555	0.22063
10	2137808851	1264538018	18	0.93997	0.42648	0.93997

Changing SEED2 for the CALL RANTRI statement, when I=5, forced the stream of the variates for X2 to deviate from the stream of the variates for X1, while changing SEED3 on the RANTRI function had no effect.

RANUNI

Random variate from a uniform distribution

Random number

HELP CALL

Syntax

RANUNI(*seed,x*)

Description

seed is an integer-valued numeric variable, with an absolute value $<2^{31}-1$. If $seed \leq 0$, the time of day is used to initialize the seed stream. A new value for *seed* is returned each time CALL RANUNI is executed.

x is a numeric variable. A new value for the random variate *x* is returned each time CALL RANUNI is executed.

The CALL RANUNI routine updates *seed* and returns a variate *x* generated from the uniform distribution on the interval (0,1), using a prime modulus multiplicative generator with modulus $2^{31}-1$ and multiplier 397204094 (Fishman and Moore 1982).

The seed must be initialized prior to the CALL RANUNI statement. The CALL RANUNI statement produces a separate stream for each seed, while the RANUNI function produces only a single stream of random variates, even with multiple RANUNI function occurrences in the same DATA step. By adjusting the seeds, streams of variates can be forced to agree or disagree for some or all of the observations in the same, or in subsequent, DATA steps.

With nonpositive seeds, when the time of day is used to initialize the seed stream, it will not be possible to duplicate the stream of variates at a later time (unless the first CALL RANUNI is only used to return a positive seed that is to be saved).

Example

The following example illustrates the use of the CALL RANUNI routine:

```
data case;
   retain seed1 seed2 seed3 45;
   do i=1 to 10;
      call ranuni(seed1,x1);
      call ranuni(seed2,x2);
      x3=ranuni(seed3);
      if i=5 then
         do;
            seed2=18;
            seed3=18;
         end;
      output;
   end;
run;

proc print;
   id i;
   var seed1-seed3 x1-x3;
run;
```

The output is shown here:

I	SEED1	SEED2	SEED3	X1	X2	X33
1	694315054	694315054	45	0.32332	0.32332	0.32332
2	1404437564	1404437564	45	0.65399	0.65399	0.65399
3	2130505156	2130505156	45	0.99209	0.99209	0.99209
4	1445125588	1445125588	45	0.67294	0.67294	0.67294
5	1013861398	18	18	0.47212	0.47212	0.47212
6	1326029789	707222751	18	0.61748	0.32933	0.61748
7	932142747	991271755	18	0.43406	0.46160	0.43406
8	1988843719	422705333	18	0.92613	0.19684	0.92613
9	516966271	1437043694	18	0.24073	0.66918	0.24073
10	2137808851	1264538018	18	0.99549	0.58885	0.99549

Changing SEED2 for the CALL RANUNI statement, when I=5, forced the stream of the variates for X2 to deviate from the stream of the variates for X1, while changing SEED3 on the RANUNI function had no effect.

SYMPUT

DATA step information to a macro variable

Special

HELP CALL

Syntax

SYMPUT(*argument-1,argument-2*)

Description

argument-1 specifies a character expression that identifies the macro variable to be assigned a value. If the macro variable does not exist, the routine creates it.

argument-2 specifies a character expression that contains the value to be assigned.

The CALL SYMPUT routine either creates a macro variable whose value is information from the DATA step or assigns a DATA step value to an existing macro variable. The CALL SYMPUT routine is listed with macro facility features in Chapter 20, "SAS Macro Facility," and it is documented in the *SAS Guide to Macro Processing, Version 6, Second Edition.*

See Also

SYMGET function in Chapter 11, "SAS Functions"

Chapter 20, "SAS Macro Facility"

SAS Guide to Macro Processing, Version 6, Second Edition

SYSTEM

Operating system commands

System command

HELP CALL

Syntax

SYSTEM(*command*)

Description

command specifies any of the following: a system command enclosed in quotes (explicit character string); an expression whose value is a system command; or the name of a character variable whose value is a system command to be executed.

The CALL SYSTEM routine issues operating system commands.

Comparisons

The CALL SYSTEM routine is similar to the X command and statement; however, it can be called.

VNAME

Variable name as value of specified variable

Variable control

HELP CALL

Syntax

VNAME(*variable-1*,*variable-2*)

Description

variable-1 specifies any valid SAS variable.

variable-2 specifies any valid SAS variable. Because SAS variable names can contain up to eight characters, the length of *variable-2* should be at least eight.

The CALL VNAME routine assigns the name of *variable-1* as the value of *variable-2*.

Example

The following example uses the CALL VNAME routine with array references to return the names of all variables in data set OLD:

```
data new;
   set old;
   array abc{*} _character_;     /* all character variables in old */
   array def{*} _numeric_;       /* all numeric variables in old   */
   length name $8;               /* name is not in either array    */
   do i=1 to dim(abc);
      call vname(abc{i},name); /* get name of character variable */
      output;                    /* write name to an observation   */
   end;
   do j=1 to dim(def);
      call vname(def{j},name); /* get name of numeric variable   */
      output;                    /* write name to an observation   */
   end;
   stop;
   keep name;
run;
```

References

Cheng, R.C.H. (1977), "The Generation of Gamma Variables," *Applied Statistics*, 26, 71–75.

Fishman, G.S. (1976), "Sampling from the Poisson Distribution on a Computer," *Computing*, 17, 145–156.

Fishman, G.S. (1978), *Principles of Discrete Event Simulation*, New York: John Wiley & Sons, Inc.

Fishman, G.S. and Moore, L.R. (1982), "A Statistical Evaluation of Multiplicative Congruential Generators with Modulus $(2^{31}-1)$," *Journal of the American Statistical Association*, 77, 129–136.

CHAPTER 13 SAS® Informats

Background information on SAS informats, including a table listing all informats, appears in Chapter 3, "Components of the SAS Language." See

Table 3.7, "SAS Informats and Aliases," and Table 3.8, "Categories and Descriptions of SAS Informats."

$ASCIIw.

Converts ASCII character data to native format

Character

Width range: 1–200

Default width: 1

HELP INFORMAT

Description

The $ASCII*w*. informat reads character data represented in ASCII and converts the data to native format. If ASCII is the native format, the $ASCII*w*. informat performs no conversion.

Comparisons

On an IBM® mainframe system, the $ASCII*w*. informat converts ASCII data to EBCDIC. On all other systems, the $ASCII*w*. informat has the same effect as the $CHAR*w*. informat.

Example

Data Lines	SAS Statement	Results *
`----+----1----+----2`		**EBCDIC**
`abc`	`input @1 name $ascii3.;`	818283
`ABC`		C1C2C3
`();`		4D5D5E
		ASCII
		616263
		414243
		28293B

* The results are hexadecimal representations of codes for characters. Each two hexadecimal digits correspond to 1 byte of binary data, and each byte corresponds to one character value.

$BINARYw.

Converts binary values to character values

Character

Width range: 1–200

Default width: 8

HELP INFORMAT

Description

The $BINARY*w*. informat converts values from binary to character representation. It does not interpret actual binary data, but rather interprets a string of characters containing only 0s or 1s as though it is actual binary information.

The *w* value specifies the width of the input field. Because 8 bits of binary information represent one character, every eight characters of input the $BINARY*w*. informat reads become one character value stored in a variable.

If the *w* value is less than 8, the $BINARY*w*. informat interprets the data as the characters you read followed by 0s. Thus, the $BINARY4. informat interprets the characters 0101 as 01010000, which translates into an EBCDIC `&` or an ASCII `P`.

If the *w* value is greater than 8 but not an even multiple of 8, the $BINARY*w*. informat reads up to the largest multiple of 8 less than *w* and converts that string to the value it represents.

Use the $BINARY*w*. informat to read representations of binary codes for unprintable characters. Enter an ASCII or EBCDIC equivalent for a particular character as a string of 0s and 1s, and use the $BINARY*w*. informat to translate and store the string as its equivalent character value.

You can use only the character digits 1 and 0 in the input, with no embedded blanks. The $BINARY*w*. informat ignores leading and trailing blanks.

Comparisons

The $BINARY*w*. informat for character data and the BINARY*w.d* informat for numeric data both read eight characters of input containing only 0s or 1s as a binary representation of 1 byte of character or numeric data. The $HEX*w*. informat reads hexadecimal digits representing the ASCII or EBCDIC equivalent of character data.

Example

Data Line	SAS Statement	Results
`----+----1----+----2`		**ASCII**
`0100110001001101`	`input @1 name $binary16.;`	`LM`
		EBCDIC
		`<(`

$CBw.

Reads standard character data from column-binary files

Character

Width range: 1–200

Default width: none

HELP INFORMAT

Description

The $CB*w*. informat reads standard character data from column-binary files, with each card column represented in 2 bytes, and translates the data into standard character codes. If the combinations are not valid punch codes, the SAS System returns blanks and sets the automatic variable _ERROR_ to 1.

Example

Data Line *	SAS Statement	Results
`12 on`	`input x $cb2.;`	**EBCDIC**
`11 off`		`+`
`0 off`		**ASCII**
`1 off`		`N`
`2 off`		
`3 off`		
`4 off`		
`5 off`		
`6 on`		
`7 off`		
`8 on`		
`9 off`		

* The data lines represent a column on a punch card, with the word *on* indicating a punch and the word *off* indicating no punch. In a column-binary file, the binary data corresponding to the card column in the example have the binary representation 0010 0000 0000 1010.

See Also

CB*w.d* informat

PUNCH.*d* informat

ROW*w.d* informat

$CHARw.

Reads character data with blanks

Character

Width range: 1–200

Default width: 1 if the length of the variable is not yet defined; otherwise, the length of the variable

HELP INFORMAT

Description

The $CHAR*w*. informat reads character data. The *w* value specifies the number of columns in the field containing the character data. The $CHAR*w*. informat does not trim leading and trailing blanks in character data before storing values.

If you use the $CHAR*w*. informat in an INFORMAT or ATTRIB statement within a DATA step that uses list input, you should remember that by default list input makes the SAS System interpret any blank embedded within data as a field delimiter, including leading blanks.

Comparisons

The $CHAR*w*. informat is almost identical to the $*w*. informat. However, the $CHAR*w*. informat does not trim leading blanks, and the $*w*. informat converts a single period in a raw data input field to a blank, while the $CHAR*w*. informat does not.

The following table compares the SAS informat $CHAR8. with notation in other programming languages:

Language	Character Notation
SAS	$CHAR8.
IBM 370 assembler	CL8
C	char [8]
COBOL	PIC x(8)
FORTRAN	A8
PL/I	CHAR(8)

Example

Data Lines	SAS Statement	Results *
`----+----1----+----2`		
`XYZ`	`input @1 name $char5.;`	`XYZbb`
` XYZ`		`bXYZb`
` X YZ`		`bXbYZ`

* The character b in the results indicates a blank space.

$CHARZBw.

Converts binary 0s to blanks

Character

Width range: 1–200

Default width: 1 if the length of the variable is not yet defined; otherwise, the length of the variable

HELP INFORMAT

Description

The $CHARZB*w*. informat reads character data and changes any byte containing a binary 0 to a blank. The *w* value specifies the number of columns in the data field. The $CHARZB*w*. informat does not trim leading and trailing blanks in character data before storing values.

Comparisons

The $CHARZB*w*. informat is identical to the $CHAR*w*. except that $CHARZB*w*. changes any byte containing a binary 0 to a blank character.

Example

Data Lines *	SAS Statement	Results
EBCDIC	`input @1 name $charzb5.;`	`XYZbb`
`E7E8E90000`		`bXYZb`
`00E7E8E900`		`bXbYZ`
`00E700E8E9`		
ASCII		
`58595A0000`		
`0058595A00`		
`005800595A`		

* The data lines are hexadecimal representations of codes for characters. Each two hexadecimal digits correspond to 1 byte of binary data, and each byte corresponds to one character. The character b in the results indicates a blank space.

$EBCDICw.

Converts EBCDIC character data to native format

Character

Width range: 1–200

Default width: 1

HELP INFORMAT

Description

The $EBCDIC*w*. informat reads character data represented in EBCDIC and converts the data to native format. If EBCDIC is the native format, the $EBCDIC*w*. informat performs no conversion.

Comparisons

On an IBM mainframe system, the $EBCDIC*w*. informat has the same effect as the $CHAR*w*. informat. On all other systems, the $EBCDIC*w*. informat converts EBCDIC to ASCII.

Example

Data Lines	SAS Statement	Results *
----+----1----+----2		**ASCII**
qrs	input @1 name $ebcdic3.;	717273
QRS		515253
+;>		2B3B3E
		EBCDIC
		9899A2
		D8D9E2
		4E5E6E

* The results are hexadecimal representations of codes for characters. Each two hexadecimal digits correspond to 1 byte of binary data, and each byte corresponds to one character value.

$HEXw.

Converts hexadecimal data to character data

Character

Width range: 1–200

Default width: 2

HELP INFORMAT

Description

The $HEX*w*. informat converts values stored as hexadecimal digits to the corresponding character representation. The *w* value specifies the number of digits of hexadecimal data. The $HEX*w*. informat converts every two digits of hexadecimal data into 1 byte of character data. If you specify 1 as the *w* value, the $HEX*w*. informat pads a trailing hexadecimal 0. If you specify an odd number greater than 1 as the *w* value, the $HEX*w*. informat reads one less hexadecimal character than you specify.

Use the $HEX*w*. informat to encode hexadecimal values into a character variable when your input method is limited to printable characters.

Comparisons

The $HEX*w*. informat for character data and the HEX*w*. informat for numeric data are similar in that they both read two digits of hexadecimal data at a time, converting them into either one digit of character data or 1 byte of numeric data.

Example

Data Line	SAS Statement	Results
----+----1----+----2		**ASCII**
6C6C	input @1 name $hex4.;	ll
		EBCDIC
		%%

$OCTAL*w*.

Converts octal data to character data

Character

Width range: 1–200

Default width: 3

HELP INFORMAT

Description

The $OCTAL*w*. informat converts octal values to character data. The *w* value specifies the width of the input field in bits, since one digit of octal data represents 3 bits of binary information. You should increment the value you specify for the *w* value by 3 for every column of octal data you read with the $OCTAL*w*. informat.

Because you need 8 bits of binary data to represent the code for one digit of character data, you need at least three digits of octal data to represent one digit of character data, which includes an extra bit. The $OCTAL*w*. informat treats every three digits of octal data as one digit of character data, ignoring the extra bit.

Use the $OCTAL*w*. informat to read octal representations of binary codes for unprintable characters. Enter an ASCII or EBCDIC equivalent for a particular character in octal notation, and use the $OCTAL*w*. informat to translate and store it as its equivalent character value.

You can use only the digits 0 through 7 in the input, with no embedded blanks. The $OCTAL*w*. informat ignores leading and trailing blanks.

Comparisons

The $OCTAL*w*. informat for character data and the OCTAL*w.d* informat for numeric data both read octal data and translate them into character or numeric equivalents.

Example

Data Line	SAS Statement	Results
`----+----1----+----2`		**EBCDIC**
`114`	`input @1 x $octal9.;`	`<`
		ASCII
		`L`

$PHEX*w*.

Converts packed hexadecimal data to character data

Character

Width range: 1–100

Default width: 2

HELP INFORMAT

Description

The $PHEX. informat converts packed hexadecimal data to character data. Packed hexadecimal data are like packed decimal data, except that all hexadecimal digits are valid. In packed hexadecimal data, the value of the low-order nibble has no meaning. In packed decimal data, the value of the low-order nibble indicates the sign of the numeric value the data represent.

The *w* value specifies the number of bytes in the input field. If you use the $PHEX*w*. informat to read packed hexadecimal data into a variable, the length of the variable is the number of bytes required to store the resulting character value, not the *w* value. In general, a character variable whose length is implicitly defined with the $PHEX*w*. informat has a length of 2*w*–1.

The $PHEX*w*. informat returns a character value, and the value of the sign nibble is treated as if it were `X'F'`, regardless of its actual value.

Comparisons

Both the PD*w.d* and the $PHEX*w.* informats read packed data, but the PD*w.d* informat returns numeric data, and the $PHEX*w.* informat returns character data.

Example

Data Line *	SAS Statement	Result
`0001111000001111`	`input @1 devaddr $phex2.;`	`1E0`

* The data line represents 2 bytes of actual binary data, with each half byte corresponding to a single hexadecimal digit. The equivalent hexadecimal representation for the data line is 1E0F.

$VARYINGw.

Reads varying length values

Character

Width range: 1–200

Default width: 8 or length of variable

HELP INFORMAT

Description

The $VARYING*w.* informat reads variable-length fields of character data. Use the $VARYING*w.* informat when the length of a character value differs from record to record. After reading a data value with the $VARYING*w.* informat, the pointer's position is the first column after the value. You can only use the $VARYING*w.* informat within a DATA step.

You can use the following terms with the $VARYING*w.* informat:

w
: specifies the maximum width of a character field for all the records in a raw file. The SAS System always associates a *w* value with the $VARYING*w.* informat. If you want to specify a *w* value, it must follow the $VARYING*w.* informat. If you do not specify a *w* value, the SAS System uses the length of the character variable into which the value is being read as the *w* value.

length-variable
: specifies a numeric variable containing the actual width of the character field in the current record. You **must** specify the name of a *length-variable* immediately after the $VARYING*w.* informat in an INPUT statement. The SAS System obtains the value of the variable by either reading it directly from a field described in an INPUT statement or by calculating its value.

If the variable's value is 0, negative, or missing for a given observation, the SAS System reads no data from the corresponding record. Thus, the $VARYING*w.* informat enables you to read both zero-length records and fields.

If the variable's value is greater than 0 but less than the *w* value, the SAS System reads the number of columns specified by *length-variable* and pads the value with trailing blanks to the maximum length when assigning it to the variable. If the value of the variable is equal to or greater than the *w* value, the SAS System reads *w* columns. *Length-variable* cannot be an array reference.

The value of *length-variable* is explicit if it exists in a numeric field in the record, or implicit if the character variable occupies the entire varying portion of a variable-length record.

Examples

Example 1: Obtaining a Current Record Length Directly

Data Lines *	SAS Statement	Results
`----+----1----+----2`		
`5shark`	`input lv 1. fi $varying9. lv;`	`shark`
`3sunfish`		`sun`
`8bluefish`		`bluefish`

* Notice the result of reading the second data line.

Example 2: Obtaining a Record Length Indirectly with the LENGTH= Option

Data Lines

```
----+----1----+----2
SMITH    CHEMISTRY
JOHNSON  GEOLOGY
WILCOX   ART
```

SAS Statements *

```
infile file-specification
       length=lg;
input @;
vlg=lg-9;
input name $ 1-9
      @10 class $varying20. vlg;
```

Results

```
SMITH   CHEMISTRY
JOHNSON GEOLOGY
WILCOX  ART
```

* The first INPUT statement enables the LENGTH= option to assign the internally stored record length to the variable LG; the trailing @ holds the record for another INPUT statement. Next, an assignment statement calculates the value of the varying-length field by subtracting the fixed-length portion of the record from the total record length. The variable VLG holds the length of the last field and becomes the *length-variable* argument to the $VARYING20. informat.

$w.

Reads standard character data

Character

Width range: 1–200

HELP INFORMAT

Description

The $*w*. informat reads standard character data. The *w* value specifies the number of columns in the field containing the character value. You must specify a *w* value because the SAS System does not supply a default value.

The $*w*. informat trims leading blanks before storing values, automatically left aligning the values. In addition, if a field contains nothing but blanks and a single period, the $*w*. informat converts the period to a blank because it interprets the period as a missing value. The $*w*. informat treats two or more periods in a field as character data.

Comparisons

The $*w*. informat is almost identical to the $CHAR*w*. informat. However, the $*w*. informat trims leading blanks and converts a single period in a raw data input field to a blank, while the $CHAR*w*. informat does not.

Example

Data Lines	SAS Statement	Results *
`----+----1----+----2`		
`XYZ`	`input @1 name $5.;`	`XYZbb`
` XYZ`		`XYZbb`
`X YZ`		`XbYZb`

* The character b in the results indicates a blank space.

BINARYw.d

Converts positive binary values to integers

Numeric

Width range: 1–64

Default width: 8

HELP INFORMAT

Description

The BINARY*w.d* informat reads the binary representation of positive numeric values, interpreting them as integer (fixed-point) values. The *w* value specifies the width of the input field. The *d* value is optional and can be greater than or equal to the *w* value. If you include a *d* value, the BINARY*w.d* informat divides the number by 10^d.

You can use only the character digits 1 and 0 in the input, with no embedded blanks. The BINARY*w.d* informat ignores leading and trailing blanks.

The BINARY*w.d* informat cannot read negative values. It treats all input values as positive (unsigned).

Example

Data Line	SAS Statement	Result
`----+----1----+----2`		
`00001111`	`input @1 value binary8.1;`	`1.5`

BITS*w.d*

Extracts bits

Numeric

Width range: 1–64

Default width: 1

HELP INFORMAT

Description

The BITS*w.d* informat extracts particular bits from an input stream, assigning the numeric equivalent of the extracted bit string to a variable. The *w* and *d* values specify the location of the string you want the BITS*w.d* informat to read. The *d* value is the zero-based offset, and the *w* value is the number of bits to read. The *d* value range is 0 through 63.

The BITS*w.d* informat is useful for extracting data from system records with many pieces of information packed into single bytes.

Example

Data Line	SAS Statement	Result *
`----+----1----+----2`		
`B`	`input @1 value bits4.4;`	`2`

* The EBCDIC binary code for a capital B is 11000010, and the ASCII binary code is 01000010. The BITS4.4 informat reads the bit string 0010 in either case and stores the numeric value 2, which is equivalent to this binary combination.

BZ*w.d*

Converts blanks to 0s

Numeric

Width range: 1–32

Default width: 1

HELP INFORMAT

Description

The BZ*w.d* informat reads numeric values and converts any trailing or embedded blanks to 0s, ignoring leading blanks. The *w* value specifies the width of the input field. The *d* value optionally specifies the number of digits to the right of the decimal point in the numeric value. The *d* value range is 0 through 31.

The BZ*w.d* informat can read numeric values located anywhere in the field. Blanks can precede or follow the numeric value, and a minus sign must precede negative values. The BZ*w.d* informat ignores blanks between a minus sign and a numeric value in an input field.

The BZ*w.d* informat interprets a single period in a field as a 0. The informat interprets multiple periods or other nonnumeric characters in a field as a missing value.

When an input value contains a decimal point, the SAS System ignores any *d* value you specify with the BZ*w.d* informat. Otherwise, when you include a *d* value, the BZ*w.d* informat divides the input values by 10^d.

To use the BZ*w.d* informat in a DATA step using list input, you must change the delimiter for list input with the DLM= option in the INFILE statement. By default, the SAS System interprets blanks between values in the data line as delimiters rather than 0s.

Comparisons

The BZ*w.d* informat is identical to the *w.d* informat except that the BZ*w.d* informat converts trailing or embedded blanks to 0s. If you do not want to convert trailing blanks to 0s (for example, when reading values in E-notation), use either the *w.d* informat or the E*w.d* informat instead.

Examples

Data Lines	SAS Statement	Results
`----+----1----+----2`		
`34`	`input @1 x bz4.;`	3400
`----+----1----+----2`		
`-2`	`input @1 y bz4.1;`	-20
`-2 1`		-20.1

CBw.d

Reads standard numeric values from column-binary files

Numeric

Width range: 1–32

Default width: none

HELP INFORMAT

Description

The CB*w.d* informat reads standard numeric values from column-binary files, translating the data into standard binary format.

The SAS System first stores each column of column-binary data you read with the CB*w.d* informat in 2 bytes, ignoring the 2 high-order bits of each byte. If the punch codes are valid, the SAS System stores the equivalent numeric value into the variable you specify. If the combinations are not valid, the SAS System assigns the variable a missing value and sets the automatic variable _ERROR_ to 1.

Example

Data Lines *	SAS Statement	Result
12 off	`input x cb8.;`	9
11 off		
0 off		
1 off		
2 off		
3 off		
4 off		
5 off		
6 off		
7 off		
8 off		
9 on		

* The data lines represent a column on a punch card, with the word *on* indicating a punch and the word *off* indicating no punch. In a column-binary file, the binary data corresponding to the card column in the example have the binary representation 0000 0000 0000 0001.

See Also

$CB*w.* informat

PUNCH.*d* informat

ROW*w.d* informat

COMMA*w.d*

Removes embedded characters

Numeric

Width range: 1–32

Default width: 1

HELP INFORMAT

Description

The COMMA*w.d* informat reads numeric values and removes embedded commas, blanks, dollar signs, percent signs, dashes, and right parentheses from the input data. The COMMA*w.d* informat converts a left parenthesis at the beginning of a field to a minus sign. The *d* value range is 0 through 31.

Example

Data Lines	SAS Statement	Results
`----+----1----+----2`		
`$1,000,000`	`input @1 x comma10.;`	1000000
`(500)`		-500

COMMAX*w.d*

Removes embedded characters

Numeric

Width range: 1–32

Default width: 1

HELP INFORMAT

Description

The COMMAX*w.d* informat reads numeric values and removes embedded periods, blanks, dollar signs, percent signs, dashes, and right parentheses from the input data. The COMMAX*w.d* informat converts a left parenthesis at the beginning of a field to a minus sign. The *d* value range is 0 through 31.

Comparisons

The COMMAX*w.d* informat operates like the COMMA*w.d* informat, but reverses the roles of the decimal point and the comma. This convention is common in European countries.

Example

Data Lines	SAS Statement	Results
`----+----1----+----2`		
`$1.000.000`	`input @1 x commax10.;`	1000000
`(500)`		-500

DATEw.

Reads date values (*ddmmmyy*)

Date and time

Width range: 7–32

Default width: 7

HELP INFORMAT

Description

The DATE*w*. informat reads date values in the form *ddmmmyy* or *ddmmmyyyy*, where *dd* is an integer from 01 through 31 representing the day of the month, *mmm* is the first three letters of the month name, and *yy* or *yyyy* is an integer representing the year. Blanks and other special characters can be placed between day, month, and year values. Width values must allow space for blanks and special characters.

Note: The SAS System defaults to a date in the 1900s if *yy* is two digits. Use the YEARCUTOFF= system option to override the system default and specify a date range of your choice.

Example

Data Lines	SAS Statement	Results
`----+----1----+----2`		
`1jan1990`	`input day date10.;`	10958
`01 jan 90`		10958
`1 jan 90`		10958
`1-jan-1990`		10958

See Also

"SAS Date and Time Values" in Chapter 4, "Rules of the SAS Language"

DATE function in Chapter 11, "SAS Functions"

DATE*w*. format in Chapter 14, "SAS Formats"

YEARCUTOFF= system option in Chapter 16, "SAS System Options"

DATETIMEw.

Reads datetime values (*ddmmmyy hh:mm:ss.ss*)

Date and time

Width range: 13–40

Default width: 18

HELP INFORMAT

Description

The DATETIME*w*. informat reads datetime values in the form *ddmmmyy*, followed by a blank or special character, and *hh:mm:ss.ss*. The value of *hh* ranges from 00 through 23 and the values of *mm* and *ss* range from 00 through 59. The value of *ss.ss* is an optional time value representing seconds and decimal fractions of seconds. With the DATETIME*w*. informat you must give a value both for the date and the time.

Note: The SAS System defaults to a date in the 1900s if *yy* is two digits. Use the YEARCUTOFF= system option to override the system default and specify a date range of your choice.

Example

Data Lines	SAS Statement	Results
`----+----1----+----2`		
`23dec89:10:03:17.2`	`input date datetime20.;`	946029797.2
`23dec1989/10:03:17.2`		946029797.2

See Also

DATE*w.* and TIME*w.* informats

"SAS Date and Time Values" in Chapter 4, "Rules of the SAS Language"

DATETIME function in Chapter 11, "SAS Functions"

DATE*w.*, DATETIME*w.d*, and TIME*w.d* formats in Chapter 14, "SAS Formats"

YEARCUTOFF= system option in Chapter 16, "SAS System Options"

DDMMYY*w.*

Reads date values (*ddmmyy*)

Date and time

Width range: 6–32

Default width: 6

HELP INFORMAT

Description

The DDMMYY*w.* informat reads date values in *ddmmyy* form, where *dd*, *mm*, and *yy* are integers representing the day, month, and year. The day, month, and year fields can be separated by blanks or special characters. However, if delimiters are used, they should be placed between all fields in the value. Blanks can also be placed before and after the date.

Note: The SAS System defaults to a date in the 1900s if *yy* is two digits. Use the YEARCUTOFF= system option to override the system default and specify a date range of your choice.

Example

Data Lines	SAS Statement	Results
`----+----1----+----2`		
`231090`	`input day ddmmyy8.;`	11253
`23/10/90`		11253
`23 10 90`		11253

See Also

DATE*w.*, MMDDYY*w.*, and YYMMDD*w.* informats

"SAS Date and Time Values" in Chapter 4, "Rules of the SAS Language"

MDY function in Chapter 11, "SAS Functions"

DATE*w.*, DDMMYY*w.*, MMDDYY*w.*, and YYMMDD*w.* formats in Chapter 14, "SAS Formats"

YEARCUTOFF= system option in Chapter 16, "SAS System Options"

E*w.d*

Reads scientific notation

Numeric

Width range: 7–32

Default width: 12

HELP INFORMAT

Description

The E*w.d* informat reads numeric values that are stored in scientific notation. The *w* value specifies the width of the field containing the numeric value. The *d* value specifies the number of digits to the right of the decimal point in the numeric value. The *d* value range is 0 through 31.

Comparisons

The E*w.d* informat is not used extensively because the SAS informat for standard numeric data, the *w.d* informat, can read numbers in scientific notation. Use the E*w.d* informat to permit only scientific notation in your input data.

Example

Data Line	SAS Statement	Result
`----+----1----+----2`		
`1.257E3`	`input @1 x e7.;`	1257

HEX*w.*

Converts hexadecimal positive binary values to fixed- or floating-point values

Numeric

Width range: 1–16

Default width: 8

HELP INFORMAT

Description

The HEX*w.* informat reads hexadecimal digits and converts them to either integer binary (fixed-point) or real binary (floating-point) values. The *w* value specifies the field width of the input value, and also specifies whether the final value is fixed-point or floating-point.

When the *w* value is less than 16, the HEX*w.* informat converts input to positive integer binary values, treating all input values as positive (unsigned).

When the *w* value is 16, the HEX*w.* informat converts input to real binary (floating-point) values, including negative values.

Note: Different computer systems store floating-point values in different ways. However, the HEX16. informat reads hexadecimal representations of floating-point values with consistent results if the values are expressed in the same way your computer system stores them.

The HEX*w.* informat ignores leading or trailing blanks.

Example

Data Line *	SAS Statement	Result
`----+----1----+----2`		
`88F 4152000000000000`	`input @1 x hex3. @5 y hex16.;`	2191 5.125

* The data line shows IBM mainframe hexadecimal data.

IBw.d

Reads integer binary (fixed-point) values

Numeric

Width range: 1–8

Default width: 4

HELP INFORMAT

Description

The IB*w.d* informat reads integer binary (fixed-point) values, including negative values represented in two's complement notation. If you use a *d* value, the IB*w.d* informat divides the number by 10 ^{d}. The *d* value range is 0 through 10.

Note: Different computer systems store integer binary values in different ways. However, the IB*w.d* informat reads integer binary values with consistent results if the values are created on the same type of computer system you use to run the SAS System.

Comparisons

Ordinarily, it is not possible to key in binary data directly from a terminal, although many programs write data in binary. The following table compares integer binary notation in several programming languages:

	Integer Binary Notation	
Language	2 Bytes	4 Bytes
FORTRAN	INTEGER*2	INTEGER*4
C	short	long
PL/1	FIXED BIN(15)	FIXED BIN(31)
COBOL	COMP PIC 9(4)	COMP PIC 9(8)
IBM 370 assembler	H	F

Example

Data Line *	SAS Statement	Result
00000080	input @1 x ib4.;	128

* The data line is a hexadecimal representation of a 4-byte integer binary number. Each byte occupies one column of the input field.

JULIANw.

Reads Julian dates (*yyddd* or *yyyyddd*)

Date and time

Width range: 5–32

Default width: 5

HELP INFORMAT

Description

The JULIAN*w.* informat reads Julian dates in the form *yyddd* or *yyyyddd*, where *yy* or *yyyy* is a two-digit or four-digit integer representing a specific year, and *ddd* is an integer from 1 through 365 (366 for a leap year), representing the day of the year. Julian dates consist of strings of contiguous numbers, which means that zeros must pad any space between the year and day value. The example below illustrates this point.

Note: Julian dates containing year values before 1582 are not valid for conversion to Gregorian dates.

Use the YEARCUTOFF= system option to override the system default and specify a date range of your choice.

Example

Data Line *	SAS Statement	Result
----+----1----+----2		
90091	input day julian8.;	11048

* The data line corresponds to the ninety-first day of 1990, or 01APR90.

See Also

JULIAN*w*. informat

"SAS Date and Time Values" in Chapter 4, "Rules of the SAS Language"

DATEJUL and JULDATE functions in Chapter 11, "SAS Functions"

JULIAN*w*. format in Chapter 14, "SAS Formats"

YEARCUTOFF= system option in Chapter 16, "SAS System Options"

MMDDYY*w*.

Reads date values (*mmddyy*)

Date and time

Width range: 6–32

Default width: 6

HELP INFORMAT

Description

The MMDDYY*w*. informat reads date values in *mmddyy* form, where *mm*, *dd*, and *yy* are integers representing the month, day, and year. The month, day, and year fields can be separated by blanks or special characters. However, if delimiters are used, they should be placed between all fields in the value. Blanks can also be placed before and after the date.

Note: The SAS System defaults to a date in the 1900s if *yy* is two digits. Use the YEARCUTOFF= system option to override the system default and specify your choice of date range.

Example

Data Lines	SAS Statement	Results
----+----1----+----2		
010190	input day mmddyy8.;	10958
1/1/90		10958
01 1 90		10958

See Also

DATE*w*., DDMMYY*w*., and YYMMDD*w*. informats

"SAS Date and Time Values" in Chapter 4, "Rules of the SAS Language"

DAY, MDY, MONTH, and YEAR functions in Chapter 11, "SAS Functions"

DATE*w*., DDMMYY*w*., MMDDYY*w*., and YYMMDD*w*. formats in Chapter 14, "SAS Formats"

YEARCUTOFF= system option in Chapter 16, "SAS System Options"

MONYY*w*.

Reads month and year date values (*mmmyy*)

Date and time

Width range: 5–32

Default width: 5

HELP INFORMAT

Description

The MONYY*w*. informat reads date values in the form *mmmyy*, where *mmm* is the first three letters of the month name, and *yy* or *yyyy* is an integer representing the year. The *mmm* and *yy* or *yyyy* values cannot be separated by blanks. A value read with the MONYY*w*. informat results in a SAS date value corresponding to the first day of the specified month.

Note: The SAS System defaults to a date in the 1900s if *yy* is two digits. Use the YEARCUTOFF= system option to override the system default and specify a date range of your choice.

Example

Data Line	SAS Statement	Result
`----+----1----+----2`		
`jun89`	`input month monyy5.;`	`10744`

See Also

DDMMYY*w*., MMDDYY*w*., and YYMMDD*w*. informats

"SAS Date and Time Values" in Chapter 4, "Rules of the SAS Language"

MONTH and YEAR functions in Chapter 11, "SAS Functions"

DDMMYY*w*., MMDDYY*w*., MONYY*w*., and YYMMDD*w*. formats in Chapter 14, "SAS Formats"

YEARCUTOFF= system option in Chapter 16, "SAS System Options"

MSEC*w*.

Reads TIME MIC values

Date and time

Width range: 8

Default width: 8

HELP INFORMAT

Description

The MSEC*w*. informat reads time values produced by IBM mainframe operating systems, converting the time values to SAS time values. The *w* value must be 8, because the OS TIME macro or the STCK System/370™ instruction on IBM mainframes each return an 8-byte value.

Comparisons

The MSEC*w*. and TODSTAMP*w*. informats both read IBM time-of-day clock values, but the MSEC*w*. informat assigns a time value to a variable, and the TODSTAMP*w*. informat assigns a datetime value. Use the MSEC*w*. informat to find the difference between two MVS TIME values, with precision to the nearest microsecond.

Example

Data Line *	SAS Statement	Result
`0000EA044E65A000`	`input btime msec8.;`	`62818.412122`

* The data line is a hexadecimal representation of a binary 8-byte time-of-day clock value. Each byte occupies one column of the input field. The result is a SAS time value corresponding to 5:26:58.41 PM.

See Also

TODSTAMP*w*. informat

NENGO*w*.

Reads Japanese date values (*r.yymmdd*)

Date and time

Width range: 7–32

Default width: 10

HELP INFORMAT

Description

The NENGO*w*. informat reads Japanese date values in the form *r.yymmdd*, where *r* is a letter representing an emperor's reign: M(Meiji), T(Taisho), S(Showa), or H(Heisei). The period is optional, and *yy*, *mm*, and *dd* are integers representing the year, month, and day. The year, month, and day values can be separated by blanks or any nonnumeric character. However, if delimiters are used, place them between all fields in the value.

See Also

"SAS Date and Time Values" in Chapter 4, "Rules of the SAS Language"

NENGO*w*. format in Chapter 14, "SAS Formats"

System/370 is a trademark of International Business Machines Corporation.

OCTAL*w.d*

Converts positive octal values to integers

Numeric

Width range: 1–24

Default width: 3

HELP INFORMAT

Description

The OCTAL*w.d* informat converts positive octal values to integer (fixed-point) values. The *w* value specifies the field width of the input value. The *d* value is optional and can be greater than or equal to the *w* value. If you include a *d* value, the OCTAL*w.d* informat divides the number by 10^d. The *d* value range is 1 through 31.

You can use only the digits 0 through 7 in the input, with no embedded blanks. The OCTAL*w.d* informat ignores leading and trailing blanks.

The OCTAL*w.d* informat cannot read negative values. It treats all input values as positive (unsigned).

Example

Data Line	SAS Statement	Result
`----+----1----+----2`		
`177`	`input @1 value octal3.1;`	`12.7`

PD*w.d*

Reads packed decimal data

Numeric

Width range: 1–16

Default width: 1

HELP INFORMAT

Description

The PD*w.d* informat reads packed decimal data. The PD*w.d* informat is useful because many programs write data in packed decimal format for storage efficiency, fitting two digits into each byte and using only a half byte for a sign. The *d* value range is 0 through 10.

Note: Different computer systems store packed decimal values in different ways. However, the PD*w.d* informat reads packed decimal values with consistent results if the values are created on the same type of computer system you use to run the SAS System.

Comparisons

This table compares packed decimal notation in several programming languages.

Language	Notation
SAS	PD4.
COBOL	COMP-3 PIC S9(7)
IBM 370 assembler	PL4
PL/I	FIXED DEC

Examples

Example 1: Reading Packed Decimal Data

Data Line *	SAS Statement	Result
`0000128C`	`input @1 x pd4.;`	128

* The data line is a hexadecimal representation of a binary number stored in packed decimal form. Each byte occupies one column of the input field.

Example 2: Creating a SAS Date with Packed Decimal Data

Data Line *	SAS Statements	Result
`0122588C`	`input mnth pd4.;` `date=input(put(mnth,6.),mmddyy6.);`	10586

* The data line is a hexadecimal representation of a binary number stored in packed decimal form on an IBM mainframe computer system. Each byte occupies one column of the input field. The result is a SAS date value corresponding to December 25, 1988.

PDTIMEw.

Reads packed decimal time of SMF and RMF records

Date and time

Default width: 4

HELP INFORMAT

Description

The PDTIME*w*. informat reads packed decimal time values contained in SMF and RMF records produced by IBM mainframe systems, converting the values to SAS time values. If a field is all 0s, the PDTIME*w*. informat treats it as a missing value.

The *w* value must be 4, because packed decimal time values in RMF and SMF records contain 4 bytes of information. The general form of a packed decimal time value in hexadecimal notation is 0*hhmmss*F, with 3 successive bytes of information representing hours, minutes and seconds, respectively, preceded by a half byte containing all 0s and followed by a half byte containing all 1s.

The PDTIME*w*. informat enables you to read packed decimal time values from files created on an IBM mainframe on any computer system.

Example

Data Line *	SAS Statement	Result
`0142225F`	`input begin pdtime4.;`	51745

* The data line is a hexadecimal representation of a binary time value stored in packed decimal form. Each byte occupies one column of the input field. The result is a SAS time value corresponding to 2:22.25 PM.

PERCENTw.

Converts percentages into numeric values

Numeric

Width range: 1–32

Default width: 6

HELP INFORMAT

Description

The PERCENT*w.* informat reads percentage values and converts them into numeric values. The PERCENT*w.* informat converts the numeric portion of the input data to a number using the same method as the COMMA*w.* informat. If a percent sign (%) follows the number in the input field, the PERCENT*w.* informat divides the number by 100.

Example

Data Line	SAS Statement	Result
`----+----1----+----2`		
`1% (20%)`	`input @1 x percent3.` `@4 y percent5.;`	`0.01 -0.2`

PIB*w.d*

Reads positive integer binary (fixed-point) values

Numeric

Width range: 1–8

Default width: 1

HELP INFORMAT

Description

The PIB*w.d* informat reads integer binary (fixed-point) values. All values are treated as positive. If you include a *d* value, the PIB*w.d* informat divides the number by 10^d. The *d* value range is 0 through 10.

Note: Different computer systems store positive integer binary values in different ways. However, the PIB*w.d* informat reads positive integer binary values with consistent results if the values are created on the same type of computer system you use to run the SAS System.

Comparisons

Positive integer binary values are the same as integer binary values except the sign bit is part of the value, which is always a positive integer. The PIB*w.d* informat treats all values as positive and includes the sign bit as part of the value.

The PIB1. informat results in a value corresponding to the binary equivalent of the contents of a byte. This is useful if your data contain values between hexadecimal 80 and hexadecimal FF, where the high-order bit can be misinterpreted as a negative sign.

Example

Data Line	SAS Statement	Results
`----+----1----+----2`		**ASCII**
`A`	`input char pib1.;`	`65`
		EBCDIC
		`193`

See Also

IB*w.d* informat

PK*w.d*

Reads unsigned packed decimal data

Numeric

Width range: 1–16

Default width: 1

HELP INFORMAT

Description

The PK*w.d* informat reads unsigned packed decimal data. The *w* value specifies the number of bytes of unsigned packed decimal data, each of which contains two digits. When you specify a *d* value, the PK*w.d* informat divides the number by 10^d. The *d* value range is 0 through 10.

Comparisons

The PK*w.d* informat is the same as the PD*w.d* informat, except PK*w.d* treats the sign half of the field's last byte as part of the value, and not as the sign of the value.

Example

Data Line *	SAS Statement	Result
`001234`	`input @1 x pk3.;`	`1234`

* The data line is a hexadecimal representation of a binary number stored in unsigned packed decimal form. Each byte occupies one column of the input field.

PUNCH.*d*

Reads whether a row of column-binary data is punched

Numeric

HELP INFORMAT

Description

The PUNCH.*d* informat reads whether a row of column-binary data is punched. The *d* value specifies which row in a card column to read. Valid values for the *d* value are 1 through 12. The PUNCH.*d* informat assigns the value 1 to the variable if row *d* of the current card column is punched, or 0 if row *d* of the current card column is not punched.

After the PUNCH.*d* informat reads a field, the pointer does not advance to the next column.

Example

Data Line *	SAS Statements	Results
`12 on`	`input x punch0.12;`	1
`11 off`	`input x punch0.11;`	0
`0 off`	`input x punch0.7;`	1
`1 off`		
`2 off`		
`3 off`		
`4 off`		
`5 off`		
`6 off`		
`7 on`		
`8 on`		
`9 off`		

* The data lines represent a column on a punch card, with the word *on* indicating a punch, and the word *off* indicating no punch. In a column-binary file, the binary data corresponding to the card column in the example have the binary representation 0010 0000 0000 0110.

See Also

$CB*w.* informat

CB*w.d* informat

ROW*w.d* informat

RBw.d

Reads real binary (floating-point) data

Numeric

Width range: 2–8

Default width: 4

HELP INFORMAT

Description

The RB*w.d* informat reads numeric data that are stored in real binary (floating-point) notation. The *d* value range is 0 through 10.

Note: Different computer systems store real binary values in different ways. However, the RB*w.d* informat reads real binary values with consistent results if the values are created on the same type of computer system you use to run the SAS System.

Comparisons

This table compares the names of real binary notation in several programming languages.

	Real Binary Notation	
Language	4 Bytes	8 Bytes
SAS	RB4.	RB8.
FORTRAN	REAL*4	REAL*8
C	float	double
IBM 370 assembler	F	D
PL/I	FLOAT BIN(21)	FLOAT BIN(53)

▶ *Caution: Using RB4. could result in truncation.*

Using RB4. to read real binary information on equipment conforming to the IEEE standard for floating-point numbers results in a truncated 8-byte number, rather than a true 4-byte floating-point number.

Example

Data Line *	SAS Statement	Result
`4280000000000000`	`input @1 x rb8.;`	128

* The data line is a hexadecimal representation of a real binary (floating-point) number on an IBM mainframe computer system. Each byte occupies one column of the input field.

RMFSTAMPw.

Reads time and date fields of RMF records

Date and time

Default width: 8

HELP INFORMAT

Description

The RMFSTAMP*w.* informat reads packed decimal time and date values of RMF records produced by IBM mainframe systems, converting the time and date values to SAS datetime values.

The *w* value must be 8 because packed decimal time and date values in RMF records contain 8 bytes of information: 4 bytes of time data followed by 4 bytes of date data. The general form of the time and date information in an RMF record in hexadecimal notation is

0*hhmmss*F00*yyddd*F

or the following:

- □ 1/2 byte containing all binary 0s
- □ 1 byte representing two digits corresponding to the hour of the day, shown as *hh*
- □ 1 byte representing two digits corresponding to minutes, shown as *mm*
- □ 1 byte representing two digits corresponding to seconds, shown as *ss*
- □ 1/2 byte containing all binary 1s, followed by 1 byte containing all binary 0s
- □ 1 byte representing two digits corresponding to the year, shown as *yy*
- □ 1-1/2 bytes containing three digits corresponding to the day of the year, shown as *ddd*
- □ 1/2 byte containing all binary 1s.

The RMFSTAMP*w.* informat enables you to read packed decimal time and date values from files created on an IBM mainframe on any computer system.

Comparisons

The RMFSTAMP*w.*informat is similar to the PDTIME*w.* informat in that both informats read packed decimal values from RMF records. The RMFSTAMP*w.* informat reads both time and date values, resulting in a SAS datetime value. The PDTIME*w.* informat reads only time values, resulting in a SAS time value.

Example

Data Line *	SAS Statement	Result
`0142225F0089286F`	`input begin rmfstamp8.;`	`939910945`

* The data line is a hexadecimal representation of a binary time and date value stored in packed decimal form as it would appear in an RMF record. Each byte occupies one column of the input field. The result is a SAS datetime value corresponding to October 13, 1989, 2:22.25 PM.

RMFDUR*w.*

Reads duration intervals of RMF records

Date and time

Default width: 4

HELP INFORMAT

Description

The RMFDUR*w.* informat reads the duration of RMF measurement intervals of RMF records produced as packed decimal data by IBM mainframe systems, converting them to SAS time values.

The *w* value must be 4, because packed decimal duration values in RMF records contain 4 bytes of information. The general form of the duration interval data in an RMF record in hexadecimal notation is *mmsstttF*, or

- □ 1 byte representing two digits corresponding to minutes, shown as *mm*
- □ 1 byte representing two digits corresponding to seconds, shown as *ss*
- □ 1-1/2 bytes representing three digits corresponding to thousandths of a second, shown as *ttt*
- □ 1/2 byte containing all binary 1s.

If the field does not contain packed decimal data, the RMFDUR*w*. informat results in a missing value.

Comparisons

The RMFDUR*w*. informat is similar to the RMFSTAMP*w*. informat in that both read packed decimal information from RMF records produced by IBM mainframe systems. The RMFDUR*w*. informat reads duration data and results in a time value. The RMFSTAMP *w*. reads time-of-day data, resulting in a datetime value.

Example

Data Line *	SAS Statement	Result **
`3552226F`	`input dura rmfdur4.;`	`2152.266`

* The data line is a hexadecimal representation of a binary duration value stored in packed decimal form as it would appear in an RMF record. Each byte occupies one column of the input field.
** The result is a SAS time value corresponding to 00:35:52.226.

See Also

RMFSTAMP*w*. and SMFSTAMP*w*. informats

ROW*w.d*

Reads a column-binary field down a card column

Numeric

HELP INFORMAT

Description

The ROW*w.d* informat reads a column-binary field down a card column. The *w* value specifies the row where the field begins. The *w* value can range from 0 through 12. The *d* value specifies the length in rows of the field. Valid values for *d* are 1 through 25. The default *d* value is 1.

The ROW*w.d* informat assigns the relative position of the punch in the field to a numeric variable.

If the field you specify has more than one punch, the ROW*w.d* informat assigns the variable a missing value and sets the automatic variable _ERROR_ to 1. If the field has no punches, the ROW*w.d* informat assigns the variable a missing value.

The ROW*w.d* informat can read fields across columns, continuing with row 12 of the new column and going down through the rest of the rows. After the ROW*w.d* informat reads a field, the pointer moves to the next row.

Example

Data Line *	SAS Statement	Result
12 off	input x row5.3;	3
11 off		
0 off		
1 off		
2 off		
3 off		
4 off		
5 off		
6 off		
7 on		
8 off		
9 off		

* The data lines represent a column on a punch card, with the word *on* indicating a punch and the word *off* indicating no punch. In a column-binary file, the binary data corresponding to the card column in the example have the binary representation 0000 0000 0000 0100.

See Also

$CB*w.* informat

CB*w.d* informat

PUNCH.*d* informat

SMFSTAMPw.

Reads time-date values of SMF records

Date and time

Default width: 8

HELP INFORMAT

Description

The SMFSTAMP*w.* informat reads integer binary time values and packed decimal date values of SMF records produced by IBM mainframe systems, converting the time and date values to SAS datetime values.

The *w* value must be 8, because time and date values in SMF records contain 8 bytes of information: 4 bytes of time data followed by 4 bytes of date data. The time portion of an SMF record is a 4-byte integer binary number that represents time as the number of hundredths of a second past midnight. The date portion of an SMF record in hexadecimal notation is

00*yyddd*F,

or the following:

- □ 1 byte containing all binary 0s
- □ 1 byte representing two digits corresponding to the year, shown as *yy*
- □ 1-1/2 bytes containing three digits corresponding to the day of the year, shown as *ddd*
- □ 1/2 byte containing all binary 1s.

The SMFSTAMP*w.* informat enables you to read integer binary time values and packed decimal date values from files created on an IBM mainframe on any computer system.

Example

Data Line *	SAS Statement	Result
`004EF5280089286F`	`input begin smfstamp8.;`	`939910945.68`

* The data line is a hexadecimal representation of a binary time and date value stored as it would appear in an SMF record. Each byte occupies one column of the input field. The result is a SAS datetime value corresponding to October 13, 1989, 2:22.25.68 PM.

S370FIB*w.d*

Reads integer binary data in IBM mainframe format

Numeric

Width range: 1–8

Default width: 4

HELP INFORMAT

Description

The S370FIB*w.d* informat reads integer binary (fixed-point) values stored in IBM mainframe format, including negative values represented in two's complement notation. The *d* value range is 0 through 10.

Use the S370FIB*w.d* informat to read integer binary data from IBM mainframe files on other computer systems.

Comparisons

This table shows the equivalent integer binary notation for several IBM 370 programming languages.

	Integer Binary Notation	
Language	4 Bytes	8 bytes
SAS	S370FIB2.	S370FIB4.
PL/I	FIXED BIN(15)	FIXED BIN(31)
FORTRAN	INTEGER*2	INTEGER*4
COBOL	COMP PIC 9(4)	COMP PIC 9(8)
assembler	H	F
C	short	long

If you use the SAS System on an IBM mainframe, the S370FIB*w.d* and the IB*w.d* informats are identical.

S370FPD*w.d*

Reads packed data in IBM mainframe format

Numeric

Width range: 1–16

Default width: 1

HELP INFORMAT

Description

The S370FPD*w.d* informat reads packed decimal values in IBM mainframe format. The last half of the last byte indicates the sign: a C or F for positive numbers and a D for negative numbers.

Packed decimal data contain two digits per byte, but only one digit in the byte contains the sign. If you specify a *d* value, the S370FPD*w.d* informat divides the number by 10^d. The *d* value range is 0 through 10.

Use the S370FPD*w.d* informat to read packed decimal data from IBM mainframe files on other computer systems.

Comparisons

The following table shows the equivalent packed decimal notation for several IBM 370 programming languages:

Language	Packed Decimal Notation
SAS	S370PD4.
PL/I	FIXED DEC(7,0)
COBOL	COMP-3 PIC S9(7)
assembler	PL4

If you use the SAS System on an IBM mainframe, the S370FPD*w.d* and the PD*w.d* informats are identical.

S370FPIB*w.d*

Reads positive integer binary data in IBM mainframe format

Numeric

Width range: 1–8

Default width: 4

HELP INFORMAT

Description

The S370FPIB*w.d* informat reads positive integer binary (fixed-point) values in IBM mainframe format. Positive integer binary values are the same as integer binary values (see the S370FIB*w.d* informat), except that all values are treated as positive. If you specify a *d* value, the S370FPIB*w.d* informat divides the number by 10^d. The *d* value range is 0 through 10.

Use the S370FPIB*w.d* informat to read positive integer binary data from IBM mainframe files on other computer systems.

If you use the SAS System on an IBM mainframe, the S370FPIB*w.d* and the PIB*w.d* informats are identical.

S370FRB*w.d*

Reads real binary (floating-point) data in IBM mainframe format

Numeric

Width range: 2–8

Default width: 6

HELP INFORMAT

Description

The S370FRB*w.d* informat reads real binary (floating-point) values in IBM 370 format. Real binary values are represented in two parts: a mantissa giving the value, and an exponent giving the value's magnitude. When you specify a *d* value, the S370FRB*w.d* informat divides the number by 10^d. The *d* value range is 0 through 10.

Use the S370FRB*w.d* informat to read real binary data from IBM mainframe files on other computer systems.

Comparisons

The following table shows the equivalent real binary notation for several IBM 370 programming languages.

	Real Binary Notation	
Language	4 Bytes	8 Bytes
SAS	S370FRB4.	S370FRB8.
PL/I	FLOAT BIN(21)	FLOAT BIN(53)
FORTRAN	REAL*4	REAL*8
COBOL	COMP-1	COMP-2
assembler	E	D
C	float	double

If you use the SAS System on an IBM mainframe, the S370FRB*w.d* and the RB*w.d* informats are identical.

TIME*w.*

Reads hours, minutes, and seconds (*hh:mm:ss.ss*)

Date and time

Width range: 5–32

Default width: 8

HELP INFORMAT

Description

The TIME*w.* informat reads time values in the form *hh:mm:ss.ss*, where *hh* and *mm* are integers representing the hour and minute, and *ss.ss* is an optional fractional field representing seconds and decimal fractions of seconds. If you do not enter a value for seconds, the SAS System assumes a value of 0.

Example

Data Line	SAS Statement	Result
`----+----1----+----2`		
`14:22:25`	`input begin time8.;`	`51745`

See Also

"SAS Date and Time Values" in Chapter 4, "Rules of the SAS Language"

HOUR, MINUTE, SECOND, and TIME functions in Chapter 11, "SAS Functions"

HHMM*w.d*, HOUR*w.d*, MMSS*w.d*, and TIME*w.d* formats in Chapter 14, "SAS Formats"

TODSTAMP*w.*

Reads 8-byte time-of-day stamp

Date and time

Default width: 8

HELP INFORMAT

Description

The TODSTAMP*w.* informat reads time-of-day clock values produced by IBM mainframe operating systems, converting the clock values to SAS datetime values.

The *w* value must be 8, because the OS TIME macro or the STCK System/370 instruction on IBM mainframes each return an 8-byte value. If the time-of-day value is all 0s, the TODSTAMP*w.* informat results in a missing value.

Use the TODSTAMP*w.* informat to read time-of-day values produced by an IBM mainframe on other computer systems.

Example

Data Line *	SAS Statement	Result
`93B200C19E7A2000`	`input btime todstamp8.;`	`704914018.41`

* The data line is a hexadecimal representation of a binary, 8-byte time-of-day clock value. Each byte occupies one column of the input field. The result is a SAS datetime value corresponding to May 3, 1982, 5:26:58.41 p.m.

TU*w.*

Reads timer units

Date and time

Width range: 4

Default width: 4

HELP INFORMAT

Description

The TU*w.* informat reads timer unit values produced by IBM mainframe operating system and OS/VS software, converting the timer unit values to SAS time values.

The *w* value must be 4 because the OS TIME macro returns a 4-byte value. There are exactly 38,400 software timer units per second. The low-order bit in a timer unit value represents approximately 26.041667 microseconds.

Use the TU*w.* informat to read timer unit values produced by an IBM mainframe on other computer systems.

Example

Data Line *	SAS Statement	Result
`8FC7A9BC`	`input btime tu4.;`	`62818.411563`

* The data line is a hexadecimal representation of a binary, 4-byte timer unit value. Each byte occupies one column of the input field. The result is a SAS time value corresponding to 5:26:58.41 p.m.

VAXRB*w.d*

Reads real binary (floating-point) data under VMS

Numeric

Width range: 2–8

Default width: 4

HELP INFORMAT

Description

The VAXRB*w.d* informat reads real binary (floating-point) numeric data stored under VMS.™ Use the VAXRB*w.d* informat to read floating-point data written under VMS on other computer systems. The *d* value range is 0 through 10.

Comparisons

If you use the SAS System running under VMS, the VAXRB*w.d* and the RB*w.d* informats are identical.

See Also

RB*w.d* informat

w.d

Reads standard numeric data

Numeric

Width Range: 1–32

HELP INFORMAT

Description

The *w.d* informat reads standard numeric values represented with 1 byte per digit. The *w* value specifies the width in columns of the field containing the numeric value. The *d* value optionally specifies the number of digits to the right of the decimal point in the numeric value. The *d* value range is 0 through 31.

The *w.d* informat reads numeric values located anywhere in the field. Blanks can precede or follow a numeric value with no effect. A minus sign with no separating blank should immediately precede a negative value. The *w.d* informat reads values with decimal points and values in scientific E-notation, and it interprets a single period as a missing value.

Include a *d* value in the *w.d* informat when you want the SAS System to insert decimal points in numeric input values. When you include a *d* value, *w.d* divides values by 10^d. The *w.d* informat interprets data that already contain a decimal point as it reads them and ignores any specified *d* value.

VMS is a trademark of Digital Equipment Corporation.

Comparisons

The *w.d* informat is identical to the BZ*w.d* informat, except that the *w.d* informat ignores trailing blanks in the numeric values. To read trailing blanks as 0s, use the BZ*w.d* informat.

The *w.d* informat can read values in scientific E-notation exactly as the E*w.d* informat does.

Example

Data Line	SAS Statement	Results	
`----+---1----+----2`			
`23       2300`	`input @1 x 6. @10 y 6.2;`	23	23
`    23 2300`		23	23
`  23     -2300`		23	-23
`  23.0     23.`		23	23
` 2.3E1   2.3`		23	2.3
`   -23  0`		-23	0

YYMMDDw.

Reads date values (*yymmdd*)

Date and time

Width range: 6–32

Default width: 6

HELP INFORMAT

Description

The YYMMDD*w.* informat reads date values in *yymmdd* form, where *yy*, *mm*, and *dd* are integers representing the year, month, and day. The month, day, and year fields can be separated by blanks or special characters. However, if delimiters are used, they should be placed between all fields in the value. Blanks can also be placed before and after the date.

Note: The SAS System defaults to a date in the 1900s if *yy* is two digits. Use the YEARCUTOFF= system option to override the system default and specify your choice of date range.

Example

Data Lines	SAS Statements	Results
`----+----1----+----2`		
`900101`	`input beg yymmdd8.;`	10958
`90 1 1`		10958
`90-01-01`		10958
`90/1/1`		10958
`19900101`		10958
`----+----1----+----2`		
`19520101`	`input date yymmdd10.;`	-2922
`1884/10/16`		-27469

See Also

DATE*w*., DDMMYY*w*., and MMDDYY*w*. informats

"SAS Date and Time Values" in Chapter 4, "Rules of the SAS Language"

DAY, MDY, MONTH, and YEAR functions in Chapter 11, "SAS Functions"

DATE*w*., DDMMYY*w*., MMDDYY*w*., and YYMMDD*w*. formats in Chapter 14, "SAS Formats"

YEARCUTOFF= system option in Chapter 16, "SAS System Options"

YYQw.

Reads quarters of the year

Date and time

Width range: 4—32

Default width: 4

HELP INFORMAT

Description

The YYQ*w*. informat reads values in the form *yyQq* or *yyyyQq*, where *yy* or *yyyy* is an integer representing the year, *Q* is the letter Q, and *q* is an integer (1, 2, 3, or 4) representing the quarter of the year. The year value, the letter Q, and the quarter value cannot be separated with blanks. A value read with the YYQ*w*. informat produces a SAS date value corresponding to the first day of the specified quarter.

Note: The SAS System defaults to a date in the 1900s if *yy* is two digits. Use the YEARCUTOFF= system option to override the system default and specify a date range of your choice.

Example

Data Line	SAS Statement	Result
`----+----1----+----2`		
`90Q2`	`input entered yyq4.;`	`11048`

See Also

"SAS Date and Time Values" in Chapter 4, "Rules of the SAS Language"

QTR, YEAR, and YYQ functions in Chapter 11, "SAS Functions"

YEARCUTOFF= system option in Chapter 16, "SAS System Options"

ZDw.d

Reads zoned decimal data

Numeric

Width range: 1—32

Default width: 1

HELP INFORMAT

Description

The ZD*w.d* informat reads zoned decimal data. The *w* value is the number of columns of the field containing a value, and the *d* value gives the number of decimal places for the value. The *d* value can range from 0 to 10 and can be larger than the *w* value, or it can be omitted.

The zoned decimal informat is similar to the standard numeric informat in that every digit requires 1 byte. However, the value's sign is in the last byte, along with the last digit.

Note: Different computer systems store zoned decimal values in different ways. However, the ZD*w.d* informat reads zoned decimal values with consistent results if the values are created on the same type of computer system you use to run the SAS System.

Positive values can be entered in zoned decimal format from a terminal. Some keying devices enable you to enter negative values by overstriking the last digit with a minus sign. The following table compares the zoned decimal informat with notation in several programming languages:

Language	Zoned Decimal Notation
SAS	ZD3.
PL/I	PICTURE'99T'
COBOL	DISPLAY PIC S 999
IBM 370 assembler	ZL3

Example

Data Line*	SAS Statement	Result
`F0F1F2C8`	`input @1 x zd4.;`	`128`

* The data line contains a hexadecimal representation of a binary number stored in zoned decimal format on an IBM mainframe computer system. Each byte occupies one column of the input field.

ZDB*w.d*

Reads zoned decimal data with blanks

Numeric

Width range: 1–32

Default width: 1

HELP INFORMAT

Description

The ZDB*w.d* informat reads zoned decimal data produced in IBM 1410, 1401, and 1620 form, where 0s are left blank rather than being punched. The *w* value specifies the number of columns of the field containing a value. The *d* value gives the number of decimal places for the value. The *d* value can range from 0 to 10 and can be larger than the *w* value.

Example

Data Line*	SAS Statement	Result
`F140C2`	`input @1 x zdb3.;`	`102`

* The data line contains a hexadecimal representation of a binary number stored in zoned decimal form, including the codes for spaces, on an IBM mainframe computer system. Each byte occupies one column of the input field.

CHAPTER 14 SAS® Formats

(continued on next page)

(continued from previous page)

Background information on SAS formats, including a table listing all formats, appears in Chapter 3, "Components of the SAS Language." See Table 3.9, "SAS Formats and Aliases" and Table 3.10, "Categories and Descriptions of SAS Formats."

$ASCIIw.

Converts native format character data to ASCII representation

Character

Width range: 1–200

Default width: 1

Alignment: left

HELP FORMAT

Description

The $ASCIIw. format converts character data to ASCII. On EBCDIC systems, the $ASCIIw. format converts EBCDIC character data to ASCII. On all other systems, the $ASCIIw. format has the same effect as the $CHARw. format.

Example

Values	SAS Statement	Results *
`abc`	`put x $ascii3.;`	`616263`
`ABC`		`414243`
`();`		`28293B`

* The results are shown as hexadecimal representations of ASCII codes for characters. Each two hexadecimal digits correspond to 1 byte of binary data, and each byte corresponds to one character.

$BINARY*w*.

Converts character values to binary representation

Character

Width range: 1–200

Default width: 8

Alignment: left

HELP FORMAT

Description

The $BINARY*w*. format converts character values to binary representation with each character generating eight binary characters.

Comparisons

The $BINARY*w*. format for character values and the BINARY*w*. format for numeric values both convert values to binary representation.

Example

Value	SAS Statement	Results

`AB`	`put @1 name $binary16.;`	**ASCII**
		`----+----1----+----2`
		`0100000101000010`
		EBCDIC
		`----+----1----+----2`
		`1100000111000010`

$CHAR*w*.

Writes standard character data

Character

Width range: 1–200

Default width: 1 if length of variable not yet defined; otherwise, the length of the variable

Alignment: left

HELP FORMAT

Description

The $CHAR*w*. format writes standard character data. The *w* value specifies the width of the output field.

Comparisons

The $CHAR*w*. format and the $*w*. format are identical, and they do not trim leading blanks.

To trim leading blanks, use the LEFT function to left justify character data prior to output, or use list output with the colon (:) format modifier and the format of your choice.

The following table compares the $CHAR*w*. format with notation in some other languages:

Language	Notation
SAS	$CHAR8.
FORTRAN	A8
C	CHAR[8]
COBOL	PIC x(8)
PL/I	A(8)

Example

Value	SAS Statement	Result
		----+----1----+----2
XYZ	`put @7 name $char4.;`	XYZ

$EBCDICw.

Converts native format character data to EBCDIC representation

Character

Width range: 1–200

Default width: 1

Alignment: left

HELP FORMAT

Description

The $EBCDIC*w*. format converts character data to EBCDIC. On ASCII systems, the $EBCDIC*w*. format converts ASCII character data to EBCDIC. On all other systems, the $EBCDIC*w*. format has the same effect as the $CHAR*w*. format. The *w* value specifies the width of the output field.

Example

Values	SAS Statement	Results *
qrs	`put x $ebcdic3.;`	9899A2
QRS		D8D9E2
+;>		4E5E6E

* The results are shown as hexadecimal representations of EBCDIC codes for characters. Each two hexadecimal digits correspond to 1 byte of binary data, and each byte corresponds to one character.

$HEXw.

Converts character values to hexadecimal representation

Character

Width range: 1–200

Default width: 4

Alignment: left

HELP FORMAT

Description

The $HEX. character format converts character values to hexadecimal representation. Each character the format converts generates two hexadecimal digits. Each blank counts as one character, including trailing blanks.

To ensure that the SAS System writes the full hexadecimal equivalent of your data, specify a *w* value twice the length of the variable or field you want to represent. If you specify a *w* value that is greater than twice the length of the variable you want to represent, the $HEX*w*. format pads with blanks.

Comparisons

The $HEX. character format is like the HEX. numeric format in that both generate the hexadecimal equivalent of values.

Example

Data Value	SAS Statement	Results
		EBCDIC
		`----+----1----+----2`
AB	`put @5 name $hex4.;`	`C1C2`
		ASCII
		`----+----1----+----2`
		`4142`

$OCTALw.

Converts character values to octal representation

Character

Width range: 1–200

Default width: 8

Alignment: left

HELP FORMAT

Description

The $OCTAL*w*. format converts character values to the octal representation of their character codes, with each character generating three octal characters. Therefore, you need to specify a *w* value three times the length of the character value.

Comparisons

The $OCTAL*w*. format for character values and the OCTAL*w*. format for numeric values both convert values to octal representation.

Example

Values	SAS Statement	Results
		EBCDIC
		`----+----1----+----2`
A	`put @10 x $octal9.;`	`301100100`
B		`302100100`
		ASCII
		`----+----1----+----2`
		`101040040`
		`102040040`

$VARYINGw.

Writes varying length values

Character

Width range: 1–200

Default width: 8 or length of variable

Alignment: left

HELP FORMAT

Description

The $VARYINGw. format writes variable-length fields of character data. Use the $VARYINGw. format when the length of a character value differs from record to record. After writing a data value with the $VARYINGw. format, the pointer's position is the first column after the value. You can only use the $VARYINGw. format within a DATA step.

You can use the following terms with the $VARYINGw. format:

w

specifies the maximum width of the output field for any output line or output file record. The SAS System always associates a *w* value with the $VARYINGw. format. If you do not specify a *w* value, the SAS System uses the length of the character variable you are writing as the *w* value.

length-variable

specifies a numeric variable containing the actual length of the current value of the character variable you are writing with the $VARYINGw. format. You must specify a *length-variable* immediately after the $VARYINGw. format in a SAS statement. The SAS System obtains the value of the *length-variable* by either reading it directly from a field described in an INPUT statement, reading the value of a variable in an existing SAS data set, or calculating its value.

If the *length-variable's* value is 0, negative, or missing for a given observation, the SAS System writes nothing to the output field. If the value is greater than 0 but less than the *w* value, the SAS System writes the number of characters specified by the length variable. If the value of the length variable is equal to or greater than the *w* value, the SAS System writes *w* columns. The value of the length variable cannot be an array reference.

Examples

Example 1: Using an Existing Variable to Specify Length

Values *		SAS Statement	Results
			`----+----1----+----2`
`New York`	`8`	`put @10 city $varying15. len;`	`New York`
`Cary`	`4`		`Cary`
`Dunmore`	`7`		`Dunmore`
`Denver`	`6`		`Denver`

* CITY is a character variable with a length of 15. It contains values varying from 1 to 15 characters in length. LEN is another variable in the data set giving the actual length of the value of CITY for the current observation.

Example 2: Using the LENGTH Function to Calculate Length

Values	SAS Statements	Results
		`----+----1----+----2`
`New York`	`len=length(city);`	`New York`
`Cary`	`put @10 city $varying15. len;`	`Cary`
`Dunmore`		`Dunmore`
`Denver`		`Denver`

$w.

Writes standard character data

Character

Width range: 1–200

Default width: 1 if length of variable not yet defined; otherwise, the length of the variable

Alignment: left

HELP FORMAT

Description

The $*w*. format writes standard character data. The *w* value specifies the width of the output field and can be explicitly specified with a number or implicitly specified with a column range.

Comparisons

The $*w*. format and the $CHAR*w*. format are identical, and they do not trim leading blanks. To trim leading blanks, use the LEFT function to left justify character data prior to output, or use list output with the colon (:) format modifier and the format of your choice.

Example

Value	SAS Statements	Result
		`----+----1----+----2`

`ABC`	`put @10 name $3.;`
	or
	`put name $ 10-12;`
		`ABC`

BEST*w*.

SAS System chooses best notation

Numeric

Width range: 1–32

Default width: 12

Alignment: right

HELP FORMAT

Description

The BEST*w*. format is the default format for writing numeric values. When there is no format specification, the SAS System chooses the format providing the most information about the value given the available field width. The SAS System always stores the complete value regardless of the format you use to represent it.

The *w* value specifies the width of the output field. When you use the BEST*w*. format, the SAS System ignores any *d* value you specify.

Example

Values	SAS Statements	Results
		----+----1----+----2
1257000	put @10 x best6.;	1.26E6
1257000	put @10 x best3.;	1E6

BINARY*w*.

Converts numeric values to binary representation

Numeric

Width range: 1–64

Default width: 8

Alignment: left

HELP FORMAT

Description

The BINARY*w*. format converts integer values to binary representation. If necessary, the BINARY*w*. format truncates numeric values to integers before converting them to binary representation. The BINARY*w*. format writes any negative numbers as all 1s.

Comparisons

The BINARY*w*. format for numeric values and the $BINARY*w*. format for character values both convert values to binary representation.

Example

Values	SAS Statement	Results
		----+----1----+----2
123.45	put @1 x binary8.;	01111011
123		01111011
-123		11111111

COMMA*w.d*

Writes numeric values with commas and decimal points

Numeric

Width range: 2—32

Default width: 6

Alignment: right

HELP FORMAT

Description

The COMMA*w.d* format writes numeric values with commas separating every three digits. The *w* value specifies the total width of the output field. The *d* value, which must be either 0 or 2, specifies whether to include decimal digits in the values. If you specify a *d* value of 2, the COMMA*w.d* format writes a decimal point and two decimal digits. If you specify a *d* value of 0, the COMMA*w.d* format does not write a decimal point or decimal digits.

Comparisons

The COMMA*w.d* format operates like the COMMAX*w.d* format, but the COMMAX*w.d* format reverses the roles of the decimal point and the comma. This convention is common in European countries.

The COMMA*w.d* format operates like the DOLLAR*w.d* format except that the COMMA*w.d* format does not print a leading dollar sign.

Example

Value	SAS Statement	Result
		`----+----1----+----2`
`23451.23`	`put @10 sales comma10.2;`	`23,451.23`

COMMAX*w.d*

Writes numeric values with commas and decimal points

Numeric

Width range: 2—32

Default width: 6

Alignment: right

HELP FORMAT

Description

The COMMAX*w.d* format writes numeric values with periods separating every three digits and a comma separating the decimal fraction. The *w* value specifies the total width of the output field. The *d* value, which must be either 0 or 2, specifies whether to include decimal digits in the values. If you specify a *d* value of 2, the COMMAX*w.d* format writes a comma and two decimal digits. If you specify a *d* value of 0, the COMMAX*w.d* format writes no comma or decimal digits.

Comparisons

The COMMAX*w.d* format operates like the COMMA*w.d* format, but reverses the roles of the decimal point and the comma. This convention is common in European countries.

The COMMAX*w.d* format operates like the DOLLARX*w.d* format except that the COMMAX*w.d* format does not print a leading dollar sign.

Example

Value	SAS Statement	Result
		`----+----1----+----2`
`23451.23`	`put @10 sales commax10.2;`	`23.451,23`

DATEw.

Writes date values (*ddmmmyy*)

Date and time

Width range: 5–9

Default width: 7

Alignment: right

HELP FORMAT

Description

The DATE*w.* format writes SAS date values in the form *ddmmmyy*, where *dd* is an integer representing the day of the month, *mmm* is the first three letters of the month name, and *yy* or *yyyy* is the year.

Example

Value	SAS Statements	Results
		`----+----1----+----2`
10847	`put day date5.;`	`12SEP`
	`put day date6.;`	` 12SEP`
	`put day date7.;`	`12SEP89`
	`put day date8.;`	` 12SEP89`
	`put day date9.;`	`12SEP1989`

See Also

"SAS Date and Time Values" in Chapter 4, "Rules of the SAS Language"

DATE function in Chapter 11, "SAS Functions"

DATE*w.* informat in Chapter 13, "SAS Informats"

DATETIME*w.d*

Writes datetime values (*ddmmmyy:hh:mm:ss.ss*)

Date and time

Width range: 7–40

Default width: 16

Alignment: right

HELP FORMAT

Description

The DATETIME*w.d* format writes SAS datetime values in the format *ddmmmyy:hh:mm:ss.ss*, representing a specific day, month, year, hour, minute, second, and decimal fraction of a second. The SAS System requires a minimum *w* value of 16 to write a SAS datetime value with the date, hour, and seconds. Add an additional two places to the width to return values with optional decimal fractions of seconds.

Note: The *d* value can range from 1 through 39, but must be less than the specified *w* value. If $w-d$ is less than 17, the SAS System truncates the decimal values.

Example

Value	SAS Statements	Results
		`----+----1----+----2`
10847	`put event datetime7.;`	`12SEP89`
	`put event datetime12.;`	`   12SEP89:03`
	`put event datetime18.;`	`   12SEP89:03:19:43`
	`put event datetime18.1;`	`12SEP89:03:19:43.0`

See Also

DATE*w*. and TIME*w.d* formats

"SAS Date and Time Values" in Chapter 4, "Rules of the SAS Language"

DATETIME function in Chapter 11, "SAS Functions"

DATE*w*., DATETIME*w*., and TIME*w*. informats in Chapter 13, "SAS Informats"

DAY*w*.

Writes day of month

Date and time

Width range: 2–32

Default width: 2

Alignment: right

HELP FORMAT

Description

The DAY*w*. format writes the day of the month from a SAS date value.

Example

Value	SAS Statement	Result
		`----+----1----+----2`
`10919`	`put date day2.;`	`23`

See Also

"SAS Date and Time Values" in Chapter 4, "Rules of the SAS Language"

DDMMYY*w*.

Writes date values (*ddmmyy*)

Date and time

Width range: 2–8

Default width: 8

Alignment: right

HELP FORMAT

Description

The DDMMYY*w*. format writes SAS date values in *ddmmyy* form, where *dd*, *mm*, and *yy* are integers representing a specific day, month, and year. When the *w* value is from 2 to 5, the SAS System prints as much of the month and day as possible. When the *w* value is 7, the date appears as a two-digit year without slashes, and the value is right aligned in the output field.

Example

Value	SAS Statements	Results
		`----+----1----+----2`
`11316`	`put date ddmmyy5.;`	`25/12`
	`put date ddmmyy6.;`	`251290`
	`put date ddmmyy7.;`	` 251290`
	`put date ddmmyy8.;`	`25/12/90`

See Also

DATE*w*., MMDDYY*w*., and YYMMDD*w*. formats

"SAS Date and Time Values" in Chapter 4, "Rules of the SAS Language"

MDY function in Chapter 11, "SAS Functions"

DATE*w*., DDMMYY*w*., MMDDYY*w*., and YYMMDD*w*. informats in Chapter 13, "SAS Informats"

DOLLAR*w.d*

Writes numeric values with dollar signs, commas, and decimal points

Numeric

Width range: 2–32

Default width: 6

Alignment: right

HELP FORMAT

Description

The DOLLAR*w.d* format writes numeric values with a leading dollar sign and a comma separating every three digits of each value. The *w* value specifies the total width of the output field. The *d* value, which must be either 0 or 2, specifies whether to include decimal digits in the value. If the *d* value is 2, the DOLLAR*w.d* format writes a decimal point and two decimal digits. If the *d* value is 0, the DOLLAR*w.d* format does not write a decimal point or decimal digits.

The hexadecimal representation of the code for the dollar sign character ($) is 5B on EBCDIC systems and 24 on ASCII systems. The monetary character these codes represent may be different in other countries, but the DOLLAR*w.d* format always produces one of these codes. If you need another monetary character, you can define your own format with the FORMAT procedure. See Chapter 18, "The FORMAT Procedure" in the *SAS Procedures Guide, Version 6, Third Edition* for more details.

Comparisons

The DOLLAR*w.d* format operates like the DOLLARX*w.d* format, but the DOLLARX*w.d* format reverses the roles of the decimal point and the comma. This convention is common in European countries.

The DOLLAR*w.d* format operates exactly like the COMMA*w.d* format except that COMMA*w.d* format does not write a leading dollar sign.

Example

Value	SAS Statement	Result
		`----+----1----+----2`
`1254.71`	`put @3 netpay dollar10.2;`	`$1,254.71`

DOLLARX*w.d*

Writes numeric values with dollar signs, periods, and commas

Numeric

Width range: 2–32

Default width: 6

Alignment: right

HELP FORMAT

Description

The DOLLARX*w.d* format writes numeric values with a leading dollar sign and a period separating every three digits of each value. The *w* value specifies the total width of the output field. The *d* value, which must be either 0 or 2, specifies whether to include decimal digits in the value. If the *d* value is 2, the DOLLARX*w.d* format writes a comma and two decimal digits. If the *d* value is 0, the DOLLARX*w.d* format writes no comma or decimal digits.

The hexadecimal representation of the code for the dollar sign character ($) is 5B on EBCDIC systems and 24 on ASCII systems. The monetary character these codes represent may be different in other countries, but the DOLLARX*w.d* format always produces one of these codes. If you need another monetary character, you can define your own format with the FORMAT procedure. See Chapter 18 in the *SAS Procedures Guide* for more details.

Comparisons

The DOLLARX*w.d* format operates like the DOLLAR*w.d* format, but reverses the roles of the decimal point and the comma. This convention is common in European countries.

The DOLLARX*w.d* format operates like the COMMAX*w.d* format except that COMMAX*w.d* does not print a leading dollar sign.

Example

Value	SAS Statement	Result
		`----+----1----+----2`
`1254.71`	`put @3 netpay dollar10.2;`	`  $1.254,71`

DOWNAME*w.*

Writes name of day of the week

Date and time

Width range: 1–32

Default width: 9

Alignment: right

HELP FORMAT

Description

The DOWNAME*w.* format writes the name of the day of the week from a SAS date value, with the first letter capitalized and the remainder of the name in lowercase letters. The name of the day is truncated to fit the format width if necessary. Thus, the format DOWNAME2. can be used to print the first two letters of the day name. If no *w* value is specified, the entire name of the day is printed.

Example

Value	SAS Statement	Result
		`----+----1----+----2`
`10621`	`put date downame.;`	`Sunday`

See Also

WEEKDAY*w.* format

"SAS Date and Time Values" in Chapter 4, "Rules of the SAS Language"

Ew.

Writes scientific notation

Numeric

Width range: 7–32

Default width: 12

Alignment: right

HELP FORMAT

Description

The E*w.* format writes numeric values in scientific notation. The *w* value specifies the width of the output field. The SAS System reserves the first column of the result for a minus sign.

Example

Values	SAS Statement	Results
		`----+----1----+----2`
`1257`	`put @1 x e10.;`	`1.257E+03`
`-1257`		`-1.257E+03`

FRACTw.

Converts values to fractions

Numeric

Width range: 4–32

Default width: 10

Alignment: right

HELP FORMAT

Description

The FRACT*w.* format converts values to fractions. The *w* value specifies the width of the output field.

Dividing the number 1 by 3 produces the value .33333333. To write this value as 1/3, use the FRACT*w.* format. FRACT*w.* writes fractions in reduced form, that is, 1/2 instead of 50/100.

Examples

Values	SAS Statements	Results
		`----+----1----+----2`
`0.6666666667`	`put @13 x fract4.;`	`2/3`
`0.2784`	`put y fract.;`	`174/625`

HEXw.

Converts real binary (floating-point) numbers to hexadecimal representation

Numeric

Width range: 1–16

Default width: 8

Alignment: left

HELP FORMAT

Description

The HEX*w*. format converts real binary (floating-point) numbers to hexadecimal representation. The *w* value specifies the width of the output field.

When the *w* value is between 1 and 15, the HEX*w*. format converts real binary numbers to fixed-point integers before writing them as hexadecimal digits. The HEX*w*. format writes negative numbers in twos complement notation, and right justifies digits when the *w* value is less than 16.

On any computer system, the least significant byte written by the HEX*w*. format is the rightmost byte. Some systems store integers with the least significant digit as the first byte. The HEX*w*. format produces consistent results regardless of the order of significance by byte on any computer system.

When the *w* value is 16, the HEX*w*. format displays floating-point values in their hexadecimal form.

Note: Different computer systems store floating-point values in different ways. However, the HEX16. format writes hexadecimal representations of floating-point values with consistent results in the same way your computer system stores them.

Comparisons

The HEX. numeric format is like the $HEX. character format in that both generate the hexadecimal equivalent of values.

Example

Values	SAS Statement	Results
		`----+----1----+----2`
35.4	`put @8 x hex8.;`	`00000023`
88		`00000058`
2.33		`00000002`
-150		`FFFFFF6A`

HHMM*w.d*

Writes hours and minutes

Date and time

Width range: 2–20

Default width: 5

Alignment: right

HELP FORMAT

Description

The HHMM*w.d* format writes the hours, minutes, and optionally, decimal fractions of minutes of a SAS time value. The SAS System rounds hours and minutes based on the value of seconds in a SAS time value. The *d* value can range from 1 through 19, but must be less than the *w* value.

Comparisons

The HHMM*w.d* format is similar to the TIME*w.d* format except that the HHMM*w.d* format does not print seconds.

Example

Value	SAS Statement	Result
		`----+----1----+----2`
`46796`	`put time hhmm.;`	`13:00`

See Also

HOUR*w.d*, MMSS*w.d*, and TIME*w.d* formats

"SAS Date and Time Values" in Chapter 4, "Rules of the SAS Language"

HMS, HOUR, MINUTE, SECOND, and TIME functions in Chapter 11, "SAS Functions"

TIME*w.* informats in Chapter 13, "SAS Informats"

HOURw.d

Writes hours and decimal fractions of hours

Date and time

Width range: 2–20

Default width: 2

Alignment: right

HELP FORMAT

Description

The HOUR*w.d* format returns the hour portion of a SAS time value. The system rounds hours based on the value of minutes in the SAS time value. If the optional *d* value is given, the SAS System prints decimal fractions of the hour. The *d* value can range from 1 through 19, but must be less than the *w* value.

Example

Value	SAS Statement	Result
		`----+----1----+----2`
`41400`	`put time hour4.1;`	`11.5`

See Also

HHMM*w.d*, MMSS*w.d*, TIME*w.d*, and TOD*w.* formats

"SAS Date and Time Values" in Chapter 4, "Rules of the SAS Language"

HMS, HOUR, MINUTE, SECOND, and TIME functions in Chapter 11, "SAS Functions"

TIME*w.* informat in Chapter 13, "SAS Informats"

IBw.d

Writes integer binary values

Numeric

Width range: 1–8

Default width: 4

Alignment: left

HELP FORMAT

Description

The IB*w.d* format writes integer binary (fixed-point) values. If you include a *d* value, the IB*w.d* format multiplies the number by 10^d.

Note: Different computer systems store integer binary values in different ways. However, the IB*w.d* format writes integer binary values with consistent results on the same kind of computer system you use to run the SAS System.

Comparisons

The following table compares integer binary notation in several programming languages:

	Integer Binary Notation	
Language	2 Bytes	4 bytes
SAS	IB2.	IB4.
FORTRAN	INTEGER*2	INTEGER*4
C	short	long

Example

Data Value	SAS Statement	Result*
128	`put x ib4.;`	00000080

* The result is a hexadecimal representation of a 4-byte integer binary number. Each byte occupies one column of the output field.

JULDAYw.

Writes Julian day of the year

Date and time

Width range: 3—32

Default width: 3

Alignment: right

HELP FORMAT

Description

The JULDAY*w*. format writes the Julian day of the year from a SAS date value.

Example

Value	SAS Statement	Result
		`----+----1----+----2`
10621 10624	`put date1 julday3. +1 date2 julday3.;`	`29  32`

See Also

"SAS Date and Time Values" in Chapter 4, "Rules of the SAS Language"

JULIANw.

Writes Julian dates (*yyddd* or *yyyyddd*)

Date and time

Width range: 5—7

Default width: 5

Alignment: left

HELP FORMAT

Description

The JULIAN*w*. format returns a Julian date from a SAS date value. The SAS System writes the Julian date with a two-digit year when the *w* value is 5. If the *w* value is 7, the Julian year value is four digits. To avoid confusion, use a four-digit year when the century is not clearly defined.

Examples

Value	SAS Statements	Results
		`----+----1----+----2`
9952	`put date julian5.;`	87091
	`put date julian6.;`	087091
	`put date julian7.;`	1987091

See Also

DATEJUL and JULDATE functions

"SAS Date and Time Values" in Chapter 4, "Rules of the SAS Language"

JULIANw. informat in Chapter 13, "SAS Informats"

MMDDYYw.

Writes date values (*mmddyy*)

Date and time

Width range: 2–8

Default width: 8

Alignment: right

HELP FORMAT

Description

The MMDDYY*w*. format writes a SAS date value in *mmddyy* form, where *mm, dd,* and *yy* are integers representing the month, day, and year.

Examples

Value	SAS Statements	Results
		`----+----1----+----2`
`10847`	`put day mmddyy2.;`	`09`
	`put day mmddyy3.;`	` 09`
	`put day mmddyy4.;`	`0912`
	`put day mmddyy5.;`	`09/12`
	`put day mmddyy6.;`	`091289`
	`put day mmddyy7.;`	` 091289`
	`put day mmddyy8.;`	`09/12/89`

See Also

DATE*w*., DDMMYY*w*., and YYMMDD*w*. formats

"SAS Date and Time Values" in Chapter 4, "Rules of the SAS Language"

DAY, MDY, MONTH, and YEAR functions in Chapter 11, "SAS Functions"

DATE*w*., DDMMYY*w*., MMDDYY*w*., and YYMMDD*w*. informats in Chapter 13, "SAS Informats"

MMSS*w.d*

Writes minutes and seconds

Date and time

Width range: 2—20

Default width: 5

Alignment: right

HELP FORMAT

Description

The MMSS*w.d* format converts a SAS time value to the number of minutes and seconds since midnight. The SAS System requires a minimum *w* value of 5 to write a value representing minutes and seconds. If the optional *d* value is specified, the SAS time value includes fractional seconds. The *d* value can range from 1 through 19, but must be less than the *w* value.

Example

Value	SAS Statement	Result
		`----+----1----+----2`
`4530`	`put time mmss.;`	`75:30`

See Also

HHMM*w.d* and TIME*w.d* formats

"SAS Date and Time Values" in Chapter 4, "Rules of the SAS Language"

HMS, MINUTE, and SECOND functions in Chapter 11, "SAS Functions"

TIME*w.* informat in Chapter 13, "SAS Informats"

MMYY*xw.*

Formats that write month and year, separated by a character

Date and time

Width range: 5—32

Default width: 7

Alignment: right

HELP FORMAT

Description

The MMYY*xw.* formats write the month (01 through 12) and year from a SAS date value, separated by colons, dashes, or other specific characters. The value of *x* can be C, D, N, P, or S, representing the type of separator; *w* represents the format width value. If the *w* value is too small to print a four-digit year, only the last two digits of the year are printed.

Example

Refer to the following table for a list of MMYYxw. formats and examples returned from an original date value of 29may1989:

Name	Separator	Example	Results
MMYY*w.*	letter M	`mmyy5.`	`05M89`
MMYYC*w.*	colon	`mmyyc7.`	`05:1989`
MMYYD*w.*	dash	`mmyyd7.`	`05-1989`
MMYYN*w.*	no separator	`mmyyn6.`	`051989`
MMYYP*w.*	period	`mmyyp6.`	`05.89`
MMYYS*w.*	slash	`mmyys7.`	`05/1989`

See Also

YYMM*xw*. formats

"SAS Date and Time Values" in Chapter 4, "Rules of the SAS Language"

MONNAME*w*.

Writes name of month

Date and time

Width range: 1–32

Default width: 9

Alignment: right

HELP FORMAT

Description

The MONNAME*w*. format writes the name of the month from a SAS date value, with the first letter capitalized and the remainder of the name in lowercase letters. The name of the month is truncated to fit the format width if necessary. Thus, the format MONNAME3. can be used to print the first three letters of the month name.

Example

Value	SAS Statements	Results
		`----+----1----+----2`
10919	`put date monname9.;`	`November`
	`put date monname1.;`	`N`

See Also

MONTH*w*. format

"SAS Date and Time Values" in Chapter 4, "Rules of the SAS Language"

MONTH*w*.

Writes month of year

Date and time

Width range: 2–32

Default width: 2

Alignment: right

HELP FORMAT

Description

The MONTH*w*. format writes the month (01 through 12) of the year from a SAS date value.

Example

Value	SAS Statement	Result
		`----+----1----+----2`
10919	`put date month.;`	`11`

See Also

MONNAME*w*. format

"SAS Date and Time Values" in Chapter 4, "Rules of the SAS Language"

MONYYw.

Writes month and year (*mmmyy* or *mmmyyyy*)

Date and time

Width range: 5–7

Default width: 5

Alignment: right

HELP FORMAT

Description

The MONYY*w*. format writes SAS date values in the form *mmmyy*, where *mmm* is the first three letters of the month name, and *yy* or *yyyy* is a two- or four-digit integer representing the year.

Example

Value	SAS Statement	Result
		`----+----1----+----2`
`10750`	`put acquired monyy7.;`	`JUN1989`

See Also

DDMMYY*w*., MMDDYY*w*., and YYMMDD*w*. formats

"SAS Date and Time Values" in Chapter 4, "Rules of the SAS Language"

MONTH and YEAR functions in Chapter 11, "SAS Functions"

MONYY*w*. informat in Chapter 13, "SAS Informats"

NEGPARENw.d

Displays negative values in parentheses

Numeric

Width range: 1–32

Default width: 6

Alignment: right

HELP FORMAT

Description

The NEGPAREN*w.d* format displays negative numbers enclosed in parentheses and nonnegative numbers with blanks instead of parentheses for proper column alignment. That is, the NEGPAREN*w.d* format reserves the last column for a right parenthesis, even when the value is positive. The NEGPAREN*w.d* format uses minus signs if a field is not wide enough for a number with parentheses.

Comparisons

The NEGPAREN*w.d* format operates just like the COMMA*w.d* format, separating every three digits of the value with a comma.

Example

Values	SAS Statement	Results
		`----+----1----+----2`
`1000`	`put @1 sales negparen10.;`	`     1,000`
`-2000`		`(    2,000)`

NENGO*w*.

Writes Japanese dates (*r.yymmdd*)

Date and time

Width range: 2–10

Default width: 10

Alignment: left

HELP FORMAT

Description

The NENGO*w*. format writes Japanese date values in the form *r.yymmdd*, where *r* is a letter representing an emperor's reign: M (Meiji), T (Taisho), S (Showa), or H (Heisei). The period is optional and *yy*, *mm*, and *dd* are integers representing the year, month, and day.

Examples

Value	SAS Statements	Results
		`----+----1----+----2`
9784 *	`put date nengo2.;`	`61`
	`put date nengo3.;`	`S61`
	`put date nengo4.;`	`S.61`
	`put date nengo5.;`	`S6110`
	`put date nengo6.;`	`S61/10`
	`put date nengo7.;`	`S611015`
	`put date nengo8.;`	`S.611015`
	`put date nengo9.;`	`S61/10/15`
	`put date nengo10.;`	`S.61/10/15`

* This corresponds to 15OCT86.

See Also

"SAS Date and Time Values" in Chapter 4, "Rules of the SAS Language"

NENGO*w*. informat in Chapter 13, "SAS Informats"

OCTAL*w*.

Converts numeric values to octal representation

Numeric

Width range: 1–24

Default width: 3

Alignment: left

HELP FORMAT

Description

The OCTAL*w*. format converts integer values to octal representation. If necessary, the OCTAL*w*. format converts numeric values to integers before displaying them in octal representation.

Comparisons

The OCTAL*w*. format for numeric values and the $OCTAL*w*. format for character values both convert values to octal representation.

Example

Value	SAS Statement	Result
		`----+----1----+----2`
3592	`put @1 x octal6.;`	`007010`

PD*w.d*

Writes packed decimal data

Numeric

Width range: 1–16

Default width: 1

Alignment: left

HELP FORMAT

Description

The PD*w.d* format writes values in packed decimal format. The *w* value specifies the number of bytes, not the number of digits. (In packed decimal data, each byte contains two digits.) If you include a *d* value, the PD*w.d* format multiplies the number by 10^d.

Note: Different computer systems store packed decimal values in different ways. However, the PD*w.d* format writes packed decimal values with consistent results on the same kind of computer system you use to run the SAS System.

Comparisons

The following table compares packed decimal notation in several programming languages:

Language	Notation
SAS	PD4.
COBOL	COMP-3 PIC S9(7)
IBM 370 assembler	PL4
PL/I	FIXED DEC

Example

Value	SAS Statement	Result*
128	put x pd4.;	0000128C

* The result is a hexadecimal representation of a binary number written in packed decimal format. Each byte occupies one column of the output field.

PERCENT*w.d*

Prints numbers as percentages

Numeric

Width range: 4—32

Default width: 6

Alignment: right

HELP FORMAT

Description

The PERCENT*w.d* format writes numeric values in percentage form. The *w* value specifies the total width of the output field. The *d* value (0 or 2) specifies the number of decimal digits the PERCENT*w.d* format writes. The PERCENT*w.d* format multiplies values by 100, formats them the same as the BEST*w.* format, and adds a percent sign (%) to the end of the formatted value, enclosing negative values in parentheses. The PERCENT*w.d* format allows room for a percent sign and parentheses, even if the value is not negative.

Example

Values	SAS Statement	Results
		----+----1----+----2
0.1	put @10 gain percent10.;	10%
1.2		120%
-0.05		(5%)

PIB*w.d*

Writes positive integer binary values

Numeric

Width range: 1—8

Default width: 1

Alignment: left

HELP FORMAT

Description

The PIB*w.d* format writes fixed-point binary values. The PIB*w.d* format treats all values as positive. If you include a *d* value, the PIB*w.d* format multiplies the number by 10^d.

Note: Different computer systems store positive integer binary values in different ways. However, the PIB*w.d* format writes positive integer binary values with consistent results on the same kind of computer system you use to run the SAS System.

Comparisons

The PIB*w.d* format operates like the IB*w.d* format except that the PIB*w.d* format treats all values as positive values.

Example

Value	SAS Statement	Result *
12	`put x pib1.;`	0C

* The result is a hexadecimal representation of a 1-byte binary number written in positive integer binary format, occupying one column of the output field.

PK*w.d*

Writes unsigned packed decimal data

Numeric

Width range: 1–16

Default width: 1

Alignment: left

HELP FORMAT

Description

The PK*w.d* format converts numeric values to unsigned packed decimal values. Each byte of unsigned packed decimal data contains two digits. The *w* value specifies the width of the output field. When you specify a *d* value, the PK*w.d* format multiplies the number by 10^d.

Comparisons

The PK*w.d* informat operates like the PD*w.d* informat except that the PK*w.d* format does not write the sign in the low-order byte.

Example

Value	SAS Statement	Result *
128	`put x pk4.;`	00000128

* The result is a hexadecimal representation of a 4-byte number written in packed decimal format. Each byte occupies one column of the output field.

QTR*w.*

Writes quarter of year

Date and time

Width range: 1–32

Default width: 1

Alignment: right

HELP FORMAT

Description

The QTR*w.* format writes the quarter of the year from a SAS date value.

Example

Value	SAS Statement	Result
		`----+----1----+----2`
10741	`put date qtr.;`	2

See Also

QTRR*w.* format

"SAS Date and Time Values" in Chapter 4, "Rules of the SAS Language"

QTRRw.

Writes quarter of year in Roman numerals

Date and time

Width range: 3—32

Default width: 3

Alignment: right

HELP FORMAT

Description

The QTRR*w*. format writes the quarter of the year from a SAS date value using Roman numerals.

Example

Value	SAS Statement	Result
		`----+----1----+----2`
`10897`	`put date qtrr3.;`	`IV`

See Also

QTR*w*. format

"SAS Date and Time Values" in Chapter 4, "Rules of the SAS Language"

RBw.d

Writes real binary (floating-point) data

Numeric

Width range: 2—8

Default width: 4

Alignment: left

HELP FORMAT

▶ ***Caution:*** *Using RB4 may result in truncation.*

Description

The RB*w.d* format writes numeric data in real binary (floating-point) notation. The *w* value specifies the width of the output field. When you specify a *d* value, the RB*w.d* format multiplies the number by 10^d.

The RB*w.d* format writes numeric data in the same way the SAS System stores them. Since it requires no data conversion, the RB*w.d* format is the most efficient method for writing data with the SAS System.

Note: Different computer systems store real binary values in different ways. However, the RB*w.d* format writes real binary values with consistent results on the same kind of computer system you use to run the SAS System.

Using RB4. to write real binary data on equipment conforming to the IEEE standard for floating-point numbers results in a truncated 8-byte number rather than a true 4-byte floating-point number.

Comparisons

The following table compares the names of real binary notation in several programming languages:

	Real Binary Notation	
Language	4 Bytes	8 bytes
SAS	RB4.	RB8.
FORTRAN	REAL*4	REAL*8
C	float	double
COBOL	COMP-1	COMP-2
IBM 370 assembler	E	D

Example

Value	SAS Statement	Result *
128	`put x rb8.;`	4280000000000000

* The result is a hexadecimal representation of an 8-byte real binary number as it looks on an IBM mainframe. Each byte occupies one column of the output field.

ROMANw.

Writes Roman numerals

Numeric

Width range: 2–32

Default width: 6

Alignment: left

HELP FORMAT

Description

The ROMAN*w*. format writes numeric values as Roman numerals. The *w* value specifies the width of the output field. The ROMAN*w*. format truncates a floating-point value to its integer component before writing.

Example

Value	SAS Statement	Result
		`----+----1----+----2`
1992	`put @5 year roman10.;`	`    MCMXCII`

SSNw.

Writes Social Security numbers

Numeric

Default width: 11

Alignment: none

HELP FORMAT

Description

The SSN*w*. format writes nine-digit numeric values as U.S. Social Security numbers, placing dashes between the third and fourth digits and between the fifth and sixth digits. The *w* value specifies the width of the output field.

If the value is missing, the SAS System writes nine single periods with dashes between the third and fourth periods and between the fifth and sixth periods. If the value contains fewer than nine digits, the SAS System right justifies the value and pads it with zeros on the left. If the value has more than nine digits, the SAS System writes it as a missing value.

Example

Value	SAS Statement	Result
		`----+----1----+----2`
263878439	`put @5 id ssn11.;`	`    263-87-8439`

S370FIB*w.d*

Writes integer binary data in IBM mainframe format

Numeric

Width range: 1—8

Default width: 4

Alignment: left

HELP FORMAT

Description

The S370FIB*w.d* format writes integer binary values in IBM mainframe format. The *w* value specifies the width of the output field. If you include a *d* value, the S370FIB*w.d* format multiplies the number by 10^d.

Use the S370FIB*w.d* format on other computer systems to write integer binary data in the same format as an IBM mainframe computer.

Comparisons

The following table shows the equivalent integer binary notation for several programming languages:

	Integer Binary Notation	
Language	4 Bytes	8 bytes
SAS	S370FIB2.	S370FIB4.
PL/I	FIXED BIN(15)	FIXED BIN(31)
FORTRAN	INTEGER*2	INTEGER*4
COBOL	COMP PIC 9(4)	COMP PIC 9(8)
IBM 370 assembler	H	F
C	short	long

S370FPD*w.d*

Writes packed decimal data in IBM mainframe format

Numeric

Width range: 1—16

Default width: 1

Alignment: left

HELP FORMAT

Description

The S370FPD*w.d* format writes packed decimal values in IBM mainframe format. The *w* value specifies the width of the output field. If you include a *d* value, the S370FPD*w.d* format multiplies the number by 10^d.

Use the S370FPD*w.d* format on other computer systems to write packed decimal data in the same format as an IBM mainframe computer.

Comparisons

The following table shows the notation for equivalent packed decimal formats in several programming languages:

Language	Packed Decimal Notation
SAS	S370FPD4.
PL/I	FIXED DEC(7,0)
COBOL	COMP-3 PIC S9(7)
IBM 370 assembler	PL4

S370FPIB*w.d*

Writes positive integer binary data in IBM mainframe format

Numeric

Width range: 1—8

Default width: 4

Alignment: left

HELP FORMAT

Description

The S370FPIB*w.d* format writes values in positive integer binary using the IBM mainframe format. The *w* value specifies the width of the output field.

Use the S370FPIB*w.d* format on other computer systems to write positive integer binary data in the same format as an IBM mainframe computer.

Comparisons

The S370FPIB*w.d* format operates like the S370FIB*w.d* format except that the S370FPIB*w.d* format treats all values as positive values.

S370FRB*w.d*

Writes real binary (floating-point) data in IBM mainframe format

Numeric

Width range: 2—8

Default width: 6

Alignment: left

HELP FORMAT

Description

The S370FRB*w.d* format writes real binary (floating-point) values in IBM mainframe format. The *w* value specifies the width of the output field. If you include a *d* value, the S370FRB*w.d* format multiplies the number by 10^d. A floating-point value consists of two parts: a mantissa giving the value and an exponent giving the value's magnitude.

Use the S370FRB*w.d* format on other computer systems to write floating-point binary data in the same format as an IBM mainframe computer.

Comparisons

The following table shows the notation for equivalent floating-point formats in several programming languages:

	Real Binary Notation	
Language	4 Bytes	8 Bytes
SAS	S370FRB4.	S370FRB8.
PL/I	FLOAT BIN(21)	FLOAT BIN(53)
FORTRAN	REAL*4	REAL*8
COBOL	COMP-1	COMP-2
IBM 370 assembler	E	D
C	float	double

TIMEw.d

Writes hours, minutes, and seconds

Date and time

Width range: 2–20

Default width: 8

Alignment: right

HELP FORMAT

Description

The TIMEw.d format writes SAS time values in the form *hh:mm:ss.ss*, where *hh, mm,* and *ss* are integers representing the hour, minute, second, and decimal fraction of a second. The *d* value can range from 1 through 19, but must be less than the *w* value.

Width values must be large enough to produce the desired results. For example, to obtain a complete time value with three decimal places, you must allow at least 12 spaces: 8 spaces to the left of the decimal point, 1 space for the decimal point itself, and 3 spaces for the decimal fraction of seconds.

Comparisons

The TIME*w.d* format is similar to the HHMM*w.d* format except that the TIME*w.d* format prints seconds.

Example

Value	SAS Statement	Result
		`----+----1----+----2`
`59083`	`put begin time.;`	`16:24:43`

See Also

HHMM*w.d*, HOUR*w.d*, MMSS*w.d*, and TIME*w.d* formats

"SAS Date and Time Values" in Chapter 4, "Rules of the SAS Language"

HOUR, MINUTE, SECOND, and TIME functions in Chapter 11, "SAS Functions"

TIME*w.* informat in Chapter 13, "SAS Informats"

TODw.

Writes the time portion of datetime values

Date and time

Width range: 2–20

Default width: 8

Alignment: right

HELP FORMAT

Description

The TOD*w.* format prints the time value from a SAS datetime value.

Example

Value	SAS Statement	Result
		`----+----1----+----2`
`956978640`	`put begin tod7.;`	`3:24:00`

See Also

TIME*w.d* format

"SAS Date and Time Values" in Chapter 4, "Rules of the SAS Language"

TIMEPART function in Chapter 11, "SAS Functions"

TIME*w.* informat in Chapter 13, "SAS Informats"

w.d

Writes standard numeric data

Numeric

Width range: 1–32

Alignment: right

HELP FORMAT

Description

The *w.d* format writes standard numeric values one digit per byte. The *w* value specifies the width of the output field. The *d* value optionally specifies the number of digits to the right of the decimal point in the numeric value. If you specify 0 for the *d* value or do not specify any *d* value, the *w.d* format writes the value without a decimal point.

The *w.d* format rounds to the nearest number that fits in the output field. If the number is too large to fit, the *w.d* format uses the BEST*w.* format. The *w.d* format writes negative numbers with leading minus signs. In addition, the *w.d* format right justifies before writing and pads with leading blanks.

When you are choosing a *w* value, remember to allow enough space to write the value, the decimal point, and a minus sign, if necessary.

Example

Value	SAS Statement	Result
		`----+----1----+----2`
`23.45`	`put @7 x 6.3;`	`23.450`

WEEKDATEw.

Writes day of week and date (*day-of-week, month-name dd, yy*)

Date and time

Width range: 3–37

Default width: 29

Alignment: right

HELP FORMAT

Description

The WEEKDATE*w.* format writes a SAS date value in the form *day-of-week, month-name dd,* and *yy* or *yyyy*. If the *w* value is too small to write the complete day of the week and month, the SAS System abbreviates as needed.

Comparisons

The WEEKDATE*w.* format is the same as the WEEKDATX*w.* format except the WEEKDATE*w.* format prints *dd* after the month's name.

Example

Value	SAS Statements	Results
		`----+----1----+----2`
`10848`	`put begin weekdate3.;`	`Wed`
	`put begin weekdate9.;`	`Wednesday`
	`put begin weekdate15.;`	`Wed, Sep 13, 89`
	`put begin weekdate17.;`	`Wed, Sep 13, 1989`

See Also

DATE*w*., DDMMYY*w*., MMDDYY*w*., TOD*w*., WEEKDATX*w*., and YYMMDD*w*. formats

"SAS Date and Time Values" in Chapter 4, "Rules of the SAS Language"

JULDATE, MDY, and WEEKDAY functions in Chapter 11, "SAS Functions"

DATE*w*., DDMMYY*w*., MMDDYY*w*., and YYMMDD*w*. informats in Chapter 13, "SAS Informats"

WEEKDATX*w*.

Writes day of week and date (*day-of-week, dd month-name yy*)

Date and time

Width range: 3–37

Default width: 29

Alignment: right

HELP FORMAT

Description

The WEEKDATX*w*. format writes a SAS date value in the form *day-of-week, dd month-name yy* or *yyyy*. If the *w* value is too small to write the complete day of the week and month, the SAS System abbreviates as needed (see the WEEKDATE*w*. format example).

Comparisons

The WEEKDATX*w*. format is the same as the WEEKDATE*w*. format except that the WEEKDATX*w*. format prints *dd* before the month's name.

Example

Value	SAS Statement	Result
		`----+----1----+----2----+`
`10869`	`put begin weekdatx.;`	`Wednesday, 4 October 1989`

See Also

WEEKDATE*w*., WORDDATE*w*., and WORDDATX*w*. formats

"SAS Date and Time Values" in Chapter 4, "Rules of the SAS Language"

TODAY and WEEKDAY functions in Chapter 11, "SAS Functions"

DATE*w*., DDMMYY*w*., MMDDYY*w*., and YYMMDD*w*. informats in Chapter 13, "SAS Informats"

WEEKDAY*w*.

Writes day of week

Date and time

Width range: 1–32

Default width: 1

Alignment: right

HELP FORMAT

Description

The WEEKDAY*w*. format writes the day of the week from a SAS date value (where 1=Sunday, 2=Monday, and so on).

Example

Value	SAS Statement	Result
		`----+----1----+----2`
`10621`	`put date weekday.;`	`1`

See Also

DOWNAME*w*. format

"SAS Date and Time Values" in Chapter 4, "Rules of the SAS Language"

WORDDATE*w*.

Writes date with name of month, day, and year (*month-name dd, yyyy*)

Date and time

Width range: 3–32

Default width: 18

Alignment: right

HELP FORMAT

Description

The WORDDATE*w*. format writes a SAS date value in the form *month-name dd, yyyy*. If the *w* value is too small to write the complete month, the SAS System abbreviates as needed.

Comparisons

The WORDDATE*w*. format is the same as the WORDDATX*w*. format except that the WORDDATE*w*. format prints *dd* after the month's name.

Example

Value	SAS Statements	Results
		`----+----1----+----2`
`11212`	`put term worddate3.;`	`Sep`
	`put term worddate9.;`	`September`
	`put term worddate12.;`	`Sep 12, 1990`
	`put term worddate18.;`	`September 12, 1990`
	`put term worddate20.;`	`  September 12, 1990`

See Also

WORDDATX*w*. format

"SAS Date and Time Values" in Chapter 4, "Rules of the SAS Language"

WORDDATX*w*.

Writes date with day, name of month, and year (*dd month-name yyyy*)

Date and time

Width range: 3–32

Default width: 18

Alignment: right

HELP FORMAT

Description

The WORDDATX*w*. format writes a SAS date value in the form *dd month-name yyyy*. If the *w* value is too small to write the complete name of the month, the SAS System abbreviates as needed.

Comparisons

The WORDDATX*w*. format is the same as the WORDDATE*w*. format except that the WORDDATX*w*. format prints *dd* before the month's name.

Example

Value	SAS Statement	Result
		`----+----1----+----2`
`10865`	`put term worddatx.;`	`30 September 1989`

See Also

WORDDATE*w*. format

"SAS Date and Time Values" in Chapter 4, "Rules of the SAS Language"

WORDF*w*.

Converts numeric values to words

Numeric

Width range: 5–200

Default width: 10

Alignment: left

HELP FORMAT

Description

The WORDF*w*. format converts numeric values to their equivalent in English words, with fractions represented numerically in hundredths. For example, 8.2 prints as eight and 20/100.

Negative numbers are preceded by the word minus. When the value's equivalent in words does not fit into the specified field, it is truncated on the right and the last character prints as an asterisk.

Comparisons

The WORDF*w*. format operates like the WORDS*w*. format except that the WORDF*w*. format prints fractions as numbers instead of words.

Example

Value	SAS Statement	Result
		`----+----1----+----2`
`2.5`	`put price wordf15.;`	`two and 50/100`

See Also

WORDS*w*. format

WORDS*w*.

Converts numeric values to words

Numeric

Width range: 5–200

Default width: 10

Alignment: left

HELP FORMAT

Description

The WORDS*w*. format converts numeric values to their equivalent in English words. For example, you might want to print checks with the amount written out below the payee line.

Negative numbers are preceded by the word minus. If the number is not an integer, the fractional portion is represented as hundredths. For example, 5.3 prints as five and thirty hundredths. When the value's equivalent in words does not fit into the specified field, it is truncated on the right and the last character prints as an asterisk.

Comparisons

The WORDS*w*. format operates like the WORDF*w*. format except that the WORDS*w*. format prints fractions as words instead of numbers.

Example

Value	SAS Statement	Result
		`----+----1----+----2---`
2.1	`put price words23.;`	`two and ten hundredths`

See Also

WORDF*w*. format

YEAR*w*.

Writes year part of date value

Date and time

Width range: 2–32

Default width: 4

Alignment: right

HELP FORMAT

Description

The YEAR*w*. format writes the year portion of a SAS date value. If the width is less than 4, the last two digits of the year are printed; otherwise, the year value is printed as four digits.

Example

The following statements return values of 1989 and 89:

```
data _null_;
   date='29JAN1989'D
   put date year4. +2 date year3.;
run;
```

See Also

"SAS Date and Time Values" in Chapter 4, "Rules of the SAS Language"

YYMMxw.

Formats that write year and month, separated by a character

Date and time

Width range: 5—32

Default width: 7

Alignment: right

HELP FORMAT

Description

The YYMM*xw*. formats write the year and month (01 through 12) from a SAS date value, separated by colons, periods, slashes, or other specific characters. If the format width is too small to print a four-digit year, only the last two digits of the year are printed.

Examples

The following table is a list of YYMM*xw*. formats and examples returned from an original date value of 29may1989:

Name	Separator	Example	Results
YYMM*w*.	letter M	`yymm7.`	`1989M05`
YYMMC*w*.	colon	`yymmc7.`	`1989:05`
YYMMD*w*.	dash	`yymmd7.`	`1989-05`
YYMMN*w*.	no separator	`yymmn6.`	`198905`
YYMMP*w*.	period	`yymmp7.`	`1989.05`
YYMMS*w*.	slash	`yymms7.`	`1989/05`

See Also

MMYY*xw*. formats

"SAS Date and Time Values" in Chapter 4, "Rules of the SAS Language"

YYMMDDw.

Writes date values (*yymmdd*)

Date and time

Width range: 2—8

Default width: 8

Alignment: right

HELP FORMAT

Description

The YYMMDD*w*. format produces a SAS date value in *yymmdd* form, where *yy* is the year, *mm* the month, and *dd* the day of the month.

Example

Value	SAS Statements	Results
		`----+----1----+----2`
`10669`	`put day yymmdd2.;`	`89`
	`put day yymmdd3.;`	` 89`
	`put day yymmdd4.;`	`8903`
	`put day yymmdd5.;`	`89-03`
	`put day yymmdd6.;`	`890318`
	`put day yymmdd7.;`	` 890318`
	`put day yymmdd8.;`	`89-03-18`

See Also

DATE*w*., DDMMYY*w*., and MMDDYY*w*. formats

"SAS Date and Time Values" in Chapter 4, "Rules of the SAS Language"

DAY, MDY, MONTH, and YEAR functions in Chapter 11, "SAS Functions"

DATE*w*., DDMMYY*w*., MMDDYY*w*., and YYMMDD*w*. informats in Chapter 13, "SAS Informats"

YYMON*w*.

Writes year and month abbreviation

Date and time

Width range: 5–32

Default width: 7

Alignment: right

HELP FORMAT

Description

The YYMON*w*. format writes the year and month of a SAS date value, with the month's name abbreviated to three characters. If the format width is too small to print a four-digit year, only the last two digits of the year are printed.

Example

Value	SAS Statement	Result
		`----+----1----+----2`
`10621`	`put date yymon7. +2 date yymon6.;`	`1989JAN  89JAN`

See Also

MMYY*xw*. formats

"SAS Date and Time Values" in Chapter 4, "Rules of the SAS Language"

YYQxw.

Formats that write year and quarter, separated by a character

Date and time

Width range: 4—32

Default width: 6

Alignment: right

HELP FORMAT

Description

The YYQ*xw*. formats write the year and quarter of a SAS date value, separated by colons, dashes, periods, or other specific characters. If the format width is too small to print a four-digit year, only the last two digits of the year are printed.

Examples

Refer to the following table for a list of YYQ*xw*. formats and examples returned from an original date value of 29may1989:

Name	Separator	Example	Results
YYQ*w*. *	letter Q	`yyq6.`	`1989Q2`
YYQC*w*.	colon	`yyqc6.`	`1989:2`
YYQD*w*.	dash	`yyqd6.`	`1989-2`
YYQN*w*.	no separator	`yyqn5.`	`19892`
YYQP*w*.	period	`yyqp6.`	`1989.2`
YYQS*w*.	slash	`yyqs6.`	`1989/2`

* For compatibility with previous versions, the width range of this format is 4-6.

See Also

YYQR*xw*. formats

"SAS Date and Time Values" in Chapter 4, "Rules of the SAS Language"

YYQRxw.

Formats that write year and quarter in Roman numerals, separated by characters

Date and time

Width range: 6—32

Default width: 8

Alignment: right

HELP FORMAT

Description

The YYQR*xw*. formats write the year and quarter of a SAS date value, with the quarter printed in Roman numerals. The date and quarter are separated by colons, dashes, or other specific characters. If the format width is too small to print a four-digit year, only the last two digits of the year are printed.

Examples

Refer to the following table for a list of YYQR*xw*. formats and examples returned from an original date value of 29may1989:

Name	Separator	Example	Results
YYQR*w*.	letter Q	`yyqr8.`	`1989QII`
YYQRC*w*.	colon	`yyqrc8.`	`1989:II`
YYQRD*w*.	dash	`yyqrd8.`	`1989-II`
YYQRN*w*.	no separator	`yyqrn7.`	`1989II`
YYQRP*w*.	period	`yyqrp8.`	`1989.II`
YYQRS*w*.	slash	`yyqrs8.`	`1989/II`

See Also

YYQ*xw.* formats

"SAS Date and Time Values" in Chapter 4, "Rules of the SAS Language"

Zw.d

Writes leading 0s

Numeric

Width range: 1–32

Default width: 1

Alignment: right

HELP FORMAT

Description

The Z*w.d* format writes standard numeric values one digit per byte and fills in 0s to the left of the data value. The *w* value specifies the width of the output field. The *d* value optionally specifies the number of digits to the right of the decimal point in the numeric value. If you specify 0 for the *d* value or do not specify any *d* value, the Z*w.d* format writes the value without a decimal point.

The Z*w.d* format rounds to the nearest number that will fit in the output field. If it is too large to fit, the Z*w.d* format uses the BEST*w.d* format. The Z*w.d* format writes negative numbers with leading minus signs. In addition, it right justifies before writing and pads with leading zeros.

When you are choosing a *w* value, remember to allow enough space to write the value, the decimal point, and a minus sign, if necessary.

Comparisons

The Z*w.d* format operates like the *w.d* format except that the Z*w.d* format pads right-justified output with 0s instead of blanks.

Example

Value	SAS Statement	Result
		`----+----1----+----2`
`1350`	`put @5 seqnum z8.`	`00001350`

ZDw.d

Writes data in zoned decimal format

Numeric

Width range: 1–32

Default width: 1

Alignment: left

HELP FORMAT

Description

The zoned decimal format is similar to standard numeric format in that every digit requires 1-byte. However, the value's sign is in the last byte, along with the last digit.

Note: Different computer systems store zoned decimal values in different ways. However, the ZD*w.d* format writes zoned decimal values with consistent results on the same kind of computer system you use to run the SAS System.

Comparisons

This table compares the zoned decimal format with notation in several programming languages:

Language	Zoned Decimal Notation
SAS	ZD3.
PL/I	PICTURE '99T'
COBOL	DISPLAY PIC S 999
IBM 370 assembler	ZL3

Example

Value	SAS Statement	Result *
120	`put x zd4.;`	F0F1F2C0

* The result is a hexadecimal representation of a binary number in zoned decimal format on an IBM mainframe computer. Each byte occupies one column of the output field.

CHAPTER 15 SAS® Data Set Options

Background information on SAS data set options, including a table listing all data set options, appears in Chapter 3, "Components of the SAS Language." See Table 3.11, "SAS Data Set Options."

Note that all data set options must be enclosed in parentheses after the data set name.

BUFNO=

Specifies the number of buffers for processing a SAS data set

DATA step and PROC steps

HELP DSOPTION

Syntax

BUFNO=*number-of-buffers*

Description

The BUFNO= data set option specifies the number of buffers to be allocated for processing a SAS data set. The buffer number is not a permanent attribute of the data set and is valid only for the current SAS session or job.

You use the following argument with the BUFNO= data set option:

number-of-buffers
: specifies a value from 1 to the maximum number of buffers available on your host system.

■ **Host Information** .... Refer to the SAS documentation for your host system for your system's default value. ■

■ **Performance Note** .... To reduce input/output operations on a small data set and speed execution time, allocate one buffer for each memory page of data to be processed. This technique is most effective if you read the same observations several times during processing. For a discussion of using the BUFNO= data set option to tune the performance of your SAS application, see "Tools for Tuning Data Set Performance" in Chapter 6, "SAS Files." ■

Comparisons

The value specified for the BUFNO= data set option overrides the value specified for the BUFNO= system option.

See Also

BUFSIZE= data set option

"Tools for Tuning Data Set Performance" in Chapter 6, "SAS Files"

BUFNO= system option in Chapter 16, "SAS System Options"

BUFSIZE=

Specifies a permanent buffer size for output SAS data sets

DATA step and PROC steps

HELP DSOPTION

Syntax

BUFSIZE=*number-of-bytes*

Description

The BUFSIZE= data set option specifies a buffer size for data sets you are creating. The BUFSIZE= data set option is valid only for output data sets, that is, data sets named in the DATA statement of a DATA step or the OUT= option of a SAS procedure.

The buffer size, or page size, determines the size of the input/output buffer the SAS System uses when transferring data during processing. A page is the number of bytes of data that the SAS System moves between external storage and memory in one logical input/output operation. Once specified, the buffer size is a permanent attribute of the data set, and the specified buffer size is used whenever the data set is processed. To change the buffer size, you must use a DATA step to copy the data set and specify a new buffer size or use the SAS System default.

You use the following argument with the BUFSIZE= data set option:

number-of-bytes
: specifies the minimum number of bytes of storage. The number of bytes can have a value from 0, the system default, to the maximum value allowed by your host system. If the value is 0, the SAS System chooses a host system default that is optimal for the SAS data set. If any value you specify is not adequate, the SAS System automatically rounds up to the next valid buffer size for the data set.

■ **Host Information** .... Refer to the SAS documentation for your host system for minimum and maximum buffer size values. ■

■ **Performance Note** .... Using the BUFSIZE= option can speed up execution time by reducing the number of times the SAS System has to read from or write to the storage medium. However, the improvement in execution time comes at the cost of increased memory consumption. See "Tools for Tuning Data Set Performance" in Chapter 6. ■

Comparisons

When used together in the same SAS session, the value specified for the BUFSIZE= data set option overrides the value specified for the BUFSIZE= system option.

See Also

BUFNO= data set option

BUFSIZE= system option in Chapter 16, "SAS System Options"

"Tools for Tuning Data Set Performance" in Chapter 6, "SAS Files"

CNTLLEV=

Specifies the level of shared access to SAS data sets

DATA step and PROC steps

HELP DSOPTION

Syntax

CNTLLEV=MEM | REC

Description

The CNTLLEV= data set option specifies the level at which shared update access to a SAS data set is denied. For Release 6.06, a SAS data set can be opened concurrently by more than one SAS session or by more than one statement, window, or procedure within a single session. For example, with the FSEDIT procedure you can request two windows on the same SAS data set in one session. With one engine for the VMS operating system, more than one user can share access to the same SAS data set.

You can use only one of the following arguments with the CNTLLEV= data set option:

MEM
: specifies that concurrent access is controlled at the SAS data set (or member) level. Member-level control restricts concurrent access to only one update access but allows read access to many sessions, procedures, or statements. For example, if you open a SAS data set with the FSVIEW command and use CNTLLEV=MEM, you cannot issue an FSEDIT command, which requires update access, on the same data set until you end the FSVIEW procedure. You can, however, issue an FSBROWSE command, which requires only read access.

REC
: specifies that concurrent access is controlled at the observation (or record) level. Record-level control allows more than one update access to the same SAS data set, but denies concurrent update of the same observation. If you use CNTLLEV=REC, you can access the same SAS data set with two FSEDIT windows.

By default, SAS procedures permit the greatest degree of concurrent access possible while guaranteeing the integrity of the data and the data analysis. Therefore, you do not normally use the CNTLLEV= option.

You can use this option when

- □ your application controls the access to the data, such as in Screen Control Language (SCL), SAS/IML software, or DATA step programming
- □ you access data through an interface engine that does not provide member-level control of the data.

If you use CNTLLEV=REC and the SAS procedure needs member-level control for integrity of the data analysis, the SAS System prints a warning to the SAS log that inaccurate or unpredictable results can occur if the data are updated by another process during the analysis.

See Also

"New Concepts: SAS Data Set Model" in Chapter 6, "SAS Files"

COMPRESS=

Compresses observations in an output SAS data set

DATA step and PROC steps

HELP DSOPTION

Syntax

COMPRESS=NO | YES

Description

The COMPRESS= data set option specifies whether observations in the data set being created are to be uncompressed (fixed-length records) or compressed (variable-length records). Compressing a data set reduces its size by reducing repeated consecutive characters or numbers to 2-byte or 3-byte representations.

The COMPRESS= data set option can be specified only for output data sets, that is, data sets named in the DATA statement of a DATA step or the OUT= option of a SAS procedure. The record type becomes a permanent attribute of the data set. To uncompress observations, you must use a DATA step to copy the data set and use COMPRESS=NO for the new data set.

You can use only one of the following arguments with the COMPRESS= data set option:

NO
: specifies that the observations are not to be compressed. By default, the SAS System stores observations as uncompressed records.

YES
: specifies that the observations are to be compressed as they are written to the output data set.

■ **Performance Note** ....

The advantages of using the COMPRESS= data set option are reduced storage requirements for the data set and fewer input/output operations necessary to read from or write to the data set during processing. ■

The following restrictions apply to data sets that have compressed observations:

- □ You cannot access observations in a compressed SAS data set by observation number; therefore, you cannot use the POINT= option in the SET statement or access observations by observation number in SAS/FSP procedures. You can use the FIRSTOBS= and OBS= data set options with compressed data sets, but processing is slower than it is with uncompressed data sets.
- □ The CPU time required to prepare observations for input/output operations is increased because of the overhead of compressing and expanding the observations.
- □ For Release 6.06, only the V606 engine can create and access compressed SAS data sets.

By default, new observations are appended to existing compressed data sets. If you want to track and reuse free space, you can use the REUSE= data set option when you create a compressed SAS data set. REUSE=YES tells the SAS System to write new observations to the space freed when you delete other observations.

Comparisons

The COMPRESS= data set option overrides the COMPRESS= system option.

See Also

REUSE= data set option

"Tools for Tuning Data Set Performance" in Chapter 6, "SAS Files"

COMPRESS= and REUSE= system options in Chapter 16, "SAS System Options"

DROP=

Excludes variables from processing or from output SAS data sets

DATA step and PROC steps

HELP DSOPTION

Syntax

DROP=*variable-list*

Description

The DROP= data set option controls which variables are processed or written to output SAS data sets during DATA and PROC steps. If the option is associated with an input data set (one specified in a SET, MERGE, or UPDATE statement in the DATA step), the variables are not available for processing. If the DROP= option is associated with an output data set (one specified in a DATA statement), the SAS System does not write the variables to the output data set, but they are available for processing.

The DROP= data set option is used in DATA or PROC steps, and it can be applied to a data set in combination with other data set options. The SAS System acts on data set options specified for input data sets before it acts on program statements or options specified for output data sets.

You use the following argument with the DROP= data set option:

variable-list specifies one or more variable names. You can list the variables in any form allowed by the SAS System. (See "Examples" later in this section.)

Comparisons

The DROP= data set option differs from the DROP statement in the following ways:

- The DROP= data set option can be used in a PROC step and the DROP statement cannot.
- The DROP= data set option can be used with input data sets to exclude variables from processing. The DROP statement only controls which variables are written to the output data set and cannot be used to exclude variables from processing.
- Using the DROP= data set option with output data sets enables you to exclude variables from some data sets but not from others. The DROP statement applies to all output data sets.

The KEEP= data set option is a parallel option that specifies a list of variables to be included in processing or written to the output data set. Use the KEEP= option if the number of variables you are including is significantly smaller than the number you are omitting.

Examples

In the following example, the variables YRSEXP and JOBCODE1 through JOBCODE4 are not included in processing. The variables COLLNAME and COLLCODE are written to the data set COLLEGE, but not to the data set HISCHOOL.

```
data college hischool(drop=collname collcode);
   set employee(drop=yrsexp jobcode1-jobcode4);
```

In Release 6.06, you can also specify variables using this form of the variable list:

```
data firstqtr;
   set yearly(drop=apr--dec);
run;
```

See Also

KEEP= data set option

DROP statement in Chapter 9, "SAS Language Statements"

FILECLOSE=

Specifies how a tape is positioned when a SAS file on the tape is closed

DATA step and PROC steps

HELP DSOPTION

Syntax

FILECLOSE=DISP | LEAVE | REREAD | REWIND

Description

The FILECLOSE= data set option enables a user to specify how a tape volume is to be positioned when a SAS file on that volume is closed.

You can use only one of the following arguments with the FILECLOSE= data set option:

DISP
: positions the tape volume according to the disposition specified in the host system's control language.

LEAVE
: leaves the tape positioned at the end of the file just processed. Use FILECLOSE=LEAVE if you are not repeatedly accessing the same files in a SAS program but are accessing one or more subsequent SAS files on the same tape.

REREAD
: leaves the tape volume postioned at the beginning of the file just processed. Use FILECLOSE=REREAD if you are accessing the same SAS data set on tape several times in a SAS program.

REWIND
: rewinds the tape volume to the beginning. Use FILECLOSE=REWIND if you are not repeatedly accessing the same files in a SAS program but are accessing one or more previous SAS files on the same tape.

■ **Host Information** ....

These values are not recognized by all host systems. Additional values are available on some host systems. Refer to the appropriate sections of the SAS documentation for your host system for more information on using SAS data libraries stored on tape.
.... ■

Comparisons

The FILECLOSE= data set option overrides the TAPECLOSE= system option.

See Also

TAPECLOSE= system option in Chapter 16, "SAS System Options"

FIRSTOBS=

Causes processing to begin at a specified observation

DATA step and PROC steps

HELP DSOPTION

Syntax

FIRSTOBS=*n*

Description

The FIRSTOBS= data set option causes processing to begin with the *n*th observation. This option is valid when reading an existing SAS data set.

You use the following argument with the FIRSTOBS= data set option:

n
: specifies a positive integer less than or equal to the number of observations in the data set.

The FIRSTOBS= option cannot be used when a WHERE statement or WHERE= data set option is specified in the same DATA or PROC step.

Comparisons

The FIRSTOBS= data set option enables you to select observations from SAS data sets. You can select observations to be read from external data files by using the FIRSTOBS= data set option in the INFILE statement.

The FIRSTOBS= data set option overrides the FIRSTOBS= system option for the individual data set.

While the FIRSTOBS= data set option specifies a starting point for processing, the OBS= data set option specifies an ending point. The two options are often used together to define a range of observations to be processed.

Examples

The following statement causes the SAS System to print data set STUDY beginning with observation 20:

```
proc print data=study(firstobs=20);
```

The following SET statement uses both FIRSTOBS= and OBS= to read only observations 5 through 10 from data set OLD:

```
data part;
   set old(firstobs=5 obs=10);
run;
```

See Also

OBS= data set option

INFILE and WHERE statements in Chapter 9, "SAS Language Statements"

FIRSTOBS= system option in Chapter 16, "SAS System Options"

IN=

Creates a variable that indicates whether the data set contributed data to the current observation

DATA step

HELP DSOPTION

Syntax

IN=*variable*

Description

The IN= data set option is used in the SET, MERGE, and UPDATE statements to create and name a variable that indicates whether the data set contributed data to the current observation. Within the DATA step, the value of the variable is 1 if the data set contributed data to the current observation, and 0 otherwise.

Specify the IN= data set option in parentheses only after a SAS data set name in the SET, MERGE, and UPDATE statements. When you use the IN= data set option with data sets sorted with BY processing and a data set contributes an observation, the IN= variable is 1 as long as that BY group is still being processed and the variable is not reset by programming logic.

Values of IN= variables are available to program statements during the DATA step, but the variables are not included in the SAS data set being created.

You use the following argument with the IN= data set option:

variable names the new variable you are creating.

Example

In this example, the IN= data set option is used in a merge operation to create a new data set containing observations with data from two existing data sets. The variable X has the value 1 when an observation is read in from data set NEW; otherwise, it has the value 0. The IF-THEN statement checks the value of X to determine if data set NEW contributed data to the current observation. If the value of X is 0, the observation is written to the data set MISSING; otherwise, the observation is written to the data set MASTER.

```
data master missing;
   merge old new(in=x);
   by id;
   if x=0 then output missing;
   else output master;
run;
```

See Also

"BY-Group Processing" in Chapter 4, "Rules of the SAS Language"

BY, MERGE, SET, and UPDATE statements in Chapter 9, "SAS Language Statements"

KEEP=

Specifies variables for processing or writing to output SAS data sets

DATA step and PROC steps

HELP DSOPTION

Syntax

KEEP=*variable-list*

Description

The KEEP= data set option controls which variables are processed or written to output SAS data sets during a DATA or PROC step. If the option is associated with an input data set (one specified in a SET, MERGE, or UPDATE statement in the DATA step), only those variables listed after the KEEP= data set option are available for processing. If the KEEP= data set option is associated with an output data set (one specified in a DATA statement), only the variables listed after the option are written to the output data set.

The KEEP= data set option can be used in DATA or PROC steps, and it can be applied in combination with other data set options. The SAS System acts on data set options specified for input data sets before it acts on program statements or options specified for output data sets.

You use the following argument with the KEEP= data set option:

variable-list
: specifies one or more variable names. You can list the variables in any form allowed by the SAS System. (See "Examples" later in this section.)

Comparisons

The KEEP= data set option differs from the KEEP statement in the following ways:

- □ The KEEP= data set option can be used in PROC steps and the KEEP statement cannot.
- □ The KEEP= data set option can be used with input data sets to specify variables for processing. The KEEP statement can be used only to specify which variables are written to the output data set.
- □ Using the KEEP= data set option with output data sets enables you to include variables in some data sets but not others. The KEEP statement applies to all output data sets.

The DROP= data set option is a parallel option that specifies variables not included in processing or omitted from the output data set. Use the DROP= option if the number of variables you are omitting is significantly smaller than the number you are including.

Examples

In the following example, the variables CROP, YIELD, INSECTS, and WEED1 through WEED3 are the only variables read into the DATA step for processing. The variables YIELD and WEED1 through WEED3 are written to the data set CORN, and only the variable YIELD is written to the data set BEANS.

```
data corn (keep=yield weed1-weed3) beans(keep=yield);
   set harvest(keep=crop yield weed1-weed3 insects);
run;
```

In Release 6.06, you can also specify variables using the following form of the variable list:

```
data period1;
   set yearly(keep=jan--may);
run;
```

See Also

DROP= data set option

KEEP statement in Chapter 9, "SAS Language Statements"

LABEL=

Specifies a label for the data set

DATA step and PROC steps

HELP DSOPTION

Syntax

LABEL=*'label'*

Description

The LABEL= data set option specifies a label for a SAS data set. The option can be used on both input and output data sets. When used on input data sets, the LABEL= option assigns a label for the file for the duration of that DATA or PROC step. When specified on an output data set, the label becomes a permanent part of that file and can be printed using the CONTENTS or DATASETS procedures.

A label assigned to a data set remains associated with that data set during SAS procedures that update a data set in place, such as the APPEND procedure. However, a label is lost if you use a data set with a previously assigned label to create a new data set in the DATA step. For example, a label previously assigned to data set ONE is lost when you create the new output data set ONE in the following DATA step:

```
data one;
   set one;
run;
```

You use the following argument with the LABEL data set option:

'label' consists of up to 40 characters and is enclosed in quotes. If the label text contains single quotes, use double quotes around the label, or use two single quotes in the label text and surround the string with single quotes.

Comparisons

The LABEL= data set option enables you to specify labels only for data sets. You can specify labels for the variables in a data set using the LABEL statement. The ATTRIB statement with the LABEL= option also enables you to assign labels to variables.

Examples

The following examples assign labels to data sets:

- □ `data w2(label='1976 W2 Info, Hourly');`
- □ `data new(label='Peter''s List');`
- □ `data new(label="Hillside's Daily Account");`
- □ `data sales(label='Sales For May(NE)');`

See Also

ATTRIB and LABEL statements in Chapter 9, "SAS Language Statements"

OBS=

Causes processing to end with the *n*th observation

DATA step and PROC steps

HELP DSOPTION

Syntax

OBS=*n*

Description

The OBS= data set option causes processing to end with the *n*th observation. (It does not specify how many observations should be processed.) This option is valid only when reading an existing SAS data set.

You use the following argument with the OBS= data set option:

n specifies a positive integer less than or equal to the number of observations in the data set or zero.

You can use OBS=0 to create an empty data set that has the structure of another data set.

The OBS= data set option cannot be used when a WHERE statement or WHERE= data set option is specified in the same DATA or PROC step.

Comparisons

The OBS= data set option enables you to select observations from SAS data sets. You can select observations to be read from external data files using the OBS= option in the INFILE statement.

The OBS= data set option overrides the OBS= system option for the individual data set.

While the OBS= option specifies an ending point for processing, the FIRSTOBS= data set option specifies a starting point. The two options are often used together to define a range of observations to be processed.

Examples

In this example, the OBS= data set option in the SET statement reads in the first ten observations from data set OLD:

```
data new;
   set old(obs=10);
run;
```

The following statement prints only observations 5 through 10 in data set STUDY:

```
proc print data=study(firstobs=5 obs=10);
```

See Also

FIRSTOBS= data set option

INFILE and WHERE statements in Chapter 9, "SAS Language Statements"

OBS= system option in Chapter 16, "SAS System Options"

RENAME=

Changes the name of a variable

DATA step and PROC steps

HELP DSOPTION

Syntax

RENAME=(*old-name-1*=*new-name-1*< . . . *old-name-n*=*new-name-n*>)

Description

The RENAME= data set option changes the name of a variable. If the RENAME= data set option is used when a data set is created, the new variable name is included in the output data set. If the RENAME= option is used on an input data set (for example, in the SET, MERGE, or UPDATE statement), the new name is used in DATA step programming statements.

If you use the RENAME= data set option on an input data set used in a SAS procedure (such as the following PRINT procedure), the SAS System changes the name of the variable in that procedure. The list of variables to rename must be enclosed in parentheses as follows:

```
proc print data=test(rename=(score1=score2));
```

You use the following arguments with the RENAME= data set option:

old-name specifies the variable you want to rename.

new-name specifies the new name of the variable.

If you use the RENAME= data set option in the same DATA step with either the DROP= or KEEP= data set option, the DROP= and KEEP= data set options are applied before the RENAME= data set option. Thus, use *old-name* in the DROP= and KEEP= data set options. You cannot drop and rename the same variable in the same statement.

Note: You cannot use a variable list (for example, X1-X10) with the RENAME= data set option.

Comparisons

The RENAME= data set option differs from the RENAME statement in the following ways:

- □ The RENAME= data set option can be used in PROC steps and the RENAME statement cannot.
- □ The RENAME statement applies to all output data sets. If you want to rename different variables in different data sets, you must use the RENAME= data set option.
- □ To rename variables before processing, you must use a RENAME= data set option on the input data set or data sets.

Use the RENAME statement or the RENAME= data set option when program logic requires that you rename variables, for example, if two input data sets have variables with the same name. To rename variables as a file management task, the DATASETS procedure or the VAR display manager window are easier and do not require DATA step processing.

Example

The following code renames variable X to a variable named KEYS. The second and third DATA steps show different placements of the RENAME= data set option and how the placement affects the program statements.

```
data one;
   input x y;
   more SAS statements
run;

data two(rename=(x=keys));
   set one;
   z=x+y;                    /* old name in program statements */
   more SAS statements
run;

data three;
   set one(rename=(x=keys));
   z=keys+y;                 /* new name in program statements */
   more SAS statements
run;
```

See Also

DROP= and KEEP= data set options

"Dropping, Keeping, and Renaming Variables" in Chapter 4, "Rules of the SAS Language"

RENAME statement in Chapter 9, "SAS Language Statements"

REPLACE=

Overrides the REPLACE= system option

DATA step and PROC steps

HELP DSOPTION

Syntax

REPLACE=NO | YES

Description

The REPLACE= data set option controls replacement of like-named temporary or permanent SAS data sets. This option is valid only when you are creating a data set.

You can use the following arguments with the REPLACE= data set option:

NO
: specifies that a new data set with a given name does not replace an existing data set with the same name.

YES
: specifies that a new data set with a given name replaces an existing data set with the same name.

Comparisons

The REPLACE= data set option overrides the REPLACE system option for the individual data set.

Example

Using the REPLACE= data set option in the following DATA statement prevents the SAS System from replacing a permanent SAS data set named ONE in a library referenced by MYLIB:

```
data mylib.one(replace=no);
```

The SAS System writes a message in the log that tells you the file has not been replaced.

See Also

REPLACE system option in Chapter 16, "SAS System Options"

REUSE=

Specifies whether new observations are written to free space in compressed SAS data sets

DATA step and PROC steps

HELP DSOPTION

Syntax

REUSE=NO | YES

Description

The REUSE= data set option specifies whether observations are appended to compressed SAS data sets or inserted in the space freed by deleting or updating other observations. By default, new observations are appended to existing compressed data sets. If you want to track and reuse free space, you can use the REUSE= data set option when you create a compressed SAS data set.

The REUSE= data set option has meaning only when you are creating new data sets with the COMPRESS=YES data set option or system option. Using the REUSE= data set option when accessing an existing SAS data set has no effect.

You can use only one of the following arguments with the REUSE= data set option:

NO
: specifies that the SAS System does not track and reuse space in compressed data sets. New observations are appended to the existing data set. Specifying the NO argument results in less efficient data storage if you delete or update many observations in the SAS data set.

YES
: specifies that the SAS System track and reuse space in compressed SAS data sets. New observations are inserted in the space freed when updating or deleting other observations.

  This fact is also true for procedures that add observations to the end of SAS data sets (for example, the APPEND and FSEDIT procedures). If you plan to use these procedures with compressed data sets, use the REUSE=NO argument. REUSE=YES causes new observations to be added wherever there is space in the file, not necessarily at the end of the file.

Comparisons

The REUSE= data set option overrides the REUSE= system option.

See Also

COMPRESS= data set option

COMPRESS= and REUSE= system options in Chapter 16, "SAS System Options"

TYPE=

Specifies the data set type for a specially structured SAS data set

DATA step and PROC steps

HELP DSOPTION

Syntax

TYPE=CORR

Description

The TYPE= data set option specifies the SAS data set type for a specially structured SAS data set. Use the TYPE= data set option in a DATA step to create a special SAS data set in the proper format.

Most SAS data sets do not have a specified type. However, there are several specially structured SAS data sets that are used by some SAS/STAT procedures. These SAS data sets contain special variables and observations, and they are usually created by SAS statistical procedures. Because most of the special SAS data sets are used with SAS/STAT software, they are described in the *SAS/STAT User's Guide, Version 6, Fourth Edition, Volume 1* and *Volume 2*.

You use the following argument with the TYPE= data set option:

CORR
: produces data sets with Pearson, Spearman, Kendall, and Hoeffding statistics.

Other values are available in other SAS software products and are described in the appropriate documentation.

See Also

Chapter 15, "The CORR Procedure," in the *SAS Procedures Guide, Version 6, Third Edition*

SAS/STAT User's Guide, Version 6, Fourth Edition, Volume 1 and *Volume 2*

WHERE=

Selects observations that meet the specified condition

DATA step and PROC steps

HELP DSOPTION

Syntax

WHERE=(*where-expression*)

Description

The WHERE= data set option enables you to select observations from a SAS data set that meet the condition specified in the WHERE expression before the SAS System brings them into the DATA or PROC step for processing. In the DATA step, the WHERE= data set option is available only with input SAS data sets listed in the SET, MERGE, and UPDATE statements. Selecting observations that meet the conditions of the WHERE expression is the first operation the SAS System performs in each iteration of the DATA step.

Like any SAS data set option, the WHERE= data set option applies only to the data set whose name it follows. It does not apply to all data sets accessed in the DATA step. Any variables specified in the WHERE expression must be part of the data set to which the WHERE= data set option applies.

You cannot use the WHERE= data set option with options that select observations by observation number, such as the FIRSTOBS= and OBS= data set options and the POINT= option in the SET statement.

If you use both the WHERE= data set option and the WHERE statement in the same DATA step, the SAS System ignores the WHERE statement for data sets with the WHERE= data set option. However, you can use the WHERE= data set option with the WHERE command in SAS/FSP software.

■ **Performance Note** ....

Using indexed SAS data sets can significantly improve performance when you are using WHERE expressions to access a subset of the observations in a SAS data set. Refer to "Release 6.06: SAS Indexes" in Chapter 6 for a complete discussion of WHERE-expression processing with indexed data sets and a list of guidelines you should consider before indexing your SAS data sets.

.... ■

You use the following argument with the WHERE= data set option:

(where-expression)
: is a valid arithmetic or logical expression that consists of a sequence of operators and operands. Note that the expression must be enclosed in parentheses. Refer to the description of the WHERE statement in Chapter 9, "SAS Language Statements," for a detailed description of the operators and operands that you can specify in a WHERE expression.

Comparisons

The WHERE statement applies to all input data sets. The WHERE= data set option selects observations only from the data set for which it is specified.

Do not confuse the purpose of the WHERE= data set option. The DROP= and KEEP= data set options select variables for processing, while the WHERE= data set option selects observations.

Example

The following example shows the correct syntax of the WHERE= data set option:

```
merge qtr1(where=(sales gt 20000)) qtr2(where=(sales gt 10000));
```

See Also

WHERE statement in Chapter 9, "SAS Language Statements"

CHAPTER 16 SAS® System Options

(continued on next page)

(continued from previous page)

Background information on SAS system options, including a table listing all system options, appears in Chapter 3, "Components of the SAS Language." See Table 3.12, "Categories and Descriptions of SAS System Options."

ALTLOG=

Specifies a destination for a copy of the SAS log

Valid as part of: configuration file, SAS invocation

HELP ALTLOG

Syntax

ALTLOG=*destination*

Description

The ALTLOG= system option specifies a destination to which a copy of the SAS log is written. Use the ALTLOG= option to capture log output for printing.

You can use the following argument with the ALTLOG= system option:

destination
: specifies either an external file or a device, depending on your host system. All messages written to the SAS log are also written to the destination.

■ **Host Information** ....

A valid destination and its syntax are host specific. Although the syntax is generally consistent with the command-line syntax of your host system, it may include additional or alternate punctuation. For details, refer to the SAS documentation for your host system.

.... ■

ALTPRINT=

Specifies a destination for a copy of the SAS procedure output file

Valid as part of: configuration file, SAS invocation

HELP ALTPRINT

Syntax

ALTPRINT=*destination*

Description

The ALTPRINT= system option specifies a destination to which a copy of the SAS procedure output file is written. Use the ALTPRINT= option to capture procedure output for printing.

You can use the following argument with the ALTPRINT= system option:

destination specifies either an external file or a device, depending on your host system. All output written to the SAS log is also written to the destination.

■ **Host Information** ....

A valid destination and its syntax are host specific. Although the syntax is generally consistent with the command-line syntax of your host system, it may include additional or alternate punctuation. For details, refer to the SAS documentation for your host system.

.... ■

AUTOEXEC=

Specifies the AUTOEXEC file

Valid as part of: configuration file, SAS invocation

HELP AUTOEXEC

Syntax

AUTOEXEC=*file-specification*

Description

The AUTOEXEC= system option specifies the autoexec file. The autoexec file contains SAS statements that are executed automatically whenever the SAS System is invoked. The autoexec file can contain any valid SAS statements. For example, you can include LIBNAME statements for SAS data libraries you access routinely in SAS sessions.

You can use the following argument with the AUTOEXEC= system option:

file-specification identifies an external file.

■ **Host Information** ....

The SAS System searches for an autoexec file whenever it is invoked. The search order depends on your host system.

A valid file specification and its syntax are host specific. Although the syntax is generally consistent with the command-line syntax of your host system, it may include additional or alternate punctuation. For details, refer to the SAS documentation for your host system.

.... ■

BATCH

Specifies the batch set of SAS system option default values

Valid as part of: configuration file, SAS invocation

HELP BATCH

Syntax

BATCH | NOBATCH

Description

The BATCH option specifies whether the batch set of SAS system option default values is in effect when the SAS System executes.

You can use the following forms of the BATCH system option:

BATCH
: specifies that the SAS System use the batch set of options. When BATCH is specified, the SAS System expects input from a file, which affects the settings of the CLEANUP, LINESIZE=, OVP, PAGESIZE=, SOURCE, and SPOOL system options. At the start of an interactive SAS session, you can use the BATCH setting to simulate the behavior of the system in batch mode.

NOBATCH
: specifies that the SAS System not use the batch set of options. While in batch mode, you can specify NOBATCH to use the nonbatch settings of the CLEANUP, LINESIZE=, OVP, PAGESIZE=, SOURCE, and SPOOL system options.

The default setting for the BATCH option depends on your host system and the SAS method of operation. Note that setting the BATCH option does not specify the method of operation. It only specifies which set of system option default values are in effect when the SAS System executes.

In addition, the BATCH system option does *not* specify the opposite of interactive methods of operation, nor does it specify whether a terminal is present. The BATCH system option only specifies whether input is coming from a file and, therefore, sets the appropriate default values for the CLEANUP, LINESIZE=, OVP, PAGESIZE=, SOURCE, and SPOOL system options.

BUFNO=

Specifies the number of buffers to use for SAS data sets

Valid as part of: configuration file, OPTIONS statement, OPTIONS window, SAS invocation

HELP BUFNO

Syntax

BUFNO=*number-of-buffers*

Description

The BUFNO= system option specifies the number of buffers to be allocated for processing a SAS data set. The number of buffers is not a permanent attribute of the data set, and it is valid only for the current SAS session or job. The BUFNO= system option applies to SAS data sets opened for input, output, or update.

You can use the following argument with the BUFNO= system option:

number-of-buffers
: specifies a value from 0 to the maximum number of buffers available on your host system.

If the number of buffers is greater than 0 when a SAS data set is opened, that number is used as the default value for the BUFNO= data set option. If the number of buffers is 0, the SAS System uses host system default values.

■ **Performance Note** ....

Using the BUFNO= system option can speed up execution time by limiting the number of input/output operations required for a particular SAS data set. (For details, see "Options for Tuning Performance" in Chapter 6, "SAS Files.") The improvement in execution time, however, comes at the expense of increased memory consumption.

■ **Host Information** ....

The syntax shown earlier applies to the OPTIONS statement. However, when you specify the BUFNO= system option on the command line or in a configuration file, the syntax is host specific and may include additional or alternate punctuation. For details, refer to the SAS documentation for your host system.

Comparisons

The BUFNO= system option can be overridden by the BUFNO= data set option.

See Also

"Options for Tuning Performance" in Chapter 6, "SAS Files"

BUFNO= data set option in Chapter 15, "SAS Data Set Options"

BUFSIZE=

Specifies permanent buffer size for output SAS data sets

Valid as part of: configuration file, OPTIONS statement, OPTIONS window, SAS invocation

HELP BUFSIZE

Syntax

BUFSIZE=*number-of-bytes*

Description

The BUFSIZE= system option specifies the size of input/output buffers for SAS data sets. The size of the input/output buffers is permanently associated with the SAS data set.

You can use the following argument for the BUFSIZE= system option:

number-of-bytes
: specifies the buffer size in bytes. The number of bytes can have a value from 0 to the maximum value allowed by your host system.

If the number of bytes is greater than 0 when a SAS data set is created, that number is used as the default value for the BUFSIZE= data set option. If the BUFSIZE= data set option is not used and the number of bytes for the BUFSIZE= system option is 0, the SAS System chooses a host system default value that is optimal for the SAS data set.

■ **Performance Note** ....

Using the BUFSIZE= system option can speed up execution time by limiting the number of input/output operations required for a particular SAS data set. (For details, see the "Performance Considerations" section in Chapter 6.) The improvement in execution time, however, comes at the expense of increased memory consumption.

■ **Host Information** ....

The syntax shown above applies to the OPTIONS statement. However, when you specify the BUFSIZE= system option on the command line or in a configuration file, the syntax is host specific and may include additional or alternate punctuation. For details, refer to the SAS documentation for your host system. ■

Comparisons

The BUFSIZE= system option can be overridden by the BUFSIZE= data set option.

See Also

"Options for Tuning Performance" in Chapter 6, "SAS Files"

BUFSIZE= data set option in Chapter 15, "SAS Data Set Options"

CAPS

Translates input to uppercase

Valid as part of: configuration file, OPTIONS statement, OPTIONS window, SAS invocation

HELP CAPS

Syntax

CAPS | NOCAPS

Description

The CAPS system option specifies whether lowercase input to the SAS System from SAS source lines, CARDS, CARDS4, and PARMCARDS statements is translated to uppercase. (Data read from external files and SAS data sets are not translated to uppercase, regardless of the setting of the CAPS system option.)

You can use the following forms of the CAPS system options:

CAPS
: specifies that the SAS System translate to uppercase all input from SAS source lines, CARDS, CARDS4, and PARMCARDS statements.

NOCAPS
: specifies that the SAS System respect the case of input from certain sources. If NOCAPS is specified, lowercase characters that occur in the following types of input are not translated to uppercase:

- □ data following CARDS, CARDS4, and PARMCARDS statements
- □ text enclosed in single or double quotes
- □ values in VALUE and INVALUE statements in the FORMAT procedure
- □ titles, footnotes, variable labels, and data set labels
- □ constant text in macro definitions
- □ values of macro variables
- □ parameter values passed to macros.

If NOCAPS is specified, all input from SAS source lines other than those listed above is translated to uppercase.

Comparisons

The CAPS system option and the CAPS command (which is available in display manager windows that allow text editing) both specify whether input is converted to uppercase. The CAPS command can act as an on/off switch or toggle. If either the CAPS system option or the CAPS command is set to translate to uppercase, all applicable input is translated to uppercase.

See Also

CAPS command in Chapter 19, "SAS Text Editor Commands"

CARDIMAGE

Processes SAS source and data lines as 80-byte cards

Valid as part of: configuration file, OPTIONS statement, OPTIONS window, SAS invocation

HELP CARDIMAGE

Syntax

CARDIMAGE | NOCARDIMAGE

Description

The CARDIMAGE system option specifies whether to process SAS source and data lines as 80-byte cards.

You can use the following forms of the CARDIMAGE system option:

CARDIMAGE
: specifies to process SAS source and data lines as if they were punched card images—all exactly 80 bytes long and padded with blanks. That is, column 1 of a line is treated as if it immediately followed column 80 of the previous line. Therefore, *tokens* can be split across lines. (A token is a character or series of characters that the SAS System treats as a discrete word. See "Tokenization" in Chapter 4, "Rules of the SAS Language," for details.) Quoted strings (literal tokens) that begin on one line and end on another are treated as if they contained blanks out to column 80 of the first line. Data lines longer than 80 bytes are split into two or more 80-byte lines. Data lines are not truncated regardless of their length.

NOCARDIMAGE
: specifies that SAS source and data lines not be treated as if they were 80-byte card images. When NOCARDIMAGE is in effect, the end of a line is always treated as the end of the last token, except for quoted strings. Quoted strings can be split across lines. All other types of tokens, such as name tokens and special character tokens, cannot be split across lines under any circumstances. Quoted strings that are split across lines are not padded with blanks.

CARDIMAGE is generally used on MVS, CMS, and VSE host systems; NOCARDIMAGE is used on other host systems.

Example

Suppose you submit the following lines:

```
data;
   x='A
   B';
run;
```

If CARDIMAGE is in effect, the variable X receives a value consisting of 78 characters: the A, 76 blanks, and the B. If NOCARDIMAGE is in effect, the variable X receives a value consisting of two characters: AB, with no intervening blanks.

CATCACHE=

Specifies the number of SAS catalogs to keep open

Valid as part of: configuration file, SAS invocation

HELP CATCACHE

Syntax

CATCACHE=*n*

Description

The CATCACHE= system option specifies the number of SAS catalogs to keep open.

You can use the following argument with the CATCACHE= system option:

n specifies any integer greater than or equal to 0.

If *n* is greater than 0, the SAS System places up to that number of open-file descriptors in cache memory instead of closing the catalogs. If *n* is 0, no open-file descriptors are kept in cache memory. You can use the CATCACHE= system option to tune an application by avoiding the overhead of repeatedly opening and closing the same SAS catalogs.

■ **Host Information** .... The syntax shown above is host specific. It is generally consistent with the command-line syntax of your host system, but may include additional or alternate punctuation. For details, refer to the SAS documentation for your host system. ■

CENTER

Centers SAS procedure output

Valid as part of: configuration file, OPTIONS statement, OPTIONS window, SAS invocation

HELP CENTER

Syntax

CENTER | NOCENTER

Description

The CENTER system option controls whether SAS procedure output is centered or left justified. The aliases for this option are CENTRE and NOCENTRE.

You can use the following forms of the CENTER system option:

CENTER specifies that SAS procedure output is centered.

NOCENTER specifies that SAS procedure output is left justified.

CHARCODE

Allows character combinations to be substituted for special characters not on the keyboard

Valid as part of: configuration file, OPTIONS statement, OPTIONS window, SAS invocation

HELP CHARCODE

Syntax

CHARCODE | NOCHARCODE

Description

The CHARCODE system option enables users to substitute character combinations for special characters that are not on the keyboard.

You can use the following forms of the CHARCODE system option:

CHARCODE
: allows substitute character combinations in place of special characters that are not on the keyboard.

NOCHARCODE
: does not allow substitute character combinations in place of special characters that are not on the keyboard.

If you do not have a backquote, a backslash, curly braces, a logical not sign, square brackets, an underscore, or a vertical bar on your keyboard, you can substitute the following character combinations for these symbols:

?: for the backquote (`)

?, for the backslash (\)

?(for the left brace ({)

?) for the right brace (})

?= for the logical not sign (¬ or ^)

?< for the left square bracket ([)

?> for the right square bracket (])

?- for the underscore (_)

?/ for the vertical bar (|).

Example

The following statement produces the output [TEST TITLE]:

```
title '?<TEST TITLE?>';
```

CLEANUP

Specifies how to handle out-of-resources condition

Valid as part of: configuration file, OPTIONS statement, OPTIONS window, SAS invocation

HELP CLEANUP

Syntax

CLEANUP | NOCLEANUP

Description

The CLEANUP system option specifies how the SAS System handles an out-of-resources condition.

You can use the following forms of the CLEANUP system option:

CLEANUP
: specifies that during the entire session the SAS System attempts to perform automatic continuous clean-up of resources that are not essential for execution. Nonessential resources include those not visible to the user (for example, cache memory) and those that are visible to the user (for example, the KEYS windows).

  When CLEANUP is in effect and an out-of-resource condition occurs (except for disk-full), a requestor window is not displayed, and no intervention is required by the user. When CLEANUP is in effect and a disk-full condition occurs, a requestor window displays allowing the user to decide how to proceed.

NOCLEANUP
: specifies that the SAS System allow the user to choose how to handle an out-of-resource condition. When NOCLEANUP is in effect and the SAS System cannot execute because of a lack of resources, the SAS System automatically attempts to clean up resources not visible to the user (for example, cache memory). However, resources visible to the user (for example, windows) are not automatically cleaned up. Instead, a requestor window is displayed that allows the user to choose how to proceed.

  The following table lists the requestor window choices:

Requester Window Choices	Action
Free windows	clears all windows not essential for execution.
Clear paste buffers	deletes paste buffer contents.
Deassign inactive librefs	prompts user for librefs to deassign.
Delete definitions of all SAS macros and macro variables	deletes all macro definitions and variables.
Delete SAS files	allows user to select files to delete.
Clear LOG window	erases LOG window contents.
Clear OUTPUT window	erases OUTPUT window contents.
Clear PROGRAM EDITOR window	erases PROGRAM EDITOR window contents.
Clear source spooling/DMS recall buffers	erases recall buffers.

(continued)

(continued)

Requester Window Choices	Action
More items to clean up	displays a list of other resources that can be cleaned up.
Clean up everything	cleans up all other options shown on the requestor window. This selection only applies to the current clean-up request, not the entire SAS session.
Continuous clean up	performs automatic continuous clean-up. When continuous clean up is selected, the SAS System cleans up as many resources as possible in order to continue execution and ceases to display the requestor window. Selecting continuous clean-up has the same effect as specifying CLEANUP. This selection applies to the current clean-up request and the remainder of the SAS session.

■ **Host Information** ....

Some host systems may also include the following choices in the requestor window:

Execute X command
: enables the user to erase files and perform other clean-up operations.

Do nothing
: specifies that the SAS system halt the clean-up request and return to the session. This selection only applies to the current clean-up request, not the entire SAS session.

If an out-of-resource condition cannot be resolved, the requestor window continues to display, in which case you should see the SAS documentation for your host system for instructions on terminating the SAS session.

When running in modes other than display manager, the operation of the CLEANUP system option depends on your host system. For details, see the SAS documentation for your host system.

.... ■

COMAMID=

Specifies the communications access method for SAS/CONNECT and SAS/SHARE software

Valid as part of: configuration file, OPTIONS statement, SAS invocation.

HELP COMAMID

Syntax

COMAMID=*access-method-id*

Description

The COMAMID= system option specifies a communications access method identifier that is used by distributed products (for example, SAS/CONNECT and SAS/SHARE software) to connect to remote partners.

You can use the following argument with the COMAMID= system option:

access-method-id
: specifies a valid communications access method ID.

■ **Host Information** ....

A valid communications access method ID and its syntax are host specific. Although the syntax is generally consistent with the command-line syntax of your host system, it may include additional or alternate punctuation. For details, refer to the SAS documentation for your host system and to *SAS/CONNECT Software: Usage and Reference, Version 6, First Edition.* ■

See Also

SAS/CONNECT Software: Usage and Reference, Version 6, First Edition

SAS/SHARE User's Guide, Version 5 Edition

COMPRESS=

Compresses observations in output SAS data sets

Valid as part of: configuration file, OPTIONS statement, OPTIONS window, SAS invocation

HELP COMPRESS

Syntax

COMPRESS=YES | NO

Description

The COMPRESS= system option specifies whether observations in a newly created SAS output data set are compressed (variable-length records) or uncompressed (fixed-length records). The record type is a permanent attribute of the data set.

You can use the following arguments with the COMPRESS= option:

YES specifies that observations are compressed.

NO specifies that observations are not compressed.

Compressing a data set reduces the size of the data set by reducing repeated consecutive characters to two- or three-byte representations. Compression of observations is not supported by all engines. To uncompress observations, you must use a DATA step to copy the data set and specify COMPRESS=NO for the new data set.

The advantages gained by using the COMPRESS= data set option include

- □ reduced storage requirements for the data set
- □ fewer input and output operations necessary to read from or write to the data set during processing.

■ **Performance Note** ....

Using the COMPRESS= system option prevents access to a SAS data set by observation number. Also, using this option increases the CPU time for reading a data set because of the overhead of compressing and uncompressing the records. In addition, some engines do not support compression of observations. Other restrictions also apply to data sets that have been compressed. For details, see the COMPRESS= data set option in Chapter 15, "SAS Data Set Options." ■

■ **Host Information** ....

The syntax shown above applies to the OPTIONS statement. However, when you specify the COMPRESS= system option on the command line or in a configuration file, the syntax is host specific and may include additional or alternate punctuation. For details, refer to the SAS documentation for your host system. ■

Comparisons

The COMPRESS= system option can be overridden by the COMPRESS= data set option.

See Also

REUSE= system option

"Options for Tuning Performance" in Chapter 6, "SAS Files"

COMPRESS= and REUSE= data set options in Chapter 15, "SAS Data Set Options"

CONFIG=

Specifies the name of the configuration file

Valid as part of: SAS invocation

HELP CONFIG

Syntax

CONFIG=*file-specification*

Description

The CONFIG= system option specifies the complete filename of your configuration file.

You can use the following argument with the CONFIG= system option:

file-specification
: specifies the name of a file containing SAS options that are executed automatically whenever the SAS System is invoked. The SAS System supplies a default configuration file, but you can create your own configuration file and store it in a location you choose.

Note that the CONFIG= system option can be specified only at SAS invocation, not in a configuration file. If you specify the CONFIG= system option in the configuration file, the option is ignored.

■ **Host Information** ....

A valid configuration filename and the syntax for specifying it are host specific. Although the syntax is generally consistent with the command-line syntax of your host system, it may include additional or alternate punctuation. For details, refer to the SAS documentation for your host system. ■

See Also

"Customizing Your Interactive SAS Session" in Chapter 1, "Essential Concepts"

DATE

Prints the date and time

Valid as part of: configuration file, OPTIONS statement, OPTIONS window, SAS invocation

HELP DATE

Syntax

DATE | NODATE

Description

The DATE system option controls whether the date and time that the SAS job began are printed at the top of each page of the SAS log and any print file created by the SAS System. (In display manager and interactive line mode sessions, the date and time appear only on procedure output.)

You can use the following forms of the DATE system option:

DATE specifies to print the date and time.

NODATE specifies not to print the date and time.

DBCS

Recognizes double-byte character sets (DBCS)

Valid as part of: configuration file, SAS invocation

HELP DBCS

Syntax

DBCS | NODBCS

Description

The DBCS system option specifies whether the SAS System recognizes double-byte character sets (DBCS). (Double-byte character sets use 2 bytes for each character in the set.)

The DBCS system option is used for various reasons including converting lowercase data that are input into the SAS System to uppercase and supporting languages such as Chinese, Japanese, Korean, and Taiwanese.

You can use the following forms of the DBCS system option:

DBCS specifies that the SAS System process double-byte character sets.

NODBCS specifies that the SAS System not process double-byte character sets.

See Also

DBCSLANG= system option

DBCSTYPE= system option

DBCSLANG=

Specifies a double-byte character set (DBCS) language

Valid as part of: configuration file, SAS invocation

HELP DBCSLANG

Syntax

DBCSLANG=*language*

Description

The DBCSLANG= system option specifies which double-byte character set (DBCS) language is being used. This option does not accept abbreviations for the value of *language*.

You can use one of the following values for *language*:

CHINESE
: specifies the Chinese language used in the People's Republic of China; the language is known as simplified Chinese.

JAPANESE
: specifies the Japanese language.

KOREAN
: specifies the Korean language.

TAIWANESE
: specifies the Chinese language used in Taiwan; the language is known as traditional Chinese.

UNKNOWN
: specifies a language that uses DBCS, but is not supported by the SAS System. When an invalid value is specified, DBCSLANG defaults to UNKNOWN. Usually, this value is not explicitly set by the user.

The proper setting for the DBCSLANG= system option depends on which setting is used for the DBCSTYPE= system option because some of the settings of DBCSTYPE= support all of the DBCSLANG= languages, while other settings of DBCSTYPE= support only Japanese.

■ **Host Information** ....

The syntax shown above is host specific. It is generally consistent with the command-line syntax of your host system but may include additional or alternate punctuation. For details, refer to the SAS documentation for your host system.

■

See Also

DBCS system option

DBCSTYPE= system option

DBCSTYPE=

Specifies a double-byte character set (DBCS) encoding method

Valid as part of: configuration file, SAS invocation

HELP DBCSTYPE

Syntax

DBCSTYPE=*encoding-method*

Description

The DBCSTYPE= system option specifies the type of double-byte character set (DBCS) encoding method. (Different hardware manufacturers use different DBCS encoding methods.)

You can use one of the following values for *encoding-method*:

DEC	specifies the DEC® encoding method.
DG	specifies the DG encoding method.
EUC	specifies the Extended UNIX® Code.
FACOM	specifies the Fujitsu® encoding method (JEF Code).
HITAC	specifies the Hitachi encoding method (KEIS Code).
HP15	specifies the HP®15 encoding method.
IBM	specifies the IBM host encoding method.
PCIBM	specifies the IBM PC encoding method.
PRIME	specifies the PRIME encoding method.
SJIS	specifies the Shift-JIS encoding method. (Valid only if the DBCSLANG=JAPANESE.)

■ **Host Information** ....

The syntax shown above is host specific. It is generally consistent with the command-line syntax of your host system but may include additional or alternate punctuation. For details, refer to the SAS documentation for your host system.

.... ■

See Also

DBCS system option

DBCSLANG= system option

DEC is a registered trademark of Digital Equipment Corporation.

UNIX is a registerd trademark of AT&T.

Fujitsu is a registered trademark of Fujitsu America, Inc.

HP is a registered trademark of Hewlett-Packard Company.

DEVICE=

Specifies a terminal device driver for SAS/GRAPH software

Valid as part of: configuration file, OPTIONS statement, OPTIONS window, SAS invocation

HELP DEVICE

Syntax

DEVICE=*device-driver-name*

Description

The DEVICE= system option specifies a terminal device driver for SAS/GRAPH software. The alias for this option is DEV=.

You can use the following argument with the DEVICE= system option:

device-driver-name
: specifies the name of a terminal device driver.

If you do not specify a device driver name at SAS invocation, you are prompted to enter a driver name when you execute a procedure that produces graphics.

■ **Host Information** ....

Valid device driver names depend on your host system. For a list of valid device driver names, refer to the SAS documentation for your host system. ■

■ **Host Information** ....

The syntax shown above applies to the OPTIONS statement. However, when you specify the DEVICE= system option on the command-line or in a configuration file, the syntax is host specific and may include additional or alternate punctuation. For details, refer to the SAS documentation for your host system. ■

DMR

Invokes a remote SAS session

Valid as part of: configuration file, SAS invocation

HELP DMR

Syntax

DMR | NODMR

Description

The DMR system option enables you to invoke a remote SAS session in order to run SAS/CONNECT software. You normally invoke the remote SAS session from a local session by including the DMR system option on the SAS command in a script TYPE statement. (A script is a text file containing statements that establish or terminate the SAS/CONNECT link between the local and the remote SAS sessions.)

You can use the following forms of the DMR system option:

DMR
: specifies that the SAS System invoke a remote session for use with SAS/CONNECT software.

NODMR
: specifies that the SAS System not invoke a remote session.

See Also

SAS/CONNECT Software: Usage and Reference, Version 6, First Edition

DMS

Invokes the SAS Display Manager System

Valid as part of: configuration file, SAS invocation

HELP DMS

Syntax

DMS | NODMS

Description

The DMS system option specifies whether the SAS Display Manager System is active in a SAS session.

You can use the following forms of the DMS system option:

DMS
: begins a display manager session.

NODMS
: begins an interactive line mode session.

DSNFERR

Generates an error message when a SAS data set is not found

Valid as part of: configuration file, OPTIONS statement, OPTIONS window, SAS invocation

HELP DSNFERR

Syntax

DSNFERR | NODSNFERR

Description

The DSNFERR system option controls whether the SAS System generates an error message when an input or update SAS data set specified in a job is not found.

You can use the following forms of the DSNFERR system option:

DSNFERR
: specifies that the SAS System issue an error message and stop processing if a reference is made to a SAS data set that does not exist.

NODSNFERR
: specifies that the SAS System ignore the error message and continue processing if a reference is made to a SAS data set that does not exist. The data set reference is treated as if _NULL_ had been specified.

ECHOAUTO

Echoes autoexec input to the log

Valid as part of: configuration file, SAS invocation

HELP ECHOAUTO

Syntax

ECHOAUTO | NOECHOAUTO

Description

The ECHOAUTO system option specifies whether autoexec input is echoed to the SAS log.

You can use the following forms of the ECHOAUTO system option:

ECHOAUTO
: specifies that SAS source lines read from the autoexec file are printed on the SAS log.

NOECHOAUTO
: specifies that SAS source lines read from the autoexec file are not printed on the SAS log. However, the SAS source lines are still executed.

Messages that result from errors in the autoexec file are printed on the SAS log regardless of how the option is set.

See Also

AUTOEXEC= system option

ENGINE=

Specifies the default access method for SAS libraries

Valid as part of: configuration file, SAS invocation

HELP ENGINE

Syntax

ENGINE=*engine-name*

Description

The ENGINE= system option specifies that a default engine name be associated with a SAS library. The default engine is used when a SAS library points to an empty directory or a new file. The default engine is also used on directory-based systems, which can store more than one SAS file type within a directory. For example, some hosts can store Version 5 and Version 6 SAS files in the same directory.

You can use the following argument with the ENGINE= system option:

engine-name specifies a valid engine name.

■ **Host Information** ....

Valid engine names depend on your host system. For details, see the SAS documentation for your host system.

.... ■

ERRORABEND

Abends for errors that normally only issue error messages

Valid as part of: configuration file, OPTIONS statement, OPTIONS window, SAS invocation

HELP ERRORABEND

Syntax

ERRORABEND | NOERRORABEND

Description

The ERRORABEND system option forces the SAS System to abend for most errors that normally cause it to issue only an error message. The aliases for this option are ERRABEND and NOERRABEND.

You can use the following forms of the ERRORABEND option:

ERRORABEND
: specifies that the SAS System abend for most errors (including syntax errors) that would normally cause it to issue an error message, set OBS=0, and go into syntax-check mode.

NOERRORABEND
: specifies that the SAS System handle errors normally, that is, issue an error message, set OBS=0, and go into syntax-check mode.

Use the ERRORABEND system option with SAS production programs, which presumably should not encounter any errors. If errors are encountered and the ERRORABEND system option is in effect, the SAS System brings the errors to your attention immediately by abending.

ERRORS=

Controls the maximum number of observations for which complete error messages are printed

Valid as part of: configuration file, OPTIONS statement, OPTIONS window, SAS invocation

HELP ERRORS

Syntax

ERRORS=*n*

Description

The ERRORS= system option controls the maximum number of observations for which complete error messages are printed.

You can use the following argument with the ERRORS= system option:

n specifies the maximum number of observations.

If data errors are detected in more than *n* observations, processing continues, but error messages do not print for the additional errors.

■ **Host Information** ....

The syntax shown above applies to the OPTIONS statement. However, when you specify the ERRORS= system option on the command line or in a configuration file, the syntax is host specific and may include additional or alternate punctuation. For details, refer to the SAS documentation for your host system.

.... ■

FIRSTOBS=

Causes the SAS System to begin reading at a specified observation

Valid as part of: configuration file, OPTIONS statement, OPTIONS window, SAS invocation

HELP FIRSTOBS

Syntax

FIRSTOBS=*n*

Description

The FIRSTOBS= system option causes the SAS System to begin reading at a specified observation in a data set. (If the SAS System is reading a file of raw data, the FIRSTOBS= system option causes the SAS System to begin reading at a specified line of data.)

You can use the following argument with the FIRSTOBS= system option:

n specifies the number of the first observation that the SAS System is to read.

By default, the SAS System begins reading with the first observation in a data set. You can override the default with the FIRSTOBS= system option. For example, if you specify FIRSTOBS=50, the SAS System begins reading with the 50th observation of the data set.

Note that this option applies to every input data set used in a program. For example, in the following code, the SAS System begins reading the eleventh observation in data sets OLD, A, and B:

```
options firstobs=11;

data a;
   set old; /* 100 observations */
run;

data b;
   set a;
run;
```

```
data c;
   set b;
run;
```

Data set OLD has 100 observations, data set A has 90, B has 80, and C has 70. To avoid decreasing the number of observations in successive data sets, reset FIRSTOBS=1 at an appropriate point between a DATA or PROC step.

You must specify FIRSTOBS=1 to use a WHERE statement or WHERE data set option.

■ **Host Information** .... The syntax shown above applies to the OPTIONS statement. However, when you specify the FIRSTOBS= system option on the command line or in a configuration file, the syntax is host specific and may include additional or alternate punctuation. For details, refer to the SAS documentation for your host system. ■

Comparisons

The FIRSTOBS= system option can be overridden by the FIRSTOBS= data set option and by using the FIRSTOBS= option as a part of the INFILE statement.

See Also

INFILE statement in Chapter 9, "SAS Language Statements"

FIRSTOBS= data set option in Chapter 15, "SAS Data Set Options"

FMTERR

Generates an error message when a format of a variable cannot be found

Valid as part of: configuration file, OPTIONS statement, OPTIONS window, SAS invocation

HELP FMTERR

Syntax

FMTERR | NOFMTERR

Description

The FMTERR system option controls whether the SAS System generates an error message when a format associated with a variable cannot be found.

You can use the following forms of the FMTERR system option:

FMTERR
: specifies that missing formats be treated as errors.

NOFMTERR
: specifies that missing formats be replaced with the *w.* or $*w.* default format.

FORMCHAR=

Specifies the default output formatting characters

Valid as part of: configuration file, OPTIONS statement, OPTIONS window, SAS invocation

HELP FORMCHAR

Syntax

FORMCHAR=*'formatting-characters'*

Description

The FORMCHAR= system option specifies the default output formatting characters for your output device. Formatting characters are used to construct tabular output outlines and dividers for various procedures, such as the CALENDAR, FREQ, and TABULATE procedures. If you do not specify formatting characters as an option in the procedure, the default specifications given in the FORMCHAR= system option are used.

You can use the following argument with the FORMCHAR= system option:

'formatting-characters'
: specifies any string or list of strings of characters up to 64 bytes long. If fewer than 64 bytes are specified, the string is padded with blanks on the right.

■ **Host Information** ....

The syntax shown above applies to the OPTIONS statement. However, when you specify the FORMCHAR= system option on the command line or in a configuration file, the syntax is host specific and may include additional or alternate punctuation. For details, see the SAS documentation for your host system.
.... ■

See Also

CALENDAR, FREQ, and TABULATE procedures in the *SAS Procedures Guide, Version 6, Third Edition*

FORMDLIM=

Specifies a character to delimit page breaks in SAS output

Valid as part of: configuration file, OPTIONS statement, OPTIONS window, SAS invocation

HELP FORMDLIM

Syntax

FORMDLIM=*'delimit-character'*

Description

The FORMDLIM= system option specifies a character that is used to delimit page breaks in SAS System output. The alias for this option is FRMDLIM=.

You can use the following argument with the FORMDLIM= system option:

'delimit-character'
: specifies a character written to delimit pages. Normally, the delimit character is null ('') as in the following statement:

```
options formdlim='';
```

When the delimit character is null, a new physical page starts whenever a page break occurs.

However, you can conserve paper by not skipping to the top of a new physical page each time. Or, you can allow multiple pages of output to appear on the same page. For example, the following statement writes a line of dashes (--) where a page break normally would occur:

```
options formdlim='-';
```

When a new page is to begin, the SAS System skips a single line, writes a line consisting of the dashes repeated across the page, and skips another single line. There is no skip to the top of a new physical page. Resetting FORMDLIM= to null causes physical pages to be written normally again.

■ **Host Information** ....

The syntax shown above applies to the OPTIONS statement. However, when you specify the FORMDLIM= system option on the command line or in a configuration file, the syntax is host specific and may include additional or alternate punctuation. For details, refer to the SAS documentation for your host system. ■

FORMS=

Specifies the default form used for interactive windowing output

Valid as part of: configuration file, OPTIONS statement, OPTIONS window, SAS invocation

HELP FORMS

Syntax

FORMS=*form-name*

Description

The FORMS= system option specifies the name of the default form used to customize the appearance of interactive windowing output. This includes output from the display manager PRINT command (when FORM= is not used) or output from interactive windowing procedures. The default form contains settings that control various aspects of interactive windowing output, including printer selection, text body, and margins. The alias for this option is FRMS=.

You can use the following argument with the FORMS= system option:

form-name specifies the name of the form. To create a customized form, use the FSFORMS command in display manager.

■ **Host Information** ....

The syntax shown above applies to the OPTIONS statement. However, when you specify the FORMS= system option on the command line or in a configuration file, the syntax is host specific and may include additional or alternate punctuation. For details, refer to the SAS documentation for your host system. ■

See Also

FORM window Chapter 17, "SAS Display Manager Windows"

FSFORMS and PRINT commands in Chapter 18, "SAS Display Manager Commands"

FSDEVICE=

Specifies the interactive windowing device driver

Valid as part of: configuration file, SAS invocation

HELP FSDEVICE

Syntax

FSDEVICE=*device-name*

Description

The FSDEVICE= system option specifies the interactive windowing device driver for your terminal. The FSDEVICE= system option specification is needed for running display manager mode and interactive windowing procedures.

You can use the following argument with the FSDEVICE= system option:

device-name specifies any valid device name.

■ **Host Information** ....

The syntax shown above is host specific. It is generally consistent with the command-line syntax of your host system, but may include additional or alternate punctuation. For information on valid device names and other details, refer to the SAS documentation for your host system.
.... ■

FULLSTIMER

Writes all system performance statistics to the SAS log

Valid as part of: configuration file, OPTIONS statement, SAS invocation

HELP FULLSTIMER

Syntax

FULLSTIMER | NOFULLSTIMER

Description

The FULLSTIMER system option specifies whether all the performance statistics of your computer system that are available to the SAS System are written to the SAS log.

You can use the following forms of the FULLSTIMER system option:

FULLSTIMER
: specifies that the SAS System write the available statistics. When FULLSTIMER is in effect, the SAS System writes to the SAS log a complete list of computer resources used for each step and the entire SAS session.

NOFULLSTIMER
: specifies that the SAS System not write performance statistics to the SAS log.

■ **Host Information** ....

Whether the FULLSTIMER system option writes to the SAS log can depend how other host-specific options are set. Also, the type of statistics written varies with host systems. For example, under some host systems, FULLSTIMER itemizes buffer I/O, direct I/O, elapsed time, page faults, and CPU time. For details, see the SAS documentation for your host system.
.... ■

Comparison

The FULLSTIMER system option specifies whether all the performance statistics of your computer system that are available to the SAS System are written to the SAS log. The STIMER system option specifies whether a subset of the performance statistics are written to the SAS log.

See Also

STIMER system option

GWINDOW

Displays SAS/GRAPH output in the GRAPH window of display manager

Valid as part of: configuration file, OPTIONS statement, OPTIONS window, SAS invocation

HELP GWINDOW

Syntax

GWINDOW | NOGWINDOW

Description

The GWINDOW system option enables you to display SAS/GRAPH software output in the GRAPH window of display manager, if your site licenses SAS/GRAPH software and if your terminal has graphics capability.

You can use the following forms of the GWINDOW system option:

GWINDOW
: specifies that the SAS System display graphics in the GRAPH window in display manager.

NOGWINDOW
: specifies that the SAS System display graphics outside of display manager.

When a graph is produced, it overwrites the display and sounds a bell. When you press RETURN, the graph disappears and your display is restored.

IMPLMAC

Allows statement-style macro calls

Valid as part of: configuration file, OPTIONS statement, OPTIONS window, SAS invocation

HELP IMPLMAC

Syntax

IMPLMAC | NOIMPLMAC

Description

The IMPLMAC system option controls whether macros defined as statement-style macros can be invoked with statement-style macro calls or if the call must be a name-style macro call. The following two statements illustrate statement-style and name-style macro calls, respectively:

- *name parameter-value-1 parameter-value-2*;
- *%name*(*parameter-value-1*, *parameter-value-2*)

You can use the following forms of the IMPLMAC system option:

IMPLMAC
: causes the macro processor to examine the first word of every statement to see if that word is a statement-style macro call.

NOIMPLMAC
: causes statement-style macro calls to be ignored. If the macro processor encounters a statement-style macro call when NOIMPLMAC is in effect, it treats the call as a SAS statement. The SAS compiler then produces an error message if the statement is not valid or is not used correctly.

Regardless of which option is in effect, you can call any macro with a name-style invocation, including those defined as statement-style macros.

■ **Performance Note** ....

When you use the IMPLMAC system option, processing time is increased because the SAS System checks every SAS statement to determine whether the beginning word is a macro call. When you use the IMPLMAC system option in conjunction with the MAUTOSOURCE system option, the MRECALL system option, or both, processing time can be increased further.

.... ■

See Also

Chapter 20, "SAS Macro Facility"

INITSTMT=

Specifies a SAS statement to be executed after any statements in the autoexec file and before any statements from the SYSIN file

Valid as part of: configuration file, SAS invocation

HELP INITSTMT

Syntax

INITSTMT=*'statement'*

Description

The INITSTMT= system option specifies a SAS statement or statements to be executed after any statements in the autoexec file and before any SAS statements from the SYSIN file. The alias for this option is IS=.

You can use the following argument with the INITSTMT= system option:

'statement' specifies any valid SAS statement or statements.

■ **Host Information** ....

The syntax shown above is host specific. It is generally consistent with the command-line syntax of your host system but may include additional or alternate punctuation. For details, refer to the SAS documentation for your host system.

.... ■

See Also

AUTOEXEC= system option

SYSIN= system option

INVALIDDATA=

Assigns a value to a variable when invalid numeric data are encountered

Valid as part of: configuration file, OPTIONS statement, OPTIONS window, SAS invocation

HELP INVALIDDATA

Syntax

INVALIDDATA=*'character'*

Description

The INVALIDDATA= system option specifies the value the SAS System is to assign to a variable when invalid numeric data are encountered with an input format, such as in an INPUT statement or the INPUT function.

You can use the following argument with the INVALIDDATA= system option:

'character' specifies the value to be assigned, which can be a letter (A through Z, a through z), a period (.), or an underscore (_). The default value is a period.

■ **Host Information** ....

The syntax shown above applies to the OPTIONS statement. However, when you specify the INVALIDDATA= system option on the command line or in a configuration file, the syntax is host specific and may include additional or alternate punctuation. For details, refer to the SAS documentation for your host system.

.... ■

LABEL

Permits SAS procedures to use labels with variables

Valid as part of: configuration file, OPTIONS statement, OPTIONS window, SAS invocation

HELP LABEL

Syntax

LABEL | NOLABEL

Description

The LABEL system option permits SAS procedures to use labels with variables. A label is a string of up to 40 characters that can be written by certain procedures in place of the variable name.

You can use the following forms of the LABEL system option:

LABEL allows procedures to use labels with variables. The LABEL system option must be in effect before the LABEL option of any procedure can be used.

NOLABEL does not allow procedures to use labels with variables. If NOLABEL is specified, the LABEL option of a procedure is ignored.

See Also

LABEL= data set option

LAST=

Specifies the most recently created data set

Valid as part of: configuration file, OPTIONS statement, OPTIONS window, SAS invocation

HELP LAST

Syntax

LAST=*SAS-data-set*

Description

The _LAST_= system option specifies the name of the most recently created data set.

You can use the following argument with the _LAST_= system option:

SAS-data-set specifies any valid SAS data set name.

By default, the SAS System includes the most recently created data set in a SAS program. Use the _LAST_= system option to override the default.

■ **Host Information** .... The syntax shown above applies to the OPTIONS statement. However, when you specify the _LAST_= system option on the command line or in a configuration file, the syntax is host specific and may include additional or alternate punctuation. For details, refer to the SAS documentation for your host system. ■

LINESIZE=

Specifies the line size of SAS procedure output

Valid as part of: configuration file, OPTIONS statement, OPTIONS window, SAS invocation

HELP LINESIZE

Syntax

LINESIZE=*width*

Description

The LINESIZE= system option specifies the line size (printer line width) for the SAS log and the SAS procedure output file used by the DATA step and procedures. The alias for this option is LS=.

You can use the following argument with the LINESIZE= system option:

width specifies the line width. Values can range from 64 through 256.

■ **Host Information** .... The syntax shown above applies to the OPTIONS statement. However, when you specify the LINESIZE= system option on the command line or in a configuration file, the syntax is host specific and may include additional or alternate punctuation. For details, refer to the SAS documentation for your host system. ■

LOG=

Specifies a destination to which the SAS log is written when executing SAS programs in modes other than display manager

Valid as part of: configuration file, SAS invocation

HELP LOG

Syntax

LOG=*destination*

Description

The LOG= system option specifies a destination to which the SAS log is written when executing SAS programs in modes other than display manager.

You can use the following argument with the LOG= system option:

destination specifies either an external file or a device, depending on your host system.

■ **Host Information** ....

A valid destination and its syntax are host specific. Although the syntax is generally consistent with the command-line syntax of your host system, it may include additional or alternate punctuation. For details, refer to the SAS documentation for your host system. ■

MACRO

Specifies whether the SAS macro language is available

Valid as part of: configuration file, SAS invocation

HELP MACRO

Syntax

MACRO | NOMACRO

Description

The MACRO system option specifies whether the SAS macro language is available. (It does not control the SYMGET function or the SYMPUT routine.)

You can use the following forms of the MACRO system option:

MACRO
: enables use of the SAS macro language.

NOMACRO
: disables use of the SAS macro language. If NOMACRO is specified and the SAS System encounters a macro statement or macro variable reference, the statement generally is not recognized, and an error message is issued.

See Also

Chapter 20, "SAS Macro Facility"

MAUTOSOURCE

Enables the macro autocall feature

Valid as part of: configuration file, OPTIONS statement, OPTIONS window, SAS invocation

HELP MAUTOSOURCE

Syntax

MAUTOSOURCE | NOMAUTOSOURCE

Description

The MAUTOSOURCE system option controls whether the macro autocall feature is available.

You can use the following forms of the MAUTOSOURCE system option:

MAUTOSOURCE
: enables the autocall feature.

NOMAUTOSOURCE
: disables the autocall feature.

If the MAUTOSOURCE option is in effect and a macro with the name requested has not been compiled, all types of macro invocations, including name-style and statement-style, cause the macro processor to search the autocall library for a file with the requested name. Any other required options, such as IMPLMAC for statement-style macros, must also be in effect.

See Also

SASAUTOS= system option

Chapter 20, "SAS Macro Facility"

MERROR

Issues a warning message when a macro-like name does not match a macro keyword

Valid as part of: configuration file, OPTIONS statement, OPTIONS window, SAS invocation

HELP MERROR

Syntax

MERROR | NOMERROR

Description

The MERROR system option controls whether the SAS macro language compiler issues a warning message if the macro processor cannot match a macro-like name (of the form %*name*) to an appropriate macro keyword.

You can use the following forms of the MERROR system option:

MERROR
: specifies that warning messages be issued.

NOMERROR
: specifies that warning messages not be issued.

Several conditions can occur that cause a macro-like name to be unmatched with an appropriate macro keyword. These conditions appear when the following occur:

- a macro keyword, including a macro call, is misspelled
- a macro is called before being defined
- strings containing percent signs are encountered.

If your program contains a percent sign in a string that could be mistaken for a macro keyword, specify NOMERROR.

See Also

Chapter 20, "SAS Macro Facility"

MISSING=

Specifies the character to print for missing numeric values

Valid as part of: configuration file, OPTIONS statement, OPTIONS window, SAS invocation

HELP MISSING

Syntax

MISSING='*character*'

Description

The MISSING= system option specifies the character to print for missing numeric variable values.

You can use the following argument with the MISSING= system option:

'*character*' specifies the value to be printed. The value can be any character.

■ **Host Information** ....

The syntax shown above applies to the OPTIONS statement. However, when you specify the MISSING= system option on the command line or in a configuration file, the syntax is host specific and may include additional or alternate punctuation. For details, see the SAS documentation for your host system.

MLOGIC

Traces execution of the macro language processor

Valid as part of: configuration file, OPTIONS statement, OPTIONS window, SAS invocation

HELP MLOGIC

Syntax

MLOGIC | NOMLOGIC

Description

The MLOGIC system option specifies whether the macro language processor traces its execution.

You can use the following forms of the MLOGIC system option:

MLOGIC
: causes tracing of macro execution and writes the trace information to the SAS log.

NOMLOGIC
: specifies no tracing.

Use the MLOGIC system option to debug macros. If MLOGIC is in effect and the macro processor encounters a macro invocation, the macro processor displays messages that identify the following:

- beginning of macro execution
- values of macro parameters at that point
- execution of each macro program statement

□ whether each %IF condition is true or false

□ ending of macro execution.

Note: Using the MLOGIC system option can produce a great deal of output.

See Also

Chapter 20, "SAS Macro Facility"

MPRINT

Displays SAS statements generated by macro execution

Valid as part of: configuration file, OPTIONS statement, OPTIONS window, SAS invocation

HELP MPRINT

Syntax

MPRINT | NOMPRINT

Description

The MPRINT system option specifies whether SAS statements generated by macro execution are displayed.

You can use the following forms of the MPRINT system option:

MPRINT
: specifies that macro-generated statements are displayed. The statements are formatted with macro variable references and macro functions resolved, with each statement beginning on a new line and with one space between words.

NOMPRINT
: specifies that no macro-generated statements are displayed.

See Also

Chapter 20, "SAS Macro Facility"

MRECALL

Searches autocall libraries for a file not found during an earlier search

Valid as part of: configuration file, OPTIONS statement, OPTIONS window, SAS invocation

HELP MRECALL

Syntax

MRECALL | NOMRECALL

Description

The MRECALL system option specifies whether the macro processor searches the autocall libraries for a file that was not found during an earlier search.

You can use the following forms of the MRECALL system option:

MRECALL
: specifies that the macro processor search the autocall libraries for an undefined macro name each time the macro is invoked.

NOMRECALL
: specifies that the macro processor search the autocall libraries only once for a requested macro name.

Use the MRECALL option primarily for the following:

- □ debugging systems that require macros in autocall libraries.
- □ recovering from errors caused by an autocall to a macro that is in an unavailable library. Use the MRECALL option to call the macro again after making the library available.

See Also

Chapter 20, "SAS Macro Facility"

NEWS=

Specifies a file that contains messages to be written to the SAS log

Valid as part of: configuration file, SAS invocation

HELP NEWS

Syntax

NEWS=*file-specification*

Description

The NEWS= system option specifies a file that contains messages to be written to the SAS log. The file can contain information for users, including news items about the SAS System.

You can use the following argument with the NEWS= system option:

file-specification specifies an external file.

■ **Host Information** ....

A valid file specification and its syntax are host specific. Although the syntax is generally consistent with the command-line syntax of your host system, it may include additional or alternate punctuation. For details, see the SAS documentation for your host system.

.... ■

See Also

SITEINFO= system option

NOTES

Writes notes to the SAS log

Valid as part of: configuration file, OPTIONS statement, OPTIONS window, SAS invocation

HELP NOTES

Syntax

NOTES | NONOTES

Description

The NOTES system option controls whether notes are written to the SAS log. The aliases for this option are LNOTES and NOLNOTES.

You can use the following forms of the NOTES system option:

NOTES
: specifies that the SAS System write notes.

NONOTES
: specifies that the SAS System not write notes. If NONOTES is specified, error and warning messages are not suppressed.

Note: NOTES must be specified on SAS programs that are sent to SAS Institute for problem determination and resolution.

NUMBER

Prints page numbers

Valid as part of: configuration file, OPTIONS statement, OPTIONS window, SAS invocation

HELP NUMBER

Syntax

NUMBER | NONUMBER

Description

The NUMBER system option controls whether the page number prints on the first title line of each page of SAS output.

You can use the following forms of the NUMBER system option:

NUMBER
: specifies that page numbers be printed.

NONUMBER
: specifies that page numbers not be printed.

OBS=

Specifies which observation the SAS System processes last

Valid as part of: configuration file, OPTIONS statement, OPTIONS window, SAS invocation

HELP OBS

Syntax

OBS=*n* | MAX

Description

The OBS= system option specifies which observation from a data set (or the last record from a raw data file) that the SAS System reads last. You can also use the OBS= system option to control analysis of SAS data sets in PROC steps.

If the SAS System is processing a file of raw data, the OBS= system option specifies the last line of data to read. The SAS System counts a line of input data as one observation, even if the raw data for several SAS data set observations are on a single line.

You can use the following arguments with the OBS= system option:

n
: specifies the number of the last observation to process.

  If OBS=0 and the NOREPLACE option is in effect, the SAS System can still take certain actions because it actually executes each DATA and PROC step in the program, using no observations. For example, the SAS System executes procedures, such as CONTENTS, and DATASETS, that process the libraries or SAS data sets. External files are also opened and closed. Therefore, even if you specify OBS=0, when your program writes to an external file with a PUT statement, an end-of-file mark is written, and any existing data in the file are deleted.

MAX
: specifies the maximum number of observations as the last to process. The default value is MAX, which is the largest signed, 4-byte integer representable on your host.

You must specify OBS=MAX to use a WHERE statement or WHERE data set option.

■ **Host Information** .... The syntax shown above applies to the OPTIONS statement. However, when you specify the OBS= system option on the command line or in a configuration file, the syntax is host specific and may include additional or alternate punctuation. For details, refer to the SAS documentation for your host system. ■

Comparisons

An OBS= specification from either a data set option or an INFILE statement option takes precedence over the OBS= system option.

Examples

The following statement causes the SAS System to read only through the 50th observation of a SAS data set:

```
options obs=50;
```

By specifying the following statement as the first statement in a program, you can check the syntax of SAS statements:

```
options obs=0 noreplace;
```

You can use the FIRSTOBS= and OBS= options together to process a set of observations from the middle of a data set. For example, the following statement processes only observations 1000 through 1100:

```
options firstobs=1000 obs=1100;
```

See Also

FIRSTOBS=, OBS=, and REPLACE data set options in Chapter 15, "SAS Data Set Options"

OPLIST

Writes the settings of SAS system options to the SAS log

Valid as part of: configuration file, SAS invocation

HELP OPLIST

Syntax

OPLIST | NOOPLIST

Description

The OPLIST system option writes to the SAS log the settings of all options specified on the command line or in the configuration file. (Some hosts may include additional information, such as the name of the configuration file.) You cannot change the settings of SAS system options with the OPLIST system option.

You can use the following forms of the OPLIST option:

OPLIST
: specifies that the SAS System write the settings of options.

NOOPLIST
: specifies that the SAS System not write the settings of options.

OVP

Overprints output lines

Valid as part of: configuration file, OPTIONS statement, OPTIONS window, SAS invocation

HELP OVP

Syntax

OVP | NOOVP

Description

The OVP system option controls whether lines output by the SAS System are overprinted.

You can use the following forms of the OVP system option:

OVP
: specifies that output lines are overprinted by the SAS System.

NOOVP
: specifies that output lines are not overprinted.

For example, if OVP is in effect when the SAS System encounters an error in a SAS statement, it prints underscores beneath the word in error. If NOOVP is in effect, the SAS System prints dashes on the next line below the error.

Note: When displaying output to a terminal, OVP is overridden and changed to NOOVP.

PAGENO=

Resets the page number

Valid as part of: configuration file, OPTIONS statement, OPTIONS window, SAS invocation

HELP PAGENO

Syntax

PAGENO=*n*

Description

The PAGENO= system option specifies a beginning page number for the next page of output produced by the SAS System. The alias for this option is PAGNO=.

You can use the following argument with the PAGENO= system option:

n specifies the page number.

Use the PAGENO= system option to reset page numbering in the middle of a SAS session.

■ **Host Information** ....

The syntax shown above applies to the OPTIONS statement. However, when you specify the PAGENO= system option on the command line or in a configuration file, the syntax is host specific and may include additional or alternate punctuation. For details, refer to the SAS documentation for your host system.
.... ■

PAGESIZE=

Specifies the pagesize of SAS output

Valid as part of: configuration file, OPTIONS statement, OPTIONS window, SAS invocation

HELP PAGESIZE

Syntax

PAGESIZE=*n*

Description

The PAGESIZE= system option specifies the number of lines that can be printed per page of SAS output. The alias for this option is PS=.

You can use the following argument with the PAGESIZE= system option:

n specifies the number of lines. Valid values are from 15 through 32767.

■ **Host Information** ....

The syntax shown above applies to the OPTIONS statement. However, when you specify the PAGESIZE= system option on the command line or in a configuration file, the syntax is host specific and may include additional or alternate punctuation. For details, refer to the SAS documentation for your host system.

■

PARM=

Specifies a parameter string passed to an external program

Valid as part of: configuration file, OPTIONS statement, OPTIONS window, SAS invocation

HELP PARM

Syntax

PARM=*'string'*

Description

The PARM= system option specifies a parameter string that can be passed to a program external to the SAS System.

You can use the following argument with the PARM= system option:

'string' specifies the string to pass to the external program.

Example

The following statements pass the parameter X=2 to an external program, EXTPGM:

```
options parm='x=2';

proc extpgm;
run;
```

■ **Host Information** ....

There are other methods of passing parameters to external programs that depend on your host system and whether you are running in interactive line or batch mode. For details, refer to the SAS documentation for your host system.

■

PARMCARDS=

Specifies the file reference to use as the PARMCARDS file

Valid as part of: configuration file, OPTIONS statement, OPTIONS window, SAS invocation

HELP PARMCARDS

Syntax

PARMCARDS=*file-reference*

Description

The PARMCARDS= system option specifies the file reference of the file that is opened when a PARMCARDS (or PARMCARDS4) statement is seen in a procedure. The alias for this system option is PRMCARDS=.

You can use the following argument with the PARMCARDS= system option:

file-reference is any valid file reference (fileref).

All data lines after the PARMCARDS (or PARMCARDS4) statement are written to the file until the delimiter line of one or four semicolons is seen. The file is closed and then made available to be read by the procedure. There is no parsing or macro expansion of the data lines.

■ **Host Information** ....

The syntax shown above applies to the OPTIONS statement. However, when you specify the PARMCARDS= system option on the command line or in a configuration file, the syntax is host specific and may include additional or alternate punctuation. For details, refer to the SAS documentation for your host system.

.... ■

PRINT=

Specifies the destination to which the SAS output file is written when executing SAS programs in modes other than display manager

Valid as part of: configuration file, SAS invocation

HELP PRINT

Syntax

PRINT=*destination*

Description

The PRINT= system option specifies the destination to which SAS output is written when executing SAS programs in modes other than interactive display manager.

You can use the following argument with the PRINT= system option:

destination specifies either an external file or a device, depending on your host system.

■ **Host Information** ....

A valid destination and its syntax are host specific. Although the syntax is generally consistent with the command-line syntax of your host system, it may include additional or alternate punctuation. For details, refer to the SAS documentation for your host system.

.... ■

PROBSIG=

Controls the number of significant digits of *p*-values in statistical procedures

Valid as part of: configuration file, OPTIONS statement, OPTIONS window, SAS invocation

HELP PROBSIG

Syntax

PROBSIG=*n*

Description

The PROBSIG= system option controls the number of significant digits of *p*-values in some statistical procedures.

You can use the following argument with the PROBSIG= system option:

n specifies the number of significant digits. The valid values are 0, 1, and 2.

When PROBSIG=0, *p*-values are written with four decimal places and truncated at .0001.

PROBSIG=1 guarantees that *p*-values are written with at least one significant digit; that is, values greater than or equal to .000095 are written with four decimal places, but values less than .000095 are written in E-notation.

PROBSIG=2 guarantees at least two significant digits so that values greater than .0000995 are written with five decimal places, and smaller values are written in E-notation.

■ **Host Information** .... The syntax shown above applies to the OPTIONS statement. However, when you specify the PROBSIG= system option on the command line or in a configuration file, the syntax is host specific and may include additional or alternate punctuation. For details, refer to the SAS documentation for your host system. ■

PROCLEAVE=

Specifies an amount of memory to leave unallocated for normal termination of a procedure

Valid as part of: OPTIONS statement, configuration file, SAS invocation

HELP PROCLEAVE

Syntax

PROCLEAVE=*value*

Description

The PROCLEAVE= system option specifies an amount of memory to leave unallocated so a procedure can terminate normally when error recovery code is initiated. If a procedure that demands large amounts of memory (such as the GLM procedure) is failing, you can increase the number of bytes specified by the PROCLEAVE= option. This forces the failing procedure to use an algorithm that demands less memory. However, the procedure is also forced to use utility data sets, thereby increasing the execution time of the procedure.

You can use the following argument with the PROCLEAVE= system option:

value specifies the amount of space to leave unallocated.

■ **Host Information** ......

Depending on your host system, *value* can specify bytes, kilobytes, or megabytes and can range from 0 to the maximum amount of available space.

The syntax shown above applies to the OPTIONS statement. However, when you specify the PROCLEAVE= system option on the command line or in a configuration file, the syntax is host specific and may include additional or alternate punctuation. For details, refer to the SAS documentation for your host system.

REMOTE=

Specifies the session ID used for SAS/CONNECT software

Valid as part of: configuration file, OPTIONS statement, OPTIONS window, SAS invocation.

HELP REMOTE

Syntax

REMOTE=*session-id*

Description

The REMOTE= system option specifies a remote session identifier to be used by SAS/CONNECT software.

You can use the following argument with the REMOTE= system option:

session-id specifies the remote session ID.

To run SAS/CONNECT software (depending on your host system configuration), you may need to include the REMOTE= system option in the following places:

- □ the local SAS session. The REMOTE= system option for the local session is valid as part of the configuration file, the OPTIONS statement, and the OPTIONS window, or at SAS invocation.
- □ the remote SAS session. The REMOTE= system option for the remote session is valid as part of the configuration file or as part of the SAS command executed to invoke the remote SAS session.

■ **Host Information** ......

Not all access methods require you to specify the REMOTE= system option for the remote SAS session. A valid session ID and its syntax are host specific.

Although the syntax is generally consistent with the command-line syntax of your host system, it may include additional or alternate punctuation. For details on access methods and appropriate values, refer to *SAS/CONNECT Software: Usage and Reference, Version 6, First Edition.* For details on host-specific syntax, refer to the SAS documentation for your host system.

See Also

SAS/CONNECT Software: Usage and Reference, Version 6, First Edition

REPLACE

Replaces permanently stored SAS data sets

Valid as part of: configuration file, OPTIONS statement, OPTIONS window, SAS invocation

HELP REPLACE

Syntax

REPLACE | NOREPLACE

Description

The REPLACE system option specifies whether permanently stored SAS data sets are replaced.

You can use the following forms of the REPLACE system option:

REPLACE
: specifies that the SAS System replace data sets.

NOREPLACE
: specifies that the SAS System not replace data sets.

If you specify NOREPLACE, a permanently stored SAS data set cannot be replaced with one of the same name. This prevents inadvertently replacing existing SAS data sets.

Comparisons

The REPLACE= data set option overrides the REPLACE system option.

See Also

REPLACE= data set option in Chapter 15, "SAS Data Set Options"

REUSE=

Specifies to reuse space when observations are added to a compressed SAS data set

Valid as part of: configuration file, OPTIONS statement, OPTIONS window, SAS invocation

HELP REUSE

Syntax

REUSE=YES | NO

Description

The REUSE= system option specifies whether free space is tracked and reused in newly created compressed SAS data sets. If space is reused, observations added to the SAS data set are inserted wherever enough free space exists instead of at the end of the SAS data set.

You can use the following arguments with the REUSE= system option:

YES
: specifies that the SAS System track free space and reuse it in a compressed SAS data set.

NO
: specifies that the SAS System not track free space and reuse it in a compressed SAS data set. Specifying REUSE=NO results in less efficient usage of space if you delete or update many observations in a SAS data set. However, the APPEND procedure, the FSEDIT procedure, and other procedures that add observations to the SAS data set continue to add observations to the end of the data set as they do for uncompressed SAS data sets.

You cannot change the REUSE= attribute of a compressed SAS data set after it is created. This means that space is tracked and reused in the compressed SAS data set according to the REUSE= value when the SAS data set was created, not when you add and delete observations.

■ **Host Information** ....

The syntax shown above applies to the OPTIONS statement. However, when you specify the REUSE= system option on the command line or in a configuration file, the syntax is host specific and may include additional or alternate punctuation. For details, refer to the SAS documentation for your host system.

Comparisons

The REUSE= data set option overrides the REUSE= system option.

See Also

COMPRESS= system option

"Options for Tuning Performance" in Chapter 6, "SAS Files"

COMPRESS= and REUSE= data set options in Chapter 15, "SAS Data Set Options"

S=

Specifies the length of statements on each line of a source statement and the length of data on lines following a CARDS statement

Valid as part of: configuration file, OPTIONS statement, OPTIONS window, SAS invocation

HELP S

Syntax

S=*n* | MAX

Description

The S= system option specifies the length of statements, exclusive of sequence numbers, on each line of SAS source statements and the length of data, exclusive of sequence numbers, on lines following a CARDS statement.

You can use the following arguments with the S= system option:

n
: specifies the length. Valid values can range from 0 to the largest signed, 4-byte integer representable on your host system.

MAX
: specifies the largest signed, 4-byte integer representable on your host system.

Input can be from either fixed- or variable-length records. Both fixed-length and variable-length records can be either unsequenced or sequenced. Unsequenced records do not contain sequence fields. Fixed-length sequenced records contain sequence fields at the end of each record. Variable-length sequenced records contain sequence fields at the beginning of each record.

Sequence fields are always eight columns wide and can contain alphabetic as well as numeric characters. For example, some editors include alphabetic information in the first few columns of the sequence field to indicate the file name. The SEQ= system option specifies the numeric portion of the sequence field, which can range from 1 through 8.

The SAS System determines whether the input contains sequence numbers based on the value of S=. If the value of S= is 0 and you have fixed-length records, the SAS System inspects the last *n* columns (where *n* is the value of the SEQ= option) of the first sequence field, which is at the end of the first line of input. If those columns contain numeric characters, the SAS System assumes the file contains sequence fields and ignores the last eight columns of each line.

If the value of S= is greater than 0 or MAX and you have fixed-length records, the SAS System uses that value as the length of the source or data to be scanned, ignores everything beyond that length on each line, and does not look for sequence numbers.

If the value of S= is 0 and you have variable-length records, the SAS System inspects the last *n* columns (where *n* is the value of the SEQ= option) of the first sequence field, which is at the beginning of the first line of input. If those columns contain numeric characters, the SAS System assumes the file contains sequence fields and ignores the first eight columns of each line.

If the value of S= is greater than 0 or MAX and you have variable-length records, the SAS System uses that value as the starting column of the source or data to be scanned, ignores everything before that length on each line, and does not look for sequence numbers.

Comparisons

The S= system option operates exactly like the S2= system option except that the S2= option only controls input from a %INCLUDE statement, an AUTOEXEC file, or an autocall macro file.

■ **Host Information** ....

The syntax shown above applies to the OPTIONS statement. However, when you specify the S= system option on the command line or in a configuration file, the syntax is host specific and may include additional or alternate punctuation. For details, refer to the SAS documentation for your host system.
.... ■

See Also

S2= system option

SEQ= system option

SASAUTOS=

Specifies the autocall library

Valid as part of: configuration file, OPTIONS statement, OPTIONS window, SAS invocation

HELP SASAUTOS

Syntax

SASAUTOS=*library-specification* |
(*library-specification-1*, . . . ,*library-specification-n*)

Description

SASAUTOS= specifies the autocall library or libraries.

You can use the following arguments with the SASAUTOS= system option:

library-specification |
(*library-specification-1*, . . . ,*library-specification-n*)
: identifies one or more aggregate storage locations, each of which can contain files or members containing definitions of SAS macros.

When you specify two or more autocall libraries, you must enclose the specifications in parentheses. You can separate multiple specifications with either a comma or a blank space.

■ **Host Information** .... The syntax shown above applies to the OPTIONS statement. However, when you specify the SASAUTOS= system option on the command line or in a configuration file, the syntax is host specific and may include additional or alternate punctuation. For details, refer to the SAS documentation for your host system. ■

SASHELP=

Specifies the location of the SASHELP library

Valid as part of: configuration file, SAS invocation

HELP SASHELP

Syntax

SASHELP=*library-specification*

Description

The SASHELP= system option specifies the location of the SASHELP library, which is where HELP files are stored.

You can use the following argument with the SASHELP= system option:

library-specification identifies an external library.

The SASHELP= system option is set during the installation process and normally is not changed after installation.

■ **Host Information** .... A valid external library specification is host specific. Although the syntax is generally consistent with the command-line syntax of your host system, it may include additional or alternate punctuation. For details, refer to the SAS documentation for your host system. ■

SASMSG=

Specifies the external library that contains SAS messages

Valid as part of: configuration file, SAS invocation

HELP SASMSG

Syntax

SASMSG=*library-specification*

Description

The SASMSG= system option specifies the external library that contains SAS error, warning, and informational messages.

You can use the following argument with the SASMSG= system option:

library-specification identifies an external library.

The SASMSG= system option is set during the installation process and normally is not changed after installation.

■ **Host Information** .... A valid external library specification is host specific. Although the syntax is generally consistent with the command-line syntax of your host system, it may include additional or alternate punctuation. For details, refer to the SAS documentation for your host system. ■

SASUSER=

Specifies the name of the SASUSER library

Valid as part of: configuration file, SAS invocation

HELP SASUSER

Syntax

SASUSER=*library-specification*

Description

The SASUSER= system option specifies the name of the SASUSER library, which contains a user's profile catalog. The library and catalog are created automatically by the SAS System; you do not have to create them explicitly.

You can use the following arguments with the SASUSER= option:

library-specification identifies an external library.

■ **Host Information** ....

A valid library specification and its syntax are host specific. Although the syntax is generally consistent with the command-line syntax of your host system, it may include additional or alternate punctuation. For details, refer to the SAS documentation for your host system.

.... ■

SEQ=

Specifies the length of the numeric portion of the sequence field

Valid as part of: configuration file, OPTIONS statement, OPTIONS window, SAS invocation

HELP SEQ

Syntax

SEQ=*n*

Description

The SEQ= system option specifies the length of the numeric portion of the sequence field.

You can use the following argument with the SEQ= system option:

n specifies the length. Valid values can range from 1 through 8.

When SEQ=8, all eight characters in the sequence field are assumed to be numeric. Unless the S= or S2= system option specifies otherwise, the SAS System assumes an eight-character sequence field; however, some editors place some alphabetic information (for example, the file name) in the first several characters. The SEQ= value specifies the number of digits that are right justified in the eight-character field. For example, if you specify SEQ=5 for the sequence field AAA00010, the SAS System looks at only the last five characters of the eight-character sequence field and, if the characters are numeric, treats the entire eight-character field as a sequence field.

■ **Host Information** ....

The syntax shown above applies to the OPTIONS statement. However, when you specify the SEQ= system option on the command line or in a configuration file, the syntax is host specific and may include additional or alternate punctuation. For details, refer to the SAS documentation for your host system.

.... ■

See Also

S= system option

S2= system option

SERROR

Issues a warning message when a macro variable reference does not match a macro variable

Valid as part of: configuration file, OPTIONS statement, OPTIONS window, SAS invocation

HELP SERROR

Syntax

SERROR | NOSERROR

Description

The SERROR system option controls whether a warning message is issued when the SAS System encounters a macro variable reference that cannot be matched with an appropriate macro variable.

You can use the following forms of the SERROR system option:

SERROR
: specifies that the SAS System issue warning messages.

NOSERROR
: specifies that the SAS System not issue warning messages.

Several conditions can occur that cause a macro variable reference to go unmatched with an appropriate macro variable. These conditions appear when the following occur:

- □ the name in a macro variable reference is misspelled.
- □ the variable is referenced before being defined.
- □ the program contains an ampersand (&) followed by a string, without intervening blanks between the ampersand and the string. For example, the following statement uses an ampersand as the symbol for the logical operator AND with no intervening blanks:

```
if x&y then do;
```

- □ the program contains an ampersand (&) that is used as a literal and is enclosed in double quotes, as in the following:

```
if buyer="Smith & Jones, Inc." then do;
```

See Also

Chapter 20, “SAS Macro Facility”

SETINIT

Allows alteration of site license information

Valid as part of: configuration file, SAS invocation

HELP SETINIT

Syntax

SETINIT | NOSETINIT

Description

The SETINIT system option enables you to alter site license information. This option is set in the installation process and is not normally changed after installation.

You can use the following forms of the SETINIT system option:

SETINIT
: enables you to alter site license information. If you are using display manager, the SETINIT command displays the SETINIT window from which you can make changes. If you are not using display manager, SETINIT enables you to change license information by running the SETINIT procedure.

NOSETINIT
: does not allow you to alter site license information.

SITEINFO=

Specifies a file containing site information to be displayed if the SITEINFO command is specified

Valid as part of: configuration file, SAS invocation

HELP SITEINFO

Syntax

SITEINFO=*file-specification*

Description

The SITEINFO= system option specifies a file that contains site-specific information. If the SITEINFO command and the SITEINFO= system option are specified, site-specific information is displayed in the SITEINFO window.

You can use the following argument with the SITEINFO= system option:

file-specification identifies an external file.

■ **Host Information** ....

A valid file specification and its syntax are host specific. Although the syntax is generally consistent with the command-line syntax of your host system, it may include additional or alternate punctuation. For details, refer to the SAS documentation for your host system.

.... ■

SORTPGM=

Specifies the name of the sort utility

Valid as part of: configuration file, OPTIONS statement, SAS invocation

HELP SORTPGM

Syntax

SORTPGM='*utility*' | BEST | HOST | SAS

Description

The SORTPGM= system option specifies the name of the system sort utility to be invoked by the SAS System.

You can use the following arguments with the SORTPGM= system option:

'*utility*' specifies the name of an accessible utility to use.

BEST specifies to use the sort utility best suited for the data.

HOST specifies to use the host sort utility available on your host system.

SAS specifies the sort utility supplied by the SAS System.

The host sort utility may be more suitable than the sort utility supplied by the SAS System for data sets that contain many observations.

■ **Host Information** ......

The syntax shown above applies to the OPTIONS statement. However, when you specify the SORTPGM= system option on the command line or in a configuration file, the syntax is host specific and may include additional or alternate punctuation. For details, refer to the SAS documentation for your host system.
.... ■

SOURCE

Writes SAS source statements to the SAS log

Valid as part of: configuration file, OPTIONS statement, OPTIONS window, SAS invocation

HELP SOURCE

Syntax

SOURCE | NOSOURCE

Description

The SOURCE system option controls whether SAS source statements are written to the SAS log.

You can use the following forms of the SOURCE system option:

SOURCE
: specifies to write SAS source statements to the SAS log.

NOSOURCE
: specifies not to write SAS source statements to the SAS log.

The SOURCE system option does not affect whether statements from the AUTOEXEC file are printed on the SAS log.

Note: SOURCE must be specified on SAS programs that are sent to SAS Institute for problem determination and resolution.

SOURCE2

Writes secondary source statements from included files

Valid as part of: configuration file, OPTIONS statement, OPTIONS window, SAS invocation

HELP SOURCE2

Syntax

SOURCE2 | NOSOURCE2

Description

The SOURCE2 system option controls whether secondary source statements from files included by %INCLUDE statements are written to the SAS log. The aliases for this option are SRC2 and NOSRC2.

You can use the following forms of the SOURCE2 system option:

SOURCE2 specifies to write secondary source statements.

NOSOURCE2 specifies not to write secondary source statements.

Note: SOURCE2 must be specified on SAS programs that are sent to SAS Institute for problem determination and resolution.

SPOOL

Writes SAS statements to a utility data set in the WORK data library

Valid as part of: configuration file, OPTIONS statement, OPTIONS window, SAS invocation

HELP SPOOL

Syntax

SPOOL | NOSPOOL

Description

The SPOOL system option controls whether SAS statements are written to a utility data set in the WORK data library for later use by a %INCLUDE or %LIST statement.

You can use the following forms of the SPOOL system option:

SPOOL
: specifies that SAS statements be saved so they can be resubmitted by a %INCLUDE or redisplayed by a %LIST statement.

NOSPOOL
: specifies that SAS statements not be saved. By specifying NOSPOOL, you can speed execution time, but you cannot use the %INCLUDE and %LIST statements to resubmit SAS statements from earlier in the session.

Examples

Specifying SPOOL is especially helpful in interactive line mode because you can resubmit a line or lines of code by referring to the line numbers. For example, suppose you submit the following lines:

```
line 1  data test;
line 2     input w x y z;
line 3     cards;
line 4  411.365 101.945 323.782 512.398
line 5  ;
```

If SPOOL is in effect, you can resubmit line number 1 by submitting the following statement:

```
%inc 1;
```

You also can resubmit a range of lines by placing a colon (:) or dash (–) between the line numbers. For example, the following statements resubmit lines 1 through 3 and 4 through 5 of the above example:

```
%inc 1:3;
%inc 4-5;
```

STIMER

Writes system performance statistics to the SAS log

Valid as part of: configuration file, OPTIONS statement, SAS invocation

HELP STIMER

Syntax

STIMER | NOSTIMER

Description

The STIMER system option specifies whether performance statistics of your computer system are written to the SAS log.

You can use the following forms of the STIMER system option:

STIMER
: specifies to write the statistics. When STIMER is in effect, the SAS System writes to the SAS log a list of computer resources used for each step and the entire SAS session.

NOSTIMER
: specifies not to write performance statistics to the SAS log.

■ **Host Information** ......

Whether the STIMER system option writes to the SAS log may depend on how other host-specific options are set. Also, the type of statistics written varies with host systems. For example, under some host systems, STIMER only itemizes the number of page faults and CPU time. Under other host systems, STIMER itemizes other resources. For details, refer to the SAS documentation for your host system. ■

Comparisons

The STIMER system option specifies whether a subset of all the performance statistics of your computer system that are available to the SAS System are written to the SAS log. The FULLSTIMER system option specifies whether all of the available performance statistics are written to the SAS log.

See Also

FULLSTIMER system option

SYMBOLGEN

Displays the results of resolving macro variable references

Valid as part of: configuration file, OPTIONS statement, OPTIONS window, SAS invocation

HELP SYMBOLGEN

Syntax

SYMBOLGEN | NOSYMBOLGEN

Description

The SYMBOLGEN system option specifies whether the macro processor displays the result of resolving macro variable references. The aliases for this option are SGEN and NOSGEN.

You can use the following forms of the SYMBOLGEN system option:

SYMBOLGEN
: specifies that the SAS System display the results in the following form:

```
SYMBOLGEN: Macro Variable name Resolves To value
```

NOSYMBOLGEN
: specifies that the SAS System not display the results.

See Also

Chapter 20, "SAS Macro Facility"

SYSIN=

Specifies a file containing a SAS program

Valid as part of: configuration file, SAS invocation

HELP SYSIN

Syntax

SYSIN=*file-specification*

Description

The SYSIN= system option specifies a file containing a SAS program. This option indicates to the SAS System you are executing in noninteractive mode and can be specified only in the SAS invocation.

You can use the following arguments with the SYSIN= system option:

file-specification identifies an external file.

■ **Host Information** ....

A valid file specification and its syntax is host specific. Although the syntax is generally consistent with the command-line syntax of your host system, it may include additional or alternate punctuation. For details, refer to the SAS documentation for your host system.

.... ■

SYSLEAVE=

Specifies an amount of memory to leave unallocated for normal SAS System termination

Valid as part of: OPTIONS statement, configuration file, SAS invocation

HELP SYSLEAVE

Syntax

SYSLEAVE=*value*

Description

The SYSLEAVE= system option specifies an amount of memory to leave unallocated so that the SAS System can attempt to terminate normally when error recovery code is initiated.

You can use the following argument with the SYSLEAVE= system option:

value specifies the amount of space to leave unallocated. Valid values are any integer from 0 to the maximum amount of available space.

■ **Host Information** ....

Depending on your host system, *value* can specify bytes, kilobytes, or megabytes and can range from 0 to the maximum amount of available space.

The syntax shown above applies to the OPTIONS statement. However, when you specify the SYSLEAVE= system option on the command line or in a configuration file, the syntax is host specific and may include additional or alternate punctuation. For details, refer to the SAS documentation for your host system.

.... ■

SYSPARM=

Specifies a character string that can be passed to SAS programs

Valid as part of: configuration file, OPTIONS statement, OPTIONS window, SAS invocation.

HELP SYSPARM

Syntax

SYSPARM=*'characters'*

Description

The SYSPARM= system option specifies a character string that can be passed to SAS programs. The character string specified can be accessed in a SAS DATA step by the SYSPARM() function or anywhere in a SAS program by using the automatic macro variable reference &SYSPARM.

You can use the following argument with the SYSPARM= system option:

'characters'
specifies a character string with a maximum length of 200.

■ **Host Information** ....

The syntax shown above applies to the OPTIONS statement. However, when you specify the SYSPARM= system option on the command line or in a configuration file, the syntax is host specific and may include additional or alternate punctuation. For details, refer to the SAS documentation for your host system.

.... ■

See Also

Chapter 20, "SAS Macro Facility"

S2=

Specifies the length of secondary source statements

Valid as part of: configuration file, OPTIONS statement, OPTIONS window, SAS invocation

HELP S2

Syntax

S2=S | *n*

Description

The S2= system option specifies the length of secondary source statements.

You can use the following arguments with the S2= system option:

S
: specifies that the current value of the S= system option be used for computing the record length of text that comes from a %INCLUDE statement, an AUTOEXEC file, or an autocall macro file.

n
: specifies that the value of *n* be used for computing the record length of text that comes from a %INCLUDE statement, an AUTOEXEC file, or an autocall macro file.

Comparisons

The S2= system option operates exactly like the S= system option except that the S2= option only controls input from a %INCLUDE statement, an AUTOEXEC file, or an autocall macro file.

■ **Host Information** ....

The syntax shown above applies to the OPTIONS statement. However, when you specify the S2= system option on the command line or in a configuration file, the syntax is host specific and may include additional or alternate punctuation. For details, refer to the SAS documentation for your host system.

■

See Also

S= system option

SEQ= system option

TAPECLOSE=

Specifies the default CLOSE disposition for a SAS data library on tape

Valid as part of: configuration file, OPTIONS statement, OPTIONS window, SAS invocation

HELP TAPECLOSE

Syntax

TAPECLOSE=REREAD | LEAVE | REWIND | DISP

Description

The TAPECLOSE= system option specifies the default CLOSE disposition (volume position) to be performed when a SAS data library on tape is closed.

You can use the following arguments with the TAPECLOSE= system option:

REREAD
: leaves the tape volume positioned at the tapemark preceding the file just closed. REREAD overrides a FREE=CLOSE specification in the control language. Specify TAPECLOSE=REREAD if you are accessing one or more tape data libraries several times in a SAS program.

LEAVE
: leaves the tape volume positioned at the tapemark following the file just closed. LEAVE overrides a FREE=CLOSE specification in the control language. Specify TAPECLOSE=LEAVE if you are not repeatedly accessing the same tape libraries in a SAS program, but are creating or accessing one or more tape libraries in a subsequent file on the same tape volume.

REWIND
: rewinds the tape volume to the beginning of the tape. A FREE=CLOSE specification in the control language overrides the REWIND specification. Specify TAPECLOSE=REWIND if you are not repeatedly accessing one or more tape libraries in a SAS program.

DISP
: positions the tape volume according to the disposition that is specified in the host system's control language.

■ **Host Information** ....

The default value for this option is host specific, except for tape libraries accessed by the COPY procedure. The only valid value for tape libraries accessed by PROC COPY is LEAVE; it cannot be overridden. Refer to the SAS documentation for your host system.

The syntax shown above applies to the OPTIONS statement. However, when you specify the TAPECLOSE= system option on the command line or in a configuration file, the syntax is host specific and may include additional or alternate punctuation. For details, refer to the SAS documentation for your host system.

.... ■

Comparisons

The FILECLOSE= data set option takes precedence over the TAPECLOSE= system option.

See Also

FILECLOSE= data set option in Chapter 15, "SAS Data Set Options"

TERMINAL

Specifies whether a terminal is attached at SAS invocation.

Valid as part of: configuration file, SAS invocation

HELP TERMINAL

Syntax

TERMINAL | NOTERMINAL

Description

The TERMINAL system option specifies whether a terminal is attached at SAS invocation. The SAS System defaults to the appropriate setting for the TERMINAL system option based on whether the session is invoked in the foreground or background.

You can use the following forms of the TERMINAL system option:

TERMINAL
: specifies that a terminal is attached.

NOTERMINAL
: specifies that a terminal is not attached. If NOTERMINAL is specified, requestor windows are not displayed.

USER=

Specifies the name of the default permanent SAS data library

Valid as part of: configuration file, OPTIONS statement, OPTIONS window, SAS invocation

HELP USER

Syntax

USER=*library-specification*

Description

The USER= system option specifies the name of the default permanent SAS data library. If this option is specified, you can use one-level names to reference permanent SAS files in SAS statements. However, if USER=WORK is specified, the SAS System assumes that files referenced with one-level names refer to temporary work files.

You can use the following argument with the USER= system option:

library-specification identifies an external library.

■ **Host Information** ....

The syntax shown above applies to the OPTIONS statement. However, when you specify the USER= system option on the command line or in a configuration file, the syntax is host specific and may include additional or alternate punctuation. For details, refer to the SAS documentation for your host system.

.... ■

VERBOSE

Writes the settings of SAS system options to either the terminal or the batch log

Valid as part of: configuration file, SAS invocation

HELP VERBOSE

Syntax

VERBOSE | NOVERBOSE

Description

The VERBOSE system option writes the settings of SAS system options that were set at SAS invocation either on the command line or as part of the configuration file. If you invoke the SAS System at a terminal, the settings are displayed at the terminal. If you invoke the SAS System as a part of a batch job, the settings are written to the batch log. (Some hosts may write additional information, such as the name of the configuration file.) You cannot change the settings of the SAS system options with the VERBOSE system option.

You can use the following forms with the VERBOSE system option:

VERBOSE
: specifies to write the settings of system options.

NOVERBOSE
: specifies not to write the settings of system options.

VNFERR

Sets the error flag for a missing variable when a _NULL_ data set is used

Valid as part of: configuration file, OPTIONS statement, OPTIONS window, SAS invocation

HELP VNFERR

Syntax

VNFERR | NOVNFERR

Description

The VNFERR system option specifies whether the SAS System sets the error flag (_ERROR_=1) for a missing variable when a _NULL_ data set (or a data set that is bypassed by the host system control language) is used in a MERGE statement of a DATA step.

You can use the following forms of the VNFERR system option:

VNFERR
: specifies that the SAS System issue a warning, set _ERROR_=1 and stop processing, or both if the error is severe enough to interrupt processing.

NOVNFERR
: specifies that the SAS System issue a warning for a variable not found, but not set _ERROR_=1 or stop processing.

WORK=

Specifies the name of the SAS WORK library

Valid as part of: configuration file, SAS invocation

HELP WORK

Syntax

WORK=*library-specification*

Description

The WORK= system option specifies the name of the SAS WORK library.

You can use the following arguments with the WORK= system option:

library-specification identifies an external library.

■ **Host Information** ....

A valid library specification and its syntax are host specific. Although the syntax is generally consistent with the command-line syntax of your host system, it may include additional or alternate punctuation. For details, refer to the SAS documentation for your host system.

.... ■

WORKINIT

Initializes the WORK data library

Valid as part of: configuration file, SAS System invocation

HELP WORKINIT

Syntax

WORKINIT | NOWORKINIT

Description

The WORKINIT system option controls whether the WORK data library is initialized at SAS System invocation. The aliases for this option are WRKINIT and NOWRKINIT.

You can use the following forms of the WORKINIT system option:

WORKINIT
: specifies to erase files from a previously existing WORK library at SAS System invocation. For example, specifying WORKINIT erases from an existing library all files that exist from a previous SAS session.

NOWORKINIT
: specifies not to erase files from the WORK library at SAS invocation.

Comparisons

Use the WORKTERM system option to control whether the WORK data library is cleared when the SAS System terminates.

See Also

WORKTERM system option

WORKTERM

Erases WORK files at the termination of a SAS session

Valid as part of: configuration file, OPTIONS statement, OPTIONS window, SAS invocation

Syntax

WORKTERM | NOWORKTERM

Description

The WORKTERM system option specifies whether SAS WORK files, such as data sets, are erased from the current SAS WORK data library at the termination of the SAS session. The aliases for this option are WRKTERM and NOWRKTERM.

You can use the following forms of the WORKTERM system option:

WORKTERM — specifies to erase the WORK files.

NOWORKTERM — specifies not to erase the WORK files.

Although NOWORKTERM prevents the WORK data sets from being deleted, it has no effect on initialization of the WORK library by the SAS System. The SAS System normally initializes the WORK library at the start of each session, which effectively destroys any pre-existing information.

Comparisons

Use the WORKINIT system option to control whether the WORK data library is cleared when the SAS System is invoked.

See Also

WORKINIT system option

YEARCUTOFF=

Specifies the first year of a 100-year span used by informats and functions

Valid as part of: configuration file, OPTIONS statement, OPTIONS window, SAS invocation

HELP YEARCUTOFF

Syntax

YEARCUTOFF=*nnnn* | *nnnnn*

Description

The YEARCUTOFF= system option specifies the first year of a 100-year span used as the default by various DATE and DATETIME informats and functions.

You can use the following argument with the YEARCUTOFF= system option:

nnnn
nnnnn — specifies the first year of the 100-year span. Valid values are from 1582 through 19900.

If the default value of *nnnn* (1900) is in effect, the 100-year span begins with 1900 and ends with 1999. Therefore, any informat or function that uses a two-digit year value assumes a prefix of 19. For example, the value 92 refers to the year 1992.

Note that the value specified in the YEARCUTOFF= system option can result in years that occur in two centuries. For example, if you specify YEARCUTOFF=1950, any two-digit value between 50 and 99 inclusive refers to the first half of the 100-year span, which is in the 1900s. Any two-digit value between 00 and 49 inclusive refers to the second half of the 100-year span, which is in the 2000s. Figure 16.1 illustrates the relationship between the 100-year span and the two centuries if YEARCUTOFF=1950.

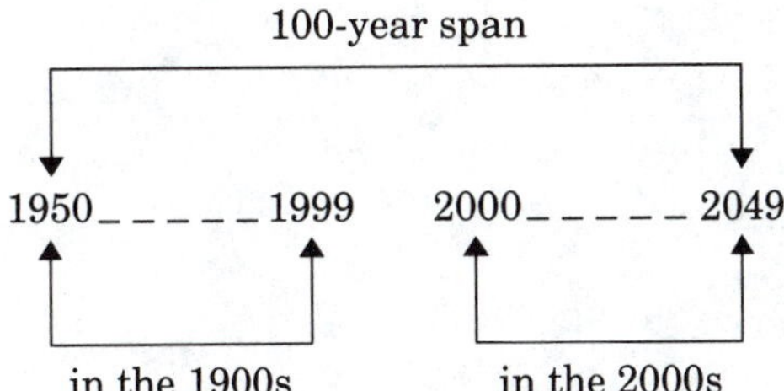

Figure 16.1 *A 100-year Span with Values in Two Centuries*

The YEARCUTOFF= system option applies to one- and two-digit years specified in the MMDDYY, YYMMDD, MONYY, DDMMYY, DATE, DATETIME, and YYQ informats and to one- and two-digit years specified in the DATEJUL, MDY, MONYY, and YYQ functions.

■ **Host Information** ....

The syntax shown above applies to the OPTIONS statement. However, when you specify the YEARCUTOFF= system option on the command line or in a configuration file, the syntax is host specific and may include additional or alternate punctuation. For details, refer to the SAS documentation for your host system.

.... ■

CHAPTER 17 SAS® Display Manager Windows

Background information on SAS display manager windows including a table listing all windows, appears in Chapter 7, "SAS Display Manager System." See Table 7.1, "Display Manager Windows."

AF

Displays windowing applications created by SAS/AF software

HELP AF

Display

```
Command ===>


                Actual text displayed in your

             AF window depends on the application

               you specify in the C= argument.
```

Invocation

AF <*arguments*>

Description

The AF window displays applications made up of catalog entries created by SAS/AF software. When you invoke the AF window, you specify the window you want to display by using the C= argument.

You can use the following arguments with the AF window:

C=*libref.catalog.entry.type*
: specifies the SAS data library, catalog, entry name, and entry type that contain the AF application.

  The C= argument is required the first time you invoke the AF window. During the same SAS session or in subsequent SAS sessions, invoking the AF window again without specifying the C= argument displays the application you called the last time you specified the C= argument. When you want to display a different application, specify the AF command again with a new C= argument.

  When you specify the C= argument, the catalog must exist, and it must contain at least one entry (the one you want to display).

  Note: Before invoking the AF window for the first time, you can use a LIBNAME statement to assign a libref to the data library containing the catalog that you want to access.

AUTORECALL=YES
: specifies that PROGRAM entry field values saved from a previous invocation are recalled when users execute the application.

AUTOSAVE=YES
saves PROGRAM entry field values when users exit from an entry.

CHECKLAST=NO
stores the name of the CBT entry at which users enter an application.

FRAME=*frame-number* | *frame-name*
specifies the number or name of the starting frame for a CBT application.

start-menu-number
specifies one or more MENU entry option numbers, which invoke the entry to display when an application executes.

Refer to the description of the AF commands in Chapter 18, "SAS Display Manager Commands," for complete information on the AF arguments.

Commands Available

Except as noted, all the commands in the following categories are available in the AF window:

- □ window-call
- □ window-management (except the PURGE command)
- □ file-management (except the COPY, DELETE, FILE, FREE, INCLUDE, and PRINT commands)
- □ window size and position (except the WSAVE command)
- □ color
- □ scrolling
- □ search (except the CHANGE and RCHANGE commands).

For information on the SAS/AF commands available in the AF window when building an application using SAS/AF software, refer to *SAS/AF Software: Usage and Reference, Version 6, First Edition.*

See Also

Chapter 18, "SAS Display Manager Commands"
SAS/AF Software: Usage and Reference, Version 6, First Edition

APPOINTMENT

Enters, updates, and displays daily calendar appointments

HELP APPOINTMENT

Display

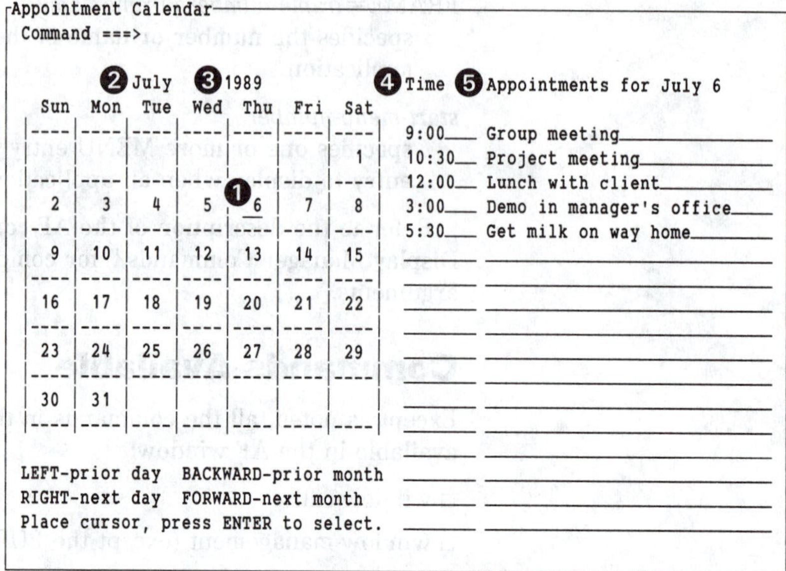

Invocation

APPOINTMENT <*libref.your-data-set* <*start-weekday*> <B>>

Description

The APPOINTMENT window enables you to enter, update, and display times and descriptors for daily appointments; store times and descriptors by date in a SAS data set; and make a list of tasks (a to-do list). The alias for invoking the APPOINTMENT window is APPT. When you invoke the APPOINTMENT window, the current month is displayed, with the current date highlighted and the cursor on it. Appointment data already entered for the current date, if any, are displayed for browsing or updating.

Note: The numbers shown in reverse video in the previous window correspond to the numbers in the following list and indicate the location of the five APPOINTMENT fields.

The five fields in the APPOINTMENT window are described below.

❶ The Day fields display the days of the current month.

❷ The Month field displays the current month. To enter, update, or browse appointment data for a different month, use the FORWARD or BACKWARD keys, or type over the current month. When typing over the Month field, you can type the entire name of the month you want to display, or you can type the first three letters, followed by a blank space. Pressing ENTER displays the appropriate calendar.

❸ The Year field displays the current year. To enter, update, or browse appointment data for a different year, type over the current year. Pressing ENTER displays the appropriate calendar.

❹ The Time field enables you to enter the time of appointments that you want to store in the APPOINTMENT window. It also enables you to make a to-do list (described later in this section).

❺ The Appointments field enables you to enter the appointments that you want to store in the APPOINTMENT window.

Arguments

You can use the following arguments with the APPOINTMENT window:

libref.your-data-set

specifies a library reference and a data set name. The data set is created if it does not already exist. If you do not specify the *libref.your-data-set* argument, your default data set (SASUSER.APPOINT) is opened.

■ **Host information** .... On most host systems, the library reference must already exist before you can specify it in the *libref.your-data-set* argument. ■

start-weekday

specifies the weekday with which you want your calendar to begin. By default, the starting day is Sunday, but you can choose a different starting day by specifying the first two letters of the calendar day, such as `mo` for Monday.

B

calls for browse mode; the Time and Appointments fields cannot be updated when this argument is specified.

Note: To use the B and *start-weekday* arguments, you must also use the *libref.your-data-set* argument; using the B and *start-weekday* arguments without the *libref.your-data-set* argument opens a WORK data set. For example, specifying APPOINT B opens the WORK.B data set.

The following example calls for the appointment data in the data set SCHEDULE.MAY to be displayed in browse mode with weeks starting on Monday (as shown by the first two letters of Monday, `mo`):

```
appt schedule.may mo b
```

Entering Appointment Data

To enter or update appointments for the current date, press ENTER. Your cursor moves to the Time field, where you type in the time. Then, move your cursor to the Appointments field and type in a description. Although the Time and Appointments fields have a fixed size, they are free-format, accepting any type of entry. You can make changes in either field by typing over already entered text.

You can also enter, update, or browse appointment data for another day. If the day you want is in the month currently displayed, move your cursor to that day and press ENTER. If the day you want is in a different month or year, you must first display the appropriate calendar. There are two ways to do this: issue the FORWARD or BACKWARD command until you reach the calendar of the month and year you want, and then press ENTER; or type over the Month or Year field, or both, with the month and year that you want, and then press ENTER. The new year or month is displayed, and the calendar configuration changes accordingly. Any

APPOINTMENT

continued

appointment data previously entered for the date selected are immediately displayed, and you can proceed as explained for the current date.

Storing Appointment Data

When you close the APPOINTMENT window, the appointment data are automatically saved to the data set you specified when you invoked the APPOINTMENT command. (If you did not use the *libref.your-data-set* argument, the data are saved to your default data set, SASUSER.APPOINT.) Saving the data enables you to recall and display them in later sessions.

Printing Appointment Data

Issue the PRINT command to print time and appointment data for the selected day and the PRINT ALL command to print all the days in the current month to the default print file. Issue the PRTFILE command to set up a print file.

Listing Tasks To Do

The APPOINTMENT window also enables you to make a list of the tasks you need to do. The list is displayed each time you invoke the APPOINTMENT window for the current day, until you mark the task as completed. Each subsequent day when you invoke your appointment data set, any incompleted items from the last date you accessed the window are copied to the current day's display.

Note: If you enter to-do items for days before the current date, they are not brought forward. If you access a future day's appointment schedule, your current list of to-do items does not appear.

To use the to-do list capability, start in column 1 of the Time field and type in either of the following text strings: TODO or TO-DO. Next, add a descriptor in the Appointments field. To mark the task as completed, change the Time field to something else, such as DONE.

Commands Available

Except as noted, all of the commands in the following categories are available in the APPOINTMENT window:

- window-call
- window-management (except the PURGE command)
- window size and position (except the WDEF and WSAVE commands)
- scrolling (except the TOP, BOTTOM, *n*, HSCROLL, and VSCROLL commands)
- file-management (except the COPY, FILE, FORMNAME, INCLUDE, and SAVE commands)
- color
- appointment.

The following commands have special meaning in the APPOINTMENT window:

CLEAR
: erases or blanks out all appointment time and description data for the current day.

DELETE
: deletes a line of appointment time and description data. The cursor must be positioned on the line when ENTER is pressed.

FORWARD
: displays the next month's calendar.

BACKWARD
: displays the previous month's calendar.

RIGHT
: displays the next day's appointments.

LEFT
: displays the previous day's appointments.

See Also

Chapter 18, "SAS Display Manager Commands"

CALCULATOR

Performs mathematical operations

HELP CALCULATOR

Display

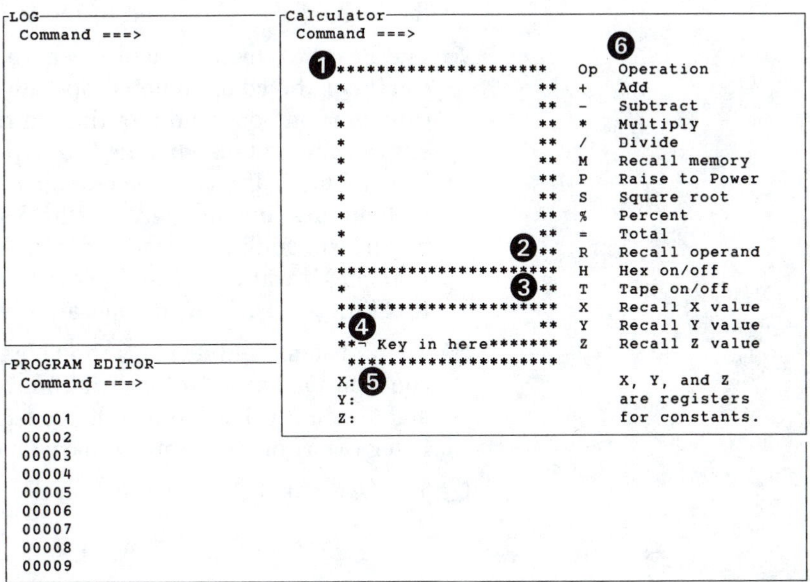

Invocation

CALCULATOR

CALCULATOR

continued

Description

The CALCULATOR window performs numerical computations such as addition, subtraction, multiplication, and division. The alias for invoking the CALCULATOR window is CALC.

When you invoke the CALCULATOR window, your cursor rests on the Primary Operand field. This is the field where you perform operations, such as multiplying two numbers. The result of an operation is displayed in the Register field, along with the operator that is in effect.

Note: The numbers shown in reverse video in the window correspond to the numbers in the following list and indicate the location of the six CALCULATOR fields.

There are six fields in the CALCULATOR window, including the Primary Operand and Register fields. All of the fields are described below.

❶ The Memory field displays the current memory contents, along with the label M: when memory contents are not zero. You can use the MEMPLUS, MEMMINUS, MEMRECALL, and MEMCLEAR commands in the Memory field.

❷ The Tape field displays the last ten operands used in operations, along with the operator used to compute each operand. This field also displays the subtotal of computations if you use the equal sign (=) operator. It is similar to an adding machine tape; it enables you to look back and see what numbers you have used in computations.

❸ The Register field displays the result of the operation most recently performed, along with the operator that is in effect. The contents of the Register field are used in the subsequent computation.

❹ The Primary Operand field is where the cursor rests and where you can enter the computational operations that you want to perform. You can enter one operand at a time in this field, or you can enter an entire computation, such as 5*3*4/8= (5 times 3 times 4 divided by 8 is equal to...). If you enter one operand at a time and press ENTER without entering an operator, the SAS System assumes that you want to perform addition because addition is the default operator. For example, if you type 4 and press ENTER and then type 2 and press ENTER, the result of the operation is 6.

❺ The Constant field displays the values of X, Y, and Z. To set up a constant for use as an operand, move the cursor to the Constant field and key in a value. To use the constant in a computation, type the letter (X, Y, or Z) in the Primary Operand field and press ENTER.

❻ The Operator field lists the operators and their meanings.

Operators

In the CALCULATOR window, if you enter several operators at once, they are evaluated in the order that they are entered, left to right, and not according to the rules of precedence for operators in SAS expressions.

The operators and their meanings are as follows:

+ add. Addition is the default operator. If you do not specify an operator and you type a number in the Primary Operand field and press ENTER, that number is added to the contents of the Register field.

– subtract.

* multiply.

/ divide.

M memory recall. The memory recall operator puts the contents of the Memory field into the Primary Operand field.

P exponentiation. The exponentiation operator raises the contents of the Register field to the power that you enter in the Primary Operand field. To use this operator, type P and the operand in the Primary Operand field and press ENTER.

S square root. If you type an S and an operand in the Primary Operand field and then press ENTER, the square root of the operand is calculated, and the result is displayed in the Register field. If you reverse the order and type an operand first and then an S in the Primary Operand field and press ENTER, the square root of the operand is calculated, and the result is displayed in the Primary Operand field. You must press ENTER a second time to move the result to the Register field.

% percent. The % (percent sign) operator calculates percentages of the contents of the Register field. To use this operator, enter an operand and % in the Primary Operand field and press ENTER. The percentage is displayed in the Primary Operand field. Pressing ENTER a second time adds the percentage to the contents of the Register field.

= equals. The = (equal sign) operator calculates a total of all the computations made since the last total. The next operand entered replaces the Register field contents and becomes the first operand of new computations.

R recall operand. The recall operator recalls the last operand you entered.

H hex. The hex operator converts the current operand; the contents of the memory; the X, Y, and Z constants; and the recall stack in the tape area to or from hexadecimal. An h is displayed to the left of the operands if there is room. The default is off. The hex operator is a toggle; issuing it a second time turns hex mode off, issuing it a third time turns it back on, and so on.

T tape. The tape operator turns the display off and on in the Tape field. The default is on. The tape operator is a toggle; issuing it a second time turns on the display, issuing it a third time turns it back off, and so on.

X recall X. The recall X operator recalls the value that you assigned to the X constant.

Y recall Y. The recall Y operator recalls the value that you assigned to the Y constant.

CALCULATOR

continued

Z recall Z. The recall Z operator recalls the value that you assigned to the Z constant.

Selecting an Operator

If you type a number in the Primary Operand field and press ENTER, that number is added by default to the contents of the Register field. To select another operation, you can do one of the following:

- □ Type the number or constant in the Primary Operand field, move the cursor to the operator you want (or to the right of it), and press ENTER. The operation is performed, and the result appears in the Register field.
- □ Type the number or constant and the operator you want in the Primary Operand field, and press ENTER. The operation is performed, and the result appears in the Register field.
- □ If you are using a mouse, point it to the operator you want, and click.

After one occurrence of the method you choose to select an operator, that operation is no longer the default; the default operation reverts to addition.

Commands Available

Except as noted, all of the commands in the following categories are available in the CALCULATOR window:

- □ window-call
- □ window-management
- □ window size and position
- □ file-management (except the COPY, FILE, FORMNAME, INCLUDE, and SAVE commands)
- □ color
- □ text-store
- □ calculator.

Note that in the CALCULATOR window, the CLEAR command clears out the Register and Primary Operand fields and erases all tape lines. Memory and constants are unchanged.

See Also

Chapter 18, "SAS Display Manager Commands"

CATALOG

Displays a directory of SAS catalog entries and enables you to manage entries

HELP CATALOG

Display

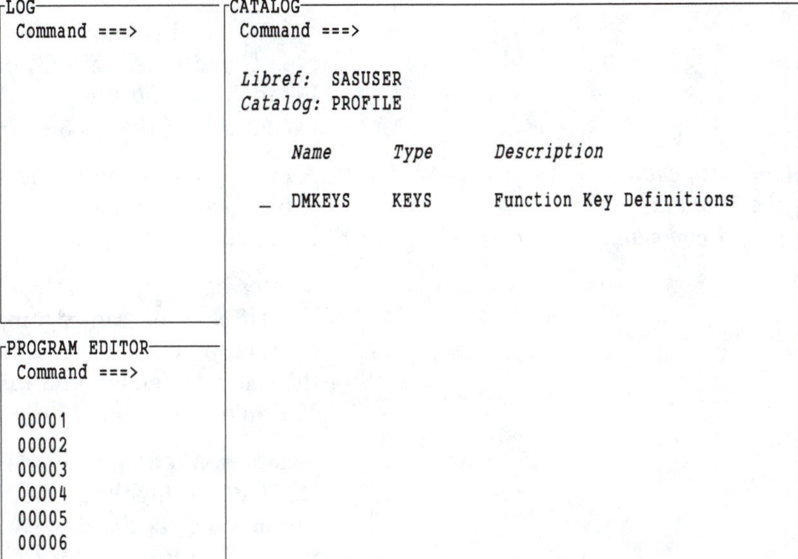

Invocation

CATALOG <*libref.catalog*>

Description

The CATALOG window displays a directory of SAS catalog entries and enables you to manage entries in SAS catalogs. The alias for invoking the CATALOG window is CAT. From the CATALOG window, you can do the following:

- □ browse a list of entries in a catalog
- □ rename, delete, and copy entries in the current catalog
- □ copy entries into the current catalog from another catalog.

Specify a libref to identify a SAS data library, as well as the name of the catalog, either in the fields displayed at the top of the window or when you invoke the window.

The CATALOG window displays a list of entries for the specified catalog; the entries can be managed in the window. Issue the COPY command to copy an entry, either from another catalog or from the current catalog to the current catalog. Issue the DELETE command to delete an entry. Use the BUILD procedure to browse or edit keys entries.

CATALOG

continued

You can also manipulate entries through the selection-field commands listed below. Move the cursor to the selection field of the entry you want. Type a command letter, and press ENTER or RETURN.

C
: cancels an R (rename) or D (delete) command. After you type C and press ENTER or RETURN, the field is no longer highlighted, and the operation is canceled. Multiple executions of the C command are allowed.

▶ ***Caution:*** *Use caution in issuing the D and V selection-field commands.*

A catalog entry cannot be restored once the request to delete it has been verified.

D
: deletes an entry. After you type D and press ENTER or RETURN, a message prompts you to type V to verify the deletion or C to cancel it. If you proceed with the deletion, the entry is deleted and disappears from the display. Multiple executions of the D command are allowed.

R
: renames an entry or its description. Press ENTER or RETURN to highlight the Name and Description fields. Type the new name, the description, or both over the old one, and press ENTER or RETURN again. The highlighting is removed, and the new name or description or both take effect. Multiple executions of the R command are allowed.

S | X
: opens the NOTEPAD window for the entry selected; entries can be of type OUTPUT, LOG, or SOURCE. If you specify another type, the entry is not displayed, and a message prompts you to select a file of type OUTPUT, LOG, or SOURCE. Multiple selections are allowed at one time. The NOTEPAD window appears for each entry selected in the order you issued the S or X command. The END command continues to activate the next NOTEPAD window until the cursor is returned to the CATALOG window.

V
: verifies a request to delete an entry. After you type V, the entry is deleted and disappears from the display. Multiple executions of the V command are allowed.

If you specify a catalog that does not exist, either when you invoke the CATALOG window or when the CATALOG window is active, a requestor window appears asking if you want to create the catalog you specified. If you answer yes, an empty catalog is created. If you answer no, you receive a message indicating that the file does not exist. If the catalog exists but cannot be opened for update, it is opened in browse mode, and you cannot make any modifications.

You can open multiple versions of the CATALOG window by specifying different libref and catalog names. Multiple selection-field commands can be selected and issued simultaneously in the CATALOG window.

Comparisons

You can also enter the CATALOG window from the DIR window. From the DIR window, select a SAS file that is a catalog. The CATALOG window then appears with the entries for that catalog.

Commands Available

Except as noted, all of the commands in the following categories are available in the CATALOG window:

□ window-call

□ window-management (except the PURGE command)

□ window size and position

□ color

□ scrolling

□ text-store

□ search (except the CHANGE and RCHANGE commands)

□ file-management (only the COPY and DELETE commands).

The following command has special meaning in the CATALOG window:

COPY
: copies one catalog entry to another catalog entry. The syntax and behavior differ from the COPY command as documented in Chapter 18. In the CATALOG window, the syntax of the COPY command is

COPY *from-spec* <*to-spec*>

where *from-spec* is the entry from which you want to copy. You can copy entries from other catalogs by specifying a three- or four-level name. The complete specification is *libref.catalog.name.type*. You must specify at least *name.type*. If you are copying from another catalog, you can omit *to-spec*; the new entry is given the same name it had in the other catalog. *To-spec* is the entry to which you want to copy. You can copy only to the current catalog, so you need specify only *name.type*. The entry types of *from-spec* and *to-spec* must match. If you omit *type* from *to-spec*, *type* is the same as that in *from-spec*.

Note that you cannot copy entries from the current catalog to another catalog.

See Also

DIR, LIBNAME, and NOTEPAD windows

Chapter 6, "SAS Files"

DIR

Displays information about SAS files

HELP DIR

Display

```
┌LOG──────────────────┐┌DIR──────────────────────────────────────────┐
│ Command ===>        ││ Command ===>                                │
│                     ││                                             │
│                     ││ Libref:  TEMP                               │
│                     ││ Type:    ALL                                │
│                     ││                                             │
│                     ││       SAS File  Type        Indexed         │
│                     ││                                             │
│                     ││    _  ARTICLE   DATA                        │
│                     ││    _  ASSIGN    DATA                        │
│                     ││    _  COMPANY   DATA                        │
│                     ││    _  EMP       DATA                        │
│                     ││    _  EMPLOYEE  DATA                        │
└─────────────────────┘│    _  FEB       DATA                        │
┌PROGRAM EDITOR───────┐│    _  FEMALES   DATA                        │
│ Command ===>        ││    _  FITNESS   DATA                        │
│                     ││    _  GRADES    DATA                        │
│ 00001               ││    _  HARVEST   DATA                        │
│ 00002               ││    _  HARVEST2  DATA                        │
│ 00003               ││    _  HEALTH    DATA                        │
│ 00004               ││    _  JAN       DATA                        │
│ 00005               ││    _  MALES     DATA                        │
│ 00006               ││    _  MEMBERS   DATA                        │
└─────────────────────┘└─────────────────────────────────────────────┘
```

Invocation

DIR <*libref.type*>

Description

The DIR window displays information about SAS files in the SAS data library you specify. If you enter the DIR window directly by issuing the DIR command, the default libref is listed as WORK and the type as ALL. Any temporary SAS files you create during your current SAS session are listed. To list all of the permanent SAS files of a particular type for a SAS data library, specify a libref and type, either in the selection fields displayed at the top of the window or, as shown in the syntax, when you invoke the window. The libref must already be assigned. Valid types are ALL, DATA, CATALOG, ACCESS, and VIEW. All of the files in that SAS data library of the specified type are listed.

The DIR window also includes the Indexed field, which indicates whether a data set is indexed. If this browse-only field is empty, either the file is not a data set or the data set is not indexed. A Yes in the Indexed field indicates the corresponding file is indexed. For more information on indexing, see "Release 6.06: SAS Indexes" in Chapter 6.

From the DIR window, you can do the following:

- □ access the VAR or CATALOG window
- □ browse a list of a data set's observations
- □ rename a file
- □ delete a file.

The files listed in the DIR window can be manipulated through several selection-field commands. Move the cursor to the selection field next to the file you want. Then type one of the following command letters, and press ENTER or RETURN:

B — opens the FSVIEW window, where you can browse the observations for the data set selected. The B selection-field command can be used only if SAS/FSP software is installed at your site. The B command is available for files of type VIEW or DATA only. Multiple executions of the B command are allowed at one time. The FSVIEW window appears for each data set in the order you issued the B command. The END command continues to activate the next FSVIEW window until the cursor is returned to the DIR window.

C — cancels an R (rename) or D (delete) command. After you type C and press ENTER or RETURN, the field is no longer highlighted, and the operation is canceled. Multiple executions of the C command are allowed.

▶ ***Caution:*** *Use caution in issuing the D and V selection-field commands.*

A file cannot be restored once the request to delete it has been verified.

D — deletes a file. After you type D and press ENTER or RETURN, a message prompts you to type V to verify the deletion or C to cancel it. If you proceed with the deletion, the file is deleted and disappears from the display. Multiple executions of the D command are allowed.

R — renames a file. Press ENTER or RETURN to highlight the SAS File field. Type in the new name, and press ENTER or RETURN again. The highlighting is removed, and the new name takes effect. Multiple executions of the R command are allowed.

S | X — depending on the type of file selected, either opens the VAR window and displays the variables for the file selected or opens the CATALOG window and displays the name, type, and description of the file selected. Multiple selections are allowed at one time. The VAR or CATALOG window appears for each selected file in the order you issued the S or X command. The END command continues to activate the next VAR or CATALOG window until the cursor is returned to the DIR window.

V — verifies a request to delete a file. After you type V, the file is deleted and disappears from the display. Multiple executions of the V command are allowed.

You can open multiple versions of the DIR window by specifying different libref names and filenames. Multiple selection-field commands can be selected and issued simultaneously in the DIR window.

Comparisons

You can also enter the DIR window from the LIBNAME window by selecting the libname of the SAS data library whose contents you want to display. Then, the DIR window appears with a list of files in that SAS data library.

DIR

continued

Commands Available

Except as noted, all of the commands in the following categories are available in the DIR window:

□ window-call

□ window-management (except the PURGE command)

□ window size and position

□ color

□ scrolling

□ text-store

□ search (except the CHANGE and RCHANGE commands).

See Also

CATALOG, LIBNAME, and VAR windows

"Release 6.06: SAS Indexes" in Chapter 6, "SAS Files"

LIBNAME statement in Chapter 9, "SAS Language Statements"

FILENAME

Displays assigned filerefs with their filenames

HELP FILENAME

Display

```
LOG
Command ===>

PROGRAM EDITOR
Command ===>

00001
00002
00003
00004
00005
00006

FILENAME
Command ===>

    Fileref    Host File Name

    F          System-specific name
    SASMSG     System-specific name
    X          System-specific name
```

Invocation

FILENAME

Description

The FILENAME window enables you to browse a listing of currently assigned filerefs and the files to which they are assigned. Filerefs are assigned with a FILENAME statement.

■ **Host Information** .... Note that the FILENAME statement and the assignment of a fileref are host-dependent. On some host systems, you can also assign filerefs with a host system command given with the X statement or with a host system command given outside a SAS session. However, only filerefs assigned with the FILENAME statement are displayed in the FILENAME window. Refer to the SAS documentation for your host system or see your SAS Software Consultant for host-specific information.
.... ■

Comparisons

Both the FILENAME and LIBNAME windows list the names of the host files and their assigned filerefs or librefs for files or groups of files. The FILENAME window, however, provides information for external files, while the LIBNAME window provides information for SAS data libraries.

For further comparison, see the documentation for the LIBNAME and FILENAME statements in Chapter 9.

Commands Available

Except as noted, all of the commands in the following categories are available in the FILENAME window:

□ window-call

□ window-management (except the PURGE command)

□ window size and position

□ color

□ scrolling

□ text-store

□ search (except the CHANGE and RCHANGE commands).

See Also

LIBNAME window

FILENAME and LIBNAME statements in Chapter 9, “SAS Language Statements”

FOOTNOTES

Enables you to browse, enter, and modify footnotes for output

HELP FOOTNOTE

Display

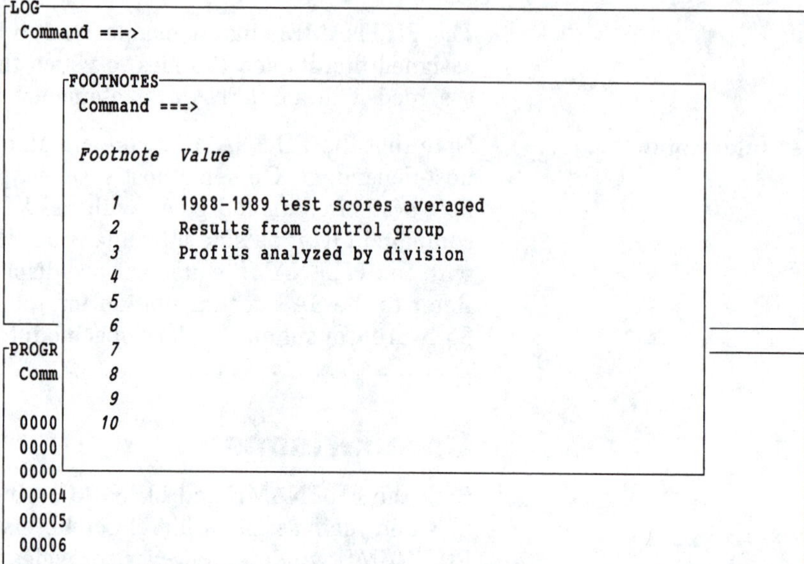

Invocation

FOOTNOTES

Description

Use the FOOTNOTES window to browse, enter, and modify footnotes for SAS procedure output. You can specify up to ten footnotes in the window. To add footnotes to the output produced by SAS procedures, enter the footnote text in the Value field beside the corresponding numbers in the window. Press ENTER or RETURN to submit the footnotes to the SAS System. The footnotes are then added to subsequent output produced during the SAS session. To modify footnotes, type over the text and press ENTER or RETURN to submit the modified footnotes to the SAS System.

Conversely, FOOTNOTE statements can be added to the program statements entered in the PROGRAM EDITOR window. After the program is issued with the SUBMIT or END command, the footnotes appear in the FOOTNOTES window, as well as on the output in the OUTPUT window. Any footnotes submitted to the SAS System in FOOTNOTE statements are added automatically to the FOOTNOTES window when the statements are executed, even if the window is closed or shown as an icon. They override footnotes previously entered either in the FOOTNOTES window or as SAS statements in the PROGRAM EDITOR window, starting with the footnote number being changed and clearing all higher numbered footnotes.

In the FOOTNOTES window, issue the CLEAR command to clear all footnotes. Issue the CANCEL command to close the window and to remove any footnotes added or modifications made since the window was activated.

Comparisons

The FOOTNOTES and TITLES windows function identically, except that one contains footnotes and the other contains titles.

Commands Available

Except as noted, all of the commands in the following categories are available in the FOOTNOTES window:

- □ window-call
- □ window-management (except the PURGE command)
- □ window size and position
- □ color
- □ scrolling
- □ text-store
- □ search (except the CHANGE and RCHANGE commands).

See Also

TITLES window
FOOTNOTE statement in Chapter 9, "SAS Language Statements"

FORM

Specifies the printer, text format, and destination for output

HELP FORM

HELP FSFORM

Display

The FORM window includes six frames, which are sometimes referred to as the FORM window subsystem. The discussion of each frame includes an example display of the frame. The information in your FORM frames may not match the displays shown in the discussions; the information in the frames varies by host system and printer selection. The displays presented in this section show an example of choosing the XEROX® 2700 as a printer selection.

Invocation

FSFORM <*catalog-name.*>*form-name*

Description

The FORM window includes six frames that enable you to create a FORM catalog entry tailored to your host system environment and printer. This entry is used in sending output from various procedures or commands to your printer. Information such as printer margins, printer control language, and font control information can be specified.

Xerox is a registered trademark of Xerox Corporation.

FORM
continued

You can create or edit a form from any display manager window by issuing the FSFORM command and a form name or from any SAS/AF or SAS/FSP window by issuing the EDIT command or the FSFORM command and a form name. Note that although the name of the window is FORM, the invocation of the FORM command is FSFORM.

Specifying *catalog-name* is optional; the default *catalog-name* is SASUSER.PROFILE. If you specify a *catalog-name* that points to a permanent library, your work is saved in that library. The *form-name* can be any name that adheres to SAS catalog naming conventions.

The following list includes names of the FORM window's six frames and the =*n* invocation for each:

Printer Selection

Text Body and Margin Information (=1)

Carriage Control Information (=2)

Print File Parameters (=3)

Font Control Information (=4)

Printer Control Language (=5).

Issue the NEXTSCR command (instead of the FORWARD command) to scroll to the next FORM frame and the PREVSCR command (instead of the BACKWARD command) to return to the previous frame. You can also issue the =*n* command to achieve the same results, where *n* is a number that corresponds with each successive FORM frame. For example, issuing =2 from the command line displays the Carriage Control Information frame. Issue the DES command to display or change the description that appears in the catalog directory.

Note: The Print File Parameters frame is optional. If it is not available, issuing =3 displays the Font Control Information frame, and issuing =4 (or a number greater than 4) displays the Printer Control Language frame.

Refer to Chapter 18 for complete information on the commands that you can use in the FORM frames.

■ **Host Information** ....

Note that the information in the FORM frames varies by host system and printer selection. Refer to the SAS documentation for your host system or see your SAS Software Consultant for details.
.... ■

Printer Selection Frame

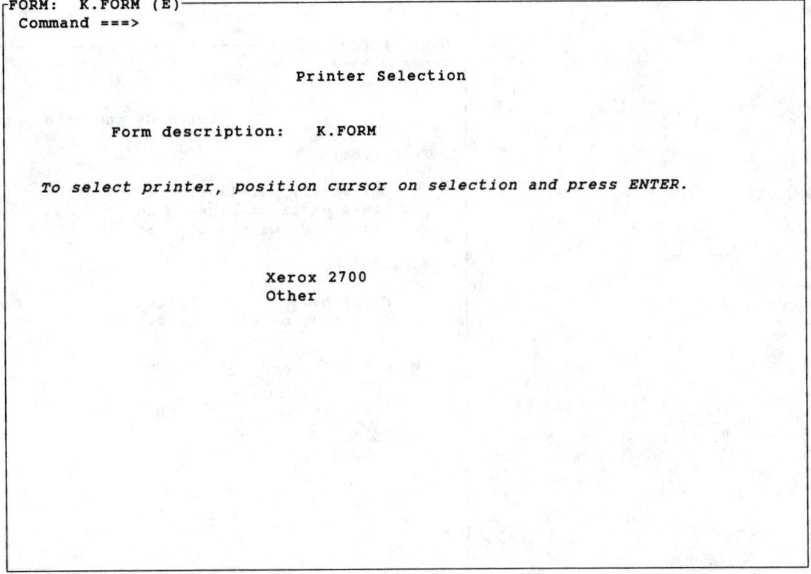

```
FORM:  K.FORM (E)
 Command ===>

                              Printer Selection

         Form description:   K.FORM

   To select printer, position cursor on selection and press ENTER.


                         Xerox 2700
                         Other
```

The Printer Selection frame appears only if you are creating a new form. By default, the Form description field contains the name and type of the entry specified at invocation. You can provide a description of up to 40 characters by typing over the name in the field; specifying a form description here is the equivalent of issuing the DES command. A list of printers is also included in this frame. Move your cursor to the printer you want and press ENTER or RETURN. Your selection takes effect, and the Text Body and Margin Information frame is displayed.

Note: You cannot display any other window from the Printer Selection frame using the =*n* command or the NEXTSCR command.

Once you have made your printer selection, you cannot return to this frame.

FORM

continued

Text Body and Margin Information Frame

```
FORM:  F.FORM (E)
Command ===>

                         Text Body and Margin Information

  Text Body:

      Characters per line:    72
      Lines on first page:    54
       Lines on following:    54

  Margins:

      First page          Left:   0          Top:    0         Bottom:   0
      Following pages     Left:   0          Top:    0         Bottom:   0
```

If you are editing an existing FORM entry, the Text Body and Margin Information frame is the first frame you see when you invoke the FORM window. You can display this frame from another FORM frame by issuing the following command:

=1

The Text Body and Margin Information frame enables you to specify page formats by entering values in the following fields:

Characters per line
: specifies the number of characters to print across the page. Base the value on the horizontal printing area of your paper and the font size.

Lines on first page
: specifies the number of lines to print on the first page. Base the number of lines on the first page on the vertical printing area of your paper and the font size.

Lines on following
: specifies the number of lines to print on each additional page. Base the number of lines on following pages on the vertical printing area of your paper and the font size.

First page
: specifies the left, top, and bottom margins. The number of characters per line determines the right margin. By default, zeros are specified for left, top, and bottom margins, indicating that the printer's default margin positions, or those specified in the Printer Control Language frame, if any, should be used. If you specify a number other than zero, the number you specify is added to the default margin position for the printer.

Following pages
: specifies the left, top, and bottom margins for additional pages. The number of characters per line determines the right margin. By default, zeros are specified for left, top, and bottom margins, indicating that the printer's default margin positions, or those specified in the Printer Control Language frame, if any, should be used. If you specify a number other than zero, the number you specify is added to the default margin position for the printer.

You can receive information on the acceptable values of a field in the Text Body and Margin Information frame by typing a question mark (?) in the field and pressing ENTER.

Carriage Control Information Frame

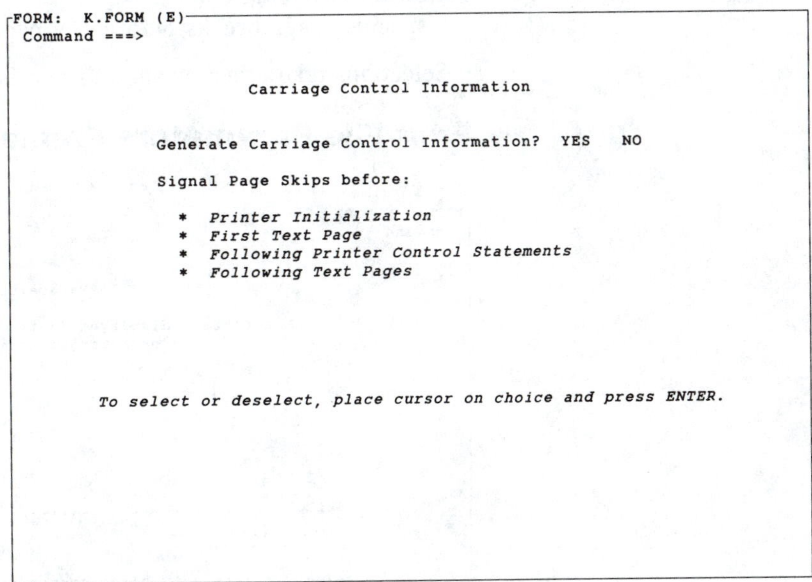

```
FORM:  K.FORM (E)
Command ===>

                    Carriage Control Information

          Generate Carriage Control Information?  YES    NO

          Signal Page Skips before:

             *  Printer Initialization
             *  First Text Page
             *  Following Printer Control Statements
             *  Following Text Pages

      To select or deselect, place cursor on choice and press ENTER.
```

The Carriage Control Information frame enables you to specify whether you want carriage control information included with the output and at which point you want to signal page breaks. You can display this frame from another FORM frame by issuing the following command:

```
=2
```

The Generate Carriage Control Information field enables you to specify whether you want to include information about page breaks. The YES field is the default. If you want to include information about page breaks with the output, keep your cursor on the YES field and press ENTER or RETURN. If you do not want this information included with the output, move your cursor to the NO field and press ENTER or RETURN. In each case, your choice is displayed in reverse video.

The other fields in the Carriage Control Information frame enable you to specify where you want page breaks and other carriage control information. To select a field, place your cursor on any of the available

FORM

continued

options and press ENTER or RETURN. Options are highlighted when selected. The fields are as follows:

Printer Initialization
: initializes the printer. Select this field if you specified the PRINT INIT label in the Printer Control Language frame.

First Text Page
: specifies a page break before the first page is printed.

Following Printer Control Statements
: specifies any other page or print labels after the PRINT INIT label. Select this field if you specified the Page *n*, PAGE LAST, or PRINT TERM label in the Printer Control Language frame.

Following Text Pages
: specifies page breaks before any pages of text following the first page.

Selections take effect as soon as you issue the END command.

Print File Parameters Frame

```
FORM:  K.FORM (E)
Command ===>

                         Print File Parameters

                  Actual text displayed in frame varies by
                              operating system.



             SELECT ..............................


        To select or deselect, place cursor on choice and press ENTER.
```

The Print File Parameters frame enables you to specify print file information based on the target host system. You can display this frame from another FORM frame by issuing the following command:

```
=3
```

You can display HELP information on each field in the Print File Parameters frame by placing your cursor on the field and pressing the function key that is set up as your HELP key.

■ **Host Information** .... Note that the information in the FORM frames varies by host system and printer selection. Refer to the SAS documentation for your host system or see your SAS Software Consultant for details.

For some host systems, a secondary frame is available as a selection from the Print File Parameters frame. A field called SELECT indicates that a secondary frame is available. You can tab to the SELECT field. For example, under the TSO host system there is a selection bar on this frame for IBM 3800 print file parameters. This selection opens a frame called IBM 3800 Print File Parameters. ■

You can receive information on the acceptable values of a field in the Print File Parameters frame by typing a question mark (?) in the field and pressing ENTER.

Font Control Information Frame

```
FORM:  L.FORM (E)
Command ===>

                         Font Control Information

Character   Number   Description        Character   Number   Description

              27     Escape                 ¬        ____    Control
    _        ____    __________             _        ____    __________
    _        ____    __________             _        ____    __________
    _        ____    __________             _        ____    __________

                                                    Scroll down for more
Color       Attribute

WHITE       REVERSE        Start:  2
                            Stop:  1
                            Desc:  Symbol font

________    HIGHLIGHT      Start:  3
                            Stop:  1
                            Desc:  Titan10 bold font

________    ________       Start:  ____________________
                            Stop:  ____________________
                            Desc:  ____________________
```

You can display the Font Control Information frame from another FORM frame by issuing the following command:

```
=4
```

Note: If the Print File Parameters frame is not available, issue the =3 command instead of the =4 command to display the Font Control Information frame.

The attributes defined in the Font Control Information frame are based on the printer you selected in the Printer Selection frame. The top part of the frame has spaces for you to define up to eight special characters that represent printer control characters. These characters are then used in the bottom portion of the frame to define text attributes. Text attributes are special colors and highlighting that you can use in your text to define printing modes. The color and highlighting attributes are associated with the control codes used by your printer for printing in the special mode.

The SAS System supplies some default text attribute definitions with the correct start and stop sequences for each special printing mode supported by printers. You can scroll through the text attribute definitions to verify

FORM

continued

the defaults available for your printer. The following default color and highlighting attributes can appear in the Font Control Information frame, depending on your printer:

Color/Highlighting	Feature
MAGENTA	underline
GREEN/HIGHLIGHT	boldface
WHITE	italics
CYAN	proportional spacing
RED	superscript
YELLOW	subscript

You can change any of these colors to another color or highlighting attribute or to a combination of color and highlighting attributes.

You can receive information on the acceptable values of a field in the Font Control Information frame by typing a question mark (?) in the field and pressing ENTER.

Control character definition In the top portion of the Font Control Information frame, you can define special characters that represent the printer control characters used in the bottom portion of the frame. Printer control characters are special characters that tell the printer that the information following the control character is a printer command. The control character specified is dependent on the printer and host system. Printer commands are not printed. By default, the tilde (~) is defined to represent the ESC key and the caret (^) to represent the CTL key. If your printer uses other characters as control characters, you can define them in this section and refer to them in the bottom portion of the frame.

You can specify up to eight control characters. For each control character you define, you specify the special character, its decimal representation, and a description, as defined in the following:

Character
: specifies the special character you use in the bottom half of this frame to specify a key or function, for example, the tilde (~).

Number
: specifies the decimal representation of the key or character as defined by your printer manual; the number 27 is the decimal representation of the ESC key.

Description
: specifies a description of the key or action.

For example, the Digital LN03 (DEC LN03) printer uses the number 155 to tell the printer to expect a command. You can select a special character, such as # (the pound sign), to represent the number in the start-stop sequence in the bottom half of the frame. It is important to choose a character that is not part of any control sequence your printer uses because the printing routines would translate it according to the information you supply and, thus, alter the printing.

Text attribute definitions The lower portion of the Font Control Information frame lets you associate a color, an attribute, or both to indicate that a printing code is used when the text is printed. You enter your text using the attributes associated with the special features to produce text using the special features available on your printer. The text attributes are defined as follows:

Color
: specifies the color to use in the text to indicate the printing mode.

Attribute
: specifies the attribute to use in the text to indicate the printing mode.

Start
: specifies the control sequence characters required by your printer to turn the printing mode on.

Stop
: specifies the control sequence characters required by your printer to turn the printing mode off.

Desc
: describes the mode you are specifying.

Control sequence characters If your printer supports boldface type you can print boldface by specifying HIGHLIGHT in the Attribute column at the bottom half of the Font Control Information frame. If your printer recognizes the sequence ESC ! to initiate boldface type and the sequence ESC " to terminate boldface, enter ~! in the Start field and ~ " in the Stop field. The description field is for your convenience and serves as documentation when you use the FORM entry. When you want text to print in boldface, enter the information using highlight. The SAS System knows that highlighted text means to print in boldface because you defined that text attribute in the frame.

■ **Host Information** ....

Because printers vary widely in the control language they use, the Font Control Information frame is particularly printer- and site-specific. Refer to your printer manual or see your SAS Software Consultant for details.

.... ■

FORM
continued

Printer Control Language Frame

```
FORM:  L.FORM (E)
Command ===>

00001 PAGE         1
00002 =UDK=  +P
00003  +X
00004 =UDK=  +P
00005  +1Titan10-P
00006  +2SymbolC10-P
00007  +3Titan10B-P
00008  +4Titan10iso-P
00009  +5Titan12iso-P
00010  m660,96,60,96,450
00011  c2
00012  1
00013  i0
00014  o
00015
00016 PAGE         2
00017  c1
00018
00019 PRINT TERM
00020  +X
00021
00022
00023
00024
00025
00026
00027
     *** END OF TEXT ***
```

You can display the Printer Control Language frame from another FORM frame by issuing the following command:

=5

Note: If the Print File Parameters frame is not available, issue the =4 command instead of the =5 command to display the Printer Control Language frame.

The Printer Control Language frame is where you compose control sequences that are sent to the printer. You can use control sequences in the following situations:

□ before text is sent

□ between pages of text

□ after all text is sent.

The Printer Control Language frame is a text editor frame and all of the text editor commands are valid in it. See Chapter 8 for a complete list of the text-editing commands.

Use the Printer Control Language frame to change the paper trays at the default font for a page or perform tasks that you cannot specify on the Font Control Information frame. Your printer manual describes the control language sequences you need. To indicate when to use a control sequence, use the following labels, placing each on a line by itself before the control sequences it sends:

PRINT INIT
: sends the control sequences that follow before sending any text to the print file. These control sequences are sent only once per print file. This enables you to print several items at a time without repeating these control sequences.

PAGE *n*

sends the control sequences that follow before sending the specified page. For example, specifying PAGE 1 sends the control sequences before the first page. The printing routines continue to send the specified control sequences before each following page until a page is reached that references another PAGE label. To stop the control sequences from repeating, specify a PAGE label with no control sequences.

PAGE LAST

sends the control sequences after all text is sent for an individual item.

PRINT TERM

sends the control sequences after all text is sent for all items.

Commands Available

Except as noted, all of the commands in the following categories are available in the FORM window:

- □ window-call
- □ window-management (except the PURGE command)
- □ color
- □ text-store (except the MARK, PCLEAR, and PLIST commands)
- □ window size and position (except the WDEF and WSAVE commands)
- □ scrolling
- □ search (except the CHANGE and RCHANGE commands)
- □ file-management (except the COPY, DELETE, FILE, INCLUDE, PRINT, and SAVE commands)
- □ forms.

See Also

Chapter 8, "SAS Text Editor"

Chapter 18, "SAS Display Manager Commands"

SAS/AF Software: Usage and Reference, Version 6, First Edition

SAS/FSP Software: Usage and Reference, Version 6, First Edition

HELP

Displays help information about the SAS System

HELP

Display

```
HELP: SAS System Help
 Command ===>

    SAS SYSTEM HELP: Main Menu

    DATA MANAGEMENT          REPORT WRITING              GRAPHICS

    TUTORIAL             MODELING & ANALYSIS TOOLS       UTILITIES

    SAS LANGUAGE             SAS GLOBAL COMMANDS         SAS WINDOWS

                             HOST INFORMATION

                                  INDEX
```

Invocation

HELP <*component-name*>

Description

Information about the SAS System is available through the HELP window, which is an online menu-driven facility that contains help information about products and features within the SAS System. Its primary window includes a menu from which you can identify the help category for which you want information. You can use the following approaches to access the HELP window:

- □ Access the primary menu for the HELP window by issuing the HELP command from one of the three primary display manager windows open by default: PROGRAM EDITOR, LOG, and OUTPUT. From that menu, you can request information for SAS software procedures, windows, and other components of SAS software.
- □ Access a specific HELP window that contains information about a particular component of SAS software by issuing the HELP command, followed by the name of the component.*
- □ Directly access a specific HELP window that contains information about a window, other than the PROGRAM EDITOR, LOG, and OUTPUT windows, by issuing the HELP command from that window.

---

* Components of SAS software for which you can obtain help information include procedures, windows, product names, statements, CALL routines, data set options, and SAS system options. For more information on obtaining help for a specific component, see the header block for that component in the appropriate chapter in this book.

The primary window contains the following categories of help information from which you can select specific information:

- □ data management
- □ report writing
- □ graphics
- □ tutorial
- □ modeling and analysis tools
- □ utilities
- □ SAS language
- □ SAS global commands
- □ SAS windows
- □ host information
- □ index.

For each component of the SAS System, the HELP window includes introductory information, complete syntax information, an index, and, if appropriate, additional topics. To select an item in the window, move the cursor to the category you want and press ENTER or RETURN, use a mouse to point and click, or use a key to tab.

Issue the END command to return to the previous window. From the primary menu, the END command closes the HELP window and returns you to the display manager window from which you started. Issue the =X command to exit the HELP window completely and return to the previously active window.

Commands Available

Except as noted, all of the commands in the following categories are available in the HELP window:

- □ window-call
- □ window-management (except the PURGE and ZOOM commands)
- □ color
- □ scrolling (except the BOTTOM, HSCROLL, TOP, and VSCROLL commands)
- □ text-store
- □ help
- □ file-management (only the FORMNAME and PRTFILE commands).

See Also

"SASHELP Library" in Chapter 6, "SAS Files"

KEYS

Enables you to browse, alter, and save function key settings

HELP KEYS

Display

```
┌LOG─────────────────────────────────┌KEYS <DMKEYS>──────────────────────┐
│ Command ===>                       │ Command ===>                      │
│                                    │                                   │
│                                    │ Key       Definition              │
│                                    │                                   │
│                                    │ F1        mark                    │
│                                    │ F2        smark                   │
│                                    │ F3        unmark                  │
│                                    │ F4        cut                     │
│                                    │ F5        paste                   │
│                                    │ F6        store                   │
│                                    │ F7        prevwind                │
│                                    │ F8        next                    │
└────────────────────────────────────│ F9        pmenu                   │
┌PROGRAM EDITOR──────────────────────│ F10       command                 │
│ Command ===>                       │ F11       keys                    │
│                                    │ F12       undo                    │
│ 00001                              │ F13       help                    │
│ 00002                              │ F14       zoom                    │
│ 00003                              │ F15       zoom off; submit        │
│ 00004                              │ F16       pgm; recall             │
│ 00005                              │ F17       rfind                   │
│ 00006                              │ F18       rchange                 │
└────────────────────────────────────└───────────────────────────────────┘
```

Invocation

KEYS

Description

To issue a command, you can use the PMENU facility, enter a command on the command line, or use function keys. Using function keys is the most efficient method if you know what each key is defined to do. The KEYS window displays function keys and their definitions.

■ **Host Information** .... Key names vary by host system and terminal. For example, in some cases function keys are numbered and in others they are not. Refer to the SAS documentation for your host system or see your SAS Software Consultant for details. ■

You can do the following in the KEYS window:

- □ browse the contents of the window without making changes
- □ change and save the key definitions.

To change a key setting, type over the definition. The new definition takes effect immediately. Issue the CANCEL command to cancel the changes and the SAVE or END command to save any changes you have made to the current key settings. The CANCEL, END, and SAVE commands affect the key settings in the current SAS session of the KEYS window and when stored in a catalog entry as follows:

- □ The END command permanently saves the key settings, both in the current session of the KEYS window and to the entry in your default catalog.
- □ The CANCEL command reinstates the key settings in the current session of the KEYS window, reversing any changes made since the most recent execution of the END command. The CANCEL command leaves the entry in the default catalog unaltered.
- □ The SAVE command permanently saves the current key settings to the entry in the default catalog. However, the key settings in the current session of the KEYS window are subject to cancellation by the CANCEL command.

Issue the COPY command to copy a previously created set of function keys into the KEYS window. Issue the PURGE command to remove key definitions not shared among devices.

▶ ***Caution:*** *The COPY command with no argument specified restores the previous settings.*

Issuing the COPY command without specifying a name cancels any changes you have made in the window and copies into the window the definitions previously stored in your default catalog.

In addition to defining a function key to issue a SAS command, you can define a function key as a text string; then you can insert that text string by positioning the cursor where you want it to appear and pressing the function key. When you define a function key to insert a text string, precede the string with a tilde (~). The tilde must appear in the first column of the key definition field. Then, position the cursor on a line where you can enter data and press the function key you defined to insert this line of text where you want it to appear. Note that the tilde is not inserted with the text string.

The KEYDEF command enables you to change function key settings temporarily. You can also use this command in conjunction with the KEYS window to change key settings permanently. After you have issued the KEYDEF command from any window, you can use one of two ways to save the temporary settings:

- □ Invoke the KEYS window, make a change in it, and issue the END command.
- □ Invoke the KEYS window and issue the SAVE command.

A requestor window appears asking you whether you want to save the settings permanently. If you type N, the temporary key settings are returned to the previous settings after you end your SAS session. If you type Y, the key settings are permanently redefined after you end your SAS session.

KEYS

continued

Commands Available

Except as noted, all of the commands in the following categories are available in the KEYS window:

□ window-call

□ window-management

□ window size and position

□ color

□ text-store

□ scrolling

□ search

□ file-management (only the COPY and SAVE commands).

The following commands have special meaning in the KEYS window:

COPY
: copies one catalog entry to another catalog entry. The syntax and behavior differ from the COPY command as documented in Chapter 18. In the KEYS window, the syntax of the COPY command is

COPY <*catalog-entry*>

where *catalog-entry* can be a one-, two-, three-, or four-level name. The complete specification is *libref.catalog.name.type*. In the KEYS window only, the COPY command works differently in two ways. First, the entry must have a type of KEYS. Second, the arguments ATTR, TABS, REPLACE, and APPEND are not valid.

SAVE
: saves the contents of the window to a catalog entry. The syntax and behavior differ from the SAVE command as documented in Chapter 18. In the KEYS window, the syntax of the SAVE command is

SAVE <*catalog-entry*>

where *catalog-entry* can be a one-, two-, three-, or four-level name. The complete specification is *libref.catalog.name.type*. In the KEYS window only, the SAVE command works differently in two ways. First, the entry must have a type of KEYS. Second, the arguments ATTR, TABS, REPLACE, and APPEND are not valid.

See Also

COPY, KEYDEF, and SAVE commands in Chapter 18, "SAS Display Manager Commands"

LIBNAME

Displays assigned librefs and their SAS data libraries and engines

HELP LIBNAME

Display

```
┌LOG──────────────────┐┌LIBNAME──────────────────────────────────────────────────┐
│ Command ===>        ││ Command ===>                                            │
│                     ││                                                         │
│                     ││      Libref    Engine    Host Path Name                 │
│                     ││                                                         │
│                     ││    _ S         V606      System-specific name           │
│                     ││    _ SASHELP   V606      System-specific name           │
│                     ││    _ SASUSER   V606      System-specific name           │
│                     ││    _ WORK      V606      System-specific name           │
│                     ││                                                         │
┌PROGRAM EDITOR───────┐│                                                         │
│ Command ===>        ││                                                         │
│                     ││                                                         │
│ 00001               ││                                                         │
│ 00002               ││                                                         │
│ 00003               ││                                                         │
│ 00004               ││                                                         │
│ 00005               ││                                                         │
│ 00006               ││                                                         │
└─────────────────────┘└─────────────────────────────────────────────────────────┘
```

Invocation

LIBNAME

Description

The LIBNAME window displays a listing of currently assigned librefs, the I/O engines, and the names of the SAS data libraries to which they are assigned. The alias for invoking the LIBNAME window is LIB. From the LIBNAME window, you can do one of the following:

- □ browse the current listing without making a selection
- □ select a libref, so you can browse or manipulate the corresponding SAS files in the DIR window.

Librefs are assigned in a LIBNAME statement.

■ **Host Information** ....

Note that the LIBNAME statement and the assignment of a libref are host-dependent. On some host systems, you can assign librefs either with a host system command issued with the X statement or a host system command issued outside of a SAS session. However, only librefs assigned with the LIBNAME statement are displayed in the LIBNAME window. Refer to the SAS documentation for your host system or see your SAS Software Consultant for host-specific information.

.... ■

To select a libref, type the selection-field command X or S in the selection field adjacent to the libref, and press ENTER or RETURN. The DIR window for that SAS data library appears. From the DIR window, you can browse or manipulate the files contained in the SAS data library. Multiple selections at one time are allowed. The DIR window appears for each file selected in the order you issue selection-field commands. The

LIBNAME

continued

END command continues to activate the next DIR window until the cursor is returned to the LIBNAME window.

Comparisons

Both the LIBNAME and FILENAME windows list the names of the host files and their assigned librefs or filerefs for the files or groups of files. The LIBNAME window, however, provides information for SAS data libraries, while the FILENAME window provides information for external files. For further comparison, see the documentation for the LIBNAME and FILENAME statements in Chapter 9.

Commands Available

Except as noted, all of the commands in the following categories are available in the LIBNAME window:

- □ window-call
- □ window-management (except the PURGE command)
- □ window size and position
- □ color
- □ scrolling
- □ text-store
- □ search (except the CHANGE and RCHANGE commands).

See Also

DIR, FILENAME, and VAR windows

LIBNAME and FILENAME statements in Chapter 9, "SAS Language Statements"

LOG

Displays messages and SAS statements for the current SAS session

HELP LOG

Display

```
LOG
Command ===>

NOTE: Copyright(c) 1985,1986,1987,1988 SAS Institute Inc., Cary, NC USA.
NOTE: SAS (r) Proprietary Software Release 6.xx
      Licensed to SAS Institute Inc., Site xxxxxxxx
```

```
PROGRAM EDITOR
Command ===>

00001
00002
00003
00004
00005
00006
```

Invocation

LOG

Description

The LOG window is one of the four primary windows. The other primary windows are the PROGRAM EDITOR, OUTPUT, and OUTPUT MANAGER windows. Like the PROGRAM EDITOR window, the LOG window is open by default and cannot be closed. It is a record of your SAS session and is helpful for debugging. When you submit SAS statements from the PROGRAM EDITOR window, the SAS log is displayed in the LOG window. The log contains all of the SAS statements submitted, as well as any notes and messages about your session. You can use various SAS system options to suppress as much or as little of your log as you choose. For more information, see Chapter 3, Chapter 5, and Chapter 16.

The default line size of the LOG window is the current terminal width, excluding the borders, unless you specify a different line size at invocation or in a configuration file. The LOG window clears itself after it contains as many lines as the maximum size of an integer on your host system, up to 99,999 lines. However, before the LOG window is cleared, the SAS System first prompts you to route a copy of the contents to a file, a catalog, or a printer.

After you browse the SAS log, you can issue the FILE command to route a copy of its contents to an external file or the SAVE command to route a copy of its contents to a catalog entry. Issue the PRINT command to print the contents of the LOG window to a print file or to a printer through the FORM subsystem. Issue the CLEAR command to clear the

LOG

continued

window. You can clear the contents of the LOG window from within that window by issuing the following command:

```
clear
```

You can clear the contents of the LOG window from another window by issuing the following command:

```
clear log
```

Commands Available

Except as noted, all of the commands in the following categories are available in the LOG window:

□ window-call

□ window-management (except the CANCEL and PURGE commands)

□ window size and position

□ color

□ scrolling

□ text-store

□ search (except the CHANGE and RCHANGE commands)

□ output (except the PAGE and PAGESIZE commands)

□ file-management (except the COPY, DELETE and INCLUDE commands)

□ text-editing (except the AUTOWRAP, BOUNDS, CAPS, CURSOR, DICT, and SPELL commands).

The AUTOSCROLL command has limited scope in the LOG window, where it can only take a numeric argument.

See Also

OUTPUT, OUTPUT MANAGER, and PROGRAM EDITOR windows

Chapter 3, "Components of the SAS Language"

Chapter 5, "SAS Output"

Chapter 16, "SAS System Options"

NOTEPAD

Creates and stores notepads of text

HELP NOTEPAD

Display

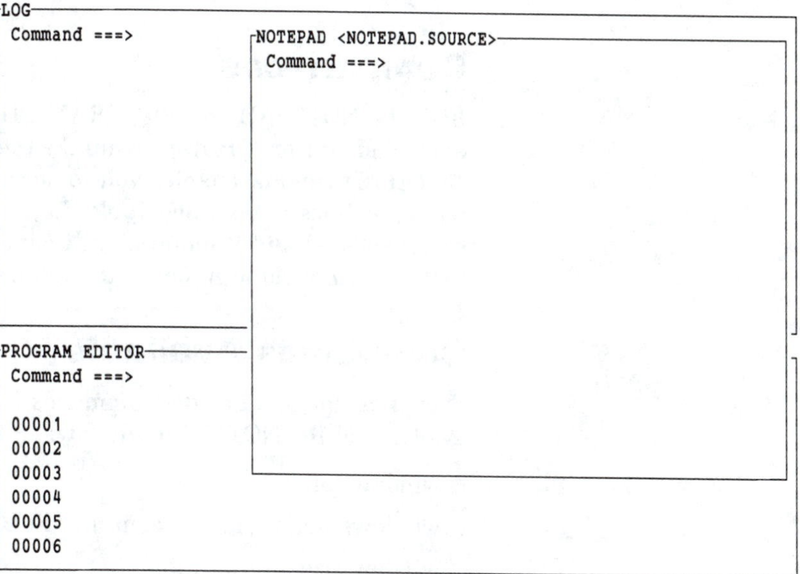

Invocation

NOTEPAD <*catalog-entry*>

Description

The NOTEPAD window is a full-screen editor for entering and altering text and for saving information from session to session. The NOTEPAD window also provides extended color and highlighting attributes that enable you to accent individual letters, words, or complete lines or blocks of text.

When you invoke the NOTEPAD window, the default notepad is displayed unless you specify a particular notepad. You can also specify notepads of types LOG and OUTPUT. Enter text with text-editing commands, as you do in the PROGRAM EDITOR window.

Issue the SAVE command to store the contents of the window in a catalog. Issue the COPY command to append the contents of a stored notepad into the NOTEPAD window. Issuing the SAVE or COPY command with no argument specified stores or copies the contents in the catalog entry most recently specified in a COPY or SAVE command. If neither command has been issued yet, the default is the origin of the notepad. Issuing the SAVE or COPY command with one- or two-level names stores or copies the contents in your SASUSER.PROFILE catalog; specifying a three-level name stores or copies the contents in the specified catalog with the libref of SASUSER.

Issue the DELETE command to delete a stored notepad, the DESCRIPTION command to add a description to catalog entries when they have been saved with the SAVE or END command, and the NTITLE command to change the window's title. As in the PROGRAM EDITOR window, issue the FILE command to route a copy of the contents of the NOTEPAD window to an external file and the INCLUDE command to copy

NOTEPAD

continued

the contents of an external file into the NOTEPAD window. You can specify the ATTR argument to store color and highlighting attributes. Issue the PRINT command to print the contents of the NOTEPAD window to a print file or to a printer through the FORM subsystem.

Comparisons

Both the NOTEPAD and PROGRAM EDITOR windows can be used to enter and edit text. However, unlike the PROGRAM EDITOR window, the NOTEPAD window enables you to accent individual letters, words, and blocks or lines of text. See Table 7.3, "Display Manager Commands—Valid Windows," in Chapter 7 for details on where the COLOR command arguments are valid.

Commands Available

Except as noted, all of the commands in the following categories are available in the NOTEPAD window:

- □ window-call
- □ window-management (except the PURGE command)
- □ window size and position
- □ color
- □ scrolling
- □ text cut-and-paste
- □ text-store
- □ search
- □ file-management
- □ text-editing
- □ notepad.

See Also

PROGRAM EDITOR window
Chapter 7, "SAS Display Manager System"

OPTIONS

Enables you to view and change some SAS system options

HELP OPTIONS

Display

```
LOG
 Command ===>
```

```
PROGRAM EDITOR
 Command ===>

 00001
 00002
 00003
 00004
 00005
 00006
```

```
OPTIONS
 Command ===>

 Option            Value

 BUFNO             3
 BUFSIZE           0
 CAPS              OFF
 CARDIMAGE         ON
 CENTER            ON
 CHARCODE          OFF
 CLEANUP           OFF
 COMPRESS          NO
 DATE              ON
 DBCS              OFF
 DEVICE
 DSNFERR           ON
 ERRORABEND        OFF
 ERRORS            20
 FIRSTOBS          1
 FMTERR            ON
 FORMCHAR          |----|+|---+=|-/\<>*
 FORMDLIM
```

Invocation

OPTIONS

Description

You can use the OPTIONS window to

□ browse the current settings of SAS system options you may want to change during your SAS session. (Note that some options can be changed only when you invoke the SAS System. These are not listed in the OPTIONS window.)

□ alter settings for the options shown in the OPTIONS window.

The Option column lists the SAS system options in alphabetic order. The Value column lists the current setting for each system option. To change an option setting, type over the value in the Value column. Use the values ON and OFF to change the value of positive and negative options.

Changes to option values take effect when you press ENTER or RETURN. You do not need to exit the OPTIONS window for the new settings to take effect. The settings remain in effect throughout your current SAS session unless you change them. Issue the CANCEL command to close the window and to return to the previous settings any settings changed since the window was activated.

If the OPTIONS window is open and you reset a system option with the OPTIONS statement, the new setting is displayed automatically in the OPTIONS window.

OPTIONS

continued

Comparisons

The OPTIONS window combines the functions of the OPTIONS procedure, which lists current option values, and the OPTIONS statement, which alters system option values. Unlike the OPTIONS statement, in which the option name is sometimes followed by an equal sign and the value, the OPTIONS window displays the option's setting in the Value column; the value can be ON, OFF, or another value. These values can be typed over to change their settings.

■ **Host Information** .... Note that the OPTIONS window does not include host options, while the OPTIONS procedure lists host options and the OPTIONS statement enables you to change their settings. Refer to the SAS documentation for your host system or see your SAS Software Consultant for details. ■

Commands Available

Except as noted, all of the commands in the following categories are available in the OPTIONS window:

- window-call
- window-management (except the PURGE command)
- window size and position
- color
- scrolling
- text-store
- search (except the CHANGE and RCHANGE commands).

See Also

OPTIONS statement in Chapter 9, "SAS Language Statements"

Chapter 16, "SAS System Options"

Chapter 22, "The OPTIONS Procedure," in *SAS Procedures Guide, Version 6, Third Edition*

OUTPUT

Displays procedure output

HELP OUTPUT

Display

```
OUTPUT
 Command ===>

                              According to Variable X by Groups                         1

 ----------------------------------- X=1 ------------------------------------

                                           OBS     Y     Z

                                             1     1     1
                                             2     1     2
                                                         -
                                             X           3

 ----------------------------------- X=2 ------------------------------------

                                           OBS     Y     Z

                                             3     1     1
                                             4     1     2
                                                         -
                                             X           3
```

Invocation

LISTING

Description

The OUTPUT, or LISTING, window is one of the four primary windows. The other primary windows are the PROGRAM EDITOR, LOG, and OUTPUT MANAGER windows. Like the PROGRAM EDITOR and LOG windows, the OUTPUT window is open by default. Unlike them, it can be closed. When you execute procedures from the PROGRAM EDITOR window, most of the output generated appears in the OUTPUT window, unless directed elsewhere. All output within a SAS session is saved by default and can be viewed by scrolling the contents of the OUTPUT window. The alias for invoking the OUTPUT window is LST.

After you browse the OUTPUT window, you can issue the FILE command to route a copy of its contents, including or excluding the attributes, to an external file. Alternatively, you can issue the SAVE command to route a copy of its contents to a catalog entry. Issue the PRINT command to print your output to a print file or to a printer through the FORM subsystem. You can clear the contents of the OUTPUT window from within the OUTPUT window by issuing the following command:

```
clear
```

You can clear the contents of the OUTPUT window from another window by issuing the following command:

```
clear output
```

See the documentation for the OUTPUT MANAGER window to determine how to clear, save, file, and print selected parts of the OUTPUT window.

OUTPUT

continued

Unless you specify a different line size and page size at invocation or in a configuration file, the OUTPUT window's default line size is the current terminal width and its default page size is the current terminal height, excluding the borders. The OUTPUT window clears itself after it contains as many lines as the maximum size of an integer on your host system, up to 99,999 lines. However, before the OUTPUT window is cleared, the SAS System first prompts you through a requestor window to save the contents to a file, a catalog entry, or a printer.

The OUTPUT window works with the OUTPUT MANAGER window. For example, when you add output to the OUTPUT window, that output is listed in the OUTPUT MANAGER window; when you clear the OUTPUT window, the OUTPUT MANAGER window is cleared also.

Either the OUTPUT window or the OUTPUT MANAGER window must be open. You can open the OUTPUT window, the OUTPUT MANAGER window, or both. Note that closing one of the two windows automatically opens the other window if it is not already open. By default, the OUTPUT window is open, but you can close it by issuing the following command:

```
listing off
```

Reopen the OUTPUT window by specifying the following command:

```
listing on
```

Commands Available

Except as noted, all of the commands in the following categories are available in the OUTPUT window:

- □ window-call
- □ window-management (except the PURGE command)
- □ window size and position
- □ color
- □ scrolling
- □ text-store
- □ search (except the CHANGE and RCHANGE commands)
- □ file-management (except the COPY, DELETE, and INCLUDE commands)
- □ output
- □ text-editing (except the AUTOWRAP, BOUNDS, CAPS, CURSOR, DICT, and SPELL commands).

See Also

LOG, OUTPUT MANAGER, and PROGRAM EDITOR windows

Chapter 5, "SAS Output"

OUTPUT MANAGER

Provides a directory of current output

HELP MANAGER

Display

```
OUTPUT MANAGER
 Command ===>

     Procedure  Page#   Pages          Description

   _ PRINT         1       1           Revenue and Expense Totals
   _ PRINT         2       1           Branch Headcount, Sales and Expenses
   _ CONTENTS      3       2           The CONTENTS Procedure
   _ PRINT         5       1           Department Sales for 1988
   _ CONTENTS      6       2           PROC CONTENTS with the NOSOURCE Option
```

Invocation

MANAGER

Description

The OUTPUT MANAGER window is one of the four primary windows. The other primary windows are the PROGRAM EDITOR, LOG, and OUTPUT windows. Unlike the other three primary windows, the OUTPUT MANAGER window is closed by default. It provides a listing of output currently displayed in the OUTPUT window. The alias for invoking the OUTPUT MANAGER window is MGR.

For each piece of procedure output, the OUTPUT MANAGER window specifies the following:

- □ the name of the procedure that created it
- □ the order in which it falls, compared to other output in the OUTPUT window
- □ the beginning page number
- □ its length in pages
- □ a description, using the first 40 characters of any titles specified. If no title is specified, the default title (The SAS System) is used.
- □ a modification to the output, if one has been made in the EDIT window.

The OUTPUT MANAGER window works with the OUTPUT window. For example, when you add output to the OUTPUT window, that output is listed in the OUTPUT MANAGER window; when you clear the OUTPUT window, the OUTPUT MANAGER window is cleared also.

OUTPUT MANAGER

continued

Either the OUTPUT window or the OUTPUT MANAGER window must be open. You can open the OUTPUT window, the OUTPUT MANAGER window, or both. Note that closing one of the two windows automatically opens the other window if it is not already open. By default, the OUTPUT window is open and the OUTPUT MANAGER window is closed. Open the OUTPUT MANAGER window by issuing the following command:

```
manager on
```

Issue the following command to close the OUTPUT MANAGER window:

```
manager off
```

You can browse and manipulate pieces of output with the selection-field commands listed below. Move the cursor to the selection field adjacent to the output you want, type a command letter, and press ENTER or RETURN.

B
: brings up a browse window, which enables you to browse the selected output.

C
: cancels any pending R (rename) or D (delete) command.

D
: deletes the output listing in the OUTPUT MANAGER window and the output in the OUTPUT window.

E
: brings up an EDIT window that enables you to make changes to a given piece of output. On the command line of the EDIT window, issue the END command to save and store in the OUTPUT window any changes made in the EDIT window. Issue the CANCEL command if you do not want to store in the OUTPUT window changes made since the invocation or last execution of the RENAME command. Issue the REPLACE command to save and store the changes in the OUTPUT window while continuing to use the EDIT window.

  You can issue the FILE command to route a copy of the contents of the EDIT window to an external file and the SAVE command to route a copy of its contents to a catalog entry. Use the INCLUDE command to copy the contents of an external file into the window and the COPY command to copy the contents of a catalog entry into the window. Issue the PRINT command to print the EDIT window's contents to a print file or to any printer through the FORM subsystem. Issue the CLEAR command to clear the contents of the EDIT window. You can use all of the text-editing commands in the EDIT window.

F
: saves a copy of the output to a file. A dialog box appears and prompts you to supply a filename. You can specify either a fileref or an external file. The fileref must have been associated with an external file in a FILENAME statement or in an appropriate host command. The external file identifies the file by its physical name. The physical name is the name by which the host system recognizes the file. The name must be enclosed in quotes. In the dialog box, you can select the REPLACE, APPEND, ATTRS, and TABS arguments. Issue the END command to complete the filing operation and the CANCEL command to cancel it.

P prints the output. As with the F selection-field command, a dialog box appears and prompts you to supply a filename and form name. Follow the same procedure as described for the F selection-field command to specify a filename. You can specify a fileref or an external file. If you do not specify a filename, your output is sent to the default printer at your site. Note that you can select the REPLACE and APPEND arguments if you direct your output to a file. Issue the END command to complete the printing operation and the CANCEL command to cancel the operation.

R renames the output's description in the OUTPUT MANAGER window only.

O saves the output to a catalog entry of OUTPUT, which can then be viewed in the NOTEPAD window. A dialog box appears and prompts you to supply a catalog entry name. You can select the REPLACE, APPEND, ATTRS, and TABS arguments. Issue the END command to complete the operation and the CANCEL command to cancel it.

V verifies a D (delete) command.

S | X switches to the OUTPUT window and forces the OUTPUT window to scroll to the output specified.

Multiple selection-field commands can be selected and issued simultaneously in the OUTPUT MANAGER window.

Commands Available

Except as noted, all of the commands in the following categories are available in the OUTPUT MANAGER window:

- window-call
- window-management (except the CANCEL and PURGE commands)
- window size and position
- color
- file-management (the FREE command only)
- scrolling
- search (except the CHANGE and RCHANGE commands)
- text-store.

Note that in the OUTPUT MANAGER's EDIT window, which is invoked by the selection-field command E, most of the commands valid in the NOTEPAD window are valid. In the OUTPUT MANAGER's BROWSE window, which is invoked by the selection-field command B, most of the commands valid in the NOTEPAD window are also valid. For details, see Table 7.3 in Chapter 7.

OUTPUT MANAGER

continued

See Also

LOG, NOTEPAD, OUTPUT, and PROGRAM EDITOR windows

Chapter 5, "SAS Output"

PROGRAM EDITOR

Enables you to enter, edit, and submit SAS statements and to save source files

HELP PROGRAM

Display

```
LOG
 Command ===>


PROGRAM EDITOR
 Command ===>

 00001
 00002
 00003
 00004
 00005
 00006
```

Invocation

PROGRAM

Description

The PROGRAM EDITOR window is one of the four primary windows. The other primary windows are the LOG, OUTPUT, and OUTPUT MANAGER windows. Like the LOG window, the PROGRAM EDITOR window is open by default and cannot be closed. The alias for invoking the PROGRAM EDITOR window is PGM. You can use the PROGRAM EDITOR window to enter and edit text, including program statements; to submit program statements to the SAS System for execution; and to save and recall source files.

After you have entered and edited your program, issue the SUBMIT command to submit your job to the SAS System. Issue the FILE command to route a copy of the window's contents to an external file or the SAVE command to route a copy to a catalog entry. Issue the INCLUDE command to copy the contents of an external file into the PROGRAM

EDITOR window or the COPY command to copy a catalog entry into the window. Issue the PRINT command to print the contents of the PROGRAM EDITOR window to a print file or to a printer through the FORM subsystem. Issue the CLEAR command to clear the window. You can clear the contents of the PROGRAM EDITOR window from within the PROGRAM EDITOR window by issuing the following command:

```
clear
```

You can clear the contents of the PROGRAM EDITOR window from another window by issuing the following command:

```
clear program
```

Note that you can use all of the text-editing commands in the PROGRAM EDITOR window. See Chapter 18 and Chapter 19 for complete information on commands.

Commands Available

Except as noted, all of the commands in the following categories are available in the PROGRAM EDITOR window:

□ window-call

□ window-management (except the CANCEL and PURGE commands)

□ window size and position

□ color

□ scrolling

□ text cut-and-paste

□ text-store

□ search

□ file-management (except the DELETE command)

□ program

□ text-editing.

See Also

LOG window

OUTPUT window

OUTPUT MANAGER window

SETINIT

Displays licensed SAS software and expiration dates

HELP SETINIT

Display

The SETINIT window includes five windows. See the discussions of each window for a display of that window.

Invocation

SETINIT

Description

Use the SETINIT window to display or alter site licensing information. Note that the SETINIT procedure also enables you to alter your site licensing information. If you invoke the SETINIT window from within display manager, you can browse the SETINIT window.

The SITEVAL Window

```
SETINIT-SITEVAL
 Command ===>



  SAS System Version: 6.06
  Operating System:   your operating system
  Site Name:          your site name
  Site Number:        your site number
  Expiration Date:    your expiration date
  System Birthdate:   your SAS System birthdate
  Grace Period:       your grace period
  Warning Period:     your warning period
  Password:
```

The SITEVAL window is the first of five windows displayed when you invoke the SETINIT command. The other windows are CPU, PROD, SEC, and REQUIRED. You activate each window by specifying its name, issuing the NEXT command, or issuing the PREVWIND command.

The SITEVAL window contains information pertinent to site licensing of SAS software. This window includes the following fields:

- □ SAS System Version, which indicates the version of the SAS System that is running
- □ Operating System, which indicates the licensed host system
- □ Site Name (also on the log)
- □ Site Number (also on the log)
- □ Expiration Date

- SAS System Birthdate
- Grace Period, which indicates how long after expiration the product runs before a warning message is issued
- Warning Period, which indicates how long after the grace period the product runs with warnings. After the warnings, the product does not run at all
- Password, which is not used by users when browsing.

The CPU Window

```
SETINIT-CPU
 Command ===>


        Model Name            Model Number           CPU Serial        E
 A  ______________      ______________      ______________     _
 B  ______________      ______________      ______________
 C  ______________      ______________      ______________
 D  ______________      ______________      ______________
 E  ______________      ______________      ______________
 F  ______________      ______________      ______________
 G  ______________      ______________      ______________
 H  ______________      ______________      ______________
 I  ______________      ______________      ______________
 U  ______________      ______________      ______________
 J  ______________      ______________      ______________
 K  ______________      ______________      ______________
 L  ______________      ______________      ______________
 M  ______________      ______________      ______________
 N  ______________      ______________      ______________
 O  ______________      ______________      ______________
```

The CPU window enables up to 16 CPUs to be licensed. Fields include Model Name, Model Number, and CPU Serial. You can edit all fields, but you cannot skip lines to add more CPUs.

SETINIT

continued

The PROD Window

```
SETINIT-PROD
 Command ===>

                         CPU:              A
                         Model Name:       your CPU model name
                         Model Number:     your CPU model number
                         CPU Serial:       your CPU serial number

                         Expiration Date: 31DEC99

                                           --------------CPU--------------
             Product            ExpDate    A . . . . . . . . . . . . . . .
           1 SAS/BASE                 *    *
           2 SAS/STAT                 *    *
           3 SAS/GRAPH                *    *
           4 SAS/ETS                  *    *
           5 SAS/FSP                  *    *
           6 SAS/OR                   *    *
           7 SAS/AF                   *    *
           8 SAS/IML                  *    *
           9 SAS/QC                   *    *
          10 SAS/PUBLISH              *    *
```

The PROD window lists expiration dates for any product and CPU. You can browse or update fields in the PROD window.

The SEC Window

```
SETINIT-SEC
 Command ===>

  SECONDARY SETINIT INFORMATION

  The following code is needed to allow changes to any of the fields below.

  SITE REPRESENTATIVE CODE:

  The identification below will be displayed on the SAS log.

  USER IDENTIFICATION:


  The information below is displayed only on this screen.

  FURTHER INFORMATION:
```

The SEC window contains secondary, optional SETINIT information. This window is typically used only when a site is running multiple copies of the SAS System, such as on microcomputers. Your SAS Site Representative can identify your copy of the SAS System with this window. If so, pertinent information is shown in the USER

IDENTIFICATION fields. If these fields are complete, the information is displayed in the SAS log. The representative can choose to enter contact information in the FURTHER INFORMATION fields. This information is contained only in the SEC window. The SITE REPRESENTATIVE CODE field is completed by the representative when initializing your copy of the SAS System. None of the information in this window can be changed without this code.

The REQUIRED Window

```
SETINIT-REQUIRED
 Command ===>


                    REQUIRED SCREEN TEXT ENTRY PANEL


   ________________________________________________________________
   ________________________________________________________________
   ________________________________________________________________
   ________________________________________________________________
   ________________________________________________________________
   ________________________________________________________________
   ________________________________________________________________
   ________________________________________________________________
   ________________________________________________________________
   ________________________________________________________________
   ________________________________________________________________
```

The REQUIRED window contains text that is displayed when the SAS System is initialized (after the SAS command is issued). The text, if any, is provided by SAS Institute before product shipment. It cannot be altered or deleted by any user, including the SAS Site Representative.

Commands Available

Except as noted, all of the commands in the following categories are available in the SETINIT window:

- □ window-call
- □ window-management (except the CANCEL, CLEAR, and PURGE commands)
- □ window size and position
- □ color
- □ scrolling (except the *n* command)
- □ file-management (except the COPY, DELETE, FILE, FORMNAME, FREE, INCLUDE, PRINT, and PRTFILE commands)
- □ text-store.

SETINIT

continued

See Also

LOG and SITEINFO windows

Chapter 16, "SAS System Options"

SITEINFO

Contains site-specific information

HELP SITEINFO

Display

```
SITEINFO
 Command ===>

            The text displayed in this window depends on

          the information your SAS Site Representative enters.
```

Invocation

SITEINFO

Description

The SITEINFO window contains free-form information about a given site, including the name of its SAS Site Representative. The alias for invoking the SITEINFO window is SITE. The window remains blank until the SAS Site Representative enters information. The SITEINFO command uses information from the SITEINFO= option. The SITEINFO= option refers to a filename whose contents are displayed in the window.

■ **Host Information** ....

The contents of the SITEINFO window vary by site and host system. Refer to the SAS documentation for your host system or see your SAS Software Consultant or SAS Site Representative for details.
■

Comparisons

Both the SITEINFO and SETINIT windows provide information about a given site. However, the information in the SITEINFO window is free-form, while the SETINIT window contains standard fields that provide specific types of information.

Commands Available

- □ window-call
- □ window-management (except the CANCEL, CLEAR, and PURGE commands)
- □ scrolling (except the *n* command)
- □ window size and position
- □ color
- □ text-store.

See Also

SETINIT window

SITEINFO= option in Chapter 16, "SAS System Options"

TITLES

Enables you to browse, enter, and modify titles for output

HELP TITLES

Display

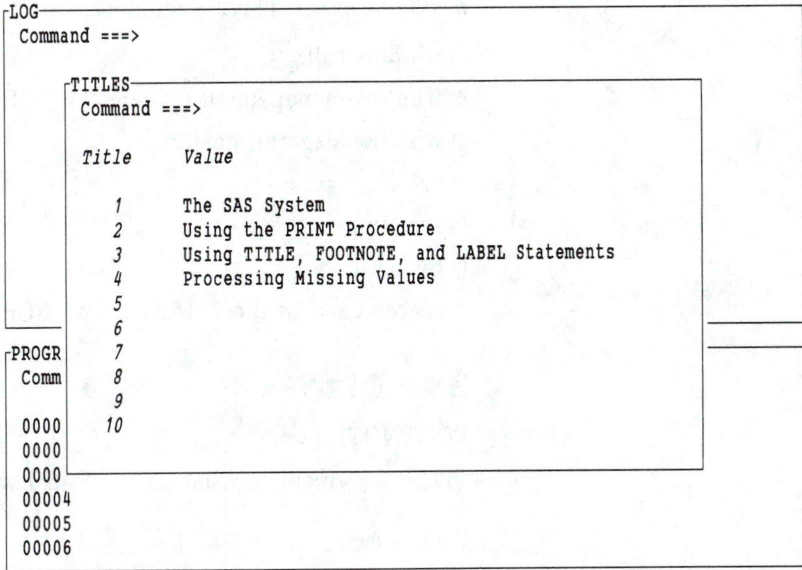
```
LOG
Command ===>

    TITLES
    Command ===>

    Title     Value

       1      The SAS System
       2      Using the PRINT Procedure
       3      Using TITLE, FOOTNOTE, and LABEL Statements
       4      Processing Missing Values
       5
       6
PROGR  7
Comm   8
       9
0000  10
0000
0000
00004
00005
00006
```

Invocation

TITLES

TITLES

continued

Description

Use the TITLES window to browse, enter, and modify titles for SAS procedure output. You can specify up to ten titles in the window. To add titles to the output produced by SAS procedures, enter the title text in the Value field beside the corresponding numbers in the window. Press ENTER or RETURN to submit the title to the SAS System. The titles are then added to subsequent output produced during the SAS session. To modify titles, type over the text and press ENTER or RETURN to submit the modified titles to the SAS System.

Conversely, TITLE statements can be added to the program statements in the PROGRAM EDITOR window. After the program is issued with the SUBMIT or END command, the titles appear in the TITLES window, as well as on the output in the OUTPUT window and in the description in the OUTPUT MANAGER window. Any titles submitted to the SAS System in TITLE statements are added automatically to the TITLES window when the statements are executed, even if the window is closed or shown as an icon. They override titles previously entered either in the TITLES window or as SAS statements in the PROGRAM EDITOR window, starting with the title number being changed and clearing all higher numbered titles.

In the TITLES window, issue the CLEAR command to clear all titles. Issue the CANCEL command to close the window and to remove any titles added or modifications made since the window was activated.

Comparisons

The TITLES and FOOTNOTES windows function identically, except that one contains footnotes and the other contains titles.

Commands Available

Except as noted, all of the commands in the following categories are available in the TITLES window:

□ window-call

□ window-management (except the PURGE command)

□ window size and position

□ color

□ scrolling

□ text-store

□ search (except the CHANGE and RCHANGE commands).

See Also

FOOTNOTES window

TITLE statement in Chapter 9, "SAS Language Statements"

VAR

Displays information about SAS data set variables and their attributes

HELP VAR

Display

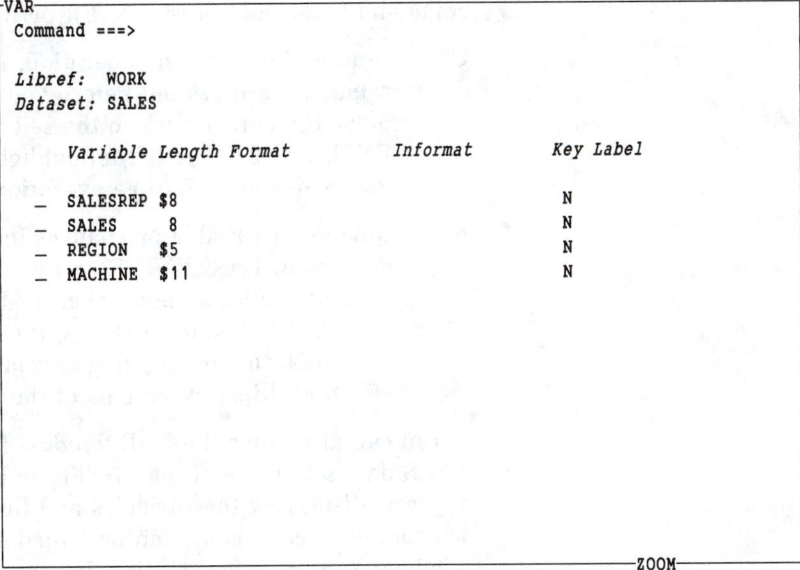

VAR
Command ===>
Libref: WORK
Dataset: SALES
Variable Length Format Informat Key Label
_ SALESREP $8 N
_ SALES 8 N
_ REGION $5 N
_ MACHINE $11 N
ZOOM

Invocation

VAR <*libref.SAS-data-set*>

Description

The VAR window displays information about variables and their attributes for the SAS data set specified, providing a quick overview of the data set's contents. It lists the variable names, types, lengths, formats, informats, key indicators, and labels.* The Key column contains a Y for variables that are included in indexes and an N for variables that are not. See "Release 6.06: SAS Indexes" in Chapter 6 for details. The VAR window also enables you to rename a variable and to change some of its attributes. You can make multiple changes at one time.

If you enter the VAR window directly by issuing the VAR command and no data set has been created during the current SAS session, the Libref and Dataset fields are empty, and a message indicates that there is no default input data set. Otherwise, the libref and data set names for the most recently created data set appear in the fields. Move the cursor to the Libref field and specify the name of a libref. (If you want to display information about the temporary data set WORK, specify WORK in the Libref field.) Then, move the cursor to the Dataset field and specify the name of a SAS data set; press ENTER or RETURN to display information about the SAS data set you selected.

* Note that the VAR window shown here is displayed with the ZOOM command set to ON.

VAR

continued

Using selection-field commands, you can rename a variable and change its format, informat, and label, or you can cancel the operation. Move the cursor to the selection field adjacent to the variable you want, type a command letter, and press ENTER or RETURN.

C cancels the renaming operation. After you have begun the renaming process but before you have pressed ENTER or RETURN, move the cursor back to the selection field, type C, and press ENTER or RETURN. The highlighting disappears, and the previous text reappears. Multiple executions of the C command are allowed.

R renames a variable or changes its format, informat, and label, or does both. Press ENTER or RETURN to highlight the Variable, Format, Informat, and Label fields. Move the cursor to each field you want to change and type the new item. Press ENTER or RETURN; the highlighting is removed, and the new value takes effect. Multiple executions of the R command are allowed.

You can also enter the VAR window from the DIR window by selecting a SAS data set and pressing ENTER or RETURN. The VAR window then appears, displaying the variables and their attributes. Multiple selection-field commands can be issued simultaneously in the VAR window. You can open multiple instances of the VAR window by specifying different libref and data set names.

Commands Available

Except as noted, all of the commands in the following categories are available in the VAR window:

- window-call
- window-management (except the PURGE command)
- window size and position
- color
- scrolling
- text-store
- search (except the CHANGE and RCHANGE commands).

See Also

DIR and LIBNAME windows

Chapter 6, "SAS Files"

CHAPTER 18 SAS® Display Manager Commands

(continued on next page)

(continued from previous page)

Background information on SAS display manager commands, including a table listing all commands, appears in Table 7.2, "Display Manager Commands—Definitions."

ADD

Adds a new line to the Time and Appointments fields

Appointment command

Syntax

ADD | INSERT

Description

The ADD (or INSERT) command inserts a line in the Time and Appointments fields in the APPOINTMENT window. There are two ways to invoke the ADD command:

- □ Position your cursor on the Commands field and type ADD or INSERT. Then move your cursor to a data field within either the Time or Appointments field and press ENTER.
- □ Find out which function key is your ADD key (you can find out your function key settings by typing KEYS on the command line and pressing ENTER). Next, move your cursor to a data field within either the Time or Appointments field and press that function key.

Whether you choose the first or the second method, a new line is added above the line where your cursor was positioned when you pressed ENTER or your function key. If all the lines displayed in the APPOINTMENT window are filled, no more lines are added; the maximum is 17 lines.

Comparisons

The ADD command is the opposite of the DELETE command.

See Also

DELETE command

APPOINTMENT window in Chapter 17, "SAS Display Manager Windows"

AF

Invokes the AF window

Window-call command

Syntax

AF <*arguments*>

Description

The AF command invokes the AF window, which displays applications developed with SAS/AF software, including CBT courses. *Arguments* specifies one or more AF command arguments.

You can use the following arguments with the AF command:

C=*library.catalog.entry.type*
: specifies the complete four-level name of a SAS catalog entry that contains an AF application.

  The first time you invoke the AF command, you must use the C= argument. You do not have to use the C= argument when you invoke the AF window again. The AF window runs the same application it ran the last time you called it.

AUTORECALL=YES
: specifies that PROGRAM entry field values saved from a previous invocation are recalled when users execute the application. Values that can be recalled have been saved with the AUTOSAVE=YES argument in the previous execution of the application. This argument works only with PROGRAM entries, whose field values are not recalled by default.

AUTOSAVE=YES
: specifies that the values in the fields of PROGRAM entries are saved when users exit from an entry. This argument works only with PROGRAM entries. By default, user field values are not saved when users exit from PROGRAM entries. You can use the AUTORECALL=YES argument to recall these values the next time the application executes.

CHECKLAST=NO
: specifies that the SAS System store the name of the CBT entry at which users enter an application.

FRAME=*frame-number* | *frame-name*
: specifies the number or name of the starting frame for a CBT application.

start-menu-number
: specifies one or more MENU entry option numbers, which invoke the entry to display when an application executes. The MENU entry can be specified by its option number on the primary menu or the option numbers on the primary menu and all submenus required to invoke the desired menu. To specify option numbers for the main menu and submenus, separate the numbers by periods (for example, 5.3.2.6). For example, if you are familiar with an application, you can specify 3.2 to display the entry called by the second choice of the submenu that is called by the third choice of the main menu.

See Also

AF window in Chapter 17, "SAS Display Manager Windows"

SAS/AF Software: Usage and Reference, Version 6, First Edition

---

APPOINTMENT

Invokes the APPOINTMENT window

Window-call command

Syntax

APPOINTMENT <*libref.your-data-set*<*start-weekday*> <B>>

Description

The APPOINTMENT command invokes the APPOINTMENT window, which enables you to display and browse a monthly calendar and to enter, update, and display times and descriptions for daily appointments. The default APPOINTMENT window is SASUSER.APPOINT. The alias for the APPOINTMENT command is APPT.

You can use the following arguments with the APPOINTMENT command:

no argument
: invokes the APPOINTMENT window with a calendar displaying the current month and year. The calendar includes columns for specifying the time and description of your daily appointments.

libref.your-data-set
: specifies a permanent SAS data set to contain your appointment data.

start-weekday
: specifies the first two letters of the weekday on which you want the calendar to start, for example, `sa` for Saturday. The default is Sunday.

  Note: The *libref.your-data-set* argument is required if you use the *start-weekday* argument.

B
: specifies that the appointment data display in browse mode. It does not allow any changes to the Time and Appointments fields.

  Note: The *libref.your-data-set* argument is required if you use the B argument.

See Also

APPOINTMENT window in Chapter 17, "SAS Display Manager Windows"

AUTOPOP

Determines whether a window is displayed when lines are written to it

Window-management command

Syntax

AUTOPOP <ON | OFF>

Description

The AUTOPOP command determines whether a window displays automatically when that window is updated by the SAS System. Within any of the primary windows you want to modify, you must have already issued the AUTOPOP command.

You can use the following arguments with the AUTOPOP command:

no argument
: acts as an on/off switch, or toggle. The first time you issue the AUTOPOP command, it reverses the current setting. If the current setting is on, issuing the AUTOPOP command changes it to off; if the current setting is off, issuing the AUTOPOP command changes it to on. When you reissue the AUTOPOP command, it returns to the previous setting.

ON
: turns on the AUTOPOP command in the window so that when lines are written to it the window displays automatically.

OFF
: turns off the AUTOPOP command in the window so that when lines are written to it the window does not display automatically.

By default, the AUTOPOP command is on in the OUTPUT window and off in other display manager windows. You can change the setting in any window for the duration of your SAS session. If you want to save the new setting permanently, issue the WSAVE command.

AUTOSCROLL

Controls the display of lines in the LOG and OUTPUT windows

Output command

Syntax

AUTOSCROLL <*n* | PAGE | MAX>

Description

The AUTOSCROLL command sets the automatic forward scroll amount in the OUTPUT and LOG windows. When the window receives a line of data and the line cannot fit in the window, the window automatically scrolls the amount specified in the command's argument. Note that issuing the AUTOSCROLL command with the PAGE argument suspends the procedure temporarily after each page of output it creates. Issuing the AUTOSCROLL command with the MAX argument suspends the execution of SAS statements at the end of each procedure that creates output. The alias for the AUTOSCROLL command is ASCROLL.

■ **Host Information** ....

The default setting of the AUTOSCROLL command varies by host system. See your SAS Software Consultant or refer to your host documentation for details.

■

You can use the following arguments with the AUTOSCROLL command:

no argument
: displays the current setting of the AUTOSCROLL command.

n
: specifies that when a new line no longer fits in the window, the window is scrolled *n* lines, and then the new line is written. If *n* is 0, no lines are written to the LOG or OUTPUT window while submitted statements are executing.

PAGE
: specifies in the OUTPUT window only that no lines are displayed until a complete page of output is written to the window. At that point, the procedure is suspended temporarily, and the OUTPUT window is activated, enabling commands to execute. Issuing the FORWARD command on the last page causes the procedure to continue. Issuing the END or SUBMIT command causes the procedure to complete executing; then the OUTPUT window suspends execution of SAS statements (as with the MAX argument), but the last page is displayed.

MAX
: specifies in the OUTPUT window only that no lines are written until the end of each procedure. At that point, the first page the procedure creates is displayed, and the OUTPUT window is activated, enabling any command to execute. Issuing the FORWARD command on the last page or issuing the END or SUBMIT command causes the SAS System to begin executing the next procedure.

See Also

END command
FORWARD command
SUBMIT command

BACKWARD

Scrolls backward

Scrolling command

Syntax

BACKWARD <*n* | HALF | PAGE | MAX | CURSOR>

Description

The BACKWARD command scrolls the contents of a window backward (toward the beginning) the amount specified by the VSCROLL command, the default. You also can override the default. The alias for the BACKWARD command is UP.

You can use the following arguments with the BACKWARD command:

no argument
: scrolls the amount specified by the VSCROLL command.

n
: scrolls *n* lines.

HALF
: scrolls half the amount shown in the window.

PAGE
: scrolls the entire amount shown in the window.

MAX
: scrolls to the first line in the window.

CURSOR
: scrolls so that the line on which the cursor is positioned becomes the bottom line in the window. If the cursor is on the last line, the BACKWARD command scrolls a page. Note that the CURSOR argument works only in windows that allow text editing.

Comparisons

The BACKWARD command with the MAX argument specified is equivalent to the TOP command and moves in the opposite direction from the FORWARD command. The BACKWARD command displays the previous month in the APPOINTMENT window only.

See Also

BOTTOM, FORWARD, HSCROLL, LEFT, *n*, RIGHT, TOP, and VSCROLL commands

BFIND

Searches for the previous occurrence of a character string

Search command

Syntax

BFIND <'*character-string*' <PREFIX | SUFFIX | WORD>>

Description

The BFIND command searches for a specified string of characters, starting at the current cursor location and moving backward. The cursor rests on the located string. If the string is not found, the SAS System issues a message to that effect. The only limit to the number of characters for which you can search is the size of the command line.

Enclose the string in quotes if it contains embedded blanks or special characters. Double quotes must be enclosed in single quotes; single quotes must be enclosed in double quotes. If you do not want lowercase letters in the search string translated into uppercase letters, enclose a character string in quotes when the CAPS command is on. (Note that windows that do not allow text editing do not recognize the CAPS command.)

In the following example, with the CAPS command on, the BFIND command finds the previous occurrence of SYSTEM instead of System:

```
bfind System
```

The following example of the BFIND command, with single quotes added, finds the previous occurrence of System instead of SYSTEM:

```
bfind 'System'
```

Note that when text is marked with the MARK command, the BFIND command searches only the marked text. You must issue the UNMARK command first to allow all text to be searched.

You can use the following arguments with the BFIND command:

no argument
: searches for the character string most recently specified in a BFIND or FIND command. If you do not specify a FIND command or a BFIND command with an argument, an error message indicates that no default search string exists.

'*character-string*'
: represents the character string that you want to find.

PREFIX
: finds a character string that is the prefix of a word, within the constraints established for the WORD argument.

SUFFIX
: finds a character string that is the suffix of a word, within the constraints established for the WORD argument.

WORD
: finds a character string within starting and ending delimiters. A delimiter is any symbol other than an uppercase or lowercase letter, a digit, a dash, or an underscore.

For example, abc123 is a word, but abc$123 is two words separated by the $ (dollar sign) delimiter. In the first example, abc123, abc can be specified as a prefix and 123 as a suffix, or the entire string can be specified as a word. In the second example, abc$123, abc and 123 are words (not a prefix and a suffix), so they must be enclosed in quotes as a character string to be found within the context of the PREFIX, SUFFIX, or WORD argument.

Comparisons

Unlike the RFIND command, which continues the search initiated by the FIND and BFIND commands, the BFIND command specifies a character string, as well as the PREFIX, SUFFIX, and WORD arguments. Issuing the BFIND command is the same as issuing the FIND PREV command and the opposite of issuing the FIND NEXT command.

See Also

CHANGE command

FIND command

MARK command

RCHANGE command

RFIND command

BOTTOM

Scrolls to the bottom line

Scrolling command

Syntax

BOTTOM

Description

The BOTTOM command scrolls to the last line of text and, in editing windows only, positions the cursor to the right of the last character.

Comparisons

The BOTTOM command is equivalent to the FORWARD command with the MAX argument specified. The BOTTOM command moves in the opposite direction from the TOP command.

See Also

BACKWARD, FORWARD, HSCROLL, LEFT, *n*, RIGHT, TOP, and VSCROLL commands

BYE

Ends a SAS session

Window-management command

Syntax

BYE

Description

The BYE command ends a SAS session from any display manager or full-screen window and returns you to your host system.

Comparisons

You can use the BYE command interchangeably with the ENDSAS command.

See Also

ENDSAS command

CALCULATOR

Invokes the CALCULATOR window

Window-call command

Syntax

CALCULATOR

Description

The CALCULATOR command invokes the CALCULATOR window, which enables you to perform mathematical operations. The alias for the CALCULATOR command is CALC.

See Also

CALCULATOR window in Chapter 17, "SAS Display Manager Windows"

CANCEL

Cancels changes in a window and removes it from the display

Window-management command

Syntax

CANCEL

Description

In some windows, the CANCEL command cancels changes in a window, closes it, and removes it from the display; in other windows, the CANCEL command closes a window and removes it from the display. See individual window descriptions for information on the command's action in a particular window.

See Also

END command

CASCADE

Creates a layered display of all open windows

Window size and position command

Syntax

CASCADE

Description

The CASCADE command displays all open windows in a layered pattern that fills the display. The layered pattern resembles an open file drawer. The name of each window is visible, but only the contents of the front window are visible. This command takes no argument. You can eliminate the layered pattern by issuing the RESIZE command or by changing to a tile pattern by issuing the TILE command.

Comparisons

The CASCADE command creates a layered display showing all window names and the contents of the front window only, while the TILE command creates a rectangular mosaic pattern displaying all windows, including their names and contents.

See Also

RESIZE command

TILE command

CATALOG

Invokes the CATALOG window

Window-call command

Syntax

CATALOG <*libref.catalog*>

Description

The CATALOG command invokes the CATALOG window, which displays the directory of a catalog and enables you to manage its entries. The alias for the CATALOG command is CAT.

You can use the CATALOG command with the following arguments:

no argument
: invokes the CATALOG window with no entries listed. You must fill in the Libref and Catalog fields to display catalog entries.

libref.catalog
: invokes the CATALOG window listing the entries for the catalog as specified, including the name, type, and description. Note that if the catalog does not exist, a requestor window appears, advising you that the catalog has not been found and asking if you want to create it.

Comparisons

You can also access the CATALOG window through the DIR window. From the DIR window, select a SAS file of type CATALOG and press ENTER or RETURN. The CATALOG window displays, listing the entries.

See Also

Chapter 6, "SAS Files"

CATALOG and DIR windows in Chapter 17, "SAS Display Manager Windows"

CHANGE

Finds and changes one character string to another

Search command

Syntax

CHANGE <*string-1 string-2* <*search-order*> <*component*>>

Description

In windows that allow text editing, the CHANGE command finds and changes a specified string of characters to another specified string of characters. The only limit to the number of characters you can specify is the size of the command line. The alias for the CHANGE command is C.

Enclose the string in quotes if it contains embedded blanks or special characters. Double quotes must be enclosed in single quotes; single quotes must be enclosed in double quotes. If you do not want lowercase letters in the search string translated into uppercase letters, enclose the character string in quotes when the CAPS command is on. When the CAPS command is on, the following occurs:

- □ If the first string is lowercased or mixed case, you must enclose it in quotes for the SAS System to find it.
- □ If the first string is lowercased or mixed case and enclosed in quotes and the second string is not enclosed in quotes, the SAS System finds the first string and changes it to the second string, uppercasing the second string in the process.
- □ If both the first and second strings are lowercased or mixed case and enclosed in quotes, the SAS System finds the first string and changes it to the second string, leaving it lowercased or mixed case.

(Note that windows that do not allow text editing do not recognize the CAPS command.) For example, with the CAPS command on, the following command not only changes the word system to platform, but uppercases the word platform as well:

```
change 'system' platform
```

The following command changes the word system to platform but leaves it lowercase:

```
change 'system' 'platform'
```

When text is marked with the MARK command, the CHANGE command searches for and alters only the marked text. You must issue the UNMARK command to allow any unmarked text to be changed.

You can use the following arguments with the CHANGE command:

no argument
: finds and changes one string to another string as specified in the previous CHANGE command.

string-1
represents the string to be changed.

string-2
represents the string to replace *string-1*.

search-order
can be one of the following arguments:

FIRST
changes the first occurrence of *string-1*, regardless of cursor position.

LAST
changes the last occurrence of *string-1*, regardless of cursor position.

NEXT
changes the next occurrence of *string-1* based on the current cursor position. If the cursor is on the command line, the NEXT argument starts at the top of the window.

PREV
changes the previous occurrence of *string-1* based on the current cursor position. If the cursor is on the command line, the PREV argument starts at the beginning of the first line of the window.

ALL
changes all occurrences of *string-1*, reports the number of occurrences as a note, and returns the cursor to the first occurrence of the string.

component
can be one of the following arguments:

PREFIX
changes *string-1*, which is the prefix of a word, within the constraints established for the WORD argument.

SUFFIX
changes *string-1*, which is the suffix of a word, within the constraints established for the WORD argument.

WORD
changes *string-1* within starting and ending delimiters. A delimiter is any symbol other than an uppercase or lowercase letter, a digit, a dash, or an underscore. Typically, a delimiter is a space.

Comparisons

The CHANGE command is often used with the RCHANGE command, which continues to change the character string most recently specified in a CHANGE command. If no argument is specified, the CHANGE command is interchangeable with the RCHANGE command.

See Also

BFIND command

FIND command

MARK command

RCHANGE command

RFIND command

CLEAR

Clears the window's contents or the display of settings

Window-management command

Syntax

CLEAR <LOG | MASK | OUTPUT | PGM | RECALL | TEXT>

Description

The CLEAR command clears a window's contents or the display of settings created with the MASK command.

You can use the following arguments with the CLEAR command. Arguments may not be valid in all windows. For example, in the LOG window the MASK argument is not applicable. Table 7.3 shows which arguments of the CLEAR command work in each display manager window.

no argument
: clears the contents of the active window. The contents vary by window. For example, issuing the CLEAR command in the TITLES or FOOTNOTES window clears the display of the titles or footnotes. If you issue the CLEAR command in the APPOINTMENT window, it clears appointment time and data for the current day. In the CALCULATOR window, issuing the CLEAR command clears the register primary operand area and all tape lines.

LOG
: clears the contents of the LOG window.

MASK
: removes the display of the mask line but does not turn off the MASK command.

OUTPUT
: clears the contents of the OUTPUT window.

PGM
: clears the contents of the PROGRAM EDITOR window.

RECALL
: clears the recall buffer.

TEXT
: clears all text in the active window.

Comparisons

Like the RESET and D commands, the CLEAR command removes the display of the mask line.

See Also

D command

MASK command

RESET command

COLOR

Changes the color and highlighting of selected portions of a window

Color command

Syntax

COLOR *field-type* <*color* | NEXT <*highlight*>>

Description

With a color monitor, issuing the COLOR command changes the color and highlighting of selected portions of a window or items within a window. If you issue the COLOR command on a monochrome monitor, only the highlighting of selected portions of a window changes. Field types vary among windows. See Table 7.3 for a table matching field types with windows and for additional information about the COLOR command. Note that support for color and highlighting attributes varies by terminal. If all colors are not available on your terminal, the SAS System matches a color to its closest counterpart.

■ **Host Information** .... Valid arguments to the COLOR command vary by host system and terminal. See your SAS Software Consultant or refer to your host documentation for details. ■

You can use the following arguments with the COLOR command:

field-type
: specifies the area of the window or the type of text whose color is to be changed. *Field-type* can be one of the following:

BACKGROUND BACK	background of the window.
BANNER	protected headings in the window, including the command-line prompt.
BORDER	lined border of the window and the window name.
BYLINE	BY statements in the OUTPUT window.
COMMAND	if the command line is present, specifying COLOR COMMAND changes the unprotected field in the command line where commands are entered. If the command line is absent, specifying COLOR COMMAND changes the foreground color of the menu.
DATA	data lines in the OUTPUT and LOG windows.

(field-type continued)

ERROR	error message lines in the LOG window.
FOOTNOTE	footnotes in the OUTPUT window.
HEADER	headings other than title headings in the OUTPUT window.
MENU	background color in pull-down menus.
MENUBORDER	border in pull-down menus.
MESSAGE	message line immediately below the command line.
MTEXT	marked string or block of text in the window.
NOTES	notes in the LOG window.
NUMBERS	all line numbers in the window.
SCROLLBAR	scroll bar in the window.
SOURCE	source lines in the LOG window.
TEXT	all text lines in the window, including lines for future text to be typed in.
TITLE	titles in the OUTPUT window.
WARNING	warnings in the LOG window.

color specifies a color for the window or for selected portions of the window. *Color* can include any of the following:

B (blue)	W (white)
R (red)	K (black)
G (green)	M (magenta)
C (cyan)	A (gray | grey)
P (pink)	N (brown)
Y (yellow)	O (orange)

NEXT changes the color to the next available color. The order of the colors depends on your monitor.

highlight specifies the highlighting attribute, which can include any of the following:

H (highlight)
U (underline)
R (reverse video)
B (blinking)

COMMAND

Reactivates or deactivates the PMENU facility in the active window

Window-management command

Syntax

COMMAND <ON | OFF>

Description

The COMMAND command reactivates or deactivates the PMENU facility in the active window only, redisplaying or removing display of the action bar. It works only after the action bar has been displayed.

You can use the following arguments with the COMMAND command:

no argument
: acts like an on/off switch, or toggle. From the Globals item on the action bar, first select the Command and then select the Command line menu items to deactivate the PMENU facility, which removes the action bar from the display. Issue the COMMAND command from the command line to reactivate the PMENU facility.

ON
: reactivates the PMENU facility in the active window alone but only after the PMENU facility has been activated and then deactivated in the active window.

OFF
: deactivates the PMENU facility in the active window but only after the PMENU facility has been activated. Note that you must use a function key with the OFF argument.

Comparisons

Like the PMENU command, the COMMAND command activates and deactivates the PMENU facility. However, to issue the COMMAND command, the action bar must already be displayed. In addition, the PMENU command affects all windows, while the COMMAND command affects only the active window.

See Also

PMENU command

PMENU facility in Chapter 7, “SAS Display Manager System,” and “Executing Commands with the PMENU Facility” in Chapter 8, “SAS Text Editor”

Chapter 26, “The PMENU Procedure,” in *SAS Procedures Guide, Version 6, Third Edition*

COPY

Copies a catalog entry into a window

File-management command

Syntax

COPY <*catalog-entry* <NOTABS> <NOATTR> <REPLACE>>

Description

The COPY command copies a catalog entry into the PROGRAM EDITOR, CATALOG, KEYS, and NOTEPAD windows, as well as into the EDIT window of the OUTPUT MANAGER window. Although the COPY command appends by default, you can use the target line commands A and B to override that default. Note that you cannot use target commands with the REPLACE argument. For more information on target commands, see Chapter 8. Note that you can interrupt the COPY command with the attention sequence in windows that allow text editing.

■ **Host Information** .... The attention sequence varies by host system and terminal. See your SAS Software Consultant or refer to your host documentation for information specific to your site. ■

You can use the following arguments with the COPY command:

no argument
: copies into the window the catalog entry previously specified in a COPY or SAVE command within the current SAS session.

catalog-entry
: specifies the SAS data library, catalog name, entry name, and entry type. You can specify one-, two-, three-, and four-level names. The complete specification for this argument is *libref.catalog.entry.type*.
  If no libref and catalog are specified, the SAS System assigns SASUSER.PROFILE as the default. Valid entry types include SOURCE, the default for the PROGRAM EDITOR and NOTEPAD windows; LOG, the default for the LOG window; OUTPUT, the default for the OUTPUT window; and KEYS, the default for the KEYS window. Any entry type is valid in the CATALOG window.

NOATTR
: specifies that stored attributes are not copied into the window with the catalog entry. Even if the attributes have been stored with the entry, you do not have to include them when the entry is copied into the window.

NOTABS
: changes any tab characters found to blanks when copied. By default, an eight-character tab is used.

REPLACE
: specifies that the contents of a catalog entry replace the contents of the window.

Comparisons

The COPY command is the opposite of the SAVE command, which writes the contents of a window to a catalog. The COPY command is similar to the INCLUDE command, which copies an external file into a window.

Note that the COPY command functions differently in the CATALOG and KEYS windows. For details, see Chapter 17.

See Also

FILE, INCLUDE, and SAVE commands

"Interrupting Execution of Commands" in Chapter 7, "SAS Display Manager System"

Chapter 8, "SAS Text Editor"

CATALOG and KEYS windows in Chapter 17, "SAS Display Manager Windows"

CUT

Removes marked text from the current window and stores it in a paste buffer

Text cut-and-paste command

Syntax

CUT <APPEND> <BUFFER=*paste-buffer-name*> <LAST | ALL>

Description

The CUT command removes marked text from the current window and stores it in a paste buffer. Issue the MARK command to mark text; the SMARK command cannot be issued with the CUT command. The CUT command is valid only in windows that allow editing with the text editor, such as PGM and NOTEPAD, as well as the EDIT window of the OUTPUT MANAGER window.

Note: Text stored in a paste buffer is not saved after you end your current SAS session.

You can use the following arguments with the CUT command:

no argument
: removes from the display any text marked in the current window and stores it in the default paste buffer. The marked text replaces any existing text in the buffer.

APPEND
: adds the marked text to the text in a paste buffer. The SAS System appends the text to the end of any text in the paste buffer.

▶ *Caution: Do not accidentally overwrite the contents of the buffer.*

If you do not specify the APPEND argument, the cut text overwrites the previous contents of the buffer.

BUFFER=*paste-buffer-name*
: creates and names a paste buffer. You can create any number of paste buffers for storing text by naming them with the BUFFER= argument in the CUT command. The rules for naming a paste buffer are the same as for naming SAS data sets and variables:

□ the name must begin with a letter (A-Z)

□ it must be from one to eight characters long

□ it can contain letters, digits, or underscores.

To insert the information stored in a named paste buffer, you must specify the buffer's name in the BUFFER= argument in the PASTE command. For example, if you create a paste buffer (*buffer1*) with the

(BUFFER= continued)

CUT command, you must also specify *buffer1* in the PASTE command to insert information stored in *buffer1*:

```
cut buffer=buffer1

paste buffer=buffer1
```

The number of paste buffers you can have in one session depends on the system-specific limitations of your host.

If you do not specify the BUFFER= argument, the SAS System uses the default paste buffer, named DEFAULT.

LAST
: cuts the most recently marked text and unmarks all other marks when more than one area of text is marked. To cut one area of text when more than one mark exists, you must use either the LAST or the ALL argument.

ALL
: cuts all current marks when more than one area of text is marked.

Cutting and Pasting Text

Use the following steps to perform cut-and-paste operations:

1. Mark the text with the MARK command. See the MARK command later in this chapter for instructions.
2. On the command line, type the word CUT and any arguments you want to specify. Then press ENTER.

   You can also use a function key to cut marked text. It is often effective to use a combination of function keys and command-line specifications. See "Executing Commands with Function Keys" in Chapter 7 for details.

   In either case, the SAS System removes the marked text from the display and stores it in the paste buffer.

A Quick Method

To store a single text string in the default paste buffer, use the following quick method of executing the MARK and CUT commands:

1. Use the MARK function key to indicate the beginning of the text string.
2. Position the cursor after the last character in the string.
3. Press the CUT function key. The text is marked automatically, the CUT command is executed, and the string is removed from the display and stored in the default paste buffer.

Comparisons

The CUT command removes marked strings from the current window and stores them in a paste buffer. The STORE command leaves the marked string in its original location and stores a copy of the text in the paste buffer. In addition, the CUT command is valid only in windows that use the full text editor, while the STORE command is valid even if the window does not use the full text editor.

See Also

MARK command

PASTE command

SMARK command

STORE command

UNMARK command

DECIMAL

Specifies the number of decimal places

Calculator command

Syntax

DECIMAL *n*

Description

In the CALCULATOR window, the DECIMAL command specifies the number of decimal places for the number calculated; you must use the numeric (*n*) argument to signify the number of decimal places. The *n* argument is convenient when you work with data containing dollar and cent values. The alias for the DECIMAL command is DEC.

Issuing the DECIMAL 0 (or DEC 0) command changes the assumed placement of the decimal point back to 0.

See Also

CALCULATOR window in Chapter 17, "SAS Display Manager Windows"

DELETE

Deletes a catalog entry

File-management command

Syntax

DELETE <<*libref.catalog.*>*entry.type*>

Description

The DELETE command can be used in the APPOINTMENT, CATALOG, and NOTEPAD windows. The *libref.catalog.entry.type* argument is not necessary in the APPOINTMENT window. In the APPOINTMENT window only, the DELETE command deletes a line in the Time and Appointments fields. The alias for the DELETE command is DEL.

There are two ways to invoke the DELETE command in the APPOINTMENT window:

- Position your cursor on the Commands field and type DELETE. Then, move your cursor to a data field in either the Time or Appointments field and press ENTER.
- Find out which function key is your DELETE key (you can find out all your function key settings by typing KEYS on the command line and pressing ENTER). Next, move your cursor to a data field in either the Time or Appointments field and press that function key.

Whether you choose the first or the second method, the line where your cursor was positioned when you pressed ENTER or your function key is deleted.

In the CATALOG and NOTEPAD windows, you can specify the *libref.catalog.entry.type* argument with the DELETE command. If the entry you are deleting is in the current catalog, you do not need to specify the *libref.catalog* argument in the CATALOG window. In the NOTEPAD window, if you do not specify the *libref.catalog* argument, SASUSER.PROFILE is the default.

In the CATALOG and NOTEPAD windows, the DELETE command deletes a catalog entry immediately without verification. In the CATALOG window, any object type can be deleted; in the NOTEPAD window, only object types of the source log and output can be deleted.

▶ ***Caution:*** *The DELETE command deletes permanently.*

A catalog entry cannot be restored once it has been deleted.

Comparisons

The DELETE command, as it functions in the APPOINTMENT window, is the opposite of the ADD command.

The DELETE command, as it functions in the CATALOG window, is the opposite of the COPY command, which copies a catalog entry. Issuing the D selection-field command in the CATALOG window to delete a catalog entry generates a request for verification.

See Also

APPOINTMENT, CATALOG, and NOTEPAD windows in Chapter 17, "SAS Display Manager Windows"

DES

Displays or changes the form's description

Forms command

Syntax

DES <'*description-string*'>

Description

Executed in the FORM window, the DES command displays or changes the description that appears in the catalog directory for the form.

You can use the following arguments with the DES command:

no argument
: displays the current description.

'*description-string*'
: replaces the current description. Note that the text string must appear in single or double quotes.

Comparisons

The DES command is similar to the NOTEPAD window's DESCRIPTION command.

See Also

DESCRIPTION command

DESCRIPTION

Assigns a description to be saved with the notepad

Notepad command

Syntax

DESCRIPTION <*description*>

Description

Executed in the NOTEPAD window, the DESCRIPTION command assigns a description to a notepad or displays the current description. You must issue the END or SAVE command to save the description.

You can use the following arguments with the DESCRIPTION command:

no argument
: generates a note that displays the currently assigned description.

description
: is the description to be saved with the notepad. The description can be up to 40 characters.

Comparisons

The DESCRIPTION command is similar to the FORM window's DES command.

See Also

DES command

NTITLE command

DIR

Invokes the DIR window

Window-call command

Syntax

DIR <*libref.type*>

Description

The DIR command invokes the DIR window, which you can use to

- □ display information about SAS files
- □ manage SAS files
- □ access the VAR and CATALOG windows.

You can use the following arguments with the DIR command:

no argument
: invokes the DIR window with the default libref WORK and the entry type ALL. Any temporary files created during the current SAS session are listed.

libref.type
invokes the DIR window listing the permanent SAS files for the SAS data library as specified, including the name, entry type, and index status.

See Also

Chapter 2, "The DATA Step"

Chapter 6, "SAS Files"

CATALOG and DIR windows in Chapter 17, "SAS Display Manager Windows"

END

Closes a window and removes it from the display

Window-management command

Syntax

END

Description

For most display manager windows, the END command closes the window, saving its contents and removing it from the display. In some cases, depending on the window, the END command closes and saves a file; in others, it enables you to exit the window and remove it from the display.

Comparisons

The END command is interchangeable with the SUBMIT command.

See Also

SUBMIT command

Chapter 17, "SAS Display Manager Windows"

ENDSAS

Ends a SAS session

Window-management command

Syntax

ENDSAS

Description

The ENDSAS command ends a SAS session from any display manager window and returns you to your host system.

Comparisons

The ENDSAS command is interchangeable with the BYE command.

See Also

BYE command

FILE

Writes the contents of a window to an external file

File-management command

Syntax

FILE <*file-specification* <ATTR> <TABS> <APPEND | REPLACE>>

Description

The FILE command writes the contents of a window to an external file.
You can use the following arguments with the FILE command:

no argument
: writes the contents of a window to the file most recently specified in the current SAS session, unless the file contains something. If it does, a requestor window appears as a safeguard, prompting you to append or replace the external file or to cancel the filing operation. If no file has been specified, an error message indicates that no default file exists.

file-specification
: can be one of the following arguments:

  fileref
  : writes the contents of the window to the external file identified by the fileref. The fileref must have previously been associated with an external file in a FILENAME statement or in an appropriate host command.

  '*external-file*'
  : writes the contents of the window to the external file as specified with the physical name. The physical name is the name by which the host system recognizes the file. The name must be enclosed in quotes.

ATTR
: stores the attributes with the file. The file is stored in a format recognized by the INCLUDE command whether or not the file has attributes.

TABS
: compresses spaces as tabs during storage, instead of storing the file with the default spacing. Multiple spaces are compressed into single tab characters wherever possible to conserve space.

APPEND
: appends the contents of the window to the contents of the external file. The APPEND argument suppresses the requestor window, which prompts you to specify A to append the file, R to replace the file, or C to cancel the operation.

REPLACE
: replaces the contents of the external file with the contents of the window. The REPLACE argument suppresses the requestor window, which prompts you to specify A to append the file, R to replace the file, or C to cancel the operation.

■ **Host Information** .... The '*external-file*' of the FILE command varies by host system. The APPEND argument is not available on all host systems. For host-specific information on these topics, refer to the SAS documentation for your host system or see your SAS Software Consultant.

.... ■

Note that you can interrupt the FILE command with the attention sequence.

■ **Host Information** .... The attention sequence varies by host system and terminal. See your SAS Software Consultant or refer to your host documentation for information specific to your site.

.... ■

Comparisons

The FILE command is similar to the SAVE command, which stores the contents of a window in a catalog entry. The FILE command is the opposite of the INCLUDE command, which copies the contents of an external file into a window.

See Also

COPY, INCLUDE, and SAVE commands

Chapter 2, "The DATA Step"

FILENAME

Invokes the FILENAME window

Window-call command

Syntax

FILENAME

Description

The FILENAME command invokes the FILENAME window, which displays assigned filerefs with their files.

Comparisons

The FILENAME statement associates a SAS fileref with an external file, while the FILENAME command opens the FILENAME window, which lists the assigned filerefs and their files.

See Also

FILENAME statement in Chapter 9, "SAS Language Statements"

FILENAME window in Chapter 17, "SAS Display Manager Windows"

FIND

Searches for a specified character string

Search command

Syntax

FIND <*'character-string'* <*search-order* > <*component*>>

Description

The FIND command searches for a specified string of characters. The cursor rests on the located string. If the string is not found, the SAS System issues a message to that effect. The only limit to the number of characters you can specify is the size of the command line. The alias for the FIND command is F.

Enclose the string in quotes if it contains embedded blanks or special characters. Double quotes must be enclosed in single quotes; single quotes must be enclosed in double quotes. When the CAPS command is on, enclose a character string in quotes or the lowercase letters in the string are translated to uppercase letters. (Note that windows that do not allow text editing do not recognize the CAPS command.) For example, with the CAPS command on, the following command finds the next occurrence of SYSTEM instead of System:

```
find System
```

The following command, with single quotes added, finds the next occurrence of System instead of SYSTEM:

```
find 'System'
```

Note that when text is marked with the MARK command, the FIND command searches only the marked text. You must issue the UNMARK command first to allow all text to be searched.

You can use the following arguments with the FIND command:

no argument
: searches for the character string most recently specified in a FIND or BFIND command. If you did not specify a FIND or BFIND command, an error message indicates that no default search string exists.

'character-string'
: represents the character string that you want to find.

search-order
: can be one of the following arguments:

  FIRST
  : finds the first occurrence of the character string, regardless of cursor position.

  LAST
  : finds the last occurrence of the character string, regardless of cursor position.

  NEXT
  : finds the next occurrence of the character string based on the current cursor position. If the cursor is on the command line, the NEXT argument starts at the top of the window.

PREV
: finds the previous occurrence of the character string based on the current cursor position. If the cursor is on the command line, the PREV argument starts at the beginning of the first line of the window.

ALL
: finds all occurrences of the character string, reports the number of occurrences as a note, and returns the cursor to the first occurrence of the string.

component
: can be one of the following arguments:

  PREFIX
  : finds a character string that is the prefix of a word, within the constraints established for the WORD argument.

  SUFFIX
  : finds a character string that is the suffix of a word, within the constraints established for the WORD argument.

  WORD
  : finds a character string within starting and ending delimiters. A delimiter is any symbol other than an uppercase or lowercase letter, a digit, a dash, or an underscore.

For example, abc123 is a word, but abc$123 is two words separated by the $ (dollar sign) delimiter. In the first example, abc123, abc can be specified as a prefix and 123 as a suffix, or the entire string can be specified as a word. In the second example, abc$123, abc and 123 are words (not a prefix and a suffix), so they must be enclosed in quotes as a character string to be found with the PREFIX, SUFFIX, or WORD argument.

Comparisons

Without an argument, the FIND command is identical to the RFIND command. Issuing the BFIND command is the same as issuing the FIND PREV command.

See Also

BFIND command

CHANGE command

MARK command

RCHANGE command

RFIND command

FOOTNOTES

Invokes the FOOTNOTES window

Window-call command

Syntax

FOOTNOTES

Description

The FOOTNOTES command invokes the FOOTNOTES window, which enables you to enter, edit, and browse up to ten lines of footnotes for procedure output.

See Also

TITLES command

FOOTNOTE statement in Chapter 9, "SAS Language Statements"

FOOTNOTES window in Chapter 17, "SAS Display Manager Windows"

FORMNAME

Sets the default form name

File-management command

Syntax

FORMNAME <*form-name* | CLEAR>

Description

The FORMNAME command sets the default form name to use with the PRINT command. The form must exist.

You can use the following arguments with the FORMNAME command:

no argument
: displays a message stating the current setting of the form name.

form-name
: identifies the form name, which can be any valid SAS name.

CLEAR
: clears the previously specified form name and returns to the original default.

Comparisons

The FORMNAME command is similar to the PRTFILE command, which sets the default print file. The FORMNAME command is also associated with the PRINT command, which prints a file using the FORM subsystem.

See Also

FSFORM, PRINT, and PRTFILE commands

FORM window in Chapter 17, "SAS Display Manager Windows"

SAS/AF Software: Usage and Reference, Version 6, First Edition

SAS/FSP Software: Usage and Reference, Version 6, First Edition

FORWARD

Scrolls forward

Scrolling command

Syntax

FORWARD <*n* | HALF | PAGE | MAX | CURSOR>

Description

The FORWARD command scrolls the contents of a window forward (toward the end) the amount specified by the VSCROLL command, the default. You can override the default. The alias for the FORWARD command is DOWN.

You can use the following arguments with the FORWARD command:

no argument
: scrolls the amount specified by the VSCROLL command.

n
: scrolls *n* lines.

HALF
: scrolls half the amount shown in the window.

PAGE
: scrolls the entire amount shown in the window.

MAX
: scrolls to the last line.

CURSOR
: scrolls so that the line on which the cursor is positioned becomes the top line in the window. If the cursor is on the top line, the FORWARD command scrolls forward a page. Note that the CURSOR argument works only in windows that allow text editing.

Comparisons

The FORWARD command with the MAX argument specified is equivalent to the BOTTOM command. The FORWARD command moves in the opposite direction from the BACKWARD command. The FORWARD command displays the next month in the APPOINTMENT window only.

See Also

BACKWARD, BOTTOM, HSCROLL, LEFT, *n*, RIGHT, TOP, and VSCROLL commands

FREE

Frees the print file

File-management command

Syntax

FREE

Description

The FREE command frees, or closes, the print file to which you are printing.

Note: You must free the print file before you can use it in another window. You cannot print to a print file from multiple windows without first freeing the print file.

The FREE command takes no arguments.

Comparisons

A file is also closed when

- □ the PRINT command is issued with any argument
- □ the current PRTFILE or FORMNAME settings are changed after issuing the PRTFILE or FORMNAME commands and then issuing the PRINT command.

See Also

FORMNAME, PRINT, and PRTFILE commands

FORM window in Chapter 17, "SAS Display Manager System"

SAS/AF Software: Usage and Reference, Version 6, First Edition

SAS/FSP Software: Usage and Reference, Version 6, First Edition

FSFORM

Invokes the FORM window

Window-call command

Syntax

FSFORM <*catalog-name.*> *form-name*

Description

The FSFORM command invokes the FORM window, which enables you to specify the type of printer, text format, and destination for your output.

You can use the following arguments with the FSFORM command:

catalog-name
: specifies the name of the SAS catalog that contains the form; the default name is SASUSER.PROFILE.

form-name
: specifies the name of the form.

See Also

FORMNAME command

Chapter 5, "SAS Output"

FORM window in Chapter 17, "SAS Display Manager Windows"

SAS/AF Software: Usage and Reference, Version 6, First Edition

SAS/FSP Software: Usage and Reference, Version 6, First Edition

HELP

Invokes the HELP window

Window-call command

Syntax

HELP <*component-name*>

Description

The HELP command invokes the HELP window, called SAS SYSTEM HELP, which displays help information about the SAS System. The results of issuing the HELP command depend on which window is active when you issue the HELP command.

You can use the following arguments with the HELP command:

no argument
: from the PROGRAM EDITOR, LOG, and OUTPUT windows, displays the primary menu of SAS System Help. From any other window, issuing the HELP command with no argument bypasses the primary menu and displays a HELP window with information specific to the previously active window.

component-name
: bypasses the primary menu and displays a specific HELP window that contains information about the specified component.

See Also

END and =X commands

HELP window in Chapter 17, "SAS Display Manager Windows"

HEX

Turns hex mode on or off

Calculator command

Syntax

HEX <ON | OFF>

Description

The HEX command turns hex mode on or off in the CALCULATOR window. When hex mode is on, it converts the current operands; the contents of memory; the X, Y, and Z constants; and the recall stack to hexadecimal. An h is displayed to the left of operands if there is space. The default is off. The alias for the HEX command is H.

Fractional hex values are not supported.

You can use the following arguments with the HEX command:

no argument
: functions like an on/off switch, or toggle.

ON
: turns hex mode on.

OFF
: turns hex mode off.

See Also

CALCULATOR window in Chapter 17, "SAS Display Manager Windows"

HOME

Moves the cursor to the command line

Window-management command

Syntax

HOME

Description

The HOME command moves the cursor to the command line or to the first input field in the window. It is designed to be issued with a function key.

■ **Host Information** ....

The HOME command can be used interchangeably with the HOME key, which is available on some terminals and host systems. Refer to your host documentation for details.

.... ■

Comparisons

The HOME command accomplishes the same result as the CURSOR command, except that the HOME command works in all windows and the CURSOR command does not.

See Also

CURSOR command

HSCROLL

Specifies the default horizontal scroll amount

Scrolling command

Syntax

HSCROLL <*n* | HALF | PAGE | MAX | CURSOR>

Description

The HSCROLL command specifies the default amount you scroll horizontally when you issue the LEFT or RIGHT scrolling command without specifying arguments.

You can use the following arguments with the HSCROLL command:

no argument
: displays the current setting.

n
: sets the default to *n* columns.

HALF
: sets the default to half the amount shown in the window.

PAGE
: sets the default to the entire amount shown in the window.

MAX
: sets the default to the leftmost or rightmost portion of the window.

CURSOR
: sets the current cursor location to the leftmost or rightmost position in the window following execution of the LEFT or RIGHT command. Note that the CURSOR argument works only in windows that allow text editing.

Comparisons

Note that the HSCROLL command sets the default, while the LEFT and RIGHT commands actually accomplish the scrolling. The HSCROLL command is the horizontal equivalent of the VSCROLL command.

See Also

BACKWARD, BOTTOM, FORWARD, LEFT, *n*, RIGHT, TOP, and VSCROLL commands

ICON

Makes the active window a smaller version of itself

Window-management command

Syntax

ICON

Description

The ICON command makes the active window a smaller square version of itself. Note that the icon does not exhibit the window's contents, nor can you do anything in it. Multiple windows that are icons can exist at one time. You return the icon to the default window configuration by pressing ENTER or RETURN within the square or entering the ICON command again.

■ **Host Information** .... Implementation of the ICON command varies by host system and terminal. Specifically, placement of icons on the display varies across host systems. See your SAS Software Consultant or refer to your host documentation for details. ■

INCLUDE

Copies the contents of an external file into a window

File-management command

Syntax

INCLUDE <*file-specification*> <NOATTR> <NOTABS> <REPLACE>
<SEQ | NOSEQ>

Description

The INCLUDE command copies the contents of an external file into a window. Although the INCLUDE command appends by default, you can use the target line commands A and B to override that default. Note that you cannot use target commands with the REPLACE argument. For more information on the target commands, see Chapter 8.

You can use the following arguments with the INCLUDE command:

no argument
: writes the contents of the file most recently specified in the current SAS session into the window. If no file has been specified, an error message indicates that no default file exists.

file-specification
: can be one of the following arguments:

  fileref
  : copies into the window the contents of an external file identified by a fileref. The fileref must have previously been associated with an external file in a FILENAME statement or in an appropriate host command.

  '*external-file*'
  : copies into the window the contents of an external file as specified with the physical name. The physical name is the name by which the host system recognizes the file. You must enclose the name in quotes.

NOATTR
: specifies that the stored attributes are not copied into the window with the file. Even if the attributes have been stored with the file, you do not have to include them when the file is copied into the window.

NOTABS
: changes any tab characters found to blanks when copied. The default is an eight-character tab.

REPLACE
: specifies that the contents of an external file replace the contents of the window.

SEQ
: specifies that any sequence numbers in the file are read in and treated as normal text.

NOSEQ
: specifies that any sequence numbers in the file are stripped out when the file is read in.

If sequence numbers exist and neither the SEQ nor the NOSEQ argument is specified, a requestor window prompts you to specify one argument or the other.

■ **Host Information** ....

The '*external-file*' of the INCLUDE command varies by host system. For host-specific information, refer to your host documentation or see your SAS Software Consultant.

.... ■

Note that you can interrupt the INCLUDE command with the attention sequence.

■ **Host Information** ....

The attention sequence varies by host system and terminal. See your SAS Software Consultant or refer to your host documentation for information specific to your site.

.... ■

Comparisons

The INCLUDE command can be compared to the %INCLUDE statement, which includes SAS statements and data lines. It is similar to the COPY command, which copies the contents of a catalog entry into a window. The INCLUDE command is the opposite of the FILE command, which stores the contents of a window in an external file.

See Also

COPY, FILE, and SAVE commands

Chapter 2, "The DATA Step"

Chapter 8, "SAS Text Editor"

KEYDEF

Redefines or identifies a function key setting outside the KEYS window

Window-management command

Syntax

KEYDEF *key-name* <*display-manager-command* | ~*text-string*>

Description

The KEYDEF command redefines a function key outside the KEYS window. By default, the new definition is in effect only for the duration of your current SAS session. You also can use the KEYDEF command to identify the setting of any given function key, whether or not it is defined with the KEYDEF command.

You can use one of two ways to save the temporary settings created with the KEYDEF command:

- □ Invoke the KEYS window, make a change in it, and issue the END command.
- □ Invoke the KEYS window and issue the SAVE command.

A requestor window appears, asking you whether you want to save the settings permanently. If you type N, the temporary key settings are returned to the previous settings after you end your session. If you type Y, the key settings are permanently redefined after you end your session.

■ **Host Information** ....

Note that function key names vary by host system and terminal. Function keys are not always numbered. See your SAS Software Consultant or refer to your host documentation for details. ■

You can use the following arguments with the KEYDEF command:

key-name
: represents any function key in the KEYS window, F1 for example. Note that if you use only the *key-name* argument with the KEYDEF command, the SAS System issues a message identifying the definition of the function key you specify.

display-manager-command | ~*text-string*
: represents any display manager command or text string to which you assign the function key specified with the KEYDEF command. A text string must be preceded by a tilde (~) to signal to the SAS System that the string is not a command, as the following example shows:

```
keydef f1 ~information needed
```

Note that the tilde does not appear with the text string when it is inserted.

Comparisons

Note that the second argument does not need to be placed in quotes. This is in contrast to the SAS System's general requirements for text strings.

Examples

Suppose you want to change your F1 key to the ZOOM command. Specify

```
keydef f1 zoom
```

The following message appears in the window:

```
F1 set to "zoom".
```

The new definition is now in effect for the duration of your session. To determine the current setting of the F1 key, specify

```
keydef f1
```

The following message appears in the window:

```
F1 set to "zoom".
```

See Also

PURGE command

KEYS window in Chapter 17, "SAS Display Manager Windows"

KEYS

Invokes the KEYS window

Window-call command

Syntax

KEYS

Description

The KEYS command invokes the KEYS window, which enables you to browse, alter, and save function key settings.

Comparisons

You can use the KEYDEF command to set a key definition without invoking the KEYS window. The new definition is not saved permanently unless you also invoke the KEYS window, make changes in it, and issue the END command or invoke the KEYS window and issue the SAVE command.

See Also

KEYDEF command

KEYS window in Chapter 17, "SAS Display Manager Windows"

LEFT

Scrolls left

Scrolling command

Syntax

LEFT <*n* | HALF | PAGE | MAX | CURSOR>

Description

The LEFT command scrolls the contents of a window left the amount specified by the HSCROLL command, the default. You can override the default.

You can use the following arguments with the LEFT command:

no argument
: scrolls the amount specified by the HSCROLL command.

n
: scrolls *n* columns.

HALF
: scrolls half the amount shown in the window.

PAGE
: scrolls the entire amount shown in the window.

MAX
: scrolls to the left margin.

CURSOR
: scrolls so that the column the cursor is on becomes the rightmost column in the window. Note that the CURSOR argument works only in windows that allow text editing.

Comparisons

The LEFT command moves in the opposite direction from the RIGHT command. The LEFT command displays the previous day's appointments in the APPOINTMENT window only.

See Also

BACKWARD, BOTTOM,FORWARD, HSCROLL, *n*, RIGHT, TOP, and VSCROLL commands

LIBNAME

Invokes the LIBNAME window

Window-call command

Syntax

LIBNAME

Description

The LIBNAME command invokes the LIBNAME window, which enables you to perform the following functions:

- □ display assigned librefs and their associated SAS data libraries and engines
- □ select a libref, which in turn displays the DIR window containing a list of SAS files associated with that libref.

The alias for the LIBNAME command is LIB.

Comparisons

The LIBNAME statement associates a libref with a SAS data library, while the LIBNAME command opens the LIBNAME window, which displays assigned librefs and their SAS data libraries and engines.

See Also

LIBNAME statement in Chapter 9, "SAS Language Statements"

DIR and LIBNAME windows in Chapter 17, "SAS Display Manager Windows"

LINESIZE

Sets or displays the line size of the active window

Output command

Syntax

LINESIZE <*n*>

Description

The LINESIZE command sets the line size or issues a message that displays the line size of the LOG or OUTPUT window, whichever is active.

You can use the following arguments with the LINESIZE command:

no argument
: issues a note that displays the current line size of the window.

n
: specifies the line size of the window. Then, a note is issued that displays the line size.

Comparisons

Line size also can be specified in the OPTIONS window or with the LINESIZE= system option. The LINESIZE command is similar to the PAGESIZE command, which displays or sets the page size in the OUTPUT window.

See Also

PAGE and PAGESIZE commands

LINESIZE= option in Chapter 16, "SAS System Options"

OPTIONS window in Chapter 17, "SAS Display Manager Windows"

LISTING

Invokes the OUTPUT window

Window-call command

Syntax

LISTING <ON | OFF>

Description

The LISTING command invokes the OUTPUT window, moving the cursor to it and activating it; it also closes the window. (The OUTPUT window displays output generated by a SAS procedure during the current SAS session.) The alias for the LISTING command is LST.

You can use the following arguments with the LISTING command:

no argument
: invokes the OUTPUT window, moving the cursor to it and activating it. If the OUTPUT window has been invoked, the LISTING command moves the cursor to the window, activating it.

ON
: opens but does not activate the OUTPUT window.

OFF
: closes the OUTPUT window and opens the OUTPUT MANAGER window, if it is not open already.

Comparisons

Note that when the OUTPUT window is open, the OUTPUT command also activates the OUTPUT window. When both the OUTPUT and OUTPUT MANAGER windows are open, the OUTPUT command acts as a toggle, moving the cursor back and forth between the two windows, activating first one and then the other. Issuing the following command achieves the same result as using the OUTPUT command as a toggle:

```
next output
```

Just as the LISTING command invokes only the OUTPUT window, the MANAGER command invokes only the OUTPUT MANAGER window. Depending on the circumstances, the OUTPUT command can activate both windows.

See Also

MANAGER, NEXT, and OUTPUT commands

Chapter 5, "SAS Output"

OUTPUT and OUTPUT MANAGER windows in Chapter 17, "SAS Display Manager Windows"

LOG

Invokes the LOG window

Window-call command

Syntax

LOG

Description

The LOG command invokes the LOG window, which displays the SAS log. The LOG window contains

- □ SAS statements you have submitted
- □ notes and messages about your SAS session
- □ output from the DATA step and from certain procedures.

See Also

Chapter 5, "SAS Output"

LOG window in Chapter 17, "SAS Display Manager Windows"

MANAGER

Invokes the OUTPUT MANAGER window

Window-call command

Syntax

MANAGER <ON | OFF>

Description

The MANAGER command invokes the OUTPUT MANAGER window, which displays a directory of SAS procedure output. It also closes the window. The alias for the MANAGER command is MGR.

You can use the following arguments with the MANAGER command:

no argument
: invokes the OUTPUT MANAGER window, moving the cursor to it and activating it. If the OUTPUT MANAGER window has been invoked, the MANAGER command moves the cursor to the window, activating it.

ON
: opens but does not activate the OUTPUT MANAGER window.

OFF
: closes the OUTPUT MANAGER window and opens the OUTPUT window, if it is not already open.

Comparisons

Note that when both the OUTPUT and OUTPUT MANAGER windows are open, the OUTPUT command can also activate the OUTPUT MANAGER window. The OUTPUT command acts as a toggle, moving the cursor back and forth between the two windows, activating first one and then the other. Issuing the following command achieves the same result as using the OUTPUT command as a toggle:

```
next output
```

Just as the MANAGER command invokes only the OUTPUT MANAGER window, the LISTING command invokes only the OUTPUT window. Depending on the circumstances, the OUTPUT command can activate both windows.

See Also

LISTING, NEXT, and OUTPUT commands

Chapter 5, "SAS Output"

OUTPUT and OUTPUT MANAGER windows in Chapter 17, "SAS Display Manager Windows"

MARK

Identifies text you want to manipulate

Text-store command

Syntax

MARK <CHAR | BLOCK>

Description

The MARK command enables you to identify text to perform the following operations:

□ cut, store, and paste operations

□ find-and-change operations.

■ **Host Information** ....

Marked text is highlighted in reverse video. However, when highlighting appears during the mark operation depends on your host system. See your host documentation for details. ■

You can use the following arguments with the MARK command:

no argument
: marks and highlights the text as a character string.

CHAR
: specifies that text marked with the MARK command is a character string. When you use the CHAR argument, marked text is highlighted on the display as a string and, if stored, is stored in a paste buffer as a text string. The CHAR argument then becomes the default for the PASTE command. When you insert this text with the PASTE command, the buffer's contents are inserted at the cursor location. Any text that follows the insert location is moved to the right, and excess text is flowed or wrapped to the next line.

  You can mark only one character string per line. In other words, you cannot highlight more than one word or phrase on one line of text.

▶ ***Caution:*** *Use care when marking every character on a line.*

If you want to mark an entire line (every character on that line), you must end the mark by placing the cursor on the first character of the next line and invoking the MARK command. Remember, however, that because two marks cannot exist on the same line you cannot mark any text on the line where you ended the previous mark.

BLOCK

specifies that text marked with the MARK command is a block of text. When you use the BLOCK argument, marked text is highlighted on the display as a rectangular block of text and, if stored, is stored in a paste buffer as a block of text. The BLOCK argument then becomes the default for the PASTE command. When you insert this text with the PASTE command, the buffer's contents are inserted as a block beginning at the current cursor location. For an example of inserting a block of text, see the PASTE command later in this chapter.

Note: You can override the CHAR or BLOCK specification in the MARK command by specifying either argument in the PASTE command.

Using the MARK Command

The following section describes marking text, cutting and pasting text, and using marked text to perform find-and-change operations.

Note: When marking text, always place the cursor in a scrollable (text) area of the display.

Marking Text with the MARK Function Key

Use the following steps to mark text with the MARK function key:

1. Place the cursor on the first character of the text you want to mark.
2. Press the MARK function key.
3. Position the cursor after the last character of the text you want to mark.
4. Press the MARK function key.

For example, if you want to mark only the DATA statement in the following statements, position the cursor over the first character (the `d` in `data`), press the function key assigned the MARK command, position the cursor after the last character you want to mark (the space after the semicolon in the example), and press the MARK function key again.

```
data example;
   input animal $ vegetble $ mineral $;
   cards;
cow carrot quartz
giraffe squash iron
;
```

Marking Text with the MARK Command

Use the following steps to mark text with the MARK command:

1. Type MARK on the command line. Do not press ENTER.
2. Move the cursor to the first character you want to mark. Press ENTER.
3. Return the cursor to the command line and type MARK. Again, do not press ENTER.
4. Position the cursor after the last character of the text you want to mark. Press ENTER.

Cutting and Pasting Text

Use the following steps to perform cut-and-paste operations:

1. Mark the text using one of the methods just described.
2. Decide whether you want to place a copy of the marked text in the paste buffer, or whether you want to cut the text out of the current window and store it in the paste buffer. To copy and store the text, issue the STORE command; to cut and store the text, issue the CUT command.

Finding and Changing Text

You can use the MARK command to look for a character or text string in a particular section of text. Follow these steps to mark text that you want to use with the find-and-change operation:

1. Mark the text using one of the methods just described.
2. Issue the FIND or CHANGE command to locate or change the text.
3. Issue the UNMARK command to clear the MARK designation.

Comparisons

The MARK command is similar to the SMARK command but with some important differences:

- □ Text marked with the MARK command can be cut or stored with the CUT or STORE command. Text marked with the SMARK command can be stored with the STORE command but cannot be cut with the CUT command.
- □ The MARK command identifies specific sections of text, while the SMARK command identifies an area on the display.
- □ You can mark only scrollable sections of the display with the MARK command. The SMARK command enables you to mark display areas that include all portions of a window, including nonscrollable sections.
- □ You can cross window borders with the SMARK command, including all or portions of multiple windows.
- □ To perform find-and-change operations, mark text using the MARK command. You cannot use the SMARK command for find-and-change operations.

■ **Host Information** .... The SMARK command is host-dependent. See the SAS documentation for your host system before using this command. ■

See Also

BFIND, CHANGE, CUT, FIND, PASTE, RCHANGE, RFIND, SMARK, STORE, and UNMARK commands

MEMCLEAR

Clears the memory register

Calculator command

Syntax

MEMCLEAR

Description

In the CALCULATOR window, the MEMCLEAR command clears the memory register.

See Also

MEMMINUS, MEMPLUS, and MEMRECALL commands

CALCULATOR window in Chapter 17, "SAS Display Manager Windows"

MEMMINUS

Subtracts register amount from the memory register

Calculator command

Syntax

MEMMINUS

Description

In the CALCULATOR window, the MEMMINUS command subtracts the last operand used in a computation (as shown in the Tape field) from the contents of the Memory field.

Comparisons

The MEMMINUS command is the opposite of the MEMPLUS command.

See Also

MEMCLEAR, MEMPLUS, and MEMRECALL commands

CALCULATOR window in Chapter 17, "SAS Display Manager Windows"

MEMPLUS

Adds register amount to the memory register

Calculator command

Syntax

MEMPLUS

Description

In the CALCULATOR window, the MEMPLUS command adds the last operand used in a computation (as shown in the Tape field) to the contents of the Memory field.

Comparisons

The MEMPLUS command is the opposite of the MEMMINUS command.

See Also

MEMCLEAR, MEMMINUS, and MEMRECALL commands

CALCULATOR window in Chapter 17, "SAS Display Manager Windows"

MEMRECALL

Puts memory contents into the primary operand area

Calculator command

Syntax

MEMRECALL

Description

In the CALCULATOR window, the MEMRECALL command places the memory contents into the primary operand area.

See Also

MEMCLEAR, MEMMINUS, and MEMPLUS commands

CALCULATOR window in Chapter 17, "SAS Display Manager Windows"

n

Scrolls to a designated line

Scrolling command

Syntax

n

Description

The *n* command scrolls line *n* to the top of the window, so that it is the first numbered line below the command line.

Comparisons

The *n* command is similar to the BACKWARD and FORWARD commands, except that it scrolls a specific line to the top of the window instead of scrolling in a general direction. It is most like the TOP and BOTTOM commands because it scrolls a specific line.

See Also

BACKWARD, BOTTOM, FORWARD, HSCROLL, LEFT, RIGHT, TOP, and VSCROLL commands

NEXT

Moves the cursor to the next window, activating it

Window-management command

Syntax

NEXT <*window-name*>

Description

The NEXT command moves the cursor to the next open window based on the order in which the windows were first opened, displaying and activating it. For example, issuing the following command in the OUTPUT and OUTPUT MANAGER windows achieves the same result as using the OUTPUT command as a toggle:

```
next output
```

The cursor moves back and forth between the OUTPUT and OUTPUT MANAGER windows, activating first one and then the other.

You can use the following arguments with the NEXT command:

no argument
: moves the cursor to the next open window, displaying and activating it.

window-name
: moves the cursor to the window specified, displaying and activating it. Even though the window is specified by name, it must already be open. You must specify the name of the window as it appears on the display. For example, specifying NEXT PROGRAM activates the PROGRAM EDITOR window, while specifying NEXT PGM does not.

Comparisons

While the NEXT command activates an already open window, a window-call command opens and activates a window. Use the PREVWIND command to return to the previous window.

See Also

PREVWIND command
Window-call commands

NEXTSCR

Scrolls to the next FORM window

Forms command

Syntax

NEXTSCR

Description

The NEXTSCR command scrolls forward to the next FORM frame and displays it. The six FORM frames are

- □ Printer Selection
- □ Text Body and Margin Information
- □ Carriage Control Information
- □ Print File Parameters (optional)

□ Font Control Information

□ Printer Control Language.

Comparisons

The NEXTSCR command is the opposite of the PREVSCR command and is similar to the =*n* command, which displays a FORM frame by numeric designation.

See Also

PREVSCR command

=*n* command

NOTEPAD

Invokes the NOTEPAD window

Window-call command

Syntax

NOTEPAD <*catalog-entry*>

Description

The NOTEPAD command invokes the NOTEPAD window, which uses the SAS text editor to create and store notepads of text.

You can use the following arguments with the NOTEPAD command:

no argument
: if any NOTEPAD windows are invoked, activates the next NOTEPAD window. Otherwise, a NOTEPAD window is invoked and the contents of SASUSER.PROFILE.NOTEPAD.SOURCE are copied into the window.

catalog-entry
: specifies the name of a notepad, either a previously created notepad in which you have already entered and saved information (with the SAVE command) or a new notepad. The notepad can be specified by a one-, two-, three-, or four-level name. The complete specification is *libref.catalog.entry.type*. Valid entry types include SOURCE, OUTPUT, and LOG.

See Also

SAVE command

NOTEPAD window in Chapter 17, “SAS Display Manager Windows”

NTITLE

Changes the displayed title of the NOTEPAD window

Notepad command

Syntax

NTITLE <*title*>

Description

The NTITLE command changes the displayed title (not the actual name) of the NOTEPAD window.

You can use the following arguments with the NTITLE command:

no argument
: deletes the NOTEPAD title and leaves the window untitled. When you subsequently close the window and then reopen it, the window is displayed with its default title.

title
: represents the name of the new title of a NOTEPAD window. Enclose the title in quotes if it contains blanks or special characters. The title can be up to 15 characters long.

Comparisons

Do not confuse the NTITLE command, which works only in the NOTEPAD window, with the TITLES command, which invokes the TITLES window. The TITLES window enables you to display and change the titles for SAS procedure output.

See Also

DESCRIPTION command

OPTIONS

Invokes the OPTIONS window

Window-call command

Syntax

OPTIONS

Description

The OPTIONS command invokes the OPTIONS window, which enables you to display and alter settings of some SAS system options.

Comparisons

The OPTIONS statement changes the value of one or more SAS system options, while the OPTIONS command invokes the OPTIONS window.

See Also

"SAS System Options" in Chapter 3, "Components of the SAS Language"

Chapter 16, "SAS System Options"

OPTIONS window in Chapter 17, "SAS Display Manager Windows"

OUTPUT

Invokes either the OUTPUT window or the OUTPUT MANAGER window

Window-call command

Syntax

OUTPUT

Description

Depending on which window has been opened, the OUTPUT command activates either the OUTPUT window (which displays output generated by a SAS procedure during the current SAS session) or the OUTPUT MANAGER window (which is a directory for output generated during the current SAS session). The OUTPUT command moves the cursor to the window, activating it.

By default, the OUTPUT window is open, and the OUTPUT command activates the OUTPUT window. If that window is closed, the OUTPUT command activates the OUTPUT MANAGER window. If both windows remain open, the OUTPUT command acts as a toggle. Issuing it moves the cursor back and forth between the two windows, activating first one and then the other.

Comparisons

When both the OUTPUT and OUTPUT MANAGER windows are open, issuing the following command achieves the same result as using the OUTPUT command as a toggle:

```
next output
```

The cursor moves back and forth between the OUTPUT and OUTPUT MANAGER windows, activating first one and then the other. Note that if you want to invoke only the OUTPUT window, specify

```
listing
```

To invoke only the OUTPUT MANAGER window, specify

```
manager
```

See Also

LISTING, MANAGER, and NEXT commands

Chapter 5, “SAS Output”

Chapter 7, “SAS Display Manager System”

OUTPUT and OUTPUT MANAGER windows in Chapter 17, “SAS Display Manager Windows”

PAGE

Specifies whether page breaks are honored

Output command

Syntax

PAGE <ON | OFF>

Description

The PAGE command specifies whether page breaks are honored in the OUTPUT window.

You can use the following arguments with the PAGE command:

no argument
: functions like an on/off switch, or toggle. The first time you issue the PAGE command, it reverses the current setting. If the current setting is on, issuing the PAGE command changes it to off; if the current setting is off, issuing the PAGE command changes it to on. When you reissue the PAGE command, it returns to the previous setting.

ON
: specifies that page breaks are honored. Nothing appears in the window following the page break.

OFF
: specifies that page breaks are not honored. A page break is displayed in the OUTPUT window as a dashed line, and more than one page of data can appear in the window simultaneously.

See Also

AUTOSCROLL command

LINESIZE command

PAGESIZE command

PAGESIZE

Sets or displays the page size of the active window

Output command

Syntax

PAGESIZE <*n*>

Description

The PAGESIZE command sets the page size or issues a message that displays the page size for the OUTPUT window only. The alias for the PAGESIZE command is PS.

You can use the following arguments with the PAGESIZE command:

no argument
: issues a note that displays the current page size of the window.

n
: specifies the page size of the window. Then, a note is issued that displays the page size.

Comparisons

Page size can also be specified in the OPTIONS window or with the PAGESIZE= system option. The PAGESIZE command is similar to the LINESIZE command, which displays or sets the line size in the OUTPUT or LOG window.

See Also

AUTOSCROLL, LINESIZE, and PAGE commands

PAGESIZE= option in Chapter 16, "SAS System Options"

OPTIONS window in Chapter 17, "SAS Display Manager Windows"

PASTE

Inserts text stored in a paste buffer at the cursor location

Text cut-and-paste command

Syntax

PASTE <CHAR | BLOCK> <BUFFER=*paste-buffer-name*>

Description

The PASTE command inserts text stored in a paste buffer at the cursor location. You can insert text stored in the default paste buffer or in any paste buffer you specified when you stored the text.

The text is inserted as either a text string or a block of text, depending on how you specified it with the MARK command. If you marked text using the CHAR argument, a text string is inserted. If you used the BLOCK argument, a text block is inserted. If you specified neither when you marked the text, the text is inserted as a text string.

Note: You can override a CHAR or BLOCK specification in the MARK command by specifying either in the PASTE command.

Text marked with the SMARK command is always inserted as a block because it is automatically stored as a block. However, you can insert this text as a string by specifying the CHAR argument in the PASTE command.

■ **Host Information** .... The SMARK command is host-dependent. See the SAS documentation for your host system before using this command. ■

You can use the following arguments with the PASTE command:

no argument
: inserts the contents of the default paste buffer into the current window after the current cursor location.

CHAR
: specifies that stored text inserted from a paste buffer be in the form of a character string. When you issue the PASTE command, the buffer's contents are inserted at the cursor location. Any text that follows the insert location moves to the right, and excess text flows or wraps to the next line.

BLOCK
specifies that stored text be inserted as a block of text. When you issue the PASTE command, the buffer's contents are inserted as a block, beginning at the current cursor location.

BUFFER=*paste-buffer-name*
retrieves the contents of the named paste buffer you created with the CUT or STORE command. If you stored your text in a paste buffer other than the default buffer, you can retrieve that text only by using the BUFFER= argument. To insert a named paste buffer, specify that buffer's name after BUFFER= in the PASTE command. You can view a list of the current paste buffer names by issuing the PLIST command from the command line. A list appears in the LOG window.

If you do not specify the BUFFER= argument, the SAS System uses the default paste buffer, named DEFAULT.

The following example demonstrates issuing the PASTE command with the CHAR and BLOCK arguments. The first two lines contain the text before the paste operation. The cursor is positioned between the two sentences on line 1.

```
00001 HERE IS TEXT. ■ MORE TEXT IS HERE.
00002 HERE IS TEXT. MORE TEXT IS HERE.
```

The contents of the paste buffer are as follows:

```
paste line one.
paste line two.
```

When you issue the PASTE command with the CHAR argument, a text string is inserted at the cursor location. The resulting text appears as follows:

```
00001 HERE IS TEXT. paste line one.
00002 paste line two. MORE TEXT IS HERE.
00003 HERE IS TEXT. MORE TEXT IS HERE.
```

When you issue the PASTE command with the BLOCK argument, a block of text is inserted at the cursor location. Instead of flowing the text as it does when you specify the PASTE CHAR command, the SAS System inserts a block of text that displaces the current text to the right. The following lines are the result:

```
00001 HERE IS TEXT. paste line one. MORE TEXT IS HERE.
00002 HERE IS TEXT. paste line two. MORE TEXT IS HERE.
00003
```

If you attempt to paste a block of text that pushes the current text past the end of the line, the PASTE command executes, but you receive a warning that text may be truncated. You can issue the UNDO command to undo the PASTE command in this case. If the paste block is wider than the distance between the current cursor position and the end of the line, the SAS System does not execute the paste, and you receive an error message stating that the block is too wide.

See Also

CUT command

MARK command

PCLEAR command

PLIST command

SMARK command

STORE command

UNMARK command

PCLEAR

Clears a paste buffer

Text-store command

Syntax

PCLEAR <BUFFER=*paste-buffer-name*>

Description

The PCLEAR command clears the contents of any paste buffer. You can enter this command on the command line of any window.

You can use the following arguments with the PCLEAR command:

no argument
: clears the contents of the default paste buffer.

BUFFER=*paste-buffer-name*
: identifies a named paste buffer whose contents you want to clear. For example, the following command clears the contents of a paste buffer named TAXPASTE:

```
pclear buffer=taxpaste
```

To view a list of named paste buffers, issue the PLIST command.

See Also

CUT command

PASTE command

PLIST command

STORE command

PLIST

Displays a list of current paste buffers in the LOG window

Text-store command

Syntax

PLIST

Description

The PLIST command displays a list of the names of all current paste buffers in the LOG window, or wherever log statements are routed.

To view the contents of paste buffers, you must insert them into a SAS display manager window by issuing the PASTE command.

See Also

PASTE command

PMENU

Activates or deactivates the PMENU facility for all windows

Window-management command

Syntax

PMENU <ON | OFF>

Description

The PMENU command activates or deactivates the PMENU facility for all windows, displaying or removing the action bar across all windows.

■ **Host Information** ....

Implementation of the PMENU command varies by host system and terminal. See your SAS Software Consultant or refer to your host documentation for details. ■

You can use the following arguments with the PMENU command:

no argument
: acts like an on/off switch, or toggle. From the command line, the PMENU command activates the PMENU facility, displaying the action bar. From the Globals item on the action bar, first select the Command and then select the Command line menu item to deactivate the PMENU facility. The action bar is removed from the display.

ON
: activates the PMENU facility, displaying the action bar.

OFF
: deactivates the PMENU facility, removing the action bar from the display. Note that the OFF argument must be used with a function key.

Comparisons

Like the COMMAND command, the PMENU command activates and deactivates the PMENU facility. However, while the COMMAND command affects only the active window, the PMENU command affects all windows.

See Also

COMMAND command

PMENU facility in Chapter 7, "SAS Display Manager System," and "Executing Commands with the PMENU Facility" in Chapter 8, "SAS Text Editor"

Chapter 26, "The PMENU Procedure," in *SAS Procedures Guide, Version 6, Third Edition*

PREVCMD

Recalls the last command issued

Window-management command

Syntax

PREVCMD

Description

The PREVCMD command recalls to the command line the last command issued in any display manager or full-screen window. You can continue to issue the PREVCMD command to recall previous commands (up to 128 characters are saved). This command is cyclic; after all previous commands have been recalled once, they are recalled again, starting with the most recent. The alias for the PREVCMD command is the question mark (?).

PREVSCR

Scrolls to the previous FORM window

Forms command

Syntax

PREVSCR

Description

The PREVSCR command scrolls backward to the previous FORM frame and displays it. The six FORM frames are

- □ Printer Selection
- □ Text Body and Margin Information
- □ Carriage Control Information
- □ Print File Parameters (optional)
- □ Font Control Information
- □ Printer Control Language.

Note: You cannot scroll back to the Printer Selection frame after you have exited from it.

Comparisons

The PREVSCR command is the opposite of the NEXTSCR command. It is similar to the =*n* command, which displays a FORM frame by numeric designation.

See Also

NEXTSCR command

=*n* command

PREVWIND

Moves the cursor to the previous window, activating it

Window-management command

Syntax

PREVWIND <*window-name*>

Description

The PREVWIND command moves the cursor to the previous open window based on the order in which the windows were opened, displaying and activating it.

You can use the following arguments with the PREVWIND command:

no argument
: moves the cursor to the previous open window, displaying and activating it.

window-name
: moves the cursor to the window specified, displaying and activating it. Even though the window is specified by name, it must be open already. You must specify the name of the window as it appears on the display. For example, specifying PREVWIND PROGRAM activates the PROGRAM EDITOR window, while specifying PREVWIND PGM does not.

Comparisons

While the PREVWIND command activates an already open window, a window-call command opens and activates a window. Issue the NEXT command to access the next window.

See Also

NEXT command

window-call commands

PRINT

Prints a file using the FORM subsystem

File-management command

Syntax

PRINT <FILE=*file-specification*> <FORM=<*catalog-name*> *form-name*> <REPLACE | APPEND>

Description

The PRINT command prints a file using the FORM subsystem.

You can use the following arguments with the PRINT command:

no argument
: causes the first execution of the PRINT command to print using the current FORMNAME setting and the current PRTFILE setting. A subsequent execution of the PRINT command with no argument specified continues to use the same *file-specification* until execution of the PRINT command with no arguments specified, the PRTFILE command with no arguments specified, or the FORMNAME command with arguments specified.

FILE=*file-specification*
: can be one of the following arguments:

  FILE=*fileref*
  : identifies the file by its fileref. The fileref must have previously been associated with an external file in a FILENAME statement or in an appropriate host command.

  FILE='*external-file*'
  : identifies the file by its physical name. The physical name is the name by which the host system recognizes the file. The name must be enclosed in quotes.

FORM=<*catalog-name*> *form-name*
: specifies the form to use in printing, where *catalog-name* specifies the name of the SAS catalog containing the form (the default is SASUSER.PROFILE) and *form-name* specifies the name of the form. If no form is specified, the form specified in the FORMNAME command or the default form is used in printing.

APPEND
: specifies that the file is to be printed, appended to its previous contents. The APPEND argument suppresses the display of a requestor window, which appears if you have not already specified the APPEND argument with the PRTFILE command. (The requestor window prompts you to specify A to append the file, R to replace the file, or C to cancel the operation.)

REPLACE
: specifies that the file is to be printed and replaces its previous contents. The REPLACE argument suppresses the display of a requestor window, which appears if you have not already specified the REPLACE argument with the PRTFILE command. (The requestor window prompts you to specify A to append the file, R to replace the file, or C to cancel the operation.)

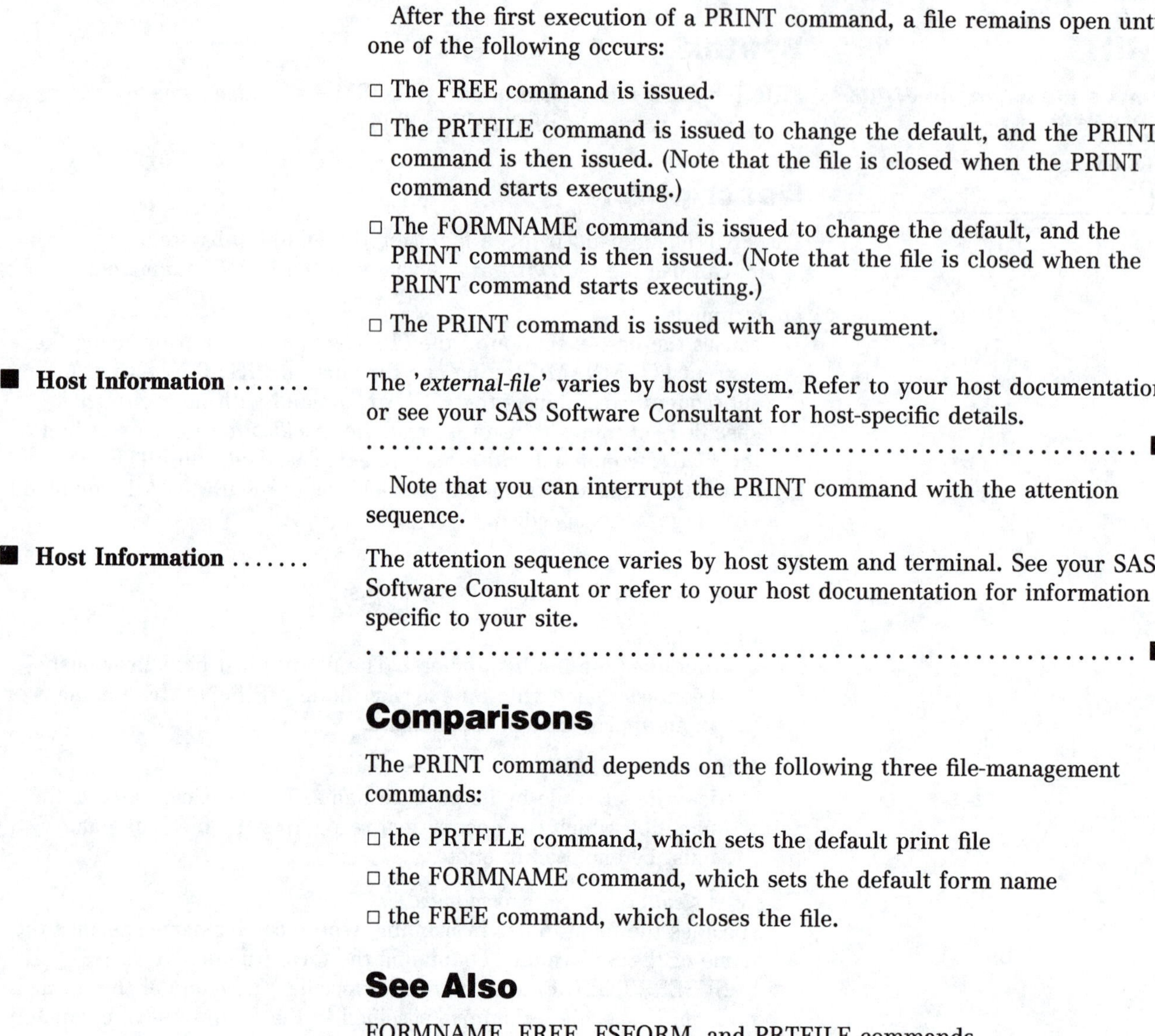

After the first execution of a PRINT command, a file remains open until one of the following occurs:

□ The FREE command is issued.

□ The PRTFILE command is issued to change the default, and the PRINT command is then issued. (Note that the file is closed when the PRINT command starts executing.)

□ The FORMNAME command is issued to change the default, and the PRINT command is then issued. (Note that the file is closed when the PRINT command starts executing.)

□ The PRINT command is issued with any argument.

■ **Host Information** .... The '*external-file*' varies by host system. Refer to your host documentation or see your SAS Software Consultant for host-specific details.

.... ■

Note that you can interrupt the PRINT command with the attention sequence.

■ **Host Information** .... The attention sequence varies by host system and terminal. See your SAS Software Consultant or refer to your host documentation for information specific to your site.

.... ■

Comparisons

The PRINT command depends on the following three file-management commands:

□ the PRTFILE command, which sets the default print file

□ the FORMNAME command, which sets the default form name

□ the FREE command, which closes the file.

See Also

FORMNAME, FREE, FSFORM, and PRTFILE commands

"Interrupting Execution of Commands" in Chapter 7, "SAS Display Manager System"

FORM window in Chapter 17, "SAS Display Manager Windows"

PRINT ALL

Prints the days in the current month

Appointment command

Syntax

PRINT ALL

Description

The PRINT ALL command prints all of the appointment lines (all of the Time and Appointments fields' data) for the days in the current month in the APPOINTMENT window. The printed listing goes to your default printer. Each day's appointments are separated from other days' appointments by three blank lines. You can issue the PRTFILE command to set the default printer.

■ **Host Information** .... The default printer varies by host system and site. Consult your SAS Software Consultant or refer to your host documentation for details. ■

See Also

FREE and PRTFILE commands

APPOINTMENT window in Chapter 17, "SAS Display Manager Windows"

PROGRAM

Invokes the PROGRAM EDITOR window

Window-call command

Syntax

PROGRAM

Description

The PROGRAM command invokes the PROGRAM EDITOR window, where you can perform the following functions:

- □ enter and edit program statements and other text
- □ submit program statements to the SAS System for execution
- □ save and include source files.

The alias for the PROGRAM command is PGM.

See Also

PROGRAM EDITOR window in Chapter 17, "SAS Display Manager Windows"

PRTFILE

Sets the default print file

File-management command

Syntax

PRTFILE <*file-specification* | CLEAR <APPEND | REPLACE >>

Description

The PRTFILE command specifies the print file where your output is sent.

■ **Host Information** .... The default print file varies by host system and site. See your SAS Software Consultant or refer to your host documentation for details. ■

You can use the following arguments with the PRTFILE command:

no argument
: displays the name of the current print file or tells you that no print file exists.

file-specification
: can be one of the following arguments:

  fileref
  : identifies the print file by its fileref. The fileref must have previously been associated with an external file in a FILENAME statement or in an appropriate host command.

  'external-file'
  : identifies the print file by its physical name. The physical name is the name by which the host system recognizes the file. The name must be enclosed in quotes.

CLEAR
: ends the association between the *file-specification* and the print file.

APPEND
: specifies that, by default, when a file is printed it is appended to the file to which it is routed. The APPEND argument suppresses the display of a requestor window, which otherwise prompts you to specify A to append the file, R to replace the file, or C to cancel the operation.

REPLACE
: specifies that, by default, when a file is printed it replaces the contents of the file to which it is routed. The REPLACE argument suppresses the display of a requestor window, which otherwise prompts you to specify A to append the file, R to replace the file, or C to cancel the operation.

■ **Host Information** .... The *'external-file'* varies by host system. For host-specific information, refer to your host documentation or see your SAS Software Consultant. ■

Comparisons

The PRTFILE command, which sets the default print file, is associated with the PRINT command, which actually prints the file. The PRTFILE command is associated with the FORMNAME command, which sets the default form name, and the FREE command, which closes the file.

See Also

FORMNAME, FREE, and PRINT commands

FORM window in Chapter 17, "SAS Display Manager Windows"

PURGE

Removes nonshared function key settings among different terminals

Window-management command

Syntax

PURGE

Description

Among different terminals, some key names are identical, or shared, while other key settings among the same group of terminals are not shared. Issuing the PURGE command removes all nonshared key names among the different terminals. The PURGE command can be used only in the KEYS window.

See Also

KEYS window in Chapter 17, "SAS Display Manager Windows"

RCHANGE

Repeats the previous CHANGE command

Search command

Syntax

RCHANGE

Description

The RCHANGE command continues to find and change one text string to another text string as most recently specified in a FIND, BFIND, or CHANGE command.

Comparisons

The RCHANGE command is used with the CHANGE command, which initiates the change of *string-1* to *string-2*.

See Also

BFIND command

CHANGE command

FIND command

MARK command

RFIND command

RECALL

Recalls submitted SAS statements

Program command

Syntax

RECALL <*n*>

Description

The RECALL command recalls to the PROGRAM EDITOR window SAS statements previously submitted in the current SAS session.

You can use the following arguments with the RECALL command:

no argument
: recalls the most recently submitted SAS statements. If you continue to issue the RECALL command with no numeric argument specified, the statements are recalled, starting with the most recently submitted or recalled and moving backward. If you issue the RECALL command after you recall all of the statements submitted during the current session, the SAS System issues the following message in the PROGRAM EDITOR window:

```
WARNING:  Nothing left to recall.
```

n
: recalls to the PROGRAM EDITOR window SAS statements submitted in the current SAS session by the numeric order in which you submitted them. The order starts with the first statement submitted and ends with the last. For example, if you issue the following command, the third block of SAS statements submitted during the current session is recalled:

```
recall 3
```

The advantage of using the numeric argument is that you can recall statements out of the order in which you submitted them.

You can also combine the two approaches, issuing the RECALL command both with and without a numeric argument. For example, suppose you have submitted five statements. Then suppose you issue the following command:

```
recall 5
```

Subsequently executing the RECALL command with no argument specified is equivalent to issuing the following command:

```
recall 4
```

See Also

SUBMIT command

SUBTOP command

RESHOW

Rebuilds the windows displayed

Window-management command

Syntax

RESHOW

Description

The RESHOW command redisplays the windows currently displayed. For example, issuing the RESHOW command removes messages from the host system, but the contents of the displayed window remain.

See Also

CLEAR command

RESIZE

Returns to the configuration prior to the tiled or cascaded pattern

Window size and position command

Syntax

RESIZE

Description

The RESIZE command eliminates the window pattern achieved with either the CASCADE or TILE command and returns to the window configuration that existed before the CASCADE or TILE command was issued. The window active immediately before execution of the CASCADE or TILE command remains the active window. Note that the RESIZE command does not resize a window after that window has been enlarged, shrunk, or moved by any method other than with the TILE or CASCADE command.

See Also

CASCADE command

TILE command

RFIND

Continues the search initiated with a FIND or BFIND command

Search command

Syntax

RFIND

Description

The RFIND command continues the search for the string of characters most recently specified in a FIND, BFIND, or CHANGE command.

Comparisons

The RFIND command is used with the FIND, BFIND, and CHANGE commands, continuing to search for the characters most recently specified.

See Also

BFIND command

CHANGE command

FIND command

MARK command

RCHANGE command

RIGHT

Scrolls right

Scrolling command

Syntax

RIGHT <*n* | HALF | PAGE | MAX | CURSOR>

Description

The RIGHT command scrolls the contents of the window right the amount specified by the HSCROLL command, the default. You can override the default.

You can use the following arguments with the RIGHT command:

no argument
: scrolls the amount specified with the HSCROLL command.

n
: scrolls *n* columns.

HALF
: scrolls half the amount shown in the window.

PAGE
: scrolls the entire amount shown in the window.

MAX
: scrolls to the right margin.

CURSOR
: scrolls so that the column the cursor is on becomes the leftmost column in the window. Note that the CURSOR argument works only in windows that allow text editing.

Comparisons

The RIGHT command moves in the opposite direction from the LEFT command. The RIGHT command displays the next day's appointments in the APPOINTMENT window only.

See Also

BACKWARD, BOTTOM, FORWARD, HSCROLL, LEFT, *n*, TOP, and VSCROLL commands

SAVE

Writes the contents of a window to a catalog entry

File-management command

Syntax

SAVE <*catalog-entry* <ATTR> <TABS> <APPEND | REPLACE>>

Description

The SAVE command writes the entire contents of the PROGRAM EDITOR, LOG, OUTPUT, NOTEPAD, and KEYS windows, as well as the BROWSE and EDIT windows of the OUTPUT MANAGER window, to a catalog entry. Note that you can interrupt the SAVE command with the attention sequence in windows that allow text editing.

■ **Host Information** .... The attention sequence varies by host system and terminal. See your SAS Software Consultant or refer to your host documentation for information specific to your site. ■

You can use the following arguments with the SAVE command:

no argument
: writes the contents of the window to the catalog entry most recently specified in a COPY or SAVE command during the current SAS session unless the entry contains something. If it does, a requestor window appears as a safeguard, prompting you to append or replace the entry or to cancel the operation.

catalog-entry
: specifies the SAS data library, catalog name, entry name, and entry type. You can specify one-, two-, three-, and four-level names. The complete specification is *libref.catalog.entry.type*. If no libref and catalog are specified, the SAS System assigns the SASUSER.PROFILE catalog as the default. Valid types are SOURCE, the default for the PROGRAM EDITOR and NOTEPAD windows; LOG, the default for the LOG window; KEYS, the default for the KEYS window; and OUTPUT, the default for the OUTPUT window.

ATTR
: stores attributes with the entry. The entry is stored in a format that is recognized whether or not the entry has attributes.

TABS
: compresses spaces as tabs during storage instead of storing the file with the default spacing. Multiple spaces are compressed into single tab characters wherever possible to conserve space.

APPEND
: appends the contents of the window to the contents of the catalog entry. The APPEND argument suppresses the requestor window, which otherwise prompts you to specify A to append the entry, R to replace the entry, or C to cancel the operation.

REPLACE
: replaces the contents of the catalog entry with the contents of the window. The REPLACE argument suppresses the requestor window, which otherwise prompts you to specify A to append the entry, R to replace the entry, or C to cancel the operation.

Comparisons

The SAVE command is similar to the FILE command, which stores the contents of a window in an external file. It is the opposite of the COPY command, which copies the contents of a catalog entry into a window.

Note that the SAVE command functions differently in the KEYS window. See Chapter 17 for details.

See Also

COPY, FILE, and INCLUDE commands

"Interrupting Execution of Commands" in Chapter 7, "SAS Display Manager System"

KEYS window in Chapter 17, "SAS Display Manager Windows"

SCROLLBAR

Activates or deactivates scroll bars

Window-management command

Syntax

SCROLLBAR <ON | OFF>

Description

The SCROLLBAR command activates scroll bars, which enable you to control scrolling either vertically or horizontally throughout the display. The alias for the SCROLLBAR command is SBAR. You can move to an absolute position or to a position relative to your current position.

Scroll bars are used to move backward and forward or left and right. You can use either the cursor or the mouse within the scroll bar to move where you want. Use either a single arrow to move through the window or a double arrow to move faster.

The SCROLLBAR command is available in all display manager windows. Unless changed, it is in effect for the duration of the SAS session. You can issue the WSAVE command to save the configuration achieved with the SCROLLBAR command beyond the current SAS session.

■ **Host Information** ...... The behavior and implementation of the SCROLLBAR command vary by host system and terminal. For details, see your SAS Software Consultant or refer to the SAS documentation for your host system. ■

You can use the following arguments with the SCROLLBAR command:

no argument
: acts like an on/off switch, or toggle. Issue it once to display the scroll bar and again to remove it from the display.

ON
: activates the scroll bar, displaying it.

OFF
: deactivates the scroll bar, removing it from the display.

See Also

PMENU command
scrolling commands

SETINIT

Invokes the SETINIT window

Window-call command

Syntax

SETINIT

Description

The SETINIT command invokes the SETINIT window, which displays SAS software products licensed by your site, as well as their expiration dates.

See Also

SETINIT window in Chapter 17, "SAS Display Manager Windows"

SITEINFO

Invokes the SITEINFO window

Window-call command

Syntax

SITEINFO

Description

The SITEINFO command invokes the SITEINFO window, which contains information about your site if your Site Installation Representative has supplied such information.

See Also

SITEINFO window in Chapter 17, "SAS Display Manager Windows"

SMARK

Identifies an area to be copied with the STORE command

Text-store command

Syntax

SMARK

Description

The SMARK command identifies an area on the display that you want to copy later with the STORE command. The areas of the display that you can mark with the SMARK command include nonscrollable sections as well as scrollable (text) areas and areas that cross window borders. When you issue the STORE command later, whatever information is in that portion of the display at the time the STORE command executes is copied, not the information displayed at the time you issued the SMARK command.

Use the SMARK command to store blocks of text as follows:

1. Identify the top corner with the cursor position, and press a function key set to issue the SMARK command.
2. Position the cursor one character to the right of the bottom corner of the block and press the same function key. The SAS System calculates the desired block from any two corners.

You also can issue the SMARK command by entering SMARK on the command line. Follow the instructions given in "Marking Text Using the MARK Command" in the MARK command in this chapter.

■ **Host information** .... The SMARK command is host-dependent. See the SAS documentation for your host system before using this command. If your system supports the SMARK command, depending on the type of hardware you are using, the SMARK command highlights the marked portion of the display using reverse video. On terminals that do not support reverse video, the SMARK command is valid; however, the marked area does not appear to be highlighted.

.... ■

Comparisons

The SMARK command is similar to the MARK command in that you use it to identify what you want to capture later with a STORE command. However, the SMARK command differs from the MARK command in the following important ways:

- □ The SMARK command identifies an area on the physical display. The MARK command identifies specific sections of text.
- □ The SMARK command enables you to mark a display area that includes all portions of a window, including nonscrollable sections. With the MARK command, you can mark only scrollable sections of the display.
- □ You can use the SMARK command to mark text across window borders, including the contents of multiple windows. You can mark only scrollable sections within a window of the display with the MARK command.
- □ You cannot use the CUT command to cut text to a paste buffer with text marked with the SMARK command. You can cut text marked with the MARK command but only in windows that use the full text editor.
- □ You cannot use the SMARK command for find-and-change operations. To perform find-and-change operations, mark text using the MARK command.

See Also

MARK command

STORE command

UNMARK command

STORE

Copies marked text in a window and stores it in a paste buffer

Text-store command

Syntax

STORE <APPEND> <BUFFER=*paste-buffer-name*> <LAST | ALL>

Description

The STORE command copies marked text in the current window and stores the copy in a paste buffer. Unlike the CUT command, the STORE command does not remove marked strings from their original location. You can use the MARK command or the SMARK command to mark the text.

■ **Host Information** .... The SMARK command is host-dependent. See the SAS documentation for your host system before using this statement. ■

Note: Text stored in a paste buffer is not saved after you end your current SAS session.

You can use the following arguments with the STORE command:

no argument
: places an exact copy of the marked text in the default paste buffer. The text replaces any existing text in that buffer.

APPEND
: adds the marked text to the text in a paste buffer. The SAS System appends the text to the end of any text in the buffer.

▶ ***Caution:** Do not accidentally overwrite the contents of the buffer.*

If you do not specify the APPEND argument, the stored text overwrites the previous contents of the buffer.

BUFFER=*paste-buffer-name*
: creates and names a paste buffer. You can create any number of paste buffers for storing text by naming them with the BUFFER= argument in the STORE command. The rules for naming a paste buffer are the same as for naming SAS data sets and variables:

- □ the name must begin with a letter (A-Z)
- □ it must be from one to eight characters long
- □ it can contain letters, digits, or underscores.

When you want to insert the information stored in a named paste buffer, you must specify the buffer's name in the BUFFER= argument in the PASTE command.

In the following example, if you create a paste buffer (*buffer1*) with the STORE command, you must specify *buffer1* in the PASTE command to insert information stored in *buffer1*:

```
store buffer=buffer1
```

```
paste buffer=buffer1
```

The number of paste buffers you can have in one session depends on the system-specific limitations of your host.

(BUFFER= continued)

If you do not specify the BUFFER= argument, the SAS System uses the default paste buffer, named DEFAULT.

LAST
: copies only the most recently marked text and unmarks all other marks when more than one area of text is marked. To store one area of text when more than one mark exists, you must use either the LAST or ALL argument.

ALL
: stores all current marks when more than one area of text has been marked.

Storing and Pasting Text

Use the following steps to store and paste text:

1. Mark the text with the MARK or SMARK command. See the MARK command and SMARK command earlier in this chapter for instructions.
2. On the command line, type the word STORE and any arguments you want to specify. Then press ENTER.

   You can also use a function key to store marked text. It is often effective to use a combination of function keys and command-line specifications. See "Executing Commands with Function Keys" in Chapter 7 for details.

   In either case, the SAS System places a copy of the marked text in the paste buffer.

A Quick Method

If only one piece of text is marked with the MARK or SMARK command, and you want to store the text in the default paste buffer, you can use the following quick method to mark and store the text:

1. Use the MARK or SMARK function key to indicate the beginning of the text string.
2. Position the cursor after the last character in the string.
3. Press the STORE function key. The text is marked automatically, the STORE command is executed, and the string is unmarked.

Comparisons

The STORE command stores a copy of the marked text in the paste buffer, leaving the marked string in its original location. The CUT command removes marked strings from the current window and stores them in a paste buffer. In addition, you can use the STORE command in windows that do not use the full text editor, while the CUT command is valid only in windows that use the full text editor.

See Also

CUT command

MARK command

PASTE command

SUBMIT

Submits SAS statements for execution

Program command

Syntax

SUBMIT <'*SAS-statement-1*; . . . *SAS-statement-n*;'>

Description

The SUBMIT command submits any program statements in the PROGRAM EDITOR window for execution to the SAS System. Lines removed from the PROGRAM EDITOR window by the execution of the SUBMIT command cannot be undone by the UNDO command. Execution can be interrupted with the attention sequence. Issue the RECALL command to return the same SAS statements previously submitted with the SUBMIT command to the PROGRAM EDITOR window.

■ **Host Information** ....

The attention sequence varies by host system and terminal. See your SAS Software Consultant for information specific to your site or refer to your host documentation. ■

▶ ***Caution:*** *The SAS System always attempts to execute text submitted by the SUBMIT command.*

If you inadvertently issue the SUBMIT command with text other than SAS statements in the PROGRAM EDITOR window, the SAS System attempts to execute whatever is submitted, which could result in numerous error messages.

You can use the following arguments with the SUBMIT command:

no argument
: submits all statements in the PROGRAM EDITOR window.

'*SAS-statement-1*; . . . *SAS-statement-n*;'
: represents SAS statements you want to submit from the command line. No other lines in the window are submitted.

Comparisons

The SUBMIT command is interchangeable with the END command. It is similar to the SUBTOP command, which submits only the top lines of SAS statements. However, the SUBTOP command is affected by the UNDO command, while the SUBMIT command is not.

See Also

END command

RECALL command

SUBTOP command

SUBTOP

Submits the top *n* lines for execution

Program command

Syntax

SUBTOP <*n*>

Description

The SUBTOP command submits the first *n* lines of SAS statements in the PROGRAM EDITOR window for execution to the SAS System. You can use the UNDO command to replace lines that the SUBTOP command removes, although it cannot actually reverse the effects of the submitted statements. Issue the RECALL command to return the same SAS statements previously submitted with the SUBTOP command to the PROGRAM EDITOR window. You can also interrupt execution of the SUBTOP command by executing the attention sequence.

■ **Host Information** .... The attention sequence varies by host system and terminal. See your SAS Software Consultant for information specific to your site or refer to your host documentation. ■

▶ ***Caution:*** *The SAS System always attempts to issue text submitted by the SUBTOP command.*

If you inadvertently issue the SUBTOP command with text other than SAS statements in the PROGRAM EDITOR window, the SAS System attempts to execute whatever is submitted, which could result in numerous error messages.

You can use the following arguments with the SUBTOP command:

no argument
: submits the top line of SAS statements in the PROGRAM EDITOR window for execution.

n
: submits the first *n* lines of SAS statements in the PROGRAM EDITOR window for execution.

Comparisons

The SUBTOP command submits the number of lines you specify, while the SUBMIT command submits all SAS statements in the PROGRAM EDITOR window. The SUBTOP command is affected by the UNDO command, while the SUBMIT command is not.

See Also

RECALL command

SUBMIT command

TAPE

Turns the tape display on and off

Calculator command

Syntax

TAPE <ON | OFF>

Description

The TAPE command turns the display of the Tape field on and off in the CALCULATOR window. When turned on (the default), the Tape field displays the last ten operands used in calculations, along with the operator used to compute each operand. The TAPE command also displays the subtotal of calculations if you use the equal sign (=) operator. This field is similar to an adding machine tape; it enables you to look back and see what numbers you have used in computations. The alias for the TAPE command is T.

You can print the tape to a file by issuing the PRINT command. Next, you can issue the FREE command to close the print file. Then you can edit the print file to see the entire tape while the CALCULATOR window is still active.

You can use the following arguments with the TAPE command:

no argument
: functions like an on/off switch, or toggle.

ON
: turns the tape display on.

OFF
: turns the tape display off.

See Also

CALCULATOR window in Chapter 17, "SAS Display Manager Windows"

TILE

Creates a mosaic of all open windows

Window size and position command

Syntax

TILE

Description

The TILE command displays all open windows in a rectangular mosaic pattern that fills the display. The size of each rectangle and the visible contents of each window depend on the number of open windows. The TILE command takes no argument. The mosaic pattern is eliminated by issuing the RESIZE command or by changing to a cascaded pattern by issuing the CASCADE command.

Comparisons

While the TILE command creates a rectangular mosaic pattern displaying all windows including their names and contents, the CASCADE command creates a layered display with all window names visible but only the contents of the front window visible.

See Also

CASCADE command

RESIZE command

TITLES

Invokes the TITLES window

Window-call command

Syntax

TITLES

Description

The TITLES command invokes the TITLES window, which enables you to enter, edit, and browse up to ten lines of titles for procedure output.

See Also

FOOTNOTES command

TITLE statement in Chapter 9, "SAS Language Statements"

TITLES window in Chapter 17, "SAS Display Manager Windows"

TOP

Scrolls to the top line

Scrolling command

Syntax

TOP

Description

The TOP command scrolls to the first line of text and positions the cursor on the first input field.

Comparisons

The TOP command is equivalent to the BACKWARD command with the MAX argument specified. The TOP command moves in the opposite direction from the BOTTOM command.

See Also

BACKWARD, BOTTOM, FORWARD, HSCROLL, LEFT, *n*, RIGHT, and VSCROLL commands

UNMARK

Returns marked text to normal status

Text-store command

Syntax

UNMARK <ALL>

Description

The UNMARK command returns marked text to normal status, removing any highlighting that results from marking the text with the MARK or SMARK command.

To unmark a section of text, press the UNMARK function key. Or, type UNMARK on the command line and then press ENTER.

If more than one area of text is highlighted, and you want to unmark all areas, type ALL on the command line and then press the UNMARK function key. To unmark just one section of marked text when the display contains several marked areas, place the cursor inside the area you want to unmark and press the UNMARK function key.

You can use the following arguments with the UNMARK command:

no argument
: unmarks a marked string or block of text in the current display. Issue the UNMARK command without specifying an argument when the text contains only one marked string or block of text.

ALL
: indicates that when there is more than one marked string or block of text, the SAS System should unmark all marked text in the current window.

See Also

CUT command

MARK command

STORE command

VAR

Invokes the VAR window

Window-call command

Syntax

VAR <*libref.SAS-data-set*>

Description

The VAR command invokes the VAR window, which enables you to

□ browse data set variables and attributes

□ rename variables

□ change a variable's format, informat, and label.

You can use the following arguments with the VAR command:

no argument
: invokes the VAR window with the default libref WORK and the data set _NULL_ if no data set has been created during the current SAS session. Otherwise, the names for the most recently created libref and data set are used.

libref.SAS-data-set
: specifies that the VAR window is invoked, listing the information about the SAS data set as specified.

See Also

Chapter 2, "The DATA Step"
VAR window in Chapter 17, "SAS Display Manager Windows"

VSCROLL

Specifies the default scroll amount forward or backward

Scrolling command

Syntax

VSCROLL <*n* | HALF | PAGE | MAX | CURSOR>

Description

The VSCROLL command specifies the default amount you scroll vertically when you issue the FORWARD or BACKWARD scrolling command with no arguments specified.

You can use the following arguments with the VSCROLL command:

no argument
: displays the current setting.

n
: sets the default to *n* lines.

HALF
: sets the default to half the amount shown in the window.

PAGE
: sets the default to the entire amount shown in the window.

MAX
: sets the default to the topmost or bottommost portion of the window.

CURSOR
: sets the current cursor location as the topmost or bottommost position in the window following execution of the FORWARD or BACKWARD command. Note that the CURSOR argument works only in windows that allow text editing.

Comparisons

Note that the VSCROLL command sets the default, while the FORWARD and BACKWARD commands actually do the scrolling. The VSCROLL command is the vertical equivalent of the HSCROLL command.

See Also

BACKWARD, BOTTOM, FORWARD, HSCROLL, LEFT, *n*, RIGHT, and TOP commands

WDEF

Redefines the active window

Window size and position command

Syntax

WDEF *starting-row starting-col nrows ncols*

Description

The WDEF command redefines the active window by specifying a new starting row and column and by specifying a size by the number of rows and columns in the window. Thus, the active window is resized and moved to a specified location on the display. The new definition is in effect until you close the window. Issue the WSAVE command to save the configuration beyond your current session.

■ **Host Information** .... Implementation of the WDEF command varies by host system and terminal. See your SAS Software Consultant or refer to your host documentation for details. ■

You must use the following arguments with the WDEF command:

starting-row
: specifies the starting row, by number, for the window border.

starting-col
: specifies the starting column, by number, for the window border.

nrows
: specifies the number of rows inside the window, including the border.

ncols
: specifies the number of columns inside the window, including the border.

Comparisons

Like the TILE and CASCADE commands, the WDEF command enables you to customize your window environment. However, the RESIZE command, which eliminates the effects of the TILE and CASCADE commands, has no effect on the WDEF command.

See Also

CASCADE command

RESIZE command

TILE command

WSAVE

Saves command settings in the window(s)

Window size and position command

Syntax

WSAVE <ALL>

Description

The WSAVE command saves the command settings put into effect for a window. After you issue the WSAVE command, the settings are retained even after you close the window or end the current SAS session unless you change them again or delete the WSAVE entries in your SASUSER.PROFILE catalog. If you do not issue the WSAVE command, the settings are in effect for that window only while the window is open.

You can issue the WSAVE command to save global settings, such as window color, window position, and the presence of scroll bars. Not all command settings can be saved with the WSAVE command. For more information about the WSAVE command, see Chapter 7.

You can use the following arguments with the WSAVE command:

no argument
: saves the settings in the active window only.

ALL
: saves all command settings that can be saved with the WSAVE command in all currently open windows.

X

Enters host system mode and allows a command to be issued

Window-management command

Syntax

X <*host-system-command*>

Description

The X command temporarily exits the SAS System to the host system. You also can use the X command to issue a host system command.

■ **Host Information** ....

The X command varies by host system and terminal. See your SAS Software Consultant or refer to your host documentation for details. ■

You can use the following arguments with the X command:

no argument
: puts you into a submode of your host system and prompts you to enter the appropriate response to return to the SAS System.

host-system-command
: issues the host system command requested.

ZOOM

Causes the active window to fill the display

Window-management command

Syntax

ZOOM <ON | OFF>

Description

The ZOOM command causes the active window to fill the entire display, concealing other windows. The alias for the ZOOM command is Z.

■ **Host Information** .... Implementation of the ZOOM command varies by host system and terminal. See your SAS Software Consultant or refer to the SAS documentation for your host system for more information. ■

You can use the following arguments with the ZOOM command:

no argument
: acts like an on/off switch, or toggle. The first time you issue the ZOOM command, it reverses the current setting. If the current setting is on, issuing the ZOOM command changes it to off; if the current setting is off, issuing the ZOOM command changes it to on. When you reissue the ZOOM command, it returns to the previous setting.

ON
: causes the window to fill the entire display.

OFF
: returns the window to its default size.

=*n*

Displays a FORM window by numeric designation

Forms command

Syntax

=*n*

Description

The =*n* command is only valid in the FORM window. The =*n* command displays one of the secondary FORM frames by numeric designation. You can use the =*n* command to move freely among all frames except the Printer Selection frame, which is the primary frame. Issue the PREVSCR command to return to the Printer Selection frame from other frames.

N is one of the following:

- □ Text Body and Margin Information
- □ Carriage Control Information
- □ Print File Parameters (optional)
- □ Font Control Information
- □ Printer Control Language.

Note: If the Print File Parameters frame is not available on your system, issuing 3 as *n* displays the Font Control Information frame and issuing 4 or a greater number as *n* displays the Printer Control Language frame.

Comparisons

The =*n* command is similar to the NEXTSCR and PREVSCR commands, which display the next frame or the previous frame from a given position. The =*n* command displays a frame, not by proximity, but by numeric designation.

See Also

NEXTSCR command

PREVSCR command

FORM window in Chapter 17, "SAS Display Manager Windows"

=X

Exits the HELP window

Help command

Syntax

=X

Description

The =X command closes the HELP window and removes it from the display, returning the cursor to the window that was active before execution of the HELP command. You can issue this command from any window in SAS System Help with the same result.

Comparisons

While the =X command exits the help facility completely, the END command returns to the previous window, even if that window is another window in SAS System Help.

See Also

END command

HELP window in Chapter 17, "SAS Display Manager Windows"

CHAPTER 19 SAS® Text Editor Commands

Background information on SAS text editor commands, including tables listing all commands, appears in Chapter 8, "SAS Text Editor." See Table 8.1, "Categories and Descriptions of SAS Text Editor Commands," and Table 8.2, "SAS Text Editor Commands—Valid Windows."

AUTOADD

Controls automatic line addition

Text-editing, command-line command

Syntax

AUTOADD <ON | OFF>

Description

The AUTOADD command controls whether blank lines are added as you scroll forward past existing text. The number of lines added is determined by the setting of the VSCROLL command, which determines the default scroll amount forward or backward. If the AUTOADD command is off, no blank lines are added, and the following message appears after the last line of text:

```
*** END OF TEXT ***
```

The AUTOADD command also controls whether blank lines are added when the cursor is on the last line and you press ENTER or RETURN. With the AUTOADD command on, one line is added; with the AUTOADD command off, no lines are added. With the AUTOADD command off, issue the I line command to insert new data lines. Note that you can save the AUTOADD command setting with the WSAVE command in the PROGRAM EDITOR and NOTEPAD windows.

You can use the following arguments with the AUTOADD command:

no argument
: acts like an on/off switch, or toggle. Issue it once to reverse the current setting. If the current setting is on, issuing the AUTOADD command changes it to off; if the current setting is off, issuing the command changes it to on. When you reissue the AUTOADD command, it returns to the previous setting.

ON
: turns on the AUTOADD command in the window, so that lines are added automatically.

OFF
: turns off the AUTOADD command in the window, so that lines are not added automatically.

See Also

AUTOFLOW, AUTOSPLIT, AUTOWRAP, and I commands

VSCROLL command in Chapter 18, "SAS Display Manager Commands"

AUTOFLOW

Controls whether text is flowed when included, copied, or pasted

Text-editing, command-line command

Syntax

AUTOFLOW <ON | OFF>

Description

The AUTOFLOW command determines whether text is automatically flowed as you bring it into a window with the INCLUDE, PASTE, or COPY command. When text is flowed, the left and right boundaries are determined by the settings specified with previous executions of the INDENT and BOUNDS commands. The AUTOFLOW command controls all text brought into the window; it does not stop at paragraph boundaries.

You can use the following arguments with the AUTOFLOW command:

no argument
: acts like an on/off switch, or toggle. The first time you issue the AUTOFLOW command, it reverses the current setting. If the current setting is on, issuing the AUTOFLOW command changes it to off; if the current setting is off, issuing the command changes it to on. When you reissue the AUTOFLOW command, it returns to the previous setting.

ON
: turns on the AUTOFLOW command in the window, so that text is flowed as it is brought into the window.

OFF
: turns off the AUTOFLOW command in the window, so that text retains its previous configuration as it is brought into the window.

Comparisons

The AUTOFLOW command determines whether text is flowed as it is brought into a window, while the TF command flows text already in a window.

See Also

AUTOSPLIT, AUTOWRAP, BOUNDS, INDENT, and TF commands

COPY, INCLUDE, and PASTE commands in Chapter 18, "SAS Display Manager Commands"

AUTOSPLIT

Determines whether text is split at carriage return or after pressing ENTER or RETURN

Text-editing, command-line command

Syntax

AUTOSPLIT <ON | OFF>

Description

The AUTOSPLIT command determines whether text is split at the cursor position wherever you enter a carriage return or press ENTER or RETURN. All text on a given line starting with the character on which the cursor is resting moves to the left margin of the next line. The cursor is repositioned also, resting on the first character of the new line.

You can use the following arguments with the AUTOSPLIT command:

no argument
: acts like an on/off switch, or toggle. The first time you issue the AUTOSPLIT command, it reverses the current setting. If the current setting is on, issuing the AUTOSPLIT command changes it to off; if the current setting is off, issuing the command changes it to on. When you reissue the AUTOSPLIT command, it returns to the previous setting.

ON
: turns on the AUTOSPLIT command in the window, so that when you enter a carriage return or press ENTER or RETURN text automatically splits at the cursor.

OFF
: turns off the AUTOSPLIT command in the window, so that when you enter a carriage return or press ENTER or RETURN text does not automatically split at the cursor.

Comparisons

Entering a carriage return with the AUTOSPLIT command on is identical to issuing the TS command with the default numeric argument of 1. The results of a carriage return with the AUTOSPLIT command on can be reversed by the TC command or undone with the UNDO command.

See Also

AUTOFLOW command

AUTOWRAP command

TF command

TS command

AUTOWRAP

Controls whether text is wrapped when it is included, copied, or filed

Text-editing, command-line command

Syntax

AUTOWRAP <ON | OFF>

Description

The AUTOWRAP command controls whether text is wrapped or truncated when it is included, copied, or filed. With the AUTOWRAP command on, you can use the INCLUDE or COPY command to bring into a window a file with a line length that exceeds the boundaries of the window without truncating the text in the file. Instead, lines are split at word boundaries. Conversely, the AUTOWRAP command allows you to use the FILE command to send to an external file text with a line length that exceeds the boundaries of the file without truncating the text. As when text is included or copied, lines are split at word boundaries. With the AUTOWRAP command off, text can be truncated depending on the line length of the text and of the window or file.

You can use the following arguments with the AUTOWRAP command:

no argument
: acts like an on/off switch, or toggle. The first time you issue the AUTOWRAP command, it reverses the current setting. If the current setting is on, issuing the AUTOWRAP command changes it to off; if the current setting is off, issuing the command changes it to on. When you reissue the AUTOWRAP command, it returns to the previous setting.

ON
: turns on the AUTOWRAP command in the window, so that text is wrapped as it is brought into the window or moved into an external file.

OFF
: turns off the AUTOWRAP command in the window so that, depending on its length, text can be truncated as it is brought into the window or moved into an external file.

See Also

AUTOFLOW and AUTOSPLIT commands

COPY, FILE, and INCLUDE commands in Chapter 18, "SAS Display Manager Commands"

BOUNDS

Sets left and right boundaries when text is flowed

Text-editing, command-line command

Syntax

BOUNDS <*left right*>

Description

The BOUNDS command resets by column position the left and right boundaries for text already in a window that is flowed with the TF command. The BOUNDS command also sets left and right boundaries for text brought into the window with the INCLUDE, COPY, and PASTE commands when the AUTOFLOW command is on. With the AUTOFLOW command on, the left boundary setting is honored when text is split with the TS command.

For example, specify the following command if you want the text flowed between columns 10 and 60, inclusive:

```
bounds 10 60
```

Each time text is flowed after this BOUNDS command is issued, it is flowed between spaces 10 and 60, inclusive, until you issue another BOUNDS command or the INDENT command is set to on.

▶ ***Caution:*** *The INDENT command overrides the BOUNDS command with text flow.*

Setting the INDENT command on always overrides the current left boundary setting. To ensure that the left boundary setting is used, set the INDENT command off. Otherwise, when text is flowed, the indention of the first line set by the INDENT command overrides the left boundary set by the BOUNDS command.

You can use the following arguments with the BOUNDS command:

no argument
: issues a note indicating the current boundary settings.

left
: sets the left boundary by column position.

right
: sets the right boundary by column position.

Comparisons

The BOUNDS command affects the behavior of the TF and TS commands. The BOUNDS command is similar to the INDENT command because both can establish the left boundary, but the BOUNDS command also determines the right boundary. When text is flowed, setting the INDENT command on always determines the left boundary, overriding the left boundary set by the BOUNDS command.

See Also

AUTOFLOW, INDENT, TF, and TS commands

COPY, INCLUDE, and PASTE commands in Chapter 18, "SAS Display Manager Commands"

C and CC

Copy one or more lines

Text-editing, line commands

Syntax

Single command:

C<*n*>
intervening text
A | B | O*

Block command:

CC
block of text
CC
intervening text
A | B | O

Description

The C (copy) and CC (copy, block) line commands copy one or more lines to a designated location anywhere in a window.

You can use the following arguments with the C and CC commands. Note that an argument must be used to indicate the target position.

A marks the target position of the line(s) to be copied, in this case *after* the line where the A argument is typed. You can place the A argument either before or after the lines to be copied.

B marks the target position of the line(s) to be copied, in this case *before* the line where the B argument is typed. You can place the B argument either before or after the lines to be copied.

n indicates the number of times the line is copied; the *n* argument can be used only with the single command. Follow *n* with a space. Without *n*, the line is copied once.

O places the line being copied on top of the line indicated (called *overlaying* the line). Blanks on the line being overlaid are replaced by any nonblank characters in corresponding positions on the line being copied. When there is more than one line being copied, those lines are overlaid on the corresponding number of target lines, beginning with the line indicated.

* In both the single and block commands, the A, B, and O can precede instead of follow the lines to be copied.

Comparisons

The C and CC commands enable you to specify a target location for the lines anywhere in the window, while the R and RR commands repeat the line or block of text immediately after it first appears.

See Also

R and RR commands

Text-cut and text-store commands in Chapter 18, "SAS Display Manager Commands"

CAPS

Changes the default case of text

Text-editing, command-line command

Syntax

CAPS <ON | OFF>

Description

The CAPS command changes the case for text not yet entered or for text modified in a window. If you specify CAPS ON and enter text, the text is converted to uppercase as soon as you press ENTER or RETURN. The setting remains in effect for a window until the session ends or until it is changed by another CAPS command. You can use the WSAVE command to save the setting of the CAPS command beyond your current SAS session.

■ **Host Information** .... On some terminals and host systems, with the CAPS command on, characters entered or modified are translated into uppercase letters when you move the cursor from the line. Others require you to press ENTER or RETURN. Refer to your host documentation for details. ■

You can use the following arguments with the CAPS command:

no argument
: acts as an on/off switch, or toggle. The first time you issue the CAPS command, it reverses the current setting. If the current setting is on, issuing the CAPS command changes it to off; if the current setting is off, issuing the command changes it to on. When you reissue the CAPS command, it returns to the previous setting.

ON
: translates characters entered or modified afterward into uppercase letters when you press ENTER or RETURN or a function key. Character strings for the FIND and CHANGE commands are also translated into uppercase unless enclosed in quotes.

OFF
: interprets characters entered or modified afterward exactly as entered.

Comparisons

The CAPS command is similar to the CU and CCU commands and to the CL and CCL commands, which alter the case of existing text. However, the CAPS command changes the default, not the case of already entered text.

See Also

CL and CCL commands

CU and CCU commands

CHANGE and FIND commands in Chapter 18, "SAS Display Manager Commands"

CL and CCL

Lowercase all characters in designated line(s)

Text-editing, line commands

Syntax

Single command:

CL<*n*>

Block command:

CCL
block of text
CCL

Description

The CL (case lower) and CCL (case lower, block) line commands lowercase all characters in a designated line or block of lines.

You can use the following arguments with the CL and CCL commands:

no argument
: lowercases only text on the line with the line command or between the two block lines, inclusive.

n
: indicates the number of lines to lowercase. Follow the *n* argument with a space. Note that the numeric argument can be used only with the single command.

Comparisons

The CL and CCL commands lowercase text already entered, while the CAPS OFF command makes the default lowercase, in essence changing the way new text is treated. Note that the CU and CCU commands, which uppercase characters, accomplish the opposite of the CL and CCL commands.

See Also

CAPS command

CU and CCU commands

COLS

Displays a line ruler that marks horizontal columns

Text-editing, line command

Syntax

COLS

Description

The COLS (columns) line command inserts a line that marks the horizontal columns in a window. This command is especially useful when you are writing a program with column input.

Issue the RESET command-line command or the D line command to remove the COLS line. Note that column lines are eliminated when text is flowed with the TF command; they are not submitted or otherwise affected by display manager and text editor commands.

See Also

D command

RESET command

CU and CCU

Uppercase all characters in designated line(s)

Text-editing, line commands

Syntax

Single command:

CU<*n*>

Block command:

CCU
block of text
CCU

Description

The CU (case upper) and CCU (case upper, block) line commands uppercase all characters in a designated line or block of lines.

You can use the following arguments with the CU and CCU commands:

no argument
: uppercases only text on the line with the line command or between the two block commands, inclusive.

n
: indicates the number of lines to uppercase. Follow the *n* argument with a space. Note that the numeric argument can be used only with the single command.

Comparisons

The CU and CCU line commands are similar to the CAPS ON command-line command. The CU and CCU commands uppercase text already entered, while the CAPS ON command makes the default uppercase, in essence changing the way new text is treated. Note that the CL and CCL commands, which lowercase characters, accomplish the opposite of the CU and CCU commands.

See Also

CAPS command

CL and CCL commands

CURSOR

Moves the cursor to the command line

Text-editing, command-line command

Syntax

CURSOR

Description

The CURSOR command moves the cursor to the command line. It is designed to be executed with a function key.

■ **Host Information** ....

The CURSOR command can be used interchangeably with the HOME key, which is available on some terminals and host systems. Refer to your host documentation for details.

.... ■

Comparisons

The CURSOR command yields the same result as the HOME command.

See Also

HOME command

D and DD

Delete one or more lines

Text-editing, line commands

Syntax

Single command:

D<*n*>

Block command:

DD
block of text
DD

Description

The D (delete) and DD (delete, block) line commands delete one or more lines of text or blank lines.

You can use the following arguments with the D and DD commands:

no argument
: deletes only the line with the line command or lines between the two block commands, inclusive.

n
: indicates the number of lines to delete. Follow the *n* argument with a space. Note that the numeric argument can be used only with the single command.

DICT

Creates, maintains, and invokes an auxiliary dictionary

Text-editing, command-line command

Syntax

DICT INCLUDE *dictionary-name* | FREE *dictionary-name* |
CREATE *dictionary-name* <*size*>

Description

The DICT command enables you to use, maintain, and create auxiliary dictionaries.

You can use the following arguments with the DICT command:

INCLUDE *dictionary-name*
: makes the auxiliary dictionary specified available in a SAS session. Only a one-level name is accepted. The SASUSER.PROFILE catalog is checked first and the SASHELP.BASE catalog second for the dictionary specified. If the auxiliary dictionary is not found, an error message is issued. If the auxiliary dictionary is included from the SASHELP.BASE catalog, no updates are saved. If it is included from the SASUSER.PROFILE catalog, updates are saved.

FREE *dictionary-name*
: releases the auxiliary dictionary specified. A newly created dictionary is not saved in your SASUSER.PROFILE catalog until you issue the DICT command with the FREE argument or end the current interactive windowing task. If the auxiliary dictionary has been modified, the changes are saved when you issue the DICT command with the FREE argument unless the dictionary has been included from the SASHELP.BASE catalog.

CREATE *dictionary-name* <*size*>
: creates a new auxiliary dictionary as specified. The dictionary is initially empty. When the dictionary is freed, it is saved in the SASUSER.PROFILE catalog. Only a one-level name is accepted. An optional size in bytes can be given to specify the size of the auxiliary dictionary. The default is 9,808 bytes.

Comparisons

The DICT command accesses existing dictionaries or creates dictionaries, and the SPELL command checks the spelling of words and flags unrecognized words. The SPELL procedure checks the spelling of words, flags unrecognized words, and creates and updates dictionaries. Use the SPELL procedure rather than the DICT command to create a permanent auxiliary dictionary since the word list used by the SPELL procedure acts as a record of the words contained in the auxiliary dictionary.

See Also

SPELL command

Chapter 33, "The SPELL Procedure," *SAS Procedures Guide, Version 6, Third Edition*

FILL

Places fill characters beginning at the current cursor position

Text-editing, command-line command

Syntax

FILL <*'fill-character'*> <*n*>

Description

The FILL command places fill characters beginning at the current cursor position. By default, the fill character is usually an underscore or dash appearing from the current cursor location either to the end of a line or to the space before the next nonblank character, whichever occurs first.

The FILL command is most easily issued with a function key. To place the fill characters at the cursor location, reset one of your function keys to issue the FILL command. Move the cursor to the data entry location and press the function key. The fill characters are then displayed.

You can also change the default. For example, issuing the following command makes the default 10 question marks:

```
fill '?' 10
```

The changed fill character is in effect for the duration of your SAS session or until you change it again. You can use the WSAVE command to save the setting permanently.

You can use the following arguments with the FILL command:

no argument
: causes one of two things to happen: If your cursor is not in the data entry field when you issue the command, a message appears indicating what the current fill character is and its number of repetitions. If the cursor is in the data entry field, the fill characters are displayed.

'fill-character'
: is a customized fill character that must appear in single quotes. This fill character remains in effect until you change it.

n
: specifies the exact number of fill characters. This number remains in effect until you change it.

I

Inserts one or more new lines

Text-editing, line command

Syntax

I<A | B><*n*>

Description

The I (insert) line command inserts one or more lines. By default, the lines are blank; you can define an initial content with the MASK command. The I command is most conveniently issued with a function key.

You can use the following arguments with the I command:

no argument
: inserts one blank line immediately after the line on which you issued the command.

A

inserts the blank lines immediately *after* the line on which the command is issued, which achieves the same results as issuing the default. Note that you cannot have any characters between the I command and the A argument.

B

inserts the blank lines immediately *before* the line on which the command is issued. Note that you cannot have any characters between the I command and the B argument.

n

indicates the number of blank lines to insert. Follow the *n* argument with a space. If the A or B argument is used, the *n* argument is specified last. For example, suppose line 00009 contains a PROC PRINT statement. The following I command indicates that you want to insert three blank lines before the current line of text:

```
ib3 9 proc print data=final.educ;
```

Comparisons

You can use the MASK line command with the I command. The I command inserts new lines, which are initialized to the value set by the MASK command.

See Also

MASK command

INDENT

Retains left-margin indention when text is flowed

Text-editing, command-line command

▶ ***Caution:*** *The INDENT ON command indents all lines.*

Syntax

INDENT <ON | OFF>

Description

The INDENT command specifies that the current indention at the left margin is used when text

- □ already in a window is flowed with the TF command
- □ is brought into a window when the AUTOFLOW command is on
- □ already in a window is split with the TS command.

With the INDENT command on, when you issue the TF command, all lines in the paragraph are indented the same amount as the first line.

You can use the following arguments with the INDENT command:

no argument

acts like an on/off switch, or toggle. The first time you issue the INDENT command, it reverses the current setting. If the current setting is on, issuing the INDENT command changes it to off; if the current setting is off, issuing the command changes it to on. When you reissue the INDENT command, it returns to the previous setting.

ON
: turns on the INDENT command in the window.

OFF
: turns off the INDENT command in the window.

Comparisons

The left boundary is affected by both the INDENT and BOUNDS commands. However, when text is flowed, turning the INDENT command on always determines the left boundary, overriding the left boundary set by the BOUNDS command.

Examples

In the first example text has been entered, and the TF command has been typed in the numbered field. The first line of the paragraph is indented. The INDENT command is on, and the default boundaries are 1 and 50.

```
tf 01      The purpose of Monday's meeting is to review
00002 the documentation plan and gather your responses. Please
00003 send a representative
00004 if you are unable to attend.
```

The next example shows the result of pressing ENTER or RETURN to issue the command. Note that the indention is used for all lines instead of the left boundary of 1, but the right boundary of 50 is used.

```
00001      The purpose of Monday's meeting is to review
00002      the documentation plan and gather your
00003      responses. Please send a representative if
00004      you are unable to attend.
```

See Also

AUTOFLOW command

BOUNDS command

TF command

TS command

JC and JJC

Center one or more designated lines of text

Text-editing, line commands

Syntax

Single command:

JC<*n*>

Block command:

JJC<*n*>
block of text
JJC<*n*>

Description

The JC (center) and JJC (center, block) line commands center a designated line or block of text. Unless you specify a numeric argument, centering is based on the current boundary setting established by the BOUNDS command. A numeric argument overrides the boundary settings.

You can use the following arguments with the JC and JJC commands:

no argument
: centers the line of text containing the line command based on the left and right boundary settings.

n
: indicates the column position at which to center the designated line(s) of text. Follow the *n* argument with a space. The numeric argument can be specified in the beginning or ending line of the block command or in both. If it is specified in both, the SAS System uses the first number.

Comparisons

Like the JL, JJL, JR, and JJR commands, the JC and JJC commands align text.

See Also

BOUNDS command

JL and JJL commands

JR and JJR commands

JL and JJL

Left align one or more designated lines of text

Text-editing, line commands

Syntax

Single command:

JL<*n*>

Block command:

JJL<*n*>
block of text
JJL<*n*>

Description

The JL (left align) and JJL (left align, block) line commands left align a designated line or block of text. Unless you specify a numeric argument, left alignment is based on the current boundary setting established by the BOUNDS command. A numeric argument overrides the boundary settings.

You can use the following arguments with the JL and JJL commands:

no argument
: left aligns the line of text containing the line command based on the left and right boundary settings.

n
: indicates the column position at which to left align the designated line(s) of text. By default, the *n* argument is the left boundary setting. Follow the *n* argument with a blank. The numeric argument can be specified in the beginning or ending line of the block command or in both. If it is specified in both, the SAS System uses the first number.

Comparisons

Like the JC, JJC, JR, and JJR commands, the JL and JJL commands align text.

See Also

BOUNDS command

JC and JJC commands

JR and JJR commands

JR and JJR

Right align one or more designated lines of text

Text-editing, line commands

Syntax

Single command:

JR<*n*>

Block command:

JJR<*n*>
block of text
JJR<*n*>

Description

The JR (right align) and JJR (right align, block) line commands right align a designated line or block of text. Unless you specify a numeric argument, right alignment is based on the current boundary setting established by the BOUNDS command. A numeric argument overrides the boundary settings.

You can use the following arguments with the JR and JJR commands:

no argument
: right aligns the line of text containing the line command based on the left and right boundary settings.

n
: indicates the column position at which to right align the designated line(s) of text. By default, the *n* argument is the right boundary setting. Follow the *n* argument with a blank. The numeric argument can be specified in the beginning or ending line of the block command or in both. If it is specified in both, the SAS System uses the first number.

Comparisons

Like the JC, JJC, JL, and JJL commands, the JR and JJR commands align text.

See Also

BOUNDS command

JC and JJC commands

JL and JJL commands

M and MM

Move one or more lines of text

Text-editing, line commands

Syntax

Single command:

M<*n*>
intervening text
A | B | O*

Block command:

MM
block of text
MM
intervening text
A | B | O

Description

The M (move) and MM (move, block) line commands move designated line(s) of text from one place to another anywhere in a window.

You can use the following arguments with the M and MM commands. Note that an argument must be used to indicate the target position.

A — marks the target position of the line(s) to be moved, in this case *after* the line where the A argument is typed. You can place the A argument either before or after the line(s) designated to be moved.

B — marks the target position of the line(s) to be moved, in this case *before* the line where the B argument is typed. You can place the B argument either before or after the line(s) designated to be moved.

n — indicates the number of lines to move. Follow the *n* argument with a space. Note that the numeric argument can be used only with the single command. Without the *n* argument, only the line containing the line command is moved.

O — places the line being moved on top of the line indicated (called *overlaying* the line). Blanks on the line being overlaid are replaced by any nonblank characters in corresponding positions on the line being moved. When there is more than one line being moved, those lines are overlaid on the corresponding number of target lines, beginning with the line indicated.

See Also

Text cut-and-paste commands and text-store commands in Chapter 18, "SAS Display Manager Commands"

* In both the single and block commands, the A, B, and O can precede instead of follow the lines to be moved.

MASK

Defines the initial contents of a new line

Text-editing, line command

Syntax

MASK

Description

The MASK command displays and allows editing of the initial contents of new lines created by the I line command. The default setting for the mask line is a blank line. To view or edit a mask line, type MASK over the line numbers on a given line and press ENTER or RETURN; the mask line is inserted. You can then edit the mask line. A line with the contents of the mask line is inserted each time you issue the I command.

The mask line remains in effect for that window throughout your current SAS session unless you change it. To redefine it or change the contents of the text, simply type over the text on the mask line.

If you want to return to the default (a blank line), do one of the following:

- □ Blank out any characters in the text field of the mask line.
- □ Issue the CLEAR command with the MASK argument:

```
clear mask
```

  The text of the mask line is cleared, and a note appears indicating that the mask line has been cleared.

You can use the RESET command or the D line command to remove the display of the MASK command. Note that the MASK command remains in effect even when you cannot see it; for example, when you have scrolled past the mask line, and it is not visible on the display or when you issue the D or RESET command without first having blanked out the mask's text.

In some windows, such as the PROGRAM EDITOR window, you can use the WSAVE command to save the mask line.

See Also

D and RESET commands

CLEAR command in Chapter 18, "SAS Display Manager Commands"

NUMBERS

Adds or removes line numbers

Text-editing, command-line command

Syntax

NUMBERS <ON | OFF>

Description

The NUMBERS command adds or removes line numbers for data lines in windows that allow text editing. When you issue the NUMBERS command to remove line numbers, the line numbers disappear and all text appears to shift left. When you issue the NUMBERS command to add line numbers, the numbers are displayed on the left, appearing to shift the text right. The alias for the NUMBERS command is NUMS.

You can use the following arguments with the NUMBERS command:

no argument
: acts like an on/off switch, or toggle. The first time you issue the NUMBERS command, it reverses the current setting. If the current setting is on, issuing the NUMBERS command changes it to off; if the current setting is off, issuing the command changes it to on. When you reissue the NUMBERS command, it returns to the previous setting.

ON
: turns on the NUMBERS command in the window, so that data lines are numbered.

OFF
: turns off the NUMBERS command in the window, so that data lines are not numbered.

R and RR

Repeat one or more designated lines

Text-editing, line commands

Syntax

Single command:

R<*n*>

Block command:

RR<*n*>
block of text
RR<*n*>

Description

The R (repeat) and RR (repeat, block) line commands repeat a designated line or block of lines immediately following the designated lines. The default is one repetition.

You can use the following arguments with the R and RR commands:

no argument
: repeats the line or lines once.

n
: indicates the number of times to repeat the designated line(s). Follow the *n* argument with a space. The numeric argument can be specified in the beginning or ending line of the block command or in both. If it is specified in both, the SAS System uses the first number.

Comparisons

The R and RR commands repeat the line or block of lines immediately after it first appears, while the C and CC commands enable you to specify a target line anywhere in a window.

See Also

C and CC commands

Text cut-and-paste commands and text-store commands in Chapter 18, "SAS Display Manager Commands"

RESET

Removes any pending line commands

Text-editing, command-line command

Syntax

RESET

Description

The RESET command removes any pending line commands. It also removes any MASK and COLS lines created when those commands were issued. Note that the display but not the setting of the mask line is removed.

Suppose you change your mind about completing a block command, such as the MM or CC command, after entering the first part of the command and scrolling forward. You can issue the RESET command to remove the pending line command.

Comparisons

You can use the RESET command to achieve the same result as using the D command to remove both the column ruler generated with the COLS command and the display of the MASK command.

See Also

D command

SPELL

Checks text for correct spelling and flags errors

Text-editing, command-line command

Syntax

SPELL <ALL <SUGGEST>>
SPELL <NEXT | PREV | SUGGEST>
SPELL <REMEMBER <*dictionary-name*>>

Description

The SPELL command flags and corrects spelling errors. You can use the SPELL command to do the following:

- □ check the spelling of words, which means the SPELL command flags words it does not recognize
- □ display suggestions for unrecognized words
- □ add unrecognized words to an auxiliary dictionary
- □ replace unrecognized words with suggested words.

The SPELL command checks words against a dictionary. By default, it uses the master dictionary, SASHELP.BASE.MASTER.DICTNARY.

However, you can specify one or more auxiliary dictionaries to use in addition to the master dictionary.

Any dictionary you create is stored in your SASUSER.PROFILE catalog. Updates to a dictionary through the REMEMBER command are saved to a temporary dictionary for use in the current SAS session only if no dictionary is specified. If a dictionary from the SASHELP.BASE catalog is specified, the word is remembered in that dictionary, but the change is not saved in the catalog when you specify the DICT command with the FREE argument to free the dictionary.

You can use the following arguments with the SPELL command:

no argument
: checks the first word if the cursor is positioned on the command line; otherwise, the SPELL command checks the word where the cursor is positioned. If the word is recognized, the message `ok` appears. Otherwise, a message appears indicating that the word is unrecognized.

ALL
: checks all words. If all words are recognized, a message appears indicating that no unrecognized words have been found. If a word is not recognized, the SPELL: Unrecognized Words window is displayed, listing the unrecognized words and their corresponding line numbers. The window also displays a blank space for the dictionary you want to specify if you issue the REMEMBER command. You can issue the SUGGEST command from this window to invoke the SPELL: Suggestions window.

  Note that the SPELL command with the ALL argument can be combined with the SUGGEST argument to bypass the SPELL: Unrecognized Words window. Specify

```
spell all suggest
```

  to invoke the SPELL: Suggestions window for each unrecognized word found.

SUGGEST
: invokes the SPELL: Suggestions window, which displays the last unrecognized word and its location, as well as suggestions for the unrecognized word. (Note that a question mark symbol (?) is an alias for the SUGGEST argument.) In this window, you can issue the REMEMBER command to store the unrecognized word in a dictionary. The window then closes, you are returned to the previous window, and a message indicates that the word is now recognized.

  You can replace the unrecognized word by moving your cursor to a suggested replacement and pressing ENTER or RETURN; the word is highlighted. On the command line, issue the REPLACE command. When you return to the previous window, the unrecognized word has been replaced, and you receive a message to that effect. If you want to replace all occurrences of the unrecognized word, first place the cursor on the phrase **ALL OCCURRENCES** and press ENTER or RETURN; the phrase **ALL OCCURRENCES** is highlighted. Then follow the same steps as if you were replacing only one occurrence of the unrecognized word.

  You can also issue the SUGGEST command in the SPELL: Unrecognized Words window by moving the cursor to an unrecognized word, pressing ENTER or RETURN to highlight it, and typing SUGGEST on the command line. The SPELL: Suggestions window then appears.

The SUGGEST argument can be combined with the ALL argument as previously explained.

NEXT
: finds the next unrecognized word, based on the current cursor position. If all words from that position to the end of the file are recognized, a message appears indicating that the end of the file has been reached. Otherwise, a message appears indicating that the word is unrecognized, and the cursor is positioned on the unrecognized word.

PREV
: finds the previous unrecognized word, based on the current cursor position. If all words from that position to the top of the file are recognized, a message appears indicating that the top of the file has been reached. Otherwise, a message appears indicating that the word is unrecognized, and the cursor is positioned on the unrecognized word.

REMEMBER <*dictionary-name*>
: adds the last unrecognized word to an auxiliary dictionary, where *dictionary-name* is the name of an auxiliary dictionary. (Note that ADD is an alias for the REMEMBER argument.) A message appears indicating that the word has been added to an auxiliary dictionary. If you are using only one auxiliary dictionary, *dictionary-name* can be omitted. If no auxiliary dictionary is specified and *dictionary-name* is omitted, the word is remembered in a temporary dictionary for the current SAS session only.

You can also issue the REMEMBER command from the spelling windows. From the SPELL: Unrecognized Words window, move the cursor to the unrecognized word and press ENTER or RETURN to highlight it; then issue the REMEMBER command from the command line. A message appears indicating that the unrecognized word is now recognized. From the SPELL: Suggestions window, issue the REMEMBER command from the command line. The window is then closed, you are returned to the previous window, and a message appears indicating that the word is recognized.

Note: Suppose you specify the name of an auxiliary dictionary with the REMEMBER command from a SPELL window. If the dictionary exists, it is automatically included. If it does not exist, it is automatically created.

To exit the spelling windows, issue the END command.

Comparisons

The SPELL command checks the spelling of words and flags unrecognized words, and the DICT command accesses existing dictionaries or creates dictionaries. The SPELL procedure checks the spelling of words, flags unrecognized words, and creates and updates dictionaries. Use the SPELL procedure to create a permanent auxiliary dictionary since the word list used by the SPELL procedure acts as a record of the words contained in the auxiliary dictionary.

See Also

DICT command

Chapter 33, "The SPELL Procedure," *SAS Procedures Guide, Version 6, Third Edition*

TC

Connects two lines of text

Text-editing, line command

Syntax

TC

Description

The TC (text connect) line command connects two lines of text. It does not truncate text. Issue it in one of the following ways:

□ Type TC in the numbered field of a line and press ENTER or RETURN. The text from the second line is moved onto the first line, with no space between any text that existed on the first line and any text that existed on the second line. To create a space between the last word of the first line and the first word of the second line, you can start the text of the second line in column two.

□ Type TC in the numbered field of a line, move the cursor to the position in the first line where you want the second line to start, and press ENTER or RETURN. The text from the second line is moved to the cursor position in the first line.

Comparisons

The TC command has the opposite effect of the TS command, which splits text at the cursor. It is similar to the TF command, except instead of flowing text in a paragraph by removing trailing blanks it breaks text at word boundaries.

See Also

TF command

TS command

TF

Flows text to a blank line or to the end of text

Text-editing, line command

Syntax

TF<A><*n*>

Description

The TF (text flow) line command removes trailing blanks from each line and flows text in one of the following ways:

□ to the end of a paragraph, as signified by a blank line

□ to the end of text.

You can use the TF command to move text into space left at the ends of lines, after you make deletions and move words to new lines following insertions. Note that the TF command never divides a word. The TF command is affected by the INDENT command; if the INDENT command is on or its equivalent toggle has been issued, the left boundary remains intact when text is flowed.

You can use the following arguments with the TF command:

no argument
: flows text to the first blank line or to the end of text, whichever comes first, honoring left and right boundary settings.

A
: flows a paragraph to the end of the text by removing trailing blanks, continuing over but not deleting blank lines. Note that this argument, like the numeric argument, must be specified on the same line as the TF command with no intermediate characters. You cannot have any characters between the TF command and the A argument.

n
: specifies a right boundary to temporarily override the right boundary set by the BOUNDS command. Follow the *n* argument with a space if possible.

Comparisons

The TF command is similar to the TC command, which connects two lines of text; it contrasts with the TS command, which splits text. While the TF command flows text in a window, the AUTOFLOW command determines whether text brought into a window is flowed. Text flowed as a result of turning the AUTOFLOW command on does not stop at paragraph boundaries but at the end of the new text.

Example

Suppose you want to flow text with extra space. The following example shows the text after you have typed the TF line command on line 00001 but before you press ENTER or RETURN:

```
tf 01 The TF command
00002      flows a paragraph
00003 by removing
00004 blanks.
```

This is the result after you have pressed ENTER or RETURN:

```
00001 The TF command flows a paragraph by removing blanks.
```

See Also

AUTOFLOW, BOUNDS, INDENT, TC, and TS commands

INCLUDE command in Chapter 18, "SAS Display Manager Commands"

TS

Splits text at the cursor

Text-editing, line command

Syntax

TS<*n*>

Description

The TS (text split) command splits text at the cursor, moving the text following and including the current cursor position to a new line starting at the left margin. If you specify a numeric argument, it moves the text down the number of lines designated. With the AUTOFLOW command on, the TS command honors the left boundary specified by the BOUNDS command or, if the INDENT command is on, the current indention at the left margin. With the AUTOFLOW command off, the left boundary and the current indention at the left margin are reset.

You can use the following arguments with the TS command:

no argument
: splits the line at the cursor position, moving remaining text to a new line.

n
: specifies how many lines down to move the remaining text. The default is 1. Follow the *n* argument with a space.

Comparisons

The TS command, with the default numeric argument of 1, is identical to entering a carriage return or pressing ENTER or RETURN with the AUTOSPLIT command on. The TS command contrasts with the TC command, which connects two lines of text, and the TF command, which flows a paragraph. With the AUTOFLOW command on, the TS command is affected by both the BOUNDS and INDENT commands.

Example

Suppose you want to split two statements of a SAS program, placing each on a separate line. The following example shows the text after you have typed the TS line command on line 00001 and positioned the cursor after the first statement but before you press ENTER or RETURN:

```
ts 01 proc print data=temp; run;
```

This is the result after you have pressed ENTER or RETURN:

```
00001 proc print data=temp;
00002 run;
```

See Also

AUTOSPLIT command

I command

TC command

TF command

UNDO

Undoes the effects of actions

Text-editing, command-line command

Syntax

UNDO

Description

The UNDO command undoes the most recent action in an active window that allows text editing. The action must be a command that modifies text or text entry. If you want to undo more than one action, you must continue to issue the UNDO command. Actions are undone one at a time, starting with the most recent and moving backward.

▶ *Caution: The UNDO command cannot undo the SUBMIT command.*

Although the UNDO command replaces lines that the SUBTOP command removes, it cannot replace lines that the SUBMIT command removes. It cannot reverse the effects of submitted SAS statements.

■ **Host Information**

On some host systems, one execution of the UNDO command undoes all text entry changes made between function key and ENTER or RETURN presses. On other host systems, one execution of the UNDO command undoes text entry for only one line of text. Refer to the SAS documentation for your host system for details. ■

Suppose, for example, that under MVS you type the following three lines in the PROGRAM EDITOR window:

```
00001 libname test final.results;
00002 proc print data=test.results;
00003 run;
```

Issuing the UNDO command removes all text from the window and generates the following message at the top of the window:

```
NOTE: 3 modified line(s) replaced.
```

Under some other host systems, you must issue the UNDO command three times to remove all three lines.

Comparisons

Although you cannot undo the SUBMIT command, you can use the RECALL command to recall submitted program statements to the PROGRAM EDITOR window.

See Also

RECALL, SUBMIT, and SUBTOP commands in Chapter 18, "SAS Display Manager Commands"

(and ((

Shift left one or more designated lines of text

Text-editing, line commands

Syntax

Single command:

(<*n*>

Block command:

((<*n*>
block of text
((<*n*>

Description

The ((shift left) and (((shift left, block) line commands shift left a designated line or block of lines one or more spaces. If the shift extends past the beginning of the current line, characters are lost. (Therefore, these commands are destructive shifts.)

You can use the following arguments with the (and ((commands:

no argument
: shifts the line or lines to the left one space.

n
: indicates the number of spaces the line shifts. The default is 1 space. Follow the *n* argument with a space. The numeric argument can be specified in both the beginning and ending lines of the block command or in either one of the two. If different arguments are specified in each, the SAS System uses the first numeric argument.

Comparisons

The) and)) commands shift text in the opposite direction from the (and ((commands. The <, <<, >, and >> commands are similar text-shift commands, but they do not destroy text to accomplish the shifts.

See Also

) and)) commands

< and << commands

> and >> commands

) and))

Shift right one or more designated lines of text

Text-editing, line commands

Syntax

Single command:

)<*n*>

Block command:

))<*n*>
block of text
))<*n*>

Description

The) (shift right) and)) (shift right, block) line commands shift right a designated line or block of lines one or more spaces. If the shift extends past the end of the current line, characters are lost. (Therefore, these commands are destructive shifts.)

You can use the following arguments with the) and)) commands:

no argument
: shifts the line or lines to the right one space.

n
: indicates the number of spaces the line shifts. The default is 1 space. Follow the *n* argument with a space. The numeric argument can be specified in both the beginning and ending lines of the block command or in either one of the two. If different arguments are specified in each, the SAS System uses the first numeric argument.

Comparisons

The (and ((commands shift text in the opposite direction from the) and)) commands. The <, <<, >, and >> commands are similar text-shift commands, but they do not destroy text to accomplish the shifts.

See Also

(and ((commands

< and << commands

> and >> commands

< and <<

Shift left one or more designated lines of text

Text-editing, line commands

Syntax

Single command:

<<*n*>

Block command:

<<<*n*>
block of text
<<<*n*>

Description

The < (shift left) and << (shift left, block) line commands shift left a designated line or block of lines one or more spaces. The lines shift the amount you specify with a numeric operand or to the left window border, whichever is less. Note that these text-shift commands do not destroy text.

You can use the following arguments with the < and << commands:

no argument
: shifts the line or lines to the left one space.

n
: indicates the number of spaces the line shifts. Follow the *n* argument with a space. The numeric argument can be specified in both the beginning and ending lines of the block command or in either one of the two. If different arguments are specified in each, the SAS System uses the first numeric argument.

Comparisons

The > and >> commands shift text in the opposite direction from the < and << commands. The),)), (, and ((commands are similar text-shift commands, which, depending on the extent of the shift, destroy text. For that reason, they are called destructive shifts.

See Also

> and >> commands

(and ((commands

) and)) commands

> and >>

Shift right one or more designated lines of text

Text-editing, line commands

Syntax

Single command:

><*n*>

Block command:

>><*n*>
block of text
>><*n*>

Description

The > (shift right) and >> (shift right, block) line commands shift right a designated line or block of lines one or more spaces. The lines shift the amount you specify with a numeric operand or to the right window border, whichever is less. Note that such text-shift commands do not destroy text.

You can use the following arguments with the > and >> commands:

no argument
: shifts the line or lines to the right one space.

n
: indicates the number of spaces the line shifts. Follow the *n* argument with a space. The numeric argument can be specified in both the beginning and ending lines of the block command or in either one of the two. If different arguments are specified in each, the SAS System uses the first numeric argument.

Comparisons

The < and << commands shift text in the opposite direction from the > and >> commands. The),)), (, and ((commands are similar text-shift commands, which, depending on the extent of the shift, can destroy text. For that reason, they are called destructive shifts.

See Also

< and << commands

(and ((commands

) and)) commands

Special Features

PART 3

CHAPTER 20 SAS® Macro Facility

Introduction

The SAS macro facility is a tool for extending and customizing the SAS System and for reducing the amount of text you must enter to do common tasks.

The features discussed in this chapter are available in the SAS macro facility in Release 6.06. The *SAS Guide to Macro Processing, Version 6, Second Edition* contains complete documentation for these features, including reference material, examples, a tutorial, processing information, and sample applications, including both short utility programs and a large macro system.

Macro Variables

Macro variables include those you create and the automatic macro variables the macro processor creates. The automatic macro variables in base SAS software are listed here. Other software products in the SAS System also provide automatic macro variables; those variables are described in the documentation for the software product that uses them.

SYSBUFFR
: receives text entered in response to a %INPUT statement that the macro processor cannot match with any variable in the statement, or all text entered when %INPUT is used with no variable name.

SYSCMD
: contains the last command from the command line of a macro window that was not recognized by display manager.

SYSDATE
: gives the date when the SAS job or session started executing.

SYSDAY
: gives the day of the week the SAS job or session started executing.

SYSDEVIC
: gives the name of the current graphics device as defined by the DEVICE= system option.

SYSDSN
: gives the name of the most recently created SAS data set as two words, *libref* and *SAS-data-set,* left aligned in eight-character fields.

SYSENV
: returns FORE or BACK to indicate whether the SAS System is running in foreground or background mode.

SYSERR
: contains the return code set by DATA or PROC steps.

SYSINDEX
: gives the number of macros that have started executing so far in the current SAS job or session.

SYSINFO
: contains information provided by some SAS procedures and documented with those procedures, in addition to the information contained in SYSERR.

SYSJOBID
: gives the name that identifies the current SAS job, session, or userid.

SYSLAST
: gives the name of the most recently created SAS data set in the form *libref.SAS-data-set.*

SYSMENV
: gives the currently active macro execution environment (that is, statements in the PROGRAM EDITOR window or on the command line of a window).

SYSMSG
: contains the message you specify to be displayed in the message area of a macro window.

SYSPARM
: contains the same character string specified with the SYSPARM= system option.

SYSPBUFF
: receives all text supplied as macro parameter values when the %MACRO statement contains the PARMBUFF option.

SYSRC
: gives the last return code set by a host system command issued within a SAS session.

SYSSCP
: returns an abbreviation for your host system.

SYSTIME
: gives the time the SAS program or session started executing.

SYSVER
: gives the release of SAS software you are using.

Macro Program Statements

The following macro program statements are available in Release 6.06:

%CMS
: executes a CMS or CP command under the CMS host system. The %CMS statement has no effect under any other host system.

%**comment*
: places comments in a macro.

%DISPLAY
: displays a macro window.

%DO
: treats text and program statements as a unit until a matching %END statement appears.

iterative %DO
: executes a portion of a macro repetitively based on the value of an index variable.

%DO %UNTIL
: executes the statements in a loop repetitively until a condition, checked at the end of the loop, becomes true.

%DO %WHILE
: executes a group of statements repetitively while a condition, checked at the beginning of the loop, is true.

%END
: ends a %DO group.

%GLOBAL
: creates global macro variables.

%GOTO | %GO TO
: causes macro execution to branch to the label specified.

%IF-%THEN/%ELSE
: executes a portion of a macro conditionally.

%INPUT
: supplies values to macro variables.

%KEYDEF
: defines display manager function keys.

%*label*:
: identifies a portion of a macro to which execution branches when a %GOTO statement executes.

%LET
: creates a macro variable and assigns it a value or changes the value of an existing macro variable.

%LOCAL
: creates local macro variables.

macro invocation
: causes the macro processor to begin executing a macro. Available are name-style invocations (%*macro-name*) and statement-style invocations (*macro-name;*).

%MACRO
begins the definition of a macro, assigns the macro a name, and can optionally include a parameter list of macro variables, the PARMBUFF option, the STMT option, or any combination of these elements.

%MEND
ends a macro definition.

%PUT
writes text to the SAS log.

%SYSEXEC
executes a host system command.

%TSO
executes a TSO command under the time-sharing option (TSO) of the MVS host system. The %TSO statement has no effect under any other host system or in batch jobs under MVS.

%WINDOW
defines a macro window.

Macro Functions

The following macro functions are available in Release 6.06:

%BQUOTE
quotes a value after resolution, including unanticipated special characters and mnemonic operators.

%EVAL
evaluates arithmetic and logical expressions.

%INDEX
finds the first occurrence of a string in another string.

%LENGTH
returns the length of an argument.

%NRBQUOTE
quotes a value after resolution, including unanticipated special characters, & (ampersand) and % (percent sign), and mnemonic operators.

%NRQUOTE
quotes a value after resolution, including the special characters % and &.

%NRSTR
quotes constant text, including % and &.

%QUOTE
quotes a value after resolution, except % and &.

%QSCAN
scans for *words* and quotes the result.

%QSUBSTR
: extracts a substring and quotes the result.

%QUPCASE
: translates lowercase characters to uppercase and quotes the result.

%SCAN
: scans for *words*.

%STR
: quotes constant text, except % and &.

%SUBSTR
: extracts a substring.

%SUPERQ
: quotes all characters in the value of the macro variable named as its argument.

%UNQUOTE
: restores significance to quoted tokens.

%UPCASE
: translates lowercase characters to uppercase.

DATA Step Interfaces

The following DATA step interfaces enable you to create macro variables, assign them values, and retrieve those values during DATA step execution rather than when the DATA step is being compiled:

SYMGET function
: returns the value of a macro variable during DATA step execution.

SYMPUT routine
: either creates a macro variable whose value is information from the DATA step or assigns a DATA step value to an existing macro variable.

Autocall Facility

The autocall facility enables you to invoke a macro without having previously defined that macro in the same SAS program. To use the autocall facility, specify the MAUTOSOURCE system option.

When autocall processing is in effect and a macro of the requested name has not been compiled, the autocall facility searches a host library for a file or file member containing the name of the macro just invoked, brings the macro source statements into the current program, and compiles and executes them.

SAS Institute supplies a library of autocall macros to each SAS site. Members in the base SAS software autocall library contain macros written at the Institute as working examples of ways the autocall facility can be used and as examples of extensions to the SAS System. Additional members may be added to the library in the future. In addition, other SAS software products could contain autocall macros. Members used with those products are described in the documentation for the products.

Autocall macros in the base SAS software library include the following:

%CMPRES
: compresses multiple blanks and removes leading and trailing blanks from an argument.

%DATATYP
: returns a value of either NUMERIC or CHAR, depending on whether the argument contains a valid numeric value or other characters.

%LEFT
: left aligns an argument by removing leading blanks.

%QCMPRES
: compresses multiple blanks, leading blanks, and trailing blanks in an argument and quotes the result.

%QLEFT
: left aligns an argument by removing leading blanks and quotes the result.

%QTRIM
: removes trailing blanks from an argument and quotes the result.

%TRIM
: removes trailing blanks from an argument.

%VERIFY
: returns the position of the first character in one argument that is not in another argument.

Macro Quoting

Macro quoting in Version 6 is more concise than in Version 5. The Version 6 %BQUOTE function combines the roles of both the %QUOTE and %BQUOTE functions in Version 5. Similarly, the Version 6 %NRBQUOTE function combines the roles of both the %NRQUOTE and %NRBQUOTE functions in Version 5. Therefore, if you are writing programs for hosts executing Version 6, you can use %BQUOTE and %NRBQUOTE exclusively and eliminate %QUOTE and %NRQUOTE. (However, %QUOTE and %NRQUOTE remain available.) If you write programs for transfer to a host executing Version 5, you must maintain the distinctions described in *SAS Guide to Macro Processing, Version 5 Edition*.

The %SUPERQ function now quotes mnemonic operators in addition to the items it quoted in Version 5.

SAS System Options Used with the Macro Facility

The following SAS system options are used with the macro facility. They are described briefly in this book. Extended descriptions and examples appear in *SAS Guide to Macro Processing, Version 6, Second Edition.*

IMPLMAC
: determines whether the macro processor recognizes statement-style macro invocations.

MACRO
: determines whether the macro facility is available to a SAS program.

MAUTOSOURCE
: controls the availability of the autocall facility.

MERROR
: controls the display of warning messages when the macro processor encounters the pattern %*name* but cannot find a macro of that name.

MLOGIC
: controls whether the macro processor displays messages that trace its execution.

MPRINT
: controls whether statements generated by macro execution are displayed in the SAS log.

MRECALL
: controls whether the macro processor searches autocall libraries for a member that was not found in a previous search.

SASAUTOS
: specifies one or more autocall libraries.

SERROR
: controls whether the macro processor issues a warning message when it encounters the pattern &*name* but cannot find a macro variable of that name.

SYMBOLGEN
: controls whether the macro processor displays the result of resolving macro variable references.

Appendices

PART *4*

Appendix 1 SAS® Notes

The SAS Notes data library currently consists of the Usage Notes data set. The Usage Notes consist of reports on known problems associated with SAS software, common user questions, and fixes available for correcting existing problems with the software.

Included in the Usage Notes data set are entries describing compatibility issues. These notes consist of incompatibilities between Version 5 and Release 6.06 and between Release 6.03 and Release 6.06.

Consult the Usage Notes whenever you encounter problems you cannot solve.

SAS Notes are distributed on all product tapes automatically and on a separate tape by request. The contents of the SAS Notes tape vary by host system.

Refer to SAS Technical Report U-112, *A Guide to the SAS Notes, Sample Library, and Online Customer Support Facility, Release 6.06*, for additional information on the SAS Notes.

Appendix 2 SAS® Sample Library

Introduction

The SAS Sample Library is a collection of SAS programs that provides users with programming examples. The sample library is included on the SAS installation tape. Each new release of SAS software includes sample programs that demonstrate new features, provide a new approach to an old problem, and illustrate specific applications of the SAS language.

The sample programs can often help you select the right procedure for a specific purpose or choose the best approach to a particular programming problem. In some cases, the data and code used in SAS documentation can also be found as a sample program.

Each SAS software product has its own sample programs. Instructions for loading these files onto your system are included in your installation package.

Data File Requirements

Many of the programs are self-contained, and you can execute them as they are without adding any data or control language. However, some sample programs do require external files.

The sample library already contains any external files listed on the DATA line in the program header, which is described later in this chapter.

You must interactively run any programs that demonstrate interactive techniques or invoke interactive graphics device drivers.

SAS Sample Library Index

The SAS Sample Library Index provides a method of referencing the sample programs in the library. The index lists major categories (for example, Analysis of Variance, Data Management, General Linear Models, or Report Writing) and the names of relevant members in each category. Refer to SAS Technical Report U-112, *A Guide to the SAS Notes, Sample Library, and Online Customer Support Facility, Release 6.06*, for a complete listing of index members for SAS products.

Consult your SAS Software Consultant for information on accessing sample programs.

Structure of a Sample Library Entry

Each entry in the SAS Sample Library contains a header describing the program's features and example code.

The Header

The header at the start of each sample program contains valuable information about the program's features. The header comments include information about the program's function, any special notes about its execution, operating system requirements, and the SAS products it uses. Figure A2.1 shows the sample library header.

Figure A2.1 *SAS Sample Library Header*

```
/****************************************************************/
/*                                                              */
/*          S A S   S A M P L E   L I B R A R Y                 */
/*                                                              */
/*    NAME:                                                     */
/*   TITLE:                                                     */
/* PRODUCT:                                                     */
/*  SYSTEM:                                                     */
/*    KEYS:                                                     */
/*   PROCS:                                                     */
/*    DATA:                                                     */
/*                                                              */
/* SUPPORT:                                                     */
/*     REF:                                                     */
/*    MISC:                                                     */
/*                                                              */
/*                                                              */
/****************************************************************/
```

The header contains the following fields:

NAME
: specifies the sample member name.

TITLE
: specifies a short description of what the sample program demonstrates.

PRODUCT
: specifies products in the SAS System that the program demonstrates. For base SAS software, the value of PRODUCT is BASE. Refer to SAS Technical Report U-112 for a listing of other products.

SYSTEM
: specifies the operating system under which you can run the sample. Sample programs representing more operating systems become available as the SAS System expands into more environments.

KEYS
: specifies category headings that the index programs use.

PROCS
: specifies procedures that the sample program invokes.

DATA
: specifies the name of an external file containing other SAS statements, data lines, or macros you must execute before you can run the sample program.

REF
: specifies documentation you can use for reference.

UPDATE
: specifies the date of the last change to the sample program.

MISC
: specifies miscellaneous information concerning the example.

Example of a SAS Sample Program

The following example is a sample program in the SAS Sample Library.

Note: Although the SAS Sample Library contains programs and some external files, it does not contain sample output.

```
/****************************************************************/
/*          S A S   S A M P L E   L I B R A R Y                 */
/*                                                              */
/*    NAME: SAMPLE                                              */
/*   TITLE: GENERATE A SAMPLE OF K OBSERVATIONS                 */
/* PRODUCT: SAS                                                 */
/*  SYSTEM: ALL                                                 */
/*    KEYS: DATMAN SSTAT                                        */
/*   PROCS: PRINT                                               */
/*    DATA:                                                     */
/*                                                              */
/* SUPPORT:                             UPDATE:                 */
/*     REF:                                                     */
/*    MISC:                                                     */
/*                                                              */
/****************************************************************/
*---------------------------RANDOM SAMPLE---------------------------*
| THIS CODE DEMONSTRATES THE LOGIC FOR TAKING A RANDOM SAMPLE OF K |
| OBSERVATIONS FROM EACH BY GROUP.                                  |
*-------------------------------------------------------------------*;

data ds;
   id=0;
   k=uniform(12345)*50+1;    /* Generate the data for this example */
   l: y=normal(12345);
   output;
   k=k-1;
   if k>0 then goto l;
   id+1;
   k=uniform(12345)*50;
   if id<10 then goto l;
   keep id y;
run;
```

```
proc print data=ds(obs=150);
run;

    /* Take a random sample of 10 from each id group */
    /* First find out how many obs in this group     */
data sample;
   scan: set ds;
         by id;
         n+1;
         if ¬last.id then goto scan;
         k=10;            /* k is the number to randomly select from */
                          /* this group. it may be a function of n,  */
                          /* e.g.: k=.05*n for a 5 percent sample    */
   loop: set ds;
         prob=k/n;        /* prob is the current select probability  */
         if uniform(12345)>prob then goto next;
         output;
         k=k-1;           /* the observation is selected             */
   next: n=n-1;
         if n>0 then goto loop;
run;

proc print;
run;
```

Appendix 3 Stored Program Facility

Introduction

The Stored Program Facility enables you to compile and store DATA step programs and then execute the stored programs at another time. You can use the Stored Program Facility to reduce processing costs for programs that are run repeatedly because the time required for compilation is eliminated. The savings are especially significant if the DATA step contains many statements. The Stored Program Facility is intended for production jobs.

Using the Stored Program Facility is a two-part process. First, you compile the SAS source program and store the compiled code. Then, you execute the compiled code, redirecting the input and output as necessary. You can redirect external files using filerefs. The facility provides the REDIRECT statement for renaming input and output SAS data sets. The following sections describe the process, provide the syntax, and list requirements and restrictions for using the Stored Program Facility.

Features of the Stored Program Facility

The Stored Program Facility is available for DATA step applications only. You can include all SAS statements and other components of the SAS language that are available to the DATA step. You cannot include the following:

- global statements, such as the FILENAME, FOOTNOTE, LIBNAME, OPTIONS, and TITLE statements
- host-specific data set options.

If you do include such statements or options in your source program statements, the SAS System does not store the compiled program. Warnings are sent to the SAS log for host-specific options, but not for global statements.

When you create a stored program from SAS source code, the SAS System processes the DATA step through the compilation phase and then stores an intermediate code representation of the program and associated data tables in a SAS file. The intermediate code is processed further when you execute the stored program. Figure A3.1 shows the process for creating a stored program.

Figure A3.1 Creating a Stored Program

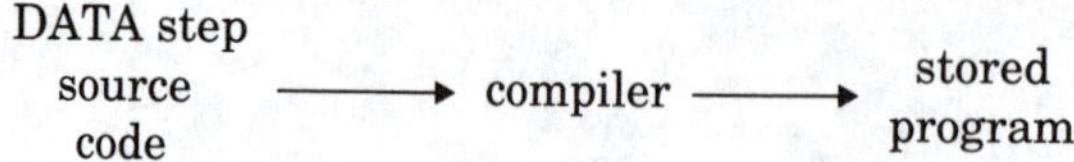

When you execute the stored program, the SAS System resolves the intermediate code produced by the compiler and generates the executable machine code for the host environment. Figure A3.2 shows the process for executing a stored program.

Figure A3.2 Executing a Stored Program

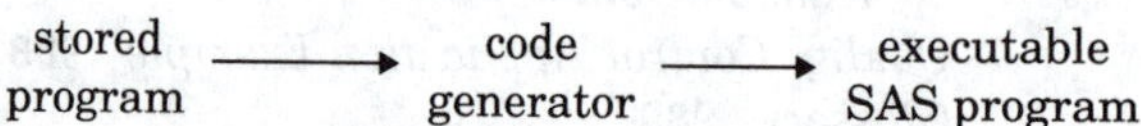

Stored compiled programs appear in your SAS data library directory and have the member type PROGRAM. To move, copy, rename, or delete stored programs, use the DATASETS procedure or the utility windows in display manager. You cannot move stored programs to another host with an incompatible machine architecture.

Compiling and Storing SAS Programs

To compile and store SAS programs, follow these steps:

1. Write, test, and debug the SAS source program carefully. The Stored Program Facility is intended for tested production jobs only. If you are reading external raw data files or if you output raw data to an external file, use a fileref rather than the actual file name in your INFILE and FILE statements so you can redirect your input and output when the stored program executes.
2. When the source program runs correctly, submit it using the PGM= option in the RUN, CARDS, or CARDS4 statement. The PGM= option tells the SAS System to compile, but not execute, the program and to store the compiled code in the SAS file named in the option. A message is sent to the SAS log when the program is stored.

▶ ***Caution:*** *Save your source code.*

The SAS System does not save the source code, and it cannot restore source code from the compiled version. You need the original source code if you attempt to move the application to another machine processing environment or if you install a new version of the SAS System. Stored programs created under Release 6.03 of the SAS System are not compatible with Release 6.06 SAS software.

Syntax

This section describes the syntax of the statements you use to compile and store SAS programs:

DATA *SAS-data-sets*;
  source program statements
RUN PGM=*stored-program-name*;

□ You must include a DATA statement, which can include the following argument:

SAS-data-sets
: specifies a valid SAS name for the output data set created by the source program. The name can be a one-level name or a two-level name. You can specify more than one data set name in the DATA statement. For more information, refer to "SAS Data Sets" in Chapter 6, "SAS Files."

□ You must include the PGM= argument in the RUN statement and specify the following value:

stored-program-name
: specifies a valid SAS name for the SAS file containing the stored program. The name can be a one-level name, but it is usually a two-level name. For more information, refer to "SAS Data Sets" in Chapter 6. Stored programs are assigned the member type PROGRAM in the SAS data library.

If your program reads data entered in the job stream, you can substitute one of the following statements for the RUN statement:

CARDS PGM=*stored-program-name*;
CARDS4 PGM=*stored-program-name*;

Example

The following example uses the information in the input SAS data set IN.SAMPLE to calculate the total number of individuals tested in an experiment. The compiled program is stored in STORED.SAMPLE.

```
libname in 'SAS-data-library';
libname out 'SAS-data-library';
libname stored 'SAS-data-library';

data out.sample;
   set in.sample;
   total=0;
   do i=1 to numreps;
      sum+numobs;
   end;
run pgm=stored.sample;
```

Executing Stored Programs

To execute a stored program, follow these steps:

1. Write an abbreviated DATA step for each execution of the stored program. In this DATA step, specify the name of the stored program in the PGM= option of the DATA statement. You can submit this DATA step as a separate program, or you can include it as part of a larger SAS program that can include other DATA and PROC steps.

   You can point to different input and output SAS data sets each time you execute the stored program by using the REDIRECT statement. The REDIRECT statement is available only in the Stored Program Facility. To redirect input and output stored in external files, include a FILENAME statement to associate the fileref in the source program with different external files.
2. Submit the abbreviated DATA steps. Be sure to end each one with a RUN statement.

Syntax

This section describes the syntax of the statements you can use to execute stored programs:

global SAS statements

DATA PGM=*stored-program-name*;
    REDIRECT INPUT | OUTPUT *old-name-1*=*new-name-1*
        <. . . *old-name-n*=*new-name-n*>;
RUN;

□ You must include a DATA statement and specify the following required value for the PGM= argument:

stored-program-name
: specifies a valid SAS name for the SAS file containing the stored program. The name can be a one-level name or a two-level name.

- □ You can point to different input and output SAS data sets each time you execute the stored program by using the REDIRECT statement.

  You can use the following arguments in the REDIRECT statement:

  INPUT | OUTPUT
  : specifies whether you are redirecting input or output data sets. When you specify INPUT, the REDIRECT statement associates the name of the input data set in the source program with the name of another SAS data set. When you specify OUTPUT, the REDIRECT statement associates the name of the output data set with the name of another SAS data set.

  old-name
  : specifies the name of the input or output data set in the source program.

  new-name
  : specifies the name of the input or output data set you want the SAS System to process for the current execution.

▶ ***Caution:*** *Use caution when redirecting input data sets.*

The number and attributes of variables in the input data sets you are reading with the REDIRECT statement should match those of the input data sets in the SET, MERGE, or UPDATE statements of the source code. If the variable type attributes are different, the stored program stops processing and an appropriate error message is sent to the SAS log. If the variable length attributes differ, the length of the variable in the source code data set determines the length of the variable in the redirected data set. Extra variables in the redirected data sets do not cause the stored program to stop processing, but the results may not be what you expect.

- □ You must use the RUN statement with no arguments to end the abbreviated DATA step.

Example

The following abbreviated DATA step executes the stored program STORED.SAMPLE created in a previous example. It includes the REDIRECT statement to specify the source of the input data as BASE.SAMPLE. The output from this execution of the program is redirected and stored in a data set named SUMS.SAMPLE.

```
libname stored 'SAS-data-library';
libname base 'SAS-data-library';
libname sums 'SAS-data-library';

data pgm=stored.sample;
   redirect input in.sample=base.sample;
   redirect output out.sample=sums.sample;
run;
```

Quality Control Application Example

This example illustrates how to use the Stored Program Facility for a simple quality control application. There are several external raw data files to be processed by this application. The source program uses the fileref DAILY in the INFILE statement. Each abbreviated DATA step used to execute the stored program includes a FILENAME statement to associate the fileref DAILY with a different external file.

To compile and store a program, issue the following statements:

```
libname stored 'SAS-data-library';

data flaws;
   infile daily;
   input station shift employee numflaws totnum;
run pgm=stored.flaws;
```

To execute a stored program, issue the following statements:

```
libname station 'SAS-data-library';
libname stored 'SAS-data-library';
filename daily 'external-file';

data pgm=stored.flaws;
   redirect output flaws=station.daily;
run;
```

Glossary

access descriptor
: a file created by SAS/ACCESS software that contains information on the data stored in a table created by a database management system product.

access method
: a set of instructions used to read from or write to a file. See also the entry for engine.

action bar
: a list of selections that appears when the PMENU command is executed. The action bar is used by placing your cursor on the selection that you want and pressing ENTER or, if you are using a mouse, by pointing and clicking on the item you want. This either executes a command or displays a pull-down menu.

aggregate storage location
: a group of distinct files on an operating system. Different host systems call an aggregate grouping of files different names, such as a directory, a maclib, or a partitioned data set. The standard form for referencing an aggregate storage location from within the SAS System is *fileref(name)*, where the *fileref* is the entire aggregate and the *(name)* is a specific file or member of that aggregate.

argument
: (1) the data values within parentheses on which a SAS function or CALL routine performs the indicated operation. (2) in syntax descriptions, any keyword in a SAS statement other than the statement name.

arithmetic operator
: an infix operator used to perform arithmetic calculations, such as addition, subtraction, multiplication, division, and exponentiation.

array
: (1) a method of grouping variables of the same type for processing under a single name. (2) a method of defining an area of memory as a unit of information.

array name
: a name selected to identify a group of variables or temporary data elements. It must be a valid SAS name that is not the name of a variable in the same DATA step.

array reference
: a description of the element to be processed in an array.

ASCII collating sequence
: an ordering of characters that follows the order of the characters in the American Standard Code for Information Interchange (ASCII) character set. The following operating systems supported by the SAS System use the ASCII collating sequence: AOS/VS, MS-DOS, OS/2, PC DOS, PRIMOS, UNIX and its derivatives, and VMS.

AUTOEXEC file
: a file containing SAS statements that are executed automatically when the SAS System is invoked. The AUTOEXEC file is usually used to specify SAS system options and librefs and filerefs that are commonly used.

automatic variable
: a variable that is created automatically by the DATA step. Every DATA step creates the _N_ and _ERROR_ variables. Some DATA step statements create additional automatic variables. The SAS macro facility also creates automatic macro variables.

base number
: in the context of numeric precision, a number raised to a power. For example, the base is 10 in the following expression:

  $.1234 \times 10^4$.

base SAS software
: software that includes a programming language that manages your data, procedures that are software tools for data analysis and reporting, a macro facility, help menus, and a windowing environment for text editing and file management.

batch mode
: on mainframes and minicomputers, a method of running SAS programs in which you prepare a file containing SAS statements and any necessary operating system control statements and submit the file to the operating system. Execution is completely separate from other operations at your terminal and is sometimes referred to as running in background. This method of running SAS programs is not available in PC and workstation environments.

bit mask
: in the SAS language, a string of 0s, 1s, and periods in single quotes that is immediately followed by the letter B. Bit masks are used in bit testing to compare internal bits in a value's representation.

Boolean operator (logical operator)
: See the entry for logical operator (Boolean operator).

buffer
: a temporary storage area reserved for holding data after they are read or before they are written.

BY group
: all observations with the same values for all BY variables.

BY-group processing
: the process of using the BY statement to process observations that are ordered, grouped, or indexed according to the values of one or more variables. Many SAS procedures and the DATA step support BY-group processing. For example, you can use BY-group processing with the PRINT procedure to print separate reports for different groups of observations in a single SAS data set.

BY value
: the value of a BY variable.

BY variable
: a variable named in a BY statement.

CALL routine
: (1) a program that can be called in the DATA step of a SAS program by issuing a CALL statement. (2) an alternate form of one of the SAS random number functions that allows more control over the seed stream and random number stream.

carriage-control character
: a specific symbol that tells the printer how many lines to advance the paper, when to begin a new page, when to skip a line, and when to hold the current line for overprint.

catalog
: See the entry for SAS catalog.

catalog entry
: See the entry for entry type.

character comparison
: a process in which character operands are compared character by character from left to right, yielding a numeric result. If the character operands are equal, the result is the value 1; if they are not equal, the result is the value 0.

character constant
: characters enclosed in quotes in a SAS statement (sometimes called a character literal). The maximum number of characters allowed is 200.

character format
: instructions to the SAS System to write character data values using a specific pattern.

character function
: a function that enables you to perform character string manipulations.

character informat
: instructions to the SAS System to read character data values into character variables using a specific pattern.

character literal
: See the entry for character constant.

character string
: See the entry for character constant.

character value
: a value that can contain alphabetic characters, numeric characters 0 through 9, and other special characters. Character values are stored in character variables.

character variable
: a variable whose values can contain alphabetic and special characters as well as numeric characters.

collating sequence
: an order assigned to characters and symbols in a character set (for example, ASCII or EBCDIC).

column-binary informat
: instructions to the SAS System to read data that are stored in column-binary or multi-punched form into character and numeric variables.

column input
: a style that gives column specifications in the INPUT statement for reading data in fixed columns.

column output
: a style that gives column specifications in the PUT statement for writing data in fixed columns.

comment
: descriptive text to explain or document a program. A comment is denoted by the symbols /* beginning the comment and the symbols */ ending the comment or by an asterisk (*) beginning the comment and a semicolon (;) ending the comment.

comparison operator
: an infix operator that tests a relationship between two values. If the comparison (or relationship) is true, the result of carrying out the operation is the value 1; if the comparison is false, the result is the value 0.

compilation
: the automatic translation of SAS statements into code.

composite index
: an index that locates observations by the values of two or more key variables.

compound expression
: an expression using more than one operator.

concatenating
: (1) a process in which the SAS System combines two or more SAS data sets, one after the other, into a single data set. (2) a process in which the SAS System combines two or more character values, one after the other, into a single character value.

condition
: one or more numeric or character expressions whose value some decision depends upon.

configuration file
: an external file containing SAS system options. The options in the file are put into effect when the SAS System is invoked.

configuration option
: a SAS option that can be specified on the command line or during invocation in a configuration file. Configuration options affect how the SAS System interfaces with the computer hardware and operating system.

constant
: a number or a character string in quotes that indicates a fixed value.

converting SAS files
: the process of changing the format of a SAS file from the format appropriate to one version of the SAS System to the format appropriate to another version under the same operating system.

data error
: a type of execution error that occurs when the data being analyzed by a SAS program contain invalid values. For example, a data error occurs if you specify numeric variables in the INPUT statement for character data. Data errors do not cause a program to stop, but instead they produce notes.

data set label
: a user-defined field in a SAS data set that can consist of up to 40 characters. It can be used for purposes of documenting the SAS data set.

data set option
: an option that appears in parentheses after a SAS data set name. Data set options specify actions that are applicable only to the processing of that SAS data set.

DATA step
: a group of statements in a SAS program that begin with a DATA statement and end with a RUN statement, another DATA statement, a PROC statement, the end of the job, or the line after in-stream input data that contains one or four semicolon(s). The DATA step enables you to read raw data or other SAS data sets and use programming logic to create a SAS data set, write a report, or write to an external file.

data value
: (1) a unit of information. (2) the intersection of a row (observation) and a column (variable) in the rectangular form of a SAS data set.

date and time format
: instructions that tell the SAS System how to write data values that represent dates, times, and datetimes.

date and time informat
: instructions that tell the SAS System how to read data values that represent dates, times, and datetimes.

date value
: See the entry for SAS date value.

declarative statement
: a statement that supplies information to the SAS System and that takes effect when the system compiles program statements.

delimiter
: a character that serves as a boundary; it separates elements of a character string, programming statement, or data line.

descriptor portion
: the descriptive information the SAS System creates and maintains about each SAS data set. It includes such information as the names of all the data set variables, the attributes of all the variables, the number of observations in the data set, and the time and date when the data set was created.

dialog box
: a feature of the PMENU facility that appears in response to an action, usually selecting a menu item. The purpose of dialog boxes is to obtain information, which you supply by filling in a field or choosing a selection from a group of fields. You can execute the CANCEL command to exit the dialog box.

directory
: (1) a list of the members and associated information in a SAS data library. (2) a list of entries and associated information in a SAS catalog.

  Note: Directory has a different meaning outside of the SAS System under some operating systems.

display manager
: See the entry for SAS Display Manager System.

display manager mode
: an interactive windowing method of running SAS programs in which you edit a group of statements, submit the statements, and then review the results of the statements in various windows.

DO group
: a sequence of statements headed by a DO statement and ended by a corresponding END statement. DO groups can be executed repeatedly in a DO loop, or they can simply be a collection of statements that are executed only when certain conditions are met.

DO loop
: the repetitive execution of the same statement or statements by use of an iterative DO, DO WHILE, or DO UNTIL statement.

double trailing at sign (@ @)
: a special symbol used to hold a line in the input buffer across iterations of the DATA step.

duration
: an integer representing the difference, in elapsed time or days, between any two time or date values.

EBCDIC collating sequence
: an ordering of characters in the Extended Binary Coded Decimal Interchange Code (EBCDIC) 8-bit character coding scheme. The following operating systems supported by the SAS System use the EBCDIC collating sequence: CMS, MVS, and VSE.

engine
: a part of the SAS System that reads from or writes to a file. Each engine allows the SAS System to access files with a particular format.

entry
: a unit of information stored in a SAS catalog.

entry type
: a part of the name for an entry in a SAS catalog that is assigned by the SAS System to identify what type of information is stored in the entry. For example, HELP is the entry type for an entry containing help information for applications developed with the BUILD procedure in SAS/AF software.

executable statement
: a SAS statement not completed after compilation and one that can be executed on an individual observation. Only executable statements can occur in a THEN or ELSE clause and can have a statement label applied to them.

execution
: (1) the process in which the SAS System carries out the statements in the DATA step for each observation or record in the step. (2) the process in which the SAS System processes items other than statements in the DATA step, such as SAS macros, procedures, and global statements.

execution mode
: See the entry for methods of running the SAS System.

explicit array
: an array that consists of an array name, an optional reference to the number of variables or temporary data elements, and an optional list of the array elements. In an explicit array, you must explicitly specify the subscript in the reference when referring to an element.

explicit array reference
: a description of the element to be processed in an explicit array. See also the entry for implicit array reference.

exponent
: the power to which a base number is raised. For example, the exponent is 4 in the following expression:

  $.1234 \times 10^4$.

expression
: a sequence of operators and operands that form a set of instructions used to produce a value.

external file
: a file created and maintained on the host operating system from which you can read data or stored SAS programming statements or to which you can write procedure output or output created by PUT statements in a DATA step.

field
: the smallest logical unit of data in an external file.

field-type of a window
: as part of the COLOR command, the area of a window or type of text where color be changed. Field types include background, banner, data, notes, and source.

file reference
: another name for fileref.

fileref
: the name used to identify an external file to the SAS System. You assign a fileref with a FILENAME statement or with operating system control language.

first-level name
: See the entry for libref.

FIRST.*variable*
: a temporary variable that the SAS System creates to identify the first observation of each BY group. It is not added to the SAS data set.

floating-point representation
: a form of storing numbers in scientific notation. On most operating systems, the base is either 2, 8, or 16, not 10.

format
: the instructions the SAS System uses to write each value of a variable. There are two types of formats: formats supplied by SAS software and user-written formats created using the FORMAT procedure.

format modifier
: a special symbol used in the INPUT and PUT statements that enables you to control the way the SAS System reads input data and writes output data.

formatted input
: a style that uses special instructions called informats for reading data in the INPUT statement.

formatted output
: a style that uses special instructions called formats for writing data in the PUT statement.

full-screen facility
: a form of screen presentation in which the contents of an entire terminal display can be displayed at once.

function
: a built-in expression that returns a value resulting from zero or more arguments.

global option
: See the entry for system option.

heading
: the text located near the beginning of each page of output. This includes lines produced by HEADER= options in FILE statements, lines written with TITLE statements, and default information such as date and page numbers.

host
: the operating system that provides facilities, computer services, and the environment for software applications.

implicit array
: an array that consists of an array name, an optional index variable, and a list of array elements. In an implicit array, you do not have to explicitly specify the subscript in the reference when referring to an element. See also the entry for explicit array.

implicit array reference
: a description of the element to be processed in an implicit array. See also the entry for explicit array reference.

inactive key
: a function key in a display manager session that is not shared, or not common, among different devices.

index
: a feature of a SAS data set that enables the SAS System to access observations in the SAS data set quickly and efficiently. The purpose of SAS indexes is to optimize WHERE-clause processing and facilitate BY-group processing.

infix operator
: an operator that appears between two operands (for example, the greater-than symbol in 8>6). There are four general kinds of infix operators: arithmetic, comparison, logical or Boolean, and others (minimum, maximum, and concatenation).

informat
: the instructions that specify how the SAS System reads raw data values to create variable values. There are two types of informats: informats supplied by SAS software and user-written informats created using the FORMAT procedure.

input buffer
: the temporary area of memory into which each record of data is read when the INPUT statement executes.

input/output operation
: the operation of physically reading data from a storage medium, such as a disk or tape, or writing data to a storage medium.

interactive facility
: a system that alternately accepts and responds to input. An interactive facility is conversational; that is, a continuous dialog exists between user and system. The SAS Display Manager System is interactive.

interactive line-mode
: a method of running SAS programs without using the SAS Display Manager System. You enter one line of a SAS program at a time. The SAS System processes each line immediately after you enter it.

interface engine
: an engine that reads and writes file formats supported by software other than the SAS System.

interleaving
: a process in which the SAS System combines two or more sorted SAS data sets into one sorted SAS data set based on the values of the BY variables.

item
: one of the choices displayed in a pull-down menu or an action bar of the PMENU facility. Selecting an item either executes a command, displays a pull-down menu, or displays a dialog box.

key variable
: a variable that is used to index SAS data sets.

label
: See the entries for data set label, statement label, and label, variable.

label, variable
: a descriptive label of up to 40 characters that can be printed by certain procedures instead of, or in addition to, the variable name.

LAST.*variable*
: a temporary variable that the SAS System creates to identify the last observation of each BY group. It is not added to the SAS data set.

length, variable
: the number of bytes used to store each of a variable's values in a SAS data set.

length variable
: (1) a numeric variable created by the LENGTH= option in the INFILE statement to store the length of the current input record. (2) a numeric variable used with the $VARYING informat or format to specify the actual length of a character variable whose length varies.

library engine
: an engine that accesses groups of files and puts them into the correct form for processing by SAS utility windows and procedures. A library engine also determines the fundamental processing characteristics of the library, presents lists of files for the library directory, and supports view engines. See also the entry for view engine.

library reference
: another name for libref.

libref (first-level name)
: the name temporarily associated with a SAS data library. You assign a libref with a LIBNAME statement or with operating system control language. The libref is the first-level name of a two-level name. For example, A is the libref in the two-level name A.B. The default libref is WORK unless the USER libref is defined. See also the entry for USER library.

line-hold specifier
: a special symbol used in INPUT statements (trailing @ or double trailing @ signs) and in PUT statements (trailing @ sign) that enables you to hold a record in the input or output buffer for further processing.

line mode
: See the entry for interactive line-mode.

list input, modified
: a style that uses special instructions called informats and format modifiers in the INPUT statement to scan input records for data values that are separated by at least one blank or other delimiter, and in some cases, by two blanks.

list input, simple
: a style that gives only variable names and dollar signs ($) in the INPUT statement to scan input records for data values that are separated by at least one blank or other delimiter.

list output
: a style in which a character string or variable is specified in a PUT statement without explicit directions that specify where the SAS System should place the string or value.

literal

(1) a SAS constant. See also the entry for constant. (2) in syntax descriptions, a part of the SAS language that you must specify using the exact set of characters that the language expects. For example, in the statement

BY *variables*;

BY is a literal because in order for the SAS System to understand the term you must spell it with the two characters B and Y. The term *variable* is not a literal because you can supply any list of valid variable names.

logical data model

a framework into which engines fit information for processing by the SAS System. It is a logical representation of data or files, not a physical structure.

logical operator (Boolean operator)

an operator used in expressions to link sequences of comparisons. The logical operators are AND, OR, and NOT.

macro facility

a tool that allows you to extend and customize features of the SAS System.

macro variable

a variable belonging to the macro language whose value is a string that remains constant until you change it.

mantissa

in floating-point representation, the number multiplied by the base raised to the power given by the exponent; the decimal part of a logarithm. For example, the mantissa is .1234 in the following expression:

$$.1234 \times 10^4 \quad .$$

master data set

in an update operation, the data set containing the information you want to update.

match-merging

a process in which the SAS System joins observations from two or more SAS data sets according to the values of the BY variables.

member

(1) a file in a SAS data library. (2) a single element of a partitioned data set under the MVS operating system.

member name

(1) the name of a file in a SAS data library. When you reference a file with a two-level name, such as A.B, the member name is the second part of the name (the libref is the first part). (2) the name of a single element of a partitioned data set under the MVS operating system.

member type

the classification of a file in a SAS data library that is assigned by the SAS System to identify what type of information is stored in the file. For example, CATALOG is the member type for catalogs.

merging
: the process of combining observations from two or more SAS data sets into a single observation in a new SAS data set.

methods of running the SAS System
: one of the following modes used to run SAS programs: display manager mode, interactive line mode, noninteractive mode, batch mode.

missing value
: incomplete SAS data. In input use a period or a blank as a placeholder for missing values of character variables, and use a period, a blank, or a special missing character (assigned with the MISSING= system option) as a placeholder for numeric variables. The SAS System displays a blank to represent a missing value for a character variable and a period or a special character to represent a missing value for a numeric variable.

mnemonic operator
: a letter abbreviation of mathematical or Boolean (logical) symbols that is used to request a comparison, logical operation, or arithmetic calculation (for example, EQ, OR, and AND).

mode of execution
: See the entry for methods of running the SAS System.

Multiple Engine Architecture (MEA)
: a feature of the SAS System that enables it to access a variety of file formats through sets of instructions called engines. See also the entry for engine.

name, variable
: the identifying attribute of a variable. A variable name must conform to SAS naming rules.

named input
: a style in which equal signs appear in the INPUT statement to read data values in the form *variable=data-value*.

named output
: a style in which equal signs appear in the PUT statement to write variable values in the form *variable=data-value*.

native engine
: an engine that accesses forms of SAS files created and processed only by the SAS System.

noninteractive mode
: a method of running SAS programs in which you prepare a file of SAS statements and submit the program to the computer system. The program runs immediately and occupies your current terminal session.

nonstandard data
: data that can be read only with the aid of informats, such as hexadecimal and binary values.

numeric constant
: a number that appears in a SAS statement.

numeric format
: instructions to the SAS System to write numeric variable values using a specific pattern.

numeric informat
: instructions to the SAS System to read numeric data values using a specific pattern to create numeric variable values.

numeric value
: a value that usually contains only numbers, including numbers in E-notation and hexadecimal notation, and sometimes a decimal point, plus sign, or minus sign. Numeric values are stored in numeric variables.

numeric variable
: a variable that can contain only numeric values. In the SAS System, all numeric variables are stored in floating-point representation.

observation
: a row in a SAS data set that contains the specific data values for an individual entity.

one-to-one matching
: the process of combining observations from two or more data sets into one observation using two or more SET statements to read observations independently from each data set.

one-to-one merging
: the process of using the MERGE statement (without a BY statement) to combine observations from two or more data sets based on the observations' positions in the data sets. See also the entry for match-merging.

operands
: the variables and constants in a comparison operation or calculation.

operator
: a symbol that requests a comparison, logical operation, or arithmetic calculation. The SAS System uses two major kinds of operators: prefix operators and infix operators.

output buffer
: in the DATA step, the area of memory to which a PUT statement writes before writing to a designated file or output device.

padding a value with blanks
: a process in which the SAS System adds blanks to the end of a character value that is shorter than the length of the variable.

page size
: (1) the size of the page of printed output. (2) the number of bytes of data that the SAS System moves between external storage and memory in one logical input/output operation.

paste buffer
: a temporary storage location that holds the contents of text stored with the STORE or CUT commands. The contents of the paste buffer remain in effect only for the current SAS session.

period
: the default character used for a missing value for a numeric variable.

permanent SAS data library
: a library that is not deleted when the SAS session terminates; it is available for subsequent SAS sessions. Unless the USER libref is defined, you use a two-level name to access a file in a permanent library. The first-level name is the libref, and the second-level name is the member name.

permanent SAS file
: a SAS file in a library that is not deleted when the SAS session or job terminates.

physical filename
: the name the operating system uses to identify a file.

PMENU facility
: a menuing system that is used instead of the command line as a way to execute commands.

pointer
: in the DATA step, a programming tool the SAS System uses to keep track of its position in the input or output buffer.

pointer control
: the process of instructing the SAS System to move the pointer before reading or writing data.

prefix operator
: an operator that is applied to the variable, constant, function, or parenthetical expression immediately following it (for example, the minus sign in -6*a).

print file
: an external file containing carriage-control (printer-control) information.

PROC step
: a group of SAS statements that call and execute a procedure, usually with a SAS data set as input.

procedures
: (1) often called SAS procedures, a collection of built-in SAS programs that are used to produce reports, manage files, and analyze data. They enable you to accept default output or to tailor your output by overriding defaults. (2) usually called user-written procedures, a self-contained user-written program, written in a language other than the SAS language, that interfaces with the SAS System and is accessed with a PROC statement.

program data vector
: the temporary area of memory, or storage area, where the SAS System builds a SAS data set, one observation at a time.

programming error
: an execution-time logic error that causes a SAS program to fail or to produce incorrect results.

propagation of missing values
: a method of treating missing values in which using a missing value in an arithmetic expression causes the SAS System to set the result of the expression to missing. Using that result in another expression causes the next result to be missing.

pull-down menu
: the list of choices that appears when you choose an item from an action bar or from another pull-down menu in the PMENU facility. The choices in the list are called items.

radix point
: in a representation of a number, the position that separates the characters of the integral part from those of the fractional part. For example, in the decimal system, the radix point is called the decimal point.

random access
: the ability to retrieve records in a file without reading previous records.

raw data
: (1) data stored in an external file that have not been read into a SAS data set. (2) in statistical analysis, data (including SAS data sets) that have not had a particular operation, such as standardization, performed on them.

record
: a unit of data in an external file that contains the specific data values for all fields of an individual entry.

requestor window
: a window that the SAS System displays so that you can confirm, cancel, or modify an action.

return code
: a code passed to the operating system that indicates whether the execution of a command or job step completed successfully.

SAS catalog
: a SAS file that stores many different kinds of information in smaller units called entries. Some catalog entries contain system information such as key definitions. Other catalog entries contain application information such as window definitions, help windows, formats, informats, macros, or graphics output.

SAS command
: a command that invokes the SAS System. This command may vary depending on operating system and site.

SAS data file
: a SAS data set that stores descriptor information and observations in the same location.

SAS data library
: a collection of one or more SAS files that are recognized by the SAS System. Each file is a member of the library.

SAS data set
: descriptor information and its related data values organized as a table of observations and variables that can be processed by the SAS System. A SAS data set can be either a SAS data file or a SAS data view.

SAS data set option
: See the entry for data set option.

SAS data view
: a SAS data set in which the descriptor portion and the observations are obtained from other files. SAS data views store the information required to retrieve data values that are stored in other files.

SAS date constant
: a date in the form *ddMMMyy* in quotes followed by the character d (for example, '06JUL89'd).

SAS date value
: the number of days between January 1, 1960, and another date.

SAS datetime constant
: a datetime in the form *ddMMMyy:hh:mm:ss* in quotes followed by the characters dt (for example, '06JUL89:09:53:22'dt).

SAS datetime value
: the number of seconds between midnight, January 1, 1960, and another date and time.

SAS Display Manager System
: an interactive windowing environment in which actions are performed with a series of commands or function keys. Within one session, multiple tasks can be accomplished. It can be used to prepare and submit programs, view and print the results, and debug and resubmit the programs.

SAS file
: a specially structured file that is created, organized, and, optionally, maintained by the SAS System. A SAS file can be a SAS data set, a catalog, a stored program, or an access descriptor.

SAS invocation
: the process of initializing a SAS session.

SAS keyword
: a literal that is a primary part of the SAS language. Keywords are the words DATA and PROC, statement names, function names, macro names, and macro function names.

SAS language
: (1) the statements that direct the execution of the SAS System. (2) as a grouping in SAS documentation, all parts of base SAS software except procedures.

SAS log
: a file that can contain the SAS statements you enter and messages about the execution of your program.

SAS name
: a name that can appear in a SAS statement, including items such as names of variables and SAS data sets. SAS names can be up to eight characters long. The first character must be a letter or an underscore. Subsequent characters can be letters, numbers, or underscores. Blanks and special characters (except the underscore) are not allowed.

SAS operator
: See the entry for operator.

SAS procedure output file
: an external file that contains the result of the analysis or the report produced. Procedures write output to the procedure output file by default. DATA step reports that contain the FILE statement with the PRINT destination also go to this file.

SAS procedures
: See the entry for procedures.

SAS program
: a sequence of related SAS statements.

SAS statement
: a string of SAS keywords, SAS names, and special characters and operators ending in a semicolon that instructs the SAS System to perform an operation or gives information to the SAS System.

SAS system option
: See the entry for system option.

SAS Text Editor
: a full-screen editing facility available in some windows of the SAS Display Manager System, as well as in windows of SAS/AF, SAS/FSP, and SAS/GRAPH software.

SAS time constant
: a time in the form *hh:mm:ss* in quotes followed by the character t (for example, '09:53:22't).

SAS time value
: the number of seconds between midnight of the current day and another time value.

SAS windowing environment
: See the entry for SAS Display Manager System.

SASHELP library
: a SAS data library supplied by SAS software that stores the text for HELP windows, default function key and window definitions, and menus.

SASUSER library
: the library that contains a profile catalog that stores the tailoring features you specify for the SAS System.

second-level name
: See the entry for member name.

seed
: an initial value used in a random number function or CALL routine to calculate a random variate.

selection field
: the portion of a display manager window (shown on the display as an underscore) where you can enter a short command to perform an action, such as B for Browse.

selection field command
: a command that enables you to perform actions from a display manager window. For example, entering the letter D in the DIRECTORY window's selection command field beside the name of a SAS data set enables you to delete that SAS data set.

sequential access
: a method of file access in which the records are read or written one after the other.

simple expression
: an expression that uses only one operator.

simple index
: an index that locates observations by the values of one variable.

site number
: the number used by SAS Institute to identify the site to which the SAS System is licensed. The site number appears near the top of the log in every SAS session.

SQL
: (1) an acronym for Structured Query Language, which is an ANSI/ISO standard language for accessing data stored in tables. (2) a procedure in base SAS software that implements this language.

standard data
: data that are stored with one digit or character per byte. Standard data can be read with all SAS input styles.

statement label
: a word that prefixes a statement in the DATA step so that execution can move to that position as necessary, bypassing other statements in the step. Statement labels follow the rules for SAS names.

statement option
: an option specified in a given SAS statement that affects only that statement.

syntax checking
: a process in which the SAS System checks each statement to be sure it is used properly, that all keywords are spelled correctly, that all names meet the requirements for SAS names, and so forth.

syntax error
: an error in the spelling or grammar of SAS statements. The SAS System finds syntax errors as it compiles each SAS step before execution.

system option
: an option that affects the appearance of SAS output, the handling of some of the files used by the SAS System, the use of system variables, the processing of observations in SAS data sets, the features of SAS System initialization, the SAS System's interface with your computer hardware, and the SAS System's interface with the operating system.

target variable
: the variable to which the result of a function or expression is assigned.

temporary file
: a SAS file in a SAS data library (usually the WORK library) that is deleted at the end of the SAS session or job.

temporary SAS data library
: a library that exists only for the current SAS session or job. The most common temporary library is the WORK library.

text editing command
: a command specific to the text editor.

title
: a heading printed at the top of each page of SAS output or log.

toggle
: the on/off switch process where you can go back and forth (switch) between two different actions.

trailing at sign (@)
: a special symbol used to hold a line for use by a later INPUT or PUT statement.

transaction data set
: in an update operation, the data set containing the information with which to update the master data set.

transport file
: a sequential file containing SAS data libraries, SAS catalogs, or SAS data sets in transport format. Because transport format is the same for all operating systems, you can use transport files to move SAS data libraries, catalogs, and data sets from one operating system or host to another.

transport format
: a machine-independent file format.

type, variable
: See the entry for variable type.

updating
: a process in which the SAS System replaces the values of variables in the master data set with values from observations in the transaction data set.

USER library
: a SAS data library defined with the libref USER. When the libref USER is defined, the SAS System uses it as the default libref for one-level names.

user-written format
: See the entry for format.

user-written informat
: See the entry for informat.

user-written procedures
See the entry for procedures.

variable
the set of data values in the program data vector or in a SAS data set that describe a given characteristic. See also the entry for macro variable.

variable attributes
the name, label, format, informat, type, and length associated with a particular variable.

variable list
a list of variables. You can use abbreviated variable lists in many SAS statements instead of listing all the variable names.

variable type
one of two divisions, numeric or character, into which the SAS System classifies variables.

view descriptor
a file created by SAS/ACCESS software that describes data values stored in database management system tables and enables the SAS System to process the data as a SAS data set.

view engine
an engine that enables the SAS System to process SAS data views. A view engine performs in a transparent manner. See also the entry for SAS data views.

window
a resizable, movable object on the display.

window field type
See the entry for *field-type* of a window.

windowing environment
See the entry for SAS Display Manager System.

WORK library
the temporary library automatically defined by the SAS System at the beginning of each SAS session or job to store temporary files. When the libref USER is not defined, the SAS System uses WORK as the default library for one-level names.

Index

A

B

C

D

E

M

N

O

P

Q

R

T

U

W

X

Y

Z

Special Characters

Your Turn

If you have comments or suggestions about base SAS software or *SAS Language: Reference, Version 6, First Edition* please send them to us on a photocopy of this page.

Please return the photocopy to the Publications Division (for comments about this book) or the Technical Support Division (for suggestions about the software) at SAS Institute Inc., SAS Campus Drive, Cary, NC 27513.

Operating System Documentation for the SAS System

Find information on performing common tasks with the SAS System under your operating system. Each operating system companion includes complete descriptions of operating system-dependent features, task-oriented sections with examples, and reference sections.

The following companions for Version 6 of the SAS System are now available:

Title	**Order Number**
SAS® Companion for the AOS/VS Environment, Version 6, First Edition	(A56104)
SAS® Companion for the CMS Environment, Version 6, First Edition	(A56103)
SAS® Companion for the MVS Environment, Version 6, First Edition	(A56101)
SAS® Companion for the OS/2® Environment, Version 6, First Edition	(A56106)
SAS® Companion for the PRIMOS Environment, Version 6, First Edition	(A56105)
SAS® Companion for the UNIX Environment and Derivatives, Version 6, First Edition	(A56107)
SAS® Companion for the VMS Environment, Version 6, First Edition	(A56102)

To order any of these books see ordering information in the back of this book.

SAS® Training from SAS Institute Inc.

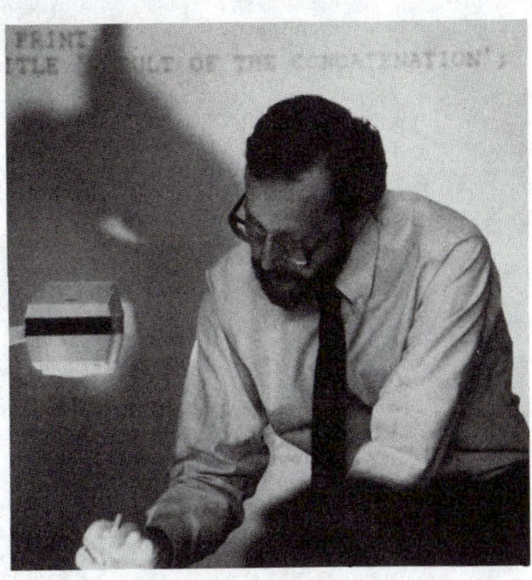

Experience Is the Best Teacher

No one knows the SAS® System and SYSTEM 2000® Data Management Software better than SAS Institute. And the experience shows in the quality and scope of our training. Whether you're developing a training program for an entire organization or choosing a course for yourself—when it comes to SAS and SYSTEM 2000 training—experience is the best teacher.

Build your own curriculum from more than 50 courses designed by professional educators working hand in hand with our software developers. Our courses are available in a number of training formats:

Instructor-based Public Training
Instructor-based On-site Training
Consortium Training
Trainer's Kits
Video-based Training
Online Training.

So you can select the best way to train users of any experience level, from novice computer user to seasoned analyst or programmer. As your needs grow and change, you may want to combine training formats to provide a complete, flexible program.

Whatever your training needs, you benefit from the experience only SAS Institute can offer. So when you consider SAS and SYSTEM 2000 training—for yourself, for your staff, or for your organization—remember who wrote the book.

For more information, call an Education Sales account representative at (919) 677-8000 or mail your completed coupon today.

SAS Institute Inc.
SAS Campus Drive
Cary, NC 27513
Phone 919-677-8000
Fax 919-677-8123

Send me a free copy of your course catalog, *SAS Training*®.

Tell me more about:

- ☐ instructor-based public training
- ☐ instructor-based on-site training
- ☐ consortium training
- ☐ trainer's kits
- ☐ video-based training
- ☐ online training.

☐ Please call me.

Mail to: SAS Institute Inc.
Education Marketing and
Sales Department
SAS Campus Drive
Cary, NC 27513

——Mr. ——Ms. ————————

Title

Company

Address

City

State ZIP

( )
Phone

Customers outside the US, contact your local distributor.

BA

Customers Outside the United States

You can order books referenced in this book by contacting the appropriate subsidiary for ordering and pricing information. Order numbers for publications follow the book titles listed on pages xxi and xxii or in the back of this book under "Operating System Documentation for the SAS System."

All orders for customers outside the United States must be placed with the appropriate subsidiary. A list of Institute subsidiaries follows:

SAS Institute NV/SA
Interleuvenlaan 10
3001 Heverlee
Belgium
Telephone (32) 16 29 09 30
Fax (32) 16 29 12 69

SAS Institute A/S
Kobmagergade 9a
1150 Copenhagen K.
Denmark
Telephone (45) 33-124233
Fax (45) 33-116155

SAS Institute Oy
Sinikalliontie 10
PL 80
02631 Espoo
Finland
Telephone (358) 0-523011
Fax (358) 0-5021198

SAS Institute s.a.
Domaine de Grégy
Boîte postale 5
77166 Grégy-sur-Yerres
France
Telephone (33) 1 60 62 11 11
Fax (33) 1 60 62 11 99

SAS Institute GmbH
PO Box 10 53 07
Neuenheimer Landstrasse, 28-30
6900 Heidelberg 1
Germany
Telephone (49) 6221-4150
Fax (49) 6221-474850

SAS Institute S.R.L.
via San Martino
della Battaglia, 17
20122 Milano
Italy
Telephone (39) 2-58300754
Fax (39) 2-58300602

SAS Institute A/S
Trollåsveien 4
1414 Trollåsen
Norway
Telephone (47) 2-805380
Fax (47) 2-800703

SAS Institute S.A.
Marbella, 19
28034 Madrid
Spain
Telephone (34) 1-372 1500
Fax (34) 1-372 1689

SAS Institute AB
Box 1249
Färögatan 2
16428 Kista
Sweden
Telephone (46) 8-793-9030
Fax (46) 8-750-5038

SAS Institute SA
Herrmann Goetz Strasse 21
8400 Winterthur
Switzerland
Telephone (052) 213 23 24
Fax (052) 213 23 74

SAS Institute BV
Koninginneweg 31
1217 KR Hilversum
Netherlands, The
Telephone (31) 35-284550
Fax (31) 35-217532

SAS Software Ltd.
Wittington House
Henley Road, Medmenham
Marlow, SL7 2EB
United Kingdom
Telephone (44) 6284-86933
Fax (44) 6284-83203

SAS Institute Australia Pty. Ltd.
Private Bag No. 52
Lane Cove, NSW 2066
Australia
Telephone (61) 2-428-0428
Fax (61) 2-418-7211

SAS Institute (NZ) Ltd.
PO Box 10-109, The Terrace
Wellington
New Zealand
Telephone (64) 4-727-595
Telex NZ31525 MED
Fax (64) 4-727-055

(continued)

Subsidiaries (continued)

SAS Institute Ltd.
Beijing Representative Office
Rm. 322, Kunlun Hotel
Chaoyang District
Beijing 100004
People's Republic of China
Telephone (86) 1 5003388-322
Fax (86) 1 5003228

SAS Institute Ltd.
Room 1403-4
Cityplaza 4
Tai Koo Shing
Hong Kong
Telephone (852) 568-4280
Telex 77467 HX
Fax (852) 568-7218

SAS Institute Japan Ltd.
Nichirei Akashi-cho Building
6-4 Akashi-cho
Chuo-ku, Tokyo 104
Japan
Telephone (81) 3-5565-8380
Fax (81) 3-5565-8389

SAS Software Korea Ltd.
#503 Wonchang-bldg.
26-3 Yoido-Dong
Youngdeungpo-Ku
Seoul 150-010
Korea
Telephone (82) 2-783-4448
Fax (82) 2-783-4449

SAS Institute Sdn. Bhd.
28th Floor Menara Maybank
100 Jalan Tun Perak
50050 Kuala Lumpur
Malaysia
Telephone (60) 3-238-3188
Fax (60) 3-238-3357

SAS Institute Ltd. (Philippines)
Strata 100, Emerald Avenue
Ortigas Center, Pasig 1600
Metro Manila
Philippines
Telephone (63) 2-632-0628
Fax (63) 2-631-2881

SAS Institute Pte. Ltd.
510 Thomson Road #16-03
Block A, SLF Complex
Singapore 1129
Telephone (65) 258-6233
Telex RS39402 SASINS
Fax (65) 258-4450

SAS Software Taiwan Ltd.
Ming Sheng E. Road, #149
Section 2, 11th Floor
Taipei
Taiwan, R.O.C.
Telephone (886) 2-507-1275
Fax (886) 2-504-1631

SAS Institute (Canada) Inc.
225 Duncan Mill Road
Suite 300
North York, Ontario
M3B 3K9
Canada
Telephone 416-443-9811
Fax 416-443-1269

United States Customers

You can order books referenced in this book by using the SAS Institute Publications Order Form on the back of this page. Order numbers for publications follow the book titles listed on pages xxi and xxii or in the back of this book under "Operating System Documentation for the SAS System." You can also place your order online using the Institute's Online Customer Support Facility. If you need faster service or need assistance with your order, call a Book Sales representative at 919-677-8000.

For United States Customers Only

SAS Institute Publications Order Form

Order Information

Mail to
SAS Institute Inc.
Book Sales Department
SAS Campus Drive
Cary, NC 27513-2414

Call
919-677-8000
Ask for Book Sales

Fax
919-677-8166

Tax & Shipping Information

Your invoice will include applicable sales taxes which, based on our understanding of your state's tax laws, SAS Institute Inc. is required to collect and remit. Shipping and handling charges will be prepaid and added to your invoice. All prices are FOB shipping point. Book orders in the continental US are shipped RPS or UPS.

Note: To determine your shipping charges for documentation, refer to the chart below. (AK, HI, Canada—call for rates.)

Total Order	Charge	Total Order	Charge
Up to $100	$5	$600.01-$700	$24
$100.01-$200	$9	$700.01-$800	$27
$200.01-$300	$12	$800.01-$900	$30
$300.01-$400	$15	$900.01-$1000	$32
$400.01-$500	$18	$1000.01+	add 3.5%
$500.01-$600	$21		

☐ Express service. Applicable shipping charges will be added.

Billing Address (if different from shipping address)

Company ____________________

ATTN: ____________________

____

Street ____________________

City ____________ State ____________ ZIP ____________

Shipping Address (street address is necessary for delivery)

Company ____________________

ATTN: ____________________

Street ____________________

City ____________ State ____________ ZIP ____________

Telephone (____) ________ - ____________ (Daytime)

Payment Information

Charge customers, please furnish:

☐ MasterCard ☐ VISA

Card account number ☐☐☐☐☐☐☐☐☐☐☐☐☐☐☐☐☐

Expiration date ☐☐ — ☐☐
Mo. Yr.

Cardholder's name ____________________
(please print)

☐ Business charge card ☐ Personal charge card

Purchase Order # ____________

Qty.	Order No.	Title	Price	Total

Prices are subject to change without notice.

Subtotal	
Sales Tax (if applicable)*	
Shipping and Handling Charges (see chart)	
Total (to be completed by Book Sales Dept.)	XXXXX

* Applicable sales tax will be charged unless a copy of your exemption certificate or certificate of resale is enclosed.